Being Human

An Introduction
to Cultural Anthropology

Second Edition

Mari Womack

**UNIVERSITY OF CALIFORNIA AT LOS ANGELES
AND SANTA MONICA COLLEGE**

Prentice
Hall

Upper Saddle River, New Jersey 07458

Library of Congress Cataloging-in-Publication Data

WOMACK, MARI.
    Being human: An introduction to cultural anthropology / Mari Womack. — 2nd ed.
      p. cm.
    Includes bibliographical references and index.
    ISBN 0-13-090296-9
    1. Ethnology. I. Title.
  GN316.W66 2001
  306—dc21   00-051041

VP, Editorial Director: Laura Pearson
AVP, Publisher: Nancy Roberts
Managing Editor: Sharon Chambliss
Director of Marketing: Beth Gillett Mejia
Project Manager: Serena Hoffman
AVP, Director of Production and Manufacturing: Barbara Kittle
Manufacturing Manager, Nick Sklitsis
Prepress and Manufacturing Buyer: Benjamin Smith
Copy Editor: Margo Quinto
Creative Design Director: Leslie Osher
Interior Designer: Kenny Beck
Cover Designer: Maria Lange
Line Art Director: Guy Ruggiero
Illustrations: Maria Piper
Photo Researcher: Karen Pugliano
Director, Image Resource Center: Melinda Reo
Interior Image Specialist: Beth Boyd
Manager, Rights and Permissions: Kay Dellosa
Cover Art: Tony Stone Images

This book was set in 10/12 Meridian
by Interactive Composition Corporation
and was printed and bound by Courier Companies, Inc.
The cover was printed by Phoenix Color Corp.

Prentice-Hall International (UK) Limited, *London*
Prentice-Hall of Australia Pty. Limited, *Sydney*
Prentice-Hall Canada Inc., *Toronto*
Prentice-Hall Hispanoamericana, S.A., *Mexico*
Prentice-Hall of India Private Limited, *New Delhi*
Prentice-Hall of Japan, Inc., *Tokyo*
Pearson Education Asia Pte. Ltd., *Singapore*
Editora Prentice-Hall do Brasil, Ltda., *Rio de Janeiro*

Brief Contents

Contents

Chapter 5   Culture in Its Material Context   98

Chapter 6   Sex, Marriage, and Family Relationships   126

PART THREE   The Question of Meaning

Chapter 7   Language and Symbols, Order and Chaos 152

Chapter 8 The Nature of Human Nature   176

Chapter 9 Natural and Supernatural Orders   206

Chapter 10   Expressive Culture   236

PART FOUR Human Ways of Life

Chapter 13 Horticulturalists   324

PART FIVE   The Adventure of Anthropology Continues

Preface

This is an exciting time to be an anthropologist. Both the people anthropologists have traditionally studied and the context of anthropological research have changed dramatically in the past few decades.

No longer is it possible for a lone anthropologist to travel to a remote area of the world to conduct ethnography among "his" or "her" people. There are no isolated areas of the world any more. We are all linked together by various kinds of technology, including satellite communications, the Internet, and international air travel. This means that the anthropologist no longer has exclusive access to an isolated group of people. Documentary filmmakers can be there first, and every schoolchild can then see a sensationalized account on "Ripley's Believe It or Not." As anthropologists no longer have exclusive dominance over this type of information, some are asking, "Is anthropology still relevant?"

This question was echoed recently in a query from one of my students. I was describing the traditional lifestyle of the !Kung of Africa's Kalahari Desert when a thin girl in platform shoes, skin-tight jeans, and a bared midriff asked, "Is this information up to date?"

The issue underlying this question was, "Is anthropology trendy enough to bother with?" After thinking it over, I replied, "The !Kung no longer live like that. But ethnographic descriptions of the !Kung will never be out of date. It's important that we know the full range of human possibilities. Otherwise, we might come to think that the way we live at any given point in time is the *only* way to live." In my response to my student, I found myself echoing the long-held anthropological wisdom that the reason we travel to the most remote areas of the world is to find out who *we* are.

Anthropology is the only scientific discipline developed for the express purpose of studying cross-cultural variation in human lifestyles. Other closely related disciplines are just beginning to recognize the importance of this research focus. Because anthropologists are 150 years ahead of the pack, anthropology is the discipline best prepared to study the rapidly changing contexts of the world's cultures. However, we must recognize the changing context of anthropology. We no longer have exclusive domain over access to a particular culture, and we must surrender the control that exclusive access to this kind of knowledge gave us.

American anthropology especially is undergoing a transition that many experience as a time of crisis. In reality, we have entered the third great era of anthropology, loosely conforming to the century mark. In the nineteenth century anthropologists framed many of the concepts that still guide the field; the twentieth century marked the era of collecting data on apparently isolated groups; the twenty-first century is ushering in an era in which anthropology must become truly international, more than simply cross-cultural. The people we have traditionally studied are now claiming the right to study us, and in so doing, they are claiming full and equal participation in the intellectual community of anthropology.

There have been attempts to internationalize American anthropology and break down the isolation of U.S. anthropologists from anthropologists in other parts of the world. The International Union of Anthropological and Ethnological Sciences is publishing a series of books that "document current theoretical developments in our discipline from a worldwide perspective." Vesna V. Godina of Slovenia, Chair of the IUAES Commission on Theoretical Anthropology, asserts: "Anthropology is either truly international or not at all!"* Anthropology is redefining itself on both the theoretical level and at the level of ethnographic research.

Being Human: An Introduction to Cultural Anthropology aims to be at the forefront of this revolution in anthropology and bring it into the classroom. From its inception, *Being Human: An Introduction to Cultural Anthropology* has presented a holistic look at cultural anthropology, framed against an understanding of the importance of gender and intracultural variation in shaping the dynamics of human groups. The success of the first edition of *Being Human* has encouraged me to venture further in attempting to develop an introductory cultural anthropology text that reflects

---

*E. L. Cerroni-Long, ed., *Anthropological Theory in North America* (Westport, CT: Bergin & Garvey, 1999).

contemporary issues in anthropology and presents them in their cultural and historical context. In this, the second edition, I have sought to:

1. *Present new research on gender and provide a consistent representation of gender roles throughout the book.* As one example, a new box in Chapter 10 addresses changing views of women's participation in sports.

2. *Incorporate recent research and developments in anthropological theory on contemporary issues, including the issue of returning control over cultural objects to the people who produced them.* A new box in Chapter 15 deals with the issue of patrimony in light of the controversy surrounding "Kennewick Man."

3. *Include material on the relationship of anthropological theory and methods to the scientific enterprise as a whole.* The discussion of anthropological theory and methods in Chapter 2 has been expanded and enhanced, and a new box in Chapter 16 addresses the power relationships inherent in anthropological research.

4. *Expand the discussions of applied anthropological theory, especially with respect to anthropology as a career.* New boxes in Chapters 2 and 16 discuss applications of anthropology in business and air traffic safety.

5. *Reorganize and reorder some chapters and utilize anthropological pedagogical devices, including videos and ethnographies.* As just one example, the discussion of types of political systems has been moved from Chapter 1 to Chapter 4, "The Political Economy."

6. *Incorporate computer technology as an aid to teaching and learning.* New Internet exercises at the end of each chapter encourage students to build on their knowledge by exploring issues related to the topics being discussed.

This second edition of *Being Human* builds on the goals that have proven successful in the first edition, in that it presents culture as a dynamic process rather than a static formula and focuses on social interaction rather than social structure. Issues of culture change are discussed where appropriate throughout the book, rather than relegated to a chapter at the end. Further, *Being Human* confronts the issue of the "we-they" dichotomy by incorporating frank discussions of ethnicity and the relationship between anthropologists and the people they study.

This text also integrates studies of American and Western culture with descriptions of non-Western societies, for both philosophical and pedagogical reasons. Focusing exclusively on studies of non-Western societies implicitly poses an oppositional relationship between the anthropologist and the people being studied, with a power balance favoring the anthropologist. Moreover, including Western examples allows North American students to relate anthropological concepts to their own lives.

Being Human is designed with both the instructor and the student in mind. As I pointed out in the preface to the first edition, introductory college courses often act as gatekeepers to the field. Many future anthropologists are "converted" to the discipline as a result of taking introductory classes. This text is organized according to a logical flow of ideas from section to section and from chapter to chapter, so that students are not required to memorize a checklist of anthropological facts. Rather, they are invited to become participants in the development of anthropological concepts.

Part One presents an overview of what it means to be human and the role of anthropology in studying this important question. Part Two examines principles of social organization. Part Three discusses the ways in which human groups reflect upon their culture and social organization through the use of language and symbols. Part Four applies concepts presented in the first four sections to specific human groups, thus combining anthropological theory and ethnographic examples in the same text. Part Five explores contemporary issues and careers in anthropology.

Part One, "The Human Perspective," consists of three chapters. Chapter 1, "We the People," discusses ways of defining humanness, the relationship between biology and culture, the "we-they" dichotomy, the importance of gender and ethnicity, and the role of European colonialism in redefining the nature of human groups. Chapter 2, "People Looking at People," focuses on anthropology as a discipline. It describes the anthropological approach and subfields, as well as anthropological methods, and discusses ethical and human factors in conducting anthropological research. Chapter 3, "The Adventure of Anthropology," provides an overview of the history of anthropology, organized according to six stages or theoretical approaches: (1) speculation about human nature arising from European colonialism; (2) formulation of theories relating to natural selection and biological evolution; (3) nineteenth century social evolutionism; (4) British social anthropology; (5) American cultural anthropology; (6) interpretive anthropology.

Part Two, "The Organization of Human Groups," consists of three chapters. Chapter 4, "The Political Economy," describes the organization of power in human groups and discusses theories—including those of Marx, neoevolutionists, and economic anthropologists—that have given rise to contemporary views on the interrelatedness of political and economic systems. Chapter 5, "Culture in Its Material Context," describes subsistence patterns and exchange systems. It concludes with a discussion of cultural materialism, drawing on the examples of Marvin Harris's perspective on the Hindu sacred cow and Michael Harner's explanation of Aztec human sacrifice. Chapter 6, "Sex, Marriage, and Family Relationships," discusses issues related to kinship, including the incest taboo, forms of marriage, economic exchange at marriage, forms of descent, residence and household formation, and kinship terminology.

Part Three, "The Question of Meaning," consists of four chapters. Chapter 7, "Language and Symbols, Order and Chaos," discusses the importance of communication in human groups. It deals with the biological basis of language, the structure and nature of human language, the relationship between language and thought, and the social context of language use. The chapter concludes with a discussion of symbols and communication based on imagery. Chapter 8, "The Nature of Human Nature," focuses on psychological anthropology: concepts of self; cross-cultural studies of perception and cognition; the anthropological debate over the Oedipal complex; the culture-and-personality school, national character studies, socialization studies, and indigenous healing systems. Chapter 9, "Natural and Supernatural Orders," discusses aspects of religion and magic, including myth, ritual, and the organization of religious communities. It also examines the role of religion in culture change, especially with respect to revitalization movements. Chapter 10, "Expressive Culture," deals with the social and cultural roles of various types of play: the visual arts, performance arts, festivals, and sports.

Part Four, "Human Ways of Life," consists of four chapters organized around subsistence patterns. Each mini-ethnography presents a holistic look at a particular group studied by anthropologists, integrates the issue of culture change, and focuses on an important anthropological concept. Chapter 11, "Foragers," takes a comparative look at three groups: the San of Africa's Kalahari Desert, the Ainu of northern Japan, and the Kwakiutl of the northwest coast of North America. The San demonstrate the importance of kinship and generalized reciprocity in gaining access to foraging rights; the Ainu represent a foraging group adapted to a rich and varied environment; the Kwakiutl provide an example of a foraging group that developed some degree of stratification and an elaborate art complex basing their subsistence on abundant and storable resources.

Chapter 12, "Pastoralists," compares Nandi cattleherders of Africa, Basseri sheepherders of Iran, and Yolmo zomo herders of Nepal. The Nandi provide an opportunity to explore gender roles, woman-woman marriage, and female circumcision; the Basseri illustrate the importance of flexible models of group formation in a nomadic pastoral society; the Yolmo illustrate the adaptability of pastoral societies to varying social and climatic conditions, as well as the interrelationship of Tibetan priestly religious organization with a shamanic healing complex.

Chapter 13, "Horticulturalists," compares the Yanomamö of Venezuela and Brazil, the Mundugumor of New Guinea, and Yap Islanders of the Pacific. The Yanomamö example illustrates the value of the holistic approach in understanding the interrelatedness of various aspects of social organization. The Mundugumor demonstrate the importance of theory in anthropology by describing a New Guinea Big Man complex from the perspective of the culture-and-personality school. The Yapese article describes a dramatic change in gender roles and lines of authority when a matrilineal horticultural society is taken over by U.S. political bureaucracy.

Chapter 14, "Agriculturalists," compares the Aztecs of central Mexico, the Nayar of southern India, and the Han of northern China. The Aztecs provide an example of a highly stratified society based on agriculture, trade, and conquest. The Nayar article, written from the perspective of a Nayar man, illustrates changes in economic status and gender roles in a matrilineal, matrilocal society resulting from English occupation and a shift to wage labor. The Han example illustrates the encounter between agricultural and pastoral groups in northern China as a result of population pressures, the effects of policy decisions made in Beijing, and the influence of various types of subsistence on gender roles.

Part Five, "The Adventure of Anthropology Continues," consists of two chapters. Chapter 15, "The People We Study," focuses on contemporary issues affecting the lives of people studied by anthropologists: political and economic subjugation by external powers, population pressures, pollution, and health issues, as well as economic and cultural colonialism. The chapter also notes ways in which indigenous people fight back against outside domination by seeking ways to control their own economic, political, and cultural lives. Chapter 16, "The People We Are," describes careers in academia, research institutions, museums, and various types of applied fields. It includes accounts by anthropologists who work in these areas. Applied areas discussed in the chapter include medicine and health care delivery systems, business, political and economic advocacy, and mass media as an educational tool.

SUPPLEMENTS

This carefully prepared supplements package is intended to give the instructor the resources needed to teach the course and the student the tools needed to successfully complete the course.

Instructor's Resource Manual This essential instructor's tool includes learning objectives, chapter outlines, teaching tips, suggestions for classroom activities, and topics for class discussion and written assignments.

Test Item File This carefully prepared manual includes over 1,400 questions in multiple-choice, true/false, and essay formats. All test questions are page-referenced to the text.

Prentice Hall Custom Test Prentice Hall's testing software program permits instructors to edit any or all items in the Test Item File and add their own questions. Other special features of this program, which is available for Windows and Macintosh, include random generation of an item set, creation of alternative versions of the same test, scrambling question sequence, and test preview before printing.

Videos A selection of high-quality, award-winning videos from the Filmmakers Library collection is available upon adoption. Please see your Prentice Hall sales representative for more information.

Transparency Acetates Taken from graphs, diagrams, and tables in this text and other sources, over 50 full-color transparencies offer an effective means of amplifying lecture topics.

The New York Times/**Prentice Hall Themes of the Times** *The New York Times* and Prentice Hall are sponsoring *Themes of the Times,* a program designed to enhance student access to current information relevant to the classroom. Through this program, the core subject matter provided in the text is supplemented by a collection of timely articles from one of the world's most distinguished newspapers, *The New York Times.* These articles demonstrate the vital, ongoing connection between what is learned in the classroom and what is happening in the world around us. To enjoy a wealth of information provided by *The New York Times* daily, a reduced subscription rate is available. For information call toll-free: 1-800-631-1222.

Prentice Hall and *The New York Times* are proud to co-sponsor *Themes of the Times.* We hope it will make the reading of both textbooks and newspapers a more dynamic, involving process.

Study Guide Designed to reinforce information in the text, the study guide includes chapter outlines and summaries, key terms, critical thinking questions, and student self-tests.

Companion Website In tandem with the text, students can now take full advantage of the World Wide Web to enrich their study of anthropology through the Womack Companion Website: **www. prenhall.com/womack**. This resource correlates the text with related material available on the Internet. Features of the Website include chapter objectives, study questions, as well as links to interesting material and information from other sites on the Web that can reinforce and enhance the content of each chapter.

Anthropology on the Internet: A Critical Thinking Guide, 2001 This guide focuses on developing the critical thinking skills necessary to evaluate and use online sources effectively. The guide also provides a brief introduction to navigating the Internet, along with complete references related specifically to the anthropology discipline and how to use the Companion Websites available for many Prentice Hall textbooks. This brief supplementary book is free to students when shrinkwrapped as a package with *any anthropology title.*

ACKNOWLEDGMENTS

I have acquired many debts in putting together this second edition of *Being Human.* Chief among them are to the dedicated staff at Prentice Hall. Nancy Roberts guided me through both the first edition and the second. Sharon Chambliss has worked almost as hard on the second edition as I have, and Serena Hoffman has probably worked even harder.

I have been greatly aided in this enterprise by comments from anthropologists who have used the first edition of *Being Human* or who would like to use the book in future courses. Foremost among these are Mary Schweitzer of Winthrop University and Susan Kirkpatrick Smith of Georgia State University. I have also been guided by comments from my own students and by their responses on exams given in my courses. I am especially grateful to Angela Bellin and other students in the Santa Monica chapter of Alpha Gamma Sigma, the student honor society, who have given me constructive feedback on my teaching style.

As all anthropologists know, kinship is the cornerstone of human relationships and formation of human groups. I have been unusually fortunate in both my consanguineal and affinal kin. Laura Womack served as editor for Chapter 15 of this book and contributed the box on patrimony. Greg and Jeff Womack provided advice, encouragement, and more tangible forms of support. Their affines—Dick Williams, Kathy Freeman Womack, and Michelle Gravatt Womack—were always there in times of crisis. And my grandchildren—Greg Womack, Jr., Aaron Womack, Michael Womack, and William Womack—contributed to this book simply by their existence.

I also have an anthropological family of great importance. My lineage can be traced to Allen W. Johnson, Jacques Maquet, Douglass Price-Williams, Philip L. Newman, and Victor Turner, who encouraged me in my study of symbols used by professional athletes. I also have a number of "siblings" who have aided me in my study of anthropology. Chief among them is E. L. Cerroni-Long, who continues to delight me with her contributions to the internationalization of anthropology. Joan Barker lured me into teaching anthropology, and Jeff Rigby kept me engaged in this important component of the anthropological enterprise. My journalistic lineage is equally illustrious, but I only have space to name a few who have contributed to my career: Ray Kabaker, Sean Kelly, Carey Pfeffer, Renee Barnett, and Candy Nall.

Most of all, I am grateful to my parents, James Truman Nall (1904–1977) and Clara Rita VanGennip Nall (1913–2000). Certainly, without them, this book could never have been written.

Mari Womack

About the Author

Dr. Mari Womack is a writer and anthropologist specializing in symbols, religion, gender, anthropological theory and methods, and American popular culture. A research scholar at the UCLA Center for the Study of Women, she is scriptwriter for the PBS television series *Faces of Culture* and co-editor of *The Other Fifty Percent,* a reader on gender. Dr. Womack hones her classroom skills by teaching at several California institutions, including UCLA and Santa Monica College. The Santa Monica College chapter of Alpha Gamma Sigma, the student honor society, presented her with its Instructional Excellence Award in spring 2000.

Formerly an international radio broadcaster for Voice of America, Dr. Womack has been quoted in *The New York Times, The Los Angeles Times,* and *The Wall Street Journal,* and has appeared on a number of television programs, including the *Today show,* applying anthropological insights to contemporary issues. As a journalist, she has reported on news events ranging from U.S. presidential elections to earthquakes. She has interviewed a number of distinguished subjects, from Benezir Bhutto of Pakistan, to Nobel Prize-winning scholars, to film stars.

Dr. Womack's current interests center on producing books on anthropology for the classroom and the general public. She has been asked to edit readers on psychological anthropology and comparative religion and has completed the writing stage for two books on symbols: *Symbols and Meaning* and *Sport as Symbol: Images of the Athlete in Art, Literature and Song.* Her book on symbols for the public will be called *Gods, Heroes, and Demons: The Importance of Symbols in Everyday Life.*

Being Human

1

We the People

In this chapter . . .

What is a human being?

As members of human groups, we define ourselves with reference to the environment, to other animals, and to outsiders. Anthropologists try to discern the social and cultural issues that underlie the great diversity and startling similarities of people in many parts of the world. Invariably, what we are is contrasted with what we are not. Humans are distinct from other animals in their ability to use tools, to communicate abstract concepts through language, and to generate and use symbols.

Culture, biology, and world view

Culture is knowledge acquired through learning, whereas biology can be either innate or shaped by the environment. In the process of learning our culture, we acquire a world view that universally appears to be organized around distinguishing between "us" and "them." Anthropologists have questioned whether the ordering of the world into binary oppositions is innate or acquired in the process of socialization. They have also questioned whether gender may play a role in world view.

Defining "Us" and "Them"

The Tiwi of Australia illustrate the way in which groups distinguish insiders from outsiders through naming customs, kinship, and use of symbols, including totems and creation myths. Among the Tiwi, territorial rights are reinforced by creation myths that link the Tiwi to ancestral wells and by beliefs that emphasize the bond between father and child as well as between living people and their ancestors.

Colonialism and the erosion of cultural boundaries

Though Europeans did not invent colonialism, which involves the subjugation of one group of people by another, the era of European colonialism obliterated many traditional cultures, changed the political map of the world, and laid the groundwork for many of the conflicts facing the world today. Cultural boundaries are also being eroded by the emergence of a global economy and technological developments in transportation and communication. The merging of world cultures presents new problems and new opportunities for learning what it means to be human.

W hat is a human being? That question has occupied thinkers of many cultures. Indeed, it is the essential question underlying the field of anthropology. Western philosophers and scientists have often addressed the issue by trying to determine what makes human beings different from other animals. The species name *Homo sapiens* identifies human beings as "thinkers" or "knowers," a concept that has some validity since the cerebral cortex, the locus of associative reasoning, is larger and more complex in humans than in any other animal.

For centuries, Western theologians speculated about whether humans are unique among animals in having a soul, or animating spirit, that transcends the material world and links them with God and angels. Some people still wonder whether there is a place for animals in heaven. The idea that only human beings have souls establishes an essential opposition between semidivine humans and an Other, which includes everything that is not human.

Anthropology is by definition the study of human beings, and anthropologists have long sought to determine what might distinguish human beings from their closest relatives on the classificatory scale: apes and monkeys. It was once thought that only humans use tools, but physical anthropologists have learned that chimpanzees use crumpled leaves to soak up water to drink and use sticks to capture termites to eat. A number of other animals also use tools. For example, sea otters use rocks to break open abalone shells so they can eat the tender flesh inside.

Language is another characteristic that has been singled out as a distinctly human trait. Animals communicate with each other through various means, including visual signals and body language, odors, and sound. However, they are unable to communicate with each other about complex and abstract concepts or objects that are remote in time and space. For example, your dog can indicate that it wants to be fed by barking and leading you to its dish, but it cannot tell you what kind of food to get at the store.

On the other hand, humans regularly communicate about complex and abstract concepts, such as those represented in the sentence "When I grow up, I want to be a doctor so I can help people." Only three words in that sentence refer to physical objects—*I, doctor,* and *people*—but even those words cannot be understood unless the listener is familiar with the abstract concepts that make up their attributes. For example, the listener must know that a doctor is someone who treats illness and that the speaker can become a doctor through education. Among humans, even a very young child can communicate such abstract information as "I want breakfast," a formulation that is beyond the capacity of any other animal.

It has been suggested that humans differ from other animals in the ability to generate and use **symbols,** which are behavior, images, or words that express ideas too complex to be stated directly. For example, the American flag stands for a wide range of concepts, including such values as democratic ideals, national solidarity, and the duties of citizenship. The flag is a badge of identity for American embassies in other countries and for American ships sailing in international waters. It is also a symbol of pride on formal occasions, as when American athletes march behind the flag during opening ceremonies for the Olympics.

The ability of human beings to use symbols is due to the development of the cerebral cortex, the part of the brain where associative thinking, including analytical reasoning and creativity, takes place. The cerebral cortex also includes the parts of the brain that govern tool use and language. The area associated with hand coordination, which is involved in tool use, is about three times larger in humans than in apes, and the differences in the areas associated with language are even greater.

Still, the dissimilarity between humans and other animals can best be understood in terms of a continuum rather than as an opposition. Humans share the attributes of a spinal column and central nervous system with other vertebrates. Like other mammals, we are warm blooded, produce live young rather than eggs, and provide nourishment for our young with secretions from mammary glands. Human blood types and chromosome structure are remarkably similar to those of chimpanzees, and humans share with those near relatives a reliance on social relationships for key aspects of survival, such as defense, finding food, and caring for offspring.

In view of such similarities between humans and other animals, why do people emphasize the differences by framing them in the form of oppositions? Let's extend the question further. Why do people—as individuals and as members of groups—view themselves as being in opposition to all other people? Why do humans organize the world into the conceptual categories of "we" and "they"?

THE WE–THEY DICHOTOMY

The concept of self as a definite "we" in opposition to a vaguely defined "they" appears to be pervasive. People who live on the northern coast of Alaska call themselves the *Inupiat,* meaning the "real people," and thus distinguish themselves from the *Tannik,* or "white people," who come to the area for visits but do not have a real commitment to the community (Chance 1966:100–101). Ironically, the word *Eskimo,* as the Inupiat are often called, was never used by the people to describe themselves. *Eskimo* is derived from a term used by their culturally distinct neighbors, the Athapaskans, and means "he who eats it raw."

Anthropologists now prefer to address indigenous people by the terms they use to describe themselves. For example, *Inupiat* refers to the people of northern and northwestern Alaska. Linguistically, the people living in the extreme far north of North America belong to two groups: the Aleuts, who live on the western part of the Alaskan peninsula and the Aleutian Islands, and the Inuits, all those peoples of the far north from Alaska to eastern Canada.

Most people make a linguistic distinction between themselves and others. Japanese refer to visitors from other countries as *gaijin,* or "outsiders." Aborigines living on the Melville and Bathurst islands off the northern coast of Australia refer to themselves as Tiwi, which means "people" in the sense of "the chosen people," as distinct from everyone else. Isolated from the Australian mainland, the Tiwi consider that dimly visible coastline as the place where Tiwi souls go after death. Outsiders "were not Tiwi and hence not real people, or at least not human enough to share the islands with the chosen people who owned them" (Hart, Pilling, and Goodale 1988:12).

Because people are dependent on their physical surroundings for food and protection, human groups tend to identify themselves with their environment even before acknowledging their relationship to outsiders. Colin Turnbull studied two very different groups of people in Africa: the Mbuti and the Ik. The Mbuti foraged for food in a rain forest where plant and animal life were abundant; the Ik hunted for game animals in the rugged mountains of northern Uganda. Both saw themselves as intimately linked to the environment, as Turnbull writes:

> In such a fluid society of hunters the environment invariably provides the central theme that holds them together, that gives them a sense of common identity; it is the hub around which their life revolves. . . . Just as the Mbuti Pygmies in their lush tropical rain forest regard the forest as a benevolent deity, so do the Ik, in their rocky mountain stronghold, think of the mountains as being peculiarly and specially theirs. People and mountains belong to each other and are inseparable. . . . The Ik, without their mountains, would no longer be the Ik and similarly, they say, the mountains without the Ik would no longer be the same mountains, if indeed they continued to exist at all. (1972:29)

The earth, on which we all depend, is often associated with human life. In the biblical book of Genesis, it is written: "And the Lord God formed man of the dust of the ground, and breathed into his nostrils the breath of life; and man became a living soul" (Gen. 2:7). People who live in agricultural societies often express a reverence for the land, imbuing it with personality and human emotions or with generative powers. The *Book of Songs,* Chinese poetry composed between 1000 and 600 B.C., includes hymns of gratitude to the Earth Spirit for a bountiful harvest:

The bows and arrows wielded by these !Kung hunters are constructed on sound technological principles that allow the men to bring down large game. The !Kung "tool kit" also includes sophisticated knowledge of animal habits, which aids them in tracking their prey.

> With our bullocks for sacrifice, and our sheep
> We come to honour the Earth Spirit, to honour
>   the quarters.
> For our fields have all done well. (Waley 1960:170)

People may also identify themselves with the animals or physical features that provide them with their livelihood. Various groups of Netsilik, Inuits who live within the Arctic Circle in the northern part of Canada, refer to themselves as the People of the Seal, the People of the Whale, or the People of the River (Balikci 1970).

The Nuer, herders in Sudan, Africa, are dependent on their cattle for a variety of needs, using virtually every part of the animal, from its horns to its milk. A man is known by the size and quality of his herd and takes one of his names from a description of one of his important animals. For example, the man's name Luerial refers both to the pattern of a cow's markings and to the tassel with which the man has decorated the cow. Young men compose songs, such as the following, for special members of their herds:

> White ox good is my mother
> And we the people of my sister,
> The people of Nyariau Bul. (Evans-Pritchard 1940:47)

Human beings are dependent on the environment—and on the plants and animals that share it—for their very existence. It is not surprising that this dependency is expressed in the way people identify themselves. Often included in this definition of self is the distinction between "us" and "them," those other people with whom we come into contact and who may be either allies or enemies, competing with us for status and resources.

The Culturally Defined Self

Children learn to identify themselves as members of groups in the process of socialization. **Socialization** is the process of transmitting culture from one generation to the next. Children are socialized by their parents and other adults, peers, and social institutions such as schools and churches.

Even before a child is born, its parents begin to prepare its social environment. In the United States, it is considered desirable for a newborn to have its own room, a custom that emphasizes the distance between the child and its parents. The room will be decorated in designs and colors that reflect the age and gender of the child—as well as the economic status of its parents. Athletic figures, trucks and automobiles, and the color blue are considered appropriate for boys. Ballerinas and the color pink are considered suitable for girls. Similarly, names are chosen on the basis of gender.

Names reflect both the unique identity of the individual and its place in a tradition of family and society. In the case of the Murngin of Australia, giving a child the name of its father's ancestor defines its place in the continuous line of generations. Among the Tiwi, a child's father or the man currently married to its mother gives the child a personal name a few weeks after its birth. This name is not permanent, and if the child's father dies and its mother remarries, it will be given a new name by its mother's new husband. Since their husbands are usually older than they are, most women are widowed several times. Consequently, a child might be known by a succession of names. Ultimately, an individual becomes known by whatever name is used when he or she first emerges

into tribal prominence (Hart et al. 1988). Thus, a name or one's individual identity may be subject to change, depending on the social context at any given time.

In American culture, upon marriage a woman traditionally changed her family name to that of her new husband. Her unmarried surname emphasized her relationship to her father; her married surname emphasized her relationship to her husband. The fact that a woman's name changed upon marriage, whereas a man's did not, indicates that her social status was dependent upon her relationship to males, whereas a man's social status was independent of his relationship to females.

Naming customs and other practices aimed at defining the relationship of the individual to the social group are determined by culture. According to the definition developed by E. B. Tylor in 1871, when anthropology was developing as a field of study, **culture** is "that complex whole which includes knowledge, belief, art, law, morals, custom and any other capabilities and habits acquired by man as a member of society." A **society** is a group of people occupying a territory and sharing a language and culture. Anthropologists also speak of **social structure,** the formal organization of group living, including politics, economics, kinship, and religion.

The concept of culture has evolved somewhat since it was first defined by Tylor, but anthropologists still stress the importance of learning in the acquisition of culture. Culture is by definition learned or acquired in the process of socialization; it is not inherent in our biological makeup.

There has been a great deal of confusion over this aspect of human behavior, in part because the concepts of culture and biology have not always been clearly defined or appropriately applied, but also because it is difficult to locate or measure the basis of human behavior. Typically, in fact, human behavior is too complex to be traced to one clearly identifiable cause.

Biology and Culture

It is a bias in American culture to assume that biology is innate and unchanging, whereas learned or cultural characteristics are mutable. However, the relationship is not so clear as all that. Biological characteristics can be either innate or shaped by environmental influences, and behavior shaped by culture is not so readily discarded as one might imagine.

Innate biological characteristics are those that are genetically encoded on DNA, the molecular basis of heredity, and include such physical attributes as eye and hair color, number of eyes and limbs, and the function of the circulatory system. Environmental influences, such as nutrition (before and after birth) and disease, can have a major impact on our biological makeup. Some obvious examples are weight gain or loss and cancer induced by smoking or exposure to the sun. And, though we tend to think of such innate characteristics as number of eyes and limbs as fixed, they too can change, as victims of automobile accidents and other disasters can attest.

Many environmental factors affecting our biology are shaped by culture. In the examples just given, smoking, acquiring a tan, and riding in a car are all cultural practices. Some cultural influences result from socialization, learning of culture through association with other people and exposure to cultural artifacts, which include everything from toothpicks to computers to cathedrals.

Even this model is not entirely neat, however. For example, taking an aspirin for a headache is both biological and cultural. Acetylsalicylic acid, the active ingredient in aspirin, acts biologically to counteract pain. However, identifying acetylsalicylic acid as a pain reliever, combining it with other substances and forming it into pills, packing the pills into bottles and then inside cardboard boxes, advertising the efficacy of aspirin in media, and taking an aspirin with a glass of water are all the result of culture. In fact, the production and transportation of aspirin are part of a much larger social and cultural context, involving medical institutions, government regulations, the marketplace, and transportation technology. Even the interpretation of pain is culturally shaped; only the circulation of acetylsalicylic acid through the bloodstream is biological.

Culture and World View

Culture shapes the way people interpret their experiences and define appropriate behavior. Anthropologists agree that cultural beliefs and values are organized according to a generally coherent world view, though there is disagreement on how consistent that world view is for all members of a particular society. One's **world view** is the culturally shaped way one sees and interprets the world. A child does not see the world in precisely the same way as an adult, and a religious specialist may not have the same view of the world as an economist. However, they are likely to share a language used to describe the world and to define their experience of the world as being similar. For example, both the religious leader and the economist may agree on the importance of being ethical, but they may not agree on what constitutes ethics.

Our world view includes implicit assumptions about the nature of the universe, and these assumptions shape our view of the natural and moral order. This view results from our socialization into a particular culture. For example, most people in the United States hold religious views developed in the Judeo-Christian tradition, so they are likely to agree that it is appropriate to speak of "God the Father." Furthermore, they are likely to share an image of this fatherly figure as having a long, flowing beard and floating on a cloud surrounded by angels, because many European artists have depicted God this way. It would be difficult for a person growing up in this tradition to have an image of God as a woman with fangs, wearing a necklace of human skulls. Yet millions of Hindus see God in precisely this way—as Kali, the demon slayer and destroyer of egocentric action. For Hindus, Kali is only one of many possible manifestations of divinity. The reasons for these differences in this aspect of world view will be discussed in Chapter 9.

Our world view necessarily limits, and is limited by, our experiences. An Inupiat woman tells the story of a mouse who one day decided to venture out of his hole and take a look at the rest of the world:

> When he stood up on his hind legs, lo and behold, to his surprise, he was able to reach the heavens! When he reached down, he felt the ground. When he reached in all directions, he was able to touch the limits of the world! He concluded that he was the largest person on the face of the earth. In reality, the poor mouse had surfaced from his hole in the ground into an old Inupiat boot sole turned upside down! (Chance 1990:13)

The mouse never realized that his heaven was the inside of an Inupiat boot. Similarly, our world view defines our perception of what options are available to us. It is as significant in shaping our behavior and appears as self-evident to us as our physical environment does. Just as it would never occur to us to try to walk through a wall or to enter a room that did not exist, we could not experience a conceptual reality that does not exist for us. The mouse will never explore the world outside the Inupiat boot and, unless something happens to change or challenge our world view, we will never venture beyond our perception of what constitutes the "real world."

DISCUSSIONS

What Is an Asian?

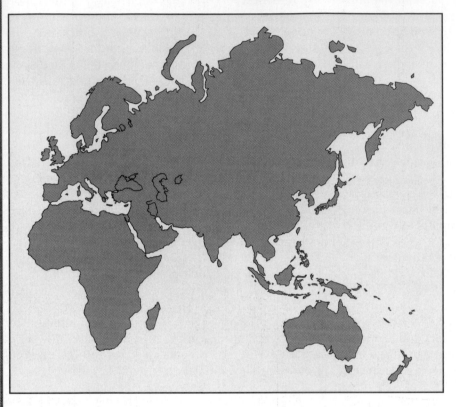

Can you trace Asia on this map? Asia is a "continent," a term that has traditionally referred to a large land mass surrounded by water. In fact, Asia shares its land mass with Europe and includes a number of islands that reach far out into the Pacific Ocean.

Who is the real we? And who is the real they? Our conceptual categories are probably less dependent on some external reality than on the meaning the reality has for us. For example, most of us take for granted the truth of the statement "Asia is a continent." Yet this statement contradicts the physical evidence. We can demonstrate the relationship of conceptual categories to physical phenomena by the following process. First, let us present a logical argument:

A. A continent is a large land mass or mainland.

B. Asia is a continent.

C. Asia is a large land mass or mainland.

This is a logical statement, but is it accurate? Pick out Asia on a map or globe, or see the map above. Now trace the boundaries of Asia with your finger. Are you sure you know where Asia ends and Europe begins? In fact, Asia and Europe together are a solidly joined land mass. Today, the dividing line between the two is usually placed at the Ural Mountains of Russia, but

For example, though our bodies are dependent on the consumption of nutrients, our world view determines what we consider to be food. People in some parts of the world classify as food animals that most North Americans consider pets. Guinea pigs are eaten in Peru, and dogs are eaten in some parts of Asia. In the United States, snails are killed to prevent them from eating garden plants; in France, snails are carefully fed on cornmeal and herbs, then cooked in garlic and butter, before being served as *escargots*. The same genus of snails that is eaten as a delicacy in France is killed as an intruder in California.

World views include implicit value judgments about what the physical and social worlds should be like. And,

in the Middle Ages, Europeans considered what we now call the Middle East to be part of Asia.

Russia is considered to be a European country even though most of its land mass is on the Asian side of the Urals. There is some justification for considering Russia a part of Europe, because Moscow, its capital, is west of the Urals. However, the designation is apt more because of historical and cultural ties between Russia and other parts of Europe. India is considered part of Asia, even though the languages of India are related to those of Europe rather than to those of Asia.

Now trace the boundaries of the eastern part of Asia. Much of what we have called a continent is in fact a number of island groups. Is Japan a part of Asia? Yes, but it is not part of the mainland. Is Indonesia? Is Australia? Is New Guinea? The United Nations classifies Indonesia as an Asian country and Australia as a distinct continent, but New Guinea poses a special problem. The western part of the island is under the control of Indonesia and thus is part of Asia, whereas the eastern part is independent (Papua New Guinea) and is considered part of Melanesia, a conceptual category designating a region of the Pacific inhabited by dark-skinned people.

Melanesia is a Pacific island group northeast of Australia and south of Micronesia, which in turn consists of islands of the West Pacific east of the Philippines and west of Polynesia. Polynesia is comprised of islands of the Central and South Pacific. Note that these islands were independent entities prior to the arrival of Europeans, though some were linked culturally, economically, and linguistically. The classification of island groups and the designation of regions of the Pacific—as well as the designation "Asia"—is a European construct.

After examining Asia on the map, do you still agree that it is a continent? In fact, it is a convention to consider Asia a continent despite evidence to the contrary, and this convention is rooted in historical circumstance. Both "Asia" and "continent" are concepts developed by Europeans to explain their experience of the world. Both terms date from the sixteenth century, when Europeans had begun their outward expansion into the world around them but had not yet charted its dimensions. Europeans used the terms to distinguish themselves from a vaguely known group of people who lived to the east of them. Because the "others" were "easterners" from the European perspective, these people came to be known as "Orientals."

It is unlikely that people from "Asia" ever thought of themselves as "Asian" until this century, after extensive exposure to European concepts. Because Americans inherited many concepts from Europeans, some people still refer to Asians as "Orientals," even though Americans must journey west to reach Asia, and the United States is geographically to the east of that "continent."

Many Asian Americans object to the term *Oriental* because it is inaccurate and typically is used to emphasize their "otherness." Obviously, "Asians" do not live east of themselves; therefore, to describe themselves as "easterners" is to validate as authentic the European perspective on themselves. To "Asians," Europeans are the "other." Asians now generally agree to the designation of Asia as a continent because it is accepted as such by the international community. However, the concept runs counter to Asians' experience of themselves as distinct and autonomous groups of people, in some cases having a history of fierce regional hostilities. Koreans do not consider themselves to be like Japanese, and Japanese do not identify themselves with Indonesians. Thus, Asians have adopted some Western conceptual categories to describe themselves even though they know themselves to be far more diverse culturally, historically, and ethnically than such categories would imply.

because world views are cultural products, they must be learned. In the process of learning our culture, we acquire values that define our own way of life as being the only or best way of life. When our parents teach us about food and the appropriate way in which to consume it, they do not give us options. If a small child growing up in the United States were to pick up an insect and try to eat it, the child's caretaker would immediately take steps to stop it. "No! Bad!" the caretaker would say, snatching the insect away from the child, while making sounds and grimaces of disgust. Yet that insect might be considered a delicacy in another culture. The insect isn't intrinsically "bad"; it is just culturally inappropriate as food in American society.

This nineteenth-century drawing shows the goddess Durga in two forms. On the left, as the demon-slayer Chandi, she advances on the demon forces in the form of a beautiful woman mounted on a lion. Standing between Chandi and the demons is Kali, Durga's more horrific form. In Hindu iconography it is conventional to portray female energy as active.

Through the process of socialization, we learn not only how to behave but also that not to behave in this way is "bad." Thus, we learn to be *ethnocentric*, to believe that our own culture is the best. Franz Boas, often called the father of American anthropology, put it this way: "It is sometimes difficult for us to recognize that the value which we attribute to our own civilization is due to the fact that we participate in this civilization and that it has been controlling all our actions from the time of our birth" (cited in Hays 1958:268 [1943]).

Bringing Order out of Chaos

Our world view is always much simpler than the "real world" which, without some form of conceptual organization, would strike us as being confused, disorderly, and "out of control." Mary Douglas suggests that it is part of human nature to attempt to impose order on a potentially chaotic universe: "Most of us indeed would feel safer if our experience could be hard-set and fixed in form. . . . It is part of our human condition to long for hard lines and clear concepts" (1966:162). Ironically, social life is seldom orderly, so the quest for order or "purity" invariably leads to new dilemmas: "The final paradox of the search for purity is that it is an attempt to force experience into logical categories of non-contradiction. But experience is not amenable and

those who make the attempt find themselves led into contradiction" (1966:162).

The French anthropologist Claude Lévi-Strauss suggests that people impose order on their experience by organizing their social and conceptual worlds into **binary oppositions**, or contrasting pairs. Such binary oppositions as up/down, male/female, nature/culture, sun/moon, father/mother, and young/old seem to be so self-evident that we assume they are part of the natural order. Yet, although there may be an affinity between these paired concepts, in most cases they are not opposites in any sense but conceptually.

For example, the sun is not opposite to the moon except by association. Both are celestial bodies when viewed from the perspective of the earth, but the sun is a flaming body at the center of our solar system, whereas the moon is a land mass that revolves around the earth. However, both appear to us as singular objects that take turns dominating the sky. They are conceptual opposites to us because the sun is associated with the day and the moon with the night.

Note that day and night are also organized as oppositions, even though each fades into the other during the periods of sunrise and sunset, which together make up several hours of the twenty-four-hour "day." Note also that we identify the twenty-four-hour period as a "day" even though a significant portion of it is

FIGURE 1.1
Binary Oppositions

The Chinese yin/yang symbol represents an ordering of the universe into binary oppositions such as masculine/feminine, light/dark, active/passive, positive/negative, and earth/heaven.

made up of "night," "dawn," and "twilight." We distinguish between night and day because organizing time into opposites reflects categories that are significant to us (see Figure 1.1). Similarly, the conceptual categories "man" and "woman," which we view as opposites, have traditionally been subsumed into the designation "man" when human beings are contrasted with other aspects of our experience such as "God" or animals. This designation reflects a world view in which "man" is assigned the significant or dominant category, the category against which "woman" is implicitly compared.

A number of scholars consider the binary opposition between "us" and "them" to be intrinsic to the experience of being human, though they differ on whether this is innate or learned. The philosopher George Herbert Mead suggested that individuals develop a sense of self through interacting with others, especially in taking on the role of others with reference to oneself. In this process of social negotiation and definition, a child comes to perceive himself as an objectified Self: "Such is the process by which a personality arises" (1934:160). Building on Mead's work, Robert Redfield (1952; 1953) asserted that the distinction between self and other is the basis for world views universally. Since the "self" is the vantage point from which the "world" is observed, our world view is never objective because its primary reference point is ourselves. Michael Kearney refines this concept:

The first requirement for a world view is the presence of a *Self*—discernibly distinct from its environment, which I refer to as the *Other*. . . . Upon analyzing the notion of the Self, we can see that it consists of two aspects. One is the "awareness" of Self as distinct from surroundings; the second is the notion of relationship between Self and surroundings. (1984:68)

Binary oppositions promote a sense of order where order may not actually exist, and they emphasize the solidarity of the in-group. Douglas notes that defining who we are as a group provides a symbol of unity: "The idea of society is a powerful image. It is potent in its own right to control or to stir men to action. This image has form; it has external boundaries, margins, internal structure. Its outlines contain power to reward conformity and repulse attack" (1966:114)

Do Women Think in Binary Oppositions?

Lévi-Strauss believes that binary oppositions reflect the deep structure of the human mind, the thought processes that determine the organization of human concepts. However, not everyone agrees that human thought is necessarily dualistic. Some scholars argue that dualism is a male form of organization that grows out of the socialization process. This view suggests that **gender,** male and female social roles, may shape the way people see the world.

Nancy Chodorow (1974) notes that the pattern of parenting in which the mother is the primary caretaker of children, while the father assumes responsibility for activities outside the home, results in a different process of self-identity for girls than for boys. Because girls are expected to model themselves after their mothers, they are provided with a role model that is continuous throughout their lives. Boys, on the other hand, identify with their mothers early in life but must later reject femininity to adhere to masculine role models. Thus, Chodorow says, the development of the masculine self-concept is based on rejection of the feminine, whereas the feminine self-concept is characterized by "embeddedness," a sense of continuity between herself and others. As a result of the differing socialization processes, a woman's ego boundaries are flexible, allowing her to nurture others. A man's ego boundaries are rigid because he has been forced to reject others to develop a distinct masculine identity.

Susan Pollak and Carol Gilligan conducted a study of gender differences in the way U.S. college students

The We–They Dichotomy

The distinction between "us" and "them" must be learned. Through the process of socialization, we learn how to distinguish between ourselves and others. Our place in a social network is defined in part by the process of acquiring a name. Our family name signifies rights and responsibilities acquired as part of a kin group. Our individual name distinguishes us from all other members of that kin group. Our name also signifies gender, indicating the importance of separating male and female roles.

Along with our social identity, we acquire a world view that shapes our experience of the natural, social, and moral order. We learn to divide the plant world into such categories as "tree," "flower," "grass," and "vegetable." We divide the animal world into "wild" and "domesticated." We

may further divide "domesticated" animals into the categories of "pets" and "potential food." These categories are not inherent in the nature of plants and animals, and people in other societies may sort them into different categories. For example, the French put snails into the "potential food" category, whereas people in the United States typically classify them as "garden pests." People of Peru classify guinea pigs both as "pets" and "potential food." People who live in cities may classify "bunny rabbits" as "pets," whereas farmers view "rabbits" as either "potential food" or "pests."

Our world view allows us to impose order onto a potentially chaotic experience, and part of that world view involves establishing a social identity that allows us to distinguish members

of our own group from outsiders. Distinguishing ourselves from outsiders can include several dimensions:

Language allows us to designate ourselves as the true people, in contrast to all other humans on the earth.

Kinship defines our affiliation as part of a descent group and allies us with others through marriage.

Names reflect our place with respect to others, as individuals and as members of kin groups.

Creation myths assert our rights to territory and affirm the value of our customs.

Insignia—such as totems, clan plaids, and gang "colors"—visually assert our membership in a particular group.

describe violence in pictures on the Thematic Apperception Test. The test is administered by showing subjects a series of ambiguous pictures and asking subjects to make up stories about the pictures. The stories are then analyzed to detect recurrent or unusual themes and for what they reveal about underlying assumptions and attitudes. Gilligan reports that men were more likely to write violence into scenes depicting intimacy, whereas women wove violence into stories about achievement:

> The danger men describe in their stories of intimacy is a danger of entrapment or betrayal, being caught in a smothering relationship or humiliated by rejection and deceit. In contrast, the danger women portray in their tales of achievement is a danger of isolation, a fear that in standing out or being set apart by success, they will be left alone. (1982:42)

This research supports the idea that the male definition of self is based on a rejection of the other, whereas the

female view of self includes the other. Thus, the women feared achievement because they associated it with being severed from the other.

In her analysis of Chinese life crisis rituals, Emily Martin (1988) suggests that the male world view demonstrates "constant efforts to separate opposites," whereas female ideology emphasizes the "unity of opposites." In other words, men think in binary oppositions, but women do not. However, Martin acknowledges that her information is incomplete, and some of her data may be interpreted as expressing either separation or unification of opposites. For example, she notes that men view marriage in terms of its potential for "a glorious addition to the social strength of the descent group," whereas women mourn their enforced separation from their own family and equate the transition with death. Women also make symbolic associations between birth, marriage, and funeral rituals.

The difference between male and female views of marriage may also be explained by differences in their social roles. The Chinese are **patrilineal,** which means that descent is traced through the male line. They are also **patrilocal,** which means that a woman leaves her natal family when she gets married, moving to her husband's household. Thus, a woman's experience of marriage is different from that of her husband. For a woman, marriage literally represents the end of all that is familiar to her; thus, it is not surprising that she would both mourn the loss and symbolically equate it with death.

For men in a patrilineal society, marriage does not represent a break with their close relatives; in fact, it reinforces their position within the family. One of a woman's primary responsibilities in marriage is to produce children so that her husband's kin group can continue. Since only women produce children, it is only through marriage that a man can fulfill one of his primary responsibilities, ensuring the perpetuation of his patrilineal line. Therefore, it is not surprising that Chinese men emphasize the formal public structure of the male descent group, whereas women are more concerned with the dramatic transitions of birth, marriage, and death that mark their lives.

Beyond Binary Oppositions

Significantly, though some scholars dispute the universality of binary oppositions, they have not challenged the basic assumption that males and females are in some sense opposites. In fact, many differences between men and women are shaped by socialization and enforced by custom, law, and religious beliefs and practices. Much of the "opposition" between males and females is socially constructed. Though in all societies the socialization and life experiences of women and men are different, females and males share more attributes than is often acknowledged. In virtually all societies, girls and boys must both separate from their mothers if they are to establish households of their own, a process that, as Chodorow acknowledges, can be fraught with hazards. And, since humans are social animals, men as well as women must be able to forge bonds with others, as well as establish separate identities.

The complexity of social life requires both females and males to negotiate rights and responsibilities with a number of other people and, in so doing, to establish a culturally appropriate balance between self and other. The context in which this balance is established can vary considerably from one culture to another, depending both on the formal organization of social interaction and on the opportunities for informal trans-

actions that may appear to run counter to publicly affirmed norms. Though binary oppositions are useful for simplifying and ordering an often chaotic and confusing universe, they must not be allowed to obscure the range and complexity of human experience.

Ironically, gender appears to be a significant factor in the organization of world view into binary oppositions among all cultures. Though different cultures vary markedly in what they consider to be feminine or masculine, there appears to be a universal assumption that the universe itself is organized into oppositions of femaleness and maleness (Womack 1993a). For example, people in almost every society believe that the sun and moon are gendered, though they may assign different genders to the two celestial bodies. In Greek mythology, the sun was male and the moon female. In Japan, the sun is female and the moon is male. Among the Maya of Central America, however, both the sun and the moon were male ball players who defeated the underworld gods of sickness and death in a sacred ball game.

Dualistic models of the universe are pervasive whether they result from universal human thought processes or are the product of socialization. Even anthropological theory has been influenced by the construction of binary oppositions. Nineteenth-century thinkers described human societies as being either "civilized" or "savage," a description that is really a refinement of the more basic dichotomy of we and they. The "we" of the European tradition was considered "civilized," whereas "they" were "savage." Although those formulations have been rejected, it is still customary to talk in terms of "Western/non-Western" and "industrial/preindustrial." This formulation obscures the real differences among such "non-Western" and "preindustrialized" people as those of mainland China, a wide variety of African cultures, and Australian Aborigines. Do we really believe that Chinese, Africans, and indigenous Australians are so similar that they can be accurately described by one inclusive term? Or that they would not be offended by such oversimplifications of their diverse and complex experiences? In fact, binary models of human groups are recodifications of the we–they dichotomy.

Defining "Us" and "Them": An Australian Example

Distinguishing "us" from "them" may traditionally have prevented people in competing groups from coming into contact with potential enemies. For example, the aboriginal people who once hunted and gathered over the rugged terrain of Australia established their social identity through an elaborate system of political alliances, kinship, and religion. The largest component of social membership for the Aborigines is the linguistic group, whose members can communicate with each other and who typically share a common history and beliefs about the nature of the physical and spiritual world.

Political allegiance among Australian Aborigines is organized through **clans,** kin groups that trace their relationship to a founding ancestor. In the case of Australians, the ancestor may be a **totem,** an animal or other figure symbolizing the unity of the kin group. The totemic ancestor and the totemic emblem identify the Aborigine with a particular kin group economically, spiritually, and politically. As foragers, the Aborigines are dependent for food on the plants and animals growing naturally around them. This dependency is expressed in religious terms, so that the group recognizes the totemic animal as kin, and members are forbidden to eat it except on special ritual occasions.

Because the Aborigines occupy territory that is unusually arid, their social system and religious beliefs center around water holes or wells, which are believed to be sacred. Clan totems live in the wells, and Aborigines believe their souls join their totemic ancestors there when they die.

A clan occupies a territory centering on a water hole. The group's claim to the land is established by a **creation myth,** a symbolic story describing how the clan came to "own" the territory. For example, among the Murngin, the Gwiyamil clan "owns," in addition to its primary territory, a small river island said to have been created when Garrawark, a legendary fish, dived underground from the well at the center of the clan's territory and, coming up in the river, made the island and awarded it to the Gwiyamil. Because the Gwiyamil "own" the land by "divine decree," it cannot be taken from them in warfare. This shared belief in divinely decreed ownership discourages neighboring groups from acquiring territory through aggression.

Belief systems of Australian Aborigines also emphasize continuity between generations. It is thought that a woman cannot conceive a child unless the father of the child "dreams" that the spirit of one of his ancestors has entered the woman's womb. The spirit enters her womb when she bathes or gets water from the ancestral well. W. Lloyd Warner reports a typical dream told to him by a Murngin man:

> I had a nice dream the other night. I dreamed that a boy child walked past all the other humpies [Australian white term for native huts] in the camp and kept coming until he got to my house. He beat on the bark wall. He called out, "Father! Father! Where are you?"
> "Here I am."
> "Where is mother?"
> I told him and wakened up.

The man interpreted his dream as a sign that his wife would become pregnant. He told the anthropologist that he later witnessed the ancestral spirit approaching his wife at the well:

> Yesterday I went fishing with my wife at the creek. I went up one side of the creek and she went up the other. By and by a bream fish came up and took her hook. He came up to it easily and quietly. My wife did not have to pull on the line, for he came in to her like he wanted to. My mielk [woman] was standing in the water only up to her ankles. He came up to her even though she was in the shallow water. Then he stopped quickly, shook himself against her leg, broke the line, and went back into the deep water. We did not see him again. I came across to her; I said, "What was that?" She said, "A bream fish." I said, "What did he do?" She told me. She said, "My father went fishing like this when my little brother was born; I think this fish shook against my leg for that." I said, "Oh you know that." "Yes." "You remember my dream I told you about?" She said, "Yes, that's what I think. I won't menstruate any longer now because that baby fish is inside me." (1969:21–22)

A child is named for the ancestor whose spirit is believed to have entered its mother's womb. In the past, anthropologists have viewed such stories as evidence that Aborigines did not understand the biological basis for conception. However, Jane Goodale (1971) discovered that Tiwi women of Australia are quite sophisticated in their knowledge about conception and childbirth. Beliefs about the importance of the father's dream and the involvement of the totemic ancestor emphasize both the relationship of father to child and the relationship of future generations to past generations.

Clan members are linked with other clans through marriage, so they may share in a political alliance that transcends the local group. For example, Warner writes of the Murngin:

> The clans are of basic importance. They are the largest units of solidarity, and open conflict never occurs within them, as it would not between a man's clan and his wife's and mother's clan. It is through his clan that a man establishes his totemic relations and identifies himself with

This man and woman of Arnhem Land in Australia are digging honey from a tree. Like the Tiwi, they are foragers, and their foraging rights to land are based on membership in a kin group that traces its descent from a totemic ancestor.

the sacred world by virtue of a mystical experience of his father. (1969:5)

Because of the elaborate system of clans, totems, and naming of generations, it is possible to quickly distinguish oneself from one's enemy even in a brief encounter.

Traditional peoples of Britain were also organized into clans identified with totemic animals. Roman soldiers who invaded the islands at the time of Julius Caesar were horrified to meet armed opponents robed in bear skins or wearing helmets adorned with the tusks of pigs. Both of these animals appear to have been totems of Scottish, Welsh, and Irish clans. We can trace the emblems of clan membership through names such as O'Sullivan and MacKenzie and through the various patterns of Scottish plaids. Traditionally, only members of the clan that "owned" a particular plaid had the right to wear it.

Similarly, members of gangs in U.S. cities use "colors" and distinctive styles of dress to distinguish friends from enemies. And just as Australian Aborigines and early Britons saw clan membership as conferring rights to a particular territory, gangs see themselves as guarding their "hood," or territory.

When a clear distinction between we and they defines the identity of groups physically isolated from each other, as were the Netsilik, the Tiwi, and the Murngin, it can be adaptive, because it separates the ingroup from outsiders who may cause harm or compete for environmental resources. Dividing the in-group from the out-group is more problematic when people

of different cultures live in the same neighborhood and interact with each other while going about their daily routines. Then the mechanisms that maintain boundaries between groups become a source of conflict and misunderstanding. As geographic isolation breaks down from a variety of causes, distinguishing us from them territorially may become a relic of the past.

The Erosion of Cultural Boundaries

Throughout history and prehistory, trade brought people of different cultures together for brief periods of time. As cities developed in areas such as Mesopotamia, Egypt, India, and China, trade and conquest made products of many cultures available to people in cosmopolitan centers. For example, Darius, Persian ruler from 521 to 486 B.C., governed an empire that included virtually all the Middle East and extended into southern Europe and parts of India. When he built his castle in the capital city of Susa, Darius wrote that he had assembled artisans and materials from all parts of his realm and beyond:

From afar its ornamentation was brought. . . . The cedar timber was brought from a mountain named Lebanon; the Assyrians brought it to Babylon, and from Babylon the Carians and Ionians brought it to Susa. Teakwood was brought from Gandara and from Carmania. The gold which was used here was brought from Sardis and from Bactria. The stone—lapis lazuli and carnelian—was brought from Sogdiana. . . . The silver and copper were brought from Egypt. The ornamentation with which the wall was adorned was brought from Ionia. The ivory was brought from Ethiopia, from India and from Arachosia. The stone pillars were brought from . . . Elam. The artisans who dressed the stone were Ionians and Sardians. The goldsmiths who wrought the gold were Medes and Egyptians. . . . Those who worked the baked brick [with figures] were Babylonians. The men who adorned the wall were Medes and Egyptians. At Susa here a splendid work was ordered; very splendid did it turn out. (Olmstead 1948:168)

Construction of such an edifice commonly took years, and it is not hard to imagine artisans so long away from their homes attempting to bring with them as many of their familiar comforts as they could carry. In this way, the people of Susa and other such cosmopolitan centers would become accustomed to seeing people of exotic appearance and habits and to hearing languages they could not comprehend.

The most pervasive form of culture contact was **European colonialism,** the military, economic, and religious expansion that began in the late fifteenth century and lasted until early in the twentieth century. Spain claimed most of South America, Central America, and a part of North America and established a foothold in Asia by uniting and colonizing the Philippines. England asserted dominance over much of North America and Africa and all of India and Australia. France carved out territories in North America, Africa, and the Pacific, while Holland established colonies in Africa and what is now Indonesia (see Figure 1.2). Europeans did not invent **colonialism**—the process in which a group captures the territory of another group and subjugates it politically, economically, culturally, and, in many cases, religiously, by establishing colonies—but they practiced it on a larger scale than any other group in history.

European colonialism is generally conceptualized as a case in which wealthy, technologically advanced nations overran poor, unsophisticated groups. One historian rejects this model, arguing instead that "Europe was driven outward not by wealth but by poverty" (Jaffe 1985:43). Though Europe was rich in agricultural resources, it was poor in minerals and other resources needed for industrialization.

As a result of their colonial expansion, Europeans dominated trade in slaves, gold, and plantation products, including sugar and coffee, thus fueling their own economic development. Proceeds from the slave trade and from African gold mines poured into Portuguese treasuries. The English forced China to open its borders to foreign trade, gaining a market for England's own lucrative opium trade and giving the English control over Hong Kong and Singapore. At the height of its power, England, a nation smaller in area than the state of Arkansas, dominated a portion of the world more than three hundred times its size.

That period of cultural upheaval redrew the world's political map and left in its wake newly formed nations that united the destinies of previously antagonistic tribal groups. Many modern conflicts, especially in Africa and Latin America, are the legacy of this period of conquest. Various political, economic, and cultural factors underlie these clashes, but virtually all involve some aspect of **ethnicity,** classification of people into groups based on their biological and cultural heritage.

THE EMERGENCE OF ETHNICITY

The complexities of ethnicity are beautifully summed up in a comment by a student who moved to the United States from Japan: "I didn't know I was Japanese until I came to the United States." As this student's experience illustrates, ethnicity is a concept of belongingness, one that often emerges out of a world-shattering encounter with an Other.

The concept of ethnicity includes biology, culture, and behavior. In general, you cannot "join" an ethnic group, nor can you leave one. And even if you don't define yourself as a member of an ethnic group, you may be defined that way by others, if your appearance or behavior conforms to their concept of ethnic identity. In his classic work *Ethnic Groups and Boundaries*, Frederik Barth identified the following characteristics of an **ethnic group:**

1. It is biologically self-perpetuating.

2. Members of the group share basic cultural values, manifest in overt cultural forms, such as language and customs.

3. Members form a community, interacting with others who share the language, customs, and values.

4. Members identify themselves, and are identified by others, as belonging to the group. ([1969]1998: 10–11)

Ethnic groups typically emerge when politically autonomous groups are subsumed within a nation,

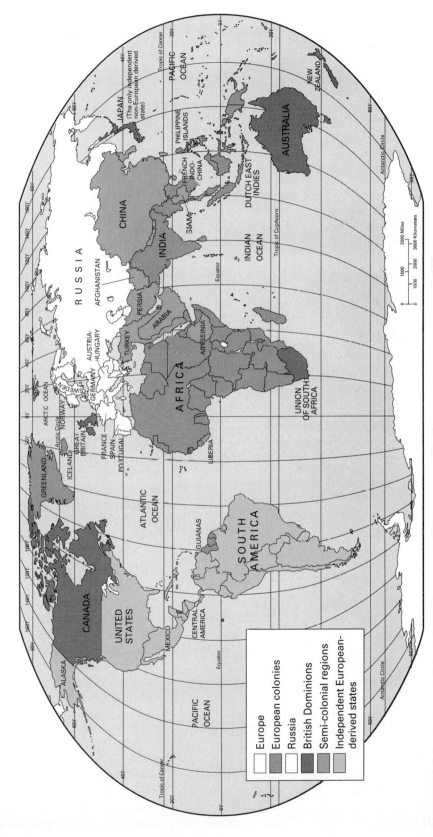

FIGURE 1.2 European Colonial Holdings as of 1910

By early in the twentieth century, a few small countries of western Europe had extended their range of influence or political control throughout the entire world. The modern cultural, economic, and political map is still dominated by five centuries of European colonial expansion.

Legend:
- Europe
- European colonies
- Russia
- British Dominions
- Semi-colonial regions
- Independent European-derived states

An image of U.S. track star Carl Lewis looms over passersby in a Tokyo street. Cities all over the world are becoming more diverse in their populations and cultures as the result of political, economic, and technological changes.

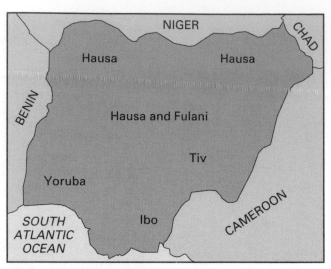

FIGURE 1.3 Ethnic Groups of Nigeria

Formerly autonomous groups, including the Hausa, Fulani, Tiv, Yoruba, and Ibo, are now joined politically in the nation of Nigeria. Ethnic conflicts sometimes emerge as the groups compete for control over national political processes.

usually as the result of conquest or colonialism or as the result of mass migration. **Autonomy** refers to the ability of a group to be self-governing. Native Americans, who had been organized into politically autonomous groups, became members of an ethnic group in the wake of European conquest and colonization of North and South America. All other ethnic groups in the United States, except native Hawaiians, resulted from migration. Ethnic groups have emerged all over the world as the result of similar processes.

The national boundaries of many countries in Africa were shaped by the territorial boundaries of colonial administration districts. For example, Nigeria includes within its territory a number of formerly autonomous groups, including the Ibo, the Hausa, the Yoruba, the Fulani, and the Tiv (see Figure 1.3). Each of these tribal groups has a distinct language and culture and is territorially based. The Hausa and Fulani occupy their traditional lands in the north; the Tiv occupy the central region; and the Ibo and Yoruba live in the south. Because ethnic groups typically emerge through loss of political autonomy, the process can lead to intense conflicts. As Nigeria moved toward independence from Britain, alliances and rivalries among these tribal groups formed the basis for political parties and, at times, fierce regional disputes.

In some cases, a dominant group may take control of the government and use its formidable resources—including the army and national economy—against its former rivals. Ethiopia includes several culturally and linguistically distinct peoples but is dominated by the Amhara of the central highlands (see Figure 1.4). From the mid-1970s, the Ethiopian government used its military, as well as troops imported from Cuba, to suppress ethnically based rebel factions—from Eritreans in the north to Somalis in the east. The extended fighting contributed to widespread hunger and forced migration.

The opposite process resulted in bloody fighting after the breakup of the eastern European nation of Yugoslavia (see Figure 1.5). Regional hostilities kept in check by the strong central Yugoslav government reemerged during a transfer of power from Croats to Serbs. Croatia and Bosnia-Herzegovina voted to dissolve the union, and Serbia, now in control of the country's military apparatus, took advantage of the op-

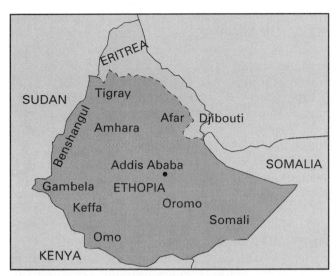

FIGURE 1.4 Ethnic Divisions in Ethiopia

Ethnic conflict in Ethiopia has resulted in periodic violence, famine, and displacement of people from their traditional homelands. Competition between groups is intensified by attempts to gain control over the national political organization, with its power to pass and enforce laws and its access to the economic base of taxation.

portunity to seize territory from the two fledgling states in the name of Serbs residing within their boundaries.

Much fighting centered on disputed geographic boundaries, but hostilities also reflected religious and ethnic differences. Bosnia-Herzegovina has a significant Muslim population, whereas Croatia is predominantly Roman Catholic, and Serbia has a mixed population that is largely Eastern Orthodox. Because of the region's eclectic ethnic and cultural mix, disputes are difficult to resolve.

At first it appeared that only Serbs were engaged in "ethnic cleansing," killing people of other ethnic groups or forcing them to leave their homes and villages. Croats retaliated with their own policies of ethnic cleansing, and finally, Muslims joined in the frenzy. The evolution of ethnic violence eventually pitted former allies and former neighbors against each other.

Ethnic groups may be formed as a result of migration for economic or political reasons. For example, the slave trade from the sixteenth to the nineteenth century transported Africans, who were culturally autonomous in their place of origin, to many parts of the

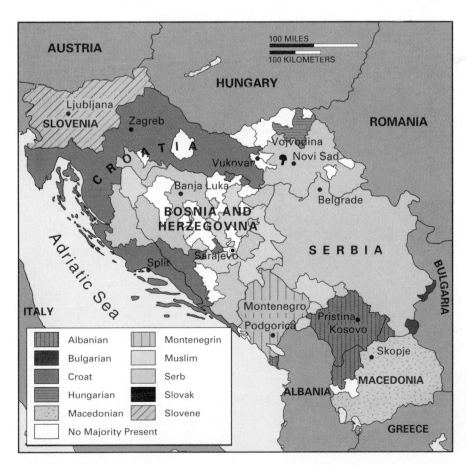

FIGURE 1.5 The Violent Birth of New Nation-States

When the strong central government of Yugoslavia collapsed, the country fragmented into new nation-states, each competing for control of territory and the apparatus of government. Conflict in these new nation-states is an expression of economic and religious competition as well as of ethnic tensions.

Western Hemisphere, including the U.S. South, where they became an ethnic minority.

Southeast Asians, allies of the United States during the Vietnam War, were displaced from their homes in Vietnam, Laos, and Cambodia when American soldiers abruptly left the region at the end of the war in 1975. Many Southeast Asians—formerly refugees—have established ethnic communities in U.S. urban centers. Vietnamese settling in Orange County, near Los Angeles, have built up a business and residential area known as Little Saigon, taking its name from the former capital of South Vietnam.

Fewer than 10 percent of the 191 nations in the world are ethnically homogeneous, and such large-scale merging of the political destinies of previously separate groups has profound implications for human physical and cultural survival. Cultural and political blending is not new; however, the process is accelerating, primarily because of three factors: (1) ethnic conflict in many parts of the world is displacing peoples who have lived in a particular region for cen-

turies; (2) the emergence of a global economy has increased the interdependence of people; and (3) technological developments in transportation and communication have eroded geographic barriers that formerly kept people distinct from each other. Today it is possible to eat a hamburger in a fast-food restaurant in New York City one day and to choose an item from a menu of the same chain in Hong Kong twenty-four hours later.

Although the we–they dichotomy may have prevented conflict in the past by drawing clear boundaries between groups of people, today there is a need for intercultural understanding as territorial borders fall or are readily crossed. It is unrealistic to try to erect rigid boundaries between groups of culturally different people who live in contiguous neighborhoods, shop in the same markets, and attend the same schools. Rather, our survival may depend on transcending cultural differences. The challenge for today is to cherish and protect the traditions of many cultures without erecting barriers to understanding.

SUMMARY

People in all societies address the question "What is a human being?" with reference to the natural resources on which they depend and in terms of their relationship to other animals and to outsiders of the same species. Scholars in Western society have attempted to distinguish human beings from other animals by emphasizing the ability of humans to use tools, language, and symbols. However, the relationship between humans and other animals—especially mammals—should be seen in terms of a continuum rather than as an opposition.

Yet, the definition of "us" as opposed to "them" may be universal in human society. People typically identify more closely with their territory or with the plants and animals they need to survive than with people defined as outsiders. Distinguishing between us and them is learned in the process of socialization into a particular society; the distinction is not biological. In the process of acquiring a social identity, we also acquire a world view that shapes our experience of the natural, social, and moral order. Our world view allows us to impose order onto a potentially chaotic experience. Mary Douglas considers the need for order to be part of human nature. Claude Lévi-Strauss suggests that it is part of the deep structure of the human mind to organize our world into binary

oppositions, contrasting pairs such as up/down and male/female.

Some scholars believe that the opposition between "us" and "them" is based on male socialization. Since both girls and boys are socialized primarily by the mother, the female role model is near and the male role model is remote. Thus, female identity involves a sense of continuity with others, whereas male identity is based on drawing clear boundaries between self and other. Dualism is present even in this model, since it is based on a binary opposition between males and females. The evidence suggests that, even if the tendency to think in binary oppositions is not "hardwired" into the human mind, it is "programmed" into us at a very early age, as part of gender role socialization.

The example of the Tiwi of Australia illustrates their definition of themselves with reference to the land and water holes on which they depend. It also shows how the solidarity of the group is reinforced through various types of kinship: the totemic animal ancestor represents the clan or descent groups; beliefs about the necessity for a man to "dream" his child before his wife can become pregnant asserts the importance of the father–child bond; naming the child after an ancestor stresses the continuity of generations; and marriage links members of different clans, thus creating cooperative networks that extend far beyond local groups.

For the Tiwi, and many other traditional people, the boundaries between "us" and "them" are clearly defined. However, trade, conquest, and the rise of cities have brought together people from many different cultures, eroding cultural boundaries. European colonialism accelerated the process of bringing disparate cultures together, usually with disastrous consequences for the peoples subjugated by the Europeans.

The process of political merging begun by colonialism is accelerating as ethnic conflict displaces indigenous people in many parts of the world, a global economy emerges, and technological advances in communication and transportation become widespread. As the boundaries fall between formerly separate groups of people, the concept of "we" and "they" is continually being redefined, and the survival of human beings may well depend on the ability of "us" to live in harmony with "them."

POWER WORDS

In any enterprise—from playing a computer game to mastering an academic discipline—it is essential to acquire the appropriate "power" objects: tools or knowledge that allow one to progress to the next level. In anthropology, the power objects are words and concepts. And just as one must not only recognize but also know how to use power objects properly, in anthropology one must not only memorize words and their meanings but also know when and how it is appropriate to use them. After reading this chapter, you should have acquired the following power words:

anthropology	creation myth	gender	society
autonomy	culture	patrilineal	symbols
binary opposition	ethnic group	patrilocal	totem
clan	ethnicity	socialization	world view
colonialism	European colonialism	social structure	

INTERNET EXERCISE

1. Find out what's new with Australian Aborigines, as reported by the Australian Institute of Aboriginal and Torres Straits Island on their website at **http://www.aiatsis.gov/index.htm**. Briefly describe current issues facing these Aborigines.

2. The U.S. Library of Congress, Federal Research Division, maintains websites specifically for studies of particular countries. The site for a profile of Yugoslavia is **http://lcweb2.loc.gov/fra/cs/yutoc.html**. Go to this site and compare what the U.S. government now considers to be Yugoslavia with the map in this chapter that includes Croatia and Bosnia/Herzegovina.

3. The modern city of Split in Croatia grew up around a summer palace erected by the Roman emperor Diocletian 1700 years ago. People still reside in the ruins of the palace, and their television antennas can be seen jutting above the palace walls. For a reconstruction of the palace as Diocletian saw it, visit **http://www.ncsa.uiuc.edu/sdg/experimental/split/split1.html**, the website maintained by Michael Greenhalgh of the Department of Art Historian at the Australian National University.

2
People Looking at People

In this chapter...

What is anthropology?

Anthropology, the study of human beings, is organized into four subfields: cultural anthropology, archaeology, linguistics, and physical anthropology. Some anthropologists are engaged in applying anthropological concepts to contemporary issues. The anthropological approach is cross-cultural and holistic. It is based on taking the insider perspective, and through cultural relativism it avoids making value judgments.

Anthropological theory and methods

Anthropology is a social science, so anthropological theories must be based on data gathered through systematic observations. The aim of anthropological research is ethnography, describing a particular culture. The anthropological method of participant observation allows the researcher to collect information through interviews and observation while living among a group of people for an extended period of time.

Encounters with the Other

Though anthropologists have developed effective fieldwork strategies, there is no one right way to conduct ethnography. Because research on human beings is a sensitive endeavor involving issues of ethics and accuracy, the American Anthropological Association has issued guidelines defining the anthropologist's responsibilities to colleagues and to the people he or she studies. The AAA notes, "Constraint, deception, and secrecy have no place in science."

Ethnography in cities

Anthropologists have traditionally conducted research at the village level in other cultures, thus facilitating the holistic approach of participant observation. Over the past few decades, anthropologists have increasingly begun to study urban populations. This shift in the fieldwork setting has required adjustments to traditional ethnographic methods. Instead of studying cultures, anthropologists may now study subcultures and include survey research techniques in their methodology.

nthropologists are fond of saying that traveling to remote parts of the world in search of the Other is really an attempt to find ourselves. When anthropologists arrive in these exotic places, they often find that the people they have come to study spend a considerable portion of *their* time trying to define who they are.

Why is the quest to know ourselves so elusive? And why is it bound up in a process of imposing rigid categories on the Other? And why is the relationship between "us" and "them" so often fraught with antagonism and anxiety? These are questions basic to the work of anthropologists because conducting fieldwork is dependent on being able to cross the boundaries between us and them. In addition, the way people define themselves, both within the group and with respect to outsiders, is an essential component of the data collected by anthropologists.

ANTHROPOLOGY AS AN INTEGRATIVE DISCIPLINE

The very word *anthropology* defines itself: *anthropos* means human being; *-ology* refers to study or science. A "Statement on Problems of Anthropological Research and Ethics" adopted by the American Anthropological Association in 1967 notes: "The human condition, past and present, is the concern of anthropologists throughout the world. The study of mankind in varying social, cultural, and ecological situations is essential to our understanding of human nature, of culture, and of society."

Anthropologists study both biology and culture, and they study cultures of both the present and the past. This is one of the distinguishing characteristics of the discipline, which is organized into four subfields according to the area of specialization: cultural anthropology, archaeology, linguistics, and physical anthropology.

Anthropological Subfields

Cultural or Sociocultural Anthropology   Cultural anthropologists study societies in existence at the time of the study. Though some people associate anthropology with the study of an exotic Other, groups studied by anthropologists have ranged from Australian Aborigines, to peasant groups in Central America, to gang members in the United States, among many others. It is the anthropological *approach*, discussed later in this chapter, rather than the group being studied, that defines anthropological research.

Cultural anthropologists study the values and belief systems of a group, as well as its marriage customs, economic transactions, and organization of power. Values and belief systems are part of the culture of a group. Institutions that order kinship, economics, politics, and religion constitute the social organization. Traditionally, American anthropologists have been interested in culture, whereas British anthropologists have focused on documenting social organization. However, it is difficult, if not impossible, to study one without the other, so the difference is primarily one of emphasis.

Archaeology   Just as cultural anthropologists study present-day cultures, archaeologists study cultures of the past. Unlike cultural anthropologists, archaeologists cannot interview the people they study or observe them as they go about their lives. Thus, archaeologists focus on **material culture** or **artifacts,** the objects produced by people in the process of living out their lives. Tools, pottery, and the remains of buildings can provide important clues to lifestyles of the past. In addition, archaeologists may analyze the physical remains of the people, including teeth and bones.

Though the popular view of archaeologists has been shaped by fictional characters like Indiana Jones, archaeology is an exacting science. Archaeologists do not simply break into tombs to collect artifacts. Not only the artifacts but also their location in relationship to each other provide the data analyzed by archaeologists. In a prehistoric animal kill site, for example, archaeologists can sometimes estimate how many hunters cooperated in the kill by the placement of arrow or spear points in relation to the animal's bones. Therefore, most objects are obtained by excavating a site laid out on an exact grid.

Linguistics   Linguists focus on human communication. Humans communicate through many different media, including posture, touch, and odor, but the form of communication most characteristic of humans is language, the organization of vocal sounds into meaningful units by means of a set of rules. Structural linguists study the organization of language. Historical linguists use the structure of language to compare different languages and determine how they might have diverged from each other or influenced each other in the past. Sociolinguists study language in its social context. Thus, sociolinguists are interested in how social relationships may be reflected in language use.

Physical or Biological Anthropology   Physical or biological anthropologists may work directly with humans or may study nonhuman primates such as monkeys and apes. **Primatologists,** anthropologists who focus on nonhuman primates, study such aspects of primate social life as parenting, aggression, the formation of dominance hierarchies, and communication. By comparing the social organization of nonhuman primates, anthropologists gain insight into many dimensions of human behavior. In working with human populations, some physical anthropologists focus on **genetics,** the study of the mechanisms underlying evolution, in an attempt to understand how biological characteristics are transmitted from one generation to the next. Others conduct research on human skeletal material, which may be all that is left of prehistoric populations. Through this research, physical anthropologists have learned how to distinguish differences in age and gender through examination of ancient teeth and bones. They have also learned a great deal about variation in human populations through time and have been able to trace the effects and distribution of such diseases as tuberculosis and syphilis.

Applied Anthropology   Many anthropologists engage in **applied anthropology,** which, as its name implies, involves the application of anthropological theories and methods to contemporary human problems. Some medical anthropologists study the efficacy of traditional healing systems, attempting to determine whether these might be integrated into Western health care systems. Others develop ways of making modern health care systems more available to people who might not otherwise have access to them. **Forensic anthropologists,** who specialize in the identification and analysis of human skeletal remains, have been called upon by law enforcement officers to identify murder victims. One prominent forensic anthropologist, Clyde C. Snow, identified the remains of convicted war criminal Josef Mengele in Brazil, settling an international dispute. Cultural anthropologists have used their knowledge of various value systems and social organizations to settle management disputes within American corporations and to protect the rights of traditional people, such as the Yanomamö of Venezuela and Brazil. Applied anthropology as a career will be discussed in greater detail in Chapter 16.

The Anthropological Approach

Anthropologists have developed a number of techniques to guide them in learning to understand the Other—in particular, a way of thinking that has come to be known as the anthropological approach. Some anthropologists believe the approach, rather than the subject matter, distinguishes the field of anthropology from other disciplines. Like anthropologists, psychologists study the way people view the world; sociologists study the way people interact with each other; economists and political scientists study the organization of material resources and power; but only anthropologists incorporate the anthropological approach as an essential part of their research. Several features are characteristics of this approach:

1. Anthropology is **cross-cultural.** From the beginnings of the discipline, anthropology has focused on the study of the Other. Though the field developed out of the European intellectual tradition, anthropologists have traveled all over the world to document

This photograph of Kristin Loftsdóttir, an anthropologist from Iceland, was taken early in her fieldwork among WoDaaBe pastoral nomads by Girgi Ganayi, a WoDaaBe. The WoDaaBe in the photograph are dressed for one of the many dance gatherings held in the Tchin-Tabaraden area of Nigeria.

ways of life that were rapidly disappearing. To understand and describe these complex patterns of behavior, anthropologists have been forced to redefine concepts that most of us—including other social scientists—take for granted. For example, it is necessary to ask: What is marriage? What is a family? What is an economic system? The answers must explain variations in these institutions all over the world. Thus, marriage may include more than two people or may involve two people of the same sex; a family may include more than parents and child; and an economic system may include activities that do not involve money.

2. Anthropology is **holistic.** As noted earlier, anthropologists study both people and nonhuman primates, in both the past and the present. They study biology, beliefs, and behavior. Cultural anthropologists further integrate the concept of holism into their research by studying groups as integrated wholes, attempting to understand attitudes and behavior within their social context. For example, a researcher who is studying religion will also learn all she or he can about the economic and political system and about the way family and kinship systems are organized.

Because anthropologists emphasize holism, cultural anthropologists typically study small groups, such as a village or, in an urban context, an ethnic community. It is difficult, if not impossible, to study a large group such as a nation holistically. Thus, anthropologists do not study anything so grand as American culture or Nigerian culture, since these are large, complex societies that resist the holistic approach. Instead, anthropologists' reports typically are based on intensive studies of smaller groups that are marked by some kind of clearly identifiable boundary.

Traditionally, anthropological research has focused on villages, since these have clear boundaries and provide an opportunity to study a range of activities, including religion, family relationships, and political and economic exchanges. As anthropologists begin more and more to study complex societies, they have sought other ways to delimit a group so that it can be studied holistically. In pursuit of this goal, anthropologists have studied groups identifiable by occupation, religion, ethnicity, or neighborhood.

3. Anthropologists try to understand the **insider perspective.** It is not enough to describe a society so that one's own colleagues can recognize its features; the anthropologist must also see the culture as the people themselves see it. This perspective facilitates the goal of holism, because the native's point of view permits the anthropologist to understand how all the parts fit together.

The insider perspective is also called the **emic** view; the outsider perspective is the **etic** view. In fact, the anthropologist moves from the etic to the emic perspective and back again as he or she journeys to the field, becomes immersed in a particular culture, and then returns to write about it. The process of moving from the etic to the emic involves initial culture shock, which gives way to increasing insight into the motivations and concerns of the people being studied. When the anthropologist leaves the field, he or she again experiences culture shock in translating those experiences into etic language in the process of producing a written description of the culture.

Although the anthropologist attempts to experience and understand a culture as the people themselves see it, he or she also remains somewhat detached from their lives, occupying a role that has been described as the "professional stranger" or the "marginal native" (Freilich 1970). This balancing act between participation and detachment distinguishes the anthropologist both from a member of the society and from a tourist or traveler. The true insider does not ask the searching questions that an anthropologist must ask, and the tourist or traveler is interested primarily in a novel experience. According to Robert B. Edgerton and L. L. Langness: "[The anthropologist] is not living among another people to enjoy their way of life. He is there to understand it and then to report his understanding to others" (1974:3).

Mariette van Tilburg enjoys a refreshing swim with her young friend Philomene in Youtou, Senegal. As this photograph illustrates, participant observation provides an opportunity to form mutually rewarding friendships.

4. Anthropologists try to apply the principle of **cultural relativism.** Perhaps even more difficult than maintaining the balancing act between insider and outsider is anthropologists' attempt to guide their studies by the principle of cultural relativism. This means that they try to avoid making value judgments about the beliefs and customs of the people they study, even though some practices may be difficult to understand. For example, Gilbert Herdt studied male initiation rites, including ceremonial male homosexuality, among the Sambia of New Guinea. Herdt explains that ritualized homosexuality practiced by the Sambia is part of a coherent cultural complex that includes warfare and strong antagonism between women and men. Herdt was aided in his understanding of such seemingly exotic customs, he says, by applying the principle of cultural relativism: "This view sees human customs as meaningful and coherent in their native social context" (1987:9).

Avoiding value judgments in conducting anthropological studies can yield rich rewards. At the time he began his study among the Sambia, Herdt notes, "Negative stereotypes and folklore pictured them as murderous guerrilla warriors, thieves, and worse" (1987:1). In living among them for two years, Herdt found the Sambia's aggressive reputation to be warranted, but he learned more: "I discovered a private side of them never hinted at in the racist stereotypes: their warmth and friendliness" (1987:1).

It is useful to distinguish between relativism as a philosophical stance and relativism as a methodological approach. The former is **philosophical relativism,** the belief that all cultures are equally valid. This belief has been criticized on the basis that it is an ethical or moral stance, rather than a scientific one. Further, it suggests that such practices as genocide or "ethnic cleansing" are as valid as providing free public education or medical care. Most people would reject this position on ethical grounds.

Methodological relativism requires the anthropologist to avoid making value judgments for the purpose of conducting research. However, it does not require the anthropologist to regard all cultural practices as being equally valid. Gananath Obeysekere suggests that anthropologists should focus on methodological relativism rather than philosophical relativism. Obeysekere asserts that relativism as a methodology supports a value-free science and "dispenses with the need to have value judgments anchored in some law of science" (1966:371). Methodological relativism provides a means of avoiding **ethnocentrism,** the view that the values of one's own group are superior to those of all other groups.

Cultural relativism is an important methodology for conducting research among people unlike ourselves. It need not include rejecting our own values or culture in favor of other ways of life. In fact, viewing the Other as morally and culturally superior to oneself is a form of cultural romanticism (Womack 1995). Although it may appear to be a position of tolerance, it actually reaffirms the we–they dichotomy. It is a disguised form of paternalism that denies the Other full participation in the complexities and contradictions of human social life. According to recent critics, "The romantic approach was and is Eurocentric in that it uses or creates images of other peoples in terms of the cognitive needs and interests of Europeans" (Joseph, Reddy, and Searle-Chatterjee 1990:17).

It is not the object of anthropology to validate or to justify other ways of life, since doing either places the researcher in the role of judge. Even if the judgment is benevolent, assuming a role that permits one to assess the value of other societies emphasizes the unequal power relationship between the anthropologist and the people being studied. As each anthropologist must discover in the process of getting to know the Other, the only real basis of tolerance is understanding.

ANTHROPOLOGICAL THEORY AND METHOD

In the academic world of North America, where the pursuit of knowledge is organized according to the subject being studied, anthropology is difficult to categorize, because it links together subjects usually sorted into different categories. Economists typically do not study the biology of economic behavior, whereas an anthropologist might. Political scientists do not examine the relationship between the allocation of power in a group and the group's religious beliefs. However, anthropologists specializing in the study of religion typically do. Anthropologists themselves sometimes debate whether anthropology should be classified with the social sciences or the humanities, since anthropological research involves both careful observation of behavior and the process of developing abstract statements about human behavior. Some physical anthropologists believe their subdiscipline would be better served if it were classified with the biological sciences.

There are no easy resolutions to any of these issues. Most anthropologists believe the discipline should continue as a holistic science, studying humanity in all its manifestations. All anthropologists agree that anthropological theory should be based on **data,** information gained through careful observation, though they may disagree on how to organize, analyze, and interpret data on what it means to be human.

Scientific Research

Science is a process for systematically gaining information about the physical world and testing this information according to a set of criteria specified in a research design. The research design is important because it specifies what types of data would be considered evidence for a particular theoretical point of view.

What counts as data differs depending on the discipline in which the research is being conducted. For example, in astronomy, the amount of light emitted by a particular star may be considered as evidence for the size of the star, its distance from the earth, and the age of the star. In biology, the ability of a cell to grow and reproduce may be taken as evidence that it is alive. In medicine, the absence of symptoms of illness may be

Though anthropology began as a Western European discipline, the scope of the discipline has become international. Anthropological research is flourishing in Asia, South America, Africa, and many other parts of the world, with each region contributing important perspectives. Here, Asian archaeologists excavate prehistoric dwelling sites on the island of Taiwan.

taken as evidence that a patient has regained health. The amount of light emitted by a star, the growth and reproduction of a cell, and illness are all **variables,** logical categories of attributes that vary according to certain conditions.

Evidence in the social sciences can be much more complicated because the variables involved are more complex, because it is difficult to isolate what variables may contribute to a particular type of behavior, and because social scientists only rarely can control conditions in the research setting with any degree of exactness. Ethical standards governing research on human subjects require that subjects give *informed consent* to any research being conducted on them and prevent scientists from exposing human subjects to conditions that might cause them physical or psychological harm. No such regulations prevent biologists from conducting controlled experiments on bacteria or fungi. Further, human behavior is typically shaped by a number of variables, including events in a subject's past that may not be known to the researcher.

Scientific research is based on **empiricism,** direct observations of the phenomena being studied. The aim of scientific research is **objectivity,** conducting observations under conditions that reduce observer bias. In fact, absolute objectivity is impossible, since all phenomena are studied from a particular perspective. In the example of astronomy given above, stars are of necessity studied from the perspective of the earth. Bacteria can only be observed through a microscope, and the degree of magnification affects the results of the observation. In the case of the social sciences, research is conducted on human beings by scientists who are also human beings. Thus, it is difficult, if not impossible, for the social scientist to remain emotionally detached from his or her subjects. In practice, the aim of the social scientist is **intersubjectivity,** conducting research in such a way that another social scientist studying the same group in the same way would arrive at the same conclusions.

Opinion versus Analysis

Students conducting studies in my anthropology courses often ask if they can include their opinions when writing up their observations. My response is a lecture on the difference between opinion and analysis. We all have opinions on a variety of subjects. We may think that one candidate for political office is preferable to another. We may think cats are more intelligent than dogs. We may think that red is a prettier color than blue. These are all opinions based on the idea that one thing is better than another.

As noted earlier, anthropologists conduct research based on the approach of cultural relativism. Science in general is conducted as a **disinterested** enterprise. That is, the aim of science is collecting information about the nature of the physical and social world rather than seeking to answer questions of a moral or ethical nature. Further, the researcher should not have a vested interest in the outcome of his or her research. In practice, disinterest is difficult to achieve. In the case of a student observing a different ethnic or religious group, maintaining a position of cultural relativism and disinterestedness may be impossible. Therefore, one's opinion is likely to be ethnocentric.

Still, scientists may have opinions about the topics they wish to research. For example, anthropologists have believed that ritual and magic are associated with conditions of risk. The difference between this type of "opinion" and opinions about the relative "goodness" of political candidates, household pets, and colors is that the scientific opinion is based on data. In the case of ritual and magic, social scientists have long noted that men going to war and people engaged in other high-risk occupations typically prepare themselves by using ritual and magic. Thus, the scientific opinion is linked to evidence rather than to subjective belief.

Certain things cannot be tested scientifically. For example, scientists cannot experimentally test whether there is a God, since this entity is not subject to objective measurement. Further, scientists cannot test whether a particular behavior is good or bad, since goodness is a value judgment, and the quality of goodness is ineffable; that is, it cannot be operationalized into discrete observable units.

Godness and goodness may unarguably enrich the human experience, but they cannot be scientifically studied, precisely *because* they are unarguable. They are a matter of opinion rather than analysis. Further, they cannot be disproved. In the scientific endeavor, analytical statements cannot be proved; they can only be disproved. In discussing this aspect of scientific inquiry with my students, I say, "After making your observations, write up your data. Then analyze the patterns of behavior that emerge from the data. Only through systematically collecting and analyzing data can you move from *opinion* to *analysis.*"

Theories and Paradigms

On the basis of observations and analyses conducted by themselves or other researchers, scientists generate theories. A **theory** is a general statement about the relationship between phenomena. It is a "systematic explanation for the observed facts and laws that relate to a particular aspect of life" (Babbie 1989:46). The example given above, the anthropological view that use of ritual and magic is associated with conditions of high risk, is a theory.

Theories do not exist in a vacuum, nor are they aimed at stating some unarguable truth. As noted earlier, they are based in data. They are also shaped by paradigms. A **paradigm** is a scientific perspective that

has been developed after an accumulation of data and theoretical formulations. Babbie describes a paradigm as a "fundamental model or scheme that organizes our view of something. Although a paradigm doesn't necessarily answer important questions, it tells us where to look for the answers" (1989:47). The unstated paradigm underlying the theoretical link between ritual and high-risk activities is that human activities serve a purpose. The anthropological paradigm framing this theoretical perspective is called *functionalism,* which will be discussed in Chapter 3.

Under ideal research conditions, theories can be tested in controlled settings. In social science research, conditions in the research setting are rarely ideal, since we cannot manipulate human beings the way we manipulate protozoa, single-celled animals. Even if we could do it, controlling the research setting would not be enough for the purposes of anthropology, which is aimed at finding out not only what patterns of behavior are characteristic of human groups but also what they *think* about their own behavior. Biologists are not interested in finding out about the world view of protozoa, only how these tiny animals behave under certain types of conditions. Anthropologists, on the other hand, attempt to learn the insider perspective of the human animals they study as well as to analyze their behavior with reference to the social group and in terms of what it says about human beings in general.

People Studying People

Anthropology developed as the study of the Other, a circumstance that can be a shock to those undertaking fieldwork for the first time. Napoleon Chagnon describes his first meeting with the Yanomamö, a group of people who live in an isolated jungle on the border of Venezuela and Brazil in South America:

I looked up and gasped when I saw a dozen burly, naked, sweaty, hideous men staring at us down the shafts of their drawn arrows! Immense wads of green tobacco were stuck between their lower teeth and lips, making them look even more hideous, and strands of dark-green slime dripped or hung from their nostrils—strands so long that they clung to their pectoral muscles or drizzled down their chins. We arrived at the village while the men were blowing a hallucinogenic drug up their noses. One of the side effects of the drug is a runny nose. The mucus is always saturated with green powder and they usually let it run freely from their nostrils. My next discovery was that there were a dozen or so vicious, underfed dogs snapping at my legs, circling me as if I were to be their next meal. I just stood there holding my notebook, helpless and pathetic. Then the stench of the decaying vegetation and

DISCUSSIONS

The Socialization of an Anthropologist

In conducting fieldwork, anthropologists often learn more than they bargained for when they first set out on the adventure of getting to know the Other. When H. B. Kimberley Cook traveled to Venezuela to study an island community, she carried with her the American cultural bias that women are not aggressive. The women of a village on the island of Margarita undertook the task of re-educating her to be a "real woman." In the process of becoming *guapa*—which, in Margariteño usage means strong and feminine—Cook developed a new understanding of female aggression in the United States.

BECOMING *GUAPA:* LEARNING TO BE A "REAL WOMAN" IN MARGARITA, VENEZUELA

H. B. Kimberley Cook

On Margarita, an island approximately twenty miles off the coast of eastern Venezuela, a "real woman" is *guapa,* strong and feminine. As a UCLA undergraduate anthropology student conducting my first fieldwork in 1979, I was subjected to an intensive course in appropriate expressions of female aggression as Margariteño women undertook to train me to become guapa. I often became the target of female aggression and was in no way equipped to compete with Margariteño women. I would inadvertently break cultural rules, such as

leaving the house at night or taking a point of view that conflicted with that of a senior townswoman.

What I considered to be independence or constructive debate was construed as inappropriate or disrespectful. As a consequence of my blunders, I suffered several tongue-lashings, occasionally delivered in front of a crowd. In one instance, I decided to walk uptown one night to visit a friend. Before I reached her house, a powerful matriarch stepped out onto the dirt road and yelled, "And where do you think you are going? You have no business leaving your house at night!"

I started to explain that I was only walking a short distance to visit a friend, but was cut off in midsentence. The woman grabbed my arm and forced me into a chair in front of her neighbor's house. She informed me: "You are not allowed to leave your house at night. I have lived in this town my whole life and I can go where I choose. But you are new here and you will not leave your house at night again."

The behavior of Margariteño women has been problematic for researchers other than myself. Although Margariteño society is generally noted for its peacefulness, women of the island are also described as aggressive and quarrelsome (McCorkle 1965:99). Having been enculturated in the

United States, where aggression and quarreling are viewed as inappropriate for well-brought-up women, I was at first oblivious to the importance of female aggression in native Margariteño society. It was only after I observed the skill and expertise with which Margariteño women use aggression to attain their goals that I focused on the topic for my master's and doctoral research. Unlike the case for U.S. and other Western societies, where female aggression is often labeled negatively as manly, abnormal, low class, or comical, in Margariteño society, aggression is considered to be appropriate gender role behavior for women. According to my Margariteño informants, "A real woman is one that is *guapa,*" meaning strong and feminine.

Margariteño women learn to use many forms of verbal, passive, indirect, and physical aggression that range in severity depending on the particular context (Cook 1992). Women may use aggression to deal with interfemale disputes over authority and paternity. They also use aggression against men to *parar el macho* (stop male misconduct). At first it seemed ironic that women would use aggression to stop intermale aggression such as fistfighting. Even more surprising is that women efficiently used aggression against men without becoming victims of male aggression.

---

filth hit me and I almost got sick. I was horrified. What kind of welcome was this for the person who came here to live with you and learn your way of life, to become friends with you? (1992:11–12)

Chagnon did manage to conduct his study, eventually spending more than three years among the Yanomamö, learning their language and, as he put it, submerging himself in their culture—up to a point. Bridging the gap

between us and them is not easy, but anthropologists have developed methods that help them achieve this aim. Chagnon's goal of living among a group of people to "learn their way of life" is the basis of the definitive anthropological method—**participant observation:**

As participant-observer, the anthropologist lives intimately as a member of the society he has chosen to study. He shares in the people's day-to-day activities, watches as

In Margarita, the main variable underlying women's ability to parar el macho is matrifocality, based on the important economic and social roles women carry out in their communities (Cook 1992). Although intense culture change on the island has diminished the contributions of women, they traditionally performed tough physical labor, including chopping wood, carrying heavy buckets of water, and, on occasion, helping with house building and fishing.

Women performed physically arduous tasks, normally associated with men's work, out of necessity. In past decades, males were frequently absent from the island for three reasons: (1) males out-migrated to the mainland because of periodic shortages of employment opportunities on the island; (2) they were occupied with fishing, an important component of Margarita subsistence that requires men to be absent from their communities for extended periods; and (3) they were away from their households owing to the cultural practice of polygyny.

By default, women became the stable social figures in their communities, responsible for the survival of themselves and their families. The concept of family is central to native Margariteño society, and male absence required women to provide the nucleus for family networks. The central role of women is reflected in Margariteño social structure. Though kinship is based on bilateral descent, many of my informants also trace descent matrilineally through ascending kin for three or four generations.

Women derive a tremendous amount of informal power in community affairs from the central roles they play in economic and social matters. This power underlies their ability to use various types of aggression both in their relations with other women and in curbing male "misconduct."

In native Margariteño society, male misconduct is relatively harmless, compared with reports of male violence in other Latin American cultures. Misconduct among Margariteño men consists primarily of disrespectful behavior, rowdy drunkenness, and fistfighting. Fistfighting is rather short-lived, since women usually step in and break up such confrontations. When I first observed women breaking up a fistfight between two males, I was frightened, fully expecting that the women would be shoved aside or injured in the course of the altercation. Instead, the two women pressed their way through the crowd that had gathered around the two men. The women took each man by the upper arm and led both of them away from the scene. With this dramatic action, the women transformed what was perceived by community members as a dangerous situation to one of comic relief.

During subsequent fieldwork in several Margariteño communities in 1980–1981, 1985, and 1987–1988, I became acculturated and felt more comfortable with culturally institutionalized patterns of female aggression. It became liberating and fun to live in a society where women had so much freedom. I was encouraged by my informants to learn how to use various forms of female aggression so that I could "become a real woman" in their culture. Not only did women my age and older take care to instruct me in aggressive acts appropriate to females, but men and young girls also gave me advice and in situ training.

One late afternoon, I was walking with a seven-year-old girl on a fishing pier in Margarita. We were alone, and it was becoming dark. We were surprised by a car that drove past us to the end of the pier, then came back around toward us. The car was filled with four "foreign" men, Venezuelans who were not from the island. They were obviously up to no good. After pulling up close to where we were walking, the driver said, "What are you doing alone out here?" The man laughed suggestively. I was nervous and suggested to my younger friend that we run down the side of the embankment and head back toward town. I was surprised by my little friend's tough response. She didn't flinch but just kept on walking. Loud

(Continued)

they eat, fight, and dance, listens to their commonplace and exciting conversations, and slowly begins to live and understand life as they do. (Edgerton and Langness 1974:2–3)

Participant observation is in fact a combination of methods adapted to a particular fieldwork context. Marjorie Shostak describes her experience of participant observation among the !Kung who live in the Kalahari Desert of southern Africa:

Upon arriving in the field, I did everything I could to understand !Kung life. I learned the language, went on gathering expeditions, followed along on hunts, ate bush foods exclusively for days at a time, lived in grass huts in !Kung villages, and sat around their fires listening to discussions, arguments, and stories. I gained an invaluable perspective, participating and watching. (1983:6)

Because of the close interaction between the anthropologist and the people he or she studies, it is

DISCUSSIONS

The Socialization of an Anthropologist (*Continued*)

enough for the men to hear, she said to me, "We are not going to run down the side of the pier. We are going to walk home down the pier. If these men give me a bad time, I am going to slam them over the head with a pole." The men just hissed and drove on.

On another occasion, I was traveling on the island with two women in their early twenties. It was early evening, dark out, and we were late getting back to our community. Before waving down a *carrito por puesto* (one of the shared cabs that operate on the island), the two women started to look around on the ground for rocks. I asked them what they were doing. They replied that, since it was dark out, if we did not know the cab driver, we had better be prepared to knock him out if he should try anything. The women did not seem afraid. Instead, their manner was practical, business-as-usual. They laughed as they selected rocks. One of the women handed me a small, round rock and said, "Here, this one will fit in your hand. It will give you more strength if you have to protect yourself." The rock fit neatly in my hand and was meant to serve as a "grip," in much the same way as brass knuckles are fitted with a hand grip to prevent one from breaking one's own knuckles when delivering a punch. When the carrito por puesto stopped, the two women recognized the driver as a local native Margariteño. They dropped their rocks, laughed, and explained their plans to him. He laughed, albeit a bit nervously.

Sometimes Margariteño men would participate in my informal enculturation by allowing themselves to be surrogate targets of my training exercises. One afternoon, when I was sitting with a well-established townswoman in her sixties, five fishermen from our community passed by our house. It was late afternoon and they were returning from a long fishing expedition, tired and dragging heavy nets. As they went by, my woman friend said, "Here, take this rock and throw it at them, and yell, *'care verga'* [a vulgar local expression]." I took the rock and threw it, winging one of the fishermen on the right arm. The other fishermen laughed. The one I hit turned around and looked at me and my woman friend (a woman well known in the community as a powerful, manipulative matriarch). With a mischievous smile, the man shook his head and mumbled that I was becoming just like the more powerful older woman.

I could not continue to enjoy the luxury of female aggression when I returned to the United States, but my experience in Margarita gave me new insights into female aggression at home. I noticed that women in the United States are more aggressive than they seem to be aware of. As the literature on female aggression has pointed out (Burbank 1994), female aggression, when it occurs, is often ignored, labeled as something else, viewed as low class, or described as pathological or nonfeminine. Nonetheless, on my return to the United States, I began to notice incidents in which women acted aggressively.

For example, I was swimming at a public pool one afternoon during scheduled lap-swimming hours. Lane lines were in place to segregate the lanes and prevent accidents. Rules were posted stating that if two people were in a lane, they must share by each taking a side. By chance, I had a lane to myself. Just as I was getting out, two people approached my lane, a man of approximately sixty years and a woman in her mid to late twenties. It was clear they would have to share the lane. The man got in first, and instead of swimming on the side of the lane, he started slowly swimming down the middle of the lane, with his head out of the water, doing the breaststroke (a stroke that takes up the entire lane). His behavior was contentious and rude. The woman swimmer and I looked at each other in mild disgust. I said to her, "Oh brother, one of those!" She nodded her head in agreement, but did not seem concerned. After putting on her bathing cap and goggles, she took off in the same lane swimming the crawl stroke. She was a fast, powerful swimmer. As she came upon the man hoarding the center of the lane, she swam straight down her side, physically bumping him aside and drenching him with her wake. She did a flip turn at the wall and headed back down the lane. The older man moved over to his side, with an expression of begrudging compliance.

Whereas Margariteño women are encouraged to be aggressive, however, I noted that when women in my own society commit acts of aggression, they usually pay for it by agonizing over their behavior and feeling self-doubt. Finally, I have noticed how hard it is for people in the United States to accept the idea that females can be openly and freely aggressive. But then, it took me nine years as an anthropologist living in a different culture to realize that myself.

When conducting fieldwork among the Yanomamö of Venezuela, Napoleon Chagnon donned ceremonial dress typical of that worn by the Yanomamö when they visit neighboring villages. In the same way, Yanomamö often don Western dress when they interact with outsiders.

important to develop a degree of trust on both sides. The anthropologist must proceed carefully in beginning fieldwork because some kinds of data are more sensitive than others. In general, rituals and religious beliefs are considered to be a more dangerous topic for discussion than preparing a meal or planting a garden, though their relative importance can vary cross-culturally. Anthropologists typically begin their research by focusing on relatively mundane topics and easily observed activities while becoming acclimated to the fieldwork setting. Becoming acclimated may involve gaining facility in the language, developing a sustainable daily routine, and finding a key informant. A **key informant** is a particularly knowledgeable member of the group who is able to articulate important concepts to outsiders.

Usually, the first questions an anthropologist asks are: How many people are there in the group? And who is related to whom? Thus, the anthropologist begins by conducting a census and compiling a genealogy. A **gene-**

alogy is a description of the kin relationships in a group. In the process of counting the people in the group and learning whom they are related to, the anthropologist builds friendships and relationships of trust.

Ethnography

The object of participant observation is to understand the world view and behavior of a group of people within their social and cultural context. The process of observing the way of life of a group of people and describing it in a systematic way is known as **ethnography:**

> Ethnography is a research process in which the anthropologist closely observes, records, and engages in the daily life of another culture—an experience labeled as the fieldwork method—and then writes accounts of this culture, emphasizing descriptive detail. (Marcus and Fischer 1986:18)

These descriptive accounts of particular cultures, often published in book or monograph form, are called **ethnographies.** They usually contain an analysis of the social structure, including kinship, economic systems and ecology, political organization, and religion. In addition, authors of ethnographies analyze cultural values and world view in an attempt to explain how the people experience their society.

Ethnographies are typically based on an extended stay in the field, usually at least a year. A lengthy stay enables the anthropologist to observe a variety of occasions, which often occur on an annual schedule. In our own society, for example, the annual cycle includes such events as New Year's, Passover, and Christmas. Most other societies also mark the year with seasonal events, which may include planting and harvest festivals or, in pastoral societies, the movement of herd animals from one pasture to another.

The usual term of fieldwork—from one to two years—allows the anthropologist to document important annual cycles but is not sufficient to allow speculation about long-term shifts within a society. Some anthropologists attempt to offset this limitation by collecting the life histories and stories of elders, material that provides clues to the development of traditions. However, data based on the memories of informants cannot be evaluated in the same way as data collected through firsthand observation. Some elders may be astute observers of their own culture, but all information stored in an individual's memory—including that of the anthropologist—is subject to a process of sorting and organizing that distinguishes it from the organizational process of systematic anthropological observation.

ENCOUNTERS WITH THE OTHER

Though the scientific stance is of necessity disinterested, people studying people encounter issues of ethics and judgment not encountered by people studying protozoa. This distinction is acknowledged in the American Anthropological Association Code of Ethics:

> Anthropological researchers, teachers and practitioners are members of many different communities, each with its own moral rules or code of ethics. . . . Furthermore, fieldworkers may develop close relationships with persons or animals with whom they work, generating an additional level of ethical considerations. In a field of such complex involvements and obligations, it is inevitable that misunderstandings, conflicts and the need to make choices among apparently incompatible values will arise. (May 1971, amended March 1, 1997)

Anthropologists have ethical responsibilities to their colleagues and students and to the discipline as a whole. Above all, anthropologists have ethical responsibilities to the subjects of their study:

> Anthropological researchers have primary ethical obligations to the people, species and materials they study and to the people with whom they work. . . . Anthropological researchers must do everything in their power to ensure that their research does not harm the safety, dignity or privacy of the people with whom they work, conduct research or perform other professional activities. (AAA Code of Ethics, amended March 1, 1997)

Unfortunately, anthropologists are neither omniscient nor omnipotent. They cannot always predict how their research and publications will affect the people they study, and even if they could, they may not have the power to prevent negative effects. Optimally, anthropologists try to anticipate any problems that might arise from their research by dealing openly and honestly with the people they study. The American Anthropological Association Code of Ethics bars anthropologists from conducting research without fully informing their subjects about the nature and purpose of the research, as well as about any possible risks involved in the study. Thus, the people being studied must give their consent to the research, and in many cases they become active participants in the research. The 1967 AAA "Statement on Problems of Anthropological Research and Ethics" notes: "Constraint, deception, and secrecy have no place in science."

Most anthropologists emphasize the importance of dealing with the people they study as fully cooperating partners in their research. In recent decades, recognition of fieldwork as a cooperative enterprise has produced a shift in the terminology used to refer to the anthropologist-subject relationship. Anthropologists once referred to their subjects as *informants,* a term that can imply secrecy and a differential power relationship favoring the anthropologist. Many anthropologists now prefer the term *consultant,* which more accurately reflects the expertise of those assisting the anthropologist in his or her research.

In addition, many anthropologists now conceal the identities of their consultants to avoid making them a target in the event of a power shift or outbreak of conflict in the group. Some anthropologists also conceal the exact location of their study, especially in areas where conflict and political upheaval are prevalent. Still, studying people is a sensitive endeavor, and no anthropologist can anticipate all the issues that might arise from his or her fieldwork. As a result, controversies often arise within the discipline about the ethics of fieldwork and whether a particular ethnography accurately reflects the data available in the field.

The Yanomamö Controversy

Chagnon's description of the Yanomamö "way of life" became controversial, in part because he calls them "the fierce people" and emphasizes the significance of warfare and other forms of violence. Chagnon writes, "The thing that impressed me most was the importance of aggression in their culture" (1992:8–9). Chagnon's critics say that his description of Yanomamö culture is distorted and that he selectively reports aggressive incidents. Certainly, Chagnon fails to describe such key aspects of Yanomamö life as the perspective of women. Unfortunately, he is not alone in this omission, as will become evident later in this chapter.

The debate goes far beyond the issue of accuracy. Some anthropologists argue that Chagnon's description of the Yanomamö has provided a justification for disrupting their traditional way of life. As are a number of other groups who live in the tropical rain forests of Venezuela and Brazil, the Yanomamö are subject to incursions of outsiders—in this case, miners and loggers—who seek control of rich resources in Yanomamö territory.

Even if the Yanomamö are fierce, fierceness is no justification for taking away their land and forcing them to abandon their customs. In fact, attempts to seize other people's resources are typically motivated by economics rather than ethics. If violence and aggression were sufficient reason to deprive groups of their resources, a significant portion of the world's land would change hands. And many American cities would be vulnerable to territorial claims on the basis that the people who live there are subject to unacceptably high levels of violence. American lands are protected from the encroachments of outsiders, not by moral superiority, but by the country's formidable political, economic, and military power. Ironically, the Yanomamö—the people Chagnon describes as fierce—are subject to incursions from people who would take their lands because they, unlike the United States, cannot defend themselves against large-scale aggression from outsiders.

The Other in Our Midst

It is not necessary to travel to exotic parts of the world to meet the Other. Many people living in the United States have been consigned to the category of "otherness," and anthropologists have conducted research among these people. Hortense Powdermaker studied the relationship between blacks and whites in Indianola, Mississippi, in the 1930s, a time when strict segregation was observed between the two groups. For a white woman, crossing the color barrier was at times fraught with social peril.

As a liberal activist who had earlier been a union organizer, Powdermaker could not bring herself to follow the prevalent white custom of stripping blacks of social status by addressing them on a first-name basis or by calling them "auntie" and "uncle." Instead, she addressed them as "Mr.," "Mrs.," or "Miss." Afraid that violation of such a serious social taboo would jeopardize her study, Powdermaker felt compelled to inform an influential white supporter of her practice of addressing blacks by their titles. She describes his reaction:

> His face, which had been smiling, froze. He stood up, as if for emphasis, and said in tones of Moses laying down the Ten Commandments, "You can't do that." I replied that I had to do it—that the Negroes were not my servants, and that I was accustomed to addressing people whom I did not know well by their proper titles. He again said sternly, "You can not do it; something terrible will happen." I asked what would happen. He could not give me a definite answer, but conveyed the idea of a catastrophe, the collapse of society, of danger to me, to him, and to everyone. (1966:153)

Such "outrageous" actions can be an advantage to an anthropologist, however. Powdermaker discovered that her behavior was so unusual for a white woman that many people assumed she must be black. She describes her first auto trip through Mississippi with an educated black woman:

> Entering the deep South with a Negro woman and seeing it, to some degree, through her eyes, was an excellent beginning; we became friends and she talked freely. I was mistaken for a Negro by colored and white people. Aware of this whenever we were in a Negro restaurant or hotel, I was amazed that my physical appearance did not count at all. My companion was quite dark but I met other Negroes lighter than I. In a few days I acquired some of the feeling tone of what it meant to be an educated Negro young woman in Mississippi. (1966:135)

Powdermaker's experience illustrates the principle that people interpret their experiences in terms of conceptual categories shaped by their world view, and they often make such interpretations even if their interpretations contradict their sense perceptions.

Anthropologists have since studied other ethnic groups in the United States, including Mexican Americans in Texas and Cajuns in Louisiana. They have also conducted research among religious groups, such as the Amish and Hare Krishnas (the Krishna Consciousness Movement), and among occupational groups, such as construction workers and police officers. Anthropologists have also charted the culture and social organization of groups considered behaviorally deviant, including drug dealers and members of gangs.

Oddly, until very recently, anthropologists have all but ignored the contribution of almost 50 percent of the world's population—women (Womack and Marti 1993). Anthropological theory is primarily based on information collected from males. The prominent scholar E. E. Evans-Pritchard questioned whether it was possible to obtain the "woman's viewpoint" and whether the contribution of women was even necessary to understanding the "native view":

> Does one get the native view about life (and about women) from men or can one get to know the women as well and see things from their viewpoint? Much depends on the people one is studying and the status of women among them. . . . The Zande [women] were almost an inferior caste, and unless elderly matrons, shy and tongue-tied. (1974:7)

Evans-Pritchard conducted his research among the Azande in the late 1920s. Fifty-five years later, Stephen

David Siemens studied the same group, traditionally an agricultural kingdom whose territory overlaps the borders of the modern states of Sudan, Zaire, and the Central African Republic. Siemens notes, "For E. E. Evans-Pritchard, the 'woman's viewpoint' was peripheral to what he considered the more important task of getting the 'native view about life,' which was virtually synonymous with the man's view" (1993:91). By overlooking the woman's viewpoint, Siemens adds, Evans-Pritchard failed to gain important information about life crisis rituals, such as rites of birth and death, which are the province of women. Ironically, those "elderly matrons" Evans-Pritchard dismissed so readily could have provided him with data that would have greatly enhanced his understanding of the Zande way of life.

The "male bias" in anthropology has led to some serious distortions in anthropological theory. Sally Slocum notes that such concepts as "man the hunter" imply that society is organized around the activities of males: "Hunting . . . is pictured as a male activity to the exclusion of females. This activity, on which we are told depends the psychology, biology, and customs of our species, is strictly male. A theory that leaves out half the human species is unbalanced" (1975:39). In fact, women are central to the economy of forager societies, providing as much as 80 percent of the daily diet (Lee 1968). And in their role as primary caretakers of children, women have a major impact on the transmission of culture from one generation to the next.

Ironically, even women anthropologists who have made significant contributions to the field often focus on information provided by males. James R. Gregory says this tendency for both male and female anthropologists to focus on males is attributable to a research bias in anthropology that defines the activities of men as important and those of women as negligible:

> Male and female ethnographers have both generally pursued research interests centered in the male world; if the female ethnographer is to achieve her primary research goals she must work with men, whereas the male ethnographer has no comparably compelling reason to work with women as a requirement for achieving his main goals. (1984:322)

There have been at least two notable exceptions to this rule. In the 1920s, Margaret Mead conducted a landmark study on socialization among adolescent girls in Samoa, and in 1971, Jane C. Goodale published a book on female Australian Aborigines, *Tiwi Wives*. Goodale's study revealed that, contrary to evidence provided by male informants, Tiwi women possessed sophisticated knowledge of the biology of childbearing, including techniques for producing abortions.

As a result of the feminist movement beginning in the United States in the 1970s, anthropologists have increasingly included the activities of women in their research. This new approach has produced an abundance of data that have forced anthropologists to rethink some of their most cherished theoretical positions.

Gender Research

One of the most significant contributions of ethnographic research focusing on gender is the discovery that men as well as women have gender. Previous studies equated men and their activities with society as a whole and relegated women and their activities to a residual category of "other." This dichotomy reflects a Western rather than a universal bias. The Western bias is expressed as an opposition between male and female attributes and roles. Recent anthropological research has indicated that the roles of women and men in most societies are seen as complementary rather than oppositional. Studies by such anthropologists as David Gilmore (1990, 1993) suggest that the "power" of males over females is not absolute, that females may exercise more real "power" in the domestic realm than previously recognized, and that males are socialized into risk taking and aggressive displays.

This is not to say that exploitation does not occur, but its dynamics are too complex to be reduced to a simple unidimensional opposition between males and females. The case of Sushma Katuwal, a Nepali woman sold into prostitution in India in the 1990s, illustrates this point.* Katuwal was fourteen years old when floods washed away her village in southern Nepal, leaving her and her impoverished family homeless. A woman of the village lured Katuwal away from her family by offering her a job working in a garment factory in Kathmandu, the capital of Nepal. Instead of bringing her to the factory, the woman took Katuwal to the Indian border and sold her for $700 to three men. The girl was taken to a city in southern India and imprisoned in a small room, where she provided sexual services to as many as thirty men a day. When she was freed in a raid by the Indian police, she was found to be HIV-positive. Katuwal now lives in a home for women rescued from the brothels. She serves on a border patrol iden-

---

*Dexter Filkins, "On Guard against a Flesh Trade," *Los Angeles Times*, June 26, 2000, p. A1.

tifying traffickers who try to smuggle Nepali girls across the border for arrest by Nepalese police.

Complex relationships of relative power and exploitation are represented in this case. Katuwal was victimized by her poverty as well as by the machination of a woman in her village. She was exploited by the three men who smuggled her out of Nepal as well as by those who paid $3.50 to $12 for sexual access to her. She was rescued by male police officers and was given refuge in a house established by a prominent woman. As a result, Katuwal was placed in a position to rescue other girls, and her effectiveness in doing so was enforced by men in the Nepalese police force. Her story and the illegal traffic in impoverished Nepali girls were made public internationally by, among others, a male journalist for the *Los Angeles Times.*

In addition to gender, other types of differential access to power and resources are reflected in Katuwal's story. The older, more knowledgeable woman has power over the younger, less experienced girl. Those who have fewer economic resources are powerless to resist those with greater access to resources. The power of governments and police is superior to that of individuals. Relatively affluent males of one country have power over impoverished women of another country. And members of mass media have the power to publicize—or ignore—information about the plight of impoverished and exploited people throughout the world.

ETHNOGRAPHY IN CITIES

Anthropologists have long expressed ambivalence about conducting research in cities. William Mangin, editor of *Peasants in Cities,* an early book on urban subcultures, writes: "Anthropologists have tended to like primitives and village peasants and dislike acculturation and the involvement of 'their' people with cities and with national and international politics" (1970:xvi). Mangin was voicing an assumption, prevalent at the time, that the work of anthropologists was to study "primitives," people whose way of life was similar to that of cultures in an earlier stage of evolution. Anthropology has come a long way since then. Anthropologists now reject the idea that any human group could accurately be called "primitive," and they recognize that all ways of life currently in existence are fully modern even if they do not fit the European model.

At the time, Mangin felt it necessary to justify urban research by focusing on subcultural groups who had migrated to cities from rural areas or who shared the characteristics of poverty and disenfranchisement with peasants (poor farmers): "Peasant and primitive culture patterns are found in cities. And city patterns, spread by radio, movies, administrators, schools, tourists, armies, and so forth, are found in the most remote rural areas, jungles, deserts, and mountains" (1970:xxiv). Articles in Mangin's book focus on the urban poor, including residents of slums in Rio de Janiero and migrants to cities in Morocco who live in *bidonvilles,* or "tin towns."

Laura Nader notes that anthropologists have tended to "study down," focusing disproportionate attention on the poor and disenfranchised. Nader suggests that part of the reason is that we have a romantic affinity for powerless people and see ourselves as champions of the oppressed. In addition, she notes that people of lower socioeconomic status have been unable to resist intrusions by social scientists because they are in a social position of powerlessness, and anthropologists have been less willing to ask penetrating questions of people of higher socioeconomic status than themselves. The failure of anthropologists to study elite power organizations such as the U.S. Senate has led to a serious lack of information about these groups. Nader points out that many American students are no more familiar with the workings of a Washington law firm than with the customs of a Mexican or New Guinea village, adding: "We anthropologists have studied the cultures of the world only to find in the end that ours is one of the most bizarre of all cultures and one, by virtue of its world influence for 'bad' or 'good,' in urgent need of study" (1974:302).

The fieldwork context for anthropologists is changing. The small-scale populations traditionally studied are rapidly becoming large-scale, part of the global economy, and linked to the outside world through the Internet, satellite television, and wage labor work. The resulting shift in the context of ethnographic fieldwork poses new problems for the ethnographer.

Is There an "American Culture"?

There have been attempts to describe "American culture" as a whole. Some examples are Margaret Mead's 1942 book *And Keep Your Powder Dry: An Anthropologist Looks at America* and Marvin Harris's 1981 book *America Now: The Anthropology of a Changing Culture.* These are generally less successful on several levels than their other books. For one thing, both of these books equate "America" with the United States, thus ignoring all the other countries in the Western Hemiphere. In addition, describing such a complex entity as the United States necessitates overgeneralization. For example, in a chapter called "Why Nothing Works," Harris writes: "America has become a land plagued by loose wires, missing screws, things that don't fit, things that don't last, things that don't work" (1981:19). But is this really true? And is it more true of the United States than of everywhere else in the world? Is this a statement that *uniquely* defines "American culture"?

These books are perhaps more important for what they say about the nature of the anthropological enterprise than for what they say about the nature of "American" life. Ironically, "American" cultural anthropologists may never be able to define "American culture." They may be too embedded in their own culture (a truism in anthropology is that "a fish doesn't know it is wet"), and the task of defining American culture overall is probably too enormous to yield to the anthropological method of ethnography.

The Problem of Access

Conducting research in small-scale societies at the level of the band or village allows the anthropologist relatively constant access to all members of the group, regardless of their age, gender, or status. The anthropologist rarely has equal access to all members of the group, but the often-public nature of much of village life allows the anthropologist to observe people as they go about their daily routines. Ceremonial or ritual occasions provide an opportunity to watch members of the group perform their assigned tasks and, often, interact with outsiders. All of these activities provide insight into the dynamics of the group.

The importance of this ability to observe a range of activities is reflected in the research of Napoleon Chagnon, who studied the Yanomamö of Venezuela over a period of years. The Yanomamö live in huts, with one side open, that encircle a central communal area. Thus, most of their daily activities, including their pattern of sleeping in hammocks, are clearly visible to other members of the group and to the ethnographer.

This ongoing daily contact is rarely available to an anthropologist conducting research in a populous urban environment. People in cities typically live in houses that are sealed off to outsiders. Unless the researcher lives with a family, he or she cannot observe people interacting in the privacy of their homes. To overcome this barrier, anthropologists often rent rooms from an established family or form a close alliance with them. This arrangement also allows the anthropologist access to others with whom the family interacts, thus overcoming another problem facing urban researchers: How can one obtain a representative sample of people and activities when these may be dispersed throughout the city?

A glance at one hypothetical household provides some insight into this problem. For the sake of illustration, let us say this household is made up of a husband who works outside the home, a wife who works at home but contributes volunteer work at a church, one child who attends grade school, one child who attends middle school, a grandmother, and a grandfather. In a single day, the husband may leave for work before the children wake up and stop at a market or gathering place for men on his way home. The children go off to separate schools, and the wife may go off for marketing or visiting with friends after completing her household tasks. The grandmother may spend the morning sewing, then go to a shop to buy thread, and stop to visit with friends on the way home. The grandfather may do household repairs, then go off to meet friends for gossip and gambling. How can one anthropologist keep track of all those people and activities?

There has been ongoing debate over whether ethnographic methods are suitable for conducting research on large-scale groups or in the urban context. Researchers in other disciplines, such as sociology, solve the problem of access by relying primarily on statistical methods and sampling populations. These methods can provide an accurate overview of a population, but they do not meet the ethnographic goals of holism and gaining access to the insider perspective. Despite these difficulties, anthropologists have managed to study a number of urban populations. Figure 2.1 identifies several of the anthropologists and sites described in this chapter.

Targeting Urban Subcultures

One way to limit the scope of urban research so that urban groups can be studied ethnographically is to focus on a particular subculture. The following examples of urban research focus on occupation, ethnicity, and specific sites as a means of defining research boundaries.

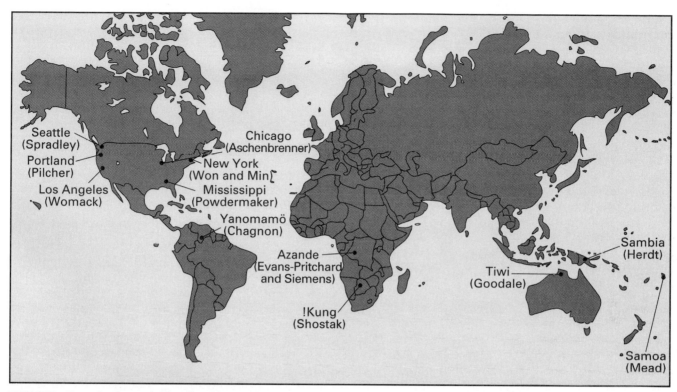

FIGURE 2.1   Anthropologists in the Field

The work of anthropologists discussed in this chapter encompasses cultures and experiences from around the world—from African Americans in Mississippi to the Tiwi, one of the aboriginal groups of Australia. Collecting information about humans in many parts of the world allows anthropologists to observe similarities and differences in the way people go about their daily lives.

Occupation   Focusing on an occupation provides the researcher with a population and a place where they can be observed. William W. Pilcher's (1972) study of longshoremen at the Port of Portland in Oregon is a classic example of this type of research. Note that he did not study the entire population of longshoremen in the United States, traveling all over the country to interview as many longshoremen as he could. Rather, he specifically studied longshoremen who loaded and unloaded ships docking at a single location. Pilcher both observed the longshoremen and participated in their activities. He had access to this group because he had worked as a longshoreman for twelve years and had grown up in a family of longshoremen. He, two of his brothers, and his father were all members of the International Longshoremen's and Warehousemen's Union. He had privileged access to this exclusive population because his father and his father's friends were prominent members of the community of Portland longshoremen.

Being an insider was not equivalent to being an ethnographer, however. Pilcher did not undertake the research phase of his association with the longshoremen until he became a graduate student at the University of Illinois. His experience of the transition from insider to ethnographer illustrates important issues with respect to the relationship between types of access and the kinds of knowledge that can be gained:

> I began this research with a large fund of knowledge gained through many years of personal experience on the waterfront. This knowledge, however, was not sufficient to allow me to prepare a descriptive and analytical treatise without extensive research into the history and present condition of the Portland longshore group, the Union, the city, and the state. In some ways my previous knowledge hindered me because I believed, when I began my research, that I knew the answers to many questions and was surprised when my own data proved me wrong. (1972:5)

Pilcher's experience illustrates a key difference between insider and outsider knowledge. The emic perspective

Polishing the Anthropological Lens:
Is Traditional Ethnography Obsolete?

As academically trained anthropologists are becoming skilled at applying anthropological theories and methods to contemporary business, medical, and other contexts, there has been increasing discussion about whether it is time to update traditional ethnographic methods. In the following article, based on a paper presented at the annual American Anthropological Association meetings and later published in *Anthropology News*, P. I. Sunderland considers time as a factor in ethnographic research. In conducting corporate research, Sunderland made use of ongoing ethnographic research and the "anthropological lens," while incorporating intensive goal-centered research using multisite data-collection techniques designed for rapid and precise data collection: videotaped interview sessions, "shadowing interviews," and the time-honored method of participant observation.

GLANCING POSSIBILITIES
P. I. Sunderland

Can meaningful anthropological research be carried out in three weeks? Not so long ago, I was commissioned by a major corporation to do just that. I had three fieldwork weeks in which to discover what child nurturing means for American parents and to understand how they accomplish it. Then another three weeks in which to analyze the data, write a report, prepare a verbal presentation, and create an accompanying video.

For a corporate research project, this time frame is entirely normative. Within the current academic anthropology paradigm, this pace is, of course, ludicrous, impossible, ridiculous, even blasphemous. What I'd like to suggest, however, is that as anthropologists we *can* carry out meaningful, anthropological research within very short periods of time. Let me first illustrate.

Fast Access

For this particular research, the fieldwork was carried out in California, Pennsylvania, and Missouri. I partnered with Ayala Fader, who was just finishing her dissertation fieldwork centered on children's language socialization. In each location, we conducted ten videotaped family interviews; eight of them lasted about two and a half hours, and two, labeled "shadowing interviews," lasted approximately four hours each. These latter two included an interview plus observational "shadowing" of parent/child activities. We accompanied parents and children to parks, prepared and ate meals with families, and watched bedtime rituals. In each location we also carried out a day of observations and informal interviews at child-centered locations such as museums or zoos.

Fader's knowledge of the language socialization literature, as well as of what was in, out, cool, and not cool with the grade school set, was of tremendous help. Her visible second-trimester pregnancy also helped us to gain instant camaraderie with parents—a critical feature of such time-dependent research.

The report, "Nurturing Nature & Crafting the Child," detailed parental conceptions of children as both flowers that naturally blossom and sculpted material, purposefully designed and crafted by the parent. The report was also able to clarify the tensions between simultaneous emphasis on the individual, sanctity of the individual and individual autonomy, and the family, both as a group and as an entity. The emphasis on the psychology of behavior and group norms while simultaneously placing value on individuality—especially individual psychological autonomy and difference—was pointed out. The ways in which child forms of everything from foods and furniture to music and videos represent accommodations to children's perceived difference and lack of competence was highlighted. The notion of cultural capital and particularly its relevance for out-of-home environments was also discussed.

But Is It "Real" Anthropology?

Yes, I was concerned whether I was doing "real" anthropology and whether the findings might have been different had we spent years rather than weeks.

When conducting fieldwork in three weeks and writing up that fieldwork in another three weeks, one cannot produce the types of ethnographic work that can be accomplished with years of endeavor. Nevertheless, work carried out from start to finish within a few months *is* something; and it is anthropological. The anthropological lens is the reason. Would I have "found" the intense focus on the norm without Foucault? Maybe, but not likely. Would I have noticed the intense accommodations made for children without having read Schieffelin or Ochs? Again, not likely. Would I have discussed "cultural capital" had I not been acquainted with Bourdieu? Almost certainly not. As anthropologists, we have a fine tradition of theoretical poaching, but we take these theories and embed them within our own ethnographic and theoretical traditions. There is an anthropological way of looking at things. In the marketplace—academic and otherwise—this anthropological lens is a large part of what we have to offer. At the moment there is an interest in anthropology and "ethnography" in the worlds of business. It is a propitious moment of opportunity for us to disseminate that specifically anthropological lens and to have an impact on the way people understand and interpret their worlds. But we cannot do so if we stick by our traditional time frame.

The Time Factor

For those involved in consumer goods, there is an important, underlying reason why taking a year or more to carry out research, plus a year or more to analyze it and write it up, is impossible: the marketplace would have changed by then. In a world where products can become outdated—if not obsolete—within six months, a multiyear study would miss entire cohorts of consumers. In our analyses, those of us in anthropological market research certainly try to introduce the cultural themes that both transcend and fuel fleeting phenomena and fashions, but if we did not deliver our analysis fast, it would be perceived as of no use.

Recent scholarship—for instance by Gupta and Ferguson, Appadurai, Marcus and Clifford—has brought the ways we fetishize fieldwork based on participant observation clearly to our attention. Yet the length of time spent conducting research is not an interrogated category in the way that matters of place, space, and participant observation are. Apart from noting the time/space compression of contemporary life or acknowledging the problematic ways traditional forms of writing and analysis serve to make time stand still, these scholars have said very little about time.

I believe we also need to bring the length of time we consider necessary to spend on a "real" study under scrutiny. We do not have to give up our goals of ethnographic work or the inductive approach. But does it have to take so long? We need to question the extent to which we are simply acting in line with an assumption that the length of time spent on something always means better, an assumption that seems to rely on metaphors of depth and excavation: more time, deeper insight, more truth.

But is this assumption appropriate for the social world in which we now live? In a very fast-paced world, is the relationship between time spent and quality of product inverted, or at least, turned and twisted on itself? Just as it has been argued that we need to find new ways to account for social relations that are not face-to-face, our methods need to take into account social relations and phenomena that speed through our lives. Multiyear research is not always the best method to use in the fast-paced world in which we live.

For those of us working in the worlds of consumer goods and services, we are in the vortex of space/time compression, the production centers of the postmodern, fast-changing pace of our lives. And we have had to develop methods appropriate to keeping up with, and being relevant for, that pace. Because of our clients' needs, we have had to learn how to understand via glancing and glimpsing. We have thereby learned the ways that, even when we are glancing through it, the anthropological lens can be a powerful tool. We are also by necessity engaged in multisited fieldwork (consumers are not in just one place), working hard to find methods appropriate to understanding people's interactions with the newest of technologies, trying to figure out the latest cultural flows from one part of the globe to another, and working with international teams. Just as the anthropological lens has something to offer business, applied anthropology has something to offer the academy.

Source: Adapted from *Anthropology News,* April 2000. Reproduced by permission of the American Anthropological Association. Not for further reproduction. P. I. Sunderland lives in New York and is a partner with the Chicago office of the B/R/S Group, Inc., a marketing research and consulting group. Other members of the B/R/S Team Mosaic include anthropologists Rita Denny and Michael Donovan.

carries with it knowledge, taken for granted by insiders, that facilitates negotiating within the group. The etic perspective, brought to the situation by an anthropologically trained researcher, provides an overview of the group dynamic.

Ethnic Groups   Just as urban anthropologists studying occupational groups must limit their observations to a particular research setting, anthropologists studying ethnic groups must define the limits of their study. Typically, they focus on members of an ethnic group residing in a specific location. Focusing on a population in a specific location reduces the risk of overgeneralizing to the ethnic group as a whole. Though it is common in mass media to represent African Americans as being a single unified community, they are not an entirely homogeneous group. Variations within the group result from differences in occupation, education, place of residence, and many other things. A family residing in an urban Chicago neighborhood would have little in common with a rural Southern family.

Joyce Aschenbrenner found socioeconomic differences within a group of black families she studied in Chicago: "Among the families in [this study] are those that are or have been relatively affluent, and others that have known only poverty" (1975:7). By including families occupying differing socioeconomic statuses, Aschenbrenner was able to identify what she called a "Black experience":

> While class differences are represented here, I have stressed the values and concepts that they share while attempting to give due recognition to individual differences and variation in social patterns. Despite differences in opinions and value conflicts, I have found similar themes in the lives of friends and informants. On the basis of these observations, I have opted for a view of the "Black experience" as a complex phenomenon in a heterogeneous society, creating in many ways a unique way of life for Black men and women in our society. (1975:7)

Studying ethnic groups poses problems of access for anthropologists, since a characteristic of ethnic groups is that they are typically closed to outsiders. Though an anthropologist could establish a base of fieldwork by arriving unannounced in a remote village, residents of most urban neighborhoods would not welcome such intrusions. Aschenbrenner gained access to the families she studied through her work at a black community center. Building on this base, she expanded her study through **network analysis,** tracing a population through the network of a particular person or sub-

group. Network analysis allows the researcher to observe the interactions of people who are geographically dispersed.

A number of studies of urban ethnic groups have been conducted by members of those groups. For example, Bernard P. Wong conducted an ethnographic study of members of New York's Chinatown (1982), and Pyong Gap Min studied Korean immigrant families in New York (1998). Min writes:

> As a Korean immigrant, I have an insider's knowledge of my own and other Korean immigrant families. My personal family experiences, my casual observations of other Korean families, my informal discussions with Korean school teachers and social workers and my reading of Korean ethnic newspaper articles have sensitized me to the pervasiveness and seriousness of conflicts and tensions in Korean immigrant families. (1998:7)

Site-Specific Research   Urban anthropologists may also conduct research centered on a particular site, aimed at gaining access to a subculture that frequents that location. In a study that has now become a classic, James P. Spradley studied "urban nomads," or tramps, in Seattle. The result was the ethnography *You Owe Yourself a Drunk: An Ethnography of Urban Nomads* (1970). In his book *Participant Observation*, Spradley identifies the importance of place for urban ethnography:

> Any physical setting can become the basis for a social situation as long as it has people present and engaged in activities. A *street* where people cross, a *bank window* where people line up and transact business, an *ocean pier* where people loiter and fish, a *bus door* through which people enter and exit the bus, and a *grocery-store check-out counter* where groceries are rung up, paid for, and bagged are all social situations. Each of these places offers rich opportunities for participant observation. (1980:40, emphasis in original)

In this type of research, the place and activity rather than the group define the kinds of data that can be obtained. When anthropologists situate themselves in villages, they gain access to a full range of activities engaged in by all members of the group, so they gain an overall picture of what village life is like. Focusing on a place rather than a group provides a piece of the picture, a fragment of the mosaic that makes up the totality of urban life.

Multimethod Research

One of my greatest adventures in the field came when I was an undergraduate anthropology major at UCLA.

Armed with a President's Fellowship provided by the University of California system, I undertook a study of other students who fit my own profile: women who had returned to college to complete their education while raising children. I wanted to determine what factors led to academic success by comparing women students raising children with other students. My population was the entire student population of the Los Angeles campus of the University of California, both graduates and undergraduates.

This was a dispersed population characteristic of a large institutional context in an urban environment. I could not observe my subjects as a group, even though they were all students at UCLA, because they would never be gathered together in the same place. Nor could I study the group through network analysis, since the students who had children were largely unaware of each other's status as parents. Further, my research question required access to this large and dispersed group overall and to data that could not be acquired through participant observation alone. I settled on a multilevel research strategy.

My grant status gave me access to statistical records maintained by the University, a form of access that lent itself to survey research. I began my study by designing a computer program that would analyze several variables I had identified as significant, on the basis of my own experience as a single mother attending the university. Those variables were age, gender, marital status, number of dependents, major, and grade level at the university. I correlated these values against grade point average, which I identified as a statistical indicator of academic success.

Note that grade point average is not the only signifier of academic success, but it is the one most accessible to statistical analysis. Other markers of success could be personal satisfaction and a rewarding career. However, those variables are much more difficult to measure and may not be available to the researcher at the time of the study.

The results of the first stage of the study indicated that the most significant variables affecting grade point average were gender, marital status, and number of dependents. Overall, single women maintained the highest grade point average in the overall population, whereas married women with children had the lowest grade point average. For male students, this relationship was almost reversed: married men maintained higher grade point averages than did single men. As I had predicted on the basis that women are the primary caregivers in U.S. society, the number of dependents was more strongly correlated with academic success for females than for males.

After determining that marital status, gender, and number of dependents were significant variables in academic success as measured by grade point average, I proceeded to the second level of the study: determining what factors in the lives of women with children shaped their college experience. I mailed a questionnaire to 10 percent of the female students with dependents, selecting every tenth name on the university's roster of students who fit that description. I did not weight the sample by age, marital status, grade point average, major, or grade level. The questionnaires included both structured and open-ended questions, which I based on my own experience as a female student with children.

The results of this part of the study were startling. I learned that many women in my sample held jobs while attending school and serving as primary caregivers for their children, as well as bearing sole responsibility for maintaining the home. Some of these women held full-time jobs in addition to their academic and domestic responsibilities. Despite their difficulties in pursuing their education, the overwhelming majority of these women listed "personal fulfillment" as their primary motivation for making the effort. "Finding a better job" came in a distant fourth.

The main difference between married women with children and single women with children lay in what they identified as their greatest difficulty in pursuing their education. Married women with children identified "finding a time and place to study" as their greatest difficulty, whereas single women with children identified "insufficient financial resources." "Finding a time and place to study" ranked much lower for single mothers than for married mothers. On the basis of my own experience as part of this population, I concluded that single mothers are better able to set priorities than are married mothers. Thus, they can make studying a higher priority than, for example, "serving family meals on time."

After analyzing the results of the questionnaires, I selected ten women for follow-up interviews. During this phase of the study, major and grade level were factored into the selection process. These open-ended interviews confirmed much of what had been learned in the questionnaire phase and also provided more in-depth information on motivations, goals, and lifestyles shaping the success of women students with children. One of these women later became my colleague on the faculty at California State University, Northridge—

she in the Psychology Department and I in the Anthropology Department—and we shared some of the same students. Thus, I inadvertently achieved a long-term look at this fascinating population.

Multimethod research is advocated for all the social sciences by John Brewer and Albert Hunter, who note that the methods used by social scientists for collecting data all have limitations:

> This multimethod strategy is simple, but powerful. . . . Each new set of data increases our confidence that the research results reflect reality rather than methodological error. And divergent findings are equally important, but for another reason. They signal the need to analyze a research problem further and to be cautious in interpreting the significance of any one set of data. (1989:17)

Ethnographic fieldwork has always been multimethod, relying on several strategies for collecting data. The multimethod approach presented as an example here illustrates ways of adapting the anthropological method and approach to the urban context, in which the target population is often elusive because it is geographically dispersed and difficult to identify.

It is common among newcomers to social science research to assume that there is only one appropriate stance from which to view the group one is studying. In fact, there are many possibilities for observing human interactions. However, the research stance shapes the kinds of data that can be gathered. There are many advantages to repeated visits to the field, including a longitudinal view of changes through time. It is also true that the position of the anthropologist vis-à-vis the people he or she studies shifts through time, and this shift affords a range of perspectives typically not available during a single visit to the field. When people study people, the calibration of the measuring instrument—the anthropologist—is rarely perfect.

SUMMARY

Anthropology is an integrative discipline that studies human beings in all their complexity: past and present; biologically, socially, and culturally. The discipline is organized into four subfields: cultural anthropology, physical anthropology, linguistics, and archaeology. In addition, some anthropologists apply the discipline's theoretical and methodological tools to contemporary issues. The anthropological approach reflects the broad scope of the discipline, so that anthropologists study cross-culturally, holistically, from the insider perspective, and taking the stance of cultural relativism.

Cultural anthropology is a social science that deals with many of the same conceptual issues as the humanities. As a science, anthropology is based in empiricism, or direct observations. The methodology of participant observation equips anthropologists for observing a range of behaviors from a variety of perspectives. The anthropological enterprise of observing and describing a group of people is called ethnography.

Because anthropologists are people studying other people, the fieldwork experience is complex. Anthropologists are guided by the American Anthropological Association Code of Ethics, which specifies that researchers must do everything in their power to avoid harm to the safety, dignity, and privacy of the people with whom they work. Because anthropology has traditionally centered on the study of the Other, we have often overlooked the others in our midst, including members of ethnic groups and women. These omissions have led to gaps in anthropological theory overall.

Anthropologists have increasingly begun to conduct research in cities. This shift in the research setting has led anthropologists to question the efficacy of ethnographic techniques, which were developed in the study of villages, for conducting research in the more socially complex environment of cities. Anthropologists have adapted ethnographic methods to cities by focusing on subcultures, such as occupational and ethnic groups. They have also conducted site-specific research, in which they conduct observations and interviews centering on an urban location where a variety of people are engaged in readily observable activities. Anthropologists have also adopted multimethod techniques that may include survey research.

Differing research populations raise a variety of issues relating to the anthropologist's ability to gain access and with respect to differing power relationships between anthropologists and the people they study. Anthropologists have traditionally "studied down," which means they are in a superior power relationship to the people they study. Some anthropologists are now beginning to "study up," so that subjects have greater power to control access to data. Under some circumstances, it is possible to conduct research in settings where anthropologists and their subjects have a balance of power with respect to each other. Differences in access and the power relationship between anthropologists and their subjects shape the kinds of data available to the anthropologist.

POWER WORDS

applied anthropology	empiricism	insider perspective	paradigm
archaeology	ethnocentrism	intersubjectivity	participant observation
artifacts	ethnographies	key informant	philosophical
cross-cultural	ethnography	linguistics	relativism
cultural anthropology	etic	material culture	physical anthropology
cultural relativism	forensic anthropology	methodological	primatology
data	genealogy	relativism	science
disinterested	genetics	network analysis	theory
emic	holistic	objectivity	variables

INTERNET EXERCISE

1. What is anthropology? For a view on the subject by the American Anthropological Association, visit **http://www.aaa.org/anthbroc.htm**. Briefly compare the description of anthropology in this chapter with that provided by the AAA.

2. Find out about the American Anthropological Association, the world's largest organization of individuals interested in anthropology. Visit their website at **http://www.aaa.org/** and select one of the following topics to explore: how to become a member; sections and interest groups; the AAA Code of Ethics; or government affairs. What does this tell you about the values and concerns of anthropologists? An online membership form is available at **http://www.aaa.org/membership_form/index.cfm/**.

3. The American Anthropological Association Guide to Departments of Anthropology provides an overview of academic resources in the field. Visit their website at **http://www.aaa.org/ guide.htm**. Note that some departments specialize in one subfield only, whereas others take a four subfields approach.

3

The Adventure of Anthropology

In this chapter...

The adventure begins—nineteenth-century evolutionists

Anthropology developed as Europeans attempted to explain differences between themselves and the people they colonized. Though early anthropology was Eurocentric and androcentric, it developed into a discipline that promoted understanding and appreciation of cultural differences. And nineteenth-century evolutionists identified many issues and institutions that continue to challenge researchers: the importance of kinship and family, the basis of law and marriage customs, and the relationship of religion to other social institutions.

The British school—the importance of structure and function

Two figures loom large in British social anthropology. Bronislaw Malinowski set the standard for fieldwork by studying all facets of Trobriand Island culture and society, from marriage customs to gardening magic. He defined the approach of functionalism, suggesting that society functions to meet human needs. The approach of A. R. Radcliffe-Brown is known as structural functionalism, which centered on the idea that social institutions promote the stability of the group.

The American school—the primacy of culture

Franz Boas, the "father of American anthropology," affirmed the value of cultural relativism and challenged the Eurocentric claims of social Darwinists. He stressed the importance of collecting information about contemporary cultures that appeared to be disappearing in the wake of European colonialism. Attempts of his students to "prove" that culture has a greater influence on behavior than biology have been criticized in recent years, but the work of Boas and his students has had a major impact both on American anthropology and on American society as a whole.

The anthropologist as Other

Behind ethnography there often lies the anthropologist's story of loneliness, frustration, and, in some cases, grief over the loss of a loved one. In his diaries, Malinowski wrote poignantly of his angst and human frailties. His experiences remained hidden until the 1960s, when his diaries were published. Now many anthropologists are telling of their fieldwork adventures, revealing an important dimension of ethnography: how the story of the anthropologist affects the story of the people being studied.

Long before crew members of the starship *Enterprise* vowed to "boldly go where no man has gone before," anthropologists were doing something very similar. Early anthropologists ventured far beyond the boundaries of their own societies in search of the Other—in this case, people who had very different ideas about what it means to be human. Unaided by intergalactic technology, anthropologists crossed vast regions of the Arctic on dogsled, suffered frostbite, cowered under mosquito nets in the tropics, and battled the effects of malaria, while pondering the meaning of life and anthropology. The journal of one such pioneer, Franz Boas (1884), records the wonder of that adventure:

> The Eskimo [Inupiat] are sitting around me, their mouths filled with raw seal liver (the spot of blood on the back of the paper shows you how I joined in). As a thinking person, for me the most important result of this trip lies in the strengthening of my point of view that the idea of a "cultured" individual is merely relative and that a person's worth should be judged by his Herzenbildung [character].

Boas wrote those lines in 1883 during an arduous trip to Baffin Island, above the Hudson Bay in the northern part of Canada. Not only might one detect the traces of seal liver blood on the original pages of Boas's notebook, but it is also possible to detect the embryonic form of the anthropological concept of cultural relativism in his enthusiastic description of "Eskimo" life.

Boas jotted down his thoughts on the relativity of culture while sitting snugly in an igloo after a difficult and dangerous expedition to Cumberland Sound, an inlet of Baffin Island, in winter, when temperatures dropped to –45°C (–49°F) and it was dark twenty-four hours a day. At that time, Boas was not technically an anthropologist. Born and educated in Germany, he was trained in physics, psychology, and geography and had journeyed to the remote north to map the region. As is true for many people who become anthropologists, Boas was drawn to the field by a transforming encounter with the Other. As many present-day anthropologists can attest, learning to understand the Other is an adventure that can precipitate a lifetime of discovery.

WHAT IS A HUMAN BEING?

Anthropology developed in the wake of the colonial expansion that brought Europeans into contact with people very unlike themselves. The "discovery" of the Americas, of East Asia, and of sub-Saharan Africa coincided with the beginnings of printing and the subsequent spread of literacy, thus providing a forum for the exchange of ideas at the same time that vast quantities of new information about the world and its people were flooding into Europe.

Because of this cataclysmic encounter with the Other, Europeans found it necessary to redefine the "we." Thus, colonialism provided the impetus for the intrinsic anthropological question posed at the beginning of Chapter 1: What is a human being? The emergence of that question as a central philosophical theme during the colonial period gave rise to many speculative and imaginative answers. In the sixteenth century, many fanciful depictions of "humanoids" appeared in European publications (see Figure 3.1). Based on travelers' descriptions, some of these representations of the incomprehensible Other portray human figures with ears the size of elephants' or with eyes in the middle of their chest.

Captives from Africa and the Americas were put on display in England and France, where observers noted that they were "clad in beasts' skins" and spoke an "unintelligible language." In fact, European royalty were often clad in beasts' skins as well, and the skin of the ermine, a large weasel, was used to decorate the garments of people of high rank. Further, the languages of those who were brought unwillingly to Europe were perfectly intelligible to members of their own group.

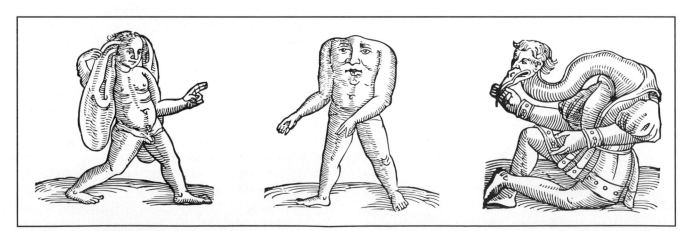

FIGURE 3.1 Woodcuts of Humanoids

During the fifteenth and sixteenth centuries, European adventurers brought reports of previously unknown people back to scholars who rarely ventured beyond their accustomed rounds. Artists rendered drawings of these "humanoids" based on travelers' accounts filtered by their own experience of European life.

In support of Robert Redfield's contention that the distinction between self and other is the universal basis of world view, writings of the colonial period indicate that Europeans considered themselves the reference point from which humanness should be defined. As Edmund Leach notes:

> From the very start of "the expansion of Europe" the invaders tended to treat all the newly discovered peoples of Southern Africa and the Americas as less than fully human, a convenient doctrine which implied that they were legitimate objects for enslavement, exploitation and extermination. (1982:66)

Though the peoples they encountered represented a range of social organizations, the Europeans followed the classic pattern of stereotyping the Other, obscuring the great differences among them. Both African and Native American groups were organized in a variety of patterns ranging from small egalitarian bands to stratified chiefdoms and states, but Europeans used similar language to describe all of them.

Europeans falsely believed that native peoples of Africa and the Americas existed in the "natural state," free of the social conventions that governed the values and behaviors of "civilized" human beings. Because they did not understand the essential order and unity underlying African and American cultures, Europeans assumed that those cultures had no rules and were existing in an "unfettered" state. Such a situation is, of course, impossible. A major contribution of anthropology is the discovery that all societies are ordered and all human beings are governed by beliefs about what is appropriate.

As Mary Douglas has pointed out, chaos or disorder is experienced as threatening, and there is no question that Europeans found their own concepts of order challenged by the "disorder" they encountered in the Other. Two main themes dominated the writings of Europeans as they attempted to order their experience of the Other. One theme centered on the concept of the debased savage; the other celebrated that of the "noble savage."

In his book *Leviathan*, published in 1651, Thomas Hobbes envisioned the life of human beings in their "natural state": "No arts; no letters; no society; and which is worst of all, continual fear and danger of violent death; and the life of man, solitary, poor, nasty, brutish, and short." On the other hand, the eighteenth-century scholar Jean Jacques Rousseau popularized the concept of the "noble savage" in his book *The Social Contract,* published in 1762. However, the term had been used nearly a century earlier by the poet John Dryden, who wrote:

> I am as free as Nature first made man,
> Ere the base laws of servitude began,
> When wild in woods the noble savage ran.
>   ("The Conquest of Granada," 1669–1670)

Thus, the conquest of the world during the colonial era produced two contradictory, and equally erroneous, concepts of the Other: that of the innocent, childlike rustic and that of the brutish "savage." Both are still with us.

Both views were reflected in the aims of an ambitious expedition to the southern coast of Australia organized by a short-lived anthropology group formed in Paris in 1800. One underlying assumption of the effort was that "savages" were superior to Europeans in health, strength, and general physical perfection but were inferior in manners, religion, and morals. A medical student on the expedition, François Péron, planned to test the hypothesis that "moral perfection must be in inverse ratio to physical perfection" (Stocking 1968:32).

Péron concluded that Australians and Tasmanians were inferior to Europeans both physically and morally, suggesting that their bountiful natural habitat had made them lethargic. It is clear, however, that Péron's views of moral attributes, at least, were subjective:

> Commenting . . . on the surprise evinced by Tasmanians at the sexual virility of a French sailor who ravished a Tasmanian woman immediately upon stepping ashore, Péron hypothesized that Tasmanian sexual desire was, like that of animals, periodic. (Stocking 1968:33)

Péron seems not to have considered the behavior of the French sailor a moral issue. French philosophy and anthropology alike would have benefited by a record of the thoughts of the Tasmanians about the "humanness" of the sailor, whose behavior violates the norms of virtually every society on the earth.

Even as Péron conducted his ill-considered investigations among the "savages," one of his senior colleagues in the group published a tract on methodology, describing a plan for the study of human societies that appears to presage modern views of the subject. In his *Considerations on the Diverse Methods to Follow in the Observation of Savage Peoples,* Joseph Marie de Gerando (known as Citizen Degerando after the French Revolution) described the "science of man" as the "noblest" of the natural sciences, a study that should be based on careful observation. From there, Degerando suggested, one would proceed to comparative analysis and, finally, to the formulation of "general laws" of human development and behavior. Degerando criticized the sweeping generalizations made by scholars and travelers of his day, noting that they tended to judge "savage" customs and motivations by analogy to their own:

> Thus, given certain actions, they suppose certain opinions or needs, because among us, such actions ordinarily result from these needs or opinions. They make the Savage reason as we do, when the Savage does not himself explain to them his reasoning. (Degerando [1883] 1969:67)

Degerando argued that it is impossible to understand the reasoning of savages without learning their language, because only with an understanding of their language could one appreciate their "manner of seeing and feeling." He added: "The best means of understanding savages is to become in a manner of speaking like one among them," thus anticipating by a century the anthropological concepts of insider perspective and participant observation.

NINETEENTH-CENTURY EVOLUTIONISTS

Among the nineteenth-century explorers was a young English naturalist named Charles Darwin, who traveled the seas of the Southern Hemisphere aboard the H.M.S. *Beagle* from 1831 to 1836. Just twenty-two years old when the *Beagle* set sail, Darwin undertook the job of studying plants and animals encountered on the voyage, much of which was along the coasts of South America and on its offshore islands. The naturalist examined tropical forests in Brazil, fossils in the pampas of Argentina, native peoples of Tierra del Fuego (the southern tip of South America), and the geology of the Andes. But Darwin's observations of variations in the animal life of the Galapagos Islands may have influenced his thinking the most.

On his journey, Darwin pored over a classic treatise by Sir Charles Lyell, *Principles of Geology*, published in 1830. Lyell discussed a theory, proposed in 1809 by the French scholar Jean Baptiste Lamarck, that one species might develop into another because of the intense desire and efforts of an individual to better adapt itself to its environment. Lamarck's observations were met with derision by many religious leaders of the day, who held to the biblical account, in which the creation of the earth and all its species took place over a period of six days.

Within this context of intellectual debate, Darwin formulated a theory to explain his observations of variation in plant and animal species. After returning to England from his voyage aboard the *Beagle*, Darwin spent more than twenty years conducting botanical and zoological studies on transmission of traits from one generation to the next. He was also familiar with efforts of British sportsmen to selectively breed for desirable traits in animals ranging from race horses to hunting dogs. Finally, on November 24, 1859, Darwin published his landmark book, *On the Origin of Species*.

Darwin is often credited with developing the concept of **evolution,** but the idea of systematic change through time had been discussed decades earlier. Darwin's greatest contribution to evolutionary theory

Charles Darwin.

is the idea that members of a particular species that are especially well suited to a particular environment will thrive and pass on their adaptive traits to their offspring, a process he called **natural selection:**

> Owing to this struggle for life, any variation, however slight and from whatever cause proceeding, if it be in any degree profitable to an individual of any species, in its infinitely complex relations to other organic beings and to external nature, will tend to the preservation of that individual, and will generally be inherited by its offspring. (1859:61)

This theory has often been called by the somewhat misleading label "survival of the fittest." It is misleading because, according to Darwin's model, "fitness" refers only to the ability of an individual to survive within a particular **econiche,** an environmental niche exploited by a particular species, not to some overall category of fitness or to what has often been misunderstood as a general moral superiority.

In themselves, the theories of evolution and natural selection do not involve value judgments. They are simply statements about the nature of the relationship among living organisms and between those organisms and their environment. For example, it would be absurd to suggest that an elephant is a "better" animal than a moose or that one is more "evolved" than the other. Each animal is adapted to its environment. Similarly, though human societies vary considerably from each other, it is inappropriate to compare them on a scale of values, yet many nineteenth-century evolutionists did exactly that.

The misinterpretation of Darwin's theory of natural selection, applied to social theory, has been called **social Darwinism.** In fact, it could more appropriately be called "social Spencerism," because Herbert Spencer helped to define the nineteenth-century model of social evolution.

How Did "We" Become So Superior?

Unlike Darwin, Spencer was not a scientist who based his theories on careful observation of species in their natural setting. Instead, he was more interested in framing general concepts that attempted to explain broad categories of phenomena. To this end, he compiled volumes of descriptions of various societies, which he used as the source for his ambitious work *Principles of Sociology,* published in 1876. Spencer, who is responsible for the concept of "survival of the fittest," also added to evolutionary theory the concept of "progress," which implies a transition from a "lesser" to a "higher" state. In his book *Social Statics,* he writes:

> Progress, therefore, is not an accident, but a necessity. Instead of civilization being artifact, it is part of nature; all of a piece with the development of the embryo or the unfolding of a flower. The modifications mankind have undergone, and are still undergoing, result from a law underlying the whole organic creation, and provided the human race continues, and the constitution of things remains the same, those modifications must end in completeness. . . . So surely must the things we call evil and immorality disappear; so surely must man become perfect. ([1850] 1883:45–46)

Spencer believed that evolution always moves from simple to complex and that human beings progress from "primitive" to "civilized" on a number of levels. The "savage" exists in a condition of subservience to the environment, he suggested, and consequently the primitive mind is closer to its environment than is the civilized mind. Therefore, the savage has acute sensory perceptions but mental processes that rarely rise above the level of sensation. The savage is credulous and is incapable of planning for the future or of framing abstract thoughts. In addition, the savage's behavior is primarily a matter of reflexive or imitative response to environmental stimuli—impulsive and nonsocial—the result of a "simpler nervous system." Because the savage lives in a simple social system, he "could not evolve these higher intellectual faculties in the absence of a fit environment" (see Stocking 1968:117–118). As society develops, Spencer believed, man progresses from behavior based on simple reflexive habit to "reflective consciousness."

As twentieth-century scientific investigations of human evolution later revealed, Spencer's assessment of the intellectual capacities of early humans was erroneous. Anatomically modern *Homo sapiens* evolved about 100,000 years ago. According to Robert Boyd and Joan B. Silk, "The qualifier 'anatomically modern' emphasizes that their bodies were very similar to modern humans, but they had not yet developed the cultural traditions, symbolic behaviors, and complex technologies that we see among later peoples" (2000:452). Thus, early humans were biologically as capable of abstract thought as was Spencer himself. The first unambiguous evidence for rituals—which are symbolic behavior and are therefore evidence of abstract thought—dates from the Upper Paleolithic, 40,000 years ago (Boyd and Silk 2000).

The most negative result of Spencer's social evolutionary theory was that it discouraged the implementation of programs aimed at helping the poor and justified European colonial expansion, even at the expense of great injury to the people being subjugated. Spencer was opposed to free public schools and to public health programs of all kinds, including licensing of doctors and nurses, because he believed that such programs were against the laws of nature, since they preserved "unfit" members of the species:

> And since preservation of the society takes precedence of individual preservation, as being a condition to it, we must, in considering social phenomena, interpret good and bad rather in their earlier senses than in their later senses; and so must regard as relatively good that which furthers survival of the society, great as may be the suffering inflicted on its members. (Spencer [1876] 1896:233)

From the perspective of more than a hundred years later, it is easy to dismiss such ideas and to question how they could have developed in the first place. However, they have found their way into many present-day theoretical formulations, including some implicit assumptions about innate differences between "Western" and "non-Western" people. As noted earlier, Spencer assumed that the "savage" is incapable of forming abstract thought and is credulous, believing in phenomena that more "sophisticated" people dismiss, such as ghosts and other spirit beings. In fact, all human groups have religion, which postulates a "reality" that transcends ordinary experience. The belief in a transcendent reality is often referred to as **mythopoetic thought.** Douglass Price-Williams writes: "Mythopoetic understanding is equally available to the individual as to the group, and cuts across all societies, technologically advanced or not" (1999:30).

Ideas that have been rejected by anthropologists have found their way into popular fiction, forming the basis for much "caveman" lore. For example, prehistoric humans, or "cavemen," are often depicted in cartoons as wearing a crude garment made of fur and carrying a crude club with which to subjugate both animals and women. However, our ancestors were shaping stone tools at least two million years ago, and there is no evidence that prehistoric women were any more "brutalized" than are modern women.

The Primacy of the Family

Despite the limitations of their data and the speculative nature of their conclusions, some early scholars identified social institutions that anthropologists still consider important to understanding the dynamics of human society. One early finding is that an analysis of public institutions, such as law, cannot be divorced from the dynamics of a seemingly private phenomenon—the family. This discovery, which still has far-reaching implications in terms of both political institutions and gender roles, was in large part due to the work of Sir Henry Maine, a teacher of law at Cambridge University. The insight was made possible by the unique combination of Maine's pedagogical interest in Roman law and his practical experience as a former member of England's colonial government in India.

As a British colonial official, Maine had noted that in certain Indian villages, property was held in common by family groups. He further observed that attempts by British administrators to break up family-owned property often resulted in depriving people of rights due them through their kin group. This was a somewhat revolutionary opinion for the time. Since property was transmitted through the male line in India (a patrilineal system), Maine theorized that males had always been dominant in all human society.

Maine's logical leap from a non-European society of his time to the origins of all human society illustrates a pervasive flaw in nineteenth-century concepts of evolution. Maine assumed that Indian society represented an earlier stage on the evolutionary scale, without considering that India's social and cultural systems had been evolving just as long as Europe's had. There is no evidence that, in the absence of military or cultural conquest, all human societies will eventually come to resemble Europe. Furthermore, there is no evidence that different present-day human institutions represent different stages of cultural development. All modern human groups have been evolving for the same period of time.

Maine combined his observations of the family in India with his scholarly knowledge of Roman law and noted that the Romans considered a group of families descended from one ancestor as a unified group (a clan). In his book *Ancient Law,* published in 1861, Maine wrote, "the unit of ancient society was the Family, of a Modern Society the Individual" (1861:121). Thus, Maine anticipated the work of several generations of anthropologists by identifying kinship as the cornerstone of society.

At the same time in the United States, a lawyer and amateur anthropologist named Lewis Henry Morgan concluded independently that kinship is central to the organization of human society. Morgan (who, like Boas, has been called the father of American anthropology) grew up in the heart of Iroquois country in

New York State. A superb organizer, as a young man, he established a secret society with elaborate costumes and ceremonies.

Morgan formed a friendship with Ely Parker, a member of the Seneca, the most populous and powerful of the confederated Iroquois tribes. With Parker, Morgan visited the Seneca reservation many times, becoming impressed with and fascinated by Seneca beliefs and way of life. His boyish secret society was now redesigned as a historical society dedicated to the purpose of recording the rapidly disappearing Native American culture.

Morgan laboriously accumulated tables of kinship terms used by many Native American groups in describing their relatives, thus distinguishing himself by assembling precise data that could be used to analyze systems for organizing kinship. He supplemented his data on Native Americans with information from a questionnaire that he sent all over the world. Such a feat in data collection still stands as a monumental effort.

One of Morgan's enduring contributions to anthropology is his identification of two concepts of kinship: consanguinity and affinity. **Consanguine** literally means "with blood" and refers to persons who are related through a biological tie. Brothers and sisters are consanguines, as are parents and children. **Affines** are relatives by marriage. Husbands and wives are affines, as are one's in-laws.

Morgan believed that his comparison of world kinship types provided evidence for an evolutionary model in which human society developed "from a state of promiscuous intercourse to final civilization." As described in his 1877 book *Ancient Society,* the trajectory of this evolutionary course was from "savagery" to "barbarism" to "civilization." Although he did not develop these concepts, Morgan refined the model to include "lower," "middle," and "upper" stages of savagery and "lower," "middle," and "upper" stages of barbarism.

From the earliest stage of savagery, "promiscuous intercourse," in which any man and any woman could have sex together, social relationships progressed through a series of stages culminating in "civilized marriage," or **monogamy,** in which one man is married to one woman. Morgan's identification of monogamy as the pinnacle of progress is typical of the perspectives of nineteenth-century European theorists, who consistently awarded European social systems the gold star for evolutionary success.

Though focusing on kinship, Morgan considered the organization of the family to be linked to patterns

Polygamy is a pattern of marriage in which an individual marries more than one mate. The most common form of polygamy is polygyny, in which a man marries more than one wife, as in this example from the Bakhtiari of Iran. The nineteenth-century evolutionist Lewis Henry Morgan suggested that types of marriage are related to the evolutionary stages of a society.

of subsistence, and his developmental stages included advances in technology. For example, the invention of the bow and arrow signaled the upper status of savagery, and the art of pottery making ushered in the lower status of barbarism. Although Morgan's model of evolutionary progression is generally rejected (and even ridiculed) today, it is a remarkable achievement and perhaps even presages the holistic approach in its implicit recognition that different aspects of social life are interrelated.

Morgan asserted that the stages of development are "substantially the same" for human beings everywhere, a concept that reinforced the idea that European society represents the pinnacle of human evolution, a **Eurocentric** perspective. As were other evolutionary models of the day, Morgan's typology was also **androcentric,** or male centered, because it assumed that patriarchy—male control of the political system—is the "natural," or "morally superior," or "most evolved" human condition. In reading these early theorists, one could easily conclude that the impetus for evolution was provided by male sexual desires and social aspirations. This theme is explicitly addressed in the writings aimed at analyzing the hypothetical evolutionary course from matriarchy to patriarchy. In patriarchy, positions of public power are reserved for males; in matriarchy, positions of public power are reserved for females.

The Primitive Horde and the Primacy of Mothers

The supposed transition from matriarchy to patriarchy is explored in a speculative work, *Das Mutterrecht* (Mother Right) (1861), by a Swiss law professor, J. J. Bachofen. A **matriarchy** is a system of government in which positions of power are reserved for females; a **patriarchy** is a system of government in which power is reserved for males. The model of evolution presented by Bachofen has been called "one of the wildest schemes from the point of view of causality" (Harris 1968:188).

As was Maine, Bachofen was interested in ancient law, and he, too, was intrigued by the social life of ancient Greece and Rome. Unlike Maine, however, Bachofen looked to mythology to explain the origins of social life, believing that myths can be analyzed for clues to ancient ways of thinking. He wrote: "Myth contains the origins, and myth alone can reveal them" ([1861] 1967:75).

Bachofen believed that the earliest human society was characterized by sexual promiscuity and that women, being nobler and more sensitive than men, would naturally be disgusted by this sexual license. On the basis of this premise, Bachofen postulated that women seized control of society by force and invented marriage to restrain men's sexuality. During this second period, or "gynocratic epoch" (a period of matriarchy), women were heads of families, children were given their mother's family name, inheritance was matrilineal, and goddesses were the supreme deities. However, Bachofen believed, this social form was based on an inferior religious principle: the biological bond between mother and child as symbolized by the Earth Mother deity.

Men tried to assert their claims through the institution of **couvade,** a childbirth custom in which the father of the child behaves as though he were giving birth, including taking to bed and observing all rituals associated with giving birth. According to Bachofen, couvade allowed men to pretend they were mothers and thus to participate in the power of motherhood.

Eventually, Bachofen reasoned, men rebelled against the authority of women, overcoming them by force. The victory of men over women marked the emergence of the Dionysian age, in which fatherhood formed the basis for the principle of divinity and the role of women was reduced to simply caring for men's offspring. Bachofen considered the principle of divine fatherhood, as expressed in the concept "God the Father," to be a "higher" evolutionary stage:

> The triumph of paternity brings with it the liberation of the spirit from the manifestations of nature, a sublimation of human existence over the laws of material life. While the principle of motherhood is common to all spheres of tellurian [earthly] life, man, by the preponderant position he accords to the begetting potency, emerges from this relationship and becomes conscious of his higher calling. Spiritual life rises over corporeal existence, and the relation with the lower spheres of existence is restricted to the physical aspect. Maternity pertains to the physical side of man, the only thing he shares with the animals: the paternal-spiritual principle belongs to him alone. Here he breaks through the bonds of tellurism and lifts his eyes to the higher regions of the cosmos. Triumphant paternity partakes of the heavenly light, while childbearing motherhood is bound up with the earth that bears all things. ([1861] 1967:109–110)

Bachofen's writings reflect several Eurocentric assumptions characteristic of nineteenth-century social evolutionist thought: (1) Mind and body are separate entities. (2) We are linked to God by our superior mental capacity, whereas we are debased by our bodies and our often unruly passions. (3) Men are intellectually superior to women. (4) Males have a stronger sex drive than women. The last assumption was fostered by the Victorian view that morally pure women should be sexually chaste, engaging in sex only to please their husbands and to bear children for the **lineage,** the line of succession in which property and status are inherited, in a patrilineal society, through the male line. Royalty and members of the nobility would be understandably reluctant to pass on their titles and wealth to the offspring of some other lineage through the infidelity of their wives. Thus, views of women as sexually reluctant and concepts of the body as impure served to maintain the "purity" of the patrilineal line.

Male sexual prowess figures prominently in the theories of a Scottish law scholar, John McLennan. As did Bachofen, McLennan drew information from

The nineteenth-century theorist John McLennan believed that bride capture represented an early stage of evolution when men acquired wives by stealing them from other men. The custom of carrying the bride across the threshold is reminiscent of bride capture. In this picture, the groom sweeps the bride down the staircase after their wedding ceremony.

classical Greek and Roman authors, but he was also one of the first anthropologists to make use of travelers' accounts of customs of non-European tribes. McLennan was particularly interested in **bride capture,** a marriage custom practiced by Greeks and Romans and some other groups, in which the groom makes a great show and pretense of stealing the bride from her family. In his book *Primitive Marriage* (1865), McLennan theorized that the custom was a remnant from an earlier evolutionary period, when men acquired wives by capturing them from other men.

Like Morgan and Bachofen, McLennan believed that sexual promiscuity was the rule among the earliest humans, whom he described as the "primitive horde." Because women were likely to have several sexual partners, it was impossible to ascertain the father of any particular woman's child. Therefore, kinship was reckoned through the mother only, and marriage customs were **endogamous,** which means that people mated within the group. Because early human populations lived under harsh conditions that subjected them to an intense struggle for existence, McLennan theorized, they practiced female **infanticide,** or killing of female infants, for the "common good":

> As braves and hunters were required and valued, it would be the interest of every horde to rear, when possible, its healthy male children. It would be less its interest to rear females, as they would be less capable of self-support, and of contributing, by their exertions to the common good. (1865:165)

McLennan lacked access to modern systematic studies of the lives of foragers, which indicate that most such groups rely primarily on the gathering done by women rather than on the hunting that is the province of men. However, like other nineteenth-century evolutionists, McLennan did not allow his theoretical formulations to be constrained by lack of data. He speculated that female infanticide led to a scarcity of women. Scarcity of women, in turn, led to the practice of polyandry, in which a woman marries more than one man. McLennan considered polyandry to be an intermediate stage in the evolution of marriage customs. Eventually, men were forced to steal wives from other groups in warfare, thus giving rise to the practice of **exogamy,** or out-marrying. As McLennan put it:

> If, then, we conceive that . . . the name of "wife" came to be synonymous with a subject and enslaved woman in the power of her captor or captors, and the name of marriage to be applied to a man's relation to such a woman as possessor of her, the origin of exogamy becomes apparent. (1865:65)

Although modern anthropologists are reluctant to view marriage as the enslavement of women, they still consider the concepts of **endogamy** (in-marrying) and exogamy to be important in explaining the role of marriage in forming political alliances.

One problem with evolutionary theories centering on the presumed sexual license of the primitive

DISCUSSIONS

Evolution and Reproduction

The importance of reproduction was acknowledged in the models generated by some nineteenth-century social evolutionists. However, these theories were centered on the male sex drive, paying little attention to the production and care of children. Survival of the group through time depends not only on the generation of offspring but also on ensuring their survival so that they might, in turn, generate offspring of their own. Since human infants are dependent on caretakers for a long period of time, theories of evolution relating to humans must also take into account biological and cultural mechanisms that promote the survival of dependent offspring.

Sarah Blaffer Hrdy (1981), a scholar focusing on biological evolution, distinguishes between mechanisms that benefit individuals and those that promote survival of the group. She notes that promoting the survival of particular individuals does not necessarily promote the survival of the group as a whole.

Hrdy provides examples from her own observations of baboons on the plains of Kenya near Mount Kilimanjaro and of Hanuman langurs in the sacred city of Mount Abu in India. Baboon and langur groups are typically composed of several females and their offspring together with a dominant male. Hrdy notes that males direct particular care toward offspring likely to be their own but are often brutal or murderous toward the offspring of other males.

Dominant males in some nonhuman primate groups kill the offspring of other males to bring the females into estrus, so the females will be sexually available. This practice promotes transmission of the dominant male's genes but compromises survival of the group because it wastes the energy necessary to produce the infant that was killed.

Reproduction represents a major investment by the entire group because producing a new primate requires energy in the form of calories. At the same time, pregnant, birthing, or nursing females may be less mobile than other individuals and, therefore, may slow the group's movements. In addition, in the case of human beings, their offspring mature more slowly than do those of other animals and must be cared for over an extended period of time. Thus, reproduction has a major impact on the dynamics of the group.

Unlike many other primates, human females do not exhibit external signs during their periods of fertility, and they are sexually receptive even when they are not fertile. Thus, sexuality is not linked directly to fertility. This has been widely explained as an adaptation that promotes monogamous pair-bonding by making a woman continuously receptive to a man and increasing the likelihood that he will be willing to invest in the offspring. Hrdy acknowledges

horde is that they are based on the assumption that the activities of prehistoric males, and the evolution of human society in general, were driven by men's prodigious sexual appetites. It is well to remember that these ideas were developed by men living in the sexually repressed Victorian era. These theories do not reflect an accurate picture of what motivates women or men, and they do not consider that the activities of most people in virtually all known societies center on providing food and shelter and creating social bonds that last through time.

These theories also do not consider that the "agenda" of evolution is to survive long enough to produce viable offspring. Thus, ensuring the survival of the next generation should be a higher social priority in terms of evolution than satisfying the sexual desires of men. A group that does not ensure the survival of its offspring is doomed to extinction.

In fact, human society is so complex that many variables interact to produce a viable constellation of values and customs. Early human beings could survive only in groups, since they were slower and weaker than many other species with which they shared an econiche. It was only by banding together, pooling their strength, outsmarting their predators, and protecting the weaker members of the group—including the helpless human infant—that human beings were able to survive as a species.

Nineteenth-century models also omit a key feature of Darwin's theory—the role of the environment as a selective factor in the evolution of a species. In the next chapter we look at some more recent theories of

that there is abundant evidence to support this view:

> Few could comfortably belittle the mutual attachment so readily observable between mated primates—particularly between human sexual partners, where the emotions of lovemaking and companionship are magnified by countless preadaptations for intelligence, subtlety, sharing, and loyalty, as well as for heightened mutual pleasure from sexual intercourse. (1981:135)

Hrdy notes, however, that evidence from nonhuman primates challenges the idea that concealed estrus and continuous sexual receptivity in humans form the basis for the monogamous pair bond. Gibbons and siamangs—both apes, and therefore genetically closer to humans than baboons and langur monkeys are—mate for life. Sexual activity among members of these two species is considerably lower than among the polygynous baboons and langurs. Breeding periods among gibbons and siamangs occur only about once every two years (Ellefson 1968, Chivers 1974, Raemakers 1977).

Among species for which seasonal or cyclical receptivity is the rule, such as among savanna baboons or Barbary macaques, females are sexually aggressive and mate repeatedly with several males. A Barbary macaque female at midcycle copulates an average of every seventeen minutes and mates at least once with every sexually mature male in the group. It is the female who initiates sexual activity (Taub 1980). Among chimpanzees, an estrous female traveling with a group of males may copulate thirty to fifty times a day (Tutin 1975).

Hrdy (1981) notes that such intense sexual activity is far more than would be necessary for insemination. She suggests that copulating repeatedly with a number of males serves to obscure paternal identity and increase the likelihood that every male in the group will extend his protection to the offspring.

Hrdy suggests that the "concealed estrus" and continual sexual receptivity of human females also serve to obscure biological paternity. Thus, females can call on protection for their offspring from a number of males, since none can be sure which child is his own. Hrdy suggests that this extension of male protection to infants who cannot be specifically identified as their own contributes to group survival. As will be discussed in Chapter 6, marriage assigns social paternity in human groups and, at the same time, defines the contribution the father must make in caring for his dependent offspring.

The forces underlying evolution—social or biological—cannot be reduced to a single mechanism. Theories of evolution must also consider such complex issues as the requirements for caring for infants born into the group.

---

evolution, which do take the environment into account. But this subtlety of Darwin's was lost on early social evolutionists, many of whom were trying to explain the "superiority" of European civilization and most of whom had not personally ventured beyond the confines of their own society.

Souls, Dreams, and the Evolution of God

One nineteenth-century evolutionist who does not fit that pattern is E. B. Tylor, who formulated the anthropological definition of culture given earlier in this volume. Tylor's interest in anthropology was sparked by a tour of Cuba and Mexico undertaken when he was twenty-four years old. He explored the remains of Aztec and Toltec civilization, writing up his adventures in a travel book called *Anahuac or Mexico and the Mexicans: Ancient and Modern* (1856). Tylor has been compared in appearance to a Greek god, and he was gifted as well with a piercing intellect, a keen sense of humor, and a talent for expressing his ideas in clear, engaging prose. He is credited with transforming anthropology into a science by applying systematic analysis to the available data. H. R. Hays writes: "A fundamental caution in all of Tylor's judgments saved him from the passionate errors of such theorists as McLennan and Morgan" (1958:63).

Tylor built on McLennan's concepts of endogamy and exogamy, postulating that the practice of outmarrying arose from the need to build alliances with potential enemies, a theory that is still important today. As Tylor put it, group survival may demand that one must "marry out or die out."

Another of Tylor's contributions was his theory of animism, described in his book *Primitive Culture* (1871). **Animism** is the belief in a spirit essence that "animates" or gives life to people, animals, plants, and, sometimes, geographic features. Tylor thought that religion developed from animistic beliefs, which were an attempt to explain such phenomena as dreams and death. He writes:

> It seems that thinking men, as yet at a low level of culture, were deeply impressed by two groups of biological problems. In the first place, what is it that makes the difference between a living body and a dead one: what causes waking, sleep, trance, disease, death? In the second place, what are those human shapes which appear in dreams and visions? (Tylor 1871, reprinted in abridged form in Lessa and Vogt 1979:12)

The answer to those two questions for "the ancient savage philosophers," Tylor argued, was the concept of a soul, or an animating spirit.

Tylor's concept of animism as the earliest form of religion has given rise to a fundamental error in classifying religion, the idea that "primitive" religions have a different conceptual basis than the "great" religious traditions. The "great" religious traditions are usually identified as Judaism, Christianity, Islam, Hinduism, and Buddhism. So-called animistic religions are seen as being linked to a "primitive" or mythopoetic mode of thought. Many scholars assume that people who believe that rocks or animals have souls just don't know any better. In fact, virtually all religions are based on the concept of animating spirits or forces. The idea that human beings have souls is an animistic belief.

The great religions achieved their distinction by having developed in large state-level societies with large armies and by the fact that they are known to Western scholars. Zoroastrianism, the state religion of ancient Persia, is not classified as a great religion, even though it contributed many ideas to the religions that are considered great, including the idea—central to many forms of Christianity—that the universe is engaged in a great battle between Good and Evil. As will be discussed in Chapter 9, the greatest factor underlying variation in religions among cultures is the social organization of the society in which each occurs.

The binary opposition between "primitive" and "civilized" religions is incorporated in the work of another scholar, Sir James Frazer, who was inspired by the religion chapter in Tylor's book *Primitive Culture* and is considered to be the last of the nineteenth-century British evolutionists. Asked to write a section for the *Encyclopaedia Britannica,* Frazer sent a questionnaire on manners, customs, and beliefs to missionaries and colonial administrators all over the world, a method reminiscent of Morgan's approach to kinship terminology.

Frazer's survey of the world's religions resulted in publication of his epic work *The Golden Bough* in 1890, in which he proposed, among many other things, that the philosophical history of the human race comprised two eras: the Age of Magic and the Age of Religion. People living in the Age of Magic—and for Frazer this included many contemporary non-European societies—could not conceive of a God as civilized people know it and were unlikely to distinguish between a god and a human being with seemingly supernatural powers, such as a king or a sorcerer. Because of this point of view, Frazer suggested, "primitive people" believe that the power of the king or sorcerer extends to nature, controlling fertility and natural abundance. Frazer did not think that "primitive people" were any different from "civilized people" in their ability to reason, but he thought that their conclusions were inevitably erroneous because they started from false assumptions.

Frazer built on the idea of spiritual associations to develop the concepts of imitative and contagious magic. **Imitative magic,** also known as **sympathetic magic,** is based on the principle that like controls like. An example of imitative magic is the voodoo doll, which is formed in the likeness of the person it is intended to control. Sticking pins in a voodoo doll is believed to bring harm to the person it represents. **Contagious magic** is based on the principle that the part controls the whole. According to this idea, nail parings and hair clippings have power over the person to whom they once belonged. Thus, love spells and other forms of magic, including voodoo dolls, may involve the use of nail parings and hair clippings. According to Frazer, contagious magic arose from the erroneous beliefs of savages that an individual's discarded hair and nail clippings retain a spiritual connection with the person.

By the end of the nineteenth century, ideas propounded by social evolutionists were being seriously questioned by Franz Boas, who rejected both their concept of European superiority and their method of armchair analysis. Boas was joined in his criticism of evolutionary models by two equally articulate scholars trained in the British tradition—Bronislaw Malinowski and A. R. Radcliffe-Brown. Together, these three ardent spokesmen for anthropology virtually redirected the field's intellectual development on both sides of the Atlantic. In the United States, Boas guided his students through an exploration of cultural variations. In Britain, Malinowski and Radcliffe-Brown focused on the structure and function of human society. Ironically, it was Frazer who inspired Malinowski to study anthropology, and it was Malinowski who eventually helped to discredit both Frazer and nineteenth-century theories of social evolution.

THE BRITISH SCHOOL: STRUCTURE AND FUNCTION

When Bronislaw Malinowski boarded an ocean liner bound for Australia, little did he know he was destined to sail into anthropological history. The year was 1914 and, as Malinowski's ship negotiated the Australian coast, World War I broke out. Malinowski was technically an enemy alien, since he was Polish by birth and therefore a citizen of the Austrian empire. The Australian government "interned" Malinowski, funding his research and allowing him to work undisturbed for the duration of the war. During the two years he spent on the Trobriand Islands off New Guinea, Malinowski invented the modern fieldwork method of participant observation and compiled an ethnographic record of the Trobrianders that remains a monument in the discipline.

The Making of an Anthropologist

Like many other pioneers in the field, Malinowski did not plan to be an anthropologist. He received his Ph.D. in mathematics in 1908 from the University of Cracow in Poland and continued to study chemistry and physics. When he was forced to discontinue his studies because of tuberculosis, he left the university with *The Golden Bough* under his arm. Frazer's cross-cultural study of religious beliefs and rituals was already a classic, and Malinowski reports that he had decided to read an English classic to take his mind off his disappointment at being unable to complete his studies. He continues:

> No sooner had I read this great work than I became immersed in it and enslaved by it. I realized then that anthropology, as presented by Sir James Frazer, is a great science, worthy of as much devotion as any of her

Bronislaw Malinowski.

elder and more exact sister studies and I became bound to the service of Frazerian anthropology. (1954:94)

Malinowski went to London to study at the London School of Economics, where he met and made friends with Frazer. Frazer later gave the inaugural address when Malinowski was installed as the holder of the first chair in anthropology at the London School of Economics in 1924. However, Malinowski later turned on his former idol, ridiculing him for what he called the "vegetable hypothesis"—the idea that "primitives" identified the power of the king or of the sorcerer with the supernatural powers of gods and with the fertility of plants and animals.

Malinowski vigorously rejected the idea that "savages" think differently from Europeans. In his book *Magic, Science and Religion and Other Essays* (1948), Malinowski noted that natives of the Trobriand Islands were as pragmatic as any Western scientist in constructing an outrigger canoe and sailing it over the open ocean. In fact, Trobrianders were so skillful at constructing and sailing these seemingly fragile

Elaborately decorated canoes are still used in Kula exchange among Trobriand Island men. The Kula ring is a system of exchange studied by Bronislaw Malinowski early in the twentieth century. Other groups studied by anthropologists have been unable to retain so much of their culture, and many rely on the accounts of anthropologists to reconstruct their traditional way of life.

craft that Malinowski described them as "argonauts of the western Pacific," in his classic ethnography of that name. Despite their formidable sailing skills, Malinowski observed, Trobrianders still saw the need for magic:

> But even with all their systematic knowledge, methodically applied, they are still at the mercy of powerful and incalculable tides, sudden gales during the monsoon season and unknown reefs. And here comes in their magic, performed over the canoe during its construction, carried out at the beginning and in the course of expeditions and resorted to in moments of real danger. ([1948] 1954:30)

Malinowski noted that modern sailors still rely on "superstition" to protect themselves from danger, and, indeed, all of us have an emotional reaction to our own death:

> Who of us really believes that his own bodily infirmities and the approaching death is a purely natural occurrence, just an insignificant event in the infinite chain of causes? To the most rational of civilized men health, disease, and the threat of death float in a hazy emotional mist, which seems to become denser and more impenetrable as the fateful forms approach. It is indeed astonishing that "savages" can achieve such a sober, dispassionate outlook in these matters as they actually do.
> Thus in his relation to nature and destiny, whether he tries to exploit the first or to dodge the second, primitive man recognizes both the natural and supernatural forces and agencies, and he tries to use them both for his benefit. ([1945] 1954:32)

This passage illustrates a perspective pervading Malinowski's work—the idea of the "calculating man." Far from being at the mercy of society, Malinowski believed, human beings negotiate within the parameters defined by social custom, ultimately using social customs to their own advantage. The passage also demonstrates perhaps the greatest benefit of Malinowski's long stay among the Trobrianders and one of his most important contributions to anthropology: a sense of the essential humanity of the Other. In his diary written in the field in 1917, Malinowski pondered the meaning of the anthropological quest:

> What is the deepest essence of my investigations? To discover what are his [the Trobriander's] main passions, the motives for his conduct, his aims. . . . His essential, deepest way of thinking. At this point we are confronted with our own problems: What is essential in ourselves? (1967:119)

The "Ethnographic Present"

Malinowski rejected attempts by evolutionists to reconstruct the social life of the past, favoring instead an intensive analysis of present-day human groups. The emphasis on the present is known as **synchronic analysis;** an analysis that attempts to understand the present in terms of the past is **diachronic analysis.** Synchronic analysis has been compared to taking a slice of a culture at a specific time and examining it through an ethnographic lens, much as one takes a slice of biological tissue for examination under a microscope. In practice, this documents a culture as though it were in isolation, thus extracting it from both its history and its surrounding social context. Studies produced by synchronic analysis are said to reflect the **ethnographic present,** the prevailing culture and social relationships existing in a group at the time the anthropologist conducted his or her study. Malinowski's focus on the present—a reaction against the speculative theories of the nineteenth-century evolutionists—is still the subject of debate. Some anthropologists charge that, as a result of its strong synchronic orientation, anthropology has failed to take account of historical developments that could help to explain present-day phenomena.

Malinowski was also a leading proponent of holism, now considered integral to the anthropological approach. One of his students, Hortense Powdermaker, writes: "No matter what institution he was describing and analyzing—the family, mortuary rites, a system of barter, or any other—he vividly demonstrated, with a mass of concrete details, the interrelationship between all elements of the culture" (1966:38).

The synchronic, holistic approach came to be known as functionalism, a designation conferred by Malinowski: "The magnificent title of the Functional School of Anthropology has been bestowed by myself, in a way on myself, and to a large extent out of my own sense of irresponsibility" (cited in Kuper 1989:1). **Functionalism** is the theoretical view that human social behavior is not random, inexplicable, or based in ignorance or superstition.

Malinowski's emphasis on synchronic, holistic analysis was shared by his contemporary and chief rival, A. R. Radcliffe-Brown. However, Radcliffe-Brown departed dramatically from Malinowski in defining the aims of anthropology. Whereas Malinowski emphasized the importance of the "calculating man" operating within the social context, Radcliffe-Brown expressed little interest in the motivation and behavior of individuals. Instead, he was dedicated to the analysis of social institutions as a basis for developing a "natural science of human society." Radcliffe-Brown vigorously rejected the title of "functionalist":

> I have been described on more than one occasion as belonging to something called the "Functional School of Social Anthropology" and even as being its leader, or one of its leaders. This Functional School does not really exist; it is a myth invented by Professor Malinowski. . . .

> I regard social anthropology as a branch of natural science. . . . I conceive of social anthropology as the theoretical natural science of human society, that is, the investigation of social phenomena by methods essentially similar to those used in the physical and biological sciences. I am quite willing to call the subject "comparative sociology," if anyone so wishes. (1952:188–189)

Malinowski and Radcliffe-Brown agreed that human societies are "functional," but they had very different views of what that "function" is. Malinowski believed that social life is aimed at serving biological needs, including providing food and shelter and producing the next generation:

> Culture thus appears first and foremost as a vast instrumental reality—the body of implements and commodities, charters of social organization, ideas and customs, beliefs and values—all of which allow man to satisfy his biological requirements through co-operation and within an environment refashioned and readjusted. ([1922] 1984:280–281).

Radcliffe-Brown, on the other hand, argued that social institutions, including religious rituals, serve the "function" of ensuring the survival of the social order:

> My own view is that the negative and positive rites of savages exist and persist because they are part of the mechanism by which an orderly society maintains itself in existence, serving as they do to establish certain fundamental social values. ([1939] 1979:56)

As others have pointed out, the theories of Malinowski and Radcliffe-Brown are not really contradictory. Social institutions may serve biological needs of individuals and stabilize the social order at the same time. The difference between the two positions is really one of emphasis rather than mutual exclusivity.

Radcliffe-Brown's insistence on viewing anthropology as a "natural science of human society" pervaded his work. Throughout his life he sought to identify elements of social organization that could be used as a basis for cross-cultural comparison. It is largely owing to his influence that most modern ethnographies are organized according to the categories of kinship, economics, political systems, and religion. Because of his emphasis on social structure, Radcliffe-Brown's approach to studying human societies came to be known as **structural functionalism,** the idea that societies function to preserve the social order. Malinowski, on the other hand,

The Development of Anthropological Concepts

The period of European colonialism—from the fifteenth to the nineteenth century—led to new formulations of what it means to be human, as Europeans compared themselves with the people they encountered in their global expansion. Anthropology developed in this atmosphere of questioning, and many of the issues that captivate the attention of anthropologists today can be traced to the origins of the discipline in the mid-nineteenth century.

Biological evolution. Charles Darwin did not invent the concept of evolution, but he did formulate the theory of natural selection, the mechanism of adaptation to the environment that underlies modern concepts of biological evolution.

Social evolutionists. Though Eurocentric and androcentric in their views, nineteenth-century social evolutionists identified many issues that continue to challenge anthropologists. The following social evolutionists

formulated concepts that continue to have an impact extending far beyond the field of anthropology.

Herbert Spencer reformulated Darwin's theory of natural selection as "survival of the fittest" and applied it to social institutions. He equated evolution with "progress" and suggested that social programs aimed at helping the poor are against the laws of nature, since they allow "unfit" members of the species to survive. Spencer's idea that evolution proceeds from simple to complex continues to be important in anthropology, but his suggestion that "savages" have a simpler nervous system than "civilized" people and therefore are incapable of abstract thought was rejected long ago.

Sir Henry Maine identified kinship and the family as the basic building block of society.

Lewis Henry Morgan traced the trajectory of evolution from

"savagery" to "barbarism" to "civilization," a typology that was rejected by anthropologists long ago. However, he made an enduring contribution to anthropology with his distinction between kinship based on consanguinity, or blood, and kinship based on affinity, or marriage.

J. J. Bachofen traced the origins of human society to a period of sexual promiscuity, supplanted by dominance by women based on the mother–child bond. He suggested that men then threw off the rule of women by force and asserted male rule based on spirituality. Though anthropologists reject this model as being unsupported by the evidence, Bachofen's theory of "mother right" is accepted by many modern feminists.

John McLennan attempted to trace social evolution through marriage customs, based on his interest in bride capture. His lasting

---

preferred to focus on understanding the lives of the people:

> What interests me really in the study of the native is his outlook on things, his Weltanschauung, the breath of life and reality which he breaths and by which he lives. Every human culture gives its members a definite vision of the world, a definite zest of life. In the roamings over human history, and over the surface of the earth, it is the possibility of seeing life and the world from the various angles, peculiar to each culture, that has always charmed me most, and inspired me with real desire to penetrate other cultures, to understand other types of life. ([1922] 1984:517)

Close Encounters with the Other

This difference in emphasis may well result from the two men's distinct personalities, as reflected in their

fieldwork experiences. Malinowski lived in close association with the Trobrianders, learning their language and sharing their triumphs and despairs. Conversely, Radcliffe-Brown despaired of learning the native language during his two-year stay among the Andaman Islanders, eventually coming to rely on a translator.

Radcliffe-Brown also had little interest in the way Andaman Islanders lived during his study, which took place after the people had been greatly affected by the establishment of a penal colony and European settlement. Instead, he spent his time drawing on the memories of informants who had lived in the islands before contact, noting, "What is really of interest to the ethnologist is the social organization of these tribes as it existed before the European occupation of the islands" (1922:22). According to one of his few

contribution to anthropology is his distinction between endogamy, or marrying within the group, and exogamy, the rule of out-marrying.

E. B. Tylor both defined the anthropological concept of culture and contributed the theory of animism, the idea that religion began with an attempt by early humans to explain dreams and changes in the body at death.

Sir James Frazer published a cross-cultural survey of religion and magic, *The Golden Bough,* still read today. Anthropologists still draw on his concepts of imitative magic, based on the idea that "like controls like," and contagious magic, based on the idea that "the part controls the whole."

British social anthropology. Established in the twentieth century, this school of thought has been dominated by two figures: Bronislaw Malinowski and A. R. Radcliffe-Brown. Both rejected nineteenth-century social evolutionary theory in favor of studying contemporary societies, and both viewed social systems as integrated wholes that serve a function in human groups. Beyond that, however, the two quarreled bitterly.

Bronislaw Malinowski set the standard for ethnography with his two-year stay in the Trobriand Islands during World War I. He designated himself a "functionalist" and viewed social organization as a means for meeting human needs.

A. R. Radcliffe-Brown came to be known as a "structural functionalist" and was interested in developing a science of anthropology that could provide the basis for cross-cultural comparison. He asserted that society functions to promote stability within the group.

American cultural anthropology. This school of thought was largely defined by "the father of American anthropology," Franz Boas. Boas was among the first to attack nineteenth-century models of social evolution. He rejected racism and asserted that culture is more important than biology in shaping behavior. Boas also trained an entire generation of influential American anthropologists, including Ruth Benedict, Margaret Mead, and Edward Sapir.

The new ethnography. In his diary, published in 1967, Malinowski recorded the self-doubt and sexual frustration he experienced during his fieldwork among the Trobriand Islanders. Though many anthropologists reacted with outrage, others welcomed the recognition that knowing the personality and fieldwork experiences of the anthropologist contributes to our understanding of the people he or she studies.

Laura Bohannan and Kenneth E. Read published accounts of their fieldwork experiences. Gilbert Herdt considered his emotional response to male puberty rites among the Sambia of New Guinea an important part of the ethnographic record. Clifford Geertz analyzed reactions of Balinese villagers to his presence among them and to his near-arrest while watching an illegal cockfight. He viewed these experiences as a means of understanding aspects of Balinese culture that would not otherwise be available to him. Renato Rosaldo notes that the death of his wife during fieldwork in the Philippines allowed him to understand an emotional component of headhunting.

colleagues who gained his confidence, Radcliffe-Brown maintained his distance from the people he studied: "[Radcliffe-Brown] had lived as a primitive autocrat, exercising a beneficent but completely authoritarian sway over the simple Andamanese, who had not been in a position to criticize his grand gestures" (E. Watson 1946:84–85).

Radcliffe-Brown was very careful of his image and position. On social occasions, he distinguished himself from lesser mortals by sweeping into a room in his voluminous black cape and top hat. On the other hand, Malinowski was something of a rebel who liked to tweak his British colleagues and generally challenge cherished beliefs. An American scholar of the time, Robert H. Lowie, remarked on what he called Malinowski's "adolescent eagerness to shock the ethnological bourgeois." He added, "Malinowski is forever engaged in two favorite pastimes. Either he is battering down wide open doors; or he is petulantly deriding work that does not personally attract him" (1937:241).

It was perhaps inevitable that these two great men would clash, given Radcliffe-Brown's inflated concern for image, Malinowski's penchant for puncturing balloons, and the arrogance of both. Their debates rang through the halls of academia during their lifetimes and continue to echo through the field of anthropology to the present day.

Between them, Malinowski and Radcliffe-Brown defined British anthropology and trained a generation of scholars whose impact continues to reverberate through the field. Malinowski dominated the British anthropological community until he accepted a teaching post in the United States in 1938, one year after Radcliffe-Brown was appointed to the first established chair in social anthropology at Oxford. Marooned in the United States by World War II—as he had been marooned in Australia by World War I—Malinowski died in 1942 without ever returning to England. The leadership of British social anthropology passed to Radcliffe-Brown, who continued to hold sway until his death in 1955. Perhaps because of their dissimilar personalities, Radcliffe-Brown and Malinowski left very different legacies to the field of anthropology. Radcliffe-Brown excelled at elucidating complex theories of social interaction, and he saw people as living examples of "social structure":

> When I pick up a particular sea shell on the beach, I recognize it as having a particular structure. . . . I examine a local group of Australian aborigines and find an arrangement of persons in a certain number of families. This, I call the social structure of that particular group at that moment of time. (cited in Tax 1953:109)

On the other hand, the people Malinowski lived among in the early decades of the twentieth century continue as vibrant actors on the anthropological stage. We feel that we know them as they go about their lives making magic for their gardens, setting sail for a perilous ocean voyage, or negotiating a marriage exchange. More than any other anthropologist of his day—with the possible exception of Boas—Malinowski was able to engage the Other. And, like Boas, he was able to share his understanding of the Other with his contemporaries and with later generations of anthropologists.

THE AMERICAN SCHOOL: THE IMPORTANCE OF CULTURE

An anthropologist can make a mark on the discipline in one of two ways: by the force of her or his ideas or by the quality of the students she or he trains. Franz Boas did both.

Boas was among the first to attack nineteenth-century models of social evolution. In a paper presented to the American Association for the Advancement of Science in 1896, he delivered one of the earliest anthropological statements against the concept of social evolution. He dismissed evolutionary models of his day on the basis that there were no data to back them up. The task of anthropology, Boas argued, is to collect data on existing populations rather than to speculate about what might have taken place in the past. He noted that Native American and other non-European cultures were rapidly disappearing as the result of colonial contact, and he asserted that it should be the highest priority of anthropologists to record all available information about them.

Boas propelled American cultural anthropology into an antievolutionary stance, just as Malinowski and Radcliffe-Brown later pushed British social anthropology into the same theoretical position. However, Boas maintained an interest in **diffusionism,** the theory that culture change takes place primarily through borrowing. Diffusionists believe that historical links between different groups can be analyzed by tracing the spread of cultural traits from one population to another. Boas's ideas on diffusion mark him as a transitional figure between evolutionary theorists, who were primarily interested in the past, and later scholars, who focused their research on present-day societies.

Boas's influence on anthropology is most pervasive because his students applied his ideas in their own research, virtually defining American anthropology as an intellectual tradition distinct from the British branch of the field. Boas trained an entire generation of innovative scholars. A complete list of his students' accomplishments would fill a textbook, but even a small sample demonstrates the scope of their influence.

Among the best known is Margaret Mead, who pioneered in studies of socialization, adapted psychological research tools for cross-cultural application, and was among the first to recognize the possibilities of visual media, including film and still photographs. Her close friend and colleague, Ruth Benedict, laid the groundwork for the study of psychological anthropology and conducted a controversial study of Japanese character during World War II, a work that is still considered a valuable resource for Japanese scholars.

Edward Sapir made a great impact on the field of linguistics by investigating the relationship between language and thought, and A. L. Kroeber established the Department of Anthropology at the University of California, Berkeley, now ranked as one of the top five in the country. Kroeber is best known among the public for his role in documenting the life of Ishi, the last living representative of a now-extinct California Indian tribe.

Anthropologists still debate the issues defined by Boas and his students, but no one denies the significance of their contribution. According to one scholar, "Boas's importance in the history of cultural anthropology . . . is attested by the brilliance of his students, who never became a school (he would have been the last man to wish it) but who were formed by the habits of his mind" (Hays 1958:260).

We have already seen that Boas helped to formulate the ideal of cultural relativism. He also added a new dimension to the anthropological concept of culture by using the term to describe specific groups of people. The concept of "cultures"—as opposed to "culture"—assumes that the beliefs and values of a particular group form a coherent conceptual orientation that pervades all aspects of the society. This theoretical assumption was carried to an extreme by some of Boas's students, who attributed greater uniformity to the behavior of individuals within groups than actually exists.

Boas's emphasis on culture fostered the development of psychological research in American anthropology, an emphasis that distinguishes the American school of anthropology from the British. Whereas British anthropologists emphasized social structure—the formal organization of a society—Americans, following the lead of Boas, stressed culture—the values, beliefs, and attitudes characteristic of a particular society.

Embracing the Other

Boas's emphasis on culture also profoundly influenced American anthropology in another, even more pervasive, way. At the time, many of his contemporaries assumed that biology determines behavior, a belief that formed the basis of racism. The idea that biology determines behavior was used to justify discrimination against people of non-European descent and discouraged implementation of programs aimed at redressing social imbalances. Boas strongly rejected racism, which he defined as the unproven assumption "that the aptitude of the European is the highest, his physical and mental type is also the highest, and every deviation from the white type necessarily represents a lower feature" (cited in Hays 1958:264).

In his book *The Mind of Primitive Man* (1944), Boas identified the socialization process of child rearing,

Franz Boas.

rather than biological traits transmitted genetically, as the key factor in transmitting world view from one generation to the next, thus laying the groundwork for the **nature-versus-nurture controversy** that would occupy his students for the next sixty years. Advocates of "nature" theories emphasize the role of biology in shaping behavior; adherents of "nurture" theories argue that socialization plays the key role. The debate is still very much with us, and psychologists are still trying to assess the relative contribution of genetics and environment.

Boas's attack against racism reached its zenith during the period between World War I and World War II, when Adolf Hitler assumed power in Germany. Boas protested Hitler's policies and Nazism in general in his writings and in radio speeches. It is fitting that Boas's last words addressed this important theme. During a luncheon for the head of the Musée de l'Homme of Paris, on December 21, 1942, at the height of World War II, Boas delivered a passionate call for eternal vigilance against racism, then fell dead of a heart attack.

In a sense, Boas's career marked a turning point in anthropology, in which the field was transformed from adventurism to systematic goal-oriented exploration, from armchair speculation to collection of evidence in support of carefully framed theories, and from a Euro-centered to a field-centered discipline. But the task of learning to understand the Other was far from solved, and it remained for anthropologists to take further steps to overcome the field's Eurocentrism.

THE ANTHROPOLOGIST AS OTHER: INTERPRETIVE ANTHROPOLOGY

When in 1967 Malinowski's widow published his diary, written during his stay among the Trobrianders, anthropologists reacted with shock and anger. The great scholar was revealed to have been beset by self-doubt and sexual frustration, often retreating from interaction with the "natives" by obsessively reading novels. With Malinowski's feet of clay revealed, it at first appeared that the entire edifice of anthropological fieldwork might crumble. In fact, publication of Malinowski's diary helped launch a whole new ethnographic form, aimed at stripping away the anthropological raiments of scientific authority and revealing the great anthropologist to be a very human instrument.

Previous books had aimed to lay bare the human element behind anthropological fieldwork. In 1954, in a book called *Return to Laughter,* the prominent anthropologist Laura Bohannan recorded her reactions to fieldwork, including her attempts to observe a wedding ceremony while at the same time participating in it:

> "Sing!" I was ordered. "Everyone else is singing." My voice trailed along uncertainly and clashed with theirs, for they were uninhibited by any doctrine of true notes and never hit just where I did. My conscience perked up. I had lost sight of the bride, but in teaching me to sing, Udama was making the words clearer and I got some of the verses of their wedding songs. My feet lost time again as I began to consider possible translations of songs that, if put into equally vernacular English, would seem unpublishable. Someone poked a finger into my ribs. I began to shuffle with renewed vigor. (Bowen [1954] 1964:124)

At the time, Bohannan felt it necessary to publish her account under a pseudonym, Elenore Smith Bowen.

Eleven years later, Kenneth E. Read recorded an intensely personal account of his encounter with the Other in *The High Valley,* based on his experiences among the Gahuku of New Guinea. He describes his reaction to a struggle in which a young woman is forcibly pulled away from her circle of agemates to be given in marriage to a man of another village:

> Like the contagion spread by panic, the violence of the emotions in the struggling throng swept over me, drawing me to the point where my own fear was indistinguishable from the distraught expressions of the girls whose circle of linked bodies rocked and staggered under the buffeting of the men. It was quite unthinkable that they could win. Not only were they badly outmatched, but also no one in the crowd intended a conscious repudiation of the impersonal order that shaped their lives. The girls' challenge was not deliberate, not undertaken from any rational objective that they hoped to gain. Yet for a brief moment I hoped for the impossible, and when the end came as Helekohe [a man of the village], breaking through the circle, grabbed Tarova by the arm and dragged her to the base of the wooden staff [where she was to be decorated for marriage], I felt so helpless, so emptied by distress that my eyes filled with unashamed tears. (1965:258–259)

How far anthropology had come from McLennan's dispassionate analysis of bride capture! Read describes the human emotion behind the formal transfer of a woman from her own kin group to that of her husband. In Read's account, the woman lives for us, as do her female and male kin. And, for the first time, we experience with the anthropologist a turbulent reaction to the inevitability of social custom. In his preface to *The High Valley,* Read laments the fact that ethnographic reports of the day reflected so little of the anthropologist's close contact with the people being studied:

> Why . . . is so much anthropological writing so antiseptic, so devoid of anything that brings a people to life? There they are, pinned like butterflies in a glass case, with the difference, however, that we often cannot tell what color these specimens are; and we are never shown them in flight, never see them soar or die except in generalities. (1965:ix)

Anthropologists have never been able to completely omit themselves from their ethnographies, because their studies are based on close involvement with the people they are describing. Still, several decades after Bohannan and Read published their "confessions," Gilbert Herdt considered it necessary to justify his emotional response to male puberty rites among the Sambia of New Guinea. Herdt observed and recorded ceremonies in which young men were the objects of ritual nosebleeding, circumcision, and ritualized homosexuality. As a young man himself, Herdt notes that he reacted to these dramatic events with strong emotions:

> I was not a cold machine—an unfeeling robot—who witnessed the ritual nose-bleedings. . . . It was my self, my feelings of shock and concern and understanding, which emerged as I recorded the events, that made this study possible. My feelings resonated to those of the Sambia themselves—their shock, fear, anger, and sorrow in the rituals. Did they not sense this? Is this not part of the reason they trusted and permitted me to be the first outsider to see their secret rites? (1987:7)

American anthropologists are not alone in noting that the discipline often takes an "antiseptic" stance, in which the anthropologist conceals his or her own human faults. Three scholars from India criticize the "fraudulently authoritative" tone of several social science disciplines, including anthropology. They say that omitting the anthropologist from the ethnography reinforces the researcher's position of superiority and may also reflect a Eurocentric bias. Although they describe anthropology as the "least ethnocentric of the social sciences," they note:

> If the subject is defined as the "particularistic" study of "others," it becomes unnecessary to incorporate the self into the analysis or recognize how the ethnography itself is socially grounded, . . . deceiving oneself into thinking that other views are socially located, but one's own are not. (Joseph, Reddy, and Searle-Chatterjee 1990:19)

Western anthropologists try to make sense of "otherness" by framing it within familiar conceptual frameworks and, in the process, impose a Eurocentric interpretation. The authors add, "The alternative, which involves redefining the self, is more challenging" (1990:17).

In recent years, anthropologists have risen to that challenge, with varying degrees of success, by acknowledging that anthropology is itself a cultural system organized around the value of trying to explain the Other. But this approach raises a new and equally important question: How can the anthropologist step into the picture without obscuring the reader's view of what she or he is trying to describe?

Deep Play

In 1971, Clifford Geertz published a seemingly innocent article that would stand as a landmark in

In his study of Bali, Clifford Geertz concluded that one can understand a group of people only by analyzing all aspects of their culture, including the way they play. In making this point, Geertz focused on the cockfight, but the Balinese are also noted for their festivals, dramatic and colorful events organized around the Hindu religion.

the development of a new type of ethnography. It begins:

> Early in April of 1958, my wife and I arrived, malarial and diffident, in a Balinese village we intended, as anthropologists, to study. A small place, about five hundred people, and relatively remote, it was its own world. We were intruders, professional ones, and the villagers dealt with us as Balinese seem always to deal with people not part of their life who yet press themselves upon them: as though we were not there. For them, and to a degree for ourselves, we were nonpersons, specters, invisible men. (1971:1)

Ten days after their arrival, Geertz and his wife, Hilda, attended a cockfight and found themselves in the middle of a crisis of culture contact greater than their own, involving Balinese, Javanese, and

Indonesian politics. After Dutch colonial powers withdrew from Southeast Asia, Bali, along with several other linguistic and cultural groups, was amalgamated into the country of Indonesia. Though the Indonesian government outlawed the cockfight, the cockfight was being held to raise money for a new school, a project desired by all members of the community. The law prohibiting cockfights was enforced by the national police, who, being largely Javanese rather than Balinese, were therefore outsiders. Despite the law and the Javanese police, the local Balinese were confident that their worthy aims would protect them from a police raid. However, as Geertz reports:

> They were wrong. In the midst of the third match, with hundreds of people, including, still transparent, myself and my wife, fused into a single body around the ring, a superorganism in the literal sense, a truck full of policemen armed with machine guns roared up. Amid great screeching cries of "pulisi! pulisi!" [police! police!] from the crowd, the policemen jumped out, and, springing into the center of the ring, began to swing their guns around like gangsters in a motion picture, though not going so far as actually to fire them. The superorganism came instantly apart as its components scattered in all directions. People raced down the road, disappeared headfirst over walls, scrambled under platforms, folded themselves behind wicker screens, scuttled up coconut trees. Cocks armed with steel spurs sharp enough to cut off a finger or run a hole through a foot were running wildly around. Everything was dust and panic. (1971:3)

Geertz and his wife fled with the Balinese. Following one fugitive into a compound, they found themselves in the courtyard of the man's house. His wife immediately set up a table, tablecloth, three chairs, and three cups of tea, and the three fugitives from justice sat down and began to sip tea as if they had been there for some time. Geertz writes:

> A few moments later, one of the policemen marched importantly into the yard, looking for the village chief. . . . Seeing me and my wife, "White Men," there in the yard, the policeman performed a classic double take. When he found his voice again he asked, approximately, what in the devil did we think we were doing there. Our host of five minutes leaped instantly to our defense, producing an impassioned description of who and what we were, so detailed and so accurate that it was my turn, having barely communicated with a living human being save my landlord and the village chief for more than a week, to be astonished. (1971:3)

The next day, Geertz discovered, he and his wife were no longer invisible. They had been accepted as temporary co-villagers.

The new ethnography puts the anthropologist into the picture and, by so doing, aims to produce a more accurate image of what life is actually like for the people being studied. Geertz's vivid description of his brush with the law in Bali conveys an immediate sense of who the Balinese are, their daily routine, and what they consider important. It is a far cry from Radcliffe-Brown's attempt to reconstruct the lives of Andaman Islanders from their memories of what it was like before the foreigners arrived. Geertz's account - clearly demonstrates that, to the Balinese, the Other included the Javanese police and, before the cockfight dramatically altered their status, the anthropologists.

Becoming the Other

Renato Rosaldo's description of his fieldwork in the Philippines reflects a more poignant process of coming to understand the Other. Rosaldo and his wife, Michelle Zimbalist Rosaldo, were faced with a seemingly insurmountable barrier; they were trying to understand why the Ilongots were headhunters:

> If you ask an older Ilongot man of northern Luzon, Philippines, why he cuts off human heads, his answer is brief, and one on which no anthropologist can readily elaborate: He says that rage, born of grief, impels him to kill his fellow human beings. He claims that he needs a place "to carry his anger." The act of severing and tossing away the victim's head enables him, he says, to vent and, he hopes, throw away the anger of his bereavement. (1989:1)

The Ilongot cope with the grief of losing their own loved ones by taking the head of someone outside their own village. But Rosaldo found this explanation "unsatisfying" from the anthropological perspective:

> When Ilongots told me, as they often did, how the rage in bereavement could impel a man to headhunt, I brushed aside their one-line accounts as too simple, thin, opaque, implausible, stereotypical, or otherwise unsatisfying. Probably I naively equated grief with sadness. Certainly no personal experience allowed me to imagine the powerful rage Ilongots claimed to find in bereavement. (1989:3)

In writing his ethnography of the Ilongot, Rosaldo drew on the anthropological concept of "exchange theory," suggesting that one death (the beheaded victim's) canceled out another (the next of kin's). Years

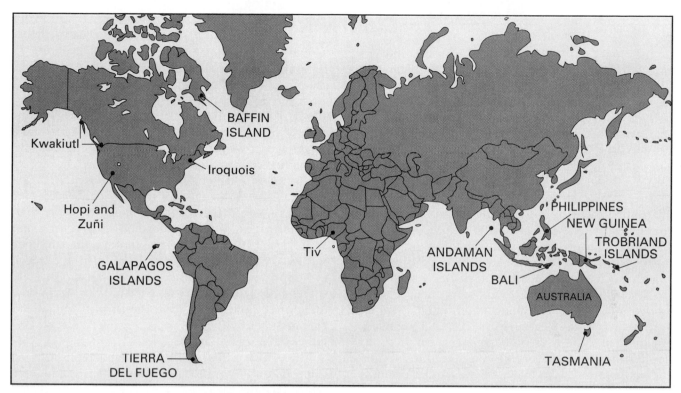

FIGURE 3.2 **The Global Reach of Anthropology**

Since Charles Darwin set sail on the H.M.S. *Beagle* in 1831, anthropologists have ventured into many regions of the world, collecting data on indigenous peoples and helping to define the discipline of anthropology. Anthropologists discussed in this chapter have studied all the areas noted on this map. If all the groups studied by anthropologists were listed on this map, the dots would virtually converge.

later, Rosaldo was forced to reconsider his facile description of the headhunter's grief:

> Not until some fourteen years after first recording the terse Ilongot statement about grief and a headhunter's rage did I begin to grasp its overwhelming force. . . . In 1981 Michelle Rosaldo and I began field research among the Ifugaos of northern Luzon, Philippines. On October 11 of that year, she was walking along a trail with two Ifugao companions when she lost her footing and fell to her death some 65 feet down a sheer precipice into a swollen river below. Immediately on finding her body I became enraged. How could she abandon me? How could she have been so stupid as to fall? I tried to cry. I sobbed, but rage blocked the tears. (1989:8–9)

In working through his grief over the death of his wife, Rosaldo engaged in battles with government officials and with insurance companies. At last, he concluded that North Americans also take heads to deal with their grief, but instead of a knife, North Americans use the legal system.

Anthropologists have long acknowledged that the reason we travel to the farthest reaches of the earth is to better understand ourselves (see Figure 3.2). And, as Renato Rosaldo suggests, it is often in sharing our common human experiences that we come at last to know the Other and to understand that the Other is none other than ourselves. The anthropological adventure begins and ends at home.

SUMMARY

In the wake of colonialism, European thinkers sought to address the question of how the morally, intellectually, and technologically "superior" European "we" differed from the "primitive" "they." Most scholars conducted this inquiry from the comfort of their armchairs and never ventured out to address the question to the "natives." Thus, they never learned that the disdained Other had much to teach Europeans about the nature of being human.

Nineteenth-century evolutionary theory was given impetus by a young English naturalist named Charles Darwin, who formulated the theory of natural selection, an important mechanism underlying evolution. The application of Darwin's theory to human societies is called "social Darwinism" but should more appropriately be called "social Spencerism." Herbert Spencer reframed Darwin's concept of natural selection as "survival of the fittest" and wedded it to the idea of "progress," so that complex European societies were considered to be superior to the more "primitive" societies under colonization.

Two other nineteenth-century evolutionists believed that social institutions were based in the family and that changes in family structure were related to change in other aspects of society. Sir Henry Maine theorized that individual ownership of property had evolved from patrilineal clans. In the United States, Lewis Henry Morgan developed a model of evolutionary stages beginning with "savagery," then passing to "barbarism," and culminating in "civilization."

J. J. Bachofen and John McLennan developed models based on the idea that humans evolved from female-centered to male-centered society—from gynocentrism to androcentrism. Bachofen focused on power relations, what he viewed as the transition from matriarchy to patriarchy. McLennan focused on inheritance rules, which he viewed as shifting from matrilineality to patrilineality.

Two other nineteenth-century theorists, E. B. Tylor and Sir James Frazer, centered their evolutionary models on religion. Tylor considered the earliest form of religion to be animism, a belief that living beings and, sometimes, geographic features are "animated" by a spirit essence. In his book *The Golden Bough*, Frazer suggested that the philosophical history of the human race consisted of two eras: the Age of Magic and the Age of Religion.

Most nineteenth-century theories of social evolution were based on armchair speculation rather than on information, and all were both Eurocentric and androcentric. By the end of the century, the emphasis shifted to data collection, and earlier theories of social evolution were discredited. Social Darwinism was successfully challenged in England by Bronislaw Malinowski and A. R. Radcliffe-Brown and in the United States by Franz Boas, often referred to as "the father of American anthropology."

The British school of anthropology emphasizes social organization and the functionalist approach, which includes the idea that all aspects of a society are interrelated. Malinowski, who defined functionalism, believed that society exists to serve the survival needs of its members. Radcliffe-Brown, a structural functionalist, argued that social organization promotes group stability.

Boas questioned the superiority of European society and formulated the principle that "the idea of a 'cultured' individual is merely relative." Boas vigorously attacked racist theories prevalent in his day and emphasized the importance of culture over biology in explaining human behavior.

The personality, experiences, and orientation of the anthropologist play an important part in the data she or he is able to collect. Among others, Clifford Geertz, Laura Bohannan, and Renato Rosaldo have described the way in which fieldwork experiences have shaped both their theoretical orientation and their understanding of what it means to be human.

POWER WORDS

affine	bride capture	couvade	econiche
androcentric	consanguine	diachronic analysis	endogamous
animism	contagious magic	diffusionism	endogamy

ethnographic present   imitative magic   mythopoetic thought   social Darwinism

Eurocentric   infanticide   natural selection   structural

evolution   lineage   nature-versus-nurture   functionalism

exogamy   matriarchy   controversy   sympathetic magic

functionalism   monogamy   patriarchy   synchronic analysis

INTERNET EXERCISE

1. Charles Darwin was much influenced in framing his theory of natural selection by Sir Charles Lyell's book *Principles of Geology,* published in 1830. Visit **http://abob.libs.uga.edu/bobk/lyellch4.html** for Chapter 4 of Lyell's book and briefly summarize his argument that forces altering the earth's strata (layers) would require long periods of time to develop.

2. Though Sir James Frazer's theories of social evolution have long been rejected, he influenced a number of poets and even filmmakers. His book *The Golden Bough* played an important role in Francis Ford Coppola's classic film *Apocalypse Now.* To learn more about Frazer's life and influence, visit the website **http://www.kirjasto.sci.fi/jfrazer.htm**.

3. Visit **http://www.aaa.org/history.htm** for a brief history of the American Anthropological Association. What does this article say about the development of anthropology as a field of study in the United States?

4

The Political Economy

In this chapter...

Evolution, environment, and economics

One flaw in nineteenth-century social evolutionary models is that they made no attempt to take adaptation to the environment into account. Twentieth-century evolutionary theorists remedied that omission. In addition, they looked to Karl Marx's idea that all social and cultural institutions have a material basis and identified technology as the key to social organization. Marx and Friedrich Engels suggested that class struggle over control of the economic system produces changes in social organization.

General and specific evolution

Leslie White revolutionized concepts of evolution by identifying energy as the resource necessary for human survival. He believed that technology, the tools and skills used in converting energy for human use, provides the basis for cultural change. White's evolutionary model is known as general evolution. Julian Steward emphasized the adaptation of a social group to a particular environment, a model known as specific evolution. Steward noted that humans adapt to the environment primarily through culture and suggested that similar patterns of exploiting the environment may result in similar cultures.

Why evolve?

Contemporary theorists note that trends in cultural evolution are toward greater complexity, though they reject the idea that this trend represents progress. John Bodley argues that complex societies are more subject than small-scale societies to collapse because of over-exploitation of the environment. Jared Diamond suggests that intensive agriculture has resulted in greater susceptibility to famine, poorer health, increased population, and social inequalities. Allen W. Johnson and Timothy Earle assert that the trend to increased complexity is an "upward spiral" launched by the shift from a subsistence economy to a political economy.

Political organization

The system for allocating power in a society is its political organization. A traditional model defines the allocation of power according to the band–tribe–chiefdom–state continuum. The political organization of bands and tribes is at the egalitarian end of the scale, whereas chiefdoms and states are stratified. The concept of nation-state has been developed to describe the emergence of large, multiethnic political entities organized around territorial claims. Human social status and behavior are reinforced through various means of social control, including joking, ostracism, and various types of conflict resolution.

I n his introduction to *The Andaman Islanders*, published in 1922, A. R. Radcliffe-Brown stated that "the study of culture is the study of adaptation to a particular environment." With this seemingly innocuous line, Radcliffe-Brown accurately identified the crucial element lacking in nineteenth-century models of social evolution. Adaptation to the environment was central to Charles Darwin's theory of natural selection but was ignored by social evolutionists of his day in their attempts to generate theories applicable to societies worldwide.

Radcliffe-Brown's statement on the importance of the environment accurately foreshadowed the emphasis of two important schools, the neo-evolutionists and the cultural materialists. **Neo-evolutionists** attempt to refine the process of analyzing change through time in human groups by isolating factors that most directly affect culture and social organization. **Cultural materialists** attempt to explain culture as a strategy for making material resources available for human use. Cultural materialism will be discussed in greater detail in Chapter 5.

Both neo-evolutionists and cultural materialists emphasize the primacy of material culture in shaping other aspects of a society, and both focus on **production,** the process of converting material resources for human use. The genealogy of this emphasis can be traced to the nineteenth-century German political theorist Karl Marx, himself influenced by evolutionists of his day.

MARX AND THE POLITICAL ECONOMY

Marx split the elements of sociocultural life into two main parts: the economic infrastructure, or base, and the "legal and political superstructure." The superstructure consists of legal-political arrangements, and "social consciousness," or ideology. Legal-political arrangements include laws and mores as well as the social institutions that support them. **Laws** are formal systems of rules; **mores** are informal, and often implicit, formulations of social values. Though laws are explicitly stated and mores often are not, the two may be equally binding. Ideology includes religion and other cultural expressions, including art and literature (see Figure 4.1).

Marx and his colleague Friedrich Engels asserted that the economic base shapes both parts of the superstructure—social organization and ideology.

Superstructure =	Ideology
	Sociopolitical Arrangements
Infrastructure =	Economic Base (means of production)

FIGURE 4.1 Marx's Model of Social Organization

Karl Marx identified economics as the key factor in social organization, a position supported by many contemporary political and economic anthropologists. According to this model, the faction that controls the means of production also controls the social and political aspects of a society. This faction can also justify its position of power through its control over the society's ideological system.

According to their model, the struggle for control over the means of production shapes society by giving rise to competing classes, a dynamic that ultimately drives the evolutionary process. As Marx and Engels wrote in *The Communist Manifesto,* published in German in 1848: "The history of all hitherto existing society is the history of class struggles" ([1848] 1964:57).

Marx and Engels believed that human social life began with "tribal ownership," associated with the "undeveloped state of production at which a people lives by hunting and fishing, by the rearing of beasts or, in the highest stage, agriculture" ([1848] 1964:122). The main feature of social structure at this stage is the family and its extensions. With an increase in population, distinctions emerge between commoners and chieftains, and slavery begins to develop.

Marx and Engels did not have available to them modern data suggesting that people who subsist by hunting and fishing have a very different form of social organization than do those who herd animals or practice agriculture. However, the two theorists were correct in associating class distinctions with an increase in population. More recent research suggests that class distinctions arise from task specialization made possible by the food surplus generated by intensive agriculture. **Task specialization** is the allocation of work on the basis of differences in status and role. **Status** refers to one's position in society. **Role** refers to the behavior associated with a particular status.

According to Marx and Engels, the second stage of social evolution is based on "ancient communal and state ownership" and is accompanied by the formation of cities through conquest and voluntary tribal mergers. Land and slaves are at first held in common, but private ownership of immovable property soon begins to be asserted. With the growth of ownership of private property in land, the tribal collective decays.

The third stage of social evolution described by Marx and Engels is based on "feudal or estate property." Feudal lords collectively own the land, which is worked not by slaves but by serfs, who are ostensibly free but are bound to the land. Serfs receive a share of the crops they produce for their lords. During the feudal stage, according to Marx and Engels, towns are organized into guilds of master craftsmen and merchants, who control the work of apprentices and journeymen.

Marx and Engels painted a grim picture of the society of their day, which they saw as a struggle between the capitalist, or moneyed, class and workers.

With industrialization, the center of production moved from the home to the factory. Karl Marx suggested that the factory worker becomes alienated from the products of his or her labor. In this factory in Idaho, women and men peel potatoes for money. They look forward to payday rather than to the satisfaction of a meal consumed in the company of their families.

This society, they maintained, "sprouted from the ruins of feudal society" ([1848] 1964:58). The merchants of the earliest towns had developed into the bourgeoisie, who, according to Marx, were locked in a struggle for power with the proletariat, or workers.

Industrialization, which dates from the middle of the eighteenth century, separates the workplace from the home and establishes the workplace as the center of production. Work traditionally conducted in the home, including production of clothing and manufacture of tools, is now carried out in factories. Thus, a domestic family-centered economy is transformed into a system driven by profits. As a result, Marx and Engels asserted, an economic system based on established social relationships is supplanted by an economic system based on exploitation. Along with this shift, workers become alienated from the products of their work and are increasingly dehumanized:

> Modern industry has converted the little workshop of the patriarchal master into the great factory of the industrial capitalist. Masses of laborers, crowded into the factory, are organized like soldiers. As privates of the industrial army they are placed under the command of a perfect hierarchy of officers and sergeants. Not only

are they slaves of the bourgeois class, and of the bourgeois state; they are daily and hourly enslaved by the machine, by the foreman, and, above all, by the individual bourgeois manufacturer himself. ([1848] 1964:69–70)

Marx and Engels stated that European colonialism accentuated the struggle between the classes because it extended the domain of the bourgeoisie throughout the world and expanded its power in the political realm. The European bourgeoisie became rich and powerful through **mercantilism,** an economic policy that favored a balance of exports over imports and established trade relationships favorable to Europe. According to Marx and Engels: "The executive of the modern state is but a committee for managing the common affairs of the whole bourgeoisie" ([1848] 1964:61). As the European bourgeoisie extended its power throughout the world and increasingly drove the machinery of its own governments, the values associated with capitalism—including the idea of profit as the ultimate good—replaced earlier ethical principles based on the concept of reciprocal relationships. **Capitalism** refers to an economic system based on private or corporate ownership, by private rather than public control of investments, and by production and distribution of goods and services based on competition in a free market.

The bleak description of industrial society Marx and Engels offered obviously includes a romanticized view of preindustrial society. That feudal lords exploited their serfs is undeniable. Serfs were bound to the land and had little say in their own destiny. Slaves were even less able to determine the course of their lives. However, it could be argued that the "freedom" of many modern workers is largely illusory, since they are subject to the whims of bosses and boards of directors as well as the need for cash to provide themselves with the basic necessities of life.

Despite Marx and Engels's strong reliance on material explanations for social phenomena, Engels scorned a simple application of Marxist theory. In a letter written in 1890 to a colleague, Engels tried to set the record straight:

> Marx and I are ourselves partly to blame for the fact that younger writers sometimes lay more stress on the economic side than is due to it. We had to emphasize this main principle in opposition to our adversaries, who denied it, and we had not always the time, the place or the opportunity to allow the other elements involved in the interaction to come into their rights. (Engels, in Selsam and Martel 1963:205–206)

Like other nineteenth-century social evolutionists, Marx and Engels did not link the development of social institutions to variations in ecology. Instead, they developed a model they felt was applicable to human societies all over the world, regardless of habitat.

GENERAL AND SPECIFIC EVOLUTION

Though social evolution took a severe beating under the combined assaults of Bronislaw Malinowski, A. R. Radcliffe-Brown, and Franz Boas, the concept of cultural evolution did not die. Instead, two twentieth-century anthropologists, Leslie White and Julian Steward, attempted to refine evolutionary theory to reflect contemporary ethnographic and archaeological research. In so doing, they identified technology as a key issue in understanding cultural variation and social organization. **Technology** refers to tools and the knowledge to make and use them.

According to White and Steward, technological advances increase the amount of energy that can be harnessed, permitting a society to increase in size, structural differentiation, and task specialization. To White and Steward, an increase in structural differentiation and task specialization is equivalent to evolution.

White and Steward agreed on a "causal chain" in which technology gives rise to other aspects of society. Furthermore, they agreed that the ability to harness energy is a reliable measure of evolution. Beyond that, White and Steward parted company on the subject of evolution. White stressed his ties to nineteenth-century theorists, who formulated general theories of evolution as a means of explaining cultural change. Steward, on the other hand, examined specific patterns of evolution as an outcome of utilizing technology in particular environments.

Leslie White: General Evolution

White developed a model of evolution that reflected Marx and Engels's emphasis on economics as the basis of culture. White's model is called **general evolution** because his purpose was to develop principles of evolution that would apply to all cultures. White

Leslie White linked cultural evolution to the ability of a society to convert energy to human use. The wood carried by this Papua New Guinea woman is a source of energy in the form of fuel for a fire, which can be used for cooking another energy source: food.

rejected the designation of "neo-evolutionist," preferring to stress his indebtedness to nineteenth-century evolutionists. His emphasis on economics as the basis for cultural evolution owes a great deal to Karl Marx. In fact, White became a convert to evolutionary theory in 1929, when he made a tour of Russia and read Marx and Engels's theories about the nature and development of civilization.

He viewed culture as an "organized, integrated system" with three subsystems: the technological, sociological, and ideological systems. The technological subsystem consists of tools, means of subsistence, and the knowledge necessary to survive; the sociological subsystem includes the organization of social relationships in the areas of kinship, economics, politics, and religion; the ideological subsystem consists of beliefs and knowledge expressed in symbolic form, including religious belief and literature.

White's three subsystems are, of course, virtually identical to Marx's model of society. And in the tradition of Marx and Engels, White insisted that "the primary role is played by the technological system" because, he said, there are three essentials to human survival: food, shelter, and defense. However, White's "technological system" focuses on tools and the techniques for using them, whereas the "material base" envisioned by Marx and Engels was a conceptual model for describing class relationships organized around control of production.

White identified energy as the basic resource necessary to promote survival:

> From a zoological standpoint, culture is but a means of carrying on the life process of a particular species, *Homo sapiens*. It is a mechanism for providing man with subsistence, protection, offense and defense, social regulation, cosmic adjustment, and recreation. But to serve these needs of man energy is required. It becomes the primary function of culture, therefore, to harness and control energy so that it may be put to work in man's service. ([1949] reprinted in Bohannan and Glazer 1988:339)

Energy, expressed in thermodynamics, is consumed in the form of calories as food and as fuel for transportation, the manufacture of tools, and other activities. The evolution of cultural systems, White contended, is related to the efficiency with which energy is converted for human use. Since tools provide a means of harvesting energy, White asserted: "The degree of cultural development varies directly as the efficiency of the tools employed, other factors remaining constant" (1988:344). White anticipated later writers in identifying subsistence, or as he puts it, the technological system, as a driving force in society:

> A social system is, as we have seen it must be, closely related to its underlying technological system. If a people are nomadic hunters . . . they will have one type of social system. If they lead a sedentary life, feeding upon rich beds of shellfish, or if they are pastoralists or intensive agriculturalists, or maritime traders, or industrialists . . . , they will have other types of social systems. ([1949] reprinted in Bohannan and Glazer 1988:345)

White noted that forager groups are relatively small and display little task specialization or "structural differentiation." He suggested that agriculture and animal husbandry led to production of a food

Early cities brought together people from many different cultures and drew on the resources of a wide area. In Rome today, ruins from an earlier period of grandeur coexist with modern buildings, providing a visual record of the cyclical nature of stratified societies.

surplus, freeing a portion of the population from subsistence work and allowing them to engage in other occupations. Thus, production of a food surplus led directly to task specialization.

Greater efficiency in food production allowed an increase in population and the development of towns and cities: "Small tribes grew into large tribes and then into nations and empires; villages grew into towns and towns into cities" (White 1949, reprinted in Bohannan and Glazer 1988:346). As population increased, kin-based political organization was no longer adequate and a new type of organization—the state—developed.

In small-scale societies, White stated, "economic organization was virtually identified with the kinship system," but as a result of task specialization, classes developed. In a class system, White argued, "property relations form the basis of social relations rather than the reverse, as was the case in tribal, kinship, society" ([1949] reprinted in Bohannan and Glazer 1988:346). As the means to accumulate property developed, the nature of warfare changed. He added:

> [In foraging societies] the factors necessary for large-scale and systematic and sustained warfare were lacking. These were supplied, however, as a consequence of the Agricultural Revolution. . . . A rich nation's possessions

together with the material and human resources that made the wealth possible would constitute a rich prize to any people who could conquer it. Warfare became a profitable occupation. ([1949] reprinted in Bohannan and Glazer 1988:347)

With widespread and chronic warfare, a professional military class emerged and populations of conquered nations were reduced to subordinate status. Within conquering nations, the imperatives of war led to the division of society into two major social classes: a small ruling group who benefited from the spoils of war and a large subordinate class who provided the "sinews of war." The subordinate class included the common soldiers and the peasants who grew the food. White's idea that foraging societies lack either the means or the necessity to conduct large-scale warfare has become an accepted component of modern anthropological theory.

White's overall model of evolution is not so widely accepted, however. Allen W. Johnson and Timothy Earle point out that White's theory lacks empirical confirmation and that White sometimes overlooked cultural practices that did not fit his theory. For example, "When important economic institutions, such as the dramatic self-aggrandizing public displays of wealth found in the 'prestige economies' . . . , failed to support his utilitarian theory, he simply dismissed them as 'social games' irrelevant to economic process" (1987:4–5).

Johnson and Earle identify a key principle in conducting social science research. All available data must be considered and none of it discarded as "irrelevant." Especially in the study of unfamiliar cultures, seemingly "irrelevant" practices may prove to be essential for understanding other apparently unrelated phenomena.

White was less concerned with analyzing the constellation of traits in a particular culture than with developing a model for comparing different cultures according to an established scale. His approach is related to an ongoing dilemma in anthropological research: whether it is better to conduct in-depth studies of particular cultures or attempt to develop general theories of culture drawing on data collected from a range of groups.

Conducting in-depth studies of particular cultures is appropriate for fulfilling the anthropological goals of holism and taking the insider perspective, which are best achieved by analyzing cultural practices within their social context. However, data generated

by this methodology are not always suitable as a basis for comparative studies. Thus, the field of anthropology continues to reverberate from the inherent conflict between theories generated by ethnographies and those generated by comparative studies. One anthropologist who attempted to reconcile these approaches was Julian Steward, White's contemporary and bitter rival.

Julian Steward: Specific Evolution

Julian Steward's theory of social evolution was based on extensive study, both archaeological and ethnographic, of American Indians in both North and South America. His research is remarkable because it

Julian Steward based his model of cultural ecology—and adaptation to the environment—on his experience studying Native American populations of both the present and the past. These petroglyphs—similar to those studied by Steward—are from Newspaper Rock in Utah. They depict the relationship of human beings to various animals that might be relied upon for food, transportation, or other uses.

combines in-depth studies of particular cultures with comparative studies of a range of cultures. Thus, Steward was uniquely positioned to view constellations of traits in different groups, a circumstance that helped shape his view of social evolution as being specific to a particular culture.

It is not surprising that archaeologists—or anthropologists trained in archaeological methods—infused new life into theories of cultural evolution. Because their studies focus on cultures of the past, archaeologists have inevitably been concerned with the processes of cultural change. They have attempted to explain the interrelated developments in styles of art, the development of stratified political institutions, religion, and such economic practices as trade and the domestication of plants and animals. Unlike nineteenth-century social evolutionists, who based their theories largely on speculations, archaeologists generate theories based on the analysis of material culture produced by human groups over long periods of time. Thus, neo-evolutionists like Steward have looked to the archaeological evidence to explain what appear to be patterns in cultural change.

According to Paul Bohannan and Mark Glazer, Steward was concerned with developing an "acceptable view of evolution without removing the 's' from 'cultures.' This problem made Steward unconventional in evolutionary theory" (1988:321). Steward wanted to avoid obscuring the important differences among groups, a position that set him apart both from White and from nineteenth-century social evolutionists.

Calling his approach **cultural ecology**, Steward emphasized the importance of environment in evolution. He noted that humans adapt to the environment through culture: "Culture, rather than genetic potential for adaptation, accommodation, and survival, explains the nature of human societies" ([1955] reprinted in Bohannan and Glazer 1988:324). Steward suggested that patterns of interaction are shaped by the type of resources available for exploitation. Steward's approach has come to be called **specific evolution.**

Steward was faced with the problem of explaining why groups geographically distant from each other may exhibit cultural uniformity in such characteristics as marriage rules, tracing of kinship, and land ownership. He suggested that they may do so because of similar exploitation of the environment.

His model of **multilinear evolution** seeks to explain parallel patterns of development in different cultures.

Energy, Evolution, and the Competition for Resources

A student and colleague of White and Steward, Marshall Sahlins, attempted to reconcile the divergent positions of the two twentieth-century cultural evolutionists. Sahlins describes a dualistic model of "specific" and "general" evolution:

> In both its biological and cultural spheres evolution moves simultaneously in two directions. On one side, it creates diversity through adaptive modification: new forms differentiate from old. On the other side, evolution generates progress: higher forms arise from, and suppress, lower. The first of these directions is Specific Evolution, and the second, General Evolution. (1960:12–13)

Sahlins departs from White's observation that evolution can be measured in terms of the efficiency with which energy is converted to human use. Instead, "The difference between higher and lower life forms . . . is not how efficiently energy is harnessed, but how much" (1960:20–21). In other words, Sahlins suggests that the amount of energy harnessed is related to the complexity of the social structure.

Anthropologists today generally agree that social evolution has proceeded in the direction of greater complexity, as expressed in task specialization and stratification. **Stratified** societies are those in which some social roles are associated with more power, higher status, and greater access to resources than others. Marvin Harris notes that both biological and cultural evolution are characterized by a tendency to larger and more efficient thermodynamic systems. However, he objects to the idea that this tendency represents "progress," a concept that implies a moral judgment. Rather, Harris says, cultural systems with techniques and tools for more efficient conversion of energy are simply alternative forms of adaptation, neither better nor worse than the ones that preceded them.

John Bodley agrees with Sahlins that complex societies, which have a great deal of social differentiation, do not necessarily use energy more efficiently than egalitarian societies:

> Specific evolution means *adaptation to local environments,* and it is clear that cultures at low levels of evolutionary

progress, as defined above, may be far more efficient in terms of energy input–output ratios, and far more stable and successfully adapted to their environments, than more "advanced" cultures. (1985:25, emphasis in original)

Bodley divides human societies into "high-energy cultures" and "low-energy cultures" according to per capita daily energy use. Nonindustrialized state societies use from two to six times more energy per capita than do farming or foraging societies, and per capita energy use almost tripled with the introduction of industrialization. Modern Americans use more than three times the daily per capita energy rate of people in early industrialized societies and nearly sixty times that of foragers. Industrialized societies have much larger populations than forager societies, so increases in energy use are two-dimensional: There are more people drawing on the world's energy sources, and each of those people consumes sixty times the energy of an individual in a forager society. Bodley argues that continued high rates of energy consumption are depleting the world's natural resources.

Bodley argues that the greater energy needs of increasingly complex societies can lead to an "environmental crisis." He notes that all organisms need energy to survive, and the earth's energy is ultimately limited, since it is derived from the sun's energy as it is transmitted to the earth. This energy is converted for use by humans and other animals by "the planet's primary producers," which are plants. The human sector, including humans and their domesticated plants and animals, competes for energy with the "natural biomass," nondomesticated plants and animals. As societies evolve, Bodley writes, an increasing proportion of the earth's **biomass,** the total amount of living matter, is transferred to the human sector, thus making it unavailable to "natural consumers":

> A clear trend in cultural evolution to date has been toward a remarkable increase in the human sector of the global biomass (humans, and domestic plants and animals) and a corresponding reduction in the earth's natural biomass. . . . As human consumers increase, natural consumers must decrease. The ultimate pinnacle of evolutionary achievement, then, should be the point when every gram of living material on earth has been transferred to the human sector and man's every natural "competitor" has been eliminated. (1985:16)

Bodley suggests that complex societies are more limited by environmental constraints because their energy demands severely tax their environments. Small-scale societies are more stable because their energy needs avoid stressing the environment. On this point Sahlins concurs:

> No one culture has a monopoly on . . . more kinds of adaptive improvements, and what is selectively advantageous for one may be simply ruinous for another. . . . Nor are those cultures that we might consider higher in general evolutionary standing necessarily more perfectly adapted to their environments than lower. Many great civilizations have fallen in the last 2,000 years, even in the midst of material plenty, while the Eskimos tenaciously maintained themselves in incomparably more difficult habitat. The race is not to the swift, nor the battle to the strong. ([1960] reprinted in Bohannan and Glazer 1988:365)

Some anthropologists have begun to focus on the disadvantages of social systems based on high energy consumption. They point out that most complex societies are characterized by a cycle involving a long era of gradual development culminating in a brief period of florescence, followed by a period of rapid decline. Archaeologists have suggested that the "mysterious" sudden collapse of the classic Mayan civilization in Central America after A.D. 790 may have been brought about by increasing demographic pressures on a limited resource base. Mayan kings appear to have conducted warfare campaigns to establish their control over a broad area, thus overtaxing the ability of the peasantry to provide for it.

Many contemporary scholars have begun to question why human beings ever settled down at all, and one anthropologist calls the development of agriculture "the worst mistake in the history of the human race" (Diamond 1987).

WHY EVOLVE?

In a symposium on foraging societies, convened in 1966 and bringing together distinguished anthropologists, Richard B. Lee noted that the !Kung, foragers of the Kalahari Desert in Africa, do not live the "nasty, brutish, and short" life ascribed to such groups by the seventeenth-century English philosopher Thomas Hobbes. Instead, Lee said, "The !Kung Bushmen have available to them some relatively abundant high-quality foods, and they do not have to walk very far or work very hard to get them"

(1968:39). Similar observations by other scholars led Marshall Sahlins, a participant at the symposium, to suggest that foragers might be described as "the original affluent society" (1968:85).

Why, then, did groups of people in many parts of the world abandon foraging in favor of food production at approximately the same time? After a period of about two million years, in which foraging provided our hominid ancestors with the means to spread throughout the globe, a shift to reliance on domesticated plants and animals began in the Middle East about ten thousand years ago. This shift has been called the "Neolithic revolution." Over the next five thousand years, similar transitions occurred in other parts of the world—probably independently. There is evidence of cultivation in Southeast Asia nearly nine thousand years ago and in sub-Saharan Africa about five thousand years ago. Cultivation of plants and animals began in Central and South America between seven and eight thousand years ago (see Figure 4.2).

Though social scientists have lauded this dramatic change in lifestyle as "progress," anthropologists have begun to question whether it has actually improved the quality of life for human beings. Evidence is accumulating to suggest that foragers work less than early agriculturalists, subsist on a more nutritious diet, and are less subject to infectious diseases.

Food producers work longer hours than modern foragers, even though foragers now subsist in the most extreme and unproductive ecological zones. The !Kung devote only twelve to nineteen hours a week to obtaining food (Lee 1968:37), and the Hadza of Tanzania spend only fourteen hours or less per week foraging. When asked why he had not emulated neighboring groups by adopting agriculture, one !Kung replied, "Why should we plant, when there are so many mongongo nuts in the world?" (Lee 1968:33).

The !Kung forager has a point. Anthropologists have determined that mongongo nuts are a rich source of protein. Lee, who studied the !Kung for several years, reports that the average daily consumption of three hundred nuts is equivalent in protein to fourteen ounces of lean beef (1968:33). The mongongo tree is also drought resistant and abundant in dry years, when cultivated crops may fail. Lee notes that "during the third year of one of the most severe droughts in South Africa's history . . . women [of neighboring pastoralist groups] were able to feed their families only by joining the Bushman women to forage for wild foods" (1968:39–40).

Anthropologists now reject the idea that evolution represents progress. They cite such problems as rapidly increasing populations, unequal access to resources, and pollution of the environment as negative consequences of the shift to increasingly elaborate systems of food production.

The !Kung provide a modern lesson in what happens when foragers are forced to settle down. Much !Kung land has been taken away for game preserves, for distribution to other indigenous people, and for white farmlands. The !Kung also lost 90 percent of their territory and were cut off from all but one of their permanent water holes when the border between Namibia and Botswana was fenced. The !Kung are now forced to rely on herding cows and cultivating limited crops. Lions kill the cows, which have been domesticated and cannot effectively run from danger. !Kung must drill wells for themselves and their animals. Ironically, though the !Kung once lived abundantly in an arid desert, enforced settling down has subjected them to the ravages of drought.

Humankind's Worst Mistake?

Recent studies, both archaeological and anthropological, refute the idea that agriculturalists command a more reliable supply of nutrients than foragers do.

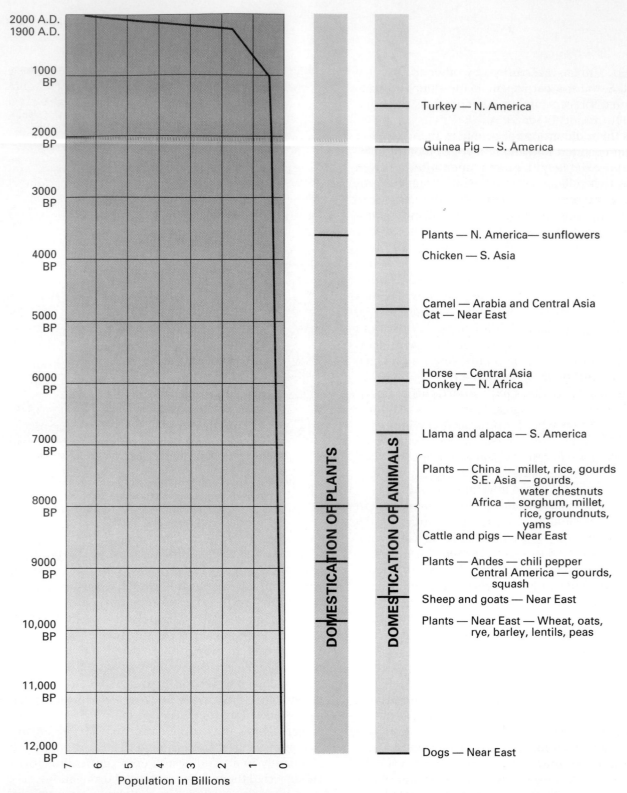

FIGURE 4.2 Population Increase with Food Production

Humans existed as foragers for more than four million years before shifting to food production. During that long period of evolution, the human population never rose above one billion. With the domestication of plants and animals beginning about twelve thousand years ago, population began to increase. In the past hundred years, there has been a precipitous rise in the world's population.

Cultivated crops—and the people who depend on them—are susceptible to changing climatic conditions and invasions of pests. In case of drought, foragers can expand their search for edible plants and animals. In addition, wild varieties of plants and animals are usually more resistant to climatic variations than are domesticated varieties. Agriculturalists typically cultivate a limited number of plants that have been bred for ease and abundance of harvest rather than for resistance to variations in climate. Because farmers depend on a limited number of crops, they run the risk of starvation in the event of crop failure. And, as Jared Diamond notes, the diet of foragers is typically better balanced than that of agriculturalists:

> While farmers concentrate on high-carbohydrate crops like rice and potatoes, the mix of wild plants and animals in the diets of surviving hunter–gatherers provides more protein and a better balance of other nutrients. In one study, the Bushmen's average daily food intake (during a month when food was plentiful) was 2,140 calories and 93 grams of protein, considerably greater than the recommended daily allowance for people of their size. It's almost inconceivable that Bushmen, who eat 75 or so wild plants, could die of starvation the way hundreds of thousands of Irish farmers and their families did during the potato famine of the 1840s. (1987, reprinted in Podolefsky and Brown 1991:73)

Though most foraging groups consume a varied diet, early farmers relied on one or a few starchy crops. As Diamond puts it, "The farmers gained cheap calories at the cost of poor nutrition." The diet of agriculturalists is still limited compared with that of foragers. Most people today subsist primarily on one of three high-carbohydrate plants—wheat, rice, or corn—even though all are deficient in certain vitamins or amino acids essential to human life.

Large fields of one type of plant—and standing water used for irrigation—provide an ideal breeding ground for populations of pests, which may afflict both crops and people. The locust swarms of biblical tradition are a product of intensive agriculture, which produced large wheat fields capable of supporting large populations of locusts. Settled people are also more susceptible than foragers to infectious diseases because they must live in their own wastes or find some means of disposing of them. In addition, the food surplus produced by intensive agriculture indirectly contributes to the spread of disease by giving rise to towns and cities. People living in crowded conditions provide a fertile breeding ground for disease-producing microbes. Diamond writes:

> Epidemics couldn't take hold when populations were scattered in small bands that constantly shifted camp. Tuberculosis and diarrhea disease had to await the rise of farming, measles and bubonic plague the appearance of large cities. (1987, reprinted in Podolefsky and Brown 1991:74)

Diamond cites the archaeological evidence to support the idea that settling down and engaging in intensive agriculture increases human health risks:

> Skeletons from Greece and Turkey show that the average height of hunter–gatherers toward the end of the ice ages was a generous 5'9" for men, 5'5" for women. With the adoption of agriculture, height crashed, and by 3000 B.C. had reached a low of only 5'3" for men, 5' for women. By classical times heights were very slowly on the rise again, but modern Greeks and Turks have still not regained the average height of their distant ancestors. (1987, reprinted in Podolefsky and Brown 1991:74)

Archaeologist George Armelagos and his colleagues document a reduction in health among Native Americans as the forager culture gave way to intensive maize farming in the Illinois and Ohio river valleys around A.D. 1150. The altered subsistence pattern negatively affected the diet, as reflected in the tooth enamel and bones of skeletons found in burial grounds:

> These early farmers paid a price for their new-found livelihood. Compared to the hunter–gatherers who preceded them, the farmers had a nearly 50 percent increase in enamel defects indicative of malnutrition, a fourfold increase in iron-deficiency anemia (evidenced by a bone condition called porotic hyperostosis), a threefold rise in bone lesions reflecting infectious disease in general, and an increase in degenerative conditions of the spine, probably reflecting a lot of hard physical labor. (Diamond 1987, reprinted in Podolefsky and Brown 1991:75)

In addition, agriculturalists in the Illinois and Ohio river valleys did not live as long as their forager predecessors.

Agriculture and Social Class

As if this litany of horrors were not enough, the food surplus generated by intensive agriculture leads to a high degree of task specialization and resulting status inequalities among settled populations. Producing a surplus allows a percentage of the population to engage in work other than food production. Historically, the numbers of people engaged in food production decreases as the efficiency of food production increases. Thus, less than 4 percent of the population in the United States today is engaged in food production. Though task specialization may seem desirable, it leads to inequality in power and access to resources.

Differences in health and diet along class lines are apparent in skeletons from Greek tombs at Mycenae dating from around 1500 B.C. Royal skeletons were two or three inches taller than were those of commoners and they had better teeth, suggesting that royals ate a better diet. The same pattern of better health for elites occurs among Chilean mummies dating from A.D. 1000. In this case, elite skeletons exhibited 75 percent fewer bone lesions caused by disease than did skeletons of commoners (Diamond 1987, reprinted in Podolefsky and Brown 1991:74–75). Among the Chilean mummies, more women than men had bone lesions from infectious disease.

In general, Diamond notes, the development of agriculture produced an elite that was better off than before, but most people were worse off. Overall, he adds, "Farming could support many more people than hunting, albeit with a poorer quality of life" (1987, reprinted in Podolefsky and Brown 1991:75).

It appears likely that foraging and other types of subsistence patterns could produce a food surplus if it were deemed desirable. The !Kung, like most foragers, did not take advantage of all the resources in their environment, selecting only those resources they considered most desirable and utilizing less desirable foodstuffs in times of drought.

Production of excess food provides no advantage at all unless the food is in a form that can be stored. Hunters of large game animals in most forager societies have no refrigeration, so they cannot store the surplus of the animals they kill. Excess meat simply rots. Thus, people like the !Kung hunted infrequently and relied primarily on plant materials, which could be stored simply by leaving them where they grew. Agricultural societies that gear production around generating a surplus generally rely on crops that deteriorate slowly in storage, such as wheat, rice, or corn.

Anthropologists disagree over the reasons for the Neolithic revolution. Diamond suggests that population densities of foragers began to rise at the end of the ice ages, and foraging bands had to choose between producing more food by taking the first steps toward agriculture or by finding ways to limit growth. Groups that chose not to limit their population drove off or killed the bands that chose to remain foragers because, as Diamond puts it, "a hundred malnourished farmers can still out-fight one healthy hunter. It's not that hunter–gatherers abandoned their life style, but that those sensible enough not to abandon it were forced out of all areas except the ones farmers didn't want" (1987, reprinted in Podolefsky and Brown 1991:75).

Diamond is correct in his position that the larger populations and stratification of settled people allow them to overpower their less numerous and more egalitarian neighbors. However, his explanation for why people switched from foraging to farming is rejected by most anthropologists. It would have taken many generations for agricultural experiments to produce sufficient food to lure foragers from their way of life. Instead, it seems likely that foragers manipulated their food supply long before they came to rely primarily on domesticated plants and animals, since foragers require a sophisticated understanding of botany and biology to survive. In fact, it seems likely that the process of settling down followed different sequences in different parts of the world. In some areas, animals may have been domesticated before plants; in other areas, plants may have been domesticated gradually as foragers followed the seasonal cycles of animals.

The change to food production took place in environmentally diverse regions where there were plants and animals suitable for domestication. In the Middle East, where the earliest-known domestication took place, there were large herds of wild sheep and goats along with large stands of wild wheat and barley. The environment ranged from the low, alluvial plains of the valley of the Tigris and Euphrates rivers to high mountain ranges, and valleys afforded easy access between the zones.

Different plants were found in different ecological zones, and, because of the difference in altitude, plants matured at different times in different zones. In summer, people moved to high altitudes to gather plants, then returned to lower altitudes in winter. Hoofed animals—deer, gazelles, wild goats, and wild sheep—suitable for domestication abounded. These were naturally **transhumant;** that is, the animals followed seasonal migration routes, and people gathered plants as they followed the animals in their migrations. Thus, the shift to food production may have taken place gradually rather than abruptly.

Evolution: The Upward Spiral

For whatever reasons human beings originally settled down, once the process began it became an upward spiral of population growth and stratification. Allen W. Johnson and Timothy Earle attempt to explain the rapid increase in complexity in their 1987 book *The Evolution of Human Societies: From Foraging Group to Agrarian State*. They distinguish between two interrelated types of economic organization, the subsistence economy and the political economy.

The subsistence economy "is organized at the household level to meet basic needs, including food, clothing, housing, and procurement technology" (1987:11). "The goal is not to maximize production but to minimize the effort expended in meeting household needs" (1987:12). Since it is not geared to producing a surplus, the subsistence economy tends to be stable. On the other hand, the political economy involves "the exchange of goods and services in an integrated society of interconnected families" (1987:13). Thus, the exchange of goods and services is no longer household- and subsistence-based but is controlled by individuals who benefit from production of a surplus.

The household economy is geared toward providing for the needs of its members, but a political economy is organized around generating a profit for a class of specialists who are not themselves involved in production. The political economy is inherently unstable, because it is geared toward growth, and some sectors of the society benefit from mobilizing a surplus from the subsistence economy. The surplus is used to finance social, political, and religious institutions that maintain the "entrepreneurs" in power. In the case of more complex societies, those in control of the surplus and social institutions are non-food-producers whose existence is justified by the need to generate and regulate a surplus:

> Such a system will grow unless checked by factors that cause declining yields. In most stratified societies we find a cyclical pattern in which the political economy expands to its limit, collapses by internal conflict, then begins to expand again. Elites recognize the limits to growth and try to overcome them by instituting major capital improvements. (Johnson and Earle 1987:13)

Johnson and Earle agree with other writers that, once under way, the evolutionary trend does not stop of its own accord. Thus, the process of social evolution follows an arc. There is a tendency toward increased population, task specialization, and stratification until intervening factors—internal conflict, conquest from outside, or exceeding the carrying capacity of the environment—force a collapse. Thus, forager societies, such as the !Kung or the Australian aborigines, supported an "affluent" lifestyle until very recently, when they were displaced by more aggressively growing settled populations. On the other hand, many more "evolved" societies, including the ancient Persians, the Egyptians, and the Incas, have long since surrendered their dominant place on the world stage.

POLITICAL ORGANIZATION

Political organization refers to the systematic allocation of power within a society. A society may be stratified or nonstratified. Stratified societies are those in which there is unequal access to power and resources. These are also called **ranked** or **hierarchical**. Stratification can occur only where there is a significant degree of task specialization. Almost inevitably it seems, task specialization leads to differences in the value placed on types of work and consequent differences in the rewards and prestige associated with them. **Complex societies** are those characterized by a great deal of task specialization. Although the United States is based on the ideal of **democracy,** or the view that every citizen should have a voice in government, it is a stratified society, because social roles are ranked and because access to power and resources differs depending on one's status.

The shadings of value placed on different types of work can be fairly complex. In the United States, jobs can be ranked according to prestige, money, and power. Some jobs rank high on all three; others rank differently according to one scale or another. The job of president of the country confers high prestige and power but is not very well paid in terms of cash. Monetary compensation is primarily in the form of perquisites, benefits that go with the job. Rock stars and professional athletes are awarded a great deal of

DISCUSSIONS

The Production of Emotion and Social Control

In Western ideology, it is generally believed that emotions arise from individual internal or biological processes. For example, it is common to attribute male "aggression" to the hormone testosterone or female "nurturance" to the hormones estrogen and progesterone. Though hormones certainly play a role in evoking emotional responses, anthropologists are increasingly discovering that expressions of emotional states are culturally patterned. In the following essay, Dennis Gaffin suggests that taunting in an effort to induce anger is a technique of social control among males of the Faeroe Islands, located in the North Atlantic midway between Norway and Iceland.

TAUNTING, ANGER, AND THE RUKKA IN THE FAEROE ISLANDS

Dennis Gaffin

For over a thousand years Faeroe Islanders have fowled for seabirds, hunted pilot whales, raised their stock of multicolored Soay sheep, and fished for cod and numerous other fish. Now advanced and large-scale, commercial fishing began after the Danish government abolished its trading monopoly in 1856. Although Faeroese now live in houses and communities with plumbing, electricity, telephone, and, recently, television, village men still jump out of their cars into the bays to communally slaughter pilot whales and clamber down long ropes over mountain cliff sides to capture fulmars, puffins, and other seabirds. Although many villagers participate in one way or another in commercial fishing enterprises, most families still participate in whale kills, fish locally, raise and slaughter their own sheep, and fowl and prepare seabirds for eating. Despite the encroachment of continental European fashion and bourgeois culture, particularly in the largest settlements, in everyday village life there is a distinctly egalitarian peasant/fisherman value system in operation both in mind and in practice.

In the Faeroe Islands, anger is not only a frequent topic of discussion and concern, but the express intent of many social encounters is to elicit anger, to prove someone's angerability. Male villagers actively ferret out and stir up anger through the practice of taunting. Such taunting is also used to create a *rukka* ("easily angered fool"; literally, "crease"). A salient feature of social differentiation in the community—perhaps second only to kinship—is along the lines of who is good or bad at controlling their anger. The Faeroese male personality is very much conceptualized as the degree of one's equanimity.

Faeroese villagers believe that everyone should control his anger—that individuals' own notions of reason can and should dominate their emotion—and that those who do not control their anger are not regulating themselves with regard to a crucial social issue. Those who fail to use their minds to limit their anger—the deviants—fail the test of being a fully "normal" member of the social group. Yet they are the ones village men use to operationalize ideas and practices of social and emotional control. The local Faeroese emotion-testing method is taunting, and in each successful taunt anger is produced. Such social/emotional interactions are the building blocks of social categorization and bases for the maintenance of community harmony.

Ridicule As Entertainment

As in many small-scale and peasant societies, Faeroese forms of entertainment historically have been primarily oral. Until the early part of this century story-telling sessions around open hearths, "evening sittings," were local forums of entertainment. Legends and indigenous satirical ballads, which rhythmically and amusingly mock local personalities, were ever-present oral literary forms. The derisive satirical ballads were often publicly sung at ring dances. Indeed, villagers have long maintained a tradition of rankling and pulling pranks on others, both on land and at sea (see Joensen 1975:110–112). Ballad singing is still popular, and wit and ridicule still form the basis of much entertainment and social control.

Like storytellers noted for their verbal facility, some people are especially skilled at knowing how to "hold [others] up for ridicule." A "jokester" is funny and skilled with "jokery" and "taunting." Many of the most outgoing villagers—councilmen, ring dance leaders, and storytellers—are also clever jokers. The vocabulary of talk about emotional and unemotional responses to ridicule or jokery, and references to anger in general, are central to Faeroese ethnopsychology and the local "politics of emotions" (Lutz and Abu-Lughod 1990).

A person who does not become "angry" at being the brunt of a taunting joke, prank, or verbal attack is "even-tempered." Such a person "knows how to tolerate" or "knows how to take [it]." He avoids becoming the frequent butt of "tricks or pranks," "artful deceit," and "roguish" or "scoundrel tricks."

The *Rukka,* or "Fool"

The *rukka,* or frequent butt of taunting, is a laughable figure to villagers and is described as a "certain kind of person." All rukkur I heard of or knew are male. This fact lends credence to the possibility that the tradition of the rukkur originated aboard Faeroese

fishing smacks, although the origin of the word *rukka* is obscure (Joensen 1975). Many villagers agree that in the nineteenth and early twentieth centuries, every ship had at least one rukka. Crewmen singled out regular butts of practical jokes, face-to-face mockery, and taunting. Such "fools" were (and are) a means of entertainment during long, difficult, nervewracking sea voyages: "In the old days they had no television, no radio. They made fun of each other. There was always one rukka."

Whether the concept arose in social life at sea and then became popular in the village or whether it originally began as a notion within village life and then extended to the smaller society aboard ship probably will never be known. In any case, the rukka functions both on land and at sea as an object of social control.

Taunting and the rukka concept emphasize the potential for anyone to become angry and act like a rukka. Talk and stories about rukkur provide cautionary tales for all villagers not to let their emotions get out of hand. One philosophical man highlights the power of ridicule: "People are more scared of being made ridiculous than they are of dying. They are not afraid of being killed in an accident if they are doing something very, very dangerous. But they are much more scared of being laughed at."

The man further suggests that individuality is somewhat stifled by the fear of ridicule, and that ridicule is dysfunctional for both him and for others with tender sensibilities. Yet from the group's perspective, from the vantage point of social control, and from the culture's lack of interest in indulging the person, such overriding of the individual may be necessary.

Ridicule and Male Social Identity

Ideally, it is the Faeroese men who are supposed to be able to joke, tease, and play pranks with one another without getting serious or becoming angry. Faeroese males are considered the unemotional sex, or at least they are less expressive of anger. As one astute observer of his own Faeroese scene put it:

> I have seen women angry more often than men. It is more permissible for women to become angry. . . . Arguing [taunting] is a kind of male humor. Women do not have the same kind of "training" in making others angry or making rukka. Men's culture and women's culture are different. Trying to get others angry is not usual for women, among themselves or between a man and a woman. A man who tried to get a woman angry would be diminished, he would lower his reputation. Arguing is men's sport.

The strong cultural value on male emotional control accords with the fact that traditionally it has been the man who works outside the home, often in cooperative, close-quarter efforts. An angry woman, working primarily in domestic spheres, does not greatly threaten economic and social order. Moreover, the village town council, church leadership, and even the dance society are composed of and led by men. A man who loses emotional control damages his role as an effective unit of the economic group as well as a unit of the whole and damages, at least symbolically, local social and sociopolitical control. As the previously quoted man stated, "If a person gets angry, he has lost control. Anger is the last way out of a situation."

Anger is the inability to negotiate with others. From the observer's or group's perspective, anger is an individual's noncollective, noncooperative, antisocial posture. Anger is self-indulgent. Also indicative of the general importance of social accommodation and outgoing, active participation in social life, Faeroese villagers consider those who do not actively participate in public life to be selfish, "for themselves" and/or "shy of people." Thus, anger indulges the individual's ego, challenges the communal spirit, and is anarchical.

Although taunting and pulling pranks might seem uncaring or unnecessarily nasty, such activity generally functions positively to keep the community viable, cohesive, and fair. It is in just this playfulness, this set of community performances, this ritualized form of communication, even with the real anger felt and displayed by the target, that this ritual mockery is valuable. It is practical in providing staged, relatively innocent, and noncrisis opportunities for taunters to express aggression and the taunted to express anger. Much more dangerous would be anger and conflict appearing spontaneously in the midst of maneuvering a boat in stormy waters, stepping along cliffside edges, or socializing with neighbors.

A central Faeroese concern is to give the appearance that everyone is content and harmonious, except through successful taunts, which themselves epitomize the very need for contentedness and harmony. Faeroese men position with and over one another through verbal interactions in taunting. Taunting operationalizes (in the negative) the value placed on negotiating social relationships and the deferring of individual psychological desires, needs, and feeling for the purpose of the common good.

Source: Adapted from Dennis Gaffin, 1995, "The Production of Emotion and Social Control: Taunting, Anger, and the Rukka in the Faeroe Islands," *Ethos* 23(2):149–172.

prestige and money but very little power. College professors are accorded a great deal of prestige but very little power or money. White-collar workers rank very low on all three scales, but they still outrank skilled manual laborers in prestige and power, though they typically earn less money.

Nonstratified, or **egalitarian,** societies also involve some degree of social specialization. In this case, social roles are allocated by gender and age but are otherwise undifferentiated. In an egalitarian society, all women perform the same tasks and are accorded approximately the same status. Similarly, though men do different work than women do, all men perform the same tasks and are accorded approximately the same status. By the same token, children are not expected to do the same work as adults, nor are they accorded the same role in decision making. And elders may do less work than vigorous young adults, but they contribute to the well-being of the group through their wise counsel.

Stratification, or the lack of it, is associated with differences in leadership roles. In general, leadership in nonstratified societies is based on ability, which means that the leader cannot coerce others to obey. Instead, the leader must persuade them to accept his guidance by demonstrating leadership qualities, such as skills in hunting or public speaking, or by providing consistently good advice. In this case, the leader cannot pass his position of influence on to his children. Each new generation must earn their positions by demonstrating leadership qualities.

In stratified societies, leadership typically resides in the office, which may be acquired through inheritance, by some form of electoral process, or by conquest. When power is vested in the office, the leader can command the labor and property of others, maintain a standing army, and exact tribute.

In stratified societies, order within the group is formally codified through laws and enforced by courts. The United States Capitol in Washington, D.C. houses Congress, the body charged with the responsibility of enacting laws that regulate many aspects of life within this nation.

Bands, Tribes, Chiefdoms, and States

In 1963, Elman Service developed a four-part typology of political organization that is still in use today: the band–tribe–chiefdom–state continuum (see Table 4.1). Both bands and tribes are nonstratified and kin-based, so that social roles are allocated according to one's membership in a kin group. In bands and tribes, the leadership position is based on ability, defined in terms

Table 4.1 The Political Organization of Human Groups			
Band	**Tribe**	**Chiefdom**	**State**
Local	Regional	Regional	Regional
Nonstratified	Nonstratified	Stratified	Stratified
Leadership based on ability	Leadership based on ability	Leadership based on office	Leadership based on office
Kin-based	Kin-based	Kin-based	Bureaucratic

of the leader's ability to persuade others to action. In the **band** form of political organization, decisions are typically made by consensus, meaning that members of the group discuss possible courses of action until everyone agrees on one plan. The !Kung are organized into bands. For most of human history, the band was the most inclusive political unit.

A **tribe** is a regional organization linking together local groups or bands. The New Guinea Big Man complex, discussed in Chapter 5, is a tribal form of organization; the Big Man forms alliances between different villages on the basis of his ability to redistribute prestigious goods. The segmentary lineage of some African cattleherder groups is also a tribal form of organization, in this case based on kinship, which links together local groups by tracing descent from a common ancestor. The segmentary lineage of African cattleherders will be discussed in Chapter 12.

A **chiefdom** is kin-based, whereas states are not. In a **state,** functions traditionally allocated on the basis of kinship are carried out by bureaucracies—formal, public bodies organized around performance of specific tasks. States and chiefdoms are hierarchical. The chief, or head of state, rules by the power of the office and can maintain an army, command the labor and property of others, and exact tribute.

As presented in Service's model, a state is a relatively homogeneous entity with shared language and cultural values. That model does not apply to the modern nations that have emerged throughout the world in the wake of European colonialism. These nations are typically polyglot entities that link together once autonomous societies—with different languages and cultural values—under a single political organization. As a result, anthropologists have been pressed to describe and define these complex entities. As it is used in the United Nations, the term **nation** refers to a political entity with territorial boundaries and a government recognized by its neighbors and by the international community. Anthropologists use the term *nation* to refer to a society that has lost its political autonomy but retains its culture and traditional lines of authority, as for example, the Navajo nation. The term **nation-state** is used to describe modern polyglot national entities.

The transition from chiefdoms and traditional states to nation-states is typically associated with a shift in the perceived base of power. Modern heads of state typically govern on the basis of authority legitimized through an impersonal political organization. On the other hand, many chiefs and traditional heads of state gained their position through descent from a ruling lineage, and they governed through a form of personal power augmented by their role as a divine representative on the earth. Chiefs such as those of Hawaii were able to exercise almost absolute power. The Hawaiian royal family was believed to possess a quality called *mana*, a sacred force that was dangerous to people of lower rank. The concept of mana conferred a kind of divinity on the chief, serving to distinguish him from his subjects and validate his power.

At one time, European monarchs were believed to govern by divine right, which reinforced their power and discouraged revolutions, since to rebel against the king was to rebel against God. Egyptian rulers were believed to be divine, as were ancient Persian kings or shahs. The Persian shahs were said to possess a quality called *farr*, a kind of personal radiance that validated their right to rule and ensured that their actions conformed to the divine will. Japanese emperors were believed to be in the direct line of descent from the sun goddess Amaterasu.

Chinese emperors ruled by the mandate of heaven, which reinforced their power when times were good and justified revolution when the country was beset by adversity. The Chinese people viewed the emperor as having the mandate of heaven as long as crops were bountiful, the country was not besieged by invaders, and there were no natural disasters. If the crops failed, or the crops were not bountiful, or the country was threatened by war, floods, or drought, the people would begin to suspect that the emperor had lost the mandate of heaven, and rival warlords would begin to plot his overthrow.

Defining Status and Role

Not just the leaders, but all members of a society are defined by status and role, and individuals may occupy a series of statuses at different times in their lives. All societies make distinctions in status and role on the basis of age and gender, though the way in which status is defined differs from one society to another. In societies at the more egalitarian end of the scale, these distinctions may be loosely defined and informally applied. Among the !Kung, for example, it is the job of women to gather mongongo

Economics and Evolution

The evolutionary models explored in this chapter are based on economic systems or material culture and each has generated debates that continue to shape anthropological theory. Understanding the issues raised by each of these theorists will help you understand the issues discussed in later chapters.

Karl Marx and Friedrich Engels: The Primacy of Economics

The cornerstone of Karl Marx and Friedrich Engels's model of society is that all aspects of society are shaped by the economic base, or infrastructure. The superstructure consists of two parts: legal-political arrangements and "social consciousness," or ideology. The dynamics of the superstructure grow out of the struggle for control of the economic base, a struggle that takes place along lines of class. As the different social classes compete for control of the infrastructure—or economic base—the society evolves through a series of stages. As noted in the following synopsis, each stage gives rise to the next:

First stage: tribal ownership. Production is organized around hunting and fishing, pastoralism, or agriculture. Society is organized around the family. An increase in population leads to distinctions between commoners and chieftains and the development of slavery.

Second stage: ancient communal and state ownership. Land and slaves are held in common. Cities develop as a result of voluntary merging of local groups and through conquest. Private ownership of property begins to develop, and the tribal collective decays.

Third stage: feudal or estate property. Feudal lords collectively own the land, which is worked by serfs who are bound to the land. In the towns, master craftsmen and merchants organized into guilds control production of goods.

Fourth stage: modern bourgeois society. The town merchants develop into the modern bourgeoisie, and the center of production moves from the home to the factory with the rise of industrialization. As factory owners, the bourgeoisie controls the capital, or money. Laborers, or the proletariat, are alienated from their work. European colonialism gives rise to mercantilism and exploitation of foreign workers and economic resources, and the profit motive replaces ongoing social relationships as the driving force of society.

Leslie White: General Evolution

In his model of general evolution, Leslie White identified food, shelter, and defense as the three essentials necessary for survival. Survival is made possible by conversion of energy through technology. Society is shaped by the pattern of converting environmental energy to human use through nomadic hunting, sedentary feeding upon shellfish, pastoralism, intensive agriculture, maritime trading, or industrialism.

Hunting societies were generally small, with little task specialization or stratification. Pastoralism and agriculture produce a food surplus, which leads to task specialization, an increase in population, and the development of towns and cities. Kin-based systems of political organization were replaced by states, classes developed, and the accumulation of property by elites gave rise to large-scale, systematic, and sustained warfare.

Julian Steward: Specific Evolution

Julian Steward's model of specific evolution is based on the idea that cultural changes result from adaptation to particular environments, an approach to the study of human groups he called "cultural ecology." Because

---

nuts, but men may gather nuts for themselves if they are away from camp on a hunt. Among the Netsilik, who live above the Arctic Circle in North America, men alone hunt seals in winter, but they are joined in the hunt by women and children when the seals are abundant in the spring.

In more hierarchical societies, status and role may be more rigidly defined. In her book *Nest in the Wind*, Martha C. Ward describes the elaborate status system in a chiefdom among the people of Pohnpei, an island in the southwestern Pacific. Pohnpeians made rigid distinctions on the basis of age, gender, position

different groups may exploit the environment in similar ways, they may develop similar social institutions, a phenomenon Steward called "multilinear evolution."

Reactions to General and Specific Evolution

In an attempt to reconcile White's model of general evolution and Steward's model of specific evolution, Marshall Sahlins suggested that adaptation to the environment (Steward's idea) creates diversity as new forms differentiate from old. The process whereby higher forms arise from and suppress lower forms is general evolution (White's model). However, Sahlins says, it is the amount of energy harnessed, not the efficiency, that provides the basis for general evolution. Marvin Harris rejects the idea that evolution constitutes progress.

John Bodley

John Bodley suggests that societies that are at "low levels" of evolution may use energy more efficiently than highly evolved societies because they are specifically adapted to their environment. He divides human groups into "high-energy cultures" and "low-energy cultures." State and industrialized societies are high-energy cultures because they have large populations, and each person in an industrialized society uses sixty times the energy of an individual in a forager society. Bodley argues that the greater energy needs of increasingly complex societies can lead to an environmental crisis as the human sector of the earth's biomass competes for energy with the natural sector.

Jared Diamond

Though settling down into food production has long been hailed as "progress," Jared Diamond notes that reliance on cultivating a limited number of crops—as is typical of agriculture—increases the risk of crop failure due to pests and climatic changes. The health of agriculturalists suffers as a result of their limited diet, contact with their own wastes, increased population, and crowding of people into cities. Production of a food surplus leads to task specialization, which gives rise to status inequities, the development of classes, and warfare.

Allen W. Johnson and Timothy Earle

Once the development of task specialization and stratification begins, it becomes an "upward spiral," as noted by Allen W. Johnson and Timothy Earle. They attribute the accelerated growth of complexity to the shift from a subsistence economy to a political economy. The subsistence economy is organized at the household level and is geared toward producing only enough to supply the needs of the family. A political economy is organized around generating a profit for a class of entrepreneurs who are not themselves engaged in production. These entrepreneurs have a vested interest in generating production of a surplus since a surplus maintains and justifies their position.

Political Organization

Societies can be stratified, meaning that access to power and resources is reserved for certain classes or individuals, or egalitarian, meaning that all members of a group potentially have access to power and resources. Formal political organization takes a number of forms:

Bands are local groups that are kin-based and egalitarian, with leadership based on demonstrated ability.

Tribes are kin-based and egalitarian, with leadership based on ability, but tribal organization links together two or more local groups.

Chiefdoms are kin-based, stratified groups, with leadership based on the power of the office.

States are stratified groups, with leadership based on the power of the office and public functions carried out by bureaucracies rather than kin groups.

Nation-states are political entities with an autonomous governing body and territorial boundaries recognized by their neighbors.

Power can also be exercised in informal contexts, in which case it is generally defined as influence, which means that an individual can persuade others to do what he or she wishes but cannot coerce them. Public positions of power are typically occupied by males, but women can often determine the course of events through private influence.

within a family, and the status of one's lineage. Ward notes that she became a member of a kin group when she funded an outboard motor for the boat of a Pohnpeian man, Sohn Alpet. To mark his acquisition, the man and his extended family held a feast to christen the motor and ratify the economic contract between himself and the anthropologist. Ward writes:

> Sohn Alpet stood up to deliver the appropriate speech and announced that by this action I had adopted him as a son. Henceforth he would address me as his mother. . . . But children have less responsibility than

parents. Mothers take care of their sons. Because he had a real mother in her nineties and a number of aunts whom he addressed as mother, this meant only one kind of responsibility. I would have financial and feasting obligations to his extended family. . . . I could not, even tactfully, disavow this honor in public, so I asked what kinship relationship this new outboard motor had. The family laughed and decided that it, too, was my son. I could assign [the motor's] elder brother [Sohn Alpet] to care for it. The family was openly pleased and instructed me to avoid eating eels, the taboo food of the Lasialap clan (1989:70).

As Ward indicates, her new status of mother to Sohn Alpet and the motor carried with it role behavior expectations that included financial and feasting obligations.

The Pohnpeian language is marked by terms of respect demarcating both the status of the person speaking and the person being addressed. English has a limited number of such terms. For example, the terms *mother* and *son* indicate the status of the individuals vis-à-vis each other as well as the appropriate behavior expected of each. Among the Pohnpeians and speakers of many other languages, status terms mark all communication events. Ward notes that she was uncomfortable about her command of the terms of respect required when she met the paramount chief of the Pohnpeians:

> I had collected dozens of examples of respect behavior and avoidance customs that were to be used in the presence of exalted persons. At one time, it was taboo to touch the Paramount Chief on pain of death. Although the extreme penalty no longer applied, the symbolic removal from direct contact with social inferiors was still in effect. Personal attendants do not look him directly in the face; they speak slowly and their intonation and vocabulary accentuate rank. (1989:78)

All societies distinguish children from adults and unmarried people from those who are married. Parenthood confers yet another status and role. In virtually all societies, changes in status are marked by rites of passage. Among the !Kung, a girl's first menstruation is marked by a ceremony conducted by adult women. When a girl is found to be menstruating for the first time, she is carried into camp and "made beautiful" (Shostak 1983:149). She is bedecked with ornaments and rubbed with oil. She is then secluded in a hut built for the ceremony, and men are not allowed to see her face, for fear that seeing it will hurt them in the hunt.

Most New Guinea horticulturalists and African cattleherders subject adolescent males to harsh puberty rituals, typically involving circumcision, intended to prepare them for life as warriors. Among East African cattleherders, boys of approximately the same age are initiated together and make up an **age set,** which bonds them together for the rest of their lives. As the men grow older, a new group of boys is initiated into the succeeding age set. All adult males are members of a named and ranked age set, with senior males at the top, followed by junior elders, senior warriors, and junior warriors. Walter Goldschmidt (1986:2) describes characteristics of the age set system:

1. The unit age sets are strongly bonded groups of men who owe one another special respect and allegiance.

2. Each set moves as a unit from one social status to another with the passage of time.

3. The age set system gives a hierarchical structure based on the principle of age seniority.

4. Men are inducted into the system through initiation in early adulthood, an initiation in which they are indoctrinated with the values of the community and in which the lessons are intensified through the shared pain of physical hazing and circumcision.

Only African cattleherders have age sets, but all societies have **age grades,** age categories associated with status and role. Some North American age grades are infant, teenager, young adult, and senior citizen.

Stratified societies make distinctions on the basis of class or caste. Both **class** and **caste** refer to a system of ranking on the basis of access to power, resources, and prestige. Class differs from caste in that some degree of social mobility is permitted in societies that observe class distinctions, whereas one's membership in a caste is determined by birth and cannot be changed. The Hindu caste system is ranked according to ideas of ritual purity, with the Brahman, or priestly caste, at the top. At the bottom on the scale of ritual purity are the outcasts, who alone can do the most polluting jobs, which include butchering cattle that have died. Though the caste system has been outlawed in India as the basis for discrimination, caste is still a dominant marker of social status.

Social mobility in a society organized around class is often more apparent than real. In England, members of the royal family obtain their position by birth, and nobility is an attribute of birth. In North America, money is a significant social marker, and money is obtained either by working or through inheritance. Jobs are ranked, and it is difficult to move upward through the social ranks. Children born into wealthy or high status either do not have to work at all or have greater access to high-paying and socially elite jobs. Historically in the United States, "old money" (money that has been inherited) is associated with higher status than "new money" (money that has been acquired by one's labors). In addition, education is both an important social marker and provides access to the more lucrative and prestigious jobs.

SOCIAL CONTROL AND CONFLICT RESOLUTION

One anthropologist has suggested that the whole point of culture is to subvert biology. This statement is in reference to the fact that human life—both biologically and culturally—is organized around learning. Unlike the behavior of other animals, human behavior is not determined by instinct; it is learned in the social context. Much of human brain development takes place after birth, when the individual is subjected to the influence of the socialization process. The long period of time humans require to reach physical maturity extends the time the individual is under the control of others.

Much of socialization is directed at teaching the individual the knowledge required for survival. Boys who grow up in forager societies must learn how to hunt and make the tools required for hunting. Girls must learn how to identify the plants that are suitable for eating and distinguish them from poisonous plants. North Americans must learn how to read and write, how to drive cars, and how to operate computers. But, by far, the most intensive socialization is aimed at teaching the skills necessary to deal with other human beings. We are taught who to cultivate as friends and who to avoid, how to acquire things from other people, and when it is necessary to give

the things we value to others. We must learn who it is appropriate to marry and how a married person is expected to behave.

Mary Douglas writes, "The whole universe is harnessed to men's attempts to force one another into good citizenship" (1966:3). Douglas was referring to the fact that behavior considered appropriate in a particular group is reinforced through beliefs that the desired behavior is essential for all good humans and has been established by some suprahuman agent or agency. It has become a truism in anthropology that laws and norms are aimed at coercing people into doing what they would rather not do or preventing them from doing what they would like to do.

Joking, ridicule, mockery, and derision are often used to enforce conformity. The egalitarian !Kung of Africa's Kalahari Desert would ridicule the game animal brought home by a successful hunter to prevent him from thinking himself better than others. According to the !Kung, a hunter who is proud of his accomplishments is likely to make trouble for others (R. Lee 1997). Asen Balikci notes that derision was an effective way of keeping deviant behavior in check among the Netsilik because people feared being laughed at. Sometimes derision took the form of song duels as a way of resolving conflicts between two men. The men would secretly compose derisive songs about each other and teach the songs to their wives. When the compositions and performers were ready, the entire group would assemble in the ceremonial igloo. Each wife sang her husband's song in turn, while the husband danced and beat a drum. In the songs, the men poetically accused each other of incest, bestiality, murder, avarice, adultery, failure at hunting, being henpecked, lacking virility, and other qualities that would reduce the status of the opponent in the eyes of the group. The man who most effectively managed to entertain the group was the winner of the song duel (Balikci 1970).

Ostracism is an effective means of social control since, unlike derision, it involves rejection of the individual by the group. Humans are social animals, dependent upon each other for comfort, resources, and mutual defense. As a result, being banned from the group can cause severe emotional and physical distress. Ostracism is often used by adolescent girls in the United States, as when girls agree to stop speaking to a member of the group. In other cases, ostracism may take extreme forms. In societies where there are sorcery beliefs, a person who had been "hexed" may be ostracized by the group or treated as though he or she were already dead. Jewish parents in the United States may sit *shiva* for a child whose transgressions they are unwilling to forgive. Sitting *shiva* is a ritual form of mourning for the dead, indicating that the errant child is dead in the eyes of his or her parents.

Physical punishment, such as beatings, may be a part of the social control mechanisms in some groups. In Singapore, flagellation is used to punish such violations of the social code as vandalism. Incarceration and capital punishment are conventional forms of punishing deviant behavior in the United States. Incarceration involves putting someone in jail or otherwise confining the person; capital punishment involves the death sentence.

Conflict resolution—resolution of disputes between individuals or factions within or between groups—can take a number of forms, as indicated by the example of song dueling among the Netsilik. Some forms of conflict resolution involve identifying a wrongdoer or assigning blame. The individual identified as a wrongdoer may be required to make reparations by apologizing or giving some item of property to the person he or she has offended. In some cases, an individual may be assigned blame because the opponent is physically stronger, has higher status, or has the support of the group. In other cases, some more formal means of assigning blame is required. **Mediation** involves calling in an impartial outsider to evaluate the issues and recommend some means of resolution, but the decision of the mediator is not binding. **Courts** are presided over by judges whose decisions are binding.

Not all conflicts are subject to assigning blame. **Wars** may be carried out to conquer territory; **raids** may be carried out to exact revenge or to capture women. The Yanomamö of Venezuela and Brazil resolve conflicts through an escalating scale of aggression. Beyond verbal aggression, which may involve arguing or making accusations, the Yanomamö engage in formal chest-pounding duels in which two men, each representing a lineage, take turns striking each other on the chest with their fists. Chest pounding can escalate into a club fight or an ax fight. Often, however, escalation of the conflict is prevented by an older and respected man or an influential leader. Napoleon Chagnon writes:

> The three most innocuous forms of violence, chest pounding, side slapping, and club fights, permit the contestants to express their hostilities in such a way that they can continue to remain on relatively peaceful terms with each other after the contest is settled. Thus, Yanomamö culture calls forth aggressive behavior, but at the same time provides a somewhat regulated system in which the expressions of violence can be controlled. (1992:185–186)

Though in most cultures it is the males who are involved in physical conflict, females fight more often than anthropologists previously assumed. Balikci describes a fist fight between two women who quarreled over the behavior of the daughter of one of the women: "They started hitting each other on the face, just like men. Soon cuts and blood covered their faces as they fought noiselessly on" (1970:173). H. B. Kimberley Cook notes that women on the island of Margarita in Venezuela are verbally and physically aggressive, even though cultural norms emphasize peacefulness for both men and women, and despite evidence that rates of crime and violence are lower for Margariteños than for other groups in the region. Of eighteen cases of physical aggression observed by Cook over a nine-month period, 44 percent involved the use of physical aggression by women (1993:63). Victoria Burbank observed 101 fights among Australian Aborigines of southeast Arnhem Land over a period of almost twenty months. She notes that forty-eight of the fights were between men and women, in most cases between family members. Women initiated the physical aggression in 46 percent of the fights in which it was possible to identify the initiator (Burbank 1991).

Political systems are not static; nor are they genetically encoded. Considerable effort must be expended to maintain the coherence of groups and to ensure that the behavior of individuals does not threaten the culturally constructed assumptions underlying the social order. Statuses and roles must be continually renegotiated. All societies have mechanisms that facilitate the ongoing process of social negotiation.

SUMMARY

Though severely battered by the combined onslaughts of Franz Boas, Bronislaw Malinowski, and A. R. Radcliffe-Brown, the concept of social evolution did not die. Nineteenth-century social evolutionary theories were inherently flawed by failure to incorporate Charles Darwin's concept of adaptation to the environment. Removed from their environmental, cross-cultural, and ethnographic context, nineteenth-century models of social evolution were Eurocentric and untestable.

In the twentieth century, neo-evolutionists and cultural materialists took another look at evolution and began to formulate new theories centering on adaptation to the environment. Neo-evolutionists are directly concerned with developing models of social evolution; for cultural materialists, the connection with evolution is indirect. Cultural materialists view culture as a strategy for converting material resources for human use.

Both neo-evolutionists and cultural materialists draw on Karl Marx's and Friedrich Engels's model of society as based in economics. Marx and Engels suggested that economic systems—the infrastructure—provide the base for social organization. Social organization—the superstructure—consists of two parts: legal-political arrangements and ideology, which includes religion.

Marx and Engels believed that society evolved from a system of "tribal ownership" organized around the family. Class distinctions emerged as a result of an increase in population, which led to the second stage, characterized by "ancient communal and state ownership." In this stage the tribal collective decays as the concept of private ownership emerges. The third stage is based on "feudal or estate property," in which feudal lords own the land that is worked by serfs. During this stage, master craftsmen and merchants become organized into guilds, controlling the work of apprentices and journeymen.

The people who controlled the guilds evolved into the bourgeoisie of today. As industrialization developed, this group gained control of the factories. Industrialization split the workplace from the home and alienated the worker from the products of labor. Mercantilism developed out of European colonialism, and the values of capitalism—profit for its own sake—replaced the value inherent in reciprocal relationships.

Two neo-evolutionists—Leslie White and Julian Steward—built on the work of Marx and Engels, identifying technology and the ability to convert environmental energy to human use as the basis for social organization. White and Steward agreed that more sophisticated technology leads to an increase in population, structural differentiation, and task specialization, which are equivalent to evolution. However, White advocated the concept of general evolution, similar stages in all societies, whereas Steward stressed the importance of specific evolution, adaptation to a particular environment.

White traced the evolutionary process to the subsistence pattern, or, in his words, the technological system, of a particular group. He suggested that a shift in the technological system resulted in production of a food surplus, which led to task specialization, an increase in population, the development of towns and cities, a shift from the kin-based to the state form of social organization, the development of classes, and the emergence of warfare as a profitable occupation.

Steward stressed the importance of culture in adapting to the environment, calling his approach to evolution "cultural ecology." He explained similar sequences of evolution in different societies as multilinear evolution, a result of similar patterns of exploiting the environment. Steward distinguished between the "culture core," which is directly related to subsistence, and "secondary features," which may be influenced by random innovations or diffusion.

Later evolutionary theorists refined White's and Steward's models, providing the basis for more contemporary models attributing culture and social organization to variations in economic systems. Marshall Sahlins suggests that specific evolution leads to greater diversity through adaptive modification, whereas general evolution is the process of progress whereby higher forms arise from lower forms. Sahlins asserts that it is the amount of energy harnessed rather than efficiency that leads to more complex, or "higher," forms of social structure.

Marvin Harris rejects the idea of evolution as progress, which implies moral judgment, and John

Bodley suggests that cultures at low levels of evolution may be more efficient than "advanced" cultures in using energy. Bodley notes there is an evolutionary trend toward increasing the biomass of the human sector, including humans and domesticated plants and animals, and that this increase eventually overtaxes the environment. Ultimately, therefore, complex societies are more subject to collapse than are small-scale societies.

Anthropologists such as Jared Diamond suggest that the shift to food production and settling down may have resulted in decreased quality of life for human beings. Diamond lists a number of negative consequences of intensive agriculture, including greater susceptibility to famine due to reliance on a limited number of crops, poorer health resulting from a more limited diet, increased population and greater population densities, and social inequalities and warfare resulting from production of a food surplus and task specialization.

Anthropologists agree that the evolutionary trends toward increased population and greater social stratification are accelerating. Allen W. Johnson and Timothy Earle suggest that this acceleration is due to a shift from a subsistence economy organized at the household level to a political economy that gives rise to "entrepreneurs," who base their existence on controlling the production of a surplus.

Political organization can be either egalitarian or stratified. In egalitarian societies, there is relatively equal access to power and resources; in stratified societies, there is unequal access to power and resources. The political organization of human groups has traditionally been described by anthropologists as being on a band–tribe–chiefdom–state continuum. Modern polyglot political systems are described by anthropologists as nation-states. The term *nation* is reserved to refer to traditional groups who retain their culture and lines of authority.

The behavior of individuals within a group is shaped or determined by status and role. Egalitarian societies are flexible in negotiating status and role, whereas hierarchical societies have rigid categories demarcating status and role. Behavior appropriate to an individual's status may be enforced by such strategies as joking, derision, ostracism, and physical punishment. Conflicts between members or factions of a group may be resolved by mediators, courts, or aggression. Conflicts between groups may be resolved by wars and raids.

POWER WORDS

age grade	general evolution	production
age set	hierarchical	raid
band	laws	ranked
biomass	mediation	role
capitalism	mercantilism	specific evolution
caste	mores	state
chiefdom	multilinear evolution	status
class	nation	stratified
complex societies	nation-state	task specialization
courts	neo-evolutionist	technology
cultural ecology	nonstratified	transhumant
cultural materialist	ostracism	tribe
democracy	political organization	war
egalitarian		

INTERNET EXERCISE

1. Petroglyphs (rock art) provide our earliest record of how prehistoric humans saw themselves, and many petroglyphs portray people interacting with animals or features of their environment. The website **http://www.geocities.com/Tokyo/ 2384/links.html**, maintained by Footsteps of Man, an organization based in Valcamonica, Italy, provides links to rock art websites all over the world. Choose rock art from two continents depicted on these web links and describe their similarities and differences. What can we know about prehistoric humans based on these self-portraits?

2. As noted in this chapter, Jared Diamond traces the ills of modern civilization back to the Agricultural Revolution of approximately 10,000 years ago. For an alternate view, visit the website **http://wcic.cioe.com/~wallyrog/innovagr.htm**, which describes innovation in agriculture as being in the "spirit of human progress." Briefly compare the evidence presented by Diamond with that presented on this website. Which view do you think more accurately represents the contribution of agriculture to human society?

3. The Netsilik Inuit traditionally settled disputes by holding drum and song duels in which men danced and drummed while their wives sang songs composed by their husbands. This form of debate has been adapted to contemporary life by the Government of the Northwest Territories, based in Hansard, Canada, in their Legislative Assembly. Visit their website at **http://www.gov. nt.ca/hansard/index.html** for a new take on this traditional debate form. Note that transcripts of assembly sessions are provided in both unedited and official edited form. How does the unofficial transcript differ from the official report?

5
Culture in Its Material Context

In this chapter...

Economic systems

Economic systems, which organize the allocation of goods and services in a society, are closely linked to political systems. Both political and economic systems are also intricately bound up with other aspects of a society, including its religion and system for reckoning kinship. Economic systems may be analyzed according to patterns of subsistence, the way environmental resources are converted for human use, or according to systems of distribution, the way goods and services are allocated within a group.

Patterns of subsistence

Subsistence patterns are considered by many anthropologists to hold the key to understanding social organization. Foragers, who do not engage in food production, generally do not develop stratification. The social organization of pastoralists varies depending on the type of animals herded. Horticulturalists, or subsistence gardeners, are more settled than either foragers or pastoralists, but they still tend to exhibit informal leadership patterns. Intensive agriculturalists tend to be settled and stratified, and some are industrialized, which means that the economic base shifts from the home to the factory. In a postindustrial society, some types of work may shift back to the home.

Systems of distribution

Systems of distribution, or exchange, reflect social relationships both by displaying status and, often, by establishing a network of obligations that reinforces social ties through time. Prestige is important in all systems of distribution, though one's ability to amass prestige through control over economic resources varies according to the social organization of one's society. In general, generalized reciprocity equalizes status by making resources available to all. Balanced reciprocity, redistribution, and the market system promote status displays.

Cultural materialism

Cultural materialists view all aspects of a culture as a means for exploiting material resources. Marvin Harris suggests that the Hindu ban on killing cows is a rational means of allocating energy produced by cows in the form of milk, dung, traction, and, eventually, meat and leather. Michael Harner argues that Aztec human sacrifice provided a source of protein where animals were scarce. An alternative explanation is that control over cows in India and over human sacrifice in Mexico provided elites with a means of reinforcing their social position in those two highly stratified societies.

Production and allocation of material goods and services make up the **economic system** of a society. Economic systems do not operate independently of other aspects of society. They are especially closely associated with political systems, which are concerned with allocation of power. In fact, some anthropologists do not distinguish between the economic and political aspects of society, referring instead to the political economy, the convention followed in the preceding chapter. This designation reflects the idea that access to economic resources often confers with it access to power.

However, economic systems are also intertwined with **kinship systems,** the social organization of biological relatedness; with patterns of marriage, which organizes reproductive and household relationships; and with systems of communication, which include language and various types of cultural expression involving the use of symbols. As indicated in our discussion of the anthropological concept of holism in Chapter 2, all aspects of a culture are interrelated.

Economic systems comprise two interrelated aspects, patterns of subsistence and systems of distribution. **Subsistence patterns** are the means by which environmental resources are converted for human use. **Distribution systems** are the means by which goods and services are made available to members of a particular group.

SUBSISTENCE PATTERNS

Patterns of subsistence are the intervening variable between culture and environment. In general, there are four basic types of subsistence: foraging (hunting, gathering, and fishing), pastoralism (herding), horticulture (subsistence gardening), and intensive agriculture. In addition, many modern societies based on intensive agriculture are also industrialized; that is, they depend heavily on manufacturing and separate the workplace from the household. Industrialization has a profound effect on culture and social institutions, especially on those aspects that depend on the allocation of resources. Because of its impact on the household and use of resources, industrialization also has a major effect on gender relations.

A society's subsistence pattern is closely linked to the formation of families. A **family** is defined as a social and economic unit organized around kinship; members of a family are economically and socially interdependent. In general there are two types of families: nuclear and extended. A **nuclear family** consists of the reproductive unit, at least one parent and dependent children. An **extended family** includes additional members of the kin group, such as the grandparents and married siblings. Extended families of China and India typically consist of three generations—grandparents, parents, and children—and include males born into the family, their wives, and their children. This is a type of extended family organized around patrilineal descent, descent through the male line.

Subsistence patterns make some types of social organization possible and preclude others. For example, it would be difficult to sustain a stratified society in the environments occupied by foragers today. However, the Kwakiutl, foragers along the western coast of Canada, maintained complex societies supported by the rich resources of forests and the seashore until European colonialists claimed their territory more than a century ago.

The modes of subsistence are loosely associated with the forms of political organization described in Chapter 4. Foraging is typically conducted within the flexible structure of the locally organized band, which allows for maximum freedom to move around in search of game and edible plants and minimal expenditure of energy toward supporting an elaborate social system. Pastoralists and horticulturalists generally are tribal; they have a regional organization for administering and defending their territories but do not need production of a food surplus to support a hierarchy.

In some cases, horticultural societies can support an economy sufficient to sustain the resource-intensive and hierarchical political organization of a chiefdom. However, horticultural societies typically are chiefdoms only when the basic horticultural economy is augmented by other economic activities, such as extensive trade. In general, only societies based on intensive agriculture have produced a food surplus sufficient to support the role specialization and social stratification of a state.

Environment helps to shape such "natural" characteristics as gender roles and marriage patterns through its effect on subsistence. Certain types of subsistence patterns are better suited to some environments than others are. For example, the traditional foraging lifestyle of the !Kung made efficient use of resources available in the Kalahari Desert of Africa, and the cultivation practices of horticulturalists appear to be well suited to rain forests in many parts of the world.

It would be inaccurate to view the interrelationship of culture and environment as a deterministic one, and it is an overstatement to suggest that subsistence patterns "cause" a particular form of social organization. However, it is certainly true that the way in which humans exploit their environment helps shape their social organization, as the following discussion of the various types of human groups will indicate.

Foragers

Foragers do not produce their own food through herding animals or cultivating plants. Instead, they rely on hunting, fishing, and gathering, basing their subsistence on the animals and plants that grow naturally in their environment. Forager groups are nomadic, moving from place to place to follow the game and to avoid overexploiting plants in a particular locale.

Foragers are characterized by small group size and a low population density. Most foragers travel in small groups of fifty to one hundred, and they range over a broad territory. Their numbers remain small through various forms of birth spacing, including postpartum sex taboos and infanticide. Postpartum sex taboos may require avoidance of sex for up to three or four years after childbirth, thus allowing a woman to nurse a child until it is three or four years old before having another child. This long period of nursing allows the child to take advantage of natural immunities provided in the mother's milk and permits gradual exposure to other foods, which may be contaminated by bacteria or be hard to digest.

If a woman gives birth while she is still nursing, she may choose to kill the newborn rather than risk the life of the older child by premature weaning. Decisions about birth control and infanticide are typically made within the family, often by the mother (Woodburn 1968). However, her decision will be consistent with the values of the group, and she will make use of techniques handed down through the generations from mother to daughter. Population control ensures the survival of the entire group by preventing overexploitation of the environment.

Because they are nomadic, foragers typically do not build permanent housing. For example, the !Kung of Africa's Kalahari desert and the Mbuti of Uganda's rain forest build temporary shelters out of sticks and leaves. Foragers also do not own land privately but share a territory in common with others of their kin group. Land ownership is not useful for foragers, since wild animals do not observe conceptual boundaries devised by human beings. Restrictions on land use may prevent hunters from pursuing and capturing their prey and may result in overexploitation of plant resources in a particular area, especially in times of drought.

Because they must carry their personal property with them, foragers typically have what anthropologists call a small tool kit, only the possessions necessary to promote their own survival. This may include bows and arrows and spears for killing game, stone knives or other implements, digging sticks for uncovering tubers, gourds for drinking water, and a string bag or other carrying device.

The most important possession of foragers is the knowledge necessary to make use of the resources in their environment. They must have a sophisticated understanding of biology and anatomy to track, kill, and butcher animals. They must know a great deal

These !Kung women are gathering various types of plant foods. Foragers typically live in small groups and are nomadic, meaning that they move from place to place hunting, gathering, and fishing. Forager subsistence is not organized around food production through herding animals or cultivating plants.

about botany to identify which plants are safe and nutritious to eat. They must have the technology to craft stone knives sharp enough to cut through the hide of an animal. And they must know enough about aerodynamics to fashion arrows and spears that will fly through the air at a speed and force sufficient to kill an animal. Foragers must also have enough medical knowledge to treat their diseases and deliver babies without the aid of modern specialists and facilities.

Because foragers live in small groups, there is little need for social differentiation. Instead, it is important that each member of the group learn all that is necessary to survive. Therefore, forager groups tend to be egalitarian, and their decisions are typically made by consensus, the process of discussing considered courses of action until general agreement is reached. No one member of the group can coerce others to do his bidding, and all, or most, members can contribute to decision making through discussion.

Of all human groups, anthropologists consider foragers the most nearly equal in terms of gender roles because there is little differentiation in the society as a whole. There is task specialization by gender and age, a characteristic that appears to be universal. Among foragers, however, all adult males perform the same tasks and all adult females do the same work. Equal participation in all the work is important for the survival of a small group, because a high degree of task specialization would place the society at risk if a specialist in an essential task were to die or become gravely ill.

In general, males hunt animals and females gather plants, but the actual situation is far more complicated. Among the Netsilik, women and children help club seals in the spring, when the animals are plentiful. In virtually all societies women "gather" small animals encountered as they move about gathering plants. Women fish, especially when the group uses nets. In any case, in most foraging societies, women may provide up to 80 to 90 percent of the diet through gathering, though this amount varies depending on the environment. For example, the Inuit of northern Alaska and Canada rely primarily on hunting; therefore, males provide the bulk of the diet.

Anthropologists traditionally thought women could not hunt because their upper body strength is not as great as that of males, so women cannot pull as large a bow or throw a spear as far as men. Also, child care is primarily the province of women. A woman carrying an infant or child would be at a disadvantage in stalking large game. However, many of the assumptions about the inability of women to hunt are based on stereotypes developed in our own industrialized society. Among the Agta of the Philippines, women hunt wild boar and deer. They carry smaller bows than men and typically hunt in groups, whereas men often hunt singly. Women also use dogs, so their kill rate is actually higher than that of men, though men provide more meat because they hunt more often.

Agta women hunters solve the problem of child care by tending each other's children. Men tend to be much more involved in child care in nonindustrialized societies, since their work does not take them very far from home. In foraging societies, as among other nonindustrialized societies, work is centered on the home or domestic unit, and men work fewer hours than do men in agricultural or industrial societies. Therefore, men in preindustrial societies are around their children much more than in North American society. The pattern of exclusive mothering considered ideal in the United States is a product of industrialization, which separates the home from the workplace, and of the nuclear family, which isolates women from each other.

Though women tend to be more nearly equal with men in most foraging societies, as compared with societies based on intensive agriculture, hunting carries with it an aura of prestige that gives men an advantage even in egalitarian societies such as that of the !Kung. Marjorie Shostak writes, "!Kung women are recognized by men and women alike as the primary economic providers of the group" (1983:240). Still, she adds, "squeals of delighted children may greet women as they return from gathering, but when men walk into the village balancing meat on sticks held high on their shoulders, everyone celebrates, young and old alike" (1983:243).

Pastoralists

The social organization of **pastoralists,** or herders, varies greatly depending on the type of animals that are domesticated, because the habits and needs of the animals shape the lives of the humans who own them. Pastoralists generally practice transhumance, a form of nomadism based on seasonal cycles. This prevents overgrazing of an area and allows pastoralists to take advantage of resources available in different ecological zones.

For example, Tirol cowherders, who inhabit the Alpine regions of western Austria and northern Italy, follow an annual cycle determined by falling and melting snow. Tiroleans move their cattle in gradual stages from winter barns and pastures in the lowlands up to summer mountain grazing areas. According to Martha C. Ward, "As grass grows scarce on the lower slopes, the cattle move higher and higher until the highest pasture is reached in the warmest season of the year, July" (1993:60). In the fall, the cattle are brought down from the pastures to be housed in barns for the winter. They are fed on hay or fodder the family has harvested during the summer. Ward says, "Farmers in Tirol tell stories about the anxiety of stretching out hay supplies until the meadows are ready to graze; they say that in the past they had to carry the winter-weak cows from the stables and lay them in the grass" (1993:60).

The Nuer, cattleherders in the flat plains of the southern Sudan in Africa, follow a pattern of transhumance based on the cycles of rainy and dry seasons. During the rainy season, which is at its peak from May through August, the cattle must be protected from the water that covers the marshy plains, because the animals quickly get diseases of the hoof if they stand in the water for long periods (Evans-Pritchard 1940:57). At this time, cattle are driven to village sites, which stand on patches of slightly elevated ground. After the rainy season, water supplies near the villages quickly dry up, and the Nuer move their cattle to camps near lakes, marshes, and rivers.

Because their migration routes follow a more predictable pattern than those of foragers, pastoralists may live in permanent or semipermanent dwellings. Tiroleans have farmhouses and barns in the lowlands and also maintain huts in the mountains for use in summer. The Nuer maintain permanent village sites on higher land but also establish temporary camps near the rivers and lakes during the dry season. During the dry season, the Nuer sleep in huts made of grass that can be erected in a few hours.

On the other hand, the Bakhtiari of the rugged mountainous regions of western Iran carry their dwellings with them. Some Bakhtiari own horses and most own donkeys, but their subsistence is based on sheep and goats. They live in black tents of goat's-hair cloth woven by the women. The Bakhtiari spend summers in the mountains, taking advantage of abundant pastures. In the fall, they load their tents and other possessions onto donkeys and drive their flocks down to the warm plains that border Iraq, where there is excellent grazing land and plenty of water. After the snows melt in the spring, the Bakhtiari return to the mountain valleys to feed their flocks on a new crop of grass.

Because they may have pack animals or semipermanent dwellings, pastoralists can accumulate more personal property than foragers can. They also own their animals and must have access to their migration routes, though they do not own land as agriculturalists do. Typically, rights to animals and migration routes are not owned by individuals but by descent groups, and pastoralists are often **unilineal,** which means they trace descent through either the male or the female line but not through both. The Bakhtiari, Nuer, and Tiroleans are patrilineal; rights to animals and migration routes are passed from father to son. The Navajo, pastoralists who herd sheep in Arizona and New Mexico, are matrilineal, so that daughters inherit important rights from their mothers and males inherit social status from their mother's brother.

As do all other known human groups, pastoralists organize their work by specialization according to gender and age. Among the Bakhtiari, men tend the flocks and do a small amount of hunting. Women cook, make cheese and butter, weave, carry fuel and water, and care for children. Among the Nuer, only women and boys are allowed to milk cattle, though a man may milk a cow if no women or boys are present. Women also make cheese and baskets and craft grindstones out of baked mud. Nuer men take their cattle out to pasture and watch over them. Young men serve as warriors.

The division of labor and the status of women vary considerably between pastoralists who herd cattle and those who herd sheep. Cattle can be fed grain to supplement their grazing, so cattleherders can be relatively more sedentary, or settled, and the work of women is important in caring for cattle. Sheep must graze over a wider area. They must be guarded against predators and carried across rivers and streams. Thus, the upper body strength of males is more valuable in sheepherder societies.

Pastoralists may practice a limited amount of agriculture. The Nuer plant millet, a cereal grass, but men gain their social status and wealth through their cattle. During the dry season, when milk production is low, the Nuer may also do a little fishing and hunting or collect wild fruits and berries. Tiroleans, who live in a richer ecological zone than the Nuer, grow a variety of cereal grains for making bread, vegetable crops for human consumption, and hay to feed their cattle in winter.

Pastoral groups vary in size from the Nuer, who live in extended families, to the Bakhtiari, who may travel in assemblages of five thousand or more. Pastoralists also vary greatly in their political organization. The Bakhtiari have tribal leaders, or *khans*, who are elected or inherit their office and can exercise formal leadership. On the other hand, the Nuer are relatively egalitarian, with respect shown to the male family head. Local Nuer villages are also linked together into lineages, or clans, who trace descent from a common ancestor. Some villages also boast a leopard skin chief, who has gained status as a result of his ritual expertise and is important in mediating disputes. The term *chief* is misleading, however, since leopard skin chiefs exercise no real political authority.

Though many pastoralists perform subsistence activities other than herding, their way of life is typically defined with respect to the animals they herd. For example, Tiroleans have a saying, "I work for my cattle" (Ward 1993:67). Nuer males take their names from their cows, sing songs to them, and gain their social status from them. In fact, the Nuer say that cattle destroy people, since "more people have died for the sake of a cow than for any other cause" (Evans-Pritchard 1940:49).

The Nuer have a story that tells how humans and cattle came to be dependent upon each other. In the beginning, all the beasts lived in a single community, but the community broke up and each species of animal went its own way. Man killed the mothers of Cow and Buffalo. Buffalo said she would avenge her mother by attacking men in the bush, but Cow said she would live alongside men and cause endless disputes about debts, bridewealth, and adultery, which would cause men to fight and kill each other. According to E. E. Evans-Pritchard, the anthropologist who first studied the Nuer, "Hence Nuer say of their cattle, 'They will be finished together with mankind,' for men will all die on account of cattle and they and cattle will cease together" (1940:49).

Horticulturalists

Horticulturalists practice small-scale agriculture in the form of subsistence gardening, which means that they do not specialize in a single crop for sale to outsiders. Horticulturalists produce a variety of foods that are sufficient to support themselves without relying on imported foodstuffs. They often raise domesticated animals, such as pigs, chickens, or dogs, and may also hunt or fish and import some specialty foods. In general, however, the food they produce is sufficient to sustain them.

Horticulture is especially well suited for the fragile soils of tropical rain forests or mountainous regions, where plow cultivation is impractical. Horticulturalists often practice a form of cultivation known as **slash-and-burn, swidden,** or **shifting agriculture.** Usually in three- to ten-year cycles, these small-scale farmers cut the forests and burn the trees, releasing nutrients to the soil. The farmers then plant a variety of crops, depending on the climate. The Yanomamö, who live in the rain forests of Venezuela and Brazil, plant bananas or plantains and various types of tubers, including sweet potatoes. The Yanomamö supplement their diet by hunting and gathering wild plants. Horticulturalists of New Guinea plant sweet potatoes and yams as well as a variety of green vegetables.

With each year of planting, the soil grows less fertile and the yield decreases. Eventually, horticulturalists abandon their exhausted gardens and clear new plots nearby. At any given time, they may maintain several gardens in various stages of fertility. Because most horticulturalists rarely move very far from their customary garden sites, they settle in semipermanent villages. Gardening rights are typically held in common by the extended family, usually on the basis of membership in a unilineal descent group. The Yanomamö are patrilineal; many New Guinea groups are matrilineal.

In horticultural societies, there is a division of labor by age and gender. Men are usually responsible for clearing the gardens. Women plant and tend the gardens and care for the domesticated animals. Men also serve as warriors and take charge of public aspects of village life, though their status typically rests on the ability of their wives to sustain the production basis on which their social position depends.

Political organization varies considerably among horticulturalists. In most cases, as among the Yanomamö, power is informal, based on the ability to influence others. At the opposite extreme, the chief of the Trobriand Islands in the South Pacific inherits his position and can coerce the labor of others:

> Not only does the chief . . . possess a high degree of authority within his own village, but his sphere of influence extends far beyond it. A number of villages are tributary to him, and in several respects subject to his authority. In case of war, they are his allies, and have to foregather in his village. When he needs men to perform some task, he can send to his subject villages, and they will supply him with workers. In all big festivities, the villages of his district will join, and the chief will act as master of ceremonies. (Malinowski [1922] 1984:63–64)

The Trobriander chief acquires much of his power through wealth, and he gains his wealth through the labor of his relatives acquired through marriage. The chief takes a wife from each of his subject villages—she will usually be a relative of the village headman—and virtually the entire community must work for him. The wealth, and therefore the power, of the Trobriander chief depends on the number of wives he has.

Intensive Agriculturalists

Intensive agriculture is a pattern of subsistence based on cultivation of a limited number of crops using the same land over and over to produce a surplus. Such concentrated land use requires technology to maintain and replenish the soil, and many agriculturalists rely on the plow, fertilizer, and irrigation. Because agriculturalists work the same land more intensively than horticulturalists do, they settle down into permanent dwellings and thus are able to accumulate personal property. Agriculturalists also need continuous access to their fields, so this type of subsistence is associated with private ownership of land.

Extended families tend to be prevalent in societies based on intensive agriculture, because the labor of all members of the family is needed on the farm. In addition, agriculture requires a major investment in land and equipment, one that is well beyond the resources of a typical individual or nuclear family. Farmers accumulate land and equipment by pooling their resources and passing property rights from one generation to the next.

Production of a food surplus permits task specialization that goes beyond age and gender. Because not everyone is engaged in food production, classes of artisans and other specialists arise. Stratification develops as different tasks become ranked, and, eventually, rights over allocation of resources pass into the hands of an elite whose main role is to keep order,

regulate production, and maintain an army to protect property and stored food surpluses. Full-time armed soldiers also maintain the position of rulers, so intensive agriculture can support chiefdoms or state forms of political organization.

As large segments of the population no longer engage in food production, there is no need for them to live near the fields, and cities arise. The growth of cities permits the development of further stratification. Specialized classes engage in trade, which further increases the power of the leaders, who can field effective armies to guard trade routes. Stratification is also associated with monumental architecture—massive public buildings that require an elite class with resources and power to command the labor of others.

Recently, anthropologists have argued that intensive agriculture reduces the status of women because they are no longer in charge of food production. With the use of the plow and other intensive farming techniques, primary responsibility for food production shifts to men. Women engage in subsidiary activities, such as care of animals. They may also be confined to the domestic sphere, caring for the home. Thus, intensive agriculture permits such institutions as *purdah*, a system in India in which women are confined to the home.

Certainly, such subsistence patterns as foraging and horticulture cannot support the seclusion of women, since all members of the society are required

In all societies, male and female economic roles are complementary. This Sinhalese woman of Sri Lanka is preparing curry for her family as part of her contribution to the household economy.

for food production. Seclusion of women is also impractical among groups who move from place to place. In Arab countries, seclusion of women in harems is largely a phenomenon of cities, since rural women are needed for food production.

In China, the practice of foot binding probably could not have developed in the absence of intensive agriculture, because it effectively prevents a woman's feet from growing naturally and hinders her ability to walk, thereby interfering with her ability to produce food. A woman hobbling about on bound feet would be a serious liability in a foraging society, where mobility is essential to survival, or in a horticultural society, where the labor of women is needed for food production.

However, generalizations about the status of women in intensive agricultural societies are hard to support because of the diverse social roles in these groups. In some agricultural societies, women in cities are less able to make choices about their lives than rural women, whose labor is essential to the economy. On the other hand, urban life may present women with more opportunities for education and income-producing work, such as selling goods in the marketplace.

Class differences also affect the status of women. In many Arab countries, women of high status are more subject to restrictions than are women of low status, because the labor of elite women is not needed for subsistence. On the other hand, in some Arab and other countries, women of high status have the freedom to obtain an education. Among the Chinese, the feet of high-status women were bound more tightly than were those of farm women, whose work in subsistence was valued. The work of high-status women was not needed, so these women could be maintained in a state of relative immobility.

Class differences in the status of women are also evident in two studies of women in the United States. Susan Ostrander (1984) conducted research among women who belonged to the "wealthiest, most powerful, and socially prominent class" in a midwestern city. She describes the upper-class women as "subservient" to their husbands, because the women were unable to make decisions affecting critical areas of their lives. They were unpaid workers in the home and worked as volunteers for charity organizations, whereas their husbands were paid for work in family firms or other businesses. The husbands objected to their wives' taking paid work outside the home, and the husbands' desires usually prevailed. As Ostrander puts it, the wives accommodated their husbands when there was a conflict between their own and their husband's interests.

On the other hand, Lillian Breslow Rubin (1976) studied gender roles among working-class men and women in the United States. In this group, women worked outside the home because of economic necessity. Men were typically employed as truckdrivers, postal clerks, or night watchmen; women worked as waitresses, salesclerks, or typists. The women expressed ambivalence about working, considering it more prestigious not to work and feeling guilty about leaving their children, but they considered paid work more satisfying than being a housewife. Men felt trapped by the working-class lifestyle:

> I'd get so mad at her, at my whole life, that I'd cut out on work a lot, and that would make things worse, because then we had more money problems. Even when I worked steady, my paycheck wasn't big enough; then when I missed days, we were really in trouble. (Rubin 1976:81–82)

There is some evidence that working-class women are more employable than their husbands but still expect men to be the primary breadwinners. The women Rubin interviewed expressed resentment toward their husbands when they were unable to fill the breadwinner role adequately. Rubin cites a statement by a twenty-nine-year-old cashier, mother of two, who had been married nine years:

> I couldn't understand how he couldn't get a job. I knew I could get a job any time I really wanted one, but I had to stay home with the baby. It seemed like he was just dumb or something that he couldn't find a good, steady job. And you know, no woman likes to think she's smarter than her husband. But I've got to admit, I did, and he didn't like it one bit. Neither did I. (Rubin 1976:91)

It is difficult for outsiders to assess the ability of women to make choices that affect their lives, since women's voices may be heard only in the domestic realm but have far-reaching repercussions. David Gilmore (1993) writes that working-class women of southern Spain virtually control not only the household but the lives of men by making decisions such as where to live and how many children to have. Since these are "domestic" decisions, men may have little voice in them but are forced to work harder and longer hours to support the decisions made by women. Gilmore notes that, as a result, women effectively have more power than men even in a society where "men rule," according to popular belief. Gilmore reports the assessment of one older man of Andalusia: "Carlos spoke candidly about the balance of power between the sexes. He allowed that the man rules in Spain, except, he added ironically, 'when he doesn't.' This latter occurs in most matters that are important to the woman" (1993:189).

Gilmore notes that, among the gentry in the same city, men may control the family purse strings by maintaining bank accounts and investments that the wife doesn't know about. And, in some landowning families, the husband may simply provide the wife with a monthly allowance. Thus, in middle- or upper-class families, the husband may be able to exert more control over his wife because he has more power in the community as a whole.

Still, power is a relative concept, one that defies easy definition. In her 1994 autobiography, *Dreams of Trespass: Tales of a Harem Girlhood,* Fatima Mernissi notes that the experience of harem life differs considerably between the city and the countryside. On the question of differences between women and men, the author describes how, as a child, she consulted Mina, a former slave woman who lived on the roof of the harem. "Why the separation [between men and women]?" the girl asked:

> Mina replied not by answering my questions but by saying that both men and women live miserable lives because of the separation. Separation creates an enormous gap in understanding. "Men do not understand women," she said, "and women do not understand men, and it all starts when little girls are separated from little boys in the hammam [communal bath]. Then a cosmic frontier splits the planet in two halves. The frontier indicates the line of power because wherever there is a frontier, there are two kinds of creatures walking on Allah's earth, the powerful on one side, and the powerless on the other."
>
> I asked Mina how would I know on which side I stood. Her answer was quick, short, and very clear: "If you can't get out, you are on the powerless side." (1994:242)

Industrialization

Industrialization could not exist without intensive agriculture. The mobilization of resources for the factory system requires the food surplus and stratification of an intensive agricultural society. However, industrialization dramatically transforms an agricultural society because it separates the home from the workplace. Under the factory system, the basis of industrialization, the center of economic life shifts from the domestic realm to the public sphere, with profound effects on every sector of society, from the family to the political system.

Industrialization contributes to the rise of the nuclear family, because an industrial economy is dependent on the labor of a geographically mobile workforce. The nuclear family is more mobile than the extended family, because small families with only one wage earner can move from place to place more readily than multiple-career families.

As young people left the farms and moved to the cities to take jobs in industry early in the twentieth century, the United States shifted from a predominantly rural nation to a predominantly urban society. The new wage earners left extended families on the farms and established nuclear families in the cities. Thus, a new model for the family emerged, one independent of the obligations of extended family ties and cut off from its history of identification with a line of ancestors. This new, rootless family is ideal for an economic system based on industrialization.

Unfortunately, the nuclear family is structurally less stable than extended families. The nuclear family is based on the marriage bond, considered by anthropologists to be more fragile than blood ties, whereas extended families are linked by a network of kin ties, both consanguineal (blood) and affinal (marriage).

The nuclear family is also more financially vulnerable than extended families, since the loss of the breadwinner in a nuclear family can impoverish the entire household. In extended families, the loss of one wage earner is compensated for by the labor of other members of the household. In addition, extended families pool their resources, so they are better able to finance such investments as a new home, a college education, or a small business.

By separating the workplace from the home and by replacing the extended family with the nuclear family, industrialization increases the need for child care from people outside the family. One or both parents must spend a significant part of the day away from home, and few family members are available to look after children and dependent elders. Typically, since men are primarily responsible for working outside the home, they are separated from their children for long hours every day. Men in forager, pastoral, horticultural, and agricultural societies work around the home, so contact between fathers and their children is rarely interrupted.

Because the North American industrial family is organized around the model of men as wage earners and women as full-time homemakers and mothers, industrialization also makes women more dependent on men. In most nonindustrialized societies, women's work is part of the general household economy. Resources and responsibilities within a domestic group are shared, and women can participate more equally in decisions. In an industrialized society, work outside the home is compensated in terms of wages; domestic labor is not. Therefore, the wage earner gains power over the domestic worker because his compensation is negotiable outside the home. Judith Marti (1993) notes that Western perceptions about the relative importance of the public sphere as opposed to the "powerlessness" of the domestic sphere are a product of industrialization.

Conclusions drawn from the dynamics of industrialized societies are not readily applicable to societies based on foraging, pastoralism, horticulture, and intensive agriculture, because those subsistence patterns typically organize the labor of women and men into complementary, interdependent roles. Although women and men perform different tasks in all societies, the distance between public and private is exaggerated in an industrial society. In many ways, this separation disempowers women by relegating them to the domestic sphere, where their work is not compensated in prestige or economic power.

On the other hand, the social, economic, and geographic mobility of industrialization may provide women with opportunities for education and work compensated by wages. However, the price women pay for these opportunities may be high, as evidenced by the experience of women who have taken their place in the public sphere of wage-compensated work. The extreme separation of workplace and home brought about by industrialization may mean that, for the first time in the history of the human animal, full participation in the economic system for most people may be incompatible with being a parent.

The Postindustrial Society

The United States is now becoming what many call a **postindustrial society.** The economy, once based on factory production, is now shifting to providing services. In some sectors of the society, the workplace and the home are once again converging. However, this development presents a range of new problems and possibilities.

The term *service economy* includes a spectrum of occupations, from working at a fast-food restaurant to consulting for a large corporation. Low-paying hourly jobs must still be performed outside the home, and the work schedule must conform to the demands of the workplace rather than to the convenience of the worker. On the other hand, work that requires specialized expertise, such as consulting, may be scheduled at the convenience of the expert. Such work also tends to be better compensated than unskilled hourly work. These differences accentuate class distinctions among workers and restrict the economic mobility of unskilled workers.

Women with specialized expertise are likely to benefit from postindustrialism because they can work at home and determine their own schedules. Their salaries are also likely to be competitive with those of men. However, unskilled workers of both sexes will have fewer opportunities to rise from the ranks of the lower classes, and the gap between rich and poor is likely to grow wider and be harder to bridge.

SYSTEMS OF DISTRIBUTION

Systems of distribution are directly related to the organization of power within a society. In some groups, control over allocation of resources provides leaders with the means to command the labor of others, amass great stores of personal wealth, or wage war. In other societies, systems of distribution are organized so that access to resources is more or less uniform throughout the group, preventing some individuals from accumulating wealth or gaining control over others, thus effectively reinforcing egalitarian relationships.

In virtually all societies, prestige is an important driving force in the allocation of resources. Marvin Harris writes, "Some of the most puzzling lifestyles on exhibit in the museum of world ethnography bear the imprint of a strange craving known as the 'drive for prestige'" (1974:94). He notes that a number of writers have remarked on the prevalence of this drive for prestige in American culture. Thorstein Veblen coined the phrase *conspicuous consumption* to describe what he called "the vicarious thrill of being mistaken for members of a class that doesn't have to work" (quoted in Harris 1974:95). However, most people in North America are unaware that prestige drives economic systems in many other parts of the world as well: "Early in the present [twentieth] century, anthropologists were surprised to discover that certain primitive tribes engaged in conspicuous consumption and conspicuous waste to a degree unmatched by even the most wasteful of modern consumer economies" (Harris 1974:95).

The degree to which prestige can be attained depends on the type of distribution system characteristic of a particular society. Systems of distribution, or exchange, include generalized reciprocity, balanced reciprocity, redistribution, and the market system. Small-scale groups, such as foragers, may be organized only around generalized reciprocity, which occurs in all societies. Groups characterized primarily by balanced reciprocity, redistribution, or the market system also practice generalized reciprocity in other contexts; within the family, virtually all societies practice generalized reciprocity.

American businesspeople are fond of saying "There's no such thing as a free lunch," and this principle appears to hold true cross-culturally. Systems of exchange establish obligations that bind members of a group in an ongoing pattern of interdependency. An individual's place in an exchange network may well determine his or her status in the society as a whole. According to Ernestine Friedl, the status of women in society is directly related to their ability to control economic resources—and to establish exchange relationships—outside the domestic sphere:

> Patriarchies are prevalent, and they appear to be strongest in societies in which men control significant goods that are exchanged with people outside the family. Regardless of who produces food, the person who gives it to others creates the obligations and alliances that are at the center of all political relations. The greater the male monopoly on the distribution of scarce items, the stronger their control of women seems to be. ([1978] 1990:231)

Systems of distribution are intricately interrelated with all other aspects of social organization, including subsistence patterns, political systems, kinship, and religion. In a sense, networks of obligation generated by exchange systems provide both the "muscle" and the motivation for ensuring that members of a society conform to group expectations of appropriate behavior. The coercive aspect of systems of exchange can be subtle, as in the case of generalized reciprocity, or the coercion can be dramatic, as in the flamboyant displays typical of redistribution. In all cases, systems of distribution define what each of us can expect

from those with whom we are united in a network of interdependency.

Generalized Reciprocity

Generalized reciprocity is a pattern of exchange in which individuals contribute without expectation of a return in kind. Instead, each person contributes goods or services appropriate for his or her age and social responsibilities. Mature young men may contribute meat from a hunt or play a musical instrument for a dance. Older men and women may provide advice based on their long experience, transmit information about the group through storytelling, or ritually heal other members of the group. Young women contribute economically through gathering and preparing plant foods and by ensuring the continuity of the group through their fertility. Children may make an economic contribution by gathering firewood or caring for siblings.

In this type of exchange system, the contribution of each individual is not tallied against the contribution of others in the group; instead, it is evaluated in terms of the contribution that could reasonably be expected of someone occupying that status and role. A system of generalized reciprocity ensures that every individual has access to resources regardless of his or her ability to contribute. It provides for the care of children and older people, women in childbirth, and people who are too sick to fend for themselves. Generalized reciprocity reinforces the solidarity of the group as a whole by establishing patterns of obligation and interdependence that continue through time.

Among foragers, allocation of resources generally follows a pattern of generalized reciprocity. Meat from hunting is distributed to the entire group according to one's place in a kinship network. Friedl notes:

> Among the !Kung San of Africa, certain parts of the animal are given to the owner of the arrow that killed the beast, to the first hunter to sight the game, to the one who threw the first spear, and to all men in the hunting party. After the meat has been divided, each hunter distributes his share to his blood relatives and his in-laws, who in turn share it with others. If an animal is large enough, every member of the band will receive some meat. ([1978] 1990:231–232)

Though women contribute up to 80 or 90 percent of the diet among most forager groups, they distribute the food they gather primarily within the nuclear family. Thus, Friedl suggests that their influence does not extend outside the family. On the other hand, men distribute meat throughout the group, and their sphere of influence may expand accordingly:

> The source of male power among hunter–gatherers lies in their control of a scarce, hard to acquire, but necessary nutrient—animal protein. . . . Vegetable foods, in contrast, are not distributed beyond the immediate household. . . . The meat distributed by the men is a public gift. Its source is widely known, and the donor expects a reciprocal gift when other men return from a successful hunt. He gains honor as a supplier of a scarce item and simultaneously obligates others to him. ([1978] 1990:231–232)

Friedl suggests that obligations created by the distribution of meat constitute a form of power or control over others, which allows skilled hunters to influence decisions, such as when and where to move the camp, and to control exchange with other groups for flint, salt, and steel axes:

> The male monopoly on hunting unites men in a system of exchange and gives them power; gathering vegetable food does not give women equal power even among foragers who live in the tropics, where the food collected by women provides more than half the hunter–gatherer diet. ([1978] 1990:231–232)

Marjorie Shostak suggests that !Kung women may actually have more control over their distribution network than men. Men are obligated to share meat from the hunt according to a predetermined system of distribution. On the other hand, women may, if they choose, extend their exchange network by distributing food outside the family:

> When a woman returns to the village, she determines how much of her gatherings, if any, will be given away, and to whom. She sets aside piles of food for those she feels inclined to give to, and places the rest in the back of her hut or beside her family's fire. The food she and her family eat that night, the next day, and perhaps even the next, will consist primarily of the things she has brought home. From start to finish, her labor and its product remain under her own control. (1983:242)

As both Friedl and Shostak point out, there are limits to how much status anyone can gain among the !Kung, who may have the most egalitarian society in the world. Richard B. Lee notes that the !Kung exercise forms of social control such as ridicule to prevent a good hunter from becoming arrogant. Lee quotes one !Kung man:

> When a young man kills much meat he comes to think of himself as a chief or a big man, and he thinks of the rest of us as his servants or inferiors. We can't accept this. We refuse one who boasts, for someday his pride will make him kill somebody. So we always speak of the meat as worthless. This way we cool his heart and make him gentle. ([1969] 1997:33)

Though forager societies such as the !Kung are organized around the principle of generalized reciprocity, this pattern of exchange is associated with certain types of relationships in all societies. For example, families, whether extended or nuclear, typically operate along the lines of generalized reciprocity, as illustrated by the pattern of interdependency and gift giving within the American nuclear family. Parents assume the burden of financial support when children are small, but children are expected to reciprocate by showing respect and obedience. As the children mature, they will be expected to contribute to the life of the family by producing grandchildren and, perhaps, by providing for the care of elderly parents.

Generalized reciprocity does not relieve anyone in a society of the burden of contributing to the maintenance of the group. Rather, it is based on the idea that, over time, all members of the group will provide some desired goods or services. They can contribute either directly through subsistence activities or indirectly through such services as mediation, counseling, or entertainment. There is no such thing as a free lunch, even in groups based on generalized reciprocity.

Balanced Reciprocity

Balanced reciprocity is the exchange of goods or services of equal value. It establishes an alliance of equality between individuals or groups, and participants in balanced reciprocity usually keep a formal or an informal record of what is exchanged. In the Trobriander **Kula ring,** the exchange of red shell necklaces for white shell armbands establishes a system of political and economic alliances that extend throughout the islands. Red shell necklaces and white shell armbands are ceremonial goods used only for trade. They cannot be hoarded, passed on to one's heirs, or traded in any context other than the Kula. Red shell necklaces must always be exchanged for white shell armbands (see Figure 5.1).

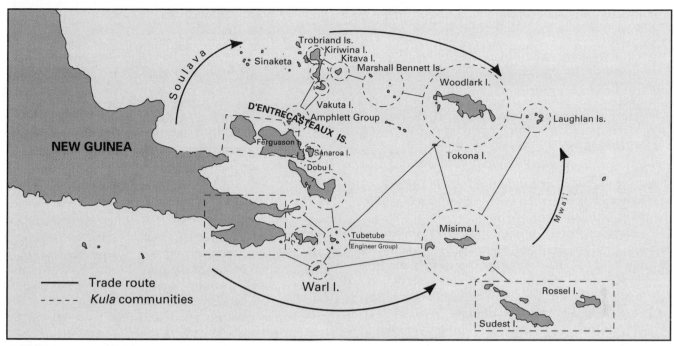

FIGURE 5.1 Kula Ring

The Kula ring is a system of balanced reciprocity engaged in by men of the Trobriand Islands. The Kula generates and reinforces alliances that last through time. Red shell necklaces, or *soulava,* move in a clockwise direction. White shell armbands, or *mwali,* are traded in a counterclockwise direction. The movement of soulava and mwali is indicated by the solid lines. The dashed circles indicate Kula communities. The area in the dashed rectangle (lower right) was indirectly affected by the Kula exchange system.

The Trobriands of Papua New Guinea are a group of islands, or atolls, formed by coral reefs around a lagoon. The Kula ring extends for a distance of about two hundred miles, linking men on different islands in exchange alliances and Trobrianders with distant island groups. To make the exchanges, men set sail in elaborately decorated ceremonial canoes, bearing red shell necklaces to trade in a clockwise direction around the islands or white shell armbands to trade in a counterclockwise direction.

When a canoe arrives for a Kula exchange, each man seeks out his trading partner. Trobrianders inherit their partners from an older relative. A commoner typically has only a few partners, but a chief can have hundreds of partners throughout the islands. The necklaces and armbands vary in value depending on their reputation. One of Bronislaw Malinowski's informants notes:

If I, an inhabitant of Sinaketa, happen to be in possession of a pair of arm-shells more than usually good, the

fame of it spreads, for it must be remembered that each one of the first-class arm-shells and necklaces has a personal name and a history of its own, and as they circulate around the big ring of the Kula, they are all well known, and their appearance in a given district always creates a sensation. Now, all my partners—whether from overseas or from within the district—compete for the favour of receiving this particular article of mine, and those who are specially keen try to obtain it by giving me [offerings and solicitary gifts]. ([1922] 1984:98–99)

A man can keep a particular item for no more than about a year, or he risks gaining a reputation for being "slow" or "hard." Thus, men in the Kula exchange remain under continual obligation to each other. According to Malinowski:

We see that all around the ring of Kula there is a network of relationships, and that naturally the whole forms one interwoven fabric. Men living at hundreds of miles' sailing distance from one another are bound together by direct or intermediate partnership, exchange with each other, know of each other, and on certain occasions meet in a larger intertribal gathering. . . . It is easy to see that in the long run, not only objects of material culture, but also customs, songs, art motives [*sic*] and general cultural influences travel along the Kula route. It is a vast, intertribal net of relationships, a big institution, consisting of thousands of men, all bound together by one common passion for Kula exchange, and secondarily, by many minor ties and interests. ([1922] 1984:92)

The system of balanced reciprocity practiced in the Kula ring serves to define and reinforce the status of males with reference to each other. Kula partners maintain a relationship of equality. However, men can gain status by acquiring particularly famous Kula articles, and they may try to use magic or their negotiating skills to "turn" their partners in their favor. Chiefs and other important men can enhance their status by establishing a network of Kula partnerships that extends throughout the islands.

The principle of balanced reciprocity also reinforces relationships between equals in the United States. On holidays and birthdays, friends must give each other objects of equal value, expressing the appropriate social distance. Gift exchange is so important that specialty goods—coffee mugs, greeting cards, and other items—have been developed as a way to meet the need for gift items between equals. By increasing or decreasing the value and intimacy of a gift, exchange partners can escalate the formation of a friendship or signal the intention to distance themselves.

Redistribution

Redistribution involves the accumulation of large amounts of goods—food and other items—with the object of giving them away in a ceremonial feast and display. The giver of the feast is rewarded by increased prestige and political influence. The best-known redistribution systems are the Kwakiutl potlatch and the pig feast, which occurs among many horticultural groups in New Guinea.

The **potlatch** was practiced by many native groups along the northwestern coast of North America. One of those groups, the Kwakiutl, lived in a rich ecological zone that made subsistence by foraging relatively easy. At the time of the arrival of the Europeans, the Kwakiutl lived on fish and shellfish from the sea; salmon from the streams; and meat, plants, and berries from the forest. The abundance of natural resources allowed the Kwakiutl to develop a system of political hierarchy with chiefs who extended their range of influence and enhanced their prestige through the potlatch. As Marvin Harris puts it:

> The object of the potlatch was to give away or destroy more wealth than one's rival. If the potlatch giver was a powerful chief, he might attempt to shame his rivals and gain everlasting admiration from his followers by destroying food, clothing, and money. Sometimes he might even seek prestige by burning down his own house. (1974:95)

The word *potlatch,* from the Chinook language of Washington and Oregon, means "gift." Preparations for the ceremonial event were elaborate, involving the accumulation of fish, animal skins, blankets, and other valuables. Among these were "coppers," sheets of pounded copper about two-and-a-half feet long. The coppers were named, and they were valued for the history associated with them. Giving the coppers a name personified them. To personify an object, place, or being is to give it a personality, which stresses its identification with humans.

On the day of the potlatch, guests ate copious quantities of food while dancers impersonating animal gods and spirits entertained them. The host and his followers arranged the piles of wealth to be given away in ceremonial display, as the host boasted about his ability to amass such abundance and derided the "poverty" of his guests. At some potlatches, blankets and other goods were not only given away, they were destroyed. The host might pour fish oil on the piles of goods and set them on fire.

To avoid humiliation, the guest chief was obligated to reciprocate by giving a potlatch twice as large as the one he and his followers had attended. In the process, the original potlatch chief received goods of greater value than those he had given away, while forcing the guest chief to strain his resources by repaying the "debt." Anthropologists have noted that politically sophisticated chiefs could use the potlatch to break their rivals, while extending their own sphere of influence.

In New Guinea, the **pig feast** can determine the political fortunes of an ambitious Big Man and unite villages of a particular region in a network of interdependency and obligation. A **Big Man** has no formal authority over others, but he can exert a great deal of influence because of his prestige. In the Elman Service model of political organization, a Big Man

People of a Papua New Guinea village host a ceremonial feast that will include redistribution of food and other valuable goods. Big Men acquire status and influence by organizing pig feasts, which demonstrate their ability to call on the economic resources of a network of relatives.

complex is a tribal form of political organization. The pig feast is organized according to the same principle as the potlatch. Most New Guinea groups are horticulturalists who produce a variety of vegetable crops and tubers for daily consumption. They also produce pigs and a special variety of yam for ceremonial distribution at the pig feast.

A man who aspires to extend his sphere of influence and to enhance his prestige—to become or remain a Big Man—must do so by hosting a pig feast. He can do this only by rallying his kinsmen to contribute yams and pigs. Most important is the labor of his wives. Most New Guinea groups are **polygynous,** which means a man may take more than one wife. Because women tend both the gardens and the pigs, a man can aspire to be a Big Man only if he is married. According to a saying among the Kawelka, a man can survive without pigs, but he would be a man of no account. He would be a "garbage man."

A Big Man cannot force his kinsmen to support his political ambitions by contributing yams and pigs, so he must rely on his oratory skills and his expertise as a mediator and negotiator. He also motivates his followers by ridicule, pleading, and haranguing.

The most prestigious goods to be distributed at the redistribution ceremony are pigs and yams. However, a large modern pig feast might also include the distribution of trucks, motorcycles, and thousands of dollars in cash. The Big Man typically hosts the pig feast for a rival Big Man and his followers. As the Big Man distributes the valuables, he extols his own ability to amass wealth and derides his guests. As Ongka, a Big Man of the Kawelka, puts it, "I have won. I have knocked you down by giving so much" (Plattner 1989).

The guest Big Man is expected to reciprocate within a reasonable period of time by inviting his host to an even bigger pig feast. This system of "payback" unites entire regions in a network of exchanges that help promote alliances that provide the framework for New Guinea's traditional system of warfare and competition between villages.

Market System

The **market system** is based on supply and demand. Unlike other exchange systems, the market system does not necessarily establish an ongoing relationship between the supplier and the recipient of the goods and services. Market systems are typically found in societies where social roles are differentiated through task specialization, since transporting goods to market, displaying them for buyers, and negotiating appropriate compensation for goods are necessarily time consuming.

The market system of exchange can be organized around a marketplace, a central area where vendors display their wares. The exchange may involve **barter,** in which goods or services of equal value are exchanged, or it may involve **cash,** a medium of exchange that has an assigned value independent of its intrinsic worth.

Cash allows exchanges to be conducted away from the marketplace, thus weakening the social bonds established by exchange. In a Western supermarket, for example, minimal social interaction is involved as customers pay for the goods they buy. Neither vendor nor customer has knowledge of the other's family or aspirations. This type of exchange focuses entirely on the exchange of goods or services and has little to do with the social relationship of the people involved. The use of credit adds yet another nonpersonal dimension to exchange, so that purchases can be made by phone, or from catalogs, or through specialists who act as go-betweens for buyer and seller. Cash

In a market system, an exchange is concluded at the time of the transaction. No ongoing relationship is established by the exchange. However, the marketplace can function as a kind of community center for the exchange of information and renewal of social ties.

and credit extend the reach of the marketplace, so that goods and services can be exchanged with minimal or no interaction between buyer and seller.

The traditional marketplace, however, is a center for multiple types of social interaction, where information is exchanged along with goods. Among the Aztecs, for example,

> the Central Mexican marketplace, or *tianquiztli,* was probably the liveliest spot of any community. There people from all walks of life congregated daily, or at least every five days, to enjoy the company of friends, the haggling over the prices of maize or cloaks, and the latest news of the region. (Berdan 1982:41)

In many societies, markets such as the tianquiztli allow low-status women to exercise economic prerogatives that would be denied to them in other contexts. Because of the economic importance of the markets, the influence of these women may extend into the political sphere. In her study of nineteenth-century Mexican women vendors, Judith Marti argues that women were often able to make government leaders submit to their demands for reduced vending fees and improved conditions. In many cases, the women were widows who would have been powerless and impoverished if they had not engaged in market exchange:

> To have an income, these poor widows had to work outside the home. They chose to run a business in the public markets. There, they found themselves in

situations neither of their choice nor of their liking, so they took actions to change them. They were successful, rather than powerless, even when fighting "city hall." (1993:223)

Modern Asante market women of western Africa display a similar capacity to control their economic destinies. These women set prices and control the exchange of produce in the marketplace, saying that selling such goods as plantains and tomatoes is not fit work for men. The women exercise exclusive domain over the marketplace, establish prices paid to farmers, maintain discipline among market vendors, and negotiate with the central government authority of Ghana.

Though the Asante are matrilineal, and the market women wield considerable economic and political power in the public domain, they continue to be subservient to their husbands in the domestic sphere. And, like market women everywhere, they continue to be viewed as people of low status by the society as a whole.

THE MATERIALIST PERSPECTIVE

Though most anthropologists acknowledge the importance of environment and subsistence patterns in shaping society, cultural materialists take what many would consider to be an extreme view. Cultural materialists suggest that all aspects of culture, including religious beliefs, can best be understood as pragmatic systems that promote optimal material advantage in a particular social and ecological context. Cultural materialists reject as idealist the position that human behavior is shaped by concepts. According to cultural materialists, it is not ideas that drive the cultural system, but material needs that shape conceptual systems, which in turn articulate and enforce rules that maintain material existence. As did Marx, cultural materialists view all social institutions as rooted in the need for generating and allocating material resources. They consider ideology as a way of explaining and reinforcing practices that arise out of material concerns.

One difference between cultural materialism and Marxism is that cultural materialists are not so wedded to the concept of class. Cultural materialists consider class relations to be critical to an understanding of economic systems, but they do not focus specifically on class conflict and class-based competition for control over the means of production, as Marxists do. Instead, cultural materialists focus on the process of converting material resources for human use. Implicit in studies conducted by cultural materialists is the idea that cultural processes "make sense" in terms of efficient allocation of material resources.

Two noted examples of analysis based on cultural materialism are Marvin Harris and Michael Harner's analyses of religious practices, which are often explained in psychological terms or are viewed as "causes" in themselves. Harris explains the Hindu ban against killing or eating cows as a system for efficient energy use; Harner argues that the Aztec practice of human sacrifice was based on the need for animal protein.

Marvin Harris's "Sacred Cow"

The best-known cultural materialist is Marvin Harris, who believes that cultural practices can best be explained as systems for making energy available for human use. Without this explanation, he writes, some cultural practices—including India's sacred cow worship—are "inexplicable." In his prologue to *Cows, Pigs, Wars and Witches*, Harris notes, "This book is about the causes of apparently irrational and inexplicable lifestyles" (1974:1).

As examples of "apparently irrational and inexplicable" behavior, Harris cites leaders of the Kwakiutl and other Northwestern coast groups as "the boastful American Indian chiefs who burn their possessions to show how rich they are," "Hindus who refuse to eat beef even though they're starving," and the "messiahs and witches who are part of the mainstream of our own civilization" (1974:1). Harris adds,

The Hindu law banning the killing of cows in India leads to an apparent surplus of these domesticated animals. Marvin Harris asserts that cows contribute to the Indian economy through production of energy in various forms: traction for plowing, milk for food, and dung for fuel.

DISCUSSIONS

Political Power and Economic Systems

In Chapter 4, we discussed Elman Service's (1962) model of political organization centering on characteristics of bands, tribes, chiefdoms, and states. That model does not consider such entities as nation-states or ethnic groups. In addition, the band–tribe–chiefdom–state model focuses on formal public systems of allocating power and overlooks the fact that power is negotiated in many different contexts.

Women are often denied power in public realms but may influence the course of events through private forms of negotiation. Max Weber (1947) defines power as the ability to carry out one's will despite resistance or opposition. On the other hand, Talcott Parsons (1963a, 1963b) defines influence as the ability to affect the behavior of others by appealing to their self-interest. Louise Lamphere considers the concept of "influence" to be directly applicable to gender:

> A woman exercises influence when she is able to bring about a decision on another's part to act in a certain way, because it is felt to be good for the other person, independent of changes in his or her situation and for positive reasons, not because of sanctions that might be imposed. (1974:99–100)

It would be a mistake to associate power with the public role of males and influence with the private role of females, however. As noted in Chapter 4, leaders of bands and tribes do not exercise power, in that they cannot impose their will on others. Instead, they must rely on their ability to persuade others as a result of their own abilities.

Anthropologist Judith Marti notes that political power cannot be divorced from economic power and that the distinction between the public and private domains is closely associated with industrialization.

POWER, PUBLIC AND PRIVATE
Judith Marti

Who holds the power in the family, in the village, in the community? Men or women? Who makes important economic decisions? Who controls the pocketbook? Power has been identified as economic power, and, by extension, it is generally assumed that men hold power because they control the economic system. Recent anthropological research challenges this view. Power and economic decision making are not strictly a male province, and the demarcation between male and female roles— generally drawn sharply in theory—are blurred in real life. The debate hinges on two conceptual distinctions: the opposition between the domestic and public domains and the division of labor along male and female lines.

The distinction between the domestic and public domains has been used to explain differences in activities associated with male and female roles. Women's activities belong to the domestic domain, which includes care of home and children and the production of necessities for family use, for example, making baskets and weaving cloth. According to this view, women stay near home and village, and their social life revolves around close female relatives.

Men's activities, on the other hand, belong to the public domain. As wage earners, men venture outside the home and interact with a wider circle that includes nonfamily members associated with business or politics (Tierney 1991). Men have access to the world at large, public cafés, distant villages and towns. Women make their way from kitchen to village bakery to general store and back and, when venturing into a public square, skirt its edges, head down, quickly crossing what is a man's world.

The idea that women and men occupy separate spheres was first formulated in Europe in the early nineteenth century and was used to describe economic life. Until that time, goods had been produced in the home, which served as both a domestic and economic unit occupied by both sexes. Industrialization forced men into factories to manufacture goods outside the home. Men became the breadwinners and carved for themselves the wider public sphere. By default, the domestic sphere became the domain of women (Tierney 1991).

"To make my point, I have deliberately chosen bizarre and controversial cases that seem like insoluble riddles" (1974:1). To solve these "insoluble riddles" Harris tries to find the underlying "rational"— that is, material—cause for practices that seem to defy pragmatic explanations.

In his most famous essay, "Mother Cow," Harris analyzes what he called his "favorite" "inexplicable lifestyle," sacred cow worship of India. Harris notes that Hindus seem to value the lives of cattle over the lives of human beings, citing Hindu riots to protest killing cattle, riots that result in loss of human life.

Contemporary research thus inherited the assumption that men, operating in the public sphere, make the important economic and political decisions and that women's input is secondary, more a matter of influence than of power. As a consequence of the distinctions between public and private and between power and influence, men have been perceived as universally dominant, powerful, and assertive; women have been seen as subservient, compliant, and acquiescent.

Recently, researchers have begun to question the validity of assumptions that assign women to the domestic domain and men to the public domain, with status and power accruing to the latter. As June Nash points out, "Even a single well-recorded case of egalitarian gender relations . . . discredits the thesis of universality of male supremacy" (Nash 1989:230).

In his study of working-class men and women of southern Spain, David Gilmore (1993) undermines the stereotype of the dominant male by demonstrating that power is not necessarily linked to the public sphere. He argues that these Andalusian women have "domestic power [that] is real and unqualified" (1993:1200). The power of Spanish women is based in residence patterns. Newlyweds typically follow the bride's choice in living close to her mother, which allows the women,

allied with other female kin, to form a base of power. In this community of women, the man is the outsider. In addition, even as men have little power in the domestic sphere, neither do they have it in the public domain. They are equal with their peers and ineffective against the power structure that controls the public realm.

Rena Lederman (1986) also challenges the myth of male dominance in her study of trade relationships among the Mendi horticulturalists of New Guinea. Many previous ethnographers had assumed that women were at the mercy of powerful male clan organizations that allocated status based on the ability of men to control exchanges of ceremonial yams and pigs. Though anthropologists have long noted that women grow the yams and tend the pigs, it was thought they had little say in how these high-prestige goods were distributed.

Lederman noted that both women and men have private exchange networks, and a woman may have exchange partners—either male or female—who are not part of her husband's or brothers' networks. She may own pigs in her own name and may act independently, and even travel great distances to conduct exchanges. A woman may choose whether to give pigs to her husband or to her brother. In the case of a serious dispute with her husband, a woman may leave him and return to

her own village to work in gardens owned by her natal kin.

Lederman concludes that it is a mistake to assume that women are restricted to the domestic domain or that male clan activities are necessarily more important than private exchange activities of both men and women. Instead, she suggests, public ceremonial exchanges organized around the clan are concerned with allocating status of males with reference to each other. Clan activities are especially important in the careers of Big Men, political leaders who hope to enhance their own renown by presiding over collective exchange events, such as pig feasts.

The idea that political and economic activities are exclusively male and that women are universally consigned to the less publicly powerful domestic sphere may well be a distorted interpretation resulting from the Western experience of industrialization. In industrialized societies, the public sphere centered on manufacturing and commerce is distinct from the domestic sphere centered on the family. In nonindustrial societies, public and private may well overlap or even merge.

Source: Adapted from Judith Marti's introduction to "Economics, Power and Gender Relations," in Mari Womack and Judith Marti, eds., *The Other Fifty Percent: Multicultural Perspectives on Gender Relations* (Prospect Heights, IL: Waveland Press, 1993).

Also, cattle may compete with humans for food. The animals are allowed to roam freely, strolling through the streets of cities, grazing on foodstuff in marketplace stalls, and snarling traffic in busy streets.

Despite the apparent overabundance of cows, Harris notes, there is a shortage of oxen. For farmers

of India, he points out, male oxen and water buffaloes provide traction necessary to pull plows, an energy need that is supplied by tractors in Western society. In the West, however, farming is part of an integrated industrial complex that produces farm machinery, motorized transport in the form of

The Material Basis of Culture

Though it would be a mistake to assume that economics or material culture determines culture and social organization, it would be equally erroneous to overlook the importance of daily subsistence activities in shaping human needs and concerns. This chapter focuses on two aspects of economic systems—subsistence patterns and systems of distribution—and examines cultural materialism, a theoretical approach that seeks to explain culture as a means of taking optimal advantage of material resources.

Subsistence Patterns

Subsistence patterns are the means by which environmental resources are converted for human use. There are generally four types of subsistence patterns: foraging, pastoralism, horticulture, and intensive agriculture. In addition, intensive agriculture can be industrialized, and the contemporary U.S. economy is often described as postindustrial.

Foraging. Foragers are small, nomadic groups who live by hunting, fishing, and gathering plants and animals.

They typically do not build permanent housing, own land privately, or accumulate many personal possessions. Political organization tends to be egalitarian, and, in most groups, gender relations tend to be relatively equal, though there is a division of labor by age and gender. In most groups, hunting animals is primarily the occupation of males, with females providing the bulk of subsistence through gathering plants. Males and females may cooperate in fishing, depending upon the type of fishing practiced.

Pastoralism. Pastoralists live by herding animals, and they practice a form of seasonal nomadism known as transhumance. In many cases, pastoralists own their herds and rights to migration routes in extended families organized around unilineal lines of descent. As do other groups, pastoralists organize their labor by age and gender, though the division of labor varies depending on the types of animals being herded.

Horticulture. Horticulturalists practice subsistence gardening, usually depending on the technique known

as slash-and-burn, swidden, or shifting agriculture. They typically live in semipermanent villages organized around unilineal kin groups. In the usual organization of labor around age and gender, men clear the gardens and women tend the gardens and care for any domesticated animals.

Intensive agriculture. Agriculturalists typically produce a food surplus through use of plows, irrigation, and, in many cases, fertilizer. They settle down in permanent dwellings, and, in some agricultural societies, production of a food surplus is sufficient for the development of cities and social stratification. Cities and social stratification are based on a division of labor that goes well beyond age and gender and results in social classes with widely differing access to resources and power.

Industrialization. With the rise of industrialization, the economic base shifts from the home to the factory. The need for a mobile workforce precipitates a shift to the nuclear family, which is structurally and economically less stable than the extended family

---

trucks, oil and gasoline, and chemical fertilizers and pesticides.

Industrialized farming is impractical for India, Harris notes. Indian farmers cannot afford to buy tractors, and India as a nation can afford neither to import industrial products nor to develop its own industrial complex organized around farming. In addition, India has one of the most severe crises of overpopulation in the world today. Industrialized farming would increase the size of farms and reduce the number of people needed to engage in agriculture, adding to India's already critical problems of unemployment and homelessness.

According to Harris, cattle contribute more to the economy of India alive than if they were slaughtered. Cattle, like humans, need large amounts of calories—

or energy—to grow to adulthood. If a cow is killed, this storehouse of energy is quickly used up, and it will take many more calories to grow another cow to adult size. Most Indian farmers cannot produce the excess of calories needed to feed cattle to maturity, only to slaughter them and use the protein up in a very short time. It takes the rich resources of a country like the United States, Harris asserts, to grow cattle primarily for their meat.

A mature cow produces calves, and the males among them can be used as draft animals for traction. Cows also produce milk, a protein source for humans. Dung, the waste product of cattle, can be watered down and used as a building material or dried and used as an energy-efficient and long-burning fuel.

characteristic of pastoral, horticultural, and agricultural societies. The shift to a nuclear family also increases the need for child care by non-family members and increases women's dependency on men, since men are most often the wage earners in industrialized societies.

Postindustrialism. The United States has been called a postindustrial society as a result of its shift from a manufacturing economy to a service-oriented economy. This shift has produced a two-tiered workforce in the service sector; jobs that require expertise are more lucrative than unskilled service sector jobs.

Systems of Distribution

Systems of exchange, or the means by which goods and services are made available to members of a society, are its systems of distribution. Prestige plays an important role in systems of distribution, though not all exchange systems offer the same opportunity for amassing status. In general, there are four systems of distribution: generalized reciprocity, balanced reciprocity, redistribution, and the market system, which can be based on either barter or cash.

Generalized reciprocity. Generalized reciprocity is based on providing goods or services without expectation of an immediate return in kind. This system usually does not enable an individual to gain prestige. It helps ensure that all members of a society receive what they need and reinforces the solidarity of the group by establishing ongoing ties of obligation.

Balanced reciprocity. Balanced reciprocity is based on the exchange of goods of equal value. In many cases, exchanges take place over a period of time; thus, this system maintains the parties to the exchange in an almost permanent state of indebtedness, thereby reinforcing alliances between equals.

Redistribution. Status is the central factor underlying systems of redistribution, the accumulation of goods for the purpose of ceremonially giving them away. The Kwakiutl potlatch and the New Guinea pig feast are the best-known examples of redistribution. Both were aimed at extending the influence of a leader throughout a region by establishing networks of mutual indebtedness, based on mobilizing the resources of large groups of kin.

Market system. The market system is based on providing goods and services on the basis of supply and demand. Whether based on barter or the use of cash, the market system typically does not establish relationships based on long-term ties of obligation between individuals and groups.

Cultural Materialism

The best known cultural materialist is Marvin Harris, who asserted that cultural practices are based on making the maximum use of energy resources. His best-known work is his analysis of the Hindu sacred cow complex, in which it is forbidden to kill cows. Harris asserts that cattle provide more energy alive through providing milk products, dung, and traction than would be available from meat if the cows were killed.

Michael Harner explains Aztec human sacrifice as based in the need for protein in an area where there were few domesticated animals and wild animals had been hunted almost to extinction. He notes that the limbs of sacrificed victims were made into soup for human consumption and that torsos were fed to animals in the zoo. He suggests that commoners were encouraged to be aggressive in warfare—which was often waged to obtain sacrificial victims—so that they could win the right to consume human flesh and thus obtain access to a much-needed source of protein.

Cattle continue to be useful after their death. When an aging cow dies, it becomes the property of the untouchables, the lowest Hindu caste, whose members have the right to dispose of the bodies of dead cattle. The untouchables eat the meat, acquiring a needed source of food. They also work the leather, a source of income. If aging cattle were sent to slaughterhouses, their meat would be sold to non-Hindus, depriving untouchables of an important food source. Throughout its life, then, and even in death, the cow contributes to the Indian economy.

Harris also notes that, ultimately, pragmatism triumphs over ideology in the Indian system. Fewer cows are needed than male oxen, so female calves are slaughtered by indirect means: "While no Hindu farmer deliberately slaughters a female calf or decrepit cow with a club or knife, he can and does get rid of them when they become truly useless from his point of view" (1974:23).

Harris says unwanted calves are killed by placing a triangular wooden yoke around their necks so they jab the cow's udder when they nurse and get kicked to death. Older animals are tethered on short ropes and allowed to starve. Finally, unknown numbers of decrepit cattle are sold secretly through a chain of Moslem and Christian middlemen and end up in the urban slaughterhouses (1974:23). Harris summarizes his position by saying:

> Do I mean to say that cow love has no effect whatsoever on the cattle sex ratio or on other aspects of the

agricultural system? No. What I am saying is that cow love is an active element in a complex, finely articulated material and cultural order. Cow love mobilizes the latent capacity of human beings to persevere in a low-energy ecosystem in which there is little room for waste or indolence. (1974:24)

Many proponents of materialist explanations for culture suggest that traditional cultures do not allow their populations to grow to the point of stressing or exceeding the carrying capacity of their environments. Harris does not attempt to explain why Indian culture has produced problems of unemployment and homelessness. Theoretically, materialist explanations should be able to address this puzzle as well. A number of anthropologists, including Jared Diamond, discussed in Chapter 4, use materialist concepts to explain the upward population spiral characteristic of intensive agricultural societies. They maintain that uncontrolled population growth in agricultural societies results from the need for labor to cultivate crops and provide defense.

That argument, however, fails to explain why pragmatic mechanisms do not kick in when carrying capacity is exceeded. One explanation could be that, in the past, expansion into underpopulated areas made it unnecessary to curtail population growth in societies based on intensive agriculture. Because of their hierarchical social organization and ability to support a standing army, agricultural societies could easily overwhelm their more egalitarian neighbors. As the world becomes more crowded, however, traditional means of resolving social and economic problems through expansion no longer suffice.

India's Sacred Cow: An Alternative View

In ancient times, cattle were sacrificed in the Indus Valley before conquest of those civilizations by the Aryans, who came sweeping in on horseback and established dominance over settled agriculturalists. The Aryans then banned ritual sacrifice of cattle, perhaps to break the authority of the early priests, who maintained their social position by mediating with the gods for rain and other favors through ritual sacrifice. In addition to banning cattle sacrifice, the Aryans drove the dark-skinned inhabitants of the region into the south of India and established a system of caste, with themselves at the pinnacle and the indigenous peoples as outcastes at the bottom.

As noted in Chapter 4, both caste and class systems are based on unequal access to power and resources.

However, a caste system differs from a system based on class in that membership in a caste is determined by birth, whereas societies with differentiated social classes allow some degree of flexibility in moving up or down the ranked system.

The ban against killing and eating cows continues to reinforce caste distinctions among Hindus by serving as a marker for "pollution." High-caste Hindus—the priestly, warrior, and landowner castes—do not kill or eat cattle or work with leather. Those practices are a means of relegating outcastes to the status of ritual "uncleanness." Traditionally, outcastes could not touch the food or water of a high-caste Hindu, and intermarrying between castes was largely forbidden. A man could marry within his own caste or one caste below, but a woman could not marry a lower-caste man. Concepts of pollution, including the killing and eating of cows, reinforced the status of high-caste Hindus.

The caste system has been outlawed in modern India, but many individuals still observe pollution laws. And the ban on killing and eating cattle distinguishes Hindus from Muslims and other outsiders. The distinction between Hindus and Muslims is so important, both ethnically and in religious terms, that when India achieved independence from Britain in 1947, the country split along religious lines, and Muslims established the new country of Pakistan. Before the partitioning of the two countries, Harris notes, "bloody communal riots aimed at preventing the Moslems from killing cows became annual occurrences" (1974:8). Though fanned by religious fervor, such displays of hostility are rooted in deep-seated political and ethnic divisions.

Thus, historically and in the present day, the sacred cow symbolizes differences in status among Hindus and provides a justification for hostilities between ethnic groups that have long been divided by competition over access to resources and power. The ban against killing and eating cattle may, as Harris asserts, provide much-needed energy resources for India's farmers. However, it also fuels divisions within India's society as a whole—both along lines of caste and between rival ethnic groups.

Michael Harner and Aztec Sacrifice

Michael Harner uses the materialist perspective to explain what he calls the "enigma" of human sacrifice among the Aztecs of Mexico before the arrival of the Spanish. Harner notes: "The extremity of Aztec sacrifice has long persisted in puzzling scholars. No human society known to history approached that of the Aztecs in the quantities of people offered as religious sacrifices: 20,000 a year is a common estimate" ([1977] 1980:209). Harner attempts to explain "why that particular form of religion should have evolved when and where it did. I suggest that the Aztec sacrifices, and the cultural patterns surrounding them, were a natural result of distinctive ecological circumstances" ([1977] 1980:209).

For Harner, the key variable explaining Aztec sacrifice was the need for animal protein. According to Harner, New World hunters had eliminated from Mesoamerica herbivores suitable for domestication by about 7200 B.C. Deer were nearly gone from the Valley of Mexico by the Aztec period. Population was increasing in the area at the same time that game was decreasing. Harner writes, "Large-scale cannibalism, disguised as sacrifice, was the natural consequence of these ecological circumstances" ([1977] 1980:211).

Harner's estimate of food resources available to the Aztecs is somewhat misleading. The Aztec Triple Alliance exacted tribute from a broad area of Mexico, controlling a range of environmental zones. Corn, beans, and squash were produced throughout Mexico, along with a number of subsidiary crops. Francis F. Berdan notes that "domesticates were few, but they were very important in the diet. Turkeys were raised for meat and eggs; dogs provided companionship and meat" (1982:25). In addition, the Aztecs hunted such animals as deer, rabbits, and wild boar. They caught fish from lakes and streams and captured a range of animals from lakeshores, including waterfowl, frogs, mollusks, and crustaceans.

According to some estimates, members of the Aztec Triple Alliance sacrificed 1 percent of the population each year. Harner writes:

> Evidence of Aztec cannibalism has been largely covered up. . . . Probably some modern Mexicans and anthropologists have been embarrassed by the topic: the former partly for nationalistic reasons; the latter partly out of a desire to portray native peoples in the best possible light. Ironically, both these attitudes may represent European ethnocentrism regarding cannibalism—a viewpoint to be expected from a culture that has had relatively abundant livestock for meat and milk. ([1977] 1980:211)

Harner adds that the Spanish conquistadors and priests who conducted ethnological research on Aztec culture shortly after the conquest amply described cannibalism. Information collected by the Spanish priest Bernardino de Sahagún from former Aztec nobles in the Aztec language, Nahuatl, sheds light on the practice:

> According to these early accounts . . . the overwhelming majority of the sacrificed captives apparently were consumed. A principal—and sometimes only—objective of Aztec war expeditions was to capture prisoners for sacrifice. While some might be sacrificed and eaten on the field of battle, most were taken to home communities or to the capital, where they were kept in wooden cages to

The Aztecs of Central Mexico sacrificed thousands of people each year by cutting out their heart and throwing their body down the temple steps, as depicted here in a drawing by Spanish conquerors. Michael Harner suggests that human sacrifice provided a needed source of animal protein.

be fattened until sacrificed by the priests at the temple-pyramids. (Harner [1977] 1980:212)

Harner argues that the means of disposing of the bodies of sacrificial victims suggests that the primary purpose of the killing was to obtain meat:

> Most of the sacrifices involved tearing out the heart, offering it to the sun and, with some blood, also to the idols. The corpse was then tumbled down the steps of the pyramid and carried off to be butchered. The head went onto the local skull rack, displayed in central plazas alongside the temple-pyramids. At least three of the limbs were the property of the captor if he had seized the prisoner without assistance in battle. Later, at a feast given at the captor's quarters, the central dish was a stew of tomatoes, peppers, and the limbs of his victim. The remaining torso, in Tenochtitlan at least, went to the royal zoo, where it was used to feed carnivorous mammals, birds, and snakes. ([1977] 1980:212)

Harner does not satisfactorily explain why the torsos of sacrificial victims were fed to animals in the zoo if protein was in critical shortage. Protein shortage also does not explain why animals, especially carnivores, which would compete with humans for protein, were kept for display in zoos.

In addition, human beings are an inefficient source of protein, since they must consume large amounts of amino acids to survive and repair body tissues. A fully grown human being will have consumed far more protein than the body would yield after butchering. The sacred cow of India is a more efficient source of protein than a human, because the cow is able to derive its sustenance from vegetable foods and yields protein while alive in the form of milk.

As Harner notes, most sacrificial victims were obtained in warfare, but certain groups of individuals, including merchants, could buy slaves for sacrifice. Particularly valued were attractive male or female slaves skilled in song and dance. The slaves were treated well, fed well, and dressed well. The owner invited distinguished guests to a series of ceremonial feasts, where the slaves, richly adorned and clothed, danced and sang. On a day chosen for its auspiciousness, the merchant walked the slave up the temple steps for sacrifice. After sacrifice, the body would be returned to the merchant for cooking and serving to his relatives at a ceremonial meal.

Nobles had access to nonhuman sources of protein not available to commoners, who subsisted mainly on domesticated plant foods such as corn and beans. Eaten together, corn and beans provide the amino acids necessary for building body tissues. However,

Harner says, "Crop failures and famines were common. . . . Poor people often could not obtain maize and beans in the same season, and hence could not rely upon these plants as a source of the essential amino acids" ([1977] 1980:213).

Despite the poor people's inability to obtain protein, only nobles were allowed to eat human flesh. Harner provides an explanation for this seeming anomaly:

> Even nobles could suffer from famines and sometimes had to sell their children into slavery in order to survive. Not surprisingly, the Aztec elite apparently reserved for themselves the right to eat human flesh, and conveniently, times of famine meant that the gods demanded appeasement through many human sacrifices. ([1977] 1980:213)

Harner acknowledges that the prohibition barring commoners from eating human flesh casts doubt on the idea that Aztec cannibalism was based on protein requirements, since the practice was forbidden to those most in need of it. However, Harner says, because successful warriors would become members of the Aztec elite and gain the right to eat human flesh, the prohibition goaded commoners to participate in wars to gain captives for sacrifice.

> Through the reward of flesh-eating rights to the group most in need of them, the Aztec rulers assured themselves [of] an aggressive war machine and were able to motivate the bulk of the population, the poor, to contribute to state and upper-class maintenance through active participation in offensive military operations. Underlying the war machine's victories, and the resultant sacrifices, were the ecological extremities of the Valley of Mexico. ([1977] 1980:213–214)

There are other explanations for the massive scale of Aztec human sacrifice, including strong indications that Aztec human sacrifice helped the Triple Alliance to maintain dominance over subjugated territories. The sacrificing of great numbers of war captives depleted opposing armies. In addition, Aztec control over ritual sacrifice—which was believed to ensure rains and protect crops—meant that rebellion against the Aztecs was equivalent to insurrection against the gods. Frances F. Berdan writes: "According to their beliefs, [Aztecs] had to ensure the continuation of the universe. The only way this could be successfully accomplished was with the continual offering of human blood" (1982:111).

Human sacrifice also appears to have been used as a means to deal with recalcitrant members of the society. During their long trek before arriving in the

Valley of Mexico, the Aztecs were led by priests and priestesses carrying the god Huitzilopochtli. The people had to submit absolutely to the will of the god as interpreted by the priests. Berdan describes the fate of a faction who opposed the will of Huitzilopochtli:

> These people were content to stay in an inviting place near Tula, even though their god, through the priests, commanded them to continue on their journey. Under cover of night, the hearts of the upstarts were torn out: The wrath of Huitzilopochtli was expressed, and the rebellious faction was eliminated. (1982:5)

Aztec Human Sacrifice: An Alternative View

A common assumption of cultural materialists is that customs such as Hindu reverence for the cow, the Kwakiutl potlatch, and Aztec human sacrifice are "inexplicable" in the absence of immediate material causes. In fact, anthropologists have explained these phenomena in terms of their relationship to other factors in the society as a whole. One common explanation is that each of these cultural phenomena permits segments of the population to exert control over others.

The Hindu sacred cow first aided the Aryans in displacing indigenous priests and later became a mark of ritual purity for the Brahmins, a hereditary priestly caste. The potlatch allowed powerful Kwakiutl chieftains to break rival upstart chiefs and establish their influence over a broad area. In the case of the Aztecs,

most human sacrifices were captured enemy soldiers; thus, sacrifice provided an effective way of eliminating dangerous military rivals and extending the domain of the Aztec empire.

It is clear that economics, as expressed both in patterns of subsistence and in systems of exchange, are central to an understanding of social dynamics. However, one must go beyond the obvious to understand why Asante market women can exercise considerable economic power in the public sphere and remain powerless in their own homes. Or why Brahmins, who occupy the highest caste in Hinduism, are often poor because their ritually pure status prevents them from taking jobs that bring them into contact with pollution. Or why Aztec priests consumed the hearts of sacrificial victims and fed their torsos to animals in the zoo. These are not "mysteries" but examples of the many varieties of human adaptation. In general, human society is too complex to support the isolation of clear-cut causal relationships.

Although cultural materialists pose provocative questions about human adaptation, human society is complicated, and it is virtually impossible to reduce explanations of social phenomena to a single variable. Yet these phenomena are far from inexplicable if examined in light of other, co-occurring practices. The value of the anthropological approach of holism is that it allows us to consider all aspects of social and cultural dynamics that might help to explain seemingly inexplicable customs.

SUMMARY

Economic systems, which are closely linked to political systems, organize the production and allocation of material goods and services. Economic systems are composed of two interrelated aspects: subsistence patterns and distribution systems. Subsistence patterns are the means by which environmental resources are converted for human use. Distribution systems are the means by which goods and services are made available to members of the group.

There are generally four types of subsistence patterns. Foragers hunt, fish, and gather animals and plants that grow naturally in their environment. Pastoralists rely primarily on herding animals. Horticulturalists are subsistence gardeners who do not produce a food surplus. Intensive agriculturalists use plows and irrigation to produce a food surplus. Some

intensive agricultural societies are also industrialized, a process that separates the workplace from the home.

Foragers are nomadic, traveling in small groups that range over a broad territory. Because the ability to move about freely is important to foragers, they do not build permanent dwellings, own land, or accumulate a great deal of personal property. The most important possession of foragers is the knowledge necessary to exploit the plant and animal resources available in their environment. Foragers tend to be relatively egalitarian, though there is task specialization by gender and age. In general, men hunt large game animals; women gather plants and small animals, though there are societies in which women hunt large animals. Women and men usually cooperate in fishing.

Pastoralists practice a form of nomadism known as transhumance, seasonal migration according to the needs of their animals. Tirol cowherders of Austria follow an annual cycle based on the falling and melting of snow. In summer, they move their cattle high on the mountains, and in the fall they bring them back down to their villages. Nuer cattleherders in Africa practice transhumance based on the annual cycle of rainy and dry seasons. During the dry season, they drive their cattle to camps near lakes, rivers, and marshes; during the wet season, they pasture their cattle near their village sites, which are on higher ground. Bakhtiari sheep and goat herders of Iran spend summers in the mountains and winters in the plains. Pastoralists typically own rights to animals and migration routes in unilineal kin groups and have a division of labor based on gender and age, though the division varies depending on the type of animal being herded.

Horticulturalists, who do not produce a food surplus for sale to outsiders, typically raise domesticated animals along with their gardens. Horticulturalists often practice a form of cultivation known as slash-and-burn, swidden, or shifting agriculture, a cyclical pattern of cutting the forest, burning it, planting crops for a few years, and then allowing the forest to reclaim the garden plot. This practice continually restores the fertility of the soil without recourse to artificial fertilizers. There is a division of labor by age and gender, with gardening tasks generally falling to women. Men clear the gardens, serve as warriors, and take charge of public aspects of village life. Political organization ranges from the informal tribal structure among the Yanomamö of Venezuela and Brazil to the chiefdoms of the Trobriand Islanders in the South Pacific.

Intensive agriculturalists produce a food surplus using plows, fertilizer, and irrigation. They settle into permanent dwellings and accumulate personal property. Task specialization based on production of a food surplus gives rise to stratification and the development of cities. Population increases dramatically owing to the need for labor and full-time soldiers. The status of women varies, depending on whether their labor is needed in subsistence and whether they are able to control resources outside the home.

Some intensive agricultural societies become industrialized, separating the home from the workplace. The need for a highly mobile workforce produces a shift from the extended family to the nuclear family. Nuclear families are less structurally stable than extended families and are more susceptible to financial disaster in the event that the main wage earner dies, becomes ill, or loses his or her job. Industrialization may reduce the status of women by making them financially dependent on a male wage earner; however, the social, economic, and geographic mobility of industrialization may also provide women with opportunities for education and wage work.

The postindustrial society developing in the United States, and the shift to a service economy, is likely to increase the gap between rich and poor. Service jobs requiring expertise are highly paid, whereas unskilled service jobs are poorly compensated and offer little opportunity for advancement.

Systems of distribution, or exchange, are related to the organization of power within a society because control over economic resources can provide a basis for differences in power. Prestige is an important component in allocating resources in all societies, and systems of distribution affect the degree to which prestige can be attained. Most systems of distribution also establish ongoing ties of obligation and indebtedness that reflect and reinforce other types of alliances. Systems of distribution include generalized reciprocity, balanced reciprocity, redistribution, and the market system.

Generalized reciprocity is based on providing goods or services without expectation of an immediate return in kind. It establishes a pattern of diffuse obligations that extends to every individual in a group and ensures that everyone has access to resources regardless of his or her ability to contribute. Generalized reciprocity is characteristically the pattern of distribution within the family in virtually all societies. In some groups, exchange based on generalized reciprocity unites the entire group in a network of ongoing obligation.

Balanced reciprocity is based on the exchange of goods or services of equal value. Among the Trobriand Islanders, the Kula ring unites men in a system of trading ceremonial goods that creates lifelong alliances. In this system, the trading of red shell necklaces for white shell armbands takes place in the context of elaborate ceremonies conducted under rigorous rules of obligation. In the United States, gift giving on holidays and birthdays follows a pattern of balanced reciprocity to reinforce relationships between equals.

Redistribution involves the accumulation of large amounts of goods with the object of giving them away in a ceremonial feast and display. This pattern is followed in the potlatch traditionally practiced by Kwakiutl chiefs of western Canada and the pig feast hosted by Big Men among New Guinea horticulturalists. The host is rewarded by an increase in status and influence, and guests must reciprocate with an even larger feast and giveaway. Potlatches and pig feasts demonstrate a leader's ability to marshal the economic resources of the group through his extensive kin network.

The market system, which may involve cash or barter, is based on supply and demand. Unlike other exchange systems, the market does not necessarily establish an ongoing relationship between the supplier and recipient of goods and services. The use of cash and credit increases the distance between the partners in an exchange by allowing transactions to take place with minimal social interaction.

Cultural materialists attempt to explain cultural practices that appear to be based in religion or some other aspect of belief as arising from the need to manage some type of material resource. Marvin Harris argues that Hindu beliefs that forbid the killing of cows are based in the need to conserve energy. He suggests that cattle provide more energy when they are alive than dead as ongoing suppliers of milk products, dung, and traction for plowing fields. In addition, the cow's meat and leather are available for use after the animal dies. Michael Harner suggests that the Aztecs of Central America practiced human sacrifice to gain a source of protein in an area where there were few domesticated animals and where many wild species had been hunted almost to extinction.

There are alternative explanations for both of these practices, including the fact that both sacred cow worship in India and human sacrifice in Central America provided an elite class with the means to control a subordinate group. Sacred cow worship allowed a priestly caste of Brahmins to enforce rules of ritual purity that placed them at the pinnacle of inherited social status. The Aztecs exacted tribute from subordinate groups over a broad region through an elaborate system of ritual and belief in which control over both gods and humans was vested in a priestly hierarchy.

In fact, culture and social organization are far too complex to be reduced to a small number of variables. Understanding the economic system of a society helps us to explain why some practices appear to promote survival of the group under certain circumstances. As we shall see in later chapters, however, it does not fully explain the rich diversity of human beliefs, economic practices, and social organization in a variety of contexts.

POWER WORDS

balanced reciprocity	foragers	market system	redistribution
barter	generalized reciprocity	nuclear family	shifting agriculture
Big Man	horticulturalists	pastoralists	slash-and-burn
cash	industrialization	pig feast	agriculture
distribution system	intensive agriculture	polygynous	subsistence pattern
economic system	kinship system	postindustrial society	swidden agriculture
extended family	Kula ring	potlatch	unilineal
family			

INTERNET EXERCISE

1. For another look at foraging societies, visit **http://www.wsu.edu:8001/vwsu/gened/learn-modules/tom_agrev/3-Hunti.../hunt-gathering1.htm**. This website asks you to compare various types of subsistence patterns. Do your best to answer.

2. Anthony Bettanin maintains a political advocacy website on behalf of the potlatch in British Columbia, Canada, that provides a great deal of information about this form of redistribution exchange. Visit the site at **http://www.anu.edu.au/~e950866/potlatch/index.html** and find out why he compares banning the potlatch to cultural genocide. Drawing on this example, briefly explain the relationship between exchange and other aspects of culture.

3. Why do Hindus regard the cow as sacred? Find out from Ram Chandran, a Hindu, on the website **http://www.hindunet.org/srh_home/1997_5/0113.html**. Briefly compare an emic Hindu view with the etic view of the anthropologist Marvin Harris.

6
Sex, Marriage, and Family Relationships

In this chapter ...

The nature of kinship

Kinship comprises two kinds of relationship, consanguinity and affinity. Consanguinity refers to ties by blood or descent; affinity refers to those created by marriage. Kin relations are important because they determine our place in a network of rights and obligations and because they shape the context in which we are socialized into our culture. Though kinship is based on a biological relationship, the organization of kin groupings varies cross-culturally, based on such related factors as economic and political organization.

Marriage: The socialization of sexuality

Procreation, or production of the next generation, is essential for all groups if they are to continue through time. In human societies, sexuality is regulated through incest taboos, which exclude certain categories of relatives as sexual partners, and through marriage rules, which determine whom one can marry and under what circumstances marriage can take place. Marriage establishes an economic partnership, defines the social identity of offspring, and establishes an alliance between kin groups.

The organization of descent and inheritance

Social status and property are passed down through the generations through various types of descent systems. Bilateral descent, found in industrialized societies and among foragers, allows individuals to claim relationship to a broad network of kin, which promotes flexibility in societies for which geographic and social mobility are important. Unilineal descent establishes a kin group with clearly defined boundaries, an advantage in societies where property is held in common by an extended family, such as among pastoralists, horticulturalists, and agriculturalists.

Residence, households, and terms of address

Kinship establishes relationships among individuals, not only in the abstract sense of belonging but also in the concrete sense of defining where one may live, the people with whom one may live, and how one addresses those with whom one shares reciprocal rights and responsibilities. The great diversity in households and kin terms cross-culturally illustrates the importance of kin relations to socialization.

Because human beings are social animals, and therefore dependent on each other for survival, the two most powerful acts one can commit are creating a human life and ending one. Birth and death are critical events in all societies. They generate shifts in economic and power relationships and dramatically alter the organization of kin groups. Reproduction has economic and political implications, and, because the long-term survival of the group is dependent on producing the next generation, gaining control over reproduction is a powerful political and economic strategy in all societies. Even among the relatively egalitarian !Kung foragers of Africa, parents try to arrange marriages for their children that will assure them of rights to desirable foraging territories.

When a child is born, it is assigned a place in a kinship network, thus ensuring that it will be cared for while in a state of dependency. The network also determines its later responsibilities in caring for others. When an individual dies, the rights, responsibilities, and property accruing to that person must be reallocated to others, and this distribution nearly always takes place along lines of kinship. **Kinship** is a social relationship formed either through consanguinity or affinity. As we learned in Chapter 3, *consanguinity* is based on blood relationships and refers to principles of descent; *affinity* refers to relationships based on marriage. Human families are organized around both types of kinship.

Human beings grow up in families, which are social and economic units organized around kinship. Families, which serve as the primary means of socialization, can be nuclear or extended. Nuclear families include a parent or parents and offspring; extended families are those in which the economically interdependent unit includes two or more related nuclear families. The extended family can be based on either the parent–child bond or on the sibling link. For example, a patrilineal extended family could include parents, sons and their wives, and their dependent children.

Being a member of a family confers certain rights and obligations, including economic cooperation. Through care of dependent individuals and production of future generations, the family is the primary means by which human beings ensure survival. Kinship and family membership order biological relationships by defining which associations will be recognized and emphasized and which will be downplayed. Though kinship is important in all societies, the way in which marriage (affinity) and descent (consanguinity) are organized differs widely from one group to another.

In this chapter, we learn how marriage organizes sexuality and production of future generations and how descent systems organize inheritance of property. We also learn how residence and family patterns are related to economic interdependence and how all these relationships of rights and responsibilities are expressed in kin terminology.

THE SOCIALIZATION OF SEXUALITY: THE INCEST TABOO

All societies have rules governing which individuals may appropriately engage in sex, and these rules are typically backed up by the strongest sanctions a group can impose. All societies have **incest taboos,** rules prohibiting sexual relations between certain categories of relatives.

There have been many attempts to explain incest taboos, but these are still the subject of intense debate. It is difficult to explain both the fact that all societies have incest taboos and that these taboos vary widely from one group to the next. In our discussion of incest taboos, we will attempt to account both for their universality and for their variations. For example, sexual relations between parents and children and between siblings are taboo in most societies, but in at least three societies—Hawaiian, Egyptian, and Inca of Peru—brother–sister marriage was the preferred practice for members of the royal family.

Instinctive Horror

The psychologist Sigmund Freud suggested that the incest taboo results from the unconscious and unacceptable attraction of a child for the parent of the opposite sex. Freud based his model on his idea of the Oedipal complex, in which the son feels sexual attraction for his mother and jealousy toward his father. However, he also formulated a concept of the Electra complex, in which a daughter is attracted to her father and jealous of her mother.

Freud believed that all children pass through a period of attraction to the opposite-sex parent and that the incest taboo developed out of a similar event that he felt must have taken place in human prehistory. In this mythical time, Freud proposed, a company of sons felt sexual desire for their mother and killed their father to eliminate him as a rival for the mother. The sons were then overcome by guilt and by fear that their own sons would rise up against them.

The sons then sacrificed an animal in honor of the father they had killed—as Freud describes it, the first religious ritual—and elevated the dead father to the status of a god. They banned all sexual relations between mother and son and, because of their great horror over their deed, extended the ban to their sisters. Thus, Freud writes, "The beginnings of religion, morals, society, and art converge in the Oedipus complex" ([1901] 1950:156).

According to Freud, the horror of that primal crime against the father remains active in the unconscious minds of contemporary humans. Freud's model is based on nineteenth-century evolutionary theories and like them is implicitly *androcentric* because it traces the origins of human society to the relations between males.

The instinctive horror theory also falls short for other reasons. There is no evidence that people instinctively recoil from sexual relations between close relatives. In fact, cross-cultural variations in incest taboos suggest that adverse reactions to incest are learned rather than innate. In addition, it is an axiom in anthropology that there is no need to impose sanctions on behavior that people would not be likely to engage in. There would be no need for an incest taboo if people were disinclined to engage in such acts.

Family Disruption Theory

Bronislaw Malinowski ([1927] 1955) theorized that incest taboos contribute to the harmony of the family by reducing sexual competition among family members. Noting that the family acts as the primary context for the socialization of children, Malinowski asserted that incest taboos provide an environment within which children can learn adult roles, free from the necessity to compete sexually with the more powerful adults who are responsible for their protection and enculturation.

One problem with Malinowski's theory is that it cannot be proved, even if it seems logical. It also suggests that sexuality necessarily implies competition, which may be a Eurocentric projection. Anthropological studies of polygamous marriages suggest that sexual jealousy becomes a factor primarily when economic competition is involved. In the case of polygynous marriages, for example, disputes among co-wives occur most frequently when the wives must compete for economic resources for their children. When the co-wives cooperate economically, as in the case of some polygynous societies such as the Masai of Africa, wives may encourage their husbands to take additional wives to assist them in their work.

Childhood Familiarity Hypothesis

Edward Westermarck (1894) suggested that boys and girls who have been in close association with each other since early childhood develop an aversion to each other, which would reduce the likelihood that they would eventually marry. He contended that incest taboos result from the sexual aversion that siblings develop toward each other.

Opponents of this explanation offer the same argument as that advanced against Freud's theory of instinctive horror. There is no reason for sanctions against behavior that people would not engage in

anyway. It also fails to explain the preference for brother–sister marriage among members of the Egyptian, Hawaiian, and Incan royal families. Brother–sister marriage within the Egyptian royal family produced some of the most moving love poems in classical literature, in which young people of both sexes declare their passion for their siblings, referring to them as "husband" or "wife."

However, there is some contemporary evidence for the childhood familiarity hypothesis. Arthur Wolf (1968) studied "minor marriage" in a northern Taiwan village still practicing *t'ung-yang-hsi*, or "daughter-in-law raised from childhood." In this Chinese custom, a girl is raised by her husband's family as a kind of sibling to her future spouse. Wolf suggested that partners in these arranged marriages were often dissatisfied sexually and romantically with their partners and were likely to become involved in extramarital affairs. These marriages produced fewer children and were more likely to end in divorce than were marriages between spouses who had not been raised together.

Results of a study of Israeli kibbutzim also support the Westermarck hypothesis. Yonina Talmon (1964) studied the second generation of three kibbutzim, collectives in which children live with members of their peer group in quarters separate from their families. Talmon discovered that, of 125 marriages, none were between individuals raised together in the same kibbutz, even though parents would have favored such a marriage. One of Talmon's subjects told her, "We are like an open book to each other. We have read the story in the book over and over again and know all about it" (1964:504). A later study of 211 kibbutzim (Shepher 1983) revealed that only 14 of 2,769 marriages were between individuals who had been raised in the same kibbutz, and all of those marriages ended in separation or divorce.

Still, the childhood familiarity explanation falls short for the same reason as the instinctive horror explanation. In the absence of other factors, incest taboos would be unnecessary if siblings or parents and children were unlikely to engage in sexual relations. It also fails to explain why, in most societies, incest taboos are extended to certain categories of cousins, who may be treated as equivalent to siblings.

Prevention of Inbreeding

By preventing intermarriage or sexual relations between closely related individuals, the incest taboo reduces the probability of pairing harmful recessive genes—those that may be fatal or impair an individual's ability to function. Because people of the same descent group are likely to carry the same genetic traits, marriage between biologically related individuals increases the probability that negative recessive genes will be paired in the next generation. Therefore, some anthropologists have theorized that the purpose of the incest taboo is to prevent inbreeding.

Though the incest taboo certainly reduces the probability of pairing negative genes, the "inbreeding" theory does not explain the great cross-cultural variability in the incest taboo. Why was brother–sister marriage the preferred form among the Hawaiian, Egyptian, and Incan royal families? And why may second cousins marry in some U.S. states but not in others? And why in some societies are certain categories of cousins the preferred marriage partners? And why are adoptive kin—including siblings and stepparents and stepchildren—legally prevented from marrying in the United States, even though they are biologically unrelated? Though inbreeding may be one explanation for the incest taboo, it does not cover all the cases known to anthropologists.

Alliance Theory

The nineteenth-century evolutionist E. B. Tylor identified the importance of alliances contracted through marriage when he asserted the principle of "marry out or die out." The incest taboo forces individuals to look for marriage partners outside their immediate families or descent groups, thus creating political and economic alliances with people who might otherwise be competitors or enemies. The alliance between kin groups is strengthened when children are born to the marriage and the affiliation continues through the next generation.

The practice of marrying outside the group is called exogamy. Exogamy can be advantageous for political entities as well as kin groups. When the countries of Europe were ruled by monarchies, political alliances were formed through marriage. In the sixteenth century, Queen Elizabeth I of England used the promise of marriage to forge advantageous pacts for her country with both France and Spain.

In-marrying, or endogamy, allows a group to consolidate its wealth and social status. Sibling marriage among the royal families of Hawaii, Egypt, and the Incas of Peru reduced claims to the throne and reinforced the power and wealth of the royal line. The

power of the royal office was reinforced by religious beliefs. Members of the Hawaiian royal family were believed to possess the quality of mana, an impersonal force residing in some persons, places, and things. Mana is beneficial to those who have the power to use it, but it is fatal to those who do not possess it. Egyptian pharaohs were believed to be divine representatives of god on the earth. Thus, the endogamous marriage customs of Egyptian and Hawaiian royal families were reinforced by religious beliefs that kept outsiders at a distance.

Exogamy and endogamy are alternative marriage strategies that can be used to shape relations between groups, whether they be kin groups or groups based on economics, power, or religious affiliation. In the United States, elite social classes tend to be endogamous, encouraging their children to marry members of their own class. Members of lower social classes may attempt to use exogamy to enhance their social position by creating a marriage alliance with someone of a higher social class. Most religious groups are endogamous, and kin groups in virtually all societies practice some degree of exogamy.

MARRIAGE

Love may be a private emotion and sex an act typically carried out in some degree of privacy, but **marriage** is a public social contract that creates an economic partnership, confers sexual rights, defines the social identity of offspring, and creates an alliance between kin groups. In biological terms, sexuality and reproduction are not dependent on marriage, but marriage is the means by which important rights and responsibilities are allocated. Networks created by marriage extend far beyond the married couple. Individuals may gain political power or increase their economic assets by arranging the marriages of members of their kin group.

An important purpose of marriage is assigning social identity to offspring. On the most immediate level, marriage ensures that an infant or developing child will be provided with kin who are responsible for his or her care. Being assured of care is essential for survival, since human young undergo a long period of dependency during which they must learn not only how to provide for their biological needs but also how to interact with others in their social group.

Humans grow up in families, which are organized around the principles of marriage and descent. In all societies, marriage defines paternal rights and obligations. This Ivory Coast father's rights to his son are established by the man's marriage to the child's mother. Through his marriage, he has acquired the right to include the child in his descent group.

On another level, marriage establishes the position of the child in a line of succession and inheritance that transmits the wealth and social status of a family to future generations.

Because of the biology of birth, maternal identity is usually known. However, the identity of the father is typically assigned through marriage. In the United States, a great deal of importance is placed on identifying the biological father because inheritance of property and family membership have a patrilateral bias, as evidenced by assigning the father's name as the child's family name. Even here, however, the father is defined legally as the man married to the child's mother. The husband of the child's mother is the social father—the one responsible for the child's care—whether or not he is the child's biological father.

This relationship is often more explicit in other societies. The Nandi, cattleherders of Kenya in Africa, practice female–female marriage. The Nandi are patrilineal, and only sons can inherit property. If a household has no male heir, its property will be destined to go to more distant relatives, so a woman may become the "female husband" of another woman and the father to the woman's children. As father, the female husband passes on her lineage affiliation to her children. The woman who becomes a female husband must become the social equivalent of a male, discontinuing sexual relations with men and assuming the rights of a husband, though she does not have sexual relations with her "wives."

The Tiwi of Australia are patrilineal and polygynous, which means that men may marry more than one wife. As is the case in most polygynous societies, only men of high status have the resources to acquire a wife, and women often marry men older than themselves. Women freely admit (though not to their husbands) to taking lovers, which is acceptable as long as they don't insult their husbands by flouting their behavior. The husbands may implicitly accede to their wives' taking lovers because their status is enhanced by their ability to control the children produced by the extramarital relationship. This reproductive strategy serves social goals rather than biological goals for the husbands involved.

The Economic Contract

When people enter into an economic agreement in the United States, the terms of the agreement are

In all societies, marriage establishes an economic contract. This young couple of Sri Lanka sign their marriage contract as members of both families look on. In North America, the marriage certificate is evidence of a social contract whose economic provisions are unspecified, though they can be upheld in a court of law. In the Sri Lanka marriage contract, the economic and other provisions are negotiated before the marriage takes place.

typically spelled out in some detail. Marriage is the only economic contract in which no details are specified, but the implied terms of marriage can be upheld in court. Depending on the state in which the couple resides, marriage may convey half of the individual's property to the other partner or transfer control over the property from one to the other. In the United States, terms of the economic contract in marriage are implicit rather than explicit.

In most other societies, marriages are arranged. The economic contract involved in these marriages is explicit, often worked out in advance by third parties. In these cases, it is believed that romantic love is not enough to build a lifetime relationship. Instead, it is believed that love grows out of the process of building a life together and that the social and financial importance of marriage is best left in the hands of people old enough to understand its implications.

Marriages can be arranged by older relatives or by an unrelated person who serves as a matchmaker. Matchmakers consider the financial and social standing of bride and groom, and in some societies they may consult omens or oracles to determine the suitability of the match and select an auspicious time for the marriage. Matchmakers also consider the personalities of the bride and groom. A poem from the Chinese *Book of Songs,* possibly written about 600 B.C., tells of the importance of the matchmaker:

> How does one cut an axe-handle?
> Without an axe it is impossible.
> How does one take a wife?
> Without a matchmaker she cannot be got.

Those who arrange the marriage work out all financial details so the marrying couple and their children will be securely provided for. In some Middle Eastern societies, marriage arrangements include provisions for the wife in case of divorce. In many groups, marriage entails a transfer of property from one kin group to the other, which usually serves to reinforce the solidarity of the marriage.

Forms of Marriage Exchange

A form of marriage payment common in many societies is **bridewealth,** also known as **brideprice.** It consists of goods given by the groom or his kin group or both to the family of the bride. Bridewealth, which usually involves a major economic commitment on the part of the groom and his family, is not a payment for a wife. Instead, it compensates the bride's family for the loss of her labor and fertility and transfers these important resources to her husband's family. Bridewealth also reinforces the alliance between the kin groups of husband and wife because it is typically paid over a number of years: when the arrangements are agreed upon, at the time of the marriage, and on the birth of a child. These ongoing economic transactions ensure continued interaction between the two kin groups. This form of exchange also contributes to the stability of the marriage, since divorce could disrupt the bridewealth arrangements.

Brideservice is another common economic transaction accompanying marriage. In this case, the groom works for the bride's family until they believe he has adequately compensated them for the loss of a daughter. In some cases, brideservice may substitute for bridewealth. Many Native American societies practiced brideservice, and the custom is familiar to readers of the Bible. Jacob acquired his wife Rachel and her older sister Leah as wives through brideservice.

In a custom known as **gift exchange,** goods or services of equivalent value may be exchanged. Among the Andaman Islanders of India, as soon as a young woman and man indicate their intention to marry, their parents cease communication and begin to send food and other gifts to each other through a third party. Alice Schlegel notes that gift exchange is often found in societies with important status differences in rank or wealth and is a way of ensuring that the intermarrying families are of the same social status (1993:125). Gift exchange reinforces the alliance between the families of the bride and groom.

Sister exchange, or **woman exchange,** occurs when a female relative is given as a bride to the family from whom a bride is sought. According to Schlegel and Herbert Barry (1986), woman exchange occurs in societies where women make a major contribution to subsistence. In some societies, such as among the Mundugumor of New Guinea, this practice takes the form of **brother–sister exchange,** in which a brother and sister arrange to marry a sister and brother from another lineage. Like some other New Guinea groups, the Mundugumor practice polygyny, in which one man marries more than one woman. Since women produce valued subsistence goods, they are much in demand as wives, and their families can demand a significant contribution in bridewealth. Young men who cannot accumulate bridewealth may arrange to marry each other's sisters, so that both are assured of wives.

Dowry is a transfer of goods or money from the bride's family to the bride. Schlegel (1993) suggests that dowry can be used to buy a high-status son-in-law, but it is conceptually based on the idea that the bride's family is paying out her share of her family's wealth. Dowry is a common economic arrangement in Europe and Asia. Traces of the dowry system are found in the U.S. custom in which the bride's family pays for the wedding. This practice is commonly expressed in terms of the family's "owing" the daughter a wedding, a reflection of the idea that dowry is the bride's claim on her family's property.

Indirect dowry combines features of bridewealth with dowry. As Schlegel writes, "Sometimes the groom's kin give goods directly to the bride, but more often they give goods to her father, who then gives goods to the new couple" (1993:125). Indirect dowry is often found in Islamic countries and, according to Schlegel, "appears to be a way of establishing the property rights of the conjugal couples that make up larger households" (1993:126). In some parts of India, the groom's family gives indirect dowry to the bride in the form of new clothing and gold jewelry.

The economic importance of marriage is downplayed in the United States, where the emphasis is on romantic love. This emphasis gives rise to the idea that marriage is primarily a sexual contract, and the success of the marriage is often measured in terms of whether the parties to the marriage are still romantically attracted to each other. Thus, responsibility for the success of the marriage is placed directly on the marrying couple, and the importance of the economic contract and the responsibilities associated with reproduction are downplayed. This emphasis seems to contribute to the instability of the family in the United States, where most marital conflict and divorces occur because of disputes over money. An older woman in the small U.S. town in which I grew up framed the economic realities much more pragmatically, saying humorously, "Kissin' don't last; cookin' do." Marrying couples in the United States increasingly resort to prenuptial agreements, but these decisions place the burden of working out financial arrangements on the marrying partners rather than on third parties, who may be less vulnerable emotionally.

Marriages in India have traditionally been arranged, and many young people still prefer to rely on their parents to choose a marriage partner, even though they are well educated and have achieved financial independence. They say they have the best of two worlds: the freedom of Western society and the security of marriage arrangements decided on by their elders. Even in societies where marriages are arranged, romantic love is not overlooked. The Chinese *Book of Songs* contains poems by women who express their satisfaction or dissatisfaction with the arrangements that have been made for them. In one case, a woman describes her plight when she rejects a marriage match:

> My heart is not a mirror,
> To reflect what others will.
> Brothers too I have;
> I cannot be snatched away.
> But lo, when I told them of my plight
> I found that they were angry with me.

The *Book of Songs* also contains poems by women who record their joy at the match made for them, including the following by an anonymous author:

> The mulberry on the lowland, how graceful!
> Its leaves, how tender!
> Now that I have seen my lord,
> Ah, what delight!
> Love that is felt in the heart,
> Why should it not be told in words?
> To the core of my heart I treasure him,
> Could not ever cease to love him.*

Types of Marriage

In virtually all industrialized nations, monogamy is the preferred marriage form. Monogamy forms an exclusive partnership between two spouses. Some scholars have suggested that, in the United States and some other countries, marriage has taken the form of **serial monogamy,** in that an individual is married to one partner at a time but may have several spouses over a lifetime. It is unclear why the shift to serial monogamy has taken place, but it is probably related to industrialization and urbanization, both of which weaken extended kin networks that provide a stabilizing force for marriage.

Serial monogamy may also be related to the increase in life span, since death has traditionally provided release from an unhappy marriage. In

---

The Book of Songs: The Ancient Chinese Classic of Poetry, trans. Arthur Waley (New York: Grove Weidenfeld, 1937).

Marriage assigns rights to a woman's fertility and labor, signified by some type of economic exchange. China is characterized by patrilineality, patrilocality, and the dowry system. A woman's fertility and labor are transferred to her husband's kin group, and rights to her own lineage's assets are paid out to her in the form of dowry. All these transactions are reflected in this wedding procession in Shandong Province, in which the bride is carried to her husband's household. The rich decorations on her litter reflect the riches she is bringing to her husband's lineage in the form of dowry, fertility, and labor.

addition, partnership needs tend to shift through time, from romantic love to the need to make a living and nurture a growing family. As children mature, the marrying couple may rediscover a need for companionship. The emphasis on romantic love in the United States may lead to unrealistic expectations, as each partner expects the other to move smoothly from one dramatically different role to another.

Helen E. Fisher (1990) notes that divorce is common in societies where men and women are relatively economically independent of each other. Among traditional foraging groups, such as the !Kung and the Hadza of Africa, women provide a large share of the daily diet through gathering, while men also provide food through hunting and gathering. When a woman becomes dissatisfied with her marriage, she is economically free to leave.

The divorce rate is also high among the Tamang of highland Nepal, where women possess livestock, corn, and money independently of their husbands, and among the Yoruba of West Africa, where women traditionally control the complex marketing system. Fisher observes that the American divorce rate began to rise as women moved into the job market, a pattern consistent with other societies in which women are financially independent:

An unhappy man will leave a wife who brings home an income long before he will desert a woman he depends on to weed his garden. And a woman with a salary may be less tolerant of marital despair than one dependent on her spouse to provide the evening meal. (1990:200)

The Economics of Polygamy No known society practices group marriage, in which more than one man is married to more than one woman at a given time, but polygamy is the most common marriage form cross-culturally. **Polygamy** has two forms: **polygyny** is the marriage of one man to more than one woman; **polyandry** is the marriage of one woman to more than one man. Many societies are polygynous; very few are polyandrous.

Even in societies that practice polygyny, most marriages are monogamous, because polygyny is beyond the economic reach of most men. Polygyny appears to be associated with societies in which there are status differences among males and in which the work of women is economically important. In many cases, polygyny is also associated with bridewealth, which makes a wife difficult to acquire. Because status and wealth accrue to older men, young men usually are unable to acquire a wife without the help of older relatives. Therefore, polygyny typically makes young men dependent on their elders.

In societies where women do much of the work of supporting a household, a woman may ask her husband to provide her with co-wives. Among the Turkana, cattleherders of Kenya, women care for

In this polyandrous wedding, among Tibetans in Nepal, a woman marries all the brothers of a family. This is fraternal polyandry, which is probably related to the need to conserve land in a mountainous region.

livestock and do much of the household labor. A man who wishes to marry an additional wife must have the support of his current wives, since they will supply the necessary cattle for bridewealth. Among the Kapauku horticulturalists of New Guinea, women tend the gardens and raise pigs and yams, which are prized for their ceremonial value. A man seeking political prestige must have the support and labor of his wife. She may urge him to take co-wives to help her with her work.

The rarity of polyandry may be due to the difficulty it creates in assigning paternity. In the few societies where it occurs, among some Tibetans, the Toda of India, and some Sinhalese of Sri Lanka, polyandry is fraternal. In **fraternal polyandry,** a woman marries her husband's brothers. This practice effectively negates the possibility that males from competing lineages will claim biological paternity, since all potential fathers are from the same descent group.

Given the difficulty in assigning paternity, one might wonder why polyandry occurs at all. Melvyn C. Goldstein (1994) studied Tibetans living in the mountainous regions of northern Nepal, where productive land is scarce. The Tibetans combine pastoralism with agriculture in a region where most families own less than an acre of cultivable land. They maintain cattle, yaks, goats, and sheep in areas too high for agriculture, which means men are gone from the household for long periods of time.

The Tibetans say polyandry makes it unnecessary to divide the land, as would eventually become necessary if each son took a separate wife (see Figure 6.1). Tibetans inherit patrilineally and follow the rule of male **primogeniture,** meaning the eldest brother has first claim on family wealth and power. In the polyandrous household, the eldest brother is dominant in terms of authority, but all the brothers share the work and participate as sexual partners. Goldstein notes that the Tibetans reject as "unstable" the idea of joint households where each brother has a separate wife:

> When I asked Tibetans about this . . . they invariably responded that such joint families are unstable because each wife is primarily oriented to her own children and interested in their success and well-being over that of the children of the other wives. . . . Thus, the children from different wives in the same generation are competing sets of heirs, and this makes such families inherently unstable. (1994:213)

Since all the brothers are married to the same wife under the Tibetan system, all their children are from the same mother, so competition among in-marrying wives is eliminated. Polyandry also controls population growth by reducing reproductive opportunities for some women. Just as polygyny prevents some men from finding wives, polyandry prevents some women from finding husbands. Goldstein notes that, though half of single women had children, they had far fewer children than married women.

The Tibetans studied by Goldstein practice fraternal polyandry. In some other societies, polygyny may

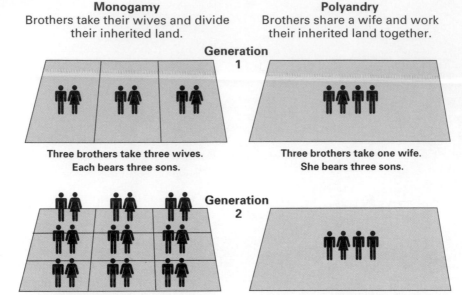

Monogamy
Brothers take their wives and divide their inherited land.

Polyandry
Brothers share a wife and work their inherited land together.

Generation 1

Three brothers take three wives. Each bears three sons.

Three brothers take one wife. She bears three sons.

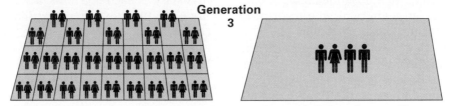

Generation 2

Nine sons take nine wives. Each bears three sons.

Three sons take one wife. She bears three sons.

Generation 3

Twenty-seven grandsons take twenty-seven wives.

Three grandsons take one wife.

FIGURE 6.1   Social Dynamics of Polyandrous Marriage

Fraternal polyandry obviates the necessity of dividing small land parcels in a patrilineal society, both by restricting population growth and by ensuring that all sons with a claim to property have a single mother. The population dynamics of fraternal polyandry are illustrated in this comparison of fraternal polyandry among Tibetans living in Nepal with monogamy.

Source: Adapted from Melvin C. Goldstein, 1987, "When Brothers Take a Wife," *Natural History.* Copyright 1987 the American Museum of Natural History.

be sororal. In **sororal polygyny** a man marries his wife's sisters. In some societies, marriage ties may continue to link kin groups even after the death of one of the partners. In the **sororate,** a woman must marry her deceased sister's husband. This means that a woman's children will be raised by her sister if she dies and her family will not be required to return her bridewealth. The **levirate** is a custom in which a widow must marry her deceased husband's brother. The levirate allows a younger son to assume the status and rights of his older brother and also allows his family to retain control over the widow and her children. These practices illustrate the importance of marriage for continuing a lineage by producing heirs and in maintaining alliance between kin groups.

KINSHIP, AFFILIATION, AND DESCENT

Marriage, which establishes affinal ties, provides a context for enculturating and assigning social identity for children. Descent, the system for organizing consanguineal links, provides a means for transmitting property and social status from one generation

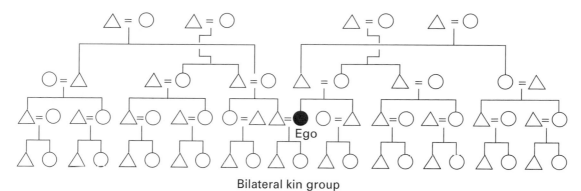

FIGURE 6.2   Bilateral Kin Group

All individuals on this diagram belong to Ego's kindred, or bilateral kin group. In a bilateral kin group, each Ego has a different kindred, a group of individuals to whom he or she claims kin. The bilateral kin group includes both consanguineal and affinal kin on both sides, so the boundaries are continually shifting through marriage, divorce, death, and birth. Because they have no fixed boundaries, bilateral kin groups are not corporate, which means they cannot make decisions or own property in common.

to the next. Just as marriage creates a set of rights and obligations centering on the marrying parties and their offspring, descent determines the ability of individuals to affiliate with kin groups and to participate in the rights and responsibilities accruing to kin group membership.

Though descent is based on biological relationships, it is far from being biologically determined. In fact, systems for figuring descent vary from one society to another, and these variations appear to be related to differing needs to control economic resources. **Bilateral descent,** in which kinship is traced through both male and female lines, affords flexibility in economic cooperation and inheritance but does little to reinforce kin group solidarity. **Unilineal descent,** in which kinship is traced either though the female or the male line but not through both, reinforces kin group solidarity and appears to be related to the ability to control economic resources beyond the nuclear family.

Bilateral Descent and Kin Group Flexibility

The literal meaning of bilateral is "two sides," a reference to the idea that kinship is figured through both male and female lines. In North America, where most descent group membership is figured bilaterally, a genealogy is called a "family tree," since bilateral descent produces kin groups that in a figurative sense branch out from an individual much like the limbs

on a tree. Bilateral descent groups have flexible boundaries, since they include consanguineal and affinal relatives on both sides. It is conceivable that one could trace kinship bilaterally to every human being on the earth if the kin network were extended indefinitely (see Figure 6.2).

In fact, members of bilateral kin groups do not trace kinship indefinitely. Instead, they recognize a limited number of kin: those who might be called upon for some purpose, including those who might be invited to a wedding or expected to attend a funeral. A bilateral kin group expands to include marriage partners of its members as well as affines linked through that marriage partner. For example, if your brother marries, you acquire not only his wife as a relative but also her parents and siblings, as well as marriage partners and children of those siblings. If the brother divorces or dies, the kin group may contract to exclude those previously acquired affinal relatives.

The bilateral kin recognized by a particular individual form a **kindred.** Because its boundaries are flexible, the kindred is different for every individual in the kin group. Thus, kindreds are **ego centered,** which means they can be figured only with reference to a specific **ego,** or individual. It does not mean that the individuals in a kindred are egocentric, which is a psychological term meaning that one is centered on oneself. However, the flexible boundaries of bilateral kin groups give rise to the "rich-relative syndrome," which means that individuals in bilateral kin groups

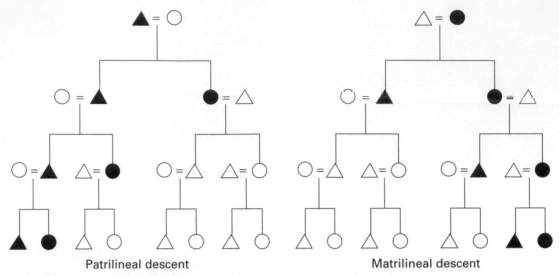

Patrilineal descent   Matrilineal descent

FIGURE 6.3 Unilineal Kin Groups

Unilineal kin groups can be either patrilineal or matrilineal. Unilineages include only consanguineal kin. They can be corporate because their boundaries are fixed, as noted in the above diagrams of patrilineal and matrilineal descent. An individual acquires membership in a unilineal kin group at birth. This membership does not change with marriage.

tend to extend the kinship tie to include all those who can provide benefits in status and economic resources and retract the kinship tie to exclude all those who are a detriment to one's status or resources. This flexibility is an advantage in a society where social and geographic mobility are desirable, as in societies based on foraging or industrialization.

With the rise of industrialization and urbanization, and in the wake of the boundless optimism for the future following World War II, the importance of descent in the United States has been downplayed. Geographic and social mobility seem more important than the ability to identify with one's ancestors. As the growth of the U.S. economy has slowed and the future seems more uncertain, many people are beginning to trace their links to their relatives through genealogies, or diagrams of kin groups.

Unilineal Descent and Kin Group Solidarity

In most societies, kinship is unilineal, which means "one line." Unilineal kin groups are those in which descent is traced through either the male or the female line, but not both. As noted in Chapter 3, most unilineal descent groups are either matrilineal

or patrilineal. Descent is traced through the female line in a **matrilineage** and through the male line in a **patrilineage.** A lineage is a unilineal descent group (see Figure 6.3).

Matrilineal descent is often confused with *matriarchy,* in which positions of public power are allocated to women. There are no known matriarchal societies; even in groups with matrilineal descent, positions of public power are typically held by men. In a matrilineal society a boy inherits his social status from his mother's brother rather than from his father. Women in matrilineal societies may have more say in group decisions, as among the Navajo and Hopi of the American Southwest, but they do not hold public positions of power. Among the matrilineal Asante of Africa, males hold positions of authority, but they are nominated to those positions by the senior female of the lineage. Among the Iroquois, who were matrilineal and the closest known society to a matriarchy, women nominated males to positions of political authority but could not hold public office themselves.

A less common form of descent is **ambilineal descent**, also known as **cognatic descent,** in which an individual may affiliate either with the matrilineal kin group or with the patrilineal kin group. Ambilineal descent provides greater flexibility than other types of unilineal descent, in that it allows individuals to affiliate with the descent group that offers greater opportunities for gaining access to resources. For example, a young man with older male siblings may affiliate with his wife's kin group if her family does not already have a male heir, an arrangement that could be beneficial for all concerned.

Unilineal descent groups have clearly defined boundaries, since all members acquire membership by birth or adoption. One does not change one's membership in a unilineal descent group by marriage, as is the case with bilateral kin groups. Because unilineages do not have fluctuating boundaries and one's right to be a member is known from birth, unilineal groups can be **corporate,** meaning they can act as a unit in making decisions or owning property. Thus, they are typically found in societies based on pastoralism, horticulture, or intensive agriculture, where there is an advantage in having clear lines of inheritance. In these groups, subsistence is based on assets that would be difficult to acquire individually: rights over animals and grazing routes; access to gardens; or ownership of land, water rights, and expensive farming equipment.

Lineages and Clans

The solidarity of unilineal descent groups can be further emphasized in the case of lineages and clans, which mark descent groups by naming customs and other insignia. Members of a lineage trace descent from a common ancestor through known links. The ability to trace one's genealogy in this way reinforces the sense of continuity in the lineage and is a means of status for individuals, who can demonstrate a direct link to a distinguished ancestor.

Members of a clan trace descent to a common ancestor, but the links to that ancestor may not be specified. For example, in the traditional clan system of Scotland, clan members are identified by the name of the founding ancestor: e.g., MacDougal. Individuals who carry the name MacDougal are presumed to have descended from that ancestor and can claim the right to wear clan identification, including MacDougal plaids. Clans based on patrilineal descent are **patriclans;** those with matrilineal descent are **matriclans.** The organization of kin groups into clans is widespread, occurring in societies as geographically dispersed as the Celts in Ireland, the Chinese, and Australian aborigines.

The solidarity of clans is typically emphasized through insignia, names, or totems. As noted in Chapter 1, a totem is a plant or animal believed to be the clan ancestor or the founder of the clan. Australian aborigines trace their ancestry to animals such as wallabies and pythons, and this clan relationship is reflected in their art, in their names, and in their ritual relationship to the totemic animal. For example, the story of the totemic ancestor will be told during important ceremonies, much as the story of the Christ child is recounted at Christmas, and the totemic ancestor will be called upon to assist in healing when a member of the clan becomes sick or suffers some misfortune. Stories of clan ancestors, emblems, names, and the rituals that commemorate them all reinforce the solidarity of the kin group.

Fictive Kin

Though unilineal and bilateral systems of descent are efficient and effective means of organizing inheritance and promoting marriage alliances in all societies, the need often arises for a means of moving individuals around on the kin chart. A patrilineal descent group may find itself without a male heir and face the loss of jointly owned assets; a nuclear family may be childless; or a lineage may need to enhance its military strength by supplementing its membership by birth with the addition of fictive kin.

Fictive kin are individuals whose membership in a kin group is assigned arbitrarily rather than through consanguinity or affinity. The relationship established by adoption is an example of fictive kinship. A patrilineal descent group without a male heir or the childless nuclear family may adopt a child to fill the desired kinship role. In Mexico, a child is provided with godparents, fictive kin who are obligated to provide assistance, through money or patronage, at key points in the child's development. If the parents die, the godparents are expected to step into the parental role.

Because of the cross-cultural importance of kinship in establishing relationships of rights and obligations, anthropologists are often assigned a fictive kin role in the societies they study. Among the Yanomamö of Venezuela, Napoleon Chagnon was called "sister's son" by one Yanomamö man and "elder brother" by another. In her study of Australian aborigines, Karen Saenz was called by one senior male by the term meaning "women who may become our wives." The individual whose membership is assigned fictively

DISCUSSIONS

Fictive Kin and Social Relationships

The organization of kinship is generally based on consanguineal, or biological, relationships or on affinal relationships, those established by marriage ties. In many cases, however, biological descent and culturally recognized marriages are inadequate to fulfill the many requirements and obligations inherent in kinship ties. In these cases, for example, when there is no male heir to a patrilineal estate or when father–daughter incest produces a socially ambiguous child, kinship is renegotiated. Fictive kin—kinship ties established by adoption or other socially recognized renegotiation of kinship—play an important role in maintaining kinship relationships when regularly constituted consanguineal or affinal ties prove to be inadequate. Where fictive kin take the place of consanguineal or affinal kin, these are typically governed by rules applicable to the more "conventional" relationships. In the following essay, Mary Weismantel examines a concept of kinship in which parenthood is defined relative to the dynamics of feeding and caring for children over extended periods of time.

MAKING KIN
Mary Weismantel

The last time I went back to Yanatoro, a scattering of farmsteads on a steep hillside above the indigenous community of Zumbagua in highland Ecuador, I found that my *achi wawa* (godchild) had a new mother. Nancy de Rocio was then ten years old; she had been born during the year and a half that I lived in Yanatoro conducting doctoral research. In those days, Heloisa was Nancy's unmarried aunt, her father Alfonso's oldest sister. During my

previous visit, in 1991, Nancy had been living with Heloisa but called her "tia" ("aunt"); two years later, the child was calling her "mama."

Heloisa, a tall, spare fifty-year-old who favors black clothing, would not find it easy to adopt a child in the United States. She lives without a husband in one windowless room, out of which she runs a small bar selling *trago* (cane liquor) on market days. During most of the 1980s her closest friend was a locally prominent white woman named Elena, who was rumored to be her lover; the two spent hours sitting together on wooden chairs in Elena's kitchen, and many nights in Elena's bed. But Elena moved from Zumbagua, leaving her friend behind. And so Heloisa brought her small niece Nancy to live with her—and to become her daughter.

Beyond "Natural" and "Unnatural" Parents

The ease of the transition contrasts sharply with conflicts over adoption, surrogate mothers, and paternity claims recounted in the U.S. media. In the United States, neither "natural" nor "unnatural" parents gain secure victories. In a diverse and unequal society, it is not surprising that individuals and communities create families that do not conform to the hegemonic ideal, or that the courtroom serves as a public spectacle in which such relationships are displayed and dismembered. What commands attention is the uncertainty of the judiciary about the ideals it should be defending; instead of reinforcing a familiar moral code, these cases and the media attention they generate exacerbate a national sense of doubt. In debates about custody,

adoption, abortion, and reproductive technologies, the public searches for a suddenly elusive definition of paternity and maternity. The United States is experiencing a crisis over consanguinity.

Heloisa's claim over her new daughter is far more secure, supported by Zumbagua belief about the nature of parenting. The social fabric of Zumbagua is made up of small households based on lifelong heterosexual marriages, a pattern that superficially resembles the conservative Euro-American ideal. In fact, however, the bonds people form with one another in the parish are based on an understanding of relatedness that differs strikingly from Euro-American principles. Absent from Zumbagua discourse are those anxieties over natural and unnatural parents that loom so large in the popular imagination of Los Angelenos. In Los Angeles, as in Latin America, poor and marginalized communities have had to create strong, flexible kinship systems in order to survive. The Zumbagua kinship system does not discriminate between mother and father in the adoption system. Birth mothers are free to give up their children if they do not wish to raise them, as are the fathers. By the same token, the choice not to raise children engendered early in life does not limit one's ability to become a parent in later years for either women or men. Other limitations do apply: the wealthy acquire children while the impoverished lose theirs, and older, established couples have a more secure claim on children than do the young. But gender is not a factor in these matters.

Heloisa exemplifies the possibilities inherent in the system. Somewhat well off by parish standards, she is nevertheless a poor woman in a peripheral rural area within Catholic Latin America; she thus lacks the elite power so often found in women who assume masculine prerogatives (e.g., Amadiume 1987). Yet Heloisa seems to have given up little or nothing in exchange for avoiding marriage and physiological motherhood, and in fact she has gained a great deal: she has a business and a child and is sexually active. Heloisa's life seems to have as its dominant theme the exertion of a powerful volition over all matters, including reproductive ones.

Feeding and Fatherhood

At the core of sensational fights between biological and adoptive parents in the United States is the courtroom drama. Adults and children enter a room in which their fates will be decided in a single pronouncement by a powerful agent of the state: a judge (and, in rare cases, a jury). Once judgment has been passed, it becomes fact: all the toys and stuffed animals the would-be parents bought, the name they chose, the time they may have spent with the child, mean nothing. Only the final statement matters, and only another judge's word, in another courtroom, could overturn its power to determine whose relationships are real and whose mere pretense.

In Zumbagua, authority is diffuse. Paternity is determined by all those directly concerned and then is confirmed—or contested—through public discourse throughout the community. No single arbiter representing an abstract political authority can grant it or take it away. By the same token, the standard for judgments is different. In Zumbaguan terms, our form of determining paternity misses a crucial dimension of materiality that people in the parish seek in judging whether relationships exist.

In the parish, any act involving food performed in the presence of others expresses important social facts. While the burden of daily cooking and feeding falls on women, men do take bowls of food and feed their children by hand in small rituals of intimacy. Those who witness these acts then affirm the relationship in words: "Look at him feeding his child," they say, or, teasing, "Look at the good father." This particular act of feeding is clearly a ritual, a symbol through which the tie between man and boy is established—especially since it is women, not men, who feed children and their fathers on a daily basis. Indeed, it is simply a different aspect of biology—eating rather than sex—that provides key parenting metaphors in the Andes.

But the act of feeding is not a disembodied ritual. If it were, a single mouthful of soup, symbolizing the parent–child bond, might be sufficient to make strangers kin. In the parish, the relationship between parent and child has more than social and spiritual dimensions: the bond is material in nature, created through corporeal means. Like those Euro-Americans who define paternity as a biological link created by the transmission of sperm, fatherhood in Zumbagua is the establishment of a concrete and irreversible link between two human bodies.

Food As a Biological Bond

In Zumbaguan eyes, engendering a child is only one component in the lengthy process of physical and social reproduction, and not necessarily the most important. Andean beliefs and practices about illness, death, and healing reveal an underlying conception of the human body as a material object built up over time through various substances and acts: ingesting food and drink, sharing emotional states with individuals or spirits, being physically close to people or objects. Bonds between people are created in the same way—gradually (Bolton 1977, Carter 1977). The two processes are interrelated: the bodies of individuals are linked through shared substances to the bodies of family members (Allen 1978, 1988).

The physical acts of intercourse, pregnancy, and birth can establish a strong bond between two adults and a child. But other adults, by taking a child into their family and nurturing its physical needs through the same substances as those eaten by the rest of the social group, can make of that child a son or daughter who is physically as well as jurally their own.

Especially critical in this process is the sharing of meals. Flesh is made from food, and especially from different grains and tubers, each of which has its own characteristic effect on the human body. Eating cooked grains raised by a household on its own land and harvested and processed through family labor results in a body and a self that have been shaped by work and skill invested in the farm. When men bring home foods bought with wages, these foods change the bodies of family members, too (Weismantel 1988,

(*continued*)

DISCUSSIONS

Fictive Kin and Social Relationships (*continued*)

1989). Those who eat together in the same household share the same flesh in a quite literal sense: they are made of the same stuff.

To feed a boy for a day does not make one a legitimate father, nor does impregnating a woman in a single night. Not enough time and effort have been invested. It is when a man lives with a woman throughout her pregnancy and birth, having sex with her repeatedly as the child grows in her womb, feeding and

caring for her and, later, for the newborn child, that he begins to be a father to the child he has engendered. It is when a woman has not only suffered through the labor of birth itself, but has also struggled to meet the incessant demands of growing children, and begun to produce recognizably socialized offspring who speak and understand, that people begin to address her with the honorific "Mama." The link between the material body and social

identity is not given and immutable from the moment of conception but is gradually and laboriously produced. Evidence of this steady, constant investment of labor by an adult in the life of the child is the only real criterion for parenthood.

Source: Adapted from Mary Weismantel, 1995, "Making Kin: Kinship Theory and Zumbagua Adoptions," *American Ethnologist* 22(4): 685–704.

---

will be considered a consanguineal or affinal relative, depending on the assigned position.

CLANS, MOIETIES, AND CROSS-COUSIN MARRIAGE

In some societies, clans may be linked together in groups called phratries or moieties. A **phratry** is a unilineal descent group composed of clans supposed to be related to each other but without specified descent links. A **moiety,** from a French word meaning "half," is a descent group divided into two primary unilineages. In societies where phratries and moieties are an important part of the descent system, clans tend to be exogamous, or out-marrying, but the preferred marriage is endogamous for the phratry or moiety to which the clan belongs. In other words, individuals may be required to marry outside their own clan but be expected to find a marriage partner within the phratry or moiety. In these systems, marriage links together closely related clans and provides a mechanism for extending political and economic alliances over a broad area.

Societies that clearly define the relationship of lineages to each other may distinguish between cross cousins and parallel cousins (Figure 6.4). **Cross cousins** are related to each other through an opposite-sex parent link. Thus, one's cross cousins are a father's sister's child or a mother's brother's child. Note

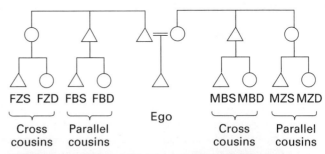

FZS FZD FBS FBD   MBS MBD MZS MZD

Cross cousins   Parallel cousins   Ego   Cross cousins   Parallel cousins

FIGURE 6.4 Cross Cousins and Parallel Cousins

Cross cousins are related by an opposite-sex link and include FZS (father's sister's son), FZD (father's sister's daughter), MBS (mother's brother's son), and MBD (mother's brother's daughter). Parallel cousins are related by a same-sex link and include FBS (father's brother's son), FBD (father's brother's daughter), MZS (mother's sister's son), and MZD (mother's sister's daughter). The distinction between cross cousins and parallel cousins is usually related to marriage rules of exogamy and endogamy.

that the sibling link between the parents is between a brother and a sister. **Parallel cousins** are related through a same-sex parent link. Thus, one's parallel cousins are a father's brother's child or a mother's sister's child, and the sibling link between the parents is between two brothers or two sisters.

The distinction between cross cousins and parallel cousins is most relevant in societies where descent is figured unilineally and marriage is used to create alliances between related lineages. In those cases, an individual may be expected to marry a cross cousin and view a parallel cousin as equivalent to a sibling. From childhood, a boy will address his female cross cousin by the term meaning "wife" and will observe incest taboos toward a female parallel cousin, whom he addresses as "sister." Similarly, a girl will address her male cross cousin as "husband" and will address her male parallel cousin as "brother," while observing the appropriate incest taboos. Cross-cousin marriage provides the mechanism that links closely related clans into phratries or moieties by extending the alliance between kin groups into succeeding generations. In societies that do not recognize phratries or moieties, cross-cousin marriage can be a means of forging political alliances between closely related clans (Figure 6.5).

Cross-cousin marriage challenges the inbreeding theory for incest taboos because cross cousins and

parallel cousins are equally closely related biologically. It supports the alliance theory, however, since cross-cousin marriage forces individuals to marry outside their own lineage into a closely related lineage. Figure 6.5, which diagrams cross-cousin marriage, illustrates the formation of alliances between closely related clans.

In some Muslim societies, the preferred marriage is between parallel cousins, specifically to a father's brother's son or daughter. This type of marriage is endogamous with respect to the patrilineage and serves to consolidate property and status within a single male line.

MARRIAGE, DESCENT, AND THE FORMATION OF HOUSEHOLDS

Kin groups are organized according to patterns of various types of interdependence. One's place on a kinship network helps shape the types of assistance one expects to receive, as well as what one must provide for others. Kinship is typically reflected in the formation of a **household,** a group of people who live together in a single dwelling or group of dwellings and are considered an economic unit. Households are often, though not always, made up of families. Families may be either nuclear, which means a marrying couple forms a new household in which to raise their children, or extended, in which several nuclear families are linked together in an economic partnership.

An extended family may be formed along generational lines or through sibling links. In the first case, married children may continue to live with the parents and raise their children in the parents' household. Extended families formed along sibling links are usually associated with unilineal descent, so that brothers, with their wives and children, may form a household organized around patrilineal descent. Extended families provide an advantage in societies where cooperation is important in sharing labor and resources, as in agricultural or pastoral societies.

Nuclear families tend to occur where geographic mobility is desirable, such as among foragers and in industrialized societies. Nuclear families offer the

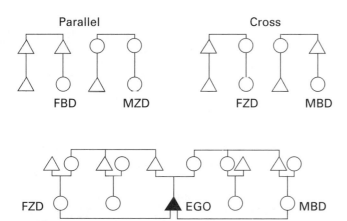

FIGURE 6.5 Cross-Cousin Marriage

Cross-cousin marriage creates alliances with closely related lineages. In this example from the Yanomamö of Venezuela and Brazil, a man has allied himself with his mother's lineage by marrying his mother's brother's daughter (MBD). Because the Yanomamö practice polygyny, the man was able to form an alliance with another closely related lineage by marrying his father's sister's daughter (FZD).

Surrogate Mothers: Redefining Parenthood

In the United States, "Mom and apple pie" have often been used as a metaphor for the good things that can be counted on. Young men have gone to war for Mom and apple pie. Politicians have built careers by singing the praises of Mom and apple pie.

But who exactly is Mom? As the discussion of kin relations in this chapter indicates, kinship is defined within a social and cultural context. Whom we call mother and the reciprocal relationship or rights and obligations established by that kin position may vary from society to society. The issue of surrogate motherhood has focused new attention on the nature of mothering. The metaphor of Mom's oven producing the warmly nurturing apple pie—an image of the womb as nurturer—has been challenged by the commercial imagery of "rent a womb." Mom went from the kitchen to the marketplace and finally to the courtroom.

In the following essay, anthropologist Helena Ragoné notes that both surrogates and commissioning couples emphasize aspects of surrogacy consistent with American kinship ideology, most notably in their emphasis on the importance of family and nurturance.

CHASING THE BLOOD TIE: LOVE AND MONEY IN SURROGATE MOTHERING
Helena Ragoné

Stated motivations for becoming surrogate mothers include the desire to help an infertile couple start a family, financial remuneration, and a love of pregnancy (Parker 1983:140). As I began my own research among surrogate mothers and commissioning couples, I soon observed a remarkable degree of uniformity in surrogates' responses to questions about their initial motivations for becoming surrogates; it was as if they had all been given a script in which they espoused culturally accepted ideas about reproduction, motherhood, and family. These motivations are fully reinforced by surrogate mother programs, which recruit surrogate mothers and match them with commissioning couples.

I also began to uncover several areas of conflict between professed motivations and actual experiences, discovering, for example, that although surrogates claim to experience "easy pregnancies" and "problem-free labor," it was not unusual for surrogates to have experienced miscarriages, ectopic pregnancies, and related difficulties. Jeannie, age thirty-six, divorced with one child and employed in the entertainment industry, described the ectopic pregnancy she experienced while she was a surrogate in this manner: "I almost bled to death; I literally almost died for my couple." Nevertheless, she was again inseminated for the same couple. Fran, age twenty-seven, divorced with one child and working as a dog trainer, described the difficulty of her delivery in this way: "I had a rough delivery, a C-section, and my lung collapsed because I had the flu, but it was worth every minute of it. If I were to die from childbirth, that's the best way to die. You died for a cause, a good one." As both these examples illustrate, some surrogates readily embrace the idea of meaningful suffering, heroism, or sacrifice.

Surrogates receive between ten thousand and fifteen thousand dollars for three to four months of insemination and nine months of pregnancy, on average. Surrogates also receive an allowance for maternity clothing, remuneration for time lost from work if they have employment outside the home, and reimbursement for all babysitting fees incurred as a result of surrogate-related activities. As one program psychologist explained, the amount paid to surrogates is intentionally held at an artificially low rate so as to screen out women who might be motivated solely by monetary gain. Surrogates frequently dismiss the suggestion that remuneration serves as a primary motivation; as expressed by Fran, "It [surrogacy] sounded so interesting and fun. The money wasn't enough to be pregnant for nine months."

Though surrogates accept monetary compensation for their reproductive work, they rarely spend the money they earn on themselves. Not one of the surrogates I interviewed spent the money she earned on herself alone; the majority spend it on their children—as a contribution for their college education funds, for example—while others spend it on home improvement, gifts for their husbands, a family vacation, or to pay off "family debts."

The money appears to serve primarily as a buffer against lean times or as a reward to their families—particularly to their husbands, who must make a number of compromises as a result of the surrogate arrangement. One of these compromises is obligatory abstention from sexual intercourse with their wives from the time insemination begins until a pregnancy has been confirmed (a period that lasts on average from three to four months but may be extended for as long as one year).

Surrogacy is viewed by surrogates as a part-time job in the sense that it allows a woman, especially a mother, to have, as one surrogate noted, "the luxury of staying at home with my children," an idea that is also attractive to their husbands. The surrogate, however, consequently spends less time with her family as a result of a new schedule that includes medical appointments, therapy sessions, and social engagements with the commissioning couple. Thus, surrogates are able to use the monetary compensations they receive as a means of procuring their husband's support when and if they become less available to the family because of their employment.

The devaluation of the amount of the surrogate payment by surrogates as insufficient to compensate for "nine months of pregnancy" serves several important purposes. This view is representative of the cultural belief that children are "priceless" (Zelizer 1985). When the largest and one of the best-established surrogate mother programs changed the wording of its advertising copy from "Help an Infertile Couple" to "Give the Gift of Life," the volume of response from potential surrogates greatly increased. The gift formulation holds particular appeal for surrogates because it reinforces the idea that having a child for someone is an act that cannot be compensated for monetarily. The "gift of life" theme is further enhanced by some surrogates to embrace the near sacrifice of their own lives in childbirth.

Fran, whose dismissal of the importance of payment has already

been noted, offered another, more revealing account of her decision to become a surrogate mother: "I wanted to do the ultimate thing for somebody, to give them the ultimate gift. Nobody can beat that, nobody can do anything nicer for them." Stella, age thirty-eight, married with two children, noted that the commissioning couples "consider it [the baby] a gift and I consider it a gift." Carolyn, age thirty-three, married with two children and the owner of a house-cleaning company, discusses her surrogacy in similar terms: "It's a gift of love. I have always been a really giving person, and it's the ultimate way to give. I've always had babies so easily. It's the ultimate gift of love."

When surrogates characterize the child they reproduce for couples as a "gift," they are also suggesting tacitly that mere monetary compensation would never be sufficient to repay the debt incurred. Although this formulation may at first appear to be a reiteration of the belief that children are culturally priceless, it also suggests that surrogates recognize that they are creating a state of enduring solidarity between themselves and their couples—precisely as in the practice of exogamy, where the end result is "more profound than the result of other gift transactions, because the relationship established is not just one of reciprocity, but one of kinship" (Rubin 1975:172). As Rubin summarizes Mauss's pioneering work on this subject, "The significance of gift giving is that [it] expresses, affirms, or creates a social link between the partners of exchange . . . confers upon its participants a special relationship of trust, solidarity and mutual aid" (1975:172).

Thus, when surrogates frame the equation as one in which a gift is being proffered, the theme serves as a counterpoint to the business aspect

of the arrangement, a reminder to them and to the commissioning couple that one of the symbolically central functions of money—the "removal of the personal element from human relationships through it[s] indifferent and objective nature" (Simmel 1978:297)—may be insufficient to erase certain kinds of relationships, and that the relational elements may continue to surface despite the monetary exchange.

On a symbolic level, remuneration detracts from the idealized cultural image of women/mothers as selfless, nurturant, and altruistic, an image that surrogates have no wish to alter. Then, too, if surrogates were to acknowledge money as adequate compensation for their reproductive work, they would lose the sense that theirs is a gift that transcends all monetary compensation. The apparent conflict between altruistic surrogacy and commercial surrogacy also underlies the public debate. In Britain, where commercial surrogacy has been declared illegal, the issue was framed often in moral terms: "The symbol of the pure surrogate who creates a child for love was pitted against the symbol of the wicked surrogate who prostitutes her maternity" (Cannell 1990:683). This dichotomous rendering in which "pure" surrogates are set in opposition to "wicked" surrogates is predicated on the idea that altruism precludes remuneration.

Although surrogates overwhelmingly cast their actions in a traditional light, couching the desire to become a surrogate mother in conservative and traditionally feminine terms, it is clear that in many respects surrogate motherhood represents a departure from traditional motherhood. It transforms private motherhood into public motherhood, and it provides women with remuneration for their

(*continued*)

Surrogate Mothers: Redefining Parenthood (*continued*)

reproductive work—work that has in American culture been done, as Schneider (1968) has noted, for "love" rather than for "money." This aspect has become one of the primary foci for state legislatures throughout the United States. The overwhelming acceptance of the idea of unpaid or noncommercial surrogacy (both in the United States and in Britain) can be attributed to the belief that it "duplicates maternity in culturally the most self-less manner" (Strathern 1991:31).

But what is perhaps even more important, the corresponding rejection of paid or commercial surrogacy may also be said to result from a cultural resistance to conflating the symbolic value of the family with the world of work, to which it has long been held in opposition. From a legal perspective, commercial surrogacy has been viewed largely by the courts as a matter of "merging the family with the world of business and commerce" (Dolgin 1993:692). This prospect presents a challenge to American cultural definitions in which the family has traditionally represented "the antithesis of the market relations of capitalism; it is also sacralized in our minds as the last stronghold against the state, as the symbolic refuge from the intrusion of a public domain that consistently threatens our sense of privacy and self-determination" (Collier et al. 1982:37).

Over time it became clear to me that many of the women who chose to become surrogate mothers did so as a way to transcend the limitations of their domestic roles as wives, mothers, and homemakers while concomitantly attesting to the importance of those roles and to the satisfaction they derived from them. That idea accounted for some of their contradictory statements. Surrogates, who are for the most part from predominantly working-class backgrounds, have often been denied access to prestigious roles and other avenues for attaining status and power. Surrogacy thus provides them with confirmation that motherhood is important and socially valued. Surrogacy also introduces them to a world of social interaction with people who are deeply appreciative of the work they do, and in this way surrogates receive validation and are rewarded for their reproductive work through their participation in this new, public, form of motherhood.

Source: Adapted from Helena Ragoné, 1996, "Chasing the Blood Tie: Surrogate Mothers, Adoptive Mothers and Fathers," *American Ethnologist* 23(2): 352–365.

---

advantage of flexibility. As noted in Chapter 5, they tend to be less stable than extended families, in which economic risk, child care, and household labor are shared by a larger number of people.

Residence Patterns

The formation of family groups is shaped by **residence patterns,** customs that determine where individuals will live after marriage. Residence is related to the degree of interdependency the marrying individuals will maintain with their kin group. In general, residence patterns are as follows:

1. **Patrilocal residence.** The son of the household brings his wife to live with or near his own parents, whereas daughters go to live with or near their husband's family. This residence pattern is found in India and China, as well as in many other parts of the world. In these cases, patrilocal residence is associated with patrilineal descent and ensures that the labor of sons, their wives, and their children is controlled by the male lineage. Patrilocal residence is also found in some matrilineal groups, however. For example, the matrilineal Asante of Ghana are patrilocal, so that a woman goes to live in her husband's village until he dies, when she returns to the village of her own matrilineage.

2. **Matrilocal residence.** The daughter of the household brings her husband home to live with or near her own parents, whereas sons go to live with or near their wife's family. This is usually associated with matrilineal descent. There are many variations on this pattern, however. David D. Gilmore (1993) notes that working-class Andalusians of southern

Spain establish neolocal residences near the wife's mother, a pattern of residence that fosters matrifocal ties—links through the female line.

3. **Ambilocal,** or **bilocal, residence.** The marrying individuals may choose which set of parents to live with or near. This system permits flexibility in economic cooperation, so that a couple may choose to ally itself with the kin group that controls the greater access to resources.

4. **Avunculocal residence.** The son of the household brings his wife to settle with or near his mother's brother. This is commonly associated with matrilineal inheritance, since a boy inherits his status and position from his mother's brother.

5. **Neolocal residence.** Individuals of both sexes establish a new residence apart from both the husband's and wife's relatives. Nuclear families are formed through neolocal residence.

The first four types of residence pattern typically continue relationships of interdependency with the extended family. Neolocal residence provides the basis for a nuclear family.

The Nayar: A Case in Household Formation

The Nayar of southern India are often referred to in the anthropological literature as "the Nayar exception" because their household organization challenges the idea that marriage is universal. Anthropologists continue to debate whether the Nayar pattern of forming sexual liaisons and households constitutes marriage. The Nayar practiced an extreme form of matrilineality and matrilocality and were organized into extended-family households. The Nayar household consisted of matrilineages, in which only consanguineal kin were permitted to reside. Because they are atypical, the case of the Nayar illustrates the way in which descent, marriage customs, and residence patterns shape relations within the family.

In the traditional caste system of what is now the state of Kerala in southern India, the Nayars were warriors and feudal landholders, typically in service to Brahmins, the priestly caste. As girls in a Nayar household neared puberty, they participated in a tali-tying ceremony, in which a man of an equal or higher caste tied a *tali*, a gold medallion on a ribbon

or gold chain, around her neck. After this ceremony, a girl was addressed by the term reserved for married women, and after her menses began she could take lovers. The lovers, who were allied with her in a *sambandham* relationship, had to be of equal or higher caste.

The woman continued to reside in her own matrilineal household and could maintain several sambandham relationships, but her lovers were not allowed to move into her household or remain with her during the day. A man could claim paternity for a woman's child by paying the midwife for the birth, but he had no say in the upbringing of his children. Children, whether male or female, were members of their mother's matrilineage and resided in their mother's household, or *taravad*. They were subject to the authority of the mother's *karanavan*, the senior male of the lineage.

Anthropologists have remarked that warrior societies tend to be patrilineal, since the most loyal army is one in which brother fights next to brother. The Nayar present an informative contrast to this idea, in that the matrilineal household they traditionally occupied is more closely allied than even the most exclusive of patrilineages. All members of the Nayar household are biologically related. There are no "in-laws," which is the kin relationship most associated with intrafamilial conflict.

The Nayar appear to have developed the most stable system of descent, marriage, and residence known to anthropologists, one in which all outsiders are excluded and each child born into the lineage is considered part of the lineage wealth. All males are potentially warriors, and all females are potentially mothers of warriors. Thus, the Nayar are in sharp contrast to patrilineal, patrilocal families in other parts of India, where daughters are not so welcome.

In the patrilineal, patrilocal system common to both India and China, daughters drain wealth from their own lineage because they leave their natal families when they marry and contribute labor to their husband's lineage. Their children continue their husband's lineage and ensure their husband's inheritance, rather than their own. In addition, much of the wealth of the wife's lineage must go to provide a dowry. Thus, in patrilocal, patrilineal systems with a dowry system, daughters enrich their husband's lineage and may impoverish their own lineage. Among the matrilineal, matrilocal Nayar, daughters enriched their own lineage by ensuring the continued survival of their kin group by providing it with sons and daughters.

KIN TERMS AND KIN RELATIONS

The organization of kin relationships is expressed in kin terms. Cross cousins are distinguished from parallel cousins through kin terminology in societies where members of one's own lineage must be clearly distinguished from outsiders for purposes of marriage or economics. Systems of kinship terminology are based on how relatives are grouped together or distinguished. Categories of relatives are generally distinguished or grouped together according to sex, generation, and lines of descent.

Among Euro-Americans, whose kinship system is bilateral, no distinction is made between father's and mother's relatives or between parallel and cross cousins. Instead, the distinction is between near and far cousins, who may be referred to as first, second, or third cousins. Euro-Americans do clearly distinguish between male and female parents (mother, father) and between male and female siblings both of Ego, the individual from whom kinship is figured (brother, sister) and of the parents' generations (aunt, uncle). Euro-Americans also distinguish the direct line of descent according to generations (grandmother and grandfather, and great-grandmother and great-grandfather). However, they do not distinguish between male and female cousins; the term *cousin* includes males and females of both sides of the family. In the case of some kin categories, such as aunt and uncle, the terminology does not distinguish consanguineal from affinal kin. An "uncle" may be either the sibling of a parent or a person married to that sibling. In this system, one's uncle may be a father's brother, a father's sister's husband, a mother's brother, or a mother's sister's husband, and the term *uncle* is usually extended to the grandparents' generation. In this system, *cousin*, *uncle*, and *aunt* are **classificatory kin terms,** which means several kinds of relatives are grouped together in the same term.

In all societies, kin terms are reciprocal, which means they reflect a relationship based on reciprocity, such as that of mother–son or father–daughter, and imply an appropriate pattern of behavior. In virtually all societies, mothers are expected to provide sons with food, and in some societies, such as the Masai, a grown son is expected to provide economically for his mother after her husband dies. Fathers are typically expected to protect and provide economically for their daughters and, in some societies, provide them with a husband. Daughters are expected to accord their fathers obedience and, in some societies, may be expected to take care of their household needs in the event of their mother's death.

Kin terms are important because they imply expected behavior, and the system of kin terminology in a particular society describes a pattern of kin relationships. Categories that may be reflected in kin terminology are the sex of the person referred to; whether the individual is related to Ego through the mother's or the father's side, by generation; and, in some cases, the sex of the person speaking.

In the following types of kin terminology, note that the Eskimo and Hawaiian systems do not distinguish between kin on the father's and kin on the mother's side. Most societies using the Eskimo and Hawaiian systems have either bilateral or cognatic descent systems. That is, they trace descent through both lines, or the individual can choose whether to align with the mother's descent group or the father's descent group. The Omaha, Crow, and Iroquois systems do distinguish mother's kin from father's kin, and the majority of societies using these systems are unilineal.

Eskimo System

Eskimo kinship terminology, the system used by Euro-Americans, emphasizes the nuclear family by identifying mother, father, brother, and sister. However, relatives outside the nuclear family tend to be grouped together, so that male and female siblings of parents are distinguished by sex, not by whether the kin link is male or female, or even by whether the link is affinal or consanguineal. Cousins may be either male or female and from either side of the family.

The Eskimo system of kin terminology is linked to bilateral descent, which centers on the nuclear family. Links to the father's and mother's kin are equally important, and either may be called upon for resources depending on whether they are "near" or "far" kin. Thus, members of the nuclear family are identified precisely, whereas those outside the nuclear family—grandparents, aunts, uncles, and cousins—are grouped together in the same classificatory term.

Hawaiian System

In **Hawaiian kinship terminology,** all relatives of the same sex in the same generation are called by the same term. All female relatives of the mother's generation, including the mother, are referred to by the same term, and all male relatives of the father's generation are referred to by the same term as the father. Thus, Ego's mother, mother's sister, and father's sister are referred to by the same term. Ego's father, father's brother, and mother's brother are referred to by the same term. All females of one's own generation are called by the term meaning "sister," and all males are called by the term meaning "brother." Grouping same-sex relatives of both sides, combined with a distinction based on generations, facilitates the process of allying oneself with either the father's or the mother's descent group, thus providing an advantage in a cognatic descent system.

Omaha System

Named after the Omaha of North America but found in many societies around the world, **Omaha kinship terminology** is usually associated with patrilineal descent. Father and father's brother are both referred to by the same term, but males of Ego's patrilineage are distinguished by generation, and both males and females of the father's lineage are distinguished from males and females of the mother's patrilineage. Mother, mother's sister, and mother's brother's daughter are all referred to by the same term. All males of the mother's patrilineage—mother's brother, mother's brother's son, and so on—are referred to by one term. Thus, members of the mother's lineage are distinguished only by sex, whereas members of the father's lineage are distinguished by sex and generation.

This system of kinship terminology emphasizes relationships within the patrilineal line and clearly distinguishes them from the matrilineal kin group.

In the Omaha system, male parallel cousins of both sides are referred to by the same terms as Ego's brother, and female parallel cousins are referred to by the term meaning "sister," which effectively eliminates parallel cousins on both sides as marriage partners. Cross-cousins on the father's side are distinguished according to their sex and the sex of the speaker. For example, a male Ego will refer to his father's sister's son as "nephew" and to his father's sister's daughter as "niece." A female Ego will refer to her father's sister's son as "son" and to her father's sister's daughter as "daughter." Since kin terms are reciprocal, the father's sister's children will refer to a male Ego as "uncle" and to a female Ego as "mother."

Crow System

Crow kinship terminology, named after another American Indian group, is the matrilineal equivalent of the Omaha system. In the Crow system, the mother and mother's sister are referred to by the same term, and females of the mother's matrilineage are distinguished by generation. Males of the father's matrilineage are referred to by the same term, as are females of the father's matrilineage. As in the Omaha system, parallel cousins of both sides are equated with brothers and sisters. In the Crow system, the father's sister's children will refer to a male Ego as "father" and to a female Ego as "father's sister."

As in the Omaha system, cross-cousins linked by the parent of one's own lineage are distinguished by sex and by the sex of the speaker. In the case of a matrilineage, these are people related through Ego's mother. Since the Crow system is the mirror image of the Omaha system, a male Ego calls the mother's brother's children "son" or "daughter," whereas a female will refer to these individuals as "nephew" or "niece."

Iroquois System

In **Iroquois kinship terminology,** also named after an American Indian group, Ego refers to father and father's brother by the same term and to mother and mother's sister by the same term but distinguishes both sets of relatives from Ego's own generation. Ego's mother's brother and father's sister are referred to in terms equivalent to "uncle" and "aunt" in English. The Iroquois system differs from the Crow and Omaha systems in that cross cousins of both sides are referred to by the same terms, distinguished by sex. That is, mother's brother's daughter and father's sister's daughter are referred to by the same term, as are mother's brother's son and father's sister's son. Parallel cousins are distinguished from cross cousins and, in many cases, equated with sisters and brothers.

SUMMARY

From birth to death, our lives are shaped by kinship, our relationship with the set of relatives with whom we share rights and responsibilities. Every child must be assigned a place in a kinship network so that it will receive the care it needs to survive. Kinship is organized according to blood, or consanguinity, and marriage, which establishes affinal, or in-law, relationships. We grow up in families, which serve as our primary means of socialization. Families may be nuclear, meaning that they are organized around a parent or parents and offspring, or they may be extended, meaning that the economically interdependent unit includes two or more related nuclear families.

Sexuality is important because it is the means for adding new members to the group. One means of socializing sexuality is through the incest taboo, which prohibits sexual relations with certain categories of relatives. Though the incest taboo is universal, it takes different forms in different societies. For example, brother–sister marriage is banned in most societies but was the preferred marriage form among members of the Hawaiian, Egyptian, and Incan royal families.

A number of explanations have been proposed for the incest taboo. Among them are Sigmund Freud's idea that incest provokes instinctive horror, Bronislaw Malinowski's idea that incest disrupts the family, and Edward Westermarck's idea that childhood familiarity is not conducive to adult sexual attraction. In most cases, incest taboos also reduce the likelihood that marriage between relatives will pair negative recessive genes. However, these are not enough to explain the variation in the incest taboo, such as brother–sister marriage. One likely explanation is alliance theory, which accounts both for brother–sister marriage and for cross-cousin marriage. Exogamy, or out-marrying, promotes alliances, whereas endogamy, or in-marrying, consolidates wealth and status.

Marriage forms an economic partnership, establishes sexual rights, assigns social identity for offspring, and creates an alliance between kin groups.

Marriage typically is accompanied by some form of economic exchange: bridewealth, brideservice, gift exchange, sister exchange, brother–sister exchange, dowry, or indirect dowry.

Types of marriage include monogamy and serial monogamy and polygamy. The two kinds of polygamy are polygyny, marriage between one man and more than one woman, and polyandry, marriage between one woman and more than one man. Both the type of marriage and the economic exchange that takes place at the time of marriage appear to be related both to the economic system and to the type of descent within a society.

Descent can be either bilateral, which promotes flexibility, or unilineal, which establishes clear boundaries that allow the kin group to function as an economic unit. Unilineal descent can be either patrilineal, through the male line, or matrilineal, through the female line. Matrilineality should not be confused with matriarchy, in which positions of power are reserved for women. Anthropologists know of no matriarchal societies, though there are many matrilineal societies. Ambilineal descent allows individuals to identify with and inherit from either the male or the female line.

The formation of households is shaped by both the descent system and the residence pattern after marriage. The marrying couple may live patrilocally, matrilocally, ambilocally or bilocally, avunculocally, or neolocally. Neolocal residence establishes a nuclear family. Patterns of interdependence established by marriage, descent, and residence are reflected in kinship terminology. The five types of kinship terminology discussed in this book are the Eskimo system, the Hawaiian system, the Omaha system, the Crow system, and the Iroquois system. Kin terminology appears to be correlated with descent. The Eskimo and Hawaiian systems, which do not distinguish matrikin from patrikin, are correlated with bilateral or ambilineal (cognatic) descent systems. The Omaha, Crow, and Iroquois systems, which do distinguish matrikin from patrikin, are correlated with unilineal descent systems.

POWER WORDS

ambilineal descent

ambilocal residence

avunculocal residence

bilateral descent

bilocal residence

brideprice

brideservice

bridewealth

brother–sister
   exchange

classificatory kin terms

cognatic descent

corporate

cross cousins

Crow kinship
   terminology

dowry

ego

ego centered

Eskimo kinship
   terminology

fictive kin

fraternal
   polyandry

gift exchange

Hawaiian kinship
   terminology

household

incest taboos

indirect dowry

Iroquois kinship
   terminology

kindred

kinship

levirate

marriage

matriclan

matrilineage

matrilocal
   residence

moiety

neolocal
   residence

Omaha kinship
   terminology

parallel cousins

patriclan

patrilineage

patrilocal
   residence

phratry

polyandry

polygamy

polygyny

primogeniture

residence
   patterns

serial monogamy

sister exchange

sororal
   polygyny

sororate

unilineal descent

woman exchange

INTERNET EXERCISE

1. For a survey of wedding customs in different countries, visit the website **http://4wedding. 4anything.com/4/0,1001,7328,00.html**. Choose one of the wedding customs described and analyze it in terms of what it says about the four characteristics of marriage cross-culturally: specifying an economic contract, assigning sexual rights, defining social identity of offspring, and establishing an alliance between kin groups.

2. As is true for other groups, descent is an important factor in the social organization of the Yanomamö of Venezuela and Brazil. Visit the website **http://www.umanitoba.ca/anthropology/ Yanomamo/lineages.html** to find out how the patrilineal descent system of the Yanomamö contrasts with that of other groups with the same system of inheritance.

3. Leela Damodara Menon, a female Nayar, provides an overview of the Nayar system of marriage and descent in terms of the advantages it offered to women. Her perspective is available on the website **http://www.freespeech.org/manushi/ gallery/matriliny.html**.

7
Language and Symbols, Order and Chaos

In this chapter . . .

The importance of communication

The ability to signal danger or the presence of food is essential to the survival of humans and virtually all other animals, but humans are remarkable for their ability to communicate precisely and effectively. Language allows us to convey information about objects that are remote in time and space and to combine a limited number of sounds to generate infinite new meanings. Language draws on rules, or grammar, to generate these new meanings.

The social context of language

Language use takes place in a social context. Terms of address may signify the social position of speakers relative to each other. Dialects—which may vary in pronunciation, vocabulary, and the rules of syntax—provide a creative source that can eventually give birth to new languages. Occupational jargon is a subcultural variation in language use that allows members of a group to distinguish themselves from outsiders and to encode concepts important to the group.

Does language shape thought?

The idea that language shapes thought is called the Sapir–Whorf hypothesis, after Edward Sapir, the originator of the idea, and his student Benjamin Whorf. Whorf discovered that Hopi language does not have terms to refer to the past or the future. He suggested that English speakers view past and future—which are abstract concepts—as "real" because the language expresses them in concrete terms. There almost certainly is an association between language and thought, but the relationship is far more complex than a simple causal statement would suggest.

Symbols: Multiple levels of communication

Because symbols communicate many levels of meaning at once, they are used to convey complex meanings that usually have emotional associations. The meaning of a symbol is arbitrary, or culturally defined, though there may be some apparently "natural" associations between a symbol and its referent. Dominant symbols encapsulate values in a particular society and are used in different contexts.

It would not be an exaggeration to suggest that the human body is adapted for communication, and that this adaptation greatly aided the survival of the species. On every level, from posture to the manipulation of sounds, the human body conveys information about mood and intent. We begin to make judgments about people from the moment they come into view, whether they are strolling across campus or stalking an animal across the veldt, or open plain.

Human beings became differentiated from other primates when their ancestors came down from the trees to forage for food. Much of hominid evolution, which led to modern humans, subsequently took place on the African veldt. Imagine the advantage of communicating across great distances as hunters coordinate their advance on a large game animal, as children recognize and rush to greet their mothers returning home with string bags filled with food, or as strangers approach the camp. We can communicate visually—with posture and gestures—across distances too great for communication by sound.

Human beings also communicate through facial expression. The musculature of the human face is the most sophisticated of all the animals and appears to be adapted for communication. The most obvious expressions are smiles, frowns, and grimaces, but people also communicate with more subtle expressions—a raised eyebrow, a sidelong glance, the direction of a gaze. We can express interest by maintaining eye contact or signal our intent to end a conversation by looking away. It may well be that the sparseness of human facial hair is related to the need to communicate nuances of meaning indirectly, without spoken language. *Posture, gestures,* and *facial expressions*—or **body language**—are studied in the branch of linguistics called **kinesics.**

Human beings also communicate through *touch,* most often employed to convey intimacy or empathy. When someone we know is depressed or has suffered a loss, touch is our most eloquent means of communication. Affection can also be conveyed through various forms of touching, including kissing and hugging.

Odors also provide a means of communication, one less developed in humans than in some other animals. Still, the effect of odors on human social life is far from negligible—as evidenced in the United States by the vast array of products designed to mask, enhance, or disguise odors emanating from the human body.

Language

But the crown jewel of human communication is language. Human beings have elaborated the use of sound to convey information beyond that of any other species, and the impact of language use on human society cannot be overestimated. **Language** is based on the human ability to encode culturally defined meanings in sound and to combine units of sound to generate infinite new meanings through the application of rules. The meanings of sounds are **arbitrary,** that is, culturally assigned. **Sign language** has the same properties as sound-based language, but in this case, meaning is coded in posture, gestures, and facial expressions. Because the meaning of sign language is coded in rules and socially assigned, or arbitrary, this form of communication is distinct from body language, which is a far less elaborate and systematic means of encoding meaning.

Many human groups have translated their sound-based language system into **writing.** Writing enables us to communicate with people across great distances of space and time. Much of what we know about the world is conveyed through writing, which also allows us to accumulate history in a form too vast to be stored in individual human brains. In a sense, writing

Through the effective use of symbols, this poster persuaded young men and women to fight for their country during World Wars I and II. Uncle Sam appears as a stern parental figure arrayed in the colors of the U.S. flag. The finger pointed directly at the viewer and the wording "I WANT YOU" both admonish the viewer and personalize the message.

allows us to expand our brain capacity so that information can be stored in an accessible form outside our bodies. Jack Goody notes that "the written tradition articulates beliefs and interests in a semipermanent form that can extend their influence independently of any particular political system" (1986:172). Goody suggests that skills required in writing accentuate class differences characteristic of a stratified society by contributing to the development of bodies of specialized knowledge.

Humans also communicate through symbolic images, which succinctly express abstract concepts that cannot be described through any other form of communication. For example, we all think we know the meaning of *patriotism,* but if called upon to define it in words, we would find ourselves bogged down in subtle shades of meaning and emotional connotations that would eventually obscure the concept rather than clarify it. It is far simpler—and more eloquent—to convey the meaning of *patriotism* in a single powerful image, such as the American flag, the eagle, or Uncle Sam. During World War II, the U.S. government did just that in a recruiting poster that influenced thousands of young Americans to sign up to fight for their country.

Linguistics

The various forms of communication allow human beings to coordinate their activities, express their needs, and exchange information about abstract concepts. Human adaptation for communication is so sophisticated, it allows us to move easily among several complex information systems. For example, we can instantly translate the concept "tree" from a sound to an image to a codified series of marks on paper. The study of the various forms of communication, in terms of their structure, history, social context, and implications for the ability to conceptualize and convey meaning, is called **linguistics.** The ability

of humans to use language is made possible by biological adaptations, both in the organization and capacity of the human brain and in the formation of the mouth and throat.

THE BIOLOGY OF HUMAN LANGUAGE

Language is a socially agreed-upon code, but the ability to communicate through language is based on biological adaptations. Human language depends on structures of the throat, mouth, and cerebral cortex. The adult human tongue is thicker than that of monkeys and apes and, unlike theirs, bends at a sharp angle into the throat. The larynx, with the vocal cords, lies farther down in the throat than the ape larynx does, and the pharynx is longer in humans than in other primates (see Figure 7.1). The pharynx anchors the tongue and serves as an opening for both the windpipe, which goes to the lungs, and the

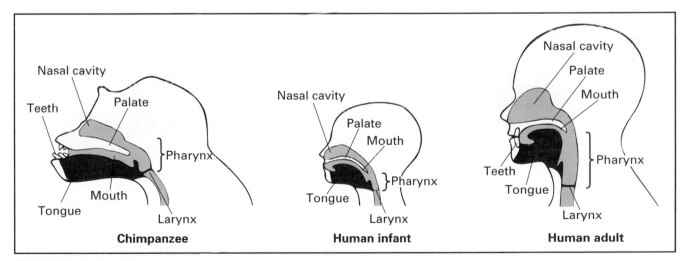

FIGURE 7.1 Vocal Apparatus

Speech is made possible by the long larynx and pharynx characteristic of humans. The larynx includes the vocal cords, which produce sound. Sound is modified in the pharynx, which also anchors the tongue. The human tongue lies lower in the throat than that of chimpanzees and other primates, giving humans greater control over sound. At birth, the vocal apparatus of the human infant resembles that of the chimpanzee. By the age of three, a child's vocal apparatus resembles that of a human adult.
Source: Adapted from Bernard G. Campbell and James D. Loy, *Humankind Emerging,* 7th ed. (New York: HarperCollins, 1996), p. 377.

esophagus, which leads to the stomach (Campbell and Loy 1996:376).

Speech occurs when wind from the lungs passes over the vocal cords, which vibrate to produce sounds. You can feel the vibration by holding your fingers against your throat near the Adam's apple, the bump formed by the largest cartilage of the larynx. Sounds produced by the vocal cords are modified by the muscles of the pharynx and the base of the tongue, which move continuously during speech. Sound is further modified and enhanced as it moves through the mouth, by the position of the tongue, lips, teeth, and the soft palate, or roof of the mouth.

Monkeys and apes vary only the shape of their mouths when they vocalize. They do not have the musculature to move the pharynx very much, and their tongues cannot form consonants. For the first six weeks of life, human infants are similarly limited. A human infant cannot make vowels because its tongue is almost entirely within its mouth and its larynx is high in the throat. The high placement of tongue and larynx allows the baby and nonhuman primates to swallow and breathe at the same time without danger of choking. By about the third year of a human infant's life, the base of the tongue and larynx have descended farther into the throat, lengthening the pharynx and making possible all of the human speech sounds.

Language Areas of the Brain

Speech involves much more than the movement of air through the larynx. Language processing would be impossible without the cerebral cortex, which has three primary areas and several areas of lesser importance in speech production (see Figure 7.2). All three primary areas are located in the dominant hemisphere, which is the left hemisphere in about 95 percent of right-handed people and 70 percent of left-handed people. The nondominant hemisphere influences such things as rhythm, emphasis, and intonation.

Researchers long thought the primary region of speech production was *Broca's area*, located in the

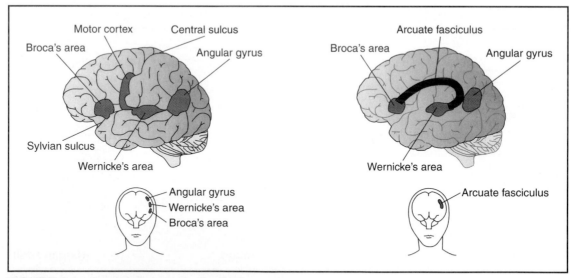

FIGURE 7.2 Speech Centers in the Brain

Human speech involves codifying thought and transmitting it to others through a string of connected sounds. Codification begins in the cerebral cortex of the brain. Primary centers of speech are usually located in the dominant hemisphere, which is the left hemisphere in about 95 percent of right-handed people and 70 percent of left-handers. Broca's area sends codes for the succession of phonemes; Wernicke's area is vital to speech comprehension. However, the production and comprehension of language depend on the coordination of a number of centers in the brain.
Source: Adapted from Bernard G. Campbell and James D. Loy, *Humankind Emerging,* 7th ed. (New York: HarperCollins, 1996), p. 378.

lower frontal lobe of the dominant hemisphere, which controls muscles of the face, jaw, tongue, pharynx, and larynx. Damage to the area has been linked to a form of aphasia—loss or impairment of speech—in which articulation is slow and labored. More recent studies have indicated that only a small portion of Broca's area is involved in speech and that other regions of the cerebral cortex behind and below Broca's area are more directly involved with speech.

Wernicke's area, located farther back in the dominant hemisphere, is vital to comprehension of speech. A bundle of nerve fibers (the *arcuate fasciculus*) transmits signals from Wernicke's area to Broca's area, permitting the articulation of a heard and memorized word (Campbell and Loy 1996:379). The connection between Broca's area and Wernicke's area is important, because language involves more than speech; one must also be able to decode sound and interpret it according to meaningful units.

Adjacent to Wernicke's area is the third primary region of the cerebral cortex, the *angular gyrus.* It is located at the juncture of the regions of the cerebral cortex connected with vision, hearing, and touch—those parts of the brain that receive sensory data from outside the body (Campbell and Loy 1996:379). The angular gyrus permits the association of sensory stimuli. It allows one to associate the word *tree,* for example, whether verbal or written, with the tree that one can see.

Language and Learning

Language involves far more associations than those linked to these three primary language centers in the brain and is much more than a reflex action. One does not automatically say "tree" when viewing a tree, as one automatically blinks when an object approaches the eye. Blinking is a reflex, a protective response coded on our genes. The sound "tree" and the written word involve a network of learned meanings, many of which have strong emotional connotations. For example, "tree" may evoke a memory of a tree climbed as a child, and "Christmas tree" may evoke a flood of emotions associated with our relations to parents, to siblings, to grandparents and peers and involving complex feelings about our own membership in the family group. "Christmas tree" is not only language; it is a symbol that draws on experiences that are no longer consciously available to us.

What Is Language?

Language is a form of communication based on sound, but human language goes far beyond the sounds produced by other animals. As far as researchers can now determine, animal communication is a **closed system,** meaning that a specific sound has only one possible meaning. For example, a dog may bark to indicate that it is hungry or may growl to indicate danger or to warn of a prowler, but it cannot combine those sounds to produce a new meaning.

On the other hand, human language is an **open system,** which means that human beings can combine a limited number of sounds to generate infinite new meanings. We can speak of a "CD" or "compact disc" or "virtual reality" without inventing new sounds or even new words to describe these new concepts. Sounds and words present in our language for thousands of years can refer to concepts that did not exist even a few decades ago.

In all languages, it is not necessary to invent new sounds when there is a need to communicate new concepts. Instead, new words are formed by recombining existing sounds. For example, the word *digital,* which refers to a process of performing operations with quantities represented electronically as digits or discrete numerical units, is formed by combining the word *digit,* referring to the Arabic number symbols 0 through 9, with *-al,* a suffix signifying an adjective. More distantly, the term *digit* derives from the Latin term *digitus,* signifying fingers and toes. The term *recording* combines a Middle English word *recorden,* meaning "to recall," with the suffix *-ing,* which can be used to convert a verb to a noun. A digital recording is a process of recording on tape or disc by breaking down sound into discrete units. Neither the word *digital* nor the word *recording* contains new sounds, though the process of recording sound digitally is relatively new. A modern music fan buying a digital recording of his or her favorite group is unknowingly paying tribute to the power of language by calling on sounds developed centuries or millennia ago and applying them to a contemporary pastime.

The Structure of Language

The ability to recombine existing sounds to form infinite new meanings is made possible through the application of rules. The study and analysis of the rules underlying language use is **structural linguistics,** also called **descriptive linguistics.** Structural linguists study **phonology** (rules for combining sounds), **morphology** (rules of word formation), and **syntax** (rules of sentence formation).

A language also includes a vocabulary of words, known as a **lexicon.** The basic building block of language is the **phoneme,** the "minimum unit of distinctive sound feature" in a language (Bloomfield 1933:78–79). Phonemes do not have meaning in and of themselves, but they have the power to change meaning. For example, the sounds phonetically expressed as *f, k^h, m, s, p^h, b,* and *h* have no meaning in the English language, but when combined with the word *at,* they change the meaning of that utterance to, respectively, *fat, cat, mat, sat, pat, bat,* and *hat.* Thus, these initial sounds are all phonemes in the English language. In Spanish, *r* and *rr* are phonemes, though they are not phonemes in English, because English speakers do not hear a significant difference between *r* and *rr.* In English, *l* and *r* are phonemes, though they are not in Japanese. Japanese speakers do not hear a significant difference between *l* and *r* and are likely to use them interchangeably.

No language uses all the sounds that can be generated by the human vocal apparatus. For example, English speakers do not make use of the "click" characteristic of people of the Kalahari Desert in Africa. The *!,* which is an essential part of the name *!Kung,* refers to a sound made by sticking the tongue against the roof of the mouth and pulling it away abruptly. The "click" sounds like a more full-bodied version of the "tsk, tsk, tsk" used by English speakers to indicate disapproval. The difference is that the !Kung click is formed against the soft palate rather than near the teeth. English speakers can form the click, but it does not have meaning in English, as it does in !Kung language. By the same token, the English language does not make use of the trilled *r* characteristic of Spanish or the throaty *h* of French.

Phonemes can be combined to produce morphemes, which link differences in sound to meaning. Henry A. Gleason (1961:53) defines a **morpheme** as the smallest meaningful unit in the structure of language. Morphemes can be **free** or **bound,** depending on whether they can stand alone or must be used as prefixes or suffixes. The word *at* is a free morpheme because it is a unit of meaning and can stand alone as a word. Similarly, the word *locate* is a free morpheme; it can stand alone or can be combined with other morphemes to generate new meanings. *Dis-* is a bound morpheme; it must be used as a prefix. Combining the bound morpheme *dis-* and the free morpheme *locate* forms the word *dislocate.* The meaning of this word can be further altered by adding the bound morpheme *-ion* to produce the word *dislocation.*

Even knowing the rules for combining phonemes and morphemes into words and for forming sentences from those words is not sufficient for producing language. The combination of words into sentences must also be perceived as meaningful by both the speaker and the one who hears the utterance. Rules for combining words to produce meaning constitute **semantics,** which relates meaning to the words and syntax of a language.

A sentence may be correct in terms of its syntax but wrong in terms of semantics. For example, the sentence "I fell down my cat" is syntactically correct but semantically incorrect. According to the semantic construction of English sentences, the speaker can fall down, her cat may fall down, or she may drop her cat or throw it down, but in English, the act of "falling" cannot be imposed onto another. In a linguistic extension of the term, however, a tree can be "felled" by a lumberjack.

All these aspects of a language—the lexicon, the rules for combining phonemes and morphemes, syntax, and semantics—make up its **grammar,** which includes everything speakers know about their language.

Error Correction

Because the rules of language use are regular and predictable, we can anticipate what others are likely to say, determine whether their utterances are "logical" or "meaningful," and correct any errors that might arise. For example, a person might say, "I fell down the stars." Because we know that this is logically impossible and semantically incorrect, we can supply the word that "makes sense." In this case, we are likely to assume that the person meant to say, "I fell down the stairs."

Logically impossible statements are not always the result of errors. They can be used for dramatic or humorous effect, as when we talk about someone's "putting his foot in his mouth" or "painting himself into a corner." These are *metaphors,* or figures of speech that draw on imagery and analogy to make a point.

The psychologist Sigmund Freud suggested that misstatements may reflect unconscious views or motivations. I almost invariably make a "Freudian slip" while talking about Freud in my psychological anthropology classes. Once, when I inadvertently referred to Freud as "Sigmund Fraud," the entire class laughed. Their ability to understand the humor of my "slip" was based on the linguistic principle of error correction and the implication that I might unconsciously consider Freud to be a "fraud."

Displacement

The ability of language to communicate concepts remote in time and space is called **displacement.** We take it for granted that we can express the idea "I had cereal for breakfast this morning, but I am getting tired of it, so I think I'll have pancakes tomorrow." Yet this simple communication is beyond the reach of other animals.

Your dog can express its displeasure with your choice of its food, but it cannot ask you to go to the store and buy the brand of dog food it saw on television. Your dog cannot even communicate this concept to another dog. Dog communication is limited to objects and experiences that are immediately accessible. For example, your dog can bark to alert you to a prowler, but it cannot inform you that a stranger came to the door while you were gone yesterday.

A dog cannot have a concept of "yesterday" or "tomorrow"—or even of "breakfast" or "food"—because it lacks a medium to discuss and refine these abstract concepts. Abstract concepts do not exist in the physical world; they are made possible by human language. No matter how hard it tries, your dog cannot say, "I have had beef every day this week and I would like to try something different tomorrow." Yet even small children can grasp and convey that kind of information.

The nearest relatives to humans, nonhuman primates, can communicate effectively using combinations of sounds, gestures, facial expressions, postures, and scents. Chimpanzees can indicate the desirability of food by varying the intensity of their food calls, and vervet monkeys can distinguish in their warning calls between danger on the ground and danger from the air. But even nonhuman primates cannot refer to an event in the past or future, and they cannot describe something that is not present. Only human language has the characteristic of displacement, of referring to something remote in time and space.

Ambiguity and Contradiction

Language sometimes appears to frustrate our attempts to communicate, as when we become bogged down in ambiguity. For example, a college student might say, "Visiting professors can be interesting." It is unclear whether the student enjoys taking classes from professors who are temporary lecturers or whether he likes paying social calls to his regular professors (Fromkin and Rodman 1988:166). Ambiguity is not a flaw in human language and can often be used to convey obliquely complex meanings that cannot be conveyed directly. Much poetry and much humor are based on the manipulation of ambiguity. For example, there is a joke about the courtier who said to his king, "Sir, the peasants are revolting tonight," to which the king replied, "Yes, and they are badly dressed, as well."

The French have a saying that "women are expensive, but men are cheap." This very expressive statement is based on the idea that traditional French gender roles require a man to support his wife financially and, before marriage, to signify his ability to provide for her by lavishing gifts and entertainment on her. The humor and cynicism of the statement arise from the contrasting meaning implicit in the second phrase. It does not mean that men are cheap to support but rather that they are disposable; they can be "thrown away" as in war or dangerous occupations.

Metaphor and Metonymy

Unlike other forms of communication, human language can communicate information with great precision. In English, I can say, "I'll meet you at the Lighthouse Deli for lunch at 12:30." This simple sentence conveys a wealth of information—about time, place, and the social context of food—with such precision that we can coordinate our movements and, coming from entirely separate locations, arrive at the same place at exactly the same time. Through language, we can meet by arrangement rather than by happenstance.

But the power of language goes well beyond that simple example. By using language to evoke imagery, we can express ideas that are not limited to time and space. Linguistic imagery consists of two general types: metaphor and metonymy. **Metaphor** is based on analogy, so that we can extend the power of words by drawing a comparison between realms of experience. When the nineteenth-century poet Fiona Macleod (pseudonym William Sharp) wrote, "My heart is a lonely hunter that hunts on a lonely hill," her personification of the heart as a "lonely hunter" evoked an image of the pathos of the human quest for love and connectedness with others. This is a much more powerful form of communication than the more precise statement, "I'm really lonely and I'd like some company."

Metonymy evokes imagery by using an attribute of a thing to stand for the thing itself. George Lakoff and Mark Johnson (1980) give the following examples of metonymy, illustrating the systematic logic underlying this type of imagery:

1. She's just a *pretty face.* (The part stands for the whole.)

2. He likes to read *Marquis de Sade.* (The producer stands for the product.)

3. The *ham sandwich* is waiting for his check. (The object stands for its user.)

4. You'll never get the *university* to agree to that. (The institution stands for the people responsible.)

5. *Wall Street* is in a panic. (The place stands for the institution.)

6. Remember the *Alamo.* (The place stands for the event.)

Lakoff and Johnson suggest that imagery expressed in language shapes the way we think and the way we experience the world: "Our concepts structure what we perceive, how we get around in the world, and how we relate to other people. Our conceptual system thus plays a central role in defining our everyday realities (1980:3).

THE SOCIAL CONTEXT OF LANGUAGE

Language use is always embedded in its social context. The Swiss linguist Ferdinand de Saussure ([1916] 1966) distinguished between **langue,** the systematic elements of a language that speakers of that language know, and **parole,** the manifestation of a language system in the speech of individuals. **Sociolinguistics** is the study of the social context of language use.

Language can be used to denote social relationships. For example, your mother may be known variously as "Mother" or "Mom" to you and your siblings, as "Jane" to her friends, as "Dr. Jones" to her patients, and as "Mrs. Jones" to the operator of the dry cleaners. These are all **terms of address,** which

Language reflects its social context. In the case of these two Buddhist monks, subcultural use of oral and body language obscures cultural differences associated with nationality. The man on the left is Tibetan; the man on the right is from the United States and follows the American custom of greater reserve in his body language. The way in which their robes are draped conveys information about their rank and affiliation to members of their subculture.

signify the social position of the speakers relative to each other.

There are also regional variations in language. Once when I traveled from Los Angeles, California, to Fort Worth, Texas, I entered a drugstore and asked where a particular product was located. The response was "il^ai." Not only her pronunciation but her soft Southern intonation sounded ambiguous to me. For a moment, I was confused, wondering if the salesperson were asking if I were from "L.A." In fact, she was instructing me that the item I wanted was on "Aisle A." We were speaking the same language, but our pronunciation and intonation were so different as to be almost mutually unintelligible. Yet both were valid expressions of the type of English spoken in the United States. Through time, such variations in accent and language use can eventually result in divergence so great that a new language is born.

A friend received an electronic dictionary for Christmas that supplied translations for English, French, Spanish, Chinese, and Japanese words. He punched in the word *subway* but could not find a translation. He called on his understanding of French to ask for the English translation of *metro* and found *underground*. That is how he discovered that his translator had been manufactured in a country familiar with the type of English spoken in England rather than in the United States.

Systematic variations in language related to geographic regions or to social class are known as **dialects.** The dialect believed to be generally spoken in the United States is **Standard American English (SAE).** It has been considered an unaccented dialect from which all other types of speech diverge. In fact, SAE is a regional dialect associated with the northern Midwest and has spread across the country owing to its prevalence among radio and television broadcasters, who seek to emulate this style.

Most U.S. speakers deviate to some degree from SAE. New Englanders speak a variety of dialects, as do people in various regions of the South. William Labov (1966) studied the use of *r* in the New York City dialect. Typically, New Yorkers drop the *r* when it is in the final position of a word or before consonants, so that the word *New Yorker* would be pronounced "New Yawkah." Labov discovered that the use of *r* is related to social class. Only the upper-middle class, the highest-ranking group in the study, regularly used the *r* in casual speech. In careful or formal speech, the lower-middle class used the *r* more often than did the upper-middle class. Robbins Burling suggests that lower-middle-class speakers may emphasize the use of the *r* in formal speech because they are in a socially uncertain position. Burling writes: "In their uncertainty they may overcompensate in trying to demonstrate prestigious forms" (1970:94). Because use of the *r* is associated with the more prestigious group, lower-middle-class speakers emulate this usage in formal public speech but not in casual talk with intimates.

Black English Vernacular

One type of dialect is **Black English,** or **Black English Vernacular (BEV),** which varies from SAE in grammatical rules and cadence. Most rules of BEV are identical to those of SAE, but others are specific to BEV. In all English dialects, speakers in normal colloquial style reduce (eliminate) the last consonant when two or more consonants occur at the end of a word and the next word begins with a consonant. For example, a speaker might say, "She came in late las' night." In BEV the last consonant is eliminated at the end of an utterance or when the next word is a vowel. For example, in BEV a speaker might say, "She come in las'" or "He was the las' one to use the phone."

As noted above, New Yorkers omit the *r* before consonants; BEV speakers may also delete the *r* between vowels, so that "Carol" may become "Ca'ol." In addition, where SAE speakers use contractions in present-tense verbs in colloquial speech, BEV permits deletion of the present-tense verb entirely. For example, "She's smart" becomes "She smart" (Bonvillain 1997).

Use of BEV varies widely within the African American community. Some speakers use the dialect in all their communication; others do not use it at all. Some may use BEV among their family and friends and switch to SAE at school or at work. "Speakers may also switch from one style to the other during any speech event, depending on topic, attitude, and co-participants" (Bonvillain 1997:150). This is called **code-switching.** The ability to switch from one dialect to another in a single conversation allows the speaker to emphasize key points or to frame them in the speech mode most appropriate for their expression. For example, BEV speakers in a context in which SAE would normally be spoken can signify a shift from a formal interaction to a more casual exchange by switching to BEV.

FIGURE 7.3   Occupational Jargon

Occupational jargon is an example of subcultural variation in language use. To a police officer, a "shoot" refers to the shooting of a suspect by an officer in the line of duty; to a photographer, a "shoot" is a photo-taking session.

Occupational Jargon

Occupational jargon is another type of variation from SAE, one that is characteristic of an occupation or a profession. To photographers, a "shoot" is a picture-taking session (see Figure 7.3). To a police officer, on the other hand, a "shoot" has a very different meaning. It refers to a situation in which a suspect is shot by an officer, and there can be "good shoots" and "bad shoots." A good shoot is one in which the suspect is armed and is shooting at the officer; a bad shoot is one in which the suspect has dropped his gun or is fleeing without shooting (Joan Barker, pers. comm., 1996).

Occupational jargon is a kind of shorthand that allows members of a group to communicate information succinctly. In the above example, *shoot* is a crisper way for a photographer to express the concept "photography session." As do other aspects of language, occupational jargon serves to mark boundaries between insiders and outsiders. Our professional competence is sometimes judged by our ability to use professional jargon. In other contexts, jargon can be used to identify members of subcultures. For example, computer buffs may talk of "surfing the 'Net," a colorful way of saying that they are interacting with a number of people linked electronically.

Language and Change

Language purists often lament what they consider the "decline" of the English language, but the continual reinvention of language in *parole,* or speech, keeps language alive and relevant, generating colorful expressions that enrich communication. English itself is a polyglot language that combines Germanic words and phrasing with strong influences from the Romance languages stemming from Latin. Thus, we draw on Germanic origins to refer to our "hand," the extension of our forearm that allows us to play the piano or to pick up a pencil, but we speak of "manual dexterity" to describe the ability to manipulate those objects skillfully. Both *manual* and *dexterity* have been adopted from French. We may also use the word *china* to refer to the fine porcelain we save for important occasions, because the technique for producing porcelain was invented in China and taken to Europe by early travelers. Similarly, the Japanese word *sushi* has found its way into our vocabulary because there is no English word to describe a food that combines raw fish, rice, and seaweed.

All languages evolve in response to changes in a society, and these linguistic shifts typically reflect divergence in geography and class. There are regional and class differences in the way English is spoken in England, the way French is spoken in France, the way German is spoken in Germany, and the way Chinese is spoken in China. Some linguists trace the evolving relationships of societies through variations in language patterns. The field of **historical linguistics** is based on the idea that systematic variations through time can be calculated to indicate when languages diverged (see Figure 7.4). By studying similarities and differences between vocabularies and grammars, linguists can also evaluate the relationship of languages to each other.

THE SAPIR–WHORF HYPOTHESIS

The idea that language shapes thought is called the **Sapir–Whorf hypothesis,** after Edward Sapir, a student of Franz Boas, and his student Benjamin Whorf. Sapir argued that every language structures the world in a particular way for its speakers. As a result,

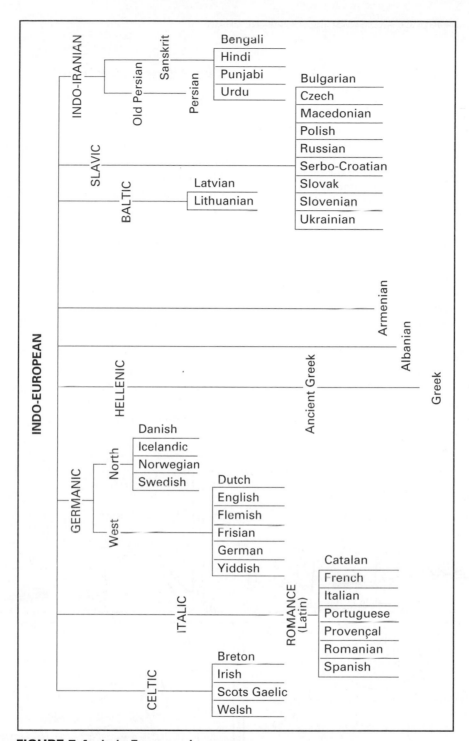

FIGURE 7.4 Indo-European Languages

Historical linguists analyze the structure of languages to determine their degree of relatedness to each other. Some historical linguists believe that the rate of language change can be statistically analyzed to determine when languages diverged from each other. This chart of Indo-European languages indicates that English is closely related to such Germanic languages as Dutch and Flemish and more distantly related to Sanskrit, a forerunner to the modern languages of India: Bengali, Hindi, Punjabi, and Urdu.

Source: Adapted from Victoria Fromkin and Robert Rodman, *An Introduction to Language,* 4th ed. Copyright © 1988 by Holt, Rinehart and Winston. Reprinted by permission of the publisher.

he said, learning a new language causes one to enter a new social reality. According to Sapir:

> Human beings do not live in the objective world alone, nor alone in the world of social activity as ordinarily understood, but are very much at the mercy of the particular language which has become the medium of expression for their society. The fact of the matter is that the "real world" is to a large extent unconsciously built up on the language habits of the group. (1949:162)

This statement expresses what Nancy Bonvillain (1997) calls the "strong version" of the Sapir–Whorf hypothesis. Some anthropologists dispute the idea that language shapes thought. Victor Barnouw notes that "languages are not always so tyrannical" (1985:172). For example, he writes, "Just because we call a ship 'she' does not mean that we actually think of the ship as being feminine" (1985:172). Barnouw and others have also noted that language differences are not necessarily correlated with cultural differences. People who speak closely related languages may have very different cultures, and people of similar cultures may belong to different language groups.

The "Weak Version"

Sapir also described what Bonvillain calls a "weak version" of the hypothesis, that "we see and hear and otherwise experience very largely as we do because the language habits of our community predispose certain choices of interpretation" (Sapir 1949:162). The difference between these two positions is obvious. In the strong version, Sapir suggests that language determines the way people experience the world; in the weak version, he suggests that language presents a range of options for interpreting peoples' experience, a position with which many anthropologists would agree.

Bonvillain notes that, taken as a body, the writings of Sapir and Whorf did not view "the relationships among language, culture, and human thinking as rigid and mechanistic but, rather, as coexisting in fluid and dynamic interactions" (Bonvillain 1997:52). The Soviet linguist V. N. Volosinov expressed a similar view of the relationship of language to experience: "There is no such thing as experience outside of embodiment in signs. . . . It is not experience that

From "Get Fuzzy," United Media/United Feature Syndicate, Inc.

Time may be a matter of perspective, rather than an absolute quantity. This cartoon illustrates three perspectives on assigning temporal priorities. The North American human perspective is that numerical time is more important than personal preference; the cat perspective assigns top priority to personal preference; the dog perspective assigns top priority to responding to a summons. The Sapir–Whorf hypothesis suggests that temporal priorities expressed in language may shape the way people experience time.

organizes expression, but the other way around—*expression organizes experience.* Expression is what first gives experience its form and specificity of direction" ([1929] 1973:85, emphasis in original).

Individuals who have experienced learning a second language and writers who must switch from oral to written expression can confirm that the form of a language shapes the type of information that can be encoded and communicated to others. While studying a group of faith healers for my master's thesis, I observed a well-dressed middle-aged man limp toward a healing circle, dragging his left foot and clutching a book entitled *Christ Heals.* I was moved to tears by the sight, which I did not write up in my thesis, though I have described the experience many times orally. It was years before I felt comfortable trying to convey in writing the man's painful clutching at hope, effectively conveyed in his expression and body language. Yet my experience of this scene profoundly affected my interpretation of the faith healers as purveyors of hope and ultimately contributed to my decision to end the study.

The Hopi View of Space and Time

The anthropologist Benjamin Whorf attempted to test what came to be known as the Sapir–Whorf hypothesis in an analysis of space and time implicit in different linguistic systems. Whorf contrasted the Hopi and what he called "Standard Average European" languages. He stated that the Hopi language contains no words, grammatical forms, or expressions that refer directly to the past, present, or future. On the other hand, English speakers apply the concept of quantity to time, as though it were a physical entity that can be counted and measured. For example, we may speak of "ten men" and also of "ten days." Though we can count ten men as physical entities, speaking of ten days requires a concept of time as being composed of countable units.

Whorf stated that the essence of Hopi life is focused on the present, on preparing for things that are capable of coming to pass. He also noted that this view of time is reasonable for an agricultural society, where the welfare of the people depends on the proper preparation of the ground and seeds for a hoped-for harvest. The Hopi also have elaborate rituals and festivals to aid the crops, which are believed to be influenced by human thought. The Hopi sing to the plants and try to cultivate happy thoughts while planting so the plants will develop in a propitious atmosphere.

Writing and Thinking

Whorf suggests that our way of thinking about time has been influenced by our system of writing, which allows us to keep records, diaries, and accounts. It is also correlated with a concern for exact sequences, as reflected in the use of calendars and clocks, and with an interest in archaeology and history. On the other hand, Whorf writes, the absence of sequencing in

Writing extends the range and durability of human communication. The Buddhist script inscribed on this birch bark transmits religious knowledge across the generations and to outsiders. Anthropologist Jack Goody (1986) suggests that, without writing, religions are confined to the local group. In societies that have writing, however, religions can convert outsiders by extending the range of communication and because the written word itself takes on the power associated with God's word.

DISCUSSIONS

Gender Differences in Conversational Styles

Language is more than syntax and grammar. Communication is inextricably bound up in its social context. Conversational styles differ both cross-culturally and within a particular culture. We adopt different conversational styles depending on whether we are conversing in the workplace, in the home, with our friends, or with strangers. In the following essay, Deborah Tannen notes that a major factor affecting conversational style is the gender of the speaker.

WHY WOMEN ASK DIRECTIONS AND MEN DON'T
Deborah Tannen

People have different conversational styles, influenced by the part of the country they grew up in, their ethnic backgrounds and those of their parents, their age, class, and gender. But conversational style is invisible. Unaware that these and other aspects of our backgrounds influence our ways of talking, we think we are simply saying what we mean.

Because we don't realize that others' styles are different, we are often frustrated in conversations. Rather than seeing the culprit as differing styles, we attribute troubles to others' intentions (she doesn't like me), abilities (he's stupid), or character (she's rude, he's inconsiderate), our own failure (what's wrong with me?), or the failure of a relationship (we just can't communicate). Few elements of our identities come as close to our sense of who we are as gender. If you mistake people's cultural background—you thought they were Greek, but they turn out to be Italian; you assumed they'd grown up in Texas, but they turn out to be Italian; you say, "Merry Christmas," and they say, "We don't celebrate

Christmas; we're Muslim"—it catches you off guard and you rearrange the mental frame through which you view them. But if someone you thought was male turns out to be female—like the jazz musician Billy Tipton, whose own adopted sons never suspected that their father was a woman until the coroner broke the news to them after his (her) death, the required adjustment is staggering. Even infants discriminate between males and females and react differently depending on which they confront.

Perhaps it is because our sense of gender is so deeply rooted that people are inclined to hear descriptions of gender patterns as statements about gender identity—in other words, as absolute differences rather than a matter of degree and percentages, and as universal rather than culturally mediated. The patterns I describe are based on observations of particular speakers in a particular place and time: mostly (but not exclusively) middle-class Americans of European background working in offices at the present time. Other cultures evince very different patterns of talk associated with gender—and correspondingly different assumptions about the "natures" of women and men. I don't put a lot of store in talk about "natures" or what is "natural." People in every culture will tell you that the behaviors common in their own cultures are "natural." I also don't put a lot of store in people's explanations that their way of talking is a natural response to their environment, as there is always an equally natural and opposite way of responding to the same environment. We all tend to regard the way things are as the way things have to be—as only natural.

The reason ways of talking, like other ways of conducting our daily lives, come to seem natural is that the behaviors that make up our lives are ritualized. Having grown up in a particular culture, we learn to do things as the people we encounter do them, so the vast majority of our decisions about how to speak become automatic. You see someone you know, you ask, "How are you?" chat, then take your leave, never pausing to ponder the many ways you could have handled this interaction differently—and would, if you lived in a different culture. Just as an American automatically extends a hand for a handshake while a Japanese automatically bows, what the American and Japanese find it natural to say is a matter of convention learned over a lifetime.

Asking Directions

. . . With regard to asking directions, women and men are keenly aware of the advantages of their own style. Women frequently observe how much time they would save if their husbands simply stopped and asked someone instead of driving around trying in vain to find a destination themselves. But I have also been told by men that it makes sense not to ask directions because you learn a lot about a neighborhood, as well as about navigation, by driving around and finding your own way.

But some situations are more risky than others. . . . An intern on duty at a hospital had a decision to make. A patient had been admitted with a condition the intern recognized, and he recalled the appropriate medication. But that medication was recommended for a number of conditions, in different dosages. He wasn't quite sure what dose was right for this condition. He had to make a quick

decision: Would he interrupt the supervising resident during a meeting to check the dose, or would he make his best guess and go for it?

What was at stake? First and foremost, the welfare, and maybe even the life, of the patient. But something else was at stake too—the reputation, and eventually the career, of the intern. If he interrupted the resident to ask about the dosage, he was making a public statement about what he didn't know, as well as making himself something of a nuisance. In this case, he went with his guess, and there were no negative effects. But . . . one wonders how many medical errors have resulted from decisions to guess rather than ask.

Asking Questions

It is clear that not asking questions can have disastrous consequences in medical settings, but asking questions can also have negative consequences. A physician wrote to me about a related experience that occurred during her medical training. She received a low grade from her supervising physician. It took her by surprise because she knew that she was one of the best interns in her group. She asked her supervisor for an explanation, and he replied that she didn't know as much as the others. She knew from her day-to-day dealings with her peers that she was one of the most knowledgeable, not the least. So she asked what evidence had led him to his conclusion. And he told her, "You ask more questions."

There is evidence that men are less likely to ask questions in a public situation, where asking will reveal their lack of knowledge. One such piece of evidence is a study done in a university classroom, where

sociolinguist Kate Remlinger noticed that women students asked the professor more questions than men students did. As part of her study, Remlinger interviewed six students at length, three men and three women. All three men told her that they would not ask questions in class if there was something they did not understand. Instead, they said they would try to find the answer later by reading the textbook, asking a friend, or, as a last resort, asking the professor in private during office hours. As one young man put it, "If it's vague to me, I usually don't ask. I'd rather go home and look it up."

The physician who asked her supervisor why he gave her a negative evaluation may be unusual in having been told directly what behavior led to the misjudgment of her skill. But in talking to doctors and doctors-in-training around the country, I have learned that there is nothing exceptional about her experience, that it is common for interns and residents to conceal their ignorance, since those who do ask are judged less capable. Yet it seems that many women who are more likely than men to ask questions (just as women are more likely to stop and ask for directions when they're lost) are unaware that they may make a negative impression at the same time that they get information. Their antennae have not been attuned to making sure they don't appear one-down.

This pattern runs counter to two stereotypes about male and female styles: that men are more focused on information and that women are more sensitive. In regard to classroom behavior, it seems that the women who ask questions are more focused on information, whereas the men who refrain from doing so are more

focused on interaction—the impression their asking will make on others. In this situation, it is the men who are more sensitive to the impression made on others by their behavior, although their concern is, ultimately, the effect on themselves rather than on others. And this sensitivity is likely to make them look better in the world of work. Realizing this puts the intern's decision in a troubling perspective. He had to choose between putting his career at risk and putting the patient's health at risk.

The reluctance to say, "I don't know," can have serious consequences for an entire company—and did: On Friday, June 17, 1994, a computer problem prevented Fidelity Investments from calculating the value of its mutual funds. Rather than report that the values for these funds were unavailable, a manager decided to report to the National Association of Securities Dealers that the values of these funds had not changed from the day before. Unfortunately, June 17 turned out to be a bad day in the financial markets, so the values of Fidelity's funds that were published in newspapers around the country stood out as noticeably higher than those of other funds. Besides the cost and inconvenience to brokerage firms who had to recompute their customers' accounts and the injustice to investors who made decisions to buy or sell based on inaccurate information, the company was mightily embarrassed and forced to apologize publicly. Clearly, this was an instance in which it would have been preferable to say, "We don't know."

Source: From *Talking from 9 to 5,* by Deborah Tannen. © 1994 by Deborah Tannen. By permission of William Morrow and Co. Inc.

Sport As Symbol

The apostle Paul often compared the Christian life to sports. In the First Epistle to the Corinthians, he writes, "Do you not know that in a race all the runners compete, but only one receives the prize? So run that you may obtain it" (1 Cor. 10:24). Paul was using sport as a metaphor to illustrate complex ideas about the appropriate approach to life. A metaphor is a symbol that explains a point by evoking an image.

Paul is not alone in making a connection between sports and moral concerns. The twelfth-century Persian poet Nizami advised his readers: "The Horizon is the boundary of your polo ground, the earth is the ball in the curve of your polo stick. Until the dust of nonexistence arises from annihilation, gallop and urge on your steed because the ground is yours."

Sport is often used as a symbol, expressing meanings that go beyond its significance as play or physical training. Sport has been called ritualized warfare, but this is only one aspect of its metaphoric role. In the art and literature of Asia, the Middle East, Europe, and the United States, there is a pervasive use of sport as a symbol for sexuality, courage, spiritual striving, and a range of other epic themes. Sport symbolism is not confined to these traditions, however. Native Americans, Africans, and the indigenous peoples of the Pacific use sport as a metaphor for various types of conflict. In fact, it would be difficult to find a culture that does not link physical contests to some form of conflict resolution. In the symbolism of sport, there is a continual conceptual flow from the playing field to everyday reality to transcendence of

the mundane world and back again. In the multivocal language of symbols, the "game" takes place on several levels at the same time. In his poem "Ballade by the Fire," Edward Arlington Robinson states, "Life is the game that must be played."

Sport and Religion

Many sports originated in religious ritual. Before the conquest of Central America by the Spanish in the sixteenth century, the ball game was part of the region's cosmology. The Maya of southern Mexico and Guatemala and the Aztecs of central Mexico developed complex civilizations marked by elaborate religious beliefs. Some of the most important of these involved the ball game.

Pok-tapok among the Maya and *tlachtli* among the Aztecs may have been ancestral to both soccer and basketball. The Spanish conquistadors were astonished to see the people of Central America playing with rubber balls that rebounded "incredibly into the ayer [air]." Europeans at that time were still playing with pig bladders or stuffed leather balls. The Central American ball game was played with a hard rubber ball in a high-walled court with two stone rings. Without using their hands, players tried to put the ball through the stone rings, a nearly impossible and hazardous enterprise. The solid heavy rubber ball, about eight inches in diameter, could be lethal when propelled at great speed. Teams of from one to four athletes bounced the ball off their bodies, much like modern soccer players. Points were scored by directing the ball into a goal area of the I-shaped court or by making

contact with a stone ring at center court (see photo on page 257). Only rarely were players able to put the ball through the stone ring.

The ball game was performed as part of religious ritual. It was closely associated with human sacrifice, and players were ritually killed to provide food for the gods. Ball courts were often located at the heart of sacred temple complexes. The ball court at the Aztec capital Tenochtitlán, near what is now Mexico City, was close to the skull rack, where heads of sacrificial victims were displayed.

The symbolic origin of the Mayan ball game is described in their creation myth, the *Popol Vuh*, which centers on the exploits of the Hero Twins. The boys, Hunapu (Hunter) and Xbalanque (Jaguar-Deer) defeated the underworld gods of sickness and death in a ball game. The twins then offered themselves as human sacrifices and after their deaths returned to kill the underworld gods named 1 Death and 7 Death. Their labors complete, the brothers then took their place in the sky as the sun and the moon. This creation myth reveals that the ritual ball game affirms the triumph of life over death and asserts the importance of human sacrifice in ensuring that life will not be conquered by the death-dealing underworld gods.

Religious Festivals

To understand sport as a religious rite, we must remove ourselves from the often austere religious observances with which we are most familiar. Contemporary rituals of most mainstream religions reflect the influence of long centuries of constraints aimed at taming religious fervor. In most cases, both historically and in the present day, religious celebrations are the setting for frenzied expressions of joy and despair.

One must imagine a great religious festival, like a fair, drawing people from all parts of the region. People from all strata of the society will intermingle, and the streets will be crowded with people calling out greetings to friends and relatives and buying wares from street vendors. Colorful banners will flutter from buildings, and there will be images of gods and goddesses writhing in agony or contorted in transports of joy. There will be feasting, dancing, ritual performances of all kinds, and theatrical enactment of traditional myths. In the midst of all this activity, arenas will be set aside where local heroes meet to wrestle, to vie against each other in races, or to compete in ball games.

Participants in these sacred sporting events often represent the forces of Good and Evil, but they do not simply act out their ritual performance, though the games contain aspects of both ritual and theater. In religious ritual and theater, the outcome is predetermined. Believers can be assured that religious ritual—properly performed—will keep their relationship with the gods and natural forces on an even keel. Audiences at theatrical performances know either that Good will triumph in the end or that the story is "only a play." But spectators at sporting events experience an added source of anxiety: No one can predict how the game will end. Good may, in fact, lose out to Evil. For the athletes, the blood and bruises are real, and the good of society rests on their performance. They must use all their strength and skill on behalf of the gods to keep Evil and Chaos from overpowering heaven and earth.

Pharisees and Captains

The Raramuri, or Tarahumara Indians, who live in a mountainous region of northern Mexico, act out a cosmic conflict between God and Satan in a stylized battle that is similar to the origins of many sports. Jesuit missionaries introduced Roman Catholicism to the Tarahumara early in the seventeenth century, but after that contact the Tarahumara remained largely isolated. In the ensuing centuries, the Tarahumara developed their own interpretation of Christian theology.

The Tarahumara believe that God is often in danger from his treacherous rival, Satan. They consider God especially vulnerable during Holy Week, just before Easter, when He must be protected from onslaughts of the Devil. Throughout the week, the Tarahumara purify themselves and their church by fasting and ritual cleansing of themselves and the church grounds. On Holy Saturday, the people spend much of the day encircling the church in a ritual procession aimed at protecting the church and, by extension, God and His wife, the Virgin Mary. William L. Merrill, an anthropologist who studied the Tarahumara ceremony, describes the tremendous responsibility felt by participants in the ritual: "The fate of the universe rests on the Raramuri's shoulders during this period, for they must prevent the Devil from vanquishing God and destroying the world" (1987:381).

The people are divided into two groups. The Pharisees represent the forces of the Devil; the Captains are charged with the responsibility of protecting God from Satan's evil power. The activities of the Pharisees reflect a complex form of role playing. They both protect God from the Devil and act on the Evil One's behalf. As representatives of the Devil, the Pharisees provide a visible, and

therefore manageable, enemy. At the same time, the dual role of the Pharisees ensures that everyone in the community is involved in protecting God, regardless of the ritual parts being played. Thus, this vital work becomes a unified effort, reinforcing the solidarity of the group while providing an opportunity to act out group conflicts.

Captains and Pharisees engage in wrestling matches, battling symbolically for control of statues of Judas and his family, believed to be relatives of Satan. Regardless of who wins, the Captains take possession of the Judas images, shooting arrows into them and setting them on fire. Thus, the evil forces that threaten the universe and the social life of the Tarahumara are vanquished for another year (Merrill 1987).

The Tarahumaras' view of Mary as God's wife and their representations of Judas's family reflect the importance of family in their own lives. It is inconceivable to the Tarahumara that anyone in God's esteemed position should be a bachelor. No male in Tarahumara society could act in a position of responsibility without taking on an adult role, which includes having a wife and children. Similarly, Judas is not likely to act without the aid of his family, so his relatives are destroyed along with him.

It is not hard to see how more secular sporting events may have arisen from just such symbolic combat. The somewhat subdued religious observances with which we are most familiar may seem far removed from the apparent chaos of these vigorously enacted religious festivals. In fact, sport and religious ritual express variations on similar symbolic themes: responsibility to one's peers, duty to one's god or moral authority, and the quest for some form of immortality.

Hopi language is reflected in their "preparing" activities of praying and the repetitive steps of ceremonial dances. Whorf suggests that, for the Hopi, repetition represents the storing up of "an invisible charge that holds over to later events" (Carroll 1956:151). Whorf writes:

> No individual is free to describe nature with absolute impartiality, but is constrained to certain modes of interpretation. . . . We are thus introduced to a new principle of relativity, which holds that all observers are not led to the same picture of the universe, unless their linguistic backgrounds are similar, or can in some way be calibrated. ([1940] 1956:214).

It is not easy to determine how well language conforms to our actual experience of the world. And even if a language is uniform, we cannot be certain whether the experiences of people within a given culture are identical. David S. Thomson notes that all languages have what he calls "dead metaphors," figures of speech that have lost their ability to evoke images. Thomson writes: "The word 'goodbye' is a dead metaphor. Once it meant 'God be with you,' but in its contracted form it conjures up no thought or picture of God" (1994:80).

The link between language and thought—though close—is probably not linear. It is more likely that language and thought are part of a dynamic relationship that includes culture and individual experience. Though the Sapir–Whorf hypothesis has contributed a great deal to analyses of **cognition,** the way people organize their experience of the world, it is ultimately impossible to prove or disprove. It is impossible to measure directly how people experience or interpret their world. Ultimately, we must rely on our interpretations of how they describe it.

THE NATURE OF SYMBOLS

Symbols are perhaps the most misunderstood medium of human communication. It is customary in the United States to dismiss something as "just a symbol," to indicate that it has no relevance to "more important" things, such as work, eating, or driving a car. In fact, symbols are the most complex and sophisticated means of encoding meaning available to

any animal, drawing on many intricate associations operating on both the conscious and unconscious levels.

Signs and Symbols

By definition, a **symbol** is a word, object, image, or behavior that encodes meaning, but not all words, objects, images, or behaviors that convey meaning are symbols. Most anthropologists distinguish between a symbol and a sign. The philosopher Suzanne Langer says of a sign: "The logical relation between a sign and its object is a very simple one. . . . They stand in a one-to-one correlation" (1942:57). That is, a **sign** has only one possible meaning. The purpose of a sign is to convey its meaning clearly and simply, so there can be no confusion.

A symbol, on the other hand, stands for a number of complex ideas. As anthropologist Victor Turner (1967) puts it, symbols are **multivocal;** they have "many voices" or meanings (see Figure 7.5). Meanings expressed by symbols tend to be complex and difficult to define in words. The anthropologist Raymond Firth notes, "Interpretation of symbols is usually a much more difficult matter than interpretation of signs" (1973:65).

FIGURE 7.5 Sign and Symbol

The meaning of the image on the left is clear: it signals to a motorist that he or she should stop before proceeding. Because it has only one possible meaning, this image is a *sign.* The image on the right has many possible meanings, all of them complex and dependent on the social context for interpretation. Because it is "multivocal," the image on the right is a *symbol.*

Symbols are difficult to interpret because they link together many complex ideas. They are designed to provoke thought. Religious symbols, such as the Star of David or the Virgin Mary, stimulate reflection on transcendence or on the nature of being human. Political symbols, such as the flag of the United States or the crown of England, emphasize the power and authority of government. Langer writes, "Symbols are not proxy for their objects, but are vehicles for the conception of objects" (1942:60–61).

The Limits of Logic

When people in Western culture boast that they "think logically," they don't realize that they are priding themselves on a relatively simple type of thinking, one in which associations can be stated in a one-to-one relationship. Logical thinking could be compared to using a calculator, which is designed to facilitate addition, subtraction, multiplication, and division of numbers. The numbers and relationship must be explicitly stated by the person operating the calculator. There can be no hidden variables.

Symbolic thinking, on the other hand, is comparable to using a computer. Each association is based on a "logical" relationship between variables, but many operations are carried out simultaneously at great speed in the "memory" of the "computer." The operations are not displayed on the "screen" until a solution has been arrived at. In the same way, symbols are processed in the cerebral cortex through the simultaneous association of many complex ideas, and most of the operations are not displayed on the "screen"—the conscious mind.

Instead, our interpretation of the symbol is experienced as a reaction—usually an emotional one—that arises from the almost instantaneous interpretation of multiple levels of meaning. The response is emotional because the interpretation draws on many levels of learning, much of which takes place in an intensely emotional context. This is why people are often moved to tears in the presence of symbols that are especially powerful for them. War veterans may be profoundly moved when saluting the national flag; Roman Catholics around the world feel strongly drawn to the Virgin Mary; and Muslims feel themselves transformed when chanting the name Allah, or God.

Symbols and Culture

The relationship between a symbol and its **referent**—what it stands for—is arbitrary. This means that it is culturally defined and learned in the process of enculturation. That is why the flags of other nations usually do not evoke an emotional response in us unless we have had a significant association with that country. People living in France will not be moved by the flag of Taiwan, but the people of mainland China certainly will. The Chinese response will be different from that of the Taiwanese, however, because both the government of Taiwan and the government of mainland China claim to be the official government of China. Thus, the people of Taiwan will respond to their flag with pride, whereas the people of China are likely to react to it with antipathy.

The fact that symbols are culturally acquired also explains why we may treat the sacred symbols of other religious faiths with contempt or casual regard but become intensely angry when someone attacks the symbols of our own religion. In the past, Christian missionaries destroyed the religious images of the people they were attempting to convert, but they considered it sacrilegious or an act of aggression when those same people attacked a cross or destroyed a church. Because the missionaries did not view indigenous symbols with the reverence they accorded their own, the religious art of many cultures has been lost to their descendants and to scholars who would like to study it.

Symbols acquire meaning within their cultural context. There is no "natural" association between the cross and Christianity. Not all crosses are sacred to Christians, and not all Christians make the same symbolic associations with the cross. The Christian cross is sacred because of its association with the death of Christ, which is viewed as Christ's sacrifice of his own life for his followers. But various Christian denominations represent the symbol of sacrifice in different ways. The death of Christ is commemorated in the Roman Catholic Mass, which is described as a sacrifice. Catholics refer to communion, in which the "body" and "blood" of Christ are ingested, as a sacrament. In Catholic churches, the cross—or crucifix—includes an image of Christ. Some Protestant churches do not ingest symbols of Christ's body and blood on a weekly basis, and they display only the cross, without the image of Christ, because they reject the representation of sacred

Symbols are powerful because they draw on public and private levels of meaning. This Christmas tree symbolizes the triumph of life over death and light over darkness. These are universal themes, and the Christmas tree unites Christian imagery with the German Celtic symbols of the evergreen tree decorated with lights. On a personal level, the Christmas tree evokes childhood memories that can be both happy and painful.

figures in this form. They view such representation as idolatry.

"Natural" Symbols

Though the relationship between a symbol and its referent is arbitrary, some symbols appear to have a "natural" association with their meaning. The Christmas tree was an important symbol in Europe long before Christianity was introduced there. Decorating an evergreen tree with lights around the time of the winter solstice in December appears to have been an old German Celtic custom affirming eternal life on the shortest day of the year, when darkness appears to reign. At that time, deciduous trees have lost their leaves and are apparently dead. Evergreen trees stand as sentinels to the persistence of the life force, and decorating their branches with lights asserts the eventual triumph of life over death and light over dark.

Though the relationship between the evergreen tree and eternal life seems obvious, or "natural," it is culturally defined. The association between the color green and life is based on cultural experiences of seasonal cycles and the reappearance of new, green leaves in the spring. Green is a symbol for life cross-culturally because most living plants contain chlorophyll for converting energy contained in light for growth. The association between green chlorophyll, which makes life possible for plants, and the life of human beings is arbitrary, or culturally assigned.

Easter is associated with the death and resurrection of Christ, but it occurs close to the vernal equinox, the spring day in which dark and light hours are almost equal. In agricultural societies in the temperate zones of the Northern Hemisphere, it is also the time when spring planting begins, and fertility rituals were conducted during this time before Christianity was introduced into Europe. The resurrection of Christ represents the triumph of life over death, just as the vitality of spring is a triumph over the "dead" winter. Eggs are a symbol of fertility, as are rabbits, since they reproduce so abundantly. In the United States, the three symbols—Christ, eggs, and bunnies—are intermingled, so that bunnies deliver eggs on the day that commemorates Christ's rising from the dead—or being "reborn."

In her book *Natural Symbols* (1970), Mary Douglas suggests that most "natural" symbols are drawn from our experience of our bodies. She notes that the left is associated with the supernatural cross-culturally, and she attributes this almost universal association to the fact that most people are right-handed. Right-handed people typically experience their left hand as being awkward, and this sense of the left's being "out of control" is extended to the supernatural. Since supernatural beings transcend the usual social order, they are also viewed as being "out of control." They must be brought under control by use of ritual, or symbolic behavior. In the United States, people often combine the symbolism of the left as being out of control with sports parlance; someone who behaves in an atypical way is described as "coming from left field."

Dominant Symbols

A **dominant symbol,** Turner states, is one that encapsulates a number of values significant in a particular society. It is used in many different contexts and may undergo shades of interpretation depending on the context in which it appears. For example, the Christian cross draws on a wide range of associations relating to the innate tendency of humans to sin against the father, the importance of expiating sin, and the virtue of sacrificing oneself for the good of society. It expresses complex concepts regarding the essential nature of human beings, relationships within the family, the importance of "paying one's debts," and the dependency of human beings on the generosity of their Creator. The cross appears in rituals in which these complex associations are ritually enacted.

For the Ndembu of Zambia in Africa, studied by Turner, a dominant symbol is the *mudyi,* or milk tree, a plant that exudes a white fluid when its thin bark is scratched. The milk tree represents the matrilineage, which Turner describes as "the backbone of Ndembu social organization" (1967:21). In a broader sense, however, the milk tree stands for the network of "interrelationships between groups and persons that makes up Ndembu society" (1967:21). At the same time, the sap of the milk tree is associated with mother's milk and instruction in traditions of the group:

> The child depends on its mother for nutriment; similarly, say the Ndembu, the tribesman drinks from the breasts of tribal custom. . . . The mother's role is the archetype of protector, nourisher, and teacher. For example, a chief is often referred to as the "mother of his people." . . . The milk tree represents harmonious, benevolent aspects of domestic and tribal life. (1967:22)

Just as among the Ndembu the milk tree represents aspects of nurturance and transmission of culture, in all societies symbols encode meaning that transcends the concrete and the ordinary. Through symbols, we learn who we are as human beings in general and as defined specifically with reference to the culture in which we develop.

SUMMARY

The ability to communicate is incorporated into our biology. In this, humans are not unique. Other animals share with us biological programming for communication through a variety of media: odors, gestures, posture, sounds, and touch. The ability of humans to communicate through odors is less well developed than that of other animals, but we are extraordinarily well equipped for communication through other media.

Body language extends our ability to convey information visually at greater distances than would be possible using the voice alone. In more intimate settings, we can express a variety of meanings through facial expressions, including smiles and frowns. We can also communicate through touch, and many of our most compelling emotions are expressed in this way—by kissing, hugging, or simply putting a hand on someone's shoulder.

The crown jewel of human communication is language, a sound-based system of conveying meaning that requires biological adaptations to the throat, mouth, and brain. Language is a system in which sounds that do not have meaning in themselves are combined according to a set of rules to generate potentially infinite new meanings. Thus, language is an open system. Meanings engendered by these sounds are culturally assigned. For example, the sound "you," which has meaning in English, may not have meaning in other languages, or the meaning may differ.

Language can convey subtle shades of meaning through ambiguity and contradiction. Language also has the characteristic of displacement, which means that it can communicate information about objects or places remote in time and space, or it can convey meanings that do not have physical reality. For example, "patriotism," "love," "country," and "greed" do not exist in the physical world. Our knowledge of them is dependent on language.

Edward Sapir suggested that language shapes thought, a concept expressed in the Sapir–Whorf hypothesis, named for Sapir and his student anthropologist Benjamin Whorf. Whorf's view of language's ability to determine our view of the world developed out of his work among the Hopi, who do not have words for past or future. Whorf argued that, because of their language the Hopi do not have a concept of time as being cumulative, as do English speakers. Whorf claimed that English expresses time in concrete terms, so that we can "save time," "spend time," "waste time," or "kill time." The Hopi can do none of those things, since their language does not objectify time.

In fact, the relationship among language, thought, and culture is extremely complex. Language makes possible certain ways of looking at the world, but language grows out of a social and cultural context that includes our experience of the physical world, our relationships with others, and our traditions.

Language codes meaning in a sound-based system. Symbols, on the other hand, encode meaning through images, words, and behaviors. Symbols are distinct from signs, which stand in a one-to-one relationship with their referent. Symbols convey many complex meanings that cannot be expressed directly in words.

The relationship between a symbol and its referent is arbitrary, or socially assigned, but symbols may draw on an attribute that appears to be inherent in the image. For example, the Virgin Mary is a symbol of idealized motherhood to Catholics, and Christmas trees are associated with eternal life because they are "ever green," green itself being a symbol for life.

Symbols extend the potential of humans to process abstract concepts and to communicate subtle shades of meaning. Human social life would be impossible without the complex communication forms made possible by language and symbols.

POWER WORDS

arbitrary	historical linguistics	phonology
Black English	kinesics	referent
Black English	language	Sapir–Whorf
Vernacular (BEV)	langue	hypothesis
body language	lexicon	semantics
bound morpheme	linguistics	sign
closed system	metaphor	sign language
code-switching	metonymy	sociolinguistics
cognition	morpheme	Standard American
descriptive linguistics	morphology	English (SAE)
dialects	multivocal	structural linguistics
displacement	occupational jargon	symbol
dominant symbol	open system	syntax
free morpheme	parole	terms of address
grammar	phoneme	writing

INTERNET EXERCISE

1. To find out more about linguistic anthropology, check the website of the Society for Linguistic Anthropology at **http://www.aaa.org/sla.htm**.

2. For a discussion of the theoretical and historical basis for the Sapir–Whorf hypothesis, check the website **http://venus.va.com.au/suggestion/sapir.html**.

3. An unusual emic view on symbols is available on the website **http://www.mgardens.org/**. It is maintained by the Lady Virgin Mary Flower Garden Medieval Catholic Folklore Society and is aimed at promoting the planting of gardens using flowers associated with the medieval iconography of the Virgin Mary.

8
The Nature of Human Nature

In this chapter . . .

Perception, cognition, and concepts of the self

Is it true, as the philosopher David Hume wrote, that "beauty in things exists in the mind which contemplates them"? Cross-cultural studies would suggest that not only beauty, but much of the way we see and think about the world — as well as our definition of selfhood — is learned in the process of enculturation. The ability of anthropologists to study variations in perception and cognition cross-culturally has been dependent on the meaning encoded in language.

Freud, Oedipus, and culture

Is there a universal pattern of childhood development? Sigmund Freud thought that all male children are subject to the Oedipal complex, in which they sexually desire the mother and resent the father. Bronislaw Malinowski suggested that the Oedipal complex is associated with patrilineal inheritance, but some anthropologists see what they consider to be Oedipal patterns cross-culturally in myths and dreams.

The culture-and-personality school

Franz Boas's emphasis on the importance of culture influenced a number of anthropologists who studied the relationship among culture, childrearing practices, and adult personality. The work of these anthropologists became known as the culture-and-personality school. Though contemporary anthropologists reject these researchers' overemphasis on uniformity within cultures and oversimplification of complex variables, the culture-and-personality school provided a basis for the development of psychological anthropology.

Defining "normal" and correcting deviance

All societies tolerate a range of behaviors considered "normal," and all societies have means for dealing with behavior that violates the norm. In some non-Western medicine, shamans or healers treat a variety of disorders, both physical and psychological. Anthropologists have noted that shamanic healing can be effective, in part because it treats underlying tensions in the group instead of isolating the individual. Shamans also treat illness through rituals similar to techniques used by Western psychotherapists.

Clifford Geertz (1973) once called human beings "the incomplete animal" because much of human development begins at birth, when the individual is dropped kicking and screaming into its culture. Unlike most other animals, the human infant is not prepared for survival by a set of encoded genetic instructions. Instead, human beings must learn virtually all of what they need to survive—how to acquire food, how to keep themselves clean and free from disease, how to recognize danger and organize a defense, and how to interact with that most subtle of organisms, other human beings. Geertz notes, "Our central nervous system— and most particularly its crowning curse and glory, the neocortex— grew up in great part in interaction with culture" (1973:49). Gail R. Benjamin writes:

> One of the important ways in which anthropologists try to obtain cultural understanding is by asking the question, How do they get to be that way? This is the question of socialization, of how infants who arrive at their birthplace with no culture, no language, and no social patterns become socialized, enculturated members of their group, passing on the thoughts and behavior patterns they have learned to new generations. (1997:23)

The process of **enculturation**—of acquiring a particular culture—is already under way by the time the infant makes its debut howl. What the mother eats during pregnancy—acquiring the nutrients that shape the developing fetus—is determined by culture. Among the Tiwi of Australia, pregnant women are prohibited from eating certain types of reptiles, and during some seasons they may not eat yams because of the belief that the sharp tips of the tubers will pierce the womb and kill the baby. Among the Aztecs, a pregnant woman was cautioned to avoid eating tamales that had become stuck to the cooking pot, because the baby would adhere to the woman's womb and she might die in childbirth. Among the Trobriand Islanders, a pregnant woman was not allowed to eat certain types of fruits, including bananas and mangoes, in the belief that the child would develop a big belly full of excrement and soon die. In the United States, pregnant women are warned to avoid drinking alcohol or smoking, and their intake of caffeine is curtailed.

A pregnant woman may also be prohibited from participating in certain events or witnessing certain sights, in the belief that doing so would harm the developing fetus. To avoid exposing the child to spirits that wander in the night, a pregnant Aztec woman was not allowed to walk around at night. To prevent the baby from being born with the umbilical cord wound around its neck, she was restrained from looking at a hanged person. Among the Tiwi, a pregnant woman is not allowed to cook or to spit into the flames of a cooking fire, in the belief that either action will cause the child to twist in the womb and give pain. She is also prohibited from bathing in the sea and in large bodies of fresh water, since this might offend the *maritji,* or rainbow spirits.

In the United States during the 1980s, a small industry developed around enculturating the fetus while it was still in utero. One entrepreneur established the University of the Unborn, a program for bombarding the fetus with classical music and recordings of good books to give it a head start on the lengthy process of formal education valued in this society.

The position of the mother during delivery, the personnel in attendance, and how soon an infant will be bathed after birth are all shaped by culture. Similarly, the name given to the child and the clothing in which it will be dressed are all the products of culture. Culture also determines whether the mother and child will be secluded after birth, who will be allowed to see the child, and whether the mother will keep the child close to her or encourage it to play independently. Culture also shapes the interaction of a child with its father and determines how much a father is able to participate in the enculturation of his child.

Enculturation and socialization practices differ widely from culture to culture. Socialization and enculturation are the processes by which an individual learns the knowledge, values, and skills—technological and social—required in a particular society. Because of the great variation in the way children are enculturated or socialized, anthropologists have asked whether people who grow up in different societies learn to see the world differently.

The complex process by which an individual acquires the traits his or her society considers desirable—or undesirable—and, in so doing, learns to experience the world in a particular way are part of the domain of psychological anthropology. **Psychological anthropology** focuses on the relationship between the individual and the group of which she or he is a part. In order to understand the complex relationship between an individual and his or her social group, we must return once again to the question posed in Chapter 1: What is a human being?

In the process of socialization into a particular culture, we are taught ways of thinking, behaving, and viewing the world that are presented as being essential to all humans, to all grown-ups, or to all "good people." So completely does the process of socialization shape our experience of the world that we come to see our own world view as representing the natural order of things. Anthropologists describe the assumption that our culturally acquired world view represents the real and only world by the axiom "The fish doesn't know it's wet."

As noted in Chapters 2 and 3, anthropologists try to counter the pervasive influence of our own cultural perspective by basing our theories and concepts on studies conducted cross-culturally. Psychological anthropologists have used cross-cultural studies as a basis for considering whether people universally perceive the world in the same way, whether they think about it in the same way, and whether concepts of the self are universal.

PERCEPTION, COGNITION, AND CONCEPTS OF THE SELF

Anthropological investigation into the nature of how people see the world focuses on the related processes of perception and cognition. **Perception** includes both the biological process of apprehending environmental stimuli and the conceptual process of interpreting those stimuli according to a set of learned expectations. **Cognition** is the process by which human beings acquire information about the world, then reorder and interpret it so that it can be used to operate within that world (Cole and Scribner 1974).

Perception

It is virtually impossible to determine how other people see the world. We share an agreed-upon reality based on language, but no one can get into someone else's head and see the world through that person's eyes. We may all agree that a particular color is blue, but we don't know if we see the color in precisely the same way. As blue shades into green, differences in perception begin to assert themselves; some people emphasize blueness and others emphasize greenness in assigning labels to a particular segment of the light spectrum.

Anthropologists have noted that what we classify as depth perception is a biological characteristic of primates, but it is also a learned skill in some respects. Depth perception is based on the binocular vision characteristic of the primate order. In primates, both eyes are oriented to look forward, so that the visual fields of the two eyes overlap, thus allowing comparison of data from both eyes. On the basis of our surroundings, we also learn to gauge distance by the relationship of objects to each other and by their relative size. For example, if one object partially obscures another, we assume that the object being obscured is behind the other. When we look at a plane in the sky, we know it is not a toy because we have seen similar planes on the ground and have watched them grow smaller as they recede in the distance.

However, foragers who have spent all their lives in the forest learn to judge distance by the relative

As viewers of this photograph, we recognize the Caterpillar to be a toy because of its size relative to the boy. Our ability to interpret what we see is based in part on the context, including the relationship of objects to each other and their relative size.

position of objects to each other and may not be so skilled at estimating distance on the basis of the size of objects. The Mbuti, who live in the Ituri rain forest of northeastern Zaire, are superb hunters, adept at sighting animals obscured by the dense growth of trees. They are less skilled at interpreting visual data when they leave the forest and travel to the plains. Colin Turnbull describes the skepticism of Kenge, a Mbuti, on his first visit to the open mountains and plains. With Turnbull and the guide, Kenge stood on a mountainside and looked out over the herds of animals on the plains below. Turnbull writes:

> On the plains, animals were grazing everywhere—a small herd of elephant to the left, about twenty antelopes staring curiously at us from straight ahead, and down to the right a gigantic herd of about a hundred and fifty buffalo. . . . [Kenge] saw the buffalo, still grazing lazily several miles away, far down below. He turned to me and said, "What insects are those?" (1962:251–252)

As one accustomed to perceiving objects at a distance and automatically correcting for the apparent reduction in size, Turnbull was confused by Kenge's question:

> At first I hardly understood; then I realized that in the forest the range of vision is so limited that there is no great need to make an automatic allowance for distance

when judging size. Out here in the plains, however, Kenge was looking for the first time over apparently unending miles of unfamiliar grasslands, with not a tree worth the name to give him any basis for comparison. The same thing happened later on when I pointed out a boat in the middle of the lake. It was a large fishing boat with a number of people in it but Kenge at first refused to believe this. He thought it was a floating piece of wood. (1962:252)

You may be able to identify with Kenge's misperception if you recall the first time you traveled to an unfamiliar country, where everything seemed strange and alien. I once traveled with a group of people from New Jersey to the eastern slopes of the Andes, in the northern part of Chile. It is the driest place on the earth—U.S. astronauts trained there for their walk on the moon—and it is the site of some of the most dramatic scenery on the earth. Golden hills rise gradually to the pink and purple Andes. Not a cloud mars the vivid blue of the sky, and not a blade of grass or a cactus can be seen in any direction. One baffled visitor exclaimed, "There's nothing here!" Accustomed to the intense greens of New Jersey, the man was unprepared for perceiving the golds, blues, pinks, and purples of the northern Chilean landscape. The color green was lacking in the landscape, so there was "nothing to see."

Cross-Cultural Studies of Perception

Though anthropologists have long presumed that there are cross-cultural differences in the way people perceive the world, investigations into the pre-cise nature of those differences have been hampered by the limitations of language and by the difficulty of developing procedures for testing perception. Even the objects used to test perception are subject to cultural interpretation. In general, two aspects of perception have been addressed in cross-cultural studies of perception: optical illusions and color categories.

Optical Illusions Since the beginning of the twentieth century, anthropologists have attempted to examine cross-cultural perceptions of optical illusions. Some perceptual responses tested by anthropologists were based on the Müller–Lyer illusion and the horizontal–vertical illusion (see Figure 8.1). Most people in Western societies see line A in the Müller–Lyer illusion as being longer than line B, even though the two lines are the same length. Susceptibility to the horizontal–vertical illusion also varies cross-culturally. People who are susceptible to the horizontal–vertical illusion see the vertical line as longer than the horizontal line even though the lines are the same length.

One of the earliest cross-cultural studies of perception was conducted in 1900 by the British psychologist and ethnologist W. H. R. Rivers. He determined that Europeans are more susceptible to the Müller–Lyer illusion than either natives of New Guinea or the Todas of southern India, but they are less susceptible to the horizontal–vertical illusion. On the basis of research among Europeans, Africans, and Filipinos, Marshall H. Segall, D. T. Campbell, and M. J. Herskovits (1966) suggest that the difference in

FIGURE 8.1 The Müller–Lyer Illusion and the Horizontal–Vertical Illusion

According to the "carpentered-world hypothesis," people who live in square or rectangular houses will be more susceptible to the Müller–Lyer illusion (that line A is longer than line B) than will those who live in round houses. On the other hand, people who live in geographic regions with broad, open vistas will be more subject to the horizontal–vertical illusion (that the vertical line is longer than the horizontal line) than will those who live in forests or cities. Cross-cultural attempts to test this hypothesis have produced mixed results.

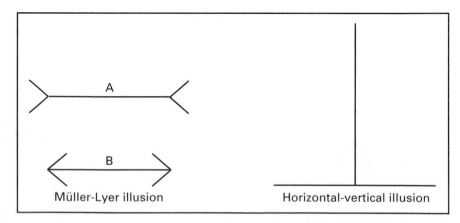

Müller-Lyer illusion   Horizontal-vertical illusion

perception is related to socialization into "carpentered environments"—in which buildings have rectangular floor plans, many straight lines, and right angles between floors, walls, and windows. The anthropologists note that Europeans, who grow up in carpentered environments, are more susceptible to the Müller–Lyer illusion than are people who grow up in round houses.

Subsequent attempts to test the carpentered-world hypothesis have produced mixed results. Gustav Jahoda (1966) tried to replicate Segall, Campbell, and Herskovits's results by comparing three groups in Ghana. He determined that people who are **literate**—able to read and write—are more susceptible to the Müller–Lyer illusion than those who are not. Jahoda suggests that literate people have learned to interpret two-dimensional space, as represented by the printed page, differently than people who are nonliterate. **Nonliterate** societies are those that do not have a written language. *Nonliterate* should not be confused with **illiterate,** which refers to members of a literate society who have not learned to read and write.

A study conducted by R. H. Pollack (1970) indicates that performance on the Müller–Lyer illusion may be related to differences in eye pigmentation. All these factors—environment, education, and the biology of the eye—have an impact on perception. It is virtually impossible, however, to manipulate such a wide range of variables with enough accuracy to produce consistently reliable results cross-culturally. As Douglass Price-Williams puts it: "One can talk broadly of the effect of culture on perception, but as soon as one fractionates that statement into exactly what element of culture corresponds to exactly what kind of perceptual process, the equation becomes vastly more complicated" (1975:11).

Color Categories   In an attempt to transcend cultural associations attached to objects and to contend with differences in perception of two-dimensional space, anthropologists have focused on color categories. There are two important aspects to cross-cultural studies comparing color designations: (1) perception, the process of receiving and organizing environmental stimuli, and (2) terminology, the words used to describe color categories. Research attempting to measure perception is limited by terminology, because the way in which people describe

things may not conform to the way stimuli are perceived.

Anthropologists have noted cross-cultural variations in the way people describe or classify color, but it is unclear whether these variations are correlated with differences in the way people perceive color. In Homeric Greek, a single term was used to designate blue, gray, and dark. Similarly, only one word was used for white and bright. In English, dark and bright are not categories of color; however, they may be expressed as such in certain other languages. The Dugum Dani, on the western part of the island of New Guinea, have only two basic color terms: *modla* translates as "light" or "bright," and *mili* translates as "dark" or "dull."

Some cultures have only three or four basic color terms for the entire spectrum visible to the human eye. Other groups have eight or nine color terms (Berlin and Kay 1969). Languages in many parts of the world do not distinguish between blue and green. English is the language with the greatest number of color terms—more than four thousand, with more being invented every day. Does this mean that English speakers "see" more colors than speakers of languages that contain only two or three color terms?

Leonard Doob (1960) conducted research among the Zulu, who have a single term for red and yellow and another term for blue and green. He compared a sample of rural Zulu women with a sample of urban Zulu women in the task of sorting deflated balloons of different colors. The sorting categories of rural women followed the color terms 50 percent of the time. The sorting categories of urban women followed traditional color terms only 23 percent of the time. This study produced two significant results: (1) the ability to classify color differences does not necessarily coincide with a culture's color terminology, and (2) urbanization affects the process of color classification. It is a given that these women would have been unable to classify colors they could not perceive.

Deflated balloons were used in the study in the hope that they would be culturally neutral and therefore would not influence the sorting categories. In other studies, subjects have been asked to sort strands of yarn by color. There are problems with this choice of objects because yarn is not culturally neutral. Weaving is an important occupation in many societies, and weavers are more likely than nonweavers to recognized subtle variations in color. Thus, the occupational category of weaver may override the influence of cross-cultural variations in color classification.

A classic study by Brent Berlin and Paul Kay (1969) challenged the view prevailing prior to their study that color categories are culturally relative. The Berlin and Kay study indicates that all languages have basic color terms drawn from a set of just eleven color categories, suggesting that color categories are universal. This finding may also imply that the physiological basis for color perception is a more important variable than the culturally learned process of paying selective attention to key indicators of color.

It is still a logical leap from discovering universal patterns of defining color categories linguistically to the assumption that a particular pattern of color perception is universal. Ian Davies and Greville Corbett (1998) tested the link between language and color perception by asking English, Russian, and Setswana speakers to sort colored tiles. Unlike English and Russian speakers, African Setswana speakers do not linguistically distinguish blue from green, and they were more likely to group blues and greens together than were English and Russian speakers. Overall, Davies and Corbett report, "The most prominent pattern in the results was that the choices of the three language samples were strikingly similar, thus supporting the universalist position" (1999:343). Studies by Davies and Corbett have produced data that support "the universalist's position but which suggest that there is also a scope for broadly universal color cognition to be modulated by local culture (including language)" (Davies and Corbett 1999:343).

Cognition Cross-Culturally

As noted in Chapter 3, Europeans have long speculated about the reasoning ability of people from cultures very different from their own. For decades, early anthropologists debated whether "primitive" people follow the same "rational" thought process of Europeans, or whether there are essential differences in the way human beings think.

Anthropologists now recognize that there is no such thing as a "primitive" person or society. All human beings and all contemporary societies are fully modern, and all are sophisticated manifestations of human ingenuity and adaptability. As noted in Chapter 1, however, our world views may differ depending on our perspective, and people of different cultures may conceptualize the world in very different ways. The debates over cognitive processes have fueled a rich tradition in the field of psychological anthropology. Dorothy Lee ([1950] 1980) suggests that some groups, such as the Trobrianders studied by Bronislaw Malinowski, may experience the world differently than people in the United States do, and this difference is reflected in their language. She describes the cognitive processes of English speakers as "lineal" and the cognitive processes of Trobrianders as "nonlineal."

Lineal and Nonlineal Thought   Lee begins with the premise that language reflects a particular way of looking at the world, or world view. It is a codification of reality. In the Trobriand language, Lee writes, there is no temporal connection between objects. That is, there is no concept of becoming, no linguistic distinction between past and present, and no arrangement of causal relationships.

For example, she says, the Trobrianders do not say that a yam becomes overripe. Becoming is a lineal concept of action expressed in the English language. In the Trobriand language, *taytu*, which designates a type of yam, implies that the yam contains a certain degree of ripeness, bigness, and roundness. An overripe yam is conceived of as something entirely different and goes by another name. It is called a *yowana*. Thus, Lee asserts, the Trobrianders do not draw a conceptual line between the various stages of yam ripening, as English speakers do. She suggests that the Trobriand language—and, by extension, Trobriand thought—is nonlineal.

On the other hand, English presumes interrelatedness between cause and effect and visualizes the process as lineal, coming from the outside, rather than as inherent, within the objects themselves. Thus, English speakers may "draw a conclusion" or trace a relationship between facts. Lee writes:

> When we see a line of trees, or a circle of stones, we assume the presence of a connecting line which is not actually visible. And we assume it metaphorically when we follow a line of thought, a course of action or the direction of an argument; when we bridge a gap in the conversation, or speak of the span of life or of teaching a course, or lament our interrupted career. ([1950] 1980:81)

Lee then asks, "But is the line present in reality?" ([1950] 1980:81). In fact, the trees and the stones are discrete units. They are not connected except in our minds. Because of their similarity and their placement adjacent to each other, we draw a conceptual line connecting the trees and the stones. Trobrianders, apparently, do not. Malinowski described the Trobriand village: "Concentrically with the circular row of yam houses there runs a ring of dwelling huts" (Lee [1950] 1980:81). Lee suggests that Malinowski's description of the village as consisting of two concentric circles does not conform to the Trobrianders' experience of their own village as being composed of discrete houses. She notes that the Trobriander word for the same village means "bump" or "aggregate of bumps." In the same way, Trobrianders describe as discrete events activities English speakers would regard as continuous and interconnected.

Lee writes: "I am not maintaining here that the Trobrianders cannot see continuity; rather, that lineal connection is not automatically made by them" ([1950] 1980:82). Lee suggests that the nonlineality of Trobriand language is reflected in their views about the efficacy of their magic. The Trobrianders do not evaluate magic in terms of the results it produces, Lee asserts, but in terms of its place in the social and cultural context. She writes: "They assumed . . . that the validity of a magical spell lay, not in its results, not in proof, but in its very being; in the appropriateness of its inheritance, in its place within the patterned activity, in its being performed by the appropriate person, in its realization of its mythical basis" ([1950] 1980:82).

In fact, Lee argues, there is no physical line connecting a "row" of trees, and there may not necessarily be a "line" connecting sequentially related events. These are interpretations of reality encoded in the English language. Thus, English speakers may "see" a line connecting a "row" of trees or a "circle" of stones or huts, whereas Trobrianders may not.

Concepts of the Body and the Self

What, exactly, *is* a human being? According to the Western model, a human being is a physical entity, a thing existing apart from other such physical entities. This view is reflected in the **medical model** of healing, in which illness is treated as a failure of organs or of bodily mechanisms. For example, an illness may

be diagnosed as a "renal failure," a failure of the kidneys to perform as they ordinarily do. Following from that diagnosis, treatment may be confined to repairing the kidney rather than treating the system that gave rise to the failure of the kidney to perform as expected. In fact, the kidneys share a relationship with every other aspect of the body, including the circulatory system, which delivers oxygen and other nutrients to the kidneys, and the lungs, which take in air and provide the oxygen that every part of the body requires.

As will be noted later in this chapter, shamans (traditional healers) typically trace the origins of illness to disrupted social relationships. This is an alien concept in Western medicine, which emphasizes the isolated, biological causes of diseases. Recent research is suggesting that the Western medical tradition is an oversimplification. Medical conditions such as cancer, hypertension, and asthma may be related to the expression or repression of emotions, which is also related to socialization and cultural expectations about the appropriate way to behave in social groups.

Logically consistent with the Western medical model is the idea that individuals are discrete units that stand in opposition to a culturally coherent group. According to the Western enculturation model, especially as framed by Sigmund Freud (1961), individuals give up their true selves to conform to the demands of the group. This view is at variance with the Chinese Confucian model of personhood, which is that the essential nature of humans is to be members of groups and that individuals can fulfill their destinies only through social interaction.

According to the Japanese view, the self is constructed in the process of socialization. One Japanese writer compared enculturation of a child to producing an article of lacquered wood: "The more coats of varnish that are laid on the foundation by laborious work throughout the years, the more valuable becomes the lacquer work as a finished product. So it is with a people" (Nohara 1936:50, quoted in Benedict 1946b:290). In her study of Japanese educational practices, Gail R. Benjamin writes:

American conceptions of personality and development tend to focus on the differences inherent in different people, to see life and education as fostering tendencies that are inborn in each individual and unique to each individual. Japanese conceptions of personality and development tend to focus on experience as the source of both the unique characteristics of the individual and of the qualities that all people have in common. Individuals are not very different [in the Japanese view], so it follows that by having common experiences, they will all learn the same things and develop the same characteristics. If they are given different experiences, they will turn out to be different kinds of people. (1997:24–25)

Since the last two decades of the twentieth century, some anthropologists studying widely differing cultures have suggested that assumptions about the nature of the self differ widely among cultures. The most recent studies have focused on factors that shape cross-cultural variations in definition of the self. On the basis of her study of French-Portuguese bilingual speakers, Michèle E. J. Koven suggests that **bilingualism**—speaking two languages—allows people to express different kinds of "selves" in each language. She writes, "Different ways of speaking, within and across languages, create socially and psychologically real effects for people, producing for the same speaker multiple expressions and experiences of socially recognizable selves" (1998:437).

Culturally negotiated constructions of the self are political, in that they reflect one's status in the group and one's ability to interact effectively. On the basis of his study of constructions of personhood in a Boston homeless shelter, Robert Desjarlais writes:

> The makings of selfhood and personhood are highly pragmatic, in that human (inter)actions, utterances, and responses can effect, for oneself or for others, and with conscious intention or not, particular understandings or representations of an individual's life, world, or presence of being in either momentary or durable ways. (2000:466–467)

Desjarlais notes that "actions and the diffuse understandings they effect are commonly rooted in relations of differential powers and authorities" (2000:467). Alice, a resident of the shelter, had represented herself as "happy on the street" until authorities—police, psychiatrists, social workers—"started to treat her badly by forcing her to take medications, confining her in psychiatric hospitals, and requiring her to heed the edicts of psychiatric and legal institutions" (2000:468). Whereas Alice had seen her life on the streets as an expression of her competence, authorities viewed Alice as mentally ill and felt they were helping Alice by preventing her from engaging in "inappropriate" social behavior.

MOTHERS, FATHERS, AND OEDIPUS

The history of psychological anthropology has been marked by an attempt to distinguish human universals from characteristics that are particular to human populations. Freud's concept of the Oedipal complex has formed an important part of this debate. The Oedipal complex takes its name from the story of the Greek hero Oedipus, who unknowingly killed his father and married his mother. Freud suggested that the Oedipal story expresses conflicts that are universal in the developmental cycle of males.

According to Freud, boys become sexually aroused by their mothers during the intimate contact occasioned by maternal nurturing and, as a result, become envious of their fathers. Melford Spiro describes the resulting conflict in the boy's mind: "As a result of his wish to possess the exclusive love of the mother, the boy moreover develops the wish to kill the father and to replace him in his relationship with the mother. (In the mind of a little boy, of course, 'to kill' means to eliminate, to banish, to be rid of.)" (1982:4). At the same time, the boy admires his father and seeks to emulate him. Freud writes: "The hatred of his father that arises in a boy from rivalry for his mother is not able to achieve uninhibited sway over his mind; it has to contend against his old-established affection and admiration for that very same person ([1901] 1950:129).

Malinowski rejected Freud's contention that the Oedipal complex is universal. Instead, he said, the tension between father and son described by Freud results from the European system of patrilineal inheritance rather than from sexual competition for the mother. Since, under the patrilineal system, a boy inherits property and social status from his father, the boy feels resentment toward his potential benefactor, who has authority over him. At the same time, the father feels ambivalence toward his son, who will eventually assume control of his status and property as the father grows older and dies.

Among the Trobriand Islanders, Malinowski noted, descent is matrilineal, which means a boy inherits status and property from his mother's brother rather than from his father. In the Trobriands, boys have warm, affectionate relationships with their fathers because they do not see them

Bronislaw Malinowski drew on his fieldwork among the Trobriand Islanders to refute Sigmund Freud's model of the Oedipus complex. Malinowski asserted that Trobriand boys do not feel antagonism toward their fathers because Trobrianders are matrilineal and boys do not inherit property or status from their father.

in an authoritarian role. "They never feel his heavy hand on themselves, he is not their kinsman, nor their owner, nor their benefactor. He has no rights, no prerogatives" (Malinowski [1927] 1955:31).

On the other hand, the relationship between a boy and his mother's brother is one of tension and conflict, since the boy will inherit status and property through his mother's line, from the senior male, his maternal uncle. At the same time, the maternal uncle is in charge of disciplining the boy and feels ambivalent toward his heir, who will eventually displace him. According to Malinowski, it is competition over authority and status, rather than over sexual access to the mother, that is the source of anxiety between a boy and the man from whom he will inherit his social position. Thus, he said, the Oedipal complex does not occur among the matrilineal Trobriand Islanders.

Trobriander Dreams

Some other anthropologists have used Malinowski's own data to challenge his view that the Oedipal complex does not occur in matrilineal societies. Malinowski, a thorough collector of data, recorded dreams of his Trobriand subjects. He learned that they never dreamed of having sexual intercourse with their mothers but did have some sexual dreams about

their sisters, despite strong sexual taboos between siblings. Brother–sister incest is also a prominent theme in Trobriand mythology. Malinowski writes:

> In the Trobriands there is no friction between father and son. . . . The ambivalent attitude of veneration and dislike is felt between a man and his mother's brother, while the repressed sexual attitude of incestuous temptation can be formed only towards his sister. Applying to each society a terse, though somewhat crude formula, we might say that in the Oedipus complex there is the repressed desire to kill the father and marry the mother, while in the matrilineal society of the Trobriands the wish is to marry the sister and kill the maternal uncle. ([1927] 1955:80)

Spiro argues that the brother–sister incest theme in Trobriand dreams and legends suggests that sexual attraction and hostility are deflected from their true objects, the mother and father, and displaced onto less threatening subjects, the sister and maternal uncle. Thus, he writes, the Oedipal complex is not absent among Trobrianders; rather, it emerges in disguised form as love for the sister and hostility toward the mother's brother.

Whether the Oedipus complex is universal continues to fuel debates in anthropology. Freud suggested that unconscious conflicts are expressed in the dreams of individuals and the myths of societies.

Allen W. Johnson and Douglass Price-Williams (1996) conducted a cross-cultural survey of myths and folktales and concluded that the Oedipal complex is indeed universally represented in these stories, which would suggest that mother–son attraction and father–son hostility is a theme in all societies. The debate over whether the Oedipal complex is universal is far from settled, however. Disagreements concerning the Oedipal complex are rooted in broader issues, such as the relative influence of socialization practices and patterns of social organization on the behavior of individuals. The debate also raises theoretical issues centering on whether myths and dreams are reliable indicators of individual motivations.

CULTURE AND PERSONALITY

Malinowski was not the only anthropologist of his day to examine psychoanalytic concepts cross-culturally. A number of Franz Boas's students also looked to Freud and other psychologists to explain cross-cultural variation in personality. The most prominent of these anthropologists formed the culture-and-personality school, which dominated the field of psychological anthropology until the 1970s.

The **culture-and-personality school** grew out of Boas's rejection of the racism of his day, expressed in biological determinism. **Biological determinism** is based on the idea that personality, including intelligence and criminal tendencies, is biologically encoded and therefore cannot be changed by education or by environment. Boas argued that culture is more important than biology in shaping behavior, and some of his students attempted to prove his contention that culture shapes personality.

Boas's students—among them Edward Sapir, Ruth Benedict, and Margaret Mead—formed an elite community. Throughout their lives they stayed in contact with each other and exchanged ideas on a variety of subjects. Sapir became best known for his contribution to linguistics, but he was an active participant in the vigorous exchange of ideas in the culture-and-personality school. Benedict played a key role in defining the relationship of culture to personality, and Mead conducted studies aimed at examining the interrelationship of culture, child-rearing practices, and personality.

Patterns of Culture

Ruth Benedict wrote what might well be considered the culture-and-personality manifesto in her book *Patterns of Culture*, first published in 1934 and still widely read. Benedict stated that culture is more than "a list of unrelated facts," and she drew on the concept of personality to describe the interrelationship of different aspects of culture. In psychological terms, **personality** is a consistent pattern in attitude and behavior through time. Culture, Benedict asserts, is personality writ large:

> A culture, like an individual, is a more or less consistent pattern of thought and action. . . . Taken up by a well-integrated culture, the most ill-assorted acts become characteristic of its peculiar goals, often by the most unlikely metamorphoses. The form that these acts take we can understand only by understanding first the emotional and intellectual mainsprings of that society. ([1934] 1946a:42)

Benedict analyzed four societies: the Pueblo Indians of New Mexico, the Plains Indians, the Dobu Islanders of Melanesia, and the Kwakiutl Indians of the northwestern coast of North America. Drawing on economic practices, family structure, political authority, religion, warfare, and folklore, Benedict classified the four societies according to what she conceived as their dominant personality type.

She described the Pueblo Indians as "Apollonian," a term taken from Nietzsche that refers to characteristics ascribed to the Greek god Apollo. According to Benedict, the Apollonian Pueblo Indians adhere to "the middle way," emphasizing cooperation, communal activities, and avoidance of all strong emotions, such as anger and jealousy.

Benedict described the Plains Indians as Dionysian, a term from Nietzsche referring to Dionysus, the Greek god of wine, whose followers celebrated him in orgiastic frenzies. Benedict suggested that the Dionysian Plains Indians "valued all violent experience, all means by which human beings may break through the usual sensory routine" ([1934] 1946a:73). Thus, they fasted and inflicted torture on themselves and used alcohol and drugs to induce religious intoxication. They also admired individuals who were fearless in warfare, gloried in their victories, and displayed wild abandon in their grief.

Benedict described the Kwakiutl as Dionysian, basing her characterization on the extravagant giveaways in the potlatch. Benedict writes, "This will to superiority they exhibited in the most uninhibited fashion. It found expression in uncensored self-glorification and ridicule of all comers" ([1934] 1946a:175). Benedict also notes that neophyte dancers in the Kwakiutl cannibal society ceremonies were expected to lose self-control, trembling and frothing at the mouth and biting spectators.

The Dobuans, who are described as assuming that any prosperous man "has thieved, killed children and his close associates by sorcery," earned the sobriquet of "paranoid" from Benedict ([1934] 1946a:155). She noted that Dobu Islanders live in an atmosphere of conflict and suspicion, and their institutions set husband against wife, neighbor against neighbor, and village against village. In psychological terms, individuals who project their own unacceptable desires onto others and are excessively suspicious of others are described as paranoid.

Benedict asserted that normality is relative to a particular culture. What is considered normal in one society would be viewed as abnormal in another. She writes, "culture may value and make socially available even highly unstable human types" ([1934] 1946a:249). She also suggested that individuals who conform to the valued personality type in a particular society will be successful, whereas those who do not conform will be unhappy failures.

Culture and Conformity

Critics of Benedict's approach note that she overlooked data that would have challenged her conclusions. Marvin Harris (1968) criticizes "the dubious factual foundation" on which *Patterns of Culture* is based. There is much variation among the different Plains Indian groups, for example, and anthropologists who have studied them consider her portrayal of Plains Indian cultures to be distorted. These anthropologists suggest that Benedict overemphasized orgiastic aspects of Plains Indian groups and downplayed the more restrained aspects of their cultures.

Benedict's own fieldwork was conducted primarily among Pueblo Indians, but she has been criticized for her analysis of even these groups. Anthropologists who have studied the Zuñi suggest that, because Benedict stayed among this group only for short periods, she did not have the opportunity to witness such events as fire walking and sword swallowing in the ceremonies of the Zuñi medicine society. Elsie Clews Parsons notes that failure to witness these events led

Benedict to "underestimate the orgiastic potentiality of Zuñi character" (1939:879). Benedict also downplayed the severity of ceremonial beatings during the male puberty rites of the neighboring Hopi (Harris 1968:407).

Benedict's model of Dionysian and Apollonian societies also assumes a high degree of cultural and psychological homogeneity within a particular society, an assumption that is at variance with evidence from later studies. Failure to conform to the norm does not necessarily lead to failure in the society as a whole. In fact, exceptional individuals are often admired, as in the case of shamans, traditional healers who often display highly deviant behavior or personalities. In U.S. society, film stars or sports heroes may be revered even though they do not conform to behavior expected of other members of society.

Patterns of Culture fueled many studies in the culture-and-personality tradition, all of which shared the following assumptions: (1) a culture is characterized by a particular configuration of values and behaviors similar to a personality type; (2) the desired

Anthropologists agree that concepts of the self may differ cross-culturally and that personhood is shaped through learning and in response to the social context. However, they disagree on the degree to which personality is shaped by culture and the importance of conformity to cultural values. The personality of the individual behind this Sri Lanka mask has been completely obscured in preparation for a cultural performance.

personality type will be rewarded, whereas nonconformists will be failures; (3) cultural values are expressed in childrearing practices, which are aimed at producing the desired personality type. These assumptions produced two types of culture-and-personality studies that were especially influential in anthropology: (1) national character studies and (2) socialization studies. Both were aimed at examining the relationship among cultural values, childrearing practices, and adult personality (see Figure 8.2).

National Character Studies

During World War II, the U.S. government financed a number of studies aimed at applying the concepts of the culture-and-personality school to analyses of "national character." **National character** studies

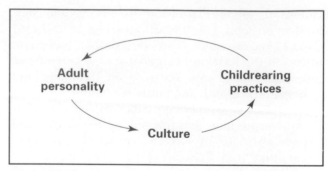

FIGURE 8.2   The Culture and Personality Model

Strongly influenced by Franz Boas, studies by the culture-and-personality school were aimed at determining the interrelationship of culture, childrearing practices, and adult personality. As the above model illustrates, these anthropologists maintained that culture gives rise to childrearing practices, which shape an adult personality that conforms to cultural values.

National character studies were aimed at determining the psychological type most characteristic of a culture. During World War II, Ruth Benedict defined the psychology of the Japanese as a contradiction between conformity to the social order—as reflected in this photograph of a Japanese wedding—and the desire to return to early childhood, when they were free to gratify their whims.

were based on the idea that there exist consistent differences between cultures that can be analyzed as psychological types. The U.S. Department of War was interested in funding such studies because it felt that understanding the psychology of wartime opponents could be useful in planning wartime operations and postwar policy. As a result, national character studies focused primarily on the U.S. enemies of the day: Japan and Germany. In addition, anthropologists analyzed the national character of the Soviets, since U.S. officials distrusted their Soviet allies because of their adherence to communism and advocacy of revolution.

Japanese National Character   Japan was perhaps the most puzzling of U.S. opponents during World War II. One seeming paradox to American observers was the "fanatical" devotion of Japanese to their emperor, expressed in Japanese soldiers' willingness to undergo great hardship or to undertake suicide missions, as opposed to their willingness, once captured, to "change sides" and work with seemingly equal devotion for their captors.

Anthropologist Clyde Kluckhohn explained this phenomenon as an example of "situational" morality, resulting from the Japanese concept of the self as defined primarily with reference to the social group. Kluckhohn suggested that a Japanese war prisoner regarded himself as socially dead and considered his relationship to his family, friends, and country as finished.

> To anthropologists who had steeped themselves in Japanese literature it was clear that Japanese morality was a situational one. As long as one was in situation A, one publicly observed the rules of the game with a fervor that impressed Americans as "fanaticism." Yet the minute one was in situation B, the rules for situation A no longer applied. (Kluckhohn 1957:137)

Japanese national character also attracted the attention of Ruth Benedict, who focused on what she saw as the contradiction in Japanese character between restrained aestheticism and fanatical militarism. The title of her 1946 book *The Chrysanthemum and the Sword* reflects what she viewed as an opposition between restraint, as expressed in the formality of Japanese flower arranging, and excess, as represented by the samurai warrior.

Benedict asserts that, to understand the Japanese, one must know what it means to "take one's proper station." Their "reliance upon order and hierarchy," she writes, pervades every aspect of society, from the family to the state and to religious and economic life (1946b:43). She suggests that through successive stages of increasingly rigorous childhood training Japanese learn that their own desires must be subordinated to those of the family and the group. A very young child is treated permissively and allowed to express aggression against its mother. When the child begins to walk, training takes the form of shaming and teasing, or the mother may threaten to give the child away if he doesn't conform to expectations.

Benedict says Japanese childrearing practices produce an adult who is torn between fear of losing face and longing for an earlier period of indulgence:

> The contradictions in Japanese male behavior which are so conspicuous to Westerners are made possible by the discontinuity of their upbringing, which leaves in their consciousness, even after all the "lacquering" they undergo, the deep imprint of a time when they were like little gods in their little world, when they were free to gratify even their aggressions, and when all satisfactions seemed possible. Because of this deeply implanted dualism, they can swing as adults from excesses of romantic love to utter submission to the family. They can indulge in pleasure and ease, no matter to what lengths they go in accepting extreme obligations. Their training in circumspection makes them in action an often timid people, but they are brave even to foolhardiness. . . . In spite of all their politeness, they can retain arrogance. (1946b:290–291)

Benedict failed to see that her characterization of Japanese male behavior as contradictory reflects a Western bias. There is, for example, no inherent contradiction in "indulging in pleasure and ease" and "accepting extreme obligations" or between being polite and arrogant. These are oppositions generated in Western culture. Rejection of "pleasure and ease" has been attributed to the Protestant work ethic pervasive in American society, and the idea that arrogance is impolite is associated with American notions of democracy and egalitarianism.

Similarly, the "contradiction" expressed in the title of her book, *The Chrysanthemum and the Sword,* is a Western construct. In Japanese culture, there is no contradiction between flower arranging and the martial arts. Both express an emphasis on artistry and discipline, as evidenced by the following advice given by the seventeenth-century Zen master Takuan Soho

(1986), teacher of swordsmanship to two generations of Japanese samurai, in a letter to Yagyu Munenori.

> Since you are a master in the martial arts without equal in past or present, you are most resplendent in rank, stipend and reputation. Waking or sleeping, you should not forget this great boon and in order to return this favor by day and by night, you should think only of fulfilling your loyalty. Total loyalty is first in making your mind correct, disciplining your body, not splitting your thoughts concerning your lord by even a hairsbreadth, and in neither resenting nor blaming others. Do not be neglectful of your daily work. At home, be filial, let nothing indecent occur between husband and wife, be correct in formality, do not love mistresses, sever yourself from the path of sensuality, be austere as a parent, and act according to the Way. In employing underlings, do not make distinctions on the basis of personal feelings. Employ men who are good and bind them to you, reflect on your own deficiencies, conduct the government of your province correctly, and put men who are not good at a distance. (1986:41)

As this passage suggests, to Japanese trained in the peaceful or martial arts, there is no opposition or contradiction between aestheticism and militarism. Both flower arranging and swordsmanship require discipline and dedication, as do parenting, governing one's province, and serving one's lord.

A Japanese anthropologist might well describe U.S. society and socialization practices as "fragmented," since individuals are forced to choose between expressing themselves artistically and defending themselves in battle. In fact, one of my students from Japan conducted an ethnography in which she described Americans as "the lonely people," since infants are forced to sleep in a room by themselves from the day they come home from the hospital, young adults are expected to leave the home where they grew up, and old people cannot live with their grown children. Loneliness—and contradiction—may well be in the eye of the beholder.

German National Character   A study of German national character by Walter C. Langer, commissioned by the U.S. intelligence service, focused on Adolf Hitler's personality. Langer concluded that Hitler had transferred his own Oedipus complex to the German nation and projected his hostility toward his father onto the Austrian Empire. The researcher noted that most Germans referred to their country as the "fatherland," but Hitler almost always called it the "motherland." Hitler's own writings express a passionate longing for Germany and a "bitter hatred against the Austrian state" (quoted in Bock 1988:83). Langer added that Hitler's writings suggest a furtive quality in his love for Germany, "where since my early youth I have been drawn by secret wishes and secret love" (quoted in Bock 1988:83). It is not difficult for psychoanalysts to see the "secret wishes and secret love" in Hitler's youthful yearnings for the "motherland" as symbolizing his secret yearning for his mother and, thus, evidence of a repressed Oedipus complex.

Erik Erikson suggested that Hitler used his own childhood story as a myth to appeal to the anger and frustrations of prewar German youths. Erikson noted that Hitler's writings drew heavily on the use of familiar images, in which his father is portrayed as harsh and autocratic and Hitler himself is presented as an idealistic son who must overthrow his father's stern authority. To German adolescents, Hitler became a kind of "glorified older brother." Erikson calls him a "gang leader who kept the boys together by demanding their admiration, by creating terror, and by shrewdly involving them in crimes from which there was no way back" (1963:337; quoted in Bock 1988:84).

In retrospect, the limitations of studies of German national character are apparent. They overemphasize uniformity within a culture; not all Germans were authoritarian or saw Hitler as a glorified older brother. Though it is true that Germans were caught up in a crisis of national identity between World War I and World War II, most opposed Hitler's rise to power, and even during the height of the Third Reich, some of Hitler's own generals tried to assassinate him because they saw him as a threat to the integrity of the German state.

Russian National Character   One of the more controversial studies to come out of the national character model was the "swaddling hypothesis," developed by Geoffrey Gorer with the aid of Margaret Mead. *Swaddling* refers to the Russian practice of wrapping an infant tightly during the early months of life. This custom, which prevents movement, was intended to help children grow straight and strong and keep them from "hurting themselves." Infants were released from their wrappings for short periods during the day so they could be cleaned and actively played with.

Gorer suggested that long periods of immobility broken by brief spurts of intense social activity produce a personality that is subject to mood swings, alternating between long periods of introspective depression and brief periods of frantic social activity. Gorer extended the correlation to Russian political life, which he described as long periods of submission to authority interrupted by brief but intense periods of revolution. This pattern, he felt, explained the violent Russian Revolution of 1917, which occurred after centuries of submission to dictatorship under the Czars.

The swaddling hypothesis is a classic among culture-and-personality studies, and criticisms of it are characteristic of those leveled against the approach as a whole. Obviously, not all Russians become depressed or suffer from mood swings as a result of swaddling, just as not all Germans are authoritarian.

Criticisms of National Character Studies   Because they were carried out during wartime, national character studies were typically conducted at a distance. Anthropologists and psychologists who analyzed the character of Japanese, Germans, or Russians never actually traveled to those parts of the world. Instead, they relied on written reports from natives of and visitors to those countries, on analyses of cultural products such as art and literature, and, in some cases, on interviews with immigrants or war prisoners from those countries.

National character studies illustrate the complexities of analyzing personality cross-culturally. Though there are certainly differences among cultures, there is also a great deal of variation within cultures, a point often overlooked by researchers in the culture-and-personality school. To describe an entire society by applying a few generalized concepts is to reduce the complexity of human social groups to an unrealistic simplicity. And the assumption that all members of a particular society conform to a single model of personality fails to hold up under the experience of anthropologists who observe diverse attitudes among people in even the smallest and most homogeneous of human groups. Finally, the link between child-rearing practices and adult personality is far too complex to reduce to a single formula.

Socialization Studies

Just as researchers of national character drew on Freudian theory to explain adult personality, anthro-pologists who studied socialization practices based their research on Freud's idea that early-childhood experiences shape adult personality. Boas's student Margaret Mead is preeminent among those who focused on the relationship between childhood training and adult personality, as shaped by the process of enculturation.

Margaret Mead   Of all the theorists in the culture-and-personality school, Margaret Mead looms largest in terms of the range of her research topics, her innovative methods, and her ability to translate anthropological concepts for the American public. She conducted research in Samoa, New Guinea, and Bali and was a critical observer of American culture. She pioneered both in adapting psychological methodology to cross-cultural studies and in visual anthropology, which uses photography as a method of data collection. Before Mead, most anthropologists viewed photography primarily as a tool for illustrating their books rather than as a valid research instrument.

Mead explored gender in *Sex and Temperament* (1935), socialization practices in *Growing Up in New Guinea* (1930) and *Coming of Age in Samoa* (1928), and trance dancing in Bali in a film she produced with her third husband, Gregory Bateson. She wrote a column in a popular women's magazine and often appeared on television to espouse her views on the role of culture in shaping personality.

Coming of Age in Samoa, her most popular book, is still in print many decades after its publication. Mead defied her mentor's wishes in choosing to study outside the United States. Boas was concerned about her health and safety in conducting a study so far from home. In exchange for his support of her journey to Samoa, Mead compromised on her research design. She wanted to study cultural change, which would have been pioneering work at the time, but Boas convinced her to focus her research on the effects of culture on adolescent identity crises. This focus was in line with Boas's belief that the most important role of anthropology was to document cultures he was convinced were rapidly disappearing, a project he recommended to all his students.

Culture and Adolescent Angst   Adolescent identity crises are considered part of normal development in American society. A youthful rebellion against authority is often attributed to the conspicuous bodily changes accompanying puberty. Following Boas's emphasis on culture rather than biology as an explanation for behavior, Mead theorized that adolescent angst is related to the stresses a particular culture places on an individual during the transition to adulthood.

She argued that adolescent Samoan girls do not undergo an identity crisis comparable to that of U.S. teenagers because Samoan culture does not precipitate dramatic behavioral changes at puberty. Specifically, she identified three aspects of Samoan childrearing practices that smooth the transition from childhood to adulthood: (1) a casual approach to emotional attachments, the result of relaxed child–parent bonds, (2) an absence of conflicting moral standards, especially those relating to sexual behavior, and (3) a limited choice of careers and adult lifestyles.

In play, this girl is already taking on roles that are assigned to women. Her "baby" lies on the floor at her feet while she "cleans" the window. House cleaning and child care are considered "feminine" jobs in this culture.

With reference to U.S. childrearing practices, Mead writes that the "close relationship between parent and child" produces a pattern in which "submission to the parent or defiance of the parent may become the dominating pattern of a lifetime" ([1928] 1968:153). In contrast, Samoan children grow up in a household that may include as many as half a dozen adult females and males, all exercising the parental roles of nurturing and discipline. As a result, she writes, Samoan children "do not distinguish their parents as sharply as our children do" ([1928] 1968:153). Thus, the Samoan child is not presented with the strictly delineated roles of a kind and nurturing mother and an authoritarian father, as is the case with the American child. Instead, she says, "The Samoan baby learns that the world is composed of a hierarchy of male and female adults, all of whom can be depended upon and must be deferred to" ([1928] 1968:153).

At the same time, Samoan adolescents do not face the bewildering array of conflicting sexual standards characteristic of U.S. society. In Samoa, Mead writes: "Sex is a natural, pleasurable thing; the freedom with which it may be indulged in is limited by just one consideration, social status" ([1928] 1968:148). She notes that the daughters and wives of chiefs are not allowed to indulge in "extra-marital experiments" and that heads of households and mothers of families "should have too many important matters on hand to leave them much time for casual amorous adventures" ([1928] 1968:148).

On the other hand, Mead notes, moral values in the United States stem from a variety of sources, including religion and various forms of media and social contexts. Divergent religious beliefs may be represented within a single family, and a growing child may also be exposed to conflicting messages about morality from a variety of sources. On Samoa, Mead writes, there is little disagreement about moral issues or about the way an individual should live his or her life: "For the explanation of the lack of conflict we must look principally to the difference between a simple, homogeneous primitive civilisation, a civilisation which changes so slowly that to each generation it appears static, and a motley, diverse, heterogeneous modern civilisation" ([1928] 1968:151).

"Cultural Determinism" Mead's work in Samoa has been both praised and criticized. Her most severe critic is Derek Freeman, who called her

approach "cultural determinism," suggesting that it was a reaction to the "biological determinism" of earlier decades. A biological determinist is one who considers behavior to be shaped by biology. Freeman argued that the parent–child bond is much stronger in Samoa than Mead portrayed. Furthermore, he writes, Samoan children are often severely punished.

Freeman also disputed Mead's claim of sexual experimentation among Samoan youths. According to Mead, easy access to sex reduced incidents of rape. However, Freeman states that "the incidence of rape in Samoa . . . is among the highest to be found anywhere in the world" (1983c:260). He describes adolescence in Samoa as a stormy and turbulent time, especially for males. Finally, he says, Mead overlooked the impact of missionaries on the traditional life of Samoans.

As did other members of the culture-and-personality school, Mead oversimplified her reports of data. However, she was not blind to the importance of biology, and in the appendixes to *Coming of Age in Samoa,* she provided details of her methodology, details of the impact of Americans on traditional society, and data on deviance that allowed later researchers to test the results of her study. In the text, however, Mead provided a colorfully written and appealing picture of life in Samoa that found a wide audience outside the cloistered halls of academia.

Collectively, Mead's research on gender and socialization practices had a profound impact on attitudes of the American public. She pioneered research techniques, defined issues that continue to be of interest, took Boas's battle against racism to the American public, and sparked an interest in other cultures that continues today. If Boas could be considered the father of American anthropology, it would not be too far-fetched to describe Mead as the mother of American anthropology.

The Six Cultures Study During the 1950s, several scholars from Cornell, Harvard, and Yale undertook a comparative study of childrearing practices in six cultures, under the direction of John W. M. Whiting. This was an ambitious attempt to systematize the study of enculturation in different cultural contexts. Six teams of researchers spent between six and fourteen months in communities of between fifty and one hundred people in East Africa, India,

Okinawa, Mexico, the Philippines, and the New England region of the United States.

In each community, researchers focused on twenty-four mothers who had children between the ages of three and ten. The mothers were interviewed according to a standard schedule, and their interactions with their children were systematically observed. Researchers were especially interested in collecting data on the behavioral systems of succorance (assistance), nurturance, self-reliance, achievement, dependence, responsibility, obedience, dominance, sociability, and aggression. Researchers also collected ethnographic data to provide information about the cultural and social context of parenting.

Culture, Social Organization, and Early-Childhood Training In analyzing results of the study, Beatrice and John Whiting (1975) found that children in the African, Mexican, and Philippine villages scored significantly higher on average for nurturance and responsibility than for dependence and dominance. The reverse was true for the children of villages in Okinawa, India, and New England. The researchers attributed these differences to variations in social complexity. The first three societies practice subsistence farming, with little economic specialization or stratification. The latter three exhibit a more pronounced division of labor, class stratification, and a centralized political system.

The Whitings suggested that, in the simpler cultures (those with lesser degrees of task specialization and stratification), children's contribution to the family in the form of work is more valued, and children are trained to be helpful and responsible. Even young children may be expected to perform such chores as carrying firewood and water, looking after younger siblings, and running errands. Because this work is of value to the family, the child will experience feelings of worth, responsibility, competence, and concern with the family welfare. Robert A. LeVine (1970) notes that punishment for disobedience or failing to perform tasks is more severe in the simpler societies.

In the more complex societies, those with greater degrees of task specialization and stratification, tasks assigned to children may seem more arbitrary, since the work is not so obviously of value. The Whitings also note that school education plays a more prominent role in more complex cultures, and school education emphasizes individual achievement and egoism rather than concern for others. School trains children for specialized roles for which the individual

The Mead–Freeman Controversy

Anthropological theory is often shaped more on the hot field of debate than in the cold corridors of academic institutions. We have already noted Bronislaw Malinowski's involvement in several debates, including his rejection of Sigmund Freud's concept of the Oedipal complex, discussed in this chapter. Derek Freeman (1983c) secured a place for himself on the time-honored turf of controversy by refuting Margaret Mead's data on Samoa.

Freeman characterized Mead's view that Samoan youths do not undergo adolescent identity crises as "cultural determinism," stating, among other things, that she overestimated the degree of sexual freedom available to unmarried Samoan females. He suggested that Mead distorted her data, omitting information that would have refuted her theory. Ironically, Paul Shankman (1996) notes that Freeman misrepresented his own sources to support his contention that adolescent identity crises are based in biology.

The issue is a significant one, hinging on whether anthropologists can look to cultural values as a reliable indicator of actual behavior. Freeman's reliance on idealized versions of appropriate behavior may have led him to misconstrue rates of premarital sex among Samoan adolescent girls. Freeman's own data indicate that 27 percent of female adolescents in a rural Western Samoan village had engaged in premarital sex; Mead's data indicate that 48 percent of the female adolescents in her sample from the Manu'a group engaged in premarital sex. It is unclear how much of a role the gender of the researcher may have played in these figures,

since we have no way of knowing whether female adolescents may have been reluctant to discuss their sexual activity with a male researcher. Shankman notes:

> During World War II in Western Samoa, Freeman . . . was given the title *manaia,* signifying that he was the nominal head of the group of untitled, unmarried men in the village. As a manaia who was fluent in Samoan, Freeman states that he was able to speak easily with young women and young men about many matters. Yet apart from a passing reference to fond memories of the young women of Sa'anapu, Freeman's only direct discussion of his findings on premarital sex among young women at that time is a statement that in 1943, "when there were rumors abroad about the loss of their virginity" (Freeman 1983b:124), girls were made to swear on the Bible in public as to whether the rumors were true or not. (Shankman 1996:565)

Researchers have long noted that actual behavior often departs significantly from idealized reports, and few scholars would accept swearing "on the Bible in public" as a reliable indicator of actual behavior.

In addition, Freeman acquired much of his data used to refute Mead's account through his association with high-ranking Samoan males. In general, high-ranking males have a vested interest in affirming idealized cultural values, since these reinforce their own position in the social order. As I note in *The Other Fifty Percent,* "male accounts present an *idealized* view of social interaction" (Womack 1993:67, emphasis in original).

In the following article, Shankman concludes that Mead came closer to the mark than Freeman did in interpreting the data on Samoan sexual conduct.

SAMOAN SEXUAL CONDUCT AND THE MEAD–FREEMAN CONTROVERSY
Paul Shankman

The Margaret Mead–Derek Freeman controversy over the nature of Samoan culture, and especially Samoan sexual conduct, has provoked popular and professional commentary for more than a decade. One reason the controversy has been so engaging is that many of the issues are not specific to Samoa but rather involve broader questions of context, rhetoric, ideology, and ethnographic authority. For anthropologists who work in other parts of the world, these general issues concerning the politics of representation have been as significant as factual issues concerning what Samoan culture was really like.

The Taupou, or "Ceremonial Virgin"
The *taupou* system and the value of virginity to Samoans are among the most important issues in the Mead–Freeman controversy. According to Freeman, the taupou, or "ceremonial virgin," was one of the "most sacrosanct traditional institutions" (1983c:253). A taupou, usually the daughter of a high-ranking chief, was required to demonstrate her chastity in a public defloration ceremony just prior to her formal arranged marriage. Freeman states that the value of virginity embodied in the taupou extended beyond these

maidens to virtually all adolescent girls (1983c:236).

Freeman's extensive discussion of the taupou system is intended to refute Margaret Mead's portrait of the taupou as a girl of high rank whose virginity was closely guarded but who was the exception rather than the cultural rule in terms of virginity. Mead argued that, apart from the taupou and other daughters of chiefs, Samoan adolescent girls could and did engage in clandestine premarital sex.

Mead argued that the hymenal blood of the virgin, traditionally displayed at the defloration ceremony, could be counterfeited with chicken's blood, a point that Freeman adamantly rejects. Freeman dismisses not only Mead's account of faking hymenal blood by using animal blood, but also that of other observers. Augustin Kramer, whose work Freeman and indeed virtually all scholars of Samoa hold in high regard, found that in the 1890s the public defloration ceremony, at least in many areas, had become virtually extinct. In large part this was because the taupou themselves were eloping so often that few true virgins remained. Kramer continues: "For a public defloration now, either the maiden is still very young, or the old women resort to other means like *chicken blood,* shark's teeth, and so forth" (1902:36; emphasis added).

While Freeman quotes Kramer as stating that proof of a bride's virginity was "indispensable" (1983c:232), he does not mention this passage about the counterfeiting of virginity. Since Kramer is often cited by Freeman in support of his critique of Mead,

Freeman's omission of this relevant passage is striking.

The Ideal of Chastity

Freeman's emphasis on the enduring value of virginity is important at the level of public ideology. But this ideology was not monolithic and did not apply equally to all segments of Samoan society. In his own work, Freeman demonstrates that for young men there was a double standard. Adolescent males were permitted and encouraged to engage in premarital sex while at the same time protecting their sisters from potential suitors. Freeman states that young men were preoccupied with the taking of virginity (1983c:245). Success in deflowering virgins was not only "deemed a personal triumph" but also a "demonstration of masculinity" (1983c:245).

For young women, however, expectations about virginity were quite different. High-ranking young women were expected to be chaste, and punishments for transgressions could be severe. If young men were shamed by their peers for failure in seduction, young women were publicly shamed if they were seduced (Freeman 1983c:23). Yet this is not the case for all young women. According to Freeman, the ideal of virginity applied "less stringently to women of lower rank" (1983c:236). Thus, Freeman himself documents multiple and conflicting values concerning virginity for both young men and women.

Freeman's emphasis on the ideology of virginity is also misleading when it comes to the explanation of actual behavior. For example, Freeman quotes Bradd Shore as

stating that chastity was "the ideal of all women before marriage" (Freeman 1983c:239), and indeed Shore does discuss this public ideal, recognizing its symbolic importance for Samoans. But Shore also states, in passages that Freeman does not cite, that the ideal of virginity is frequently unrealized and that premarital sex, carefully hidden from public view, is "not uncommon" (Shore 1982:229–230). In an earlier piece, Shore found that "premarital sex is part of growing up for many Samoan boys and girls. . . . Privately, at least, many Samoan youth see sex as an important part of youthful adventure" (1981:197).

Freeman's own data on adolescent sexual activity do not support his claim that in Samoa, "the cult of virginity is probably carried to a greater extreme than [in] any other culture known to anthropology" (1983c:250). Referring to the virginity of female adolescents, Freeman notes that in a rural western Samoan village he studied, about 20 percent of fourteen-year-olds, about 30 percent of sixteen-year-olds, and almost 40 percent of seventeen-year-olds had engaged in premarital intercourse (1983b:124; 1983c:238–240). For Freeman, these percentages are not "inconsiderable," but he views them as "deviations" (1983a:7) or "departures" (1983b:124) from a strict public morality. These deviations, according to Freeman, are also viewed by Samoans as illicit and, if detected, are subject to social disapproval and punishment (1983b:124). Nevertheless, they are surprisingly common.

Conclusion

Whatever Mead's shortcomings, it is now apparent that Freeman's own history of sexual conduct in Samoa is

(continued)

DISCUSSIONS

The Mead–Freeman Controversy (*continued*)

open to criticism and that his argument is not well supported by many of the very sources that he uses to criticize Mead. Freeman's reading of the literature on Samoan sexual conduct is selective, and he omits passages that are not in accord with his restrictive characterization of Samoan sexual conduct.

Margaret Mead's argument is more in accord with the data available from a number of sources on Samoa than Freeman's. Yet Mead's account of the attenuation of the taupou system is very brief, and *Coming of Age* does contain errors of fact and interpretation, as well as overstatements. Given that it was a popular book initially published in 1928, this is not surprising. What is more surprising is how a senior scholar like Freeman, with his exten-

sive knowledge of Samoa, could allow serious omissions and overstatements to mar the work he had contemplated and researched for almost forty years.

Source: Adapted from Paul Shankman, 1996, "The History of Samoan Sexual Conduct and the Mead–Freeman Controversy," *American Anthropologist* 98:555–567.

---

may have to compete, so such attributes as "seeking attention" and "seeking dominance" may be more appropriate in these cultures.

Culture and Class One problem with the Six Cultures Study is that it oversimplified complex variables such as "aggression" and "nurturance" and obscured important differences within groups. In a later study of children in India, Susan Seymour (1992) observes that the Indian component of the Whiting and Whiting study represented only one caste and status group, a high-caste group of Rajputs from a northern Indian village. Seymour sampled households from a range of castes and socioeconomic statuses and noted that training of children from lower-class Indian families more closely fit the profile of the "simpler" societies in the Six Cultures Study, even though Indian society as a whole is complex in terms of task specialization and stratification. The household tasks lower-status Indian children are expected to perform prepare them for similar work that will have to be performed in their adult lives.

Seymour agrees that upper-class Indian children are not expected to perform household tasks such as carrying loads or caring for younger siblings, but she rejects the idea that training of upper-class children is lower in "responsibility." Upper-class boys and girls are expected to entertain guests and to perform well in school. Far from fostering egoistism, such tasks

train them in the behavior necessary to reinforce their family's place in the community. Upper-class children perform no routine household tasks because they will not be performing those tasks as adults. Seymour writes:

> Nonetheless, higher-status children in Bhubaneswar are expected to acquire other kinds of responsible behavior—namely, studiousness and the complex etiquette associated with hospitality. . . . They are being oriented to the world outside the family—not just for their own individual achievement but for the well-being of their families. (1992:366)

What about Fathers? Though brilliantly conceived for its era and scope, the Six Cultures Study was influenced by Western assumptions. For example, researchers did not systematically observe interactions between fathers and children or the influence of peer groups. The Western research bias excluding fathers from socialization studies is based on a family pattern developed in industrialized societies, in which working for wages separates fathers from their children. In nonindustrial societies, men's work may be performed in or around the home, so fathers interact with their children more consistently than fathers in industrial societies do.

L. L. Langness writes, "Fathers and husbands are far more absent from the ethnographic literature (indeed, they are amazingly absent from it) than they

Researchers in the culture-and-personality school were interested in the process of socialization, in which a child learns values and behaviors that shape his or her adult life. Socialization studies often reflect a Western bias by focusing on the interaction between mother and child, ignoring the role of the father and other members of the community. In this scene from Laos, a father bathes his son.

probably were from their families" (1993:46). Langness's observation is supported by his own research among the Bena Bena of New Guinea and is confirmed by Barry S. Hewlett's quantitative study of paternal child care among the Aka Pygmies of central Africa. Hewlett suggests that Aka fathers are intimately involved in child rearing: "The Aka are exceptional in comparison to other societies in that fathers are actively involved with infants and are second only to mothers in the amount of direct care to their infants" (1992:5).

Though the mother may be the primary caretaker in traditional societies, infants may also be cared for, and even suckled, by other women in the group. And nonparents, both men and women, take a more active part in caring for children than is the case in the United States, where children are considered in some sense to be the property of the parents. J. B. Watson (1983) describes this more generalized pattern of child rearing as **collective nurturance** or **community-as-parent.** In his ethnography of the Siane of New Guinea, R. F. Salisbury notes:

> After a relatively short period when young children are looked after exclusively by their mother, and when

they visit their father for fondling and affection, the training of children is undertaken by males and females generally, rather than by the elementary families. (1962:18)

The process of child rearing involves many variables, including the various aspects of parenting, the influence of peers, biological factors such as nutrition and illness, and extraordinary events such as the death of a parent or a natural disaster. The personality of a developing child is subject to a variety of influences, both internal and external to the individual and the group.

Anthropologists and psychologists no longer look upon a child as a "blank slate," a generic human on which an infinite array of possibilities can be imposed. Rather, learning—becoming enculturated—is a dynamic process in which experiences are selectively perceived and evaluated in light of associations with similar events. No matter how vigilant, a parent cannot control the variety of influences that may shape the experiences of a developing child. And no culture, however seemingly uniform, produces individuals who are stamped out of a mold.

CONFORMITY, DEVIANCE, AND TRADITIONAL HEALING

The culture-and-personality school has been criticized for many reasons—including oversimplifying the variables involved in studying culture—but one of the most pervasive criticisms is that it overestimated the degree of conformity within a culture. Anthropologists now know that in all cultures the range of tolerable behavior is broader than might be expected. Values and norms are idealized guidelines, and most people do not follow them exactly.

In all societies, values may be contradictory. How does one explain, for example, the fact that societies with the value "Thou shalt not kill" engage in long periods of continuous warfare in which many people are killed? During the Christian Crusades in the eleventh, twelfth, and thirteenth centuries, Europeans went to war for the stated purpose of defending their religion by winning the Holy Land from the Muslims. The Holy Land—or Middle East—is still

The Significance of Symbols in Vodou Ritual Trance Possession

"Blood-maddened, sex-maddened, god-maddened" is the way W. R. Seabrook described practitioners of Haitian *vodou* (voodoo or *vodun*) in 1929. Seabrook's evaluation was prompted by his observations of trance possession, a prominent feature of nearly all vodou ritual. An individual experiencing trance possession loses consciousness and engages in behavior considered bizarre by sedate observers. Contrary to Seabrook's lurid description, vodou trance possession is far from uncontrolled. The behavior expected of *possedés* (persons being possessed) is culturally prescribed and is reinforced by ritual instruction and social sanctions. Vodou symbols, expressed in a complex pantheon and acted out in rituals of trance possession, provide a means of coping with stress in a social context of poverty and powerlessness.

The Social Context

Vodou is a syncretic religion, which means that it combines two or more religious traditions. Reflecting Haiti's dual cultural heritage, vodou is a product of slavery and French colonialism. By the time France had acquired Haiti from Spain in 1697, the native population had been virtually eliminated. France repopulated Haiti with slaves brought from Africa. The population of Haiti today is composed primarily of the descendants of slaves and early French colonists, and the two-caste system generated by slavery is still evident in the social structure and in vodou symbolism.

Much has been written about the brutal poverty and depressing lifestyle of the Haitian peasant. Population pressure increasingly results in impoverishment of the land through overcultivation, and encroachment on forest lands causes erosion during the rainy season. Alfred Métraux (1958:32) describes how, while watching soil being washed away by a river, a peasant said to him: *"Voila notre vie qui s'en va"* ("That is our life going away," trans. Womack).

Roman Catholicism is the official religion of Haiti, as well as the religion of the elite. Peasants usually practice both vodou and Catholicism. Métraux (1958:287) was told by his informants: *"Il faut être catholique pour servir les loa"* ("One must be Catholic to serve the loa [possessing spirits]," trans. Womack). Vodou ceremonies are preceded by several Catholic prayers followed by hymns to the Virgin Mary and the saints.

Possession

At the top of the vodou pantheon is a supreme God, creator of the universe, an impersonal and vague force similar to "fate" or "nature." Vodou practitioners also worship a number of lesser deities, including twins, ancestral spirits, and *loa* (Iwa). The loa are derived from African deities, but their ranks have been augmented by spirits that first appeared in Haitian vodou. The loa can cure illness or cause it, can prevent misfortune or cause it, and can provide counsel and encouragement to their followers.

Possession occurs when a loa "enters the head" of an individual. In vodou terminology, the loa "mounts" his *cheval*, or "horse," the person being possessed. From the moment of possession, the thoughts and behaviors of the *possedé* (person being possessed) are attributed to the loa, and the possedé is not held liable for anything the loa does while in possession of his or her body. When the possedé's conscious self returns, he or she claims to remember nothing of the events that took place during the possession.

The identification with the loa is so complete that the possedé's physiological response is consistent with that of the loa rather than with his or her unpossessed state. "A person who is made ill by alcohol is possessed by deities who drink freely; a person crippled by rheumatism will dance with agility" (Bourguignon 1965:47). "[If] a male loa mounts a female devotee . . . she is addressed by a male name, wears male clothes, eats and drinks the things her loa prefers (no matter how distasteful to her ordinarily), and otherwise manifests his characteristics" (Leyburn 1966:150).

Individuals may become possessed outside the ceremonial context, usually during times of stress. "Storms, accidents, and medical emergencies often precipitate possession" (Ravenscroft 1965:179). At these times, the loa may function as a kind of guardian spirit or counselor. Under normal circumstances, however, the loa are not supposed to appear outside the ritual setting. "People whose spirits appear erratically are considered to be deranged and in need of treatment by a vodou specialist: clearly, something is wrong in the relationship between human and spirit" (Bourguignon 1976:17). La *folie*, or madness, is always considered to be sent by the loa, usually as punishment for neglecting them. Similarly, an individual who has unusually bad luck may be suspected of being negligent toward his or her family loa.

The Loa

Rada loa, whose origins can be traced to the Dahomean religion of West Africa, are considered to be tolerant and forgiving. *Pétro loa,* more violent than their Rada counterparts, developed under Spanish rule in Haiti. The two groups should not be interpreted as personifications of a dichotomy between "good" and "evil." It is a matter of style and degree rather than opposition: "The Rada loa are never called 'man-eaters.' They may kill to punish, but never, like some Pétro, simply for malice. . . . On the other hand, in the Pétro family, along with helpful and decent loa, there are some that eat humans" (Métraux 1958:78; trans. Womack).

One of the most striking aspects of vodou is the clearly defined character of each loa. "Each loa engages in a characteristic behavior pattern during possession. The *houngan* [vodou shaman] . . . can say at once what god possesses a person present" (Hurston 1938:142). No one has compiled a catalog of Haitian loa, and it is unlikely that such an endeavor could ever be completed. Every major region of Haiti has its own local variations, and new loa manifest themselves from time to time. However, a few loa are known throughout Haiti. Among these are Ogoun and Erzulie, both of whom illustrate the importance of possession in transcending the impoverished and powerless condition of most Haitian peasants.

Ogoun is patron of war, fire, and the power of recognized authority. It is said that he can protect his petitioners against bullets and other weapons. People possessed by Ogoun may demonstrate their invulnerability to wounds or burns by washing their hands in flaming rum or handling glowing bars of iron. Ogoun may manifest himself as a soldier or a politician; he also represents male fertility: "Women wishing children prostrated themselves before Ogoun and . . . he danced with them in a way to symbolize sex and procreation" (Hurston 1938:178).

Erzulie is a beautiful, rich woman of lavish tastes. She is light-skinned, and, when she possesses dark-skinned people, they cover their face with white powder. During possession, Erzulie's first act is to prepare a meticulous and time-consuming toilette. Then, sumptuously arrayed, she goes out to the gathering, escorted by several of the handsomest men. She walks languidly and gracefully, flirting with the men and snubbing all the women who are not her special devotees. "She has . . . been known to say—when there was no water to sprinkle on the earthen floor to settle the dust and cool the room—'Sprinkle perfume instead!'" (Deren 1970:141).

A vodou practitioner may be possessed by any number of loa during his or her lifetime or by a succession of loa during a single vodou ceremony. This built-in flexibility of the vodou pantheon allows the individual to act out various aspects of his or her personality in a number of ways. The possedé may take on the behavior of one of several clearly developed loa "types," most of which can manifest themselves in either the Rada or Pétro aspect. Since women can be possessed by male loa and vice versa, and because the loa are powerful, the possedé can transcend gender roles and class limitations by being possessed by a loa of the opposite sex or of a higher social class.

At the same time, each possessing loa has a recognizable, well-delineated personality and a place in the vodou pantheon in relationship to other loa. Thus, the loa embodies (or "enspirits") for the possedé an individual personality type within the framework of a clearly defined social role. Continuity in personality and social role is reinforced by the possession career, in which an individual learns how to "tame the loa" by establishing a close relationship of interdependency with a particular loa known as the *maît-tête,* or "master of the head."

Taming the Loa

From infancy, the Haitian peasant is exposed to vodou. He or she may be carried to ceremonies or dances and witness trance possession many times. By observing trance possession and overhearing adult conversations, a child learns vodou beliefs and expectations about appropriate behavior during possession. First possessions usually occur when the individual begins to take on adult responsibilities or in adolescence. First possessions are considered to be more violent than subsequent possessions, because the loa is *bossal,* or "wild." "Bossal possessions involve rolling about on the ground, because the loa, it is said, have not yet learned to stand or to dance" (Ravenscroft 1965:49).

At the time of a first possession, the possedé is carefully watched by the houngan or, if the possession takes place outside the ceremonial context, a houngan may be called to identify the possessing loa. This is a matter of vital importance, because the loa that first possesses the individual becomes his or her maît-tête. This loa will serve as the individual's protector and counselor, and there is believed to be an equivalence between the personality of the individual and that of his or her maît-tête.

A *laver-tête,* or head-washing ceremony, is performed soon after the first

(*continued*)

The Significance of Symbols in Vodou Ritual Trance Possession (*continued*)

possession to give the individual a measure of control over his or her maît-tête. The laver-tête is described as a baptism of the loa. It is a three-day ritual that begins with offerings of food and sacrifices to the loa who is maît-tête. The object of the laver-tête is to teach the devotee "how to marre, or 'tie,' his spirit, so as to enjoy the social aspects of a vodun dance without fear that his loa will come unbidden" (Herskovits 1937:146). As the "horse" becomes accustomed to his or her loa, transition to the possessed state becomes smoother and calmer, and the individual is supposed to acquire increasing control over the loa.

After the onset of possession during young adulthood, individuals maintain a steady and characteristic rate of possession throughout their active adult years. Some time between the ages of forty-five and sixty, individuals undergo a decline in frequency of possession and soon cease to become possessed at all: "Elderly people are rarely possessed, because, it is said, they have gained much knowledge and because the spirits are considerate in not imposing the fatigue of a possession trance,

with its dancing and sometimes acrobatics, on the elderly" (Bourguignon 1976:17). Kent Ravenscroft says the decline of trance possession coincides with a time of life when Haitians become "physically and socially dependent on their middle-aged sons and daughters, who traditionally serve them with great respect and attention" (1965:175). That is, Haitian vodou practitioners are most likely to experience regular trance possession when their adult responsibilities are greatest.

Symbolism and the Social Personality

In childhood, the individual is presented with a number of acceptable loa personalities. During the first trance possession, he or she experiences the loa in an intensely personal and impressive way. The loa is named with the assistance of the houngan. In naming the loa, the individual acquires a symbolic personality that provides an identity and position both in the vodou pantheon and with relationship to fellow vodou practitioners.

The affinity between the devotee and his or her loa is strengthened

during the laver-tête ceremony and in subsequent ritual possessions, as the individual learns to "tie" his or her loa. In the process, the possédé learns the importance of conforming to culturally appropriate standards of behavior, while at the same time gaining access to a culturally approved way of acting out turbulent emotions at a time when his or her social responsibilities are likely to be greatest.

In vodou, folie-like behavior is first encouraged and exploited for its psychotherapeutic value. It is then brought under control and finally extinguished through manipulation of symbols in the ritual of trance possession. The vodou pantheon permits unambiguous labeling of the social personalities of possédés. These named personalities are manipulated through the ritual of trance possession for the treatment of stress and personality disorders. The pantheon of possessing spirits is a symbolic representation of personality "types," through which the Haitian peasant expresses individual strivings and needs and learns to bring them into line with values of the group.

---

the site of much armed conflict among Christians, Jews, and Muslims, all of whom follow the commandment handed down through Moses: "Thou shalt not kill."

In fact, the commandment is interpreted by all concerned as relative—as it was also interpreted by Moses. According to the relative interpretation, the commandment is, "Thou shalt not kill except when

killing is deemed necessary to protect oneself, the family, members of the group, and/or the principles on which the group is established." "Thou shalt not kill" is the explicit value. The addendum "except when it is deemed necessary" is the implicit norm, and in Christian, Jewish, and Muslim countries, soldiers who refuse to fight are customarily executed as traitors.

Deviance and Healing

Human society is complex, and the values that shape a culture are complicated and contradictory. Individuals do not simply memorize rules for behavior; they learn often-elusive guidelines and gradually gain an understanding of the context in which the guidelines are appropriately applied. Yet, though values are mutable and subject to interpretation, all societies impose limits on the range of behavior that will be tolerated. In general, behavior is likely to be classified as **deviant** when it is so counter to norms that it is considered disruptive to the harmonious functioning of the group.

In Western societies, it is common to distinguish between intentional deviance (crimes) and unintentional deviance, which is viewed as being due to ignorance, accident, or illness. According to the Western medical model, illness may be classified as either physical or mental. In the United States, deviance is believed to result from some action or attitude of the deviant person and is treated as an individual problem rather than as an affliction of the group as a whole.

Most societies do not distinguish between physical and mental illness, nor do they necessarily draw a boundary between intentional and unintentional deviance. Treatment is usually aimed at identifying problematic relationships within the group. In these societies, the source of the problem is often attributed to outside agencies, such as ghosts or malevolent spirits. Traditional healers, or **shamans,** frame their diagnoses and treatments in symbolic terms. The use of symbols, which express complex ideas in simple, dramatic forms, allows the indirect expression of powerful emotional issues.

By attributing illness or problematic behavior to ghosts or demons, the shaman can defuse the powerful emotions generated by competing social interests and use symbols to treat a disorder within the social context. For example, a shaman may attribute the cause of an illness to "soul loss" and will then attempt to determine whether some enemy of the afflicted person has stolen the individual's soul through magical means. In so doing, the shaman diagnoses tensions underlying the illness or inappropriate behavior and treats the affliction by "healing" conflicts within the group.

Anthropologists have noted that indigenous healing systems, or traditional non-Western medical practices, make use of techniques similar to those used in Western psychotherapy. However, whereas in the Western medical model diagnoses and treatment are typically expressed in scientific or medical terminology, indigenous healing practices frame diagnoses and treatment in symbolic terms.

For example, a Western psychologist may use psychodrama to help a patient understand a problem by acting it out. A shaman, on the other hand, may enact a ritual drama by "journeying" into the world of spirits to battle the demons that afflict the patient. The "journey" is typically accompanied by drumming and dancing, ringing of bells, chanting, or other flamboyant actions, and the battle with malevolent spirits may be vigorously dramatized with gestures. The entire community often comes to watch, and the patient becomes both spectator and

Many traditional healers—such as this shaman from Borneo—use techniques similar to those of Western therapists, including psychodrama and catharsis. However, shamans make more direct use of symbolic images and language, often attributing bouts of illness to supernatural causes.

fully involved participant in the ritual, which symbolizes internal conflicts or problematic relationships with others, or both.

The Shamanic Journey

The shaman does not physically leave the room. Instead, the journey is through the unconscious mind, both that of the shaman and that of the patient, as well as through the unconscious attitudes of members of the group who may be present at the healing ceremony. Unconscious or subconscious thoughts are those that are below the surface of the individual's awareness or conscious mind. Claude Lévi-Strauss, whose theory of the binary organization of the human mind was discussed in Chapter 1, explains the effectiveness of shamanic healing in his book *Structural Anthropology*. Lévi-Strauss describes the case of a shaman among the Cuna Indians of Panama who guides a woman through a difficult and potentially fatal childbirth through the ritual use of symbols.

The shaman was called in after the midwife, a woman who normally attends births in many societies, determined that the woman in labor was in danger of dying. The shaman made ritual figures, chanted invocations, and purified the birthing room by burning herbs. At no time did he touch the woman's body. Instead, he crouched under the hammock where the woman was lying and chanted the story of his journey to the abode of Muu, the female power responsible for forming the fetus. The shaman "determined" that Muu had exceeded her function and captured the soul of the mother-to-be. If the shaman could not persuade or force Muu to release the woman's soul, she and her child would die.

The shaman then called on animal assistants to aid him in his journey to the abode of Muu and exhorted his spirit figures to help him rescue the soul of the woman's uterus:

> The (sick) woman lies in the hammock in front of you.
> Her white tissue lies in her lap, her white tissues move softly.
> The (sick) woman's body lies weak.
> When they light up (along) Muu's way, it runs over with exudations and like blood.

> Her exudations drip down below the hammock all like blood, all red.
> The inner white tissue extends to the bosom of the earth.
> Into the middle of the woman's white tissue a human being descends. (Lévi-Strauss 1963:190)

Lévi-Strauss suggests that the shaman's account of his journey into the abode of Muu is a description of the landscape of the woman's body, and that she understands this on a subconscious level. The woman then relaxes and allows the birth to take place unimpeded by her reactions to what Lévi-Strauss describes as "incoherent and arbitrary pains, which are an alien element in her system but which the shaman, calling upon myth, will re-integrate within a whole where everything is meaningful" (1963:197). Lévi-Strauss adds:

> The shaman provides the sick woman with a language, by means of which unexpressed, and otherwise inexpressible, psychic states can be immediately expressed. And it is the transition to this verbal expression—at the same time making it possible to undergo in an ordered and intelligible form a real experience that would otherwise be chaotic and inexpressible—which induces the release of the physiological process, that is, the reorganization, in a favorable direction, of the process to which the sick woman is subjected. (Lévi-Strauss 1963:198)

The journey described by the shaman is, in fact, the symbolic landscape of the woman's body. In her mind, the woman "followed" the shaman on his journey, and her unconscious understood the "landscape" to be the birth canal. Guided by the shaman, she relaxed in the terrain of her own body and allowed the child to be born. Or as the shaman put it, "Into the middle of the woman's white tissue a human being descends."

Altered States of Consciousness

To "journey" into the unconscious, shamans typically undergo an **altered state of consciousness,** a state of perceiving the world through a lens unlike that of ordinary consciousness. Some anthropologists prefer the term *alternative state of consciousness*, on the basis that the "normal" state of consciousness is a cultural construct, since we see what we are culturally programmed to see.

Everyone experiences altered states of consciousness in the form of dreams. One may also enter an altered state of consciousness through sleep deprivation, extreme states of joy, meditation, fasting, and consuming various types of chemical substances. Alcohol, tobacco, marijuana, peyote, LSD, and other types of chemicals induce an altered state of consciousness.

Shamans do not induce an altered state of consciousness for recreational purposes, as is often the case in the United States, because they are entering a world peopled by spirits that may be either beneficial or harmful. Just as one does not attempt to pilot an aircraft without learning to fly or to travel across the country without a road map, one does not enter the unconscious—the most dangerous terrain humans can explore—without a flight plan or the assistance of helpers.

Shamans are typically aided by animal or spirit beings, guides to the spirit world acquired during long years of training. The shamanic career usually begins with what Western psychotherapists would call a psychotic episode. The would-be shaman may be subject to delusions, confusion, or acute physical illness. In the United States, an individual undergoing such acute distress would be treated with medications and might be hospitalized. In non-Western societies, distraught relatives of the suffering individual would be more likely to call in an experienced shaman, who might diagnose the episode as a call from the spirits.

The neophyte shaman then undergoes a long period of training, often as long as twelve or fifteen years—the same amount of time as required for a medical degree in the United States—exploring his or her own subconscious terrain under the guidance of the experienced shaman. In the process, the shaman-in-training learns how to call on his or her experience of illness to heal the distress of others.

Not all individuals suffering a psychotic episode are diagnosed as potential shamans, just as not all such phenomena are treated successfully by Western therapists. However, anthropologists have noted that, in societies that have a shamanic complex, schizophrenia-like symptoms are considered treatable through shamanic training. In the United States, schizophrenia is considered a progressive disorder—that is, one that worsens over the lifetime of the individual—which has led some anthropologists to suggest that schizophrenics may be "failed shamans," in that they have not acquired the necessary training to manage their disorder in a way that could be used to heal others.

It should be noted that shamans are deviant in the sense that they do not fit the profile of "normal" individuals in a society. This fact illustrates the point that deviant, or exceptional, individuals may not be "failures," as members of the culture-and-personality school suggested. In fact, most outstanding individuals typically are deviant—including artists and other creative people, religious specialists, and exceptional leaders—in that they do not fit the profile of the **normative** person, one who conforms to the majority. "Deviants" quite often operate on the "dangerous" margins of society, where they critique, challenge, and often "heal" their more "normal" fellows.

SUMMARY

Culture begins to shape our lives even before we are born, since customs associated with pregnancy and childbirth affect our development in utero, and we are born into a world already shaped by cultural expectations about the nature of being human. We learn to "see" in the context of culture, which profoundly affects the way in which we perceive and order our world cognitively.

Cross-cultural differences in perception seem to exist, but they are difficult to measure objectively, since we cannot study perception directly and must rely instead on language—descriptions of what people consider relevant. There are differences in how people react to optical illusions and in how they order colors, and these differences probably are related to differences in socialization.

There is no such thing as "primitive" thought or a "primitive" culture, since people in all cultures must process complex information about their natural environment and their relationships with other people. However, anthropologists have identified some cognitive differences cross-culturally that may be related to the use of language. There are also cross-cultural differences in the way people conceive of the self, which is typically defined in a social context. Concepts of the self extend to perceptions of the body and may be used to negotiate a social role with varying degrees of power or autonomy.

Anthropologists have attempted to test Sigmund Freud's idea of the Oedipal complex cross-culturally. In the Oedipal complex, a boy develops a sexual desire for his mother and becomes jealous of his father. Bronislaw Malinowski argued that the Oedipal complex is related to the patrilineal inheritance patterns of Europeans and does not occur among the matrilineal Trobrianders. Instead, Malinowski noted, relations between Trobriand fathers and sons are warm and cordial, whereas a boy feels hostility toward his mother's brother, from whom he inherits property. Other scholars— including Melford Spiro, Allen W. Johnson, and Douglass Price-Williams—note that conflicts resembling the Oedipal complex show up in dreams of Trobrianders and myths of cultures universally.

The culture-and-personality school, developed by students of Franz Boas as a reaction to racism, asserts the importance of culture over biology in shaping behavior. During World War II, national character studies were conducted on the Japanese, Germans, and Russians. These were conducted at a distance. In addition, they tended to oversimplify the variables involved in studying cultures and to overestimate the degree of uniformity within a culture. Margaret Mead pioneered the study of socialization with her research among Samoan adolescent girls. This study has been labeled an example of "cultural determinism" and has been criticized for its oversimplification of data. However, it stands as a classic among culture-and-personality studies.

The Six Cultures Study, conducted by John and Beatrice Whiting, is a more systematic attempt to examine socialization cross-culturally, but it, too, is flawed by oversimplification of complex variables. In general, anthropologists agree that there is a relationship among childrearing practices, adult personality, and culture, but the relationship is difficult to define.

In recent years, through studies of indigenous healing systems, anthropologists have examined cross-cultural definitions of deviance and attempts to integrate deviant individuals into the society. These studies have revealed that shamans, or healers, use many techniques viewed as effective by Western psychotherapists, but shamans typically couch their diagnoses and treatment in the symbolic language of ritual. Shamans also treat the social group and do not isolate the deviant individual, as is common in Western practice. Shamans "journey" through the unconscious by means of altered states of consciousness, cognitive states in which ordinary ways of perceiving the world are suspended.

POWER WORDS

altered state of
   consciousness
bilingualism
biological
   determinism
cognition
collective
   nurturance
community-as-parent

culture-and-personality
   school
deviant
enculturation
illiterate
literate
medical model
national
   character

nonliterate
normative
perception
personality
psychological
   anthropology
shaman

INTERNET EXERCISE

1. To learn more about Margaret Mead's contribution to anthropology, check the website maintained by the American Museum of Natural History, where Mead worked from 1927 until her death in 1978: **http://www.amnh.org/Exhibition/ Expedition/Treasures/Margaret_Mead/mead. html.**

2. For an emic view of contemporary shamanic practice, consult the website Dancing Bear Way at **http://www.dancing-bear.com/shaman.htm.** Note that neither the author nor the publisher of *Being Human* endorses any particular form of shamanism, healing, or religious practice. For anthropological purposes, you should view a visit to this website as an ethnographic enterprise rather than a spiritual quest.

3. For an analysis of psychological disorders from the perspective of the Western medical model, visit the website on schizophrenia maintained by the National Institute of Mental Health (**http://www. nimh.nih.gov/publicat/schizoph.htm**). How does this differ from a shamanic or symbolic perspective in terms of explaining the causes for the disorder? In terms of treatment?

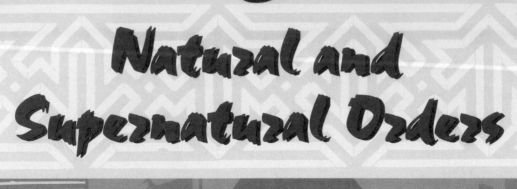

9
Natural and Supernatural Orders

In this chapter...

Myth: Symbolic view of the universe

Religious belief—or myth—describes the universe in symbolic terms. Creation myths provide a charter for society by explaining the origin of the world and the place of human beings in it. Cosmologies depict the universe, its landscape, and the human, animal, and spirit beings that inhabit it. Religious myths reflect the cultural values, social organization, and subsistence patterns of the society that produced them.

Ritual: The behavioral aspect of religion

Ritual is the symbolic behavior associated with religion. As do myths, rituals reflect the allocation of power and other social relationships within society. Rites of passage, which include rituals accompanying birth, puberty, marriage, and death, help ease the transition from one social state to another. Rites of intensification, including celebrations such as Christmas, Easter, Ramadan, and Passover, reinforce social solidarity. Divination aids in decision making and restores the social order in times of crisis.

Community: The social organization of religion

Religion operates within its social context, reflecting the organization of society as a whole and providing a microcosm of that society within the religious community. Leadership within religious groups is consistent with that of the larger society. Stratified societies give rise to priesthoods, which confer formal authority onto religious officials. Shamans, who base their power on their ability to contact spirits, are found in small-scale societies and in the interstices of complex societies. Demons and witches reflect tensions and conflicts characteristic of all social groups.

Religion and social change

Religion generally reinforces social stability, but all societies change, and religion can be a powerful agent for transformation. Periods of intense social crisis can produce revitalization movements, conscious attempts to promote culture change according to a coded value system. Though they are organized around social change, revitalization movements typically look to tradition for validation of their goals. European colonialism produced revitalization movements in many parts of the world; among the best known are the "cargo cults" of Melanesia.

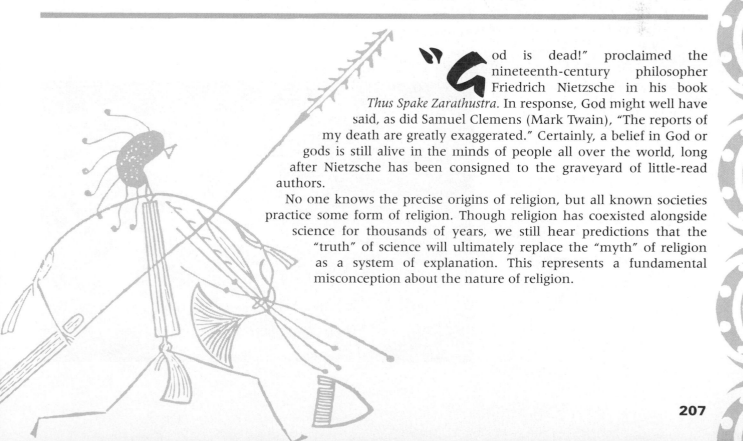

"God is dead!" proclaimed the nineteenth-century philosopher Friedrich Nietzsche in his book *Thus Spake Zarathustra*. In response, God might well have said, as did Samuel Clemens (Mark Twain), "The reports of my death are greatly exaggerated." Certainly, a belief in God or gods is still alive in the minds of people all over the world, long after Nietzsche has been consigned to the graveyard of little-read authors.

No one knows the precise origins of religion, but all known societies practice some form of religion. Though religion has coexisted alongside science for thousands of years, we still hear predictions that the "truth" of science will ultimately replace the "myth" of religion as a system of explanation. This represents a fundamental misconception about the nature of religion.

WHAT IS RELIGION?

Religion is defined as a set of beliefs and practices aimed at ordering the relationship of human beings to the supernatural. Though generally accurate, this definition is a little misleading, since the concept of "supernatural" has a Western bias. It suggests that the realm of gods and spirits is outside of or in opposition to the "natural," or physical, world. According to Judeo-Christian tradition, having once set the world in motion, God is constrained by "natural" laws from further intervention, except in rare cases when the natural laws are set aside so that miracles can be performed.

In most other societies, the existence and actions of gods and spirits are part of the natural order. Spirits have their place in the physical world just as humans do. In Japanese Shinto, for example, virtually every feature of the natural landscape, including trees, streams, mountains, caves, and rocks, is the abode of a spirit, or *kami*. In gardening, traveling, or going about their daily lives, people who practice Shinto must respect the rights of the kami who dwell among them. Australian Aborigines say that Westerners "sit" on the land; that is, Westerners are unaware that the land is alive and extends all the way to the sky and down to the center of the earth (Saenz 1994:395–397). In Western thought, the land is inanimate, or "dead," and consists only of that which can be seen.

Western theologians often speak derisively of beliefs that all of nature is living or contains a living essence. They dismiss such beliefs as "superstition." Anthropologists do not use the term *superstition*, an ethnocentric term that fails to consider the vitality and utility of non-Western religions. Symbolic views of the land as living reflect the experience of the people who depend on it for resources. The Australian Aboriginal view of the land as living is consonant with their kinship system, which links descent groups to foraging rights in a particular territory, as discussed in Chapter 1. The land plays a vital part in the material and social well-being of the people; therefore it is "alive."

Japanese beliefs about the importance of respecting the kami have allowed them to continue practicing intensive agriculture on islands where land is in short supply without destroying the natural beauty of the environment. Europeans, on the other hand, resorted to colonial expansion when their consumer needs overran the productivity of their land. And Europeans believe in many things that cannot be seen or proved—such as gravity.

Religion and Science

Religion and science are not competing belief systems (Table 9.1). Religious explanation is encoded in

Tibetan mandalas, or sacred circles, depict a universe centered on a particular Buddha manifestation. They unite the physical universe with a conceptual universe and the individual consciousness with mystic realms presided over by Buddhas, deities, and guardian spirits. Within the mandala, states of awareness are represented by the four directions—north, east, south, and west—which converge at the center of the mandala. Here, Tibetan monks have constructed a mandala dedicated to Kalachakra, who presides over time. After months of painstaking work, the monks are preparing to sweep the sand painting away, representing release from attachment to time.

Table 9.1 Parallel Domains of Religion and Science			
Systems of Meaning (Symbolic Systems)		**Systems of Information**	
Religion	Explanation	Science	Explanation
Magic	Manipulation/control	Technology	Manipulation/control

symbols, and religion is a system of meaning. Science provides a framework for systematically acquiring information about the physical world and testing that information through controlled observations. When applied to solving practical problems such as building a bridge or designing an airplane, science manifests as technology. Applied religion is magic. Both religion and magic are symbolic systems, but religion emphasizes explanation, whereas **magic** is a means of manipulation. In fact, the relationship between religion and magic falls on a continuum. All religions contain some magic, and all magical systems include some type of explanation.

In his study of the Trobriand Islands, Bronislaw Malinowski argues that all societies have technology, and all societies have religion and magic. However, not all societies have science, the self-conscious pursuit of information about the physical world. In *Magic, Science and Religion and Other Essays* ([1928] 1954), Malinowski notes that no society could survive without the technology necessary to provide for basic biological needs.

As noted in Chapter 3, Malinowski observed that Trobrianders are experts at the art of sailing. They can build outrigger canoes sturdy enough to sail across tumultuous ocean waves, and they can navigate by the stars. According to Malinowski, Trobrianders have "a whole system of principles of sailing, embodied in a complex and rich terminology, traditionally handed on and obeyed as rationally and consistently as is modern science by modern sailors" ([1928] 1954:30). However, no canoe is built or sailed without magic to ensure the safety of the craft. According to Malinowski, technology and magic are complementary systems that ensure the safety of Trobriand sailors on two fronts: technology is aimed at ensuring their physical safety; magic addresses their psychological safety, allowing them to perform their tasks without the distraction of fears for their personal safety.

My study of magic used by professional athletes (1982, 1992) confirms Malinowski's assertion that technology and magic are complementary approaches to performing tasks under conditions of physical and psychological danger. Professional and Olympic-level athletes are continually subjected to stress that most people encounter only in times of crisis. Auto racers risk their lives in every competition; a number of Grand Prix drivers I interviewed are now dead, killed in competition. Hockey players and football players risk serious injury every time they take to the ice or the field. At the same time, these athletes are subjected to public ridicule and scorn if they do not perform at levels beyond ordinary human capacities. I note: "[Magic] helps the player focus his attention on the task at hand. It can be used . . . to prevent anxiety or . . . the chanting of fans . . . from interrupting his concentration" (Womack 1982:200).

At the same time, my study confirms A. R. Radcliffe-Brown's (1939) view that religion and magic serve to maintain the stability of the social group. I write: "[Magic] helps establish a rank order among team members" and "directs individual motivations and needs toward achieving group goals" (Womack 1982:200). My study concludes that magic used by professional athletes mediates among a variety of concerns—including relationships with fans and other team members, physical danger, and risks associated with winning and losing—thereby reducing anxiety and allowing the athlete to focus on performance.

In keeping with his emphasis on the role of religion and magic in coping with psychological danger, Malinowski suggests that religion addresses the universal fear of death and the need to explain the importance of human life. He adds that religion is not escapist, but provides a positive force for self-preservation by affirming the continuation of life:

Man's conviction of continued life is one of the supreme gifts of religion, which judges and selects the better of the two alternatives suggested by self-preservation—the hope of continued life and the fear of annihilation. The belief in spirits is the result of the belief in immortality.

The substance of which the spirits are made is the full-blooded passion and desire for life, rather than the shadowy stuff which haunts his dreams and illusions. ([1928] 1954:51)

Religion, Magic, and Technology

Religion and magic do not replace technology in any society. People in the United States who thank God for their daily bread do not expect the Supreme Being to grow the wheat, grind it into flour, bake it into bread, and bring it to the table. They are well aware that those tasks must be performed by human hands. Instead, the prayer of thanksgiving acknowledges the limitations of human enterprise, which is dependent on vagaries of weather, economics, and social relationships.

The athletes I interviewed did not use ritual in place of practice or as a substitute for technological expertise. As one baseball player put it, "You can't just take somebody out of the stands and give them a ritual. You have to be a good athlete." Players were also sophisticated about the relationship between ritual and psychological preparedness. When I asked athletes why they used ritual, they almost invariably replied, "Because it helps me concentrate" (Womack 1982).

Similarly, the beliefs and rituals of Shinto priests, Australian Aborigines, Trobrianders, and others are not used in place of technology or as a substitute for subsistence skills. Rather, religion and magic call on forces that appear to transcend human limitations. Elsewhere, I write that religion is not "simply a mistaken attempt to deal with questions which can now be answered more accurately by science. . . . This view attributes too much power to science and too little to religion and, in so doing, shortchanges both" (1982:2):

Science is not framed in such a way as to address the global themes and moral concerns that are within the domain of religion. If religion makes an unacceptably biased science, science would be a hopelessly impoverished religion. (Womack 1982:2)

MYTH

Religious beliefs are *myths*, a term used differently in anthropology than in common parlance. **Myths** are symbolic stories about the nature of the world and the role of human beings in it. Whether or not myths are historically true—and some do contain important historical information—they are "true" in the symbolic sense. That is, they encode information about values and social relationships. Myths define the essential nature of human beings as seen by a particular culture.

Creation Myths

Creation myths describe the origins of the world and serve as a **social charter** to explain the organization of human relationships. For example, the second story of Genesis in the Bible, verses 2:1–25, which describes how humans came to be, states that Eve was created from Adam's rib. This is sometimes used to justify domination of females by males, but this interpretation ignores the first story of Genesis, which indicates that males and females were created at the same time: "God created [man] in [his] image . . . male and female [He] created them" (Gen. 1:27). Furthermore, the use of pronouns in English translations conveys the idea that God is masculine, whereas pronouns in the original Hebrew are often indeterminate or plural.

An anthropological analysis would note that the male emphasis is consistent with the fact that the people of the Bible were patrilineal, and the creation myth emphasizes the importance of the male line in patrilineal systems. Patrilineality is further expressed in later verses of the Bible, in which the line of descent is traced from father to son, and the names of mothers and sisters are rarely mentioned. This omission of women as co-genitors and siblings does not suggest that biblical chroniclers were ignorant of the importance of women in conceiving a child. Rather, it illustrates the importance of myth in defining relevant social relationships. Wives were acquired from outside the patrilineage, and sisters married outside their patrilineage. Therefore, they were less socially significant than males, who had the power and responsibility to carry forward membership in the lineage.

This issue is important because, for many years, anthropologists asserted that Australian Aborigines did not understand the role of biology in conception, on the basis that their stories of conception emphasized the importance of a woman's bathing in the ancestral waters and the father's dreaming of the child (see Chapter 1). In her study of the Tiwi of northern Australia, Jane Goodale (1971) noted that Tiwi women were quite sophisticated in their understanding of the biological aspects of conception, paternity, and childbirth. In fact, the average female Tiwi adolescent was apparently more knowledgeable about biological conception than most U.S. teenagers. Tiwi conception myths did not address biological conception, which they took for granted. Instead, their conception beliefs reflected the importance of the matrilineal descent group and the social importance of fathers in the lives of their children.

Among Masai cattleherders of Africa, women are not allowed to own cattle, though they tend cattle, which are owned by men. The Masai are polygynous, and each co-wife tends a portion of her husband's cattle in trust for her son. If a woman does not have a son, she may become impoverished when her husband dies. The Masai justify this system, which seems unfair to women, by saying that women lost the right to own cattle through carelessness. According to the Masai creation myth, cattle that once belonged to women—wildebeests and other hooved animals—now run wild in the bush because women were too lazy to take care of them. This creation myth justifies ownership of cattle by men and attributes women's economic dependence on men to women's own shortcomings. Women, as well as men, accept this explanation for their dependent social role.

Cosmology and Society

Creation myths typically include a **cosmology,** a symbolic description of the universe. The cosmology describes a landscape and the beings—animal, human, and spirit—that inhabit it. The nature of the symbolic universe and the relationship of humans to other beings are shaped by the subsistence pattern and social organization of the culture in which the cosmology developed.

The part of the Bible often called the Old Testament developed among pastoral nomads who figured their descent patrilineally and engaged in warfare with settled agriculturalists. We know much of this from their creation myths and their cosmology, as well as from their accounts of their travels and their poetic descriptions of their relationship to God.

When King David sings, "The Lord is my shepherd; I shall not want. He maketh me to lie down in green pastures; he leadeth me beside the still waters" (Ps. 23), he is using metaphors characteristic of pastoralists: the Lord takes care of us as we take care of

our sheep. In the book of Genesis, God gives Adam dominion over "the fish of the sea, the birds of the air, and all the living things that move on the earth." This represents a world view in which animals are either dependent upon human beings or in competition with us.

This concept would not be found among foragers, who do not have dominion over animals or plants. The Ainu of northern Japan called bears, wolves, foxes, and owls "mountain people" and viewed them as deities. Animals, like people, were seen as having souls. After an animal was killed and eaten, its bones had to be treated with the same respect accorded to a human corpse. The animals were given a ceremony much like a funeral, and their bones were saved in a bone pile much as human bodies in Western society are consigned to cemeteries (Ohnuki-Tierney 1974).

Foragers typically view animals as equal or even superior to themselves and often consider them to have human characteristics. There are many stories among traditional forager groups in North America that describe the transformation of an animal into a human being or vice versa. In many cases, the close association between humans and animals allows humans to acquire animal guides or helpers. A story of the Inupiat of Alaska relates how a poor hunter is transformed into a good hunter because of the aid he gives a wounded polar bear. The man sees a polar bear on the ice and prepares to kill it, but the bear says, "Don't shoot me. If you follow me and do what I say, I will make it so you will always be able to get whatever animals you think about." The man climbs on the bear's back and is taken under the sea. They eventually emerge onto the ice and arrive at an igloo, where a second polar bear lies injured with a spear in its haunch. The first bear takes off the "parka" it is wearing and becomes a man. The hunter removes the spear from the second bear and heals its injury. The first bear then dons its bearskin "parka" again and transports the hunter back to the place of their first encounter. From that day on, the man was always successful in the hunt (Chance 1966). This story emphasizes a characteristic of the forager way of life: the interdependency of humans and animals. In other forager societies, such as the Tiwi, people may consider themselves descendants of a totemic animal ancestor, another view of the world that stresses the close association of animals and people.

Many **agrarian,** or agricultural, people see life as a cyclical process that duplicates the planting cycle. The

Hopi Pueblo people of the U.S. Southwest compare the life of humans to the life of corn, their staple crop. When planting the corn, and during its early life, the Hopi talk to the corn and sing to it so it will grow up in a cheerful environment. When the corn stalk develops tassels, it is considered to be a young maiden, and when it ripens, the ears of corn are thought to be its children.

When a Hopi woman marries, her garment is decorated with tassels like that of the corn, and her wedding gown will eventually become her shroud, symbolic of her role in passing on life to her children. Similarly, the women in the bride's family weave a basket for her husband that will be used to "spin him up to the clouds" when he dies. The Hopi believe that when they die they join the *kachinas,* spirit figures who come back to the earth with the rain. Throughout their lives, the Hopi see their own lives reflected in the life cycle of the corn, and when they die, they give life to the corn—and therefore to their people—through rain.

The Hindus of India are among the first settled agriculturalists, and their belief in reincarnation, or rebirth through a series of lives, is related to the apparent death and rebirth of the plants they cultivate. Hindus also see the "life" of the universe itself as a cycle of creation and destruction. This process is symbolized in three powerful male gods: Brahma the creator, Vishnu the sustainer, and Siva the destroyer. Since Hindus believe that all the universe is the play of the gods, Vishnu is often worshipped in the form of Krishna, who expresses playfulness through such manifestations as a mischievous child, a flute player, and an ardent lover. The symbolism of Siva appears dualistic to the Western eye. He is both destroyer and creator. This apparent dualism is less problematic for Hindus, who consider destruction the essential first step to creation. Just as the fields must be cleared for planting, the crumbling universe must be cleared of debris before creation can begin.

Agriculturalists are concerned with fertility, so each Hindu god must have a female counterpart. Brahma's consort is Saraswati, the goddess of learning. Krishna is linked romantically with several females, but his relationship with Radha epitomizes romance in Hindu mythology. Radha and Krishna are believed to incarnate as human lovers in each generation and are often linked as Radha-Krishna. In Vishnu's incarnation as Rama, his wife is Sita, goddess of agriculture. Siva is both the great ascetic and the symbol of virility, represented in the *lingam,* the male sex organ. His consort is Sakti, the essence of female power.

Female gods characteristically play an important part in the cosmology of agricultural societies because of women's ability to bear children, which is associated with the fertility of the land. In Hindu mythology, the earth is female and is fertilized by rain, which falls from the male sky. The Hopi associate the swelling of the earth when seeds are about to break through the ground with the swelling of a woman's belly when she is pregnant.

Female gods are also important in the lives of foragers, who are aware that the fertility of female animals is essential to abundant supplies of game animals. One of the most important deities among the Ainu was Grandmother Hearth, also known as Fire Grandmother, who was not only protector of the household but also mediator between the Ainu and all the other gods. In the Ainu pantheon, Grandmother Hearth was second only to the bear deities, who were important to Ainu subsistence.

Spirit Beings and Forces

The French sociologist Emile Durkheim once suggested that religion is social organization projected into the heavens. As Durkheim puts it, "Religion is something eminently social. Religious representations are collective representations that express collective realities" (1915:22). This reasoning explains why David, the warrior king of the Bible, declared God to be "mighty in battle" and "the Lord of hosts; he is the king of glory" (Ps. 24). David was comparing the dominion of God with his own reign and the "hosts" of the Lord with his own armies. After a defeat in battle, David laments: "O God, you have rejected us and broken our defenses" (Ps. 60).

It would be an overstatement to suggest that social organization determines cosmology. However, it would be difficult for a forager, whose world view is shaped by relatively egalitarian social relationships, small group size, and sporadic quarrels rather than large-scale warfare, to envision an all-powerful god who commands huge, well-disciplined armies. Among !Kung foragers of Africa, for example, a variety of gods with varying degrees of power are thought to maintain the delicate balance between life and death, sickness and health, rain and drought, abundance and scarcity. Marjorie Shostak writes:

> Both the greater and lesser deities are modeled on humans, and their characteristics reflect the multitude of possibilities inherent in the human spirit. Sometimes they are kind, humane, and generous; at other times, whimsical, vindictive, or cruel. Their often erratic behavior is thought responsible for the unpredictability of human life and death. (1981:291)

All social groups are sometimes afflicted by quarrels and factional disputes, and these apparent disruptions of the social order are often personified as demons. Our lives are also troubled by what appear to be whimsical forces in nature, which find expression as cosmic personalities. In most societies, the world is "peopled" with supernatural beings of many types. Among them are gods, demons, ghosts, and ancestor spirits.

In addition, our bodies are inhabited by souls, often considered to be the essential element of human life. Beliefs about spirit beings vary considerably from one society to another, so that it is virtually impossible to sort into neat categories the vast array of spirit beings known to people throughout the world. It is possible, however, to make some qualified generalizations about the characteristics of the supernatural.

Supernatural Power and Natural Forces Gods, or **deities,** are spirit beings who have varying degrees of power to affect human life. Their interest in doing so may differ considerably from one society to the next. Even within a single society, some gods may be more closely involved in human life than others. Concepts regarding the power of gods are related to the amount of power individuals can exercise within a particular society. Gods with considerable ability to exercise power are found in stratified societies. Thus, the power of the Judeo-Christian God is absolute, and the Hindu god Siva can summon up the force to destroy the world. These characterizations are consistent with the power of rulers in a stratified society.

The Greek god Zeus, on the other hand, was able to exercise only the power accruing to the head of an extended family. He was constrained by the wishes of his wife, Hera; his children, including Artemis and Apollo, often went their own unruly ways. The interrelationships of the gods in the Greek pantheon are consistent with the dynamics of the Greek extended family. The *kami*, or gods of Japanese Shinto, are even more limited in their powers, in many cases

In the world view of Tibetan Buddhism, the universe contains powerful forces, both malevolent and beneficent. The horrific mien of this deity marks it as extremely powerful, able to drive away demons or to burn away the confines of the human ego.

presiding over a single natural feature, such as a mountain or a stream.

Gods who preside over a limited area or feature are often called **nature spirits.** Philip L. Newman describes nature spirits among the Gururumba of New Guinea: "They are male, and occur in a number of fantastic human forms such as half-men, bats with human heads, or with long hair covering their bodies. They may also change from one form to another even including the fully human form" (1965:63). Nature spirits are rarely seen since Gururumba believe they are transparent like smoke or mist.

The Gururumba are horticulturalists whose subsistence centers on growing yams and tending pigs. Gururumba men are cautious when venturing through an area believed to be inhabited by a nature spirit, because the spirit may attack to defend its territory, just as humans can be expected to attack if an intruder enters their territory. An attack by a nature spirit may cause illness or death. Gururumba may also enlist the aid of a nature spirit to ensure good health or productive gardens by entering into a reciprocal exchange agreement. Newman writes:

> The man provides the spirit with a house, food from each of the gift exchanges he initiates, and information about his gardening activities and the disposition of his pig herd. In return the spirit takes a proprietary interest in the man's gardens and pigs. It protects the gardens against theft and rides herd on the pigs when they are not under human supervision. It may even "doctor" the pigs if they are ill or receive an injury. (1965:63)

Reciprocal exchange agreements between men and nature spirits mirror those between human males who wish to form alliances.

Gods serve a number of functions in human life. They may be creators of the universe, serve as protectors, provide resources necessary for human survival, or maintain order in society through their power to punish humans for wrongdoing.

Personifications of Conflict and Danger   Demons are negative forces. In many cases, they challenge the power of the gods, as in the case of Satan, who in Christian theology challenges God's dominion over the earth. Religious scholars have traced the origins of Satan to Zoroastrianism, the state religion of the old Persian Empire. Zoroastrians visualize the world as the scene of a great battle between Good and Evil. The armies of Good are commanded by Spenta Mainyu, and the forces of Evil are commanded by Angra Mainyu, also known as Ahriman. Both spirits emanate from the one true god, Ahura Mazda. The battle between Spenta Mainyu and Angra Mainyu mirrored the ongoing wars between the Persians and their neighbors, especially the Turks. Persian rulers were depicted as fighting on behalf of Good, whereas opposing rulers were seen as fighting on behalf of Evil. The eleventh-century Persian poet Ferdowsi often referred to Turkish rulers as "Ahriman," the human manifestation of the Evil Spirit.

In Hindu theology, the armies of demons once rose up against the gods. Finding themselves sorely challenged, the gods pooled all their energies to create a new being capable of doing battle with the demons. In Hindu belief, active energy is feminine and latent energy is masculine, so the new god was female. Durga was a beautiful woman who rode into battle on the back of her lion and killed the demon army with the aid of her violent aspect, Kali, who sprang from Durga's forehead in the heat of battle.

Satan, Ahriman, and Durga are all products of stratified societies, which are able to do battle with great armies. More egalitarian societies, such as those found among foragers and horticulturalists, typically cannot maintain a standing army, and their demons are correspondingly more limited in their powers. The Wamirans, horticulturalists who live on the southeastern coast of New Guinea, attribute food shortages to Tamodukorokoro, a "monster" who lived among them in a past time. Tamodukorokoro was a "hairy, ugly ogre" who once supplied the people with abundant food. According to legend, the Wamirans feared the ogre, so they chased him away and have been cursed with a shortage of food ever since (Kahn 1994). Tamodukorokoro, like most people, has both good and bad characteristics. He provides food, but he commands no armies and lays waste to no cities. Like humans, whose powers are limited, Tamodukorokoro has only a limited, though often frustrating and negative, influence.

Animating Spirits   Souls are the animating spirit of humans. In some societies, animals and plants may also have souls. The number of souls animating human beings varies from one society to another. The Yanomamö of Venezuela and Brazil believe that humans have three souls and an animal counterpart or alter ego. If an individual's animal alter ego is killed, the human dies also. Practitioners of Haitian vodou (voodoo) believe that humans have two souls: a *'tit bon ange* that animates the body and a *gros bon ange* that is the source of conscious awareness. Because the body is animated by a different spirit than the consciousness, a person or being who captures the *gros bon ange* can control the person's body.

Having one's body possessed by another can be either positive or negative. In spirit possession, a *loa* (conceived of as either a deity or an ancestor spirit) displaces an individual's *gros bon ange* and inhabits the person's body. The possessing spirit can then enjoy the company of humans, dance with them, and accept their gifts. By surrendering her or his body to a possessing loa, a vodou practitioner gains favors and protection from the spirit.

There is a negative aspect to having two animating spirits, however. If one's *gros bon ange* is captured by another human, one who is skilled in the art of vodun and has malevolent intent, the individual becomes a zombie whose body is subject to that person's command.

Spirit possession, the idea that one's body can be controlled by a spirit being other than one's own soul or souls, is a common religious belief cross-culturally, though the experience can be viewed as either positive or negative. Born-again Christians believe that they can be saved from eternal damnation only by being "slain in the spirit." Typically, this involves surrendering oneself to the Holy Spirit, which may manifest through convulsions and "speaking in tongues," or glossalalia. A possessing spirit may also manifest itself in a negative sense by causing illness in the possessed person or by causing that person to behave in inappropriate ways.

Many societies attribute illness to *soul loss.* It is believed that the soul can either be captured by a malevolent being, through sorcery, or when the soul goes wandering in one's dreams. If the soul is captured or does not return, the person sickens and dies. In Chapter 8, we described the journey of a shaman into the spirit world to rescue the soul of a woman who was having a difficult childbirth.

Among the Aymara of Bolivia, diseases may be attributed to soul loss, or *susto,* magical fright. The *animo,* one of three souls a person possesses, is lured back into the body by placing an article of the patient's clothing a short distance from his or her house, along with the contents of llama entrails, gall stones diluted in holy water, and ritual foods. The shaman and his assistant, at least one friend or relative of the patient, then retreats to the patient's house, where they call the animo, while offering it libations of alcohol and tossing pieces of wool that has been spun in reverse to the wind. The patient is supposed to be asleep during this time to allow the animo to enter his or her body. When the person's animo arrives, the shaman and his assistant immediately envelop it in the patient's clothing and place the clothing by the patient, while making him drink some of the holy water and washing his face. Then the patient is dressed in the clothing (Buechler and Buechler 1971:102).

Spirits of the Dead   In all societies, when a soul leaves the body, it takes on another kind of social identity, depending on whether the spirit is believed to maintain its relationship of interdependence with the social group or whether it detaches itself from society. Spirits of dead relatives who maintain their social relationships are **ancestor spirits.** Those who surrender their social responsibilities are **ghosts,** especially if they stay around and trouble the living. The ghosts' lingering is usually believed to be due to some unresolved conflict or some unfulfilled responsibility. The Yanomamö believe that one aspect of the soul travels to an upper layer of the world after the death of the body, whereas another aspect goes to live a wandering life in the rain forest. Some of the wandering spirits become malevolent and attack people who travel in the forest at night (Chagnon 1992).

Lyle B. Steadman and colleagues (1996) argue that beliefs that spirits of the dead continue to interact with living human beings, either to aid or to harass them, are universal. They also state that "claims of communication between the living and the dead appear to occur universally," adding that ancestors are also the source of an indigenous society's traditions, providing guidance on "how to relate to one's physical and social environment" (1996:73).

Spirits of the dead may be described by a variety of terms, including *ghosts, shades, spirits, souls, totemic plants and animals,* or merely *the dead,* depending on the cosmology of the particular society. Steadman and his colleagues suggest that totemic plants and animals are "clearly ancestral in that they identify a person with a line of ancestors" (1996:63). Ancestors reflect the importance of kinship in human life. Just as kinship rules establish important relationships of interdependency among living human beings, ancestral beliefs extend the network of interdependency to the realm of the dead. For example, the belief in a founding totemic animal ancestor among Australian aborigines reinforces the solidarity of a particular descent group and validates its claim to a particular territory.

Impersonal Forces   Not all aspects of the supernatural world are personified. **Mana** is a Polynesian concept that power resides in certain persons, places, and objects. Whereas gods, demons, and other spirit beings are believed to have human or animal characteristics, mana is impersonal. It is conceived of as a formless force that is neither good nor evil in and of itself. There can also be differing degrees of power residing in humans, places, and objects. A person with little mana can be harmed by coming into contact with a person, place, or object that has a great deal of mana.

The belief that members of the Hawaiian royal family had mana helped to reinforce the power of the chief. Hawaiian lineages were ranked in social importance according to how closely they were related to the chiefly lineage. According to the same criterion, lineages were ranked with respect to mana. Members of lineages closely related to the chiefly lineage were believed to have more mana than members of lineages more distantly related. Members of the chiefly lineage were believed to have a great deal of mana, whereas commoners were believed to have very little. It was believed that a commoner who touched a member of the chiefly lineage would sicken and die. Thus, the chief was set apart from his subjects in terms of both secular and sacred power.

More recently, the idea that mana is associated with certain places has helped the Hawaiians, who have lost most of their land to descendants of missionaries and colonizing merchants, fight back against those they view as outsiders. When a modern hotel or high-rise building suffers some disaster, such as a fire or damage from flooding, indigenous Hawaiians may suggest that builders have offended a local spirit. In retaliation, the mana of the spirit or place has attacked the offending building.

One of the most powerful places in Hawaii in terms of mana is the volcano Mauna Loa, which is sacred to the goddess Pele. The site is now administered by the National Park Service, and it is illegal to take chunks of lava away from the park. It is also "dangerous" to steal from a goddess or a place with so much mana. According to U.S. park rangers, they receive shipments of lava daily from all over the world accompanied by notes that read: "I took this from Mauna Loa and I have had bad luck ever since. Please return this to the volcano" (Michael O'Sullivan, pers. comm., 1988). Thus, people who flout the power of secular authorities eventually submit to the mana of Mauna Loa.

The Mutability of Spirit Beings and Forces

Mana is an impersonal force, but, in general, most symbolic representations of the supernatural are personified. Spirits are seen as conscious beings with motivations and attributes much like those of humans. For example, the God of the Bible proclaims in the Ten Commandments: "I the Lord thy God am a jealous God" (Exod. 20:5). And many Christians and Jews envision God as an old man with a flowing beard.

However, the Judeo-Christian God, the Islamic Allah, and the Hindu Brahman (the creative force underlying all reality; not to be confused with Brahma, the creator god) defy simple representation, appearing to have both personal and impersonal aspects. The esteemed twelfth-century Jewish scholar Maimonides cautioned against attempting to define God's attributes, stating that the true nature of God transcends the ability of humans to conceptualize it:

> He is a simple essence, without any additional element whatsoever; He created the universe, and knows it, but not by any extraneous force. There is no difference whether these various attributes refer to His actions or to relations between Him and His works; in fact, these relations . . . exist only in the thoughts of men. (1956:74)

References to the Creator in Genesis often make use of Hebraic pronouns that are equivalent to *it* or *they*. The commonly used pronoun *he* in English translations reflects the limitations of the English language with reference to nongendered pronouns. Maimonides anticipated by eight centuries the view of anthropologists that spirit beings are symbolic entities whose form represents the realities of human experience.

Islamic conventions reject personifications of Allah, though this entity is seen as having such attributes as generosity. The Hindu concept of Brahman, or Ultimate Reality, is explicitly nonpersonal. It is neither male nor female. Instead, it is the creative force underlying the universe. The manifest universe is feminine, sometimes referred to as *Mahamaya*, the Sanskrit term for "great illusion." The "great illusion" is the idea that form is "real" in a limited sense. In Hindu belief, all physical manifestations—humans, animals, the earth, air, and even the great gods—ultimately are Brahman.

The Hindu view of Ultimate Reality, or Brahman, is similar to the theory of Western physicists that all matter is ultimately energy. The difference is that Hindus see energy as conscious—or self-aware—whereas physicists view energy as merely "physical." This distinction reflects the difference between religion and science discussed earlier in this chapter. Though Hindu theology and scientific theory conceptualize the nature of the universe in virtually identical terms—as energy—the religious view emphasizes Ultimate Reality in terms of its meaning and relevance for human life. The scientific view of energy, on the other hand, is concerned not with what it means for human life but with its utility for explaining natural phenomena.

RITUAL

For most people, religion comes alive through the practice of ritual, or symbolic behavior. **Ritual** is behavior that is repetitive, sequential, nonordinary, and "powerful." Because ritual is *repetitive,* innovation is generally not tolerated. Ritual is expected to conform to tradition and to be performed the same way each time. Some Roman Catholics in the United States are still unhappy over the church's decision in the 1960s to hold religious services in English. They feel that because of this change the ritual of the Mass has lost much of its meaning. In this case, "meaning" is experienced as the emotive power of the ritual. It has little or nothing to do with the "meaning" of the words used in the ritual. It matters less that devotees understand the words than that they understand the "meaning" of the Mass.

Ritual is *sequential,* which means it has an order of performance that must be adhered to. "Amen" must be recited at the end of a prayer, not at the beginning. Even though people who recite the prayer may not know the literal meaning of *amen,* they know its symbolic meaning, which is to underscore the importance of the prayer. Similarly, in reciting the Lord's Prayer, one must say it in proper order: "Our Father which art in heaven, Hallowed be thy name. Thy kingdom come . . ." It is inappropriate and even disrespectful to transpose or omit any part of the prayer.

Ritual is *nonordinary,* which means it is set apart from ordinary reality by time, space, or exaggeration. It takes place in a sacred place at a sacred time. Most Christian services take place in a church on Sunday. The Jewish Shabbat, or sabbath, is observed in the home on Friday night and at temple on Saturday. Ritual may also be distinguished from mundane reality through exaggeration. The ritual meal eaten by Jews on Friday night in observance of Shabbat is set apart from ordinary meals by prayer, the types of foods eaten, and the stylized participation of all members of the family.

Ritual is considered to be *powerful* by those who perform it. There is no such thing as "just a ritual." Rituals are neither empty nor meaningless. They have the "power" to change the world, either by intervention of supernatural entities or by transformation of the participant. Chinese Buddhists pray for help from Kuan Yin, often called the goddess of mercy, in times of danger or need, and they believe she will always come to their aid. One prays to a god or gods in expectation that those entities will hear the prayer. In any event, the prayer transforms the relationship of the individual to the deity and, in many cases, to the people around him or her.

Religious ritual takes place within a social context. It reflects the values of a particular society and provides a means of transmitting those values through the generations. According to Victor Turner, "Ritual . . . is precisely a mechanism that periodically

Religion is a symbolic system, which means that religious beliefs and customs evoke emotion and define boundaries between groups. The Israeli women in this photo are praying at Jerusalem's Western Wall, known as the Wailing Wall or *Kotel.* The practice of praying out loud is traditionally taboo for women, but the Israeli Supreme Court had earlier ruled that women could pray out loud, read from the Torah, and wear the prayer shawl known as the *tallit.* The ultra-Orthodox woman at the right is heckling them, and Orthodox men and women accused the women of "destroying the people of Israel."

converts the obligatory into the desirable" (1967:30). He adds:

> In the action situation of ritual, with its social excitement and directly physiological stimuli, such as music, singing, dancing, alcohol, incense, and bizarre modes of dress, the ritual symbol . . . effects an interchange of qualities between its poles of meaning." (1967:30)

Rituals vary according to function. Rites of passage accompany a change from one social state to another. Rites of intensification typically occur on a cyclical basis and serve to reinforce the solidarity of the group. Divination is aimed at diagnosing the cause of illness within individuals and times of crisis within the group. All three types of ritual serve to enhance the smooth functioning of the group and to provide for remedies in times of danger.

Rites of Passage

According to Arnold van Gennep, **rites of passage** are "ceremonial patterns which accompany a passage from one situation to another or from one cosmic or social world to another" (1960:10). In the lives of individuals, changes of state include birth, puberty, marriage, and death. According to Turner (1967), such periods of transition are socially "dangerous" because they involve a realignment of the position of the individual with respect to society. Societies may also undergo a "dangerous" change of state, as when a group goes to war or is conquered by another group.

Times of social, psychological, and physical danger are typically rendered "safe" through ritual. Van Gennep suggests that all rites of passage can be divided into three phases: *separation*, *marginality* (or *liminality*), and *incorporation* or *aggregation*. In the first phase, the individual or group is ritually separated—or torn away—from the previous state. In some cases this separation is literal, as in the practice of bride capture, in which a bride is ritually "stolen" from her family. In other cases, the tearing away of status is symbolic, as when initiates into religious groups submit to shaving of the head and surrender secular status by giving up clothing and attire associated with the secular life.

Following Mary Douglas's idea of purity and danger, Turner (1967) notes that the middle, or liminal, phase of rites of passage is the most socially and

A lama, or Buddhist priest, conducts a cremation ceremony in Nepal. This is a rite of passage; it marks the transition from one social state to another. Rites of passage include baptisms, naming ceremonies, and various types of puberty rituals, as well as marriages, initiations, and funerals.

symbolically dangerous because the individual or group in transition is "betwixt and between," belonging to no clearly defined social category. Douglas writes, "If uncleanness is matter out of place, we must approach it through order" (1966:40). In times of social danger, ritual symbols impose order on the chaos of uncertain social status—as is characteristic of the liminal phase of rites of passage—by encoding cultural values.

In his study of puberty rites among the Ndembu of Africa, Turner notes that initiates in the middle phase of these rites of passage are structurally "invisible." They have no social identity, since a "society's secular definitions do not allow for the existence of a not-boy–not-man, which is what a novice in a male puberty rite is" (1967:95). Thus, an initiate may be treated as though he is dead:

> The neophyte may be buried, forced to lie motionless in the posture and direction of customary burial, may be stained black, or may be forced to live for a while in the company of masked and monstrous mummers representing . . . the dead, or worse still, the un-dead. (Turner 1967:96)

Virtually all rites of passage include a period of seclusion when the individual in transition is considered unclean or "dangerous." In many societies, women undergo a period of seclusion after giving birth. In the United States, it is considered unlucky for anyone outside the immediate family to see the bride on the morning of her wedding. At this time, she is "betwixt and between," neither married nor single. The bride remains in seclusion—typically with females of her family or with close female friends—until she walks down the aisle. She remains veiled until her new husband lifts the veil after their marriage has been officially proclaimed.

During incorporation or aggregation, the third phase of rites of passage, the initiate assumes a new social identity, often symbolized by taking a new name. Among the Sambia of New Guinea, the names of initiates in male puberty rites are changed near the end of the seven-day ceremony after completion of purification rites, which include a public ritual beating and nose-bleeding ceremony (Herdt 1987). With the assumption of a new social identity, the initiate is once again "pure" and "safe," able to take his place within the society.

Not all rites of passage are so formal. Some rites of passage attend a significant event in the life of the

Critical periods in the lifetime of a society's members are commonly marked by rites of passage. Shown here are youths of the Xavante people, in South America, during their initiation into adult status.

individual. The Barabaig of Tanzania, of East Africa, traditionally celebrated a young man who killed an "enemy of the people." Enemies of the people included lions, elephants, rhinos, cape buffalo, and members of other tribes. A killer of an "enemy of the people," or *ghadyirochand,* was rewarded by "gifts of livestock from his relatives and people living in the vicinity of the kill" (Klima 1970:58). The man was also adorned with regalia celebrating his new status as a "killer," including a "heavily beaded leather cap with a long curving strip of brass symbolizing the tail of a lion (Klima 1970:59). Klima writes:

> Upon making a kill, the young man returns to his parents' kraal and sits down outside the gate, singing his kill-song, *ranginod,* while waiting for his father and mother to give him cows. Having received offers of cows, he walks through the kraal gate and his head is anointed with butter. The next day he goes out to collect his lover and her girl friends who will accompany him on his journey to solicit gifts. (Klima 1970:59)

The killer of an enemy of the people is symbolically equated to a woman who has given birth. He wears ornaments customarily worn by women, including brass neck coils, ear coils, and finger rings. He also observes a period of convalescence after having given "birth" and must observe taboos associated with birth. He must not touch food or do any work. Klima writes:

> As he goes from place to place, he sings his kill-song and waves his shield in front of his mouth, giving his voice a quavering sound. People honor him by throwing butter that spatters his shield, his face and clothes. After about one month, he removes most of his female ornamentation, with the exception of the brass finger-rings. These will be worn for a lifetime as visual evidence of his status. (Klima 1970:59–60)

Among anthropologists, taboos associated with birth are often considered evidence of beliefs in the pollution and lowered status of women. This is a view that reflects North American economic realities rather than indigenous views. In North America, children are an economic liability because of the economic realities of the nuclear family, the emphasis on romantic love as the basis of marriage, and the economics of industrialization. After investing heavily in children, parents must surrender them to their spouses.

For the Barabaig and other groups in nonindustrialized societies, children are an economic asset. A lineage cannot continue without children, male children in a patrilineage and female children in a matrilineage. The Barabaig are patrilineal, so having sons is a necessity. Children of both sexes contribute to the lineage through their labor, and a daughter brings bridewealth into the lineage upon her marriage.

Thus, women who give birth are heroes to the lineage, as are men who kill enemies of the people.

Rites of Intensification

Whereas rites of passage ease the transition from one social state to another and are therefore associated with change, **rites of intensification** occur on a cyclical basis and are aimed at reinforcing the solidarity of the group (Wallace 1966). In religions of the Judeo-Christian–Islamic tradition, rites of intensification take place weekly and are associated with the day of rest decreed by God at the time of creation.

Rites of intensification may also occur on a seasonal basis. These are usually associated with the cycle of planting in agricultural societies. Spring is an especially fertile time for religious ritual, since this is when planting takes place and many animals give birth. Easter and Passover both occur at about the time of the vernal equinox, when night and day are approximately equal. The Islamic Ramadan occurs a little earlier, and the celebration of Buddha's birthday takes place in late spring.

Among the Raramuri Indians of northern Mexico, Easter ceremonies introduced by Catholic Jesuit missionaries in the seventeenth century have been combined with local customs relating to purification. Called *Tarahumara* by outsiders, the Raramuri interpret Christian theology according to their own

Religious belief is intensified through regularly occurring rituals, such as this Roman Catholic Mass. The performance of a ritual and the personnel involved reflect the culture and social organization of the society in which the ritual occurs. In this case, social stratification is evidenced by the rich ceremonial vessels, the ornate cathedral, and the hierarchical priesthood. The power of the priesthood is analogous to the power of the political hierarchy in the same society.

concepts of kinship and community. The Raramuri consider God to be their father and associate him with the sun. God's wife, their mother, is the Virgin Mary, and they associate her with the moon. The Devil is God's elder brother and therefore the uncle of the Raramuri. The Devil is the father of all non-Indians and cares for them just as God cares for the Raramuri.

The Raramuri acknowledge their relationship with God through religious festivals that include dancing, chanting, feasting, and offerings of food and maize beer. During these festivals, or fiestas, bits of food are also buried to deflect the Devil and to placate his malevolence. William L. Merrill writes:

> Any Raramuri with the resources and inclination can stage a fiesta any time of the year. People sometimes sponsor fiestas because God instructs them in their dreams to do so or because they feel in special need of his protection. They also hold [fiestas] to send food, tools, clothing and other goods to recently deceased relatives; to compensate Raramuri doctors for curing the living; or to petition God to end a drought. (1987:375)

The Raramuri also hold festivals at points in the life cycle of the maize (corn), the central component of Raramuri subsistence. Prominent holy days in the Catholic ritual calendar are also observed through festivals.

In agricultural societies, the harvest is typically marked by rites of intensification. Halloween, which occurs on October 31, marks both the "death" of summer and a time when dead spirits can frolic among the living. In the United States, newly harvested pumpkins take on the fearsome faces of jack-o'-lanterns, and sedate suburban homeowners display images of witches on broomsticks and black cats, which in this society are associated with bad luck.

Halloween suspends "laws" that normally govern relationships between the living and the dead, allowing spirits considered dangerous and normally held in check to enjoy a brief period of time among the living. This is an example of **ritual inversion,** a symbolic observance when ordinary relationships are reversed. Ritual inversion does not challenge or attack the social order; instead, it affirms ordinary reality by providing a glimpse into extraordinary possibilities. Halloween ultimately confirms the ascendency of ordinary life by temporarily opening its boundaries to the extraordinary and the dead.

New Year is also an important ritual in many societies, marking the "death" of the old year and the birth of a new cycle. In the United States, New Year is celebrated just after the winter solstice, the shortest day of the year. The old year is represented as an old man with a sickle, associated with the grim reaper described by the poet Henry Wadsworth Longfellow:

> There is a Reaper whose name is Death,
> And, with his sickle keen,
> He reaps the bearded grain at a breath,
> And the flowers that grow between.

The baby New Year arrives wearing a diaper, beginning anew the cycle of birth and death symbolized by the passing year (Figure 9.1). In the United States, New Year's Day has become a secular celebration, but among the Aymara of Bolivia, New Year's Day is celebrated as a fertility ritual, during which small quantities of produce and animal figures made from grain meal are sold (Buechler and Buechler 1971:68–69).

Symbols associated with rites of intensification reinforce group membership and affirm the importance of social relationships. Rites of intensification

FIGURE 9.1   Father Time and Baby New Year

Rites of intensification based on an annual cycle often draw on imagery of the human life cycle. In agricultural societies, this imagery may be related to the planting cycle. Just as plants emerge from the earth, grow to a peak of abundance, and then wither away, humans appear to do the same. In Western tradition, the old, dying year is personified as an old man with a sickle. In the same symbolism, death is portrayed as the Grim Reaper. The new year is depicted as an exuberant infant in a diaper and banner.

DISCUSSIONS

Visions of the Divine Feminine

Vietnamese "boat people" who left Southeast Asia to escape political and economic turmoil after the withdrawal of U.S. troops from the South Vietnamese capital of Saigon in 1975 set out across the South China Sea in small, overloaded fishing boats, with inadequate food or water. An estimated 50 percent of the boat people died as a result of hunger, storms, capsized boats, or brutalization and rape by pirates. Driven to despair by the unaccustomed terrors of the open sea, many boat people jumped overboard, summoned by "calls" from dead relatives whom they seemed to see in the turbulent waves.

Many boat people who survived attribute their deliverance to their visions of Kuan Yin, the "goddess of mercy," or the Virgin Mary at key moments when they were subjected to grave danger from storms or pirates. Though culturally and politically autonomous, Vietnam has historically been strongly influenced by Chinese Buddhist traditions. Kuan Yin is a Bodhisattva, or enlightened being committed to aiding all sentient beings. In Indian Buddhist tradition, Kuan Yin appears in male form as Avalokitesvara. As a female Bodhisattva, Kuan Yin's attributes are described in the Lotus Sutra:

> To hear her name and see her form
> Delivers beings from every woe.

Kuan Yin is the benefactor of all who are in danger or need, but she is the special patron of sailors and fishermen. She shares many attributes with the Virgin Mary of Christian tradition; for example, in Portugal,

Mary is viewed as the patron of fishermen. The iconography, or visual imagery, of Mary and Kuan Yin are similar, in both China and Vietnam. Under French colonial rule, many Vietnamese converted to Catholicism. Catholicized Vietnamese boat people saw visions of the Virgin Mary in the moments before they were saved from what appeared to be certain disaster, whereas Buddhists saw Kuan Yin. These are culturally appropriate symbolic variations on imagery of a divine protectress prevalent in many societies. In the following essay, Lex Hixon, a noted Sanskrit scholar and author of seven books on religion, suggests that imagery of the Divine Feminine is virtually universal.

THE NATURE OF MOTHER WISDOM

Lex Hixon

The Great Mother is humanity's most primordial, pervasive, and fruitful image of reality. Either secretly or openly, she appears with extraordinary power, wisdom, and tenderness at the core of every culture. She illuminates the entire universe, because she is not some local or limited goddess but our Universal Mother. She expresses herself fluently through and within every sacred tradition, without needing to call attention to her feminine nature.

Various feminine expressions of the Divine abounded in the ancient world. The many appearances of Virgin Mary—at Tepeyac in Mexico, Fatima in Portugal, Gerabondal in Spain, and Lourdes in France, and contemporary apparitions in Egypt,

Yugoslavia, and various parts of America—are special revelations of her reality for the modern world. Through the Goddess tradition, alive everywhere on the planet, she guides, protects, terrifies, chastens, heals, liberates, and illuminates. Her relation as Great Mother to the cosmos and its innumerable life forms is as tender as her relation with each human soul. It is a relation so intimate as to be free from subject or object, that is to say, a relationship that is intrinsically mystical.

The Goddess always remains the uncompromising Warrior of Truth—not primarily a nurturing mother figure but a Wisdom Mother who educates and liberates, gradually removing all limits. Her teaching is that of indivisible oneness, expressed by the diversity of her cosmic dance through countless civilizations and religions.

The Divine Mother is not distinct in essence from the inscrutable Yahweh of Jewish tradition, God the Hidden Father of Christianity, or Allah Most High of Islam, who is beyond all conceptions and descriptions. She is recognized in Mahayana Buddhism as Prajnaparamita, the depth of unthinkability, Mother of all Buddhas. From the radiant blackness of the womb of Mother Reality emerge numerous messengers of truth, profoundly mature women and men who have graced every culture throughout history. Also from her reality emerge cruel and arrogant human beings who create dramas of suffering and conflict that the Mother uses to awaken, purify, and elevate the soul. From her alone

flow cosmic harmony and cosmic dissent.

The Goddess tradition appears to exist in its most undiluted practice today within the ancient tantric lineages of Hinduism and Buddhism, which are being passed on intact, even to the present generation. Some observers note that the majority of teachers and advanced practitioners of these ancient traditions are male. This fact does not present any obstacle to the functioning of goddess energy, and the balance is rapidly changing, as the largest movement on the planet today is the women's movement. This change is already evident as a great prominence of modern women in the realm of spiritual practice.

The primordial worship of the Great Goddess in the Middle East and Europe is indirectly reflected now as the veneration of the Virgin Mary and the sublime women saints of the Catholic Church. But since the Divine Mother is all-pervading, we can find her presence as well within religions that have been dominated by the masculine metaphor. Consider the Divine Presence experienced as the feminine Shekhinah and the Sabbath Queen in Jewish tradition. Another instance is the universal veneration among Muslims of the Virgin Mary and of Fatima, daughter of the Prophet of Islam. The principal names of Allah—Compassionate and Merciful, Rahman and Rahim—both derive from the Arabic root that signifies "womb."

Indeed, everywhere we look in ancient or modern life, the nurturing, maturing, educating, and liberating power of the Divine Feminine can be seen in operation at the deepest levels of culture wisdom. She operates directly through humanity, primarily through women but also through men; neopagan, feminist, wise woman, traditional native, tantric, ecological, green, and creation-centered movements in contemporary society are reestablishing conscious communion with the Goddess on an increasingly wide scale.

From the most simple, basic point of view, for several years during infancy and early childhood, both female and male children relate in essentially the same mode and with the same intensity to the mother love at the core of their daily existence. The one we call father is at first simply mother number two, with bearded or abrasive face. Every longing is for mother. All sustenance is mother. Even the infant's landscape, before and after birth, is simply mother. For nine months, her heartbeat is our rhythm, our primal music. This is the original ground, prior to gender differentiation and sharp individuation, to which Goddess tradition gives us access, not as an infantile regression but as the fruitful soil of reconciliation, harmony, tenderness without boundary, unitive wisdom, and totality. That the great Indian poet of the Mother, Ramprasad, blossomed through a male body only shows that the ecstatic sensitivity, the all-embracing heart, the merciless honesty and diamond courage of Mother's most intimate companions are not fundamentally dependent on the biologically and culturally conditioned abstractions masculine and feminine.

The basic cry of Ramprasad is "Ma! Ma! Ma!" What child is not crying out something like this wherever she or he may be on the planet or in planetary history? Is not Mother Reality always at the core of human experience, at the center of our spiritual hunger and thirst, and therefore at the heart of our integrity?

Goddess tradition is much richer than any stereotypical notion of mother worship. Its practitioners are not interested in projecting a cosmic mother figure any more than they would project a cosmic father figure. The goal of spirituality is to realize truth, not to engage in projection and fantasy. Through Ramprasad's songs, the Goddess reveals herself as Woman Warrior, Teacher, Mother, and Consort. In different moods, she appears youthful, ancient, or ageless. These are actual dimensions of experience that can be entered by her devotees. She is divine creativity, evolutionary energy, timeless awareness, transcendent reality, and, in a special tantric sense, she is every woman. She constitutes the feminine principle within male and female persons and also manifests the gender-free feminine—self-luminous Mother Wisdom, nondual awareness and bliss.

Source: Adapted from Lex Hixon, *Mother of the Universe: Visions of the Goddess and Tantric Hymns of Enlightenment* (Wheaton, IL: Quest Books, 1994).

organized around an annual cycle typically associate the "birth" and "death" of the year with the lives of individuals. Symbols associated with these rituals and festivals give expression to the anxieties all people feel about "dangerous" events such as birth and death. Acting out these anxieties with the people who share our lives transforms potentially disruptive emotions into the "glue" that holds the social group together.

Divination

Despite the power of rites of passage and rites of intensification to reinforce group solidarity, all societies go through times of crisis when the fragile social bonds seem about to break apart. Illness or natural disaster may threaten the ability of group members to interact with each other. At these times, it may become necessary to identify the source of tensions and restore order. **Divination** is a process of gaining secret knowledge about the past, present, or future by calling on the aid of spirits or by looking for supernatural signs. Divination is used both for diagnosis of social conflict and for social control.

When tragedy strikes an individual in a small group, it affects the life of everyone. Unexpected illness or death, especially that of a prominent member of the group, threatens the security of all. In an economy based on cattle herding, drought or disease affecting the herd can endanger everyone. Through divination, social tensions and anxiety over seemingly unpreventable disasters are deflected away from the group by attributing the danger to supernatural agents.

In his study of the Azande, horticulturalists in the southern Sudan, E. E. Evans-Pritchard says the Azande distinguish between "secondary" causation and "ultimate" causation. "Secondary causes" are the observable causes of an event; the "ultimate cause" of an event is the supernatural agency responsible. The anthropologist notes that an Azande may say that a person who committed suicide was killed by witchcraft. However, Evans-Pritchard writes, the Azande is "telling you the ultimate cause of his death and not the secondary causes":

> You can ask him "How did he kill himself" and [the Azande] will tell you that [the dead man] committed suicide by hanging himself from the branch of a tree. You can also ask: "Why did he kill himself?" and he will tell you that it was because he was angry with his brothers. The cause of his death was hanging from a tree, and

the cause of his hanging from a tree was his anger with his brothers. ([1937] 1976:24)

To the Azande, however, the anger and the hanging are secondary causes. The ultimate cause is witchcraft, because "only crazy people commit suicide, and . . . if everyone who was angry with his brothers committed suicide there would soon be no people left in the world" ([1937] 1976:24).

The family may then call upon a shaman, who can determine the source of witchcraft by various means of divination. In one divination ceremony described by Evans-Pritchard, the headman of a village engaged a group of shamans to conduct a *séance*, a form of divination in which the diviners are possessed by the spirits of the dead. In a dramatic ceremony, the shamans accused four men of slandering a headman either because they were jealous or felt they had been wronged. An old man at the séance asked about the success of his crops and was told that his crops were in danger because two of his wives were jealous of his chief wife. The shamans told the man that the jealous co-wives must make restitution by blowing water onto the plants.

Evans-Pritchard notes that séances provide an "open investigation" into "delicate personal matters" ([1937] 1976:77). They allow people to air their private grievances and to gain compensation for them or to alleviate their guilt by making restitution to their neighbors. Thus, this type of divination enacts a social drama that allows participants to express their differences and come to some form of settlement.

Not all divination is aimed at restoring order in the group. Anthony F. C. Wallace (1966) points out that divination facilitates decision making when a group is faced with two equally desirable choices. Many forager groups rely on some form of divination when deciding where to hunt. The Algonkian Indians, who lived in the area around Lake Ontario, used *scapulimancy,* the reading of bones, to decide where to seek herds of caribou. Omar K. Moore (1957) suggests that the Algonkians' divination randomized decision making and helped to prevent overhunting of caribou in a particular area.

As have many other groups, Chinese have traditionally relied on *geomancy*—"reading the earth"—to determine where to build their houses, how to place the rooms, and how to orient the doors and windows. This process, called *feng shui* (wind–water), is based on reading geological signs to determine where the natural forces would be most propitious for wealth, health, and a long life. This divination process reflects the importance of land in an agricultural society and provides a way of transmitting folk wisdom about climate and geological features.

COMMUNITY

A religion is ultimately shaped by the society of which it is a part and by the community of people who make up its membership. A key factor in the organization of religion is whether the society that produced it is egalitarian or stratified. As noted in Chapter 4, egalitarian societies are characterized by relatively equal access to power and resources, whereas stratified societies are characterized by unequal access to power and resources.

The degree of social differentiation is related to task specialization. In societies at the egalitarian end of the scale, there is task specialization by age and gender, and all adult members are engaged in food production as long as they are physically able. In stratified societies, only a segment of the population is engaged in food production, and they are able to produce a food surplus that gives rise to a great deal of task specialization. In stratified societies, there are many kinds of specialized roles, including that of leader or ruler, tax collectors, soldiers, various kinds of artisans, and many others. An artisan is one who is skilled in some kind of craft, such as making shoes or fashioning jewelry out of gold and precious stones.

In stratified societies, the ruler has power that is vested in the office, which gives him or her the authority to command others. In an egalitarian society, leadership is based not in a social role but in the ability of the leader to persuade others. These differences in the sources and dynamics of power are reflected in the social organization of religion. Though religious experience is shaped by the dynamics of the group as a whole, certain personnel play key roles in the social enactment of religion.

Priests

A **priest** is a religious leader whose authority is conferred by the office. *Priest* is the sociological and anthropological term that refers to any religious office that confers authority based in the position, including rabbis, priests, imams, monks, nuns, popes, lamas, and bishops. Since the social organization of religion reflects that of the group as a whole and since the power of priests is public and formal, they typically are found in societies with some degree of stratification. Societies having no formal political authority typically do not have a concept of religious authority.

The primary responsibility of the priest is to maintain relationships with the gods or other spirit beings on behalf of the group. Priests reinforce the stability of the group by performing the rituals that maintain the reciprocal relationship between humans and spirit beings. Priests are responsible for observing the ritual calendar by conducting rites of intensification and for presiding over rites of passage, such as baptisms, weddings, and funerals.

Just as formal political office is a male prerogative in all known societies, the priesthood is typically male-centered and most priests are male. Women may be priests in some agricultural societies, however, reflecting the symbolic importance of female fertility. Frederique Apffel Marglin (1985) conducted a study of *devadasis*, female priests associated with a Hindu temple in Puri, in the state of Orissa on the northeastern coast of India. Male priests conduct most rituals of the temple, which is dedicated to a number of important Hindu gods. The temple is associated with the king of Puri, who is viewed as a living deity. The devadasis are consecrated to the main deity of the temple in a marriage ceremony that entitles them to dance and sing in temple rituals:

> The devadasis are a very specialized, unusual group of women. They do not marry any mortal man and their dedication to temple service is regarded as constituting a marriage with the main deity, Jagannath, a form of Vishnu. . . . They are the only women who participate in the rituals and festivals of Puri as ritual specialists. (Marglin 1985:18)

The status of the devadasis is not so clear as that of male ritual specialists, partly because of their sexual role. As wives of the god-king, devadasis are expected to have sexual relations with the king, but they can also receive other men in their own homes. The devadasis are called by titles that mean variously "courtesan" and "auspicious woman." Under the traditional system, devadasis had important status

Chasing the Comet: Technology As a Symbol for the Third Millennium

In March 1997, 39 members of the Heaven's Gate cult of San Diego, California—wearing tennis shoes and bearing "passports"—boarded a space ship they believed was traveling in the wake of the Halle Bopp comet. They undertook the journey by committing mass suicide. This event earned me the reputation of a prophet among some of my cultural anthropology students, since I had been predicting such an event—including the theme of technology as symbol—for several years.

My ability to predict this event owes less to a crystal ball—which I don't have, in any event—than to the ability of social science to predict probable events and courses of action given adequate theory and evidence. As is the case with the physical sciences, social scientists cannot expect to predict the behavior of individual cases. Rather, we can predict that a specific type of event is likely to occur in a particular set of circumstances.

I was able to predict this event on the basis of anthropological analyses of revitalization movements, especially those occurring in the wake of colonialism. In recent times, anthropologists have noted the emergence of revitalization movements in various parts of the world, including North America, in response to culture change. William O. Beeman describes American militia groups as revitalization movements that hark back to what members see as a Golden Age "when being white, male, and having a gun really meant something

in American society" (1997:332). Beeman notes that members of the militia groups view their values as representing a Golden Age in U.S. society: "The militia groups see the growth of government regulation and the rise of legislation that overturns the social order of the past as debilitating for American life. Indeed, for many members life under present social conditions is increasingly losing its meaning" (1997:332).

Anthropologists such as Anthony F. C. Wallace (1956, 1969) have linked the emergence of revitalization movements to social crises. In addition to various types of social crises identified in media, members of the U.S. public faced a culturally significant crisis in the late 1990s: the approach of the year 2000, identified with the end of the second millennium. Historically, the end of a millennium has been conceptually associated with apocalyptic visions of the end of the world and has given rise to millenarian movements.

Millenarian movements typically follow the model of a messianic cult and display a characteristic pattern. Movement members are disaffected by their social condition; they believe the world is about to end; and they attribute the end of the world to conditions of moral decay. Further, members believe that, though most people will be destroyed in this Armageddon, true believers can be saved by a messiah, god, or hero if they follow a path of purification.

Typically, symbols associated with a millenarian movement and the type of purification to be undertaken are defined by a charismatic leader. Max Weber used the term *charismatic leader* to describe an individual whose control over his followers was based on his personality rather than on his achievements:

> The term "charisma" will be applied to a certain quality of an individual personality by virtue of which he is considered extraordinary and treated as endowed with supernatural, superhuman, or at least specifically exceptional powers or qualities. (Weber 1978:241)

In the case of revitalization movements, symbols and the types of ritual purification practiced are validated by linking them to tradition, even though these symbols are typically developed by the leader of the movement.

Viewing the millennium as an important symbolic event is not a maverick notion particular to Western culture or to religious radicals. Culturally significant markers of time are often attended by anxiety and a sense of crisis. The annual cycle of the death of the old year followed by the birth of the new year is significant in all cultures. In societies that assign numbers to their years, the death of some years is viewed as more powerful than the death of others. The death of a decade, for example, is more significant than that of a year ending in mid-cycle. Frances F. Berdan (1982) notes that the end of the 52-year calendrical cycle of the Aztecs was marked by a sense of crisis and possible doom. Vulnerable people, including pregnant women and children, covered their faces with maguey-leaf masks. The thousand-year cycle for those who guide their days by the Gregorian calendar is of vital significance, made even more important by its rarity in human experience.

The emergence of technological symbols as a culturally defining theme in North America today is based both in history and in a changing cultural context. In the year 999, at the end of the first millennium, western Europeans following the Julian calendar—now the Gregorian calendar—framed their anxiety over the approaching millennial marker in Judeo-Christian, and especially Christian, terms. Symbols focused on the personification of Good and Evil in the forms of God and Satan, and the awaited Messiah was Christ, believed to be coming to the earth for the second time.

Since that turn of the millennium, the European Enlightenment of the eighteenth century drew sharp boundaries between sacred and secular in the areas of politics and the arts. This demarcation had an especially important impact on the development of science and scientific methods, and the Western intellectual tradition has been framed in terms of an opposition between science and religion. In the 1960s, in the United States, the emphasis on verifiable knowledge received an impetus with John F. Kennedy's formulation of a technology battle with the Soviet Union, and this emphasis on a verifiable science has continued into the present.

Many contemporary North Americans are skeptical of the idea of a rescue by a spirit being. In their everyday lives, they look to rescue by the medical or scientific establishment. People in the United States are more likely to ask Congress to allocate funds for research on a terminal illness than to ask God for a cure. We create babies in a petri dish and implant the embryo in a rented womb. We prolong life not by prayer, but by measuring caloric and fat intake.

Technology emerged as an important symbolic image in American popular culture during the industrial revolution, and the mythology of technology as messiah or savior has since been elaborated. In 1977, the Stephen Spielberg movie *Close Encounters of the Third Kind* framed a millenarian movement in technological terms. The hero of this film, Roy Neary, played by Richard Dreyfuss, desperately tries to persuade U.S. military and political leaders to prepare for a visit by creatures from outer space. His pleas are rejected, and he is increasingly marginalized as he takes on the U.S. military establishment. In the end, Neary's efforts are justified by the arrival of benevolent space beings, who are depicted as arriving on a mother ship amid rays of light and clouds of glory, much as God and angels were depicted in paintings by Raphael and Michelangelo. The space beings reject the overtures of the official greeting committee and meet first with Neary, an ordinary man who had the courage to defy conventional wisdom.

There are many other examples of use of technological symbols to portray cultural perspectives relating to change and the millennium. The *Los Angeles Times Special Millennium Issue/Fashion* of August 1999 portrays the approach of the third millennium in millenarian terms. The millennium is portrayed as Doomsday. The editor, Alice Short, writes: "The van carrying the clothes was very late. By the time the models finally emerged from the artificial chill of their motor home in platinum wigs and the winter whites of Ralph Lauren, dark clouds were cutting in front of the sun. Beautiful. Photographer Steve Shaw could not have Photoshopped a more menacing sky for his fashion send-up of "Village of the Damned," the 1960 sci-fi thriller about 12 strangely malevolent children living in the same tiny town. Our 'town' is actually a movie set, built in the early '90s and dubbed Club Ed, outside of Lancaster. It seemed an ideal mood for our issue on fashion at the millennium."

The "ideal mood" for millennial fashion is described in technological and menacing imagery: artificial chill, motor home, platinum wigs, winter whites, dark clouds, menacing sky, village of the damned, strangely malevolent children. The defining image of humans is as robots, or machines. The models are expressionless, identical, and mechanically posed. They are posed with gas station pumps, in booths at anonymous cafés, with motel signs, or grouped around a telephone booth. The technology represented is decades old, suggesting a retrograde tie to what is viewed as a look to the future.

The concept of the year 2000 as Doomsday and technology as symbol also became apparent in the public attention focused on the Y2K computer glitch, the inability of some computer hardware and software to read four-digit year dates. Some media figures predicted widespread airline delays, the failure of home appliances and transportation, the

(*continued*)

Chasing the Comet: Technology As a Symbol for the Third Millennium (*continued*)

loss of bank records, as well as the obvious inability of non-Y2K-compliant computers to accurately process programs that are date sensitive. Some imaginative minds projected this as a kind of technological Armageddon in which life as we know it in the United States might come to an end.

In the case of the Heaven's Gate cult, members were computer programmers and other technologically sophisticated people. They lived in an affluent community outside San Diego. Those who "boarded the mother ship" ranged in age from 18 to 24 and carried "passports" that entitled them to entry into the Next World. The group ran a company that designed websites, and leaders recruited members through websites. Members of the group who were not present at the "departure" declared that they had nothing else to live for, and the mother of a woman who had "boarded the space ship" said she was happy for her daughter and envied her.

For members of the Heaven's Gate cult, the journey was seen as transcending everyday reality in twentieth-century United States. For members of the American public, the incident was shocking, because it challenged the idea that affluence and technological proficiency are a protective barrier against despair and delusion. The mass suicide demonstrated that people who are among the technological elite can view themselves as disenfranchised.

The Heaven's Gate cult was a syncretic millenarian movement, combining the symbolism of computer technology with that of Christianity. The leader of the group, Do, represented himself as the heir to a community of beings that transcended ordinary reality. He compared himself to Christ, stating that transcendent beings of his type descended to the earth in 2000-year cycles. He also juxtaposed the superior awareness of himself and his followers to that of what he called Luciferians, members of the divine fraternity who failed to make the cut. Do also drew on Christian symbolism by referring to his place of origin and ultimate destiny as the Kingdom of Heaven.

Do constructed a cosmology that combined Christian symbolism with technological symbolism, especially the symbolism of computer technology. He described the human brain as a "comparatively primitive computer" and spoke of knowledge and learning as programming and reprogramming.

The creation myth of the Heaven's Gate cult also emphasized technology. Do asserted that he had arrived on the earth from an evolutionary level above human (the Kingdom of Heaven). He added that he and his "task partner," Ti, had arrived on the earth in one of a number of unreported "UFO crashes." According to this story of creation, Ti and Do took over two human bodies by being deposited in the human bodies as "chips," a term that draws on the imagery of computer chips. Ti emerged in this new form as female; Do became incarnated as male.

In preparing his followers to board the space ship that was supposedly following in the wake of the Halle Bopp comet, Do advised them that they must "disconnect or separate from the physical container or body to enter the Next World." Drawing on Christian symbolism and the analogy of his own incarnation with that of Christ, Do wrote on the group's website, "I am about to return to my Father's Kingdom."

Though the mass suicide of the Heaven's Gate movement was shocking to the public, it was predictable, given the sense of social crisis and anxiety over the approaching millennium prevalent among the public. The use of technological symbolism was consistent with the use of technological metaphors throughout the twentieth century. The form of millenarian movements remains the same cross-culturally, but the symbols called upon are embedded in differing social and cultural contexts. People who have lost faith in the world of spirits and the supernatural must call on the world of science for symbols. We must rely on comets and space ships. In a world where passports are required to travel from one country to another, we must have a "passport" to transport us to a world of meaning.

Source: Adapted from a paper presented by Mari Womack at the 98th Annual Meeting of the American Anthropological Association, November 17–21, 1999, Chicago, Illinois. © 1999 Mari Womack.

and freedoms unavailable to other women. They were the only women allowed to learn to read, to sing, and to dance. The devadasi system has eroded, though not disappeared, in large part because of vigorous moral condemnation by British colonial rulers and writers.

Among the Aztecs of Central Mexico, infant girls and boys could be dedicated to the priesthood by their parents. Unlike male priests, female priests often left the priesthood to marry while still young, with permission of their parents and town leaders. Women who made the priesthood a lifelong career performed many important ritual functions, often participating in religious ceremonies alongside the men (Berdan 1982).

Among Roman Catholics and many Buddhist groups, women may become nuns, a priestly role. The status of nuns differs, depending on the groups. Depending on the order, Catholic nuns may teach at all educational levels, from kindergarten to university. In many parishes, they are the primary means of providing religious instruction. Nuns may also serve as missionaries, as nurses, and as hospital administrators.

In most cases, among both Catholics and Buddhists, nuns play a secondary role to priests and monks. There are exceptions, however. The Hsi Lai Temple in Hacienda Heights, California, is presided over by nuns at all levels of administration. The temple, which reflects the culture of Chinese Buddhism, is headed by an abbess, whose authority is second only to the head of the Pure Land Buddhist organization in Taiwan. Women may also head churches among some Protestant groups in North America, including Episcopalians.

Among Hindus of India, some male followers of Bahuchara Mata may dress and act like women to serve in a specialized form of priesthood. Bahuchara Mata is "one of the many versions of the Mother Goddess worshiped throughout India" (Nanda 1999:ix). These men dedicated to the worship of Bahuchara Mata are known as *hijras,* and they undergo an operation in which the penis and testicles are removed. Serena Nanda (1999) notes that they are socially defined as a third gender, which is neither male nor female.

Hijras perform at marriages, though they do not preside over them. However, Nanda writes, "The most important traditional role for the hijras in Indian society is that of performing at homes where a male child has been born" (1999:1). Nanda notes that the birth of a son is an auspicious occasion and cause for great celebration. Dancing and performing often bawdy songs, the hijras call on the Mother Goddess to bestow fertility, prosperity, and a long life on the child. Thus, the hijras, who have divested themselves of generating life, give to the child the power to continue his patrilineal line (Nanda 1999:3).

Shamans

Whereas the power of a priest resides in the office, the power of a **shaman** resides in the demonstrated ability to control spirits or supernatural forces. The shaman typically uses these powers to heal or to restore harmony to the community after disaster has struck. C. Von Furer-Haimendorf describes the differing roles of priests and shamans this way:

> While [the priest] follows the broad and well-trodden path of long-established ritual, the [shaman] must battle through the wilderness of the supernatural world to discover the cause of disease and threatening disaster, and must devise the means of placating the wrath of malignant spirits. The priests acts . . . while all is well;

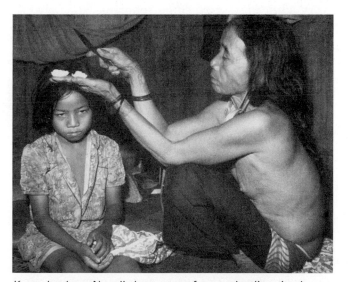

Karpu bonbo, a Nepali shaman, performs a healing ritual. Unlike priests, shamans attain their position by their demonstrated ability to contact spirits. Both priests and shamans serve the village of Melemchi. A priestly lineage of lamas maintains the social order through their performance of rites of passage and rites of intensification; shamans look after everyday concerns through healing rituals and other types of spirit intervention.

his offerings are tendered to gods while their mood is benevolent, and his prayers are designed to solicit their favor for the welfare of the community, and their protection against dangers not yet arisen. It is only when misfortune is rife that the [shaman] is called in to restore the disturbed relations with supernatural powers, to draw the sick from the jaws of death or to counteract the black magic of an enemy. ([1970] 1997:87)

The shaman may inherit a shamanic gift but cannot undertake shamanic training until called by the spirits to serve them. The call usually comes in the form of a life-threatening illness or psychological crisis that Western doctors might diagnose as schizophrenia or some other form of psychosis.

Not all such illness episodes are considered to be a call from the spirits. The disturbed individual may suffer for months or even years before the call to be a shaman is clear, at which time the long shamanic training begins. During apprenticeship to an established shaman, the aspiring shaman learns to enter the spirit world by means of trance induced by drugs, fasting, dancing, or other means. As the young shaman gains expertise, she or he may acquire spirit helpers and, along with them, increasing power to heal.

In small-scale societies, such as the !Kung of Africa, every adult may serve some shamanic functions. In most groups, women are able to become shamans, reflecting the more equal access to power and resources of egalitarian societies. In stratified or complex societies, women may be shamans even where the role of priest is closed to them. Women are allowed to become shamans because the shamanic role has little formal authority associated with it, and the shamanic functions of healing and of purification in birth and death rituals are typically associated with women.

Complex societies may have both priests and shamans, as in the case of the Saora, horticulturalists of Orissa in India. The functions of the village priest are to maintain shrines to local gods and to guard the village lands from hostile spirits. The shaman diagnoses the source of trouble or disease and has the power to cure it. The priest and shaman hold complementary positions. When a new priest is to be appointed, a shaman falls into a trance and asks the gods and ancestors whether the candidate is acceptable to them. If these spirit beings agree with the choice of living humans, the shaman summons the ghost of the last priest who held office in the village. If he approves, the shaman—possessed by the dead

priest and acting as his representative—signifies that approval by placing his hands on the head of the new priest and telling him to do his work well (Von Furer-Haimendorf [1970] 1997:81).

Sorcerers and Witches

Sorcerers are similar to shamans, both in their call to the spirits and in the course of their training. However, sorcerers use their power to kill or to cause harm. In some societies, shamans may also be sorcerers. In Haiti, vodun practitioners known as houngans are said to "work with both hands"; that is, they are both shamans and sorcerers. Vodun (vodou or voodoo) adepts believe that the most effective healers are those who can control the evil forces as well as the beneficial spirits. In most societies that have sorcery beliefs, both men and women can be sorcerers.

The term *witch* is used differently in anthropology than in everyday English. In anthropological usage, **witches** are powerless people who channel evil into society because they cannot obtain what they want through their social relationships. An individual may inherit the tendency to be a witch, but the capacity to cause evil may lie dormant until it is activated by jealousy, anger, or some other antisocial emotion (Evans-Pritchard [1937] 1976). Witchcraft charges are most likely to be leveled against people whose behavior is out of the ordinary or whose personality brings them into conflict with other people.

People are believed to resort to witchcraft when they lack the ability to meet their needs or to satisfy their desires through socially acceptable means. Thus, people who lack power in a society are the ones most likely to be accused of witchcraft, and women, who are less able than men to exert social power in most groups, are most subject to witchcraft accusations. Witchcraft accusations serve to ensure social conformity, since most people prefer not to be subjected to vilification by their neighbors or to be forced to pay damages for someone else's illness or misfortune. The concept of witchcraft also allows people to personify tensions and conflict arising naturally out of social interaction and to project their anger or frustration onto less powerful members of the group.

The Wiccan Movement

In the United States, the concept of "witch" includes the functions of shamans, sorcerers, and witches. All these aspects of informal supernatural power have been expressed in witchcraft beliefs at some point in Western history. The dynamics of the seventeenth-century witchcraft trials in Salem, Massachusetts, are closest to the anthropological concept of witch. Charges of witchcraft were leveled against people—mostly women—who did not conform to their neighbors' standards of appropriate behavior. Even today, the American public occasionally becomes titillated by rumors of "black magic" or "satanic cults," which are a variant on the anthropological concept of sorcery. Like sorcerers in some other societies, practitioners of evil in the United States are presumed to act with some degree of secrecy.

In recent decades, members of the feminist movement have drawn on medieval or pre-Christian European shamanic healing practices to develop new religions that do not reflect the male bias—in myth, hierarchy, and control over ritual—of modern Christianity. Matilda Joslyn Gage was one of the earliest feminist writers to look to "witchcraft" as a charter for developing a new religion for women. In her book *Woman, Church, and State* (1893), Gage lays the intellectual groundwork for the twentieth-century witchcraft movement:

> Whatever the pretext made for witchcraft persecutions, we have abundant proof that the so-called "witch" was among the most profoundly scientific persons of the age. The church, having forbidden its offices and all external methods of knowledge to woman, was profoundly stirred with indignation at her having through her own wisdom, penetrated into some of the most deeply subtle secrets of nature: and it was a subject of debate during the middle ages if learning for woman was not an additional capacity for evil, as owing to her, knowledge had first been introduced into the world.

The last part of the passage refers to the Christian story of Adam and Eve, in which Eve stole fruit from the Tree of the Knowledge of Good and Evil. Thus, according to Gage, woman introduced "knowledge" into the world.

Modern witches, or members of the wiccan movement, often refer to themselves as "neopagans," an implicit rejection of Christian dominance over medieval European shamanism. The following prescription for a neopagan ritual, adapted from Margot Adler's book *Drawing Down the Moon* (1979), illustrates the emphasis on feminine imagery:

> A circle should be marked on the floor, surrounding those who will participate in the ceremony. An altar is

to be set up at the center of the circle. At the center of the altar shall be placed an image of the Goddess, and an incense burner placed in front of it. (Quoted in Young 1993:429)

Modern wicca and other neopaganist organizations are political movements that draw their "charter" from the traditional ability of women to perform shamanic rituals and to preside over fertility. They have much in common with revitalization movements, religious movements aimed at bringing about social change or "revitalizing" religion or society.

REVITALIZATION MOVEMENTS

Religion generally reinforces cultural values and social organization, but it can also be an effective form of rebellion. Anthony F. C. Wallace defines a **revitalization movement** as "any conscious, organized effort by members of a society to construct a more satisfying culture" (1966:30). Not all revitalization movements are religious. In the United States during the 1960s, civil activists sought to reform what they saw as a materialist culture centered on the military-industrial complex.

However, revitalization movements involve a committed philosophical viewpoint, and many are centered on some form of religion. Revitalization movements based on religion can be especially effective because they can draw on powerful cultural symbols and claim the support of supernatural beings. In many cases, leaders of revitalization movements claim to receive guidance through **revelation,** communications from the spirit world.

Social Stress

Wallace suggests that revitalization movements are a response to social stress. He proposes a five-stage model for the course of these attempts to reconstruct the cultural world: steady state, increased individual stress, a period of cultural distortion, a period of revitalization, and a new steady state.

During the initial steady state, culture change is relatively slow and involves a low degree of stress for most individuals. Wallace writes that, during the period of increased individual stress, "The sociocultural system is being 'pushed' progressively out of equilibrium by various forces, such as climatic and biotic change, epidemic disease, war and conquest, social subordination, or acculturation" (1966:159). Increasingly large numbers of individuals are placed under stress, and disillusionment becomes widespread. Crime, illness, and asocial responses to stress increase.

During the period of cultural distortion, individual breaches of social mores become institutionalized, so that interest groups assail what they consider the evil effects of "the system" or "the Establishment." Scapegoating, in the form of attacks on other groups, becomes commonplace. At this point, Wallace says, "it is difficult to return to a steady state without the institution of a revitalization process" (1966:159).

During the revitalization stage, an individual or group constructs a new, idealistic image of the culture and transmits it to others. As the movement grows, it becomes organized into a coherent social unit. With success in communicating the new values and forming an organization, the revitalization movement adapts to existing institutions and its message becomes routinized. At this point a new steady state arises.

Nativistic Movements

Though revitalization movements are aimed at changing the status quo, they often draw on cultural traditions for validation. For example, leaders of new Christian movements often say they are returning to what Christ really meant. Leaders of **nativistic movements,** who seek to overthrow colonial domination, often look to their ancestors as a symbol of continuity in a changing world. The Ghost Dance religion, which spread among several Native American groups in the late nineteenth century, centered on the idea that the dead would return, whites would be expelled, and the old ways would return. As are many other revitalization movements, the Ghost Dance religion was a **millenarian movement,** based on the belief that the present, imperfect world would end and a new ideal society would be instituted by supernatural beings.

During the first half of the twentieth century, a number of millenarian movements sprang up in Melanesia, including New Guinea and some Pacific islands, in response to colonial domination of the region. Called **cargo cults,** these movements were generally organized around the idea that the world was about to end and that the ancestors would return and restore the riches controlled by whites to their rightful owners, the Melanesians. The word *cargo* is the Pidgin English term for trade goods, and it refers to the cargo carried on ships and planes invading the area during World War II. Peter Worsley writes:

> Troops on both sides in World War II found their arrival in Melanesia heralded as a sign of the Apocalypse. The G.I.'s who landed in the New Hebrides, moving up for the bloody fighting on Guadalcanal, found the natives furiously at work preparing airfields, roads and docks for the magic ships and planes that they believed were coming from "Rusefel" (Roosevelt), the friendly king of America. ([1959] 1994:364)

The arrival of U.S. soldiers in the Pacific especially influenced the development of cargo cults, since dark-skinned Melanesians saw American blacks living on equal terms with whites. This dramatic departure from colonial policy of racial separation in the region was taken as a sign that old prophecies foretelling the end of the world were about to come true.

Though framed in religious metaphor, cargo cults had a major political impact. Native people refused to work for colonial powers or pay taxes. In some cases, they destroyed their own property. The people also turned away from the political rule of whites to follow their own leaders of cargo cults. This development allowed local leaders to establish a base of power and reduced the authority of colonial governors. Eventually, some cargo cults developed into independence movements that brought an end to colonial rule over many Pacific island groups.

CHINESE ANCESTOR REVERENCE: A CASE STUDY IN MYTH, RITUAL, AND COMMUNITY

Virtually all societies have some form of belief in spirit survival after death, but Chinese **ancestor reverence** is perhaps the most formal system of paying respect to dead relatives. Appropriate behavior

Table 9.2 The Five Relationships for Fulfillment	
Father	Son
Older brother	Younger brother
Husband	Wife
Ruler	Subject
Friend	Friend

within the family—including dead relatives—is formally encoded in the Confucian concept of social relationships. According to Confucian philosophy, humans have the quality *jen*, which compels them to live in the company of others. An individual isolated from others cannot fulfill human potential.

Five relationships are most important for the fulfillment of this potential: father–son, older brother–younger brother, husband–wife, ruler–subject, friend–friend (Table 9.2). The first person in each pair occupies the position of responsibility; the second person is in the position of obedience. Only the fifth relationship—friend–friend—is based on equality.

Relationships within the family continue after death in a system of ritual observance that unites land ownership, the patrilineal inheritance system, and clan membership. China is traditionally an agricultural society, which means that land ownership is central to the economic system. Before 1949, when a social system based on Confucian ideals was replaced by a Communist system, each village was occupied by a patrilineage that maintained land ownership in the extended family.

Clan membership is indicated by the family name, a designation of such importance that it precedes the individual name. The importance of family and succession is also suggested by the fact that the second name indicates the generation into which one is born. The Chinese name is written as follows: family name–generation name–individual name.

Younger generations are expected to show respect for older generations, a responsibility that is not terminated by death. The oldest son is expected to "feed" his parents even after they are dead by maintaining an ancestral altar in the family home and by ritual observances at the ancestral graveyard, which is supposed to occupy the most auspicious position on the land. Failure to perform rituals for the ancestors will bring misfortune and dishonor to the entire family.

Spirits of the dead who are not "fed" by family members become "hungry ghosts" who prey upon the unwary and bring mischief upon the entire village. Each August, Chinese in Hong Kong, Taiwan, and Singapore hold a Hungry Ghost Festival, in which they provide food and paper spirit money for dead spirits who do not have family to take care of them.

Ancestor reverence reinforces the responsibility of the individual to the family and extends that responsibility to the community as a whole in the practice of feeding hungry ghosts. Though Chinese belief and practice represent an unusually formal version of ancestor reverence, they are not far removed from the North American practice of holding elaborate funerals and placing flowers on the graves of dead relatives or of observing Memorial Day and Halloween. Both systems of recognizing the continuing importance of dead relatives stem from the obligations of family members to each other. The formality of the Chinese system is related to patrilineal inheritance and extended-family ownership of land; the informality of the Western system is related to the emergence of the nuclear family in association with industrialization.

SUMMARY

Religion is universal. Though no one knows how or when religion began, it is an integral part of all known societies. In Western society, it is common to view religion as an attempt to understand the workings of the universe on the basis of an inadequate knowledge of the physical world. However, the ethnographic evidence suggests that our forager ancestors were sophisticated in their knowledge of plants and animals, as are people of present-day forager societies.

Based on his study of Trobriand Islanders in the Western Pacific, Bronislaw Malinowski argued that

all societies have technology, magic, and religion. Technology—the ability to manipulate the physical world through practical knowledge and skills—is essential to all human groups. Magic—symbolic manipulation of the physical world—is called upon to ensure success in conditions of risk that defy technology. Religion—a symbolic system of explanation—defines the relationship of human beings to the supernatural and addresses questions about the meaning of human life.

Religious beliefs are encoded in myths, symbolic stories about the origin and organization of the universe. Creation myths describe the symbolic origin of the universe and provide a social charter for present-day social organization. Cosmology describes the universe symbolically, in terms of its landscape and the plant, animal, human, and spirit beings that inhabit it. Myths reflect the social organization and subsistence pattern of the society that produced them.

Ritual—the symbolic behavior characteristic of a religion—is repetitive, sequential, nonordinary, and powerful. It is believed to reinforce or change the relationship of the individual or group to the supernatural. Rites of passage ease the transition from one social state to another, a period when ordinary social status is suspended and the individual is considered "dangerous." Rites of intensification reinforce social solidarity through periodic observance of some event of symbolic importance to the group. Divination aids in decision making and restores order when an individual—or the group as a whole—is threatened by illness or misfortune.

The organization of the religious community reflects the organization of the society in which it occurs. Priests, whose authority resides in their office, are characteristic of stratified societies, where political officials wield formal authority. Shamans are typical of small-scale or egalitarian societies, in which all members of the group have access to resources and power. Shamans may also operate in stratified societies alongside priests because of their ability to heal or to settle social conflicts through access to spirits. Sorcerers and witches dramatize social conflicts and provide a means of enforcing conformity and addressing grievances that fall outside the purview of usual channels for redress.

Revitalization movements may develop during times of dramatic social change, when tensions may produce dissatisfaction with prevailing values or institutions. In the wake of European colonialism, revitalization movements developed in many parts of the world. Nativistic movements represent a call for restoration of the older order, whereas millenarian movements anticipate the end of the present unsatisfactory world and the beginning of a new, idealized social order.

POWER WORDS

agrarian	magic	rites of intensification
ancestor reverence	mana	rites of passage
ancestor spirits	millenarian movement	ritual
cargo cults	myths	ritual inversion
cosmology	nativistic movement	shaman
creation myth	nature spirits	social charter
deities	priest	sorcerer
demons	religion	souls
divination	revelation	spirit possession
ghosts	revitalization	witch
gods	movement	

INTERNET EXERCISE

1. As noted in Chapter 2, the anthropological approach to analyzing social groups is holistic. For a look at the relationship between religion and other aspects of social organization among the people of Fiji, visit the website **http://www.moon.com/travel_matters/hot_off_the_press/people_of_fiji.html**. What role do ethnicity and gender play in the social organization of Fiji?

2. Yutaka Yamada, a symbolic anthropologist, has explored life history narratives or autobiographies of members of Japanese new religions who report religious experiences such as possession, trance, visions, dreams, miraculous healing, dramatic forms of conversion, and shamanic experiences. To learn more about this relationship between religion and altered states of consciousness, check the website **http://www.anthja.com/exersymb3.html**.

3. CNN maintains a website analyzing the role of the Internet in the mass suicide of the Heaven's Gate cult in southern California in March 1997. Based on information provided at **http://www.cnn.com/US/9803/25/heavens.gate/**, do you think the Internet could contribute to the formation of cults like Heaven's Gate? Why or why not?

10

Expressive Culture

In this chapter . . .

The visual arts

People in all societies adorn objects with visual designs. Depending on the culture, the objects of their adornment may include their bodies, their utensils, their homes, their public buildings, and their ritual objects. Like other forms of expressive culture, the visual arts provide a means of depicting and reflecting upon cultural themes. The visual arts reflect the social context in which they are produced and "consumed." In stratified societies, the production of art may be controlled by elites. In less stratified societies, the production and consumption of the visual arts may be a communal activity.

Performance arts: Story telling and theater

Much cultural knowledge is transmitted through legends and folktales, which may be acted out by storytellers or in theatrical performances. When legends and folktales from one group are introduced into another, they lose much of their social and cultural context. In all societies, however, the performance of culturally meaningful stories allows us to reflect upon the human condition, both in general and with reference to our specific social group.

Performance arts: Music and dance

In Western societies, musical performances are often distinguished from dance performances, and the sacred is distinguished from the secular. In other societies, these boundaries may not be so strictly defined. In all societies, music and dance reflect social organization, especially gender roles. In a number of societies, such instruments as trumpets and flutes may be associated with male potency, and one anthropologist asserts that dance is an explicitly sexual expression of the importance of fertility and relations between females and males.

Play, sport, and festivals

Play is set apart from the "real world" conceptually, linguistically, behaviorally, and spatially. In the "protected" world of play, children learn adult roles. Games and sports reflect the social organization and economic activities of the societies in which they develop. Play may also be an exuberant and spontaneous approach to social life. Cultural values and social organization may be acted out in festivals, sacred or secular times of celebration.

Expressive culture is inextricably linked to every other aspect of social life. In his article "Art As a Cultural System," Clifford Geertz writes: "The feeling . . . a people has for life appears . . . in a great many other places than in their art. It appears in their religion, their morality, their science, their commerce, their technology, their politics, their amusements, their law, even in the way they organize their everyday practical existence" (1997:110).

Most social institutions affirm cultural values. For example, the importance of cooperation and interdependence among foragers is reflected in the division of labor along lines of age and gender, exchange based on generalized reciprocity, equal access to resources, informal leadership, and religious ritual performed by shamans who can be either male or female.

Expressive culture provides a context in which cultural values and social institutions are reflected upon and reinforced or challenged. **Expressive culture** includes the visual arts, theater, music, dance, and various forms of play— from children's play to organized sports. These are the creative wellspring from which culture is created, acted out, criticized, and affirmed or rejected.

A number of scholars use the term *play* to designate the activities described in this chapter as "expressive culture." In fact, the term *play* refers to a broad range of activities and attributes. One can "play ball," watch a "play," engage in "swordplay," or "play around." Though scholars have interpreted play in various ways depending on their usage of the term, they are unanimous in associating play with creativity. In his 1950 book *Homo Ludens* (Man the Player), the Swiss philosopher Johan Huizinga suggests that all of culture—including language, law, war, and the various forms of art—originate in play:

> Culture arises in the form of play. . . . It is played from the very beginning. Even those activities which aim at the immediate satisfaction of vital needs—hunting, for instance—tend, in archaic society, to take on the play-form. . . . In the twin union of play and culture, play is primary. (1950:46)

Structure and Antistructure

The anthropologist Victor Turner developed an extensive analysis of the relationship of play-forms to social structure. As do many other anthropologists, Turner notes that social "structure" is dynamic rather than static: "Cultural systems . . . depend not only for their meaning but also for their existence upon the participation of conscious, volitional human agents and upon men's continuing and potentially changing relations with one another" (1974:32).

Turner differentiates between "structure," which affirms pragmatic ideals, and "antistructure," which generates imagery and philosophical concepts that encourage people to reflect upon what the structure actually means. *Symbols* are the language of antistructure, the purpose of which is to pose creative alternatives to ordinary reality. Turner writes: "Rules that abolish minutiae of structural differentiation in, for example, the domains of kinship, economics, and political structure liberate the human structural propensity and give it free reign in the cultural realm of myth, ritual, and symbol" (1969:133).

There is a continual feedback loop between a society's structure and its antistructure through its expressive culture. Turner notes that he is concerned with "the constant cross-looping of social history with the numerous genres of cultural performance—ranging from ritual, through theater, the novel, folk drama, art exhibitions, ballet, modern dance, poetry readings, to film and television" (1987:77). In other words, *all* these symbolic forms have something to tell us about the nature of the society in which we live.

Turner includes in his concept of antistructure what he calls "social dramas"—real-life events that take on the symbolic importance of myth: "Each feeds and draws on the other: in this way people try to assign meaning to their 'behavior,' turning it into 'conduct.' They become reflexive, at once their own subject and object. One of the modes in which they do this is play—including games and sports, as well as festivals" (1987:77).

The meaning of our everyday lives—especially our relationships with others—is told to us through the works of those who live on the margins of society—artists, musicians, actors, and sports figures. These interpreters of the social "drama" become more important as society becomes more secularized. To some extent, Turner suggests, artists, musicians, actors, and sports figures assume the role of shamans in more traditional societies. Artists, musicians, and actors force us to question the validity of our values and institutions, whereas athletes confirm them. Scholars consider sport to be the most conservative play-form, in that it does not challenge the prevailing social order.

> Play paradoxically has become a more serious matter with the decline of ritual and the contraction of the religious sphere—in which people used to become morally reflexive, relating their lives to the values handed down in sacred traditions. The play frame, where events are scrutinized in the leisure time of the social process, has to some extent inherited the function of the ritual frame. (Turner 1987:77)

Play-forms derive much of their power from the fact that they are defined as "not real." Businesspeople engaged in hard-fought negotiations may deflect their tension or anger into a safe arena by discussing sports over lunch. War can be conducted safely on the chessboard or the football field. In the arts, social criticism is most palatable when it is combined with humor, as when comedians ridicule political leaders or social customs.

Culture is continually created and re-created in every act of human interaction, from talking "baby talk" to a child, to deciding who should be invited to a wedding, to performing a religious ritual. Nothing in human social life is a precise repetition of what has gone before, even though a particular act may be justified by tradition, as in "we've always done it

The United States' Brandi Chastain is greeted by teammates after kicking the game-winning overtime penalty shootout kick against China during the Women's World Cup Final at the Rose Bowl in Pasadena, California, July 10, 1999. The U.S. won the shootout 5–4 after the game ended in a 0–0 tie.

this way." It is in the negotiation of what we have "always done" that social organization and cultural values are continually reinvented and, in most cases, reaffirmed.

Expressive Culture and Social Organization

Expressive culture mirrors what we believe our values and social institutions "really" are. The performers, the style of performance, the audience, and the physical context are all shaped by culture and social organization. In the most undifferentiated societies, in which there is equal access to power and resources, expressive culture is open to all. Among the !Kung, for example, everyone may act out culture in dance, just as everyone may eat by gathering mongongo nuts.

Among the Netsilik, foragers above the Arctic Circle in northern Canada, all men have the option of acting out their disputes through song duels, in which they compose insulting songs about their opponents and stage their performance before a group of interested onlookers. Just as wives prepare the seal meat their husbands bring home from a hunt, the women also perform their husbands' songs. The man whose songs most entertain onlookers wins both the song duel and the dispute.

As societies become more socially differentiated, task specialization is reflected in the expressive culture. In the most complex societies, where task specialization is marked and rulers have absolute power over their subjects, actors, musicians, artists, and athletes may be full-time specialists who act out the values of their culture in their various arenas.

When expressive culture is controlled by professionals, most of the public participates primarily as spectators, or onlookers. In the United States, for example, baseball, basketball, and football teams represent their cities on the playing field, a symbolic form of competition that takes the place of more hostile rivalries between cities. Just as professional armies represent the country on the battlefield, professional athletes represent the public on the playing field. When spectators try to participate in the "warfare," they are ejected from the "game." A child may draw in kindergarten, but the picture is unlikely to be displayed in the Metropolitan Museum of Art in New York or the Louvre in Paris. The walls of art galleries are reserved for the works of recognized professional artists. You may sing in your shower, but you must pay to hear your favorite musician perform.

In the following sections, we explore the cultural and social context of four types of expressive culture: (1) the visual arts, (2) the performance arts of story telling and theater, (3) the performance arts of music and dance, and (4) the various forms of play, including sports and festivals.

VISUAL ARTS

People in all societies adorn objects with visual designs. Depending on the purpose and the social context, people may decorate their bodies, their utensils, their homes, their public buildings, and their ritual objects. All the world is a "canvas," to paraphrase William Shakespeare, and the most commonly decorated canvas is the human body. It is variously painted, etched, pierced, stretched, shrunk, split, or spliced, depending on the aesthetic prevailing in a particular culture. The body may also be decorated with jewelry or clothing.

Body Art

In different cultures, various parts of the body are painted, and the pattern of painting may reflect age, gender, or social status. In India and Morocco, among other places, a bride's hands are decorated with henna, an orange-red dye. In the United States, women may decorate their faces with cosmetics after they reach puberty. In many societies, men mark their adult status by painting designs on their bodies. Babies and children may also be adorned by painting designs on their bodies or faces.

Scarification is practiced in many societies. This is a process of decorating the body by inflicting wounds and allowing the wounds to heal. The wounds typically result in raised bumps similar to welts left by

Body decoration occurs in all societies. Among the Paiwan, aboriginal people of Taiwan, tattooing is considered a mark of beauty. This Paiwanese woman displays her tattoos for her fellow villagers and for the camera.

mosquito bites, but the marks caused by scarification are permanent. Scarification is performed by people trained in the art. The marks can be of different shapes and form a decorative pattern. Nuba girls of the southern Sudan are scarified on their abdomen and torso at puberty. The skin is repeatedly hooked with a sharp thorn, pulled away from a woman's body and sliced with a small metal knife (Faris 1972). The scarification is extended after a woman has given birth and weaned her first child. Males are also scarified in some other African groups.

Tattooing is also widely practiced. Among Samoans, both women and men are tattooed as a mark of adult status. Combs made from a polished section of boar's tusk are dipped into ink made from kerosene soot and water and then hammered into the skin. The process is extremely painful, and extensive tattoos are a mark of stoicism. Men are tattooed in a dense pattern that covers the entire body, except for the pubic area, from midtorso to just below the knee. Women are tattooed in a less dense pattern around the thighs to just below the knees. Before Western contact, tattooing was a mark of chiefly status.

Various parts of the body may also be pierced or otherwise surgically altered. In Western cultures, the ear lobes are most commonly pierced. Lip discs, or *labrets*, are worn by some South American Indian groups, such as the Kayapo of Brazil. The nobility among the Aztecs of Central Mexico wore lip pendants, lip plugs, and ear plugs. Commoners were not permitted to display these luxury items.

Anthropomorphic Imagery

In addition to the human body, various types of utilitarian objects are artistically enhanced. Nicholas David, Judy Sterner, and Kodzo Gavua suggest that the widespread practice of decorating clay pots is due to their association with the human body: "We shall argue that pots 'are' persons and that concepts of the body are closely related to and partly determinative of decorative expression on pots (and sometimes other media also)" (1988:365). In his response to this analysis, Warren DeBoer notes that archaeologists "regularly use the anthropomorphic terminology of 'mouth,' 'lip,' 'neck,' 'shoulder,' 'body,' 'leg,' and 'foot' in describing ceramic vessels" (1988:381).

Anthropomorphism is the practice of attributing human characteristics to a nonhuman being or object. It is a form of symbolic imagery known as *metaphor,* in which meaning is evoked by analogy or comparison. For example, the assertion by David, Sterner, and Gavua that "pots 'are' persons" is a metaphor. Similarly, in the statement "life is a journey, not a destination," the terms *journey* and *destination* are metaphors that make a symbolic analogy or comparison between our experience of life and the process of traveling from one place to another.

Attributing "life" or "spirit" to decorated objects is widespread among the people who make the objects. Many woodcarvers believe that the design of the finished object is inherent in the wood, and they are simply liberating its spirit. Some Hopi potters dream the designs they apply to their pots, which they view as being imbued with spirit. As depicted in the film about Hopi symbolism *Songs of the Fourth World,* a pot made by one craftswoman and used for holding corn was viewed as a metaphor for the womb, which holds life in the form of a child. For the Hopi, a woman's ability to transmit life by bearing children is symbolically linked to corn, which sustains life for the Hopi.

David, Sterner, and Gavua analyze the symbolism of pottery produced by the Mafa and Bulahay, two horticulturalist groups in the highlands of northern Cameroon in Africa. They note that, in these societies, pots are viewed as representing God or human beings, either dead or living:

> God pots are equipped with a head and a left arm and hand and may, as do those representing males, have a stylized bearded chin and moustache. Occasionally a stylized penis appears on male ancestor pots, female ones have breasts and a vulva. The Mafa pot representing twins . . . has two bodies joined in one mouth, corresponding to the belief that twins' souls or spirits are indissolubly linked. (1988:371)

The various forms of the visual arts—from pots to paintings—often express or reflect religious beliefs. For example, vodou (voodoo) artists of Haiti take their inspiration from the loa, or spirits. The artists believe themselves to be possessed by the loa, who then direct the execution of a painting or a mural. Nelson H. H. Graburn writes:

> Indeed, it has often been said that traditional religions are the raison d'être [reason for being] for local art traditions, and though this is not universally true (for secular beliefs such as rank and power are also expressed), the death of the local religion often coincides with the demise of the functional arts. (1976:12)

The human affinity for adornment is universal. People in all societies decorate their bodies, their tools and utensils, and their abodes. Where they exist, public buildings also provide a "canvas" for the artistic touch. Here, a Hopi woman carefully removes a decorated pot from its mold.

Much of the art of India and ancient Greece and Rome depicts the gods, both male and female. Religious themes and images are also prevalent in European art. The sixteenth-century Italian artist Michelangelo is among the most famous practitioners of this form of art. In some cases, religious art is believed to embody sacred power. These images or objects are known as **icons.** In archaeology, **iconography** is the analysis of conventional images, either sacred or secular, used to decorate pots, baskets, and other objects within a culture.

Art and Society

Jacques Maquet (1986) distinguishes between art and aesthetics. He notes that all societies have an aesthetic tradition, in that all known groups decorate their bodies, tools, and living quarters. However, Maquet suggests that not all societies have art, which he defines as objects produced specifically for artistic purposes. Production of these objects, which include paintings and sculptures, is associated with task specialization. By implication, making art objects is also associated with stratification, in that it requires a class of elites who can commission such works and a class of artisans who can produce them. **Artisans** are specialized craftspeople who may produce items from leather, gold, silver, precious or semiprecious stones, feathers, stone, or many other objects.

In the Western tradition, art is "owned," either by the artist or by the consumer. This sense of possessing a work of art may be associated with stratification; it is not a universal characteristic of the artistic process. Paul Bohannan observes that among the Tiv of Africa, making an artistic design may be a communal activity. He describes the process of carving walking sticks:

> The most astounding feature, to me, was that comparatively few of the designs were by a single individual. As I sat watching a young man of about thirty carve a stick one day, he was called away. He laid aside his stick and the double-edged knives with which he was cutting the design. A guest came in a few moments later, picked up the stick and added a few designs. A little later, he handed it to someone else. Four men put designs on that stick before the owner returned and finished it. ([1961] 1968:741)

Figure carving may be an individual activity, but art criticism is communal. Men feel free to comment on another man's creative work and help to shape its design: "In Tivland, almost every man is a critic. Because there are no specialists in taste and only a few in the manufacture of art, every man is free to know what he likes and to make it if he can" (Bohannan [1961] 1968:745).

In stratified societies, artistic taste and expression are controlled by elites and the artists they employ. Some analysts distinguish between "fine art," produced by specialists employed by elites, and "folk art," objects produced by members of the lower classes for their own use (Graburn 1976). However, many anthropologists consider this distinction to reflect a Western, elitist bias. Objects made by artists from the lower classes or from non-Western societies become folk art when they are purchased for display by elite Western art consumers. Graburn writes:

> In stratified societies that consist of dominant and conquered strata, the arts of the latter peoples may be of two major types: (1) Those arts—the inwardly directed arts—that are made for, appreciated, and used by peoples within their own part-society; these arts have important functions in maintaining ethnic identity and social structure, and in didactically instilling the important values in group members. (2) Those arts made for an external, dominant world; these have often been despised by connoisseurs as unimportant, and are sometimes called "tourist" or "airport" arts. (1976:4–5)

Graburn adds that, though "tourist" art may be despised by connoisseurs, it is "important in presenting to the outside world an ethnic image that must be maintained and projected as part of the all-important boundary-defining system" (1976:5).

The visual arts—whatever their source or "canvas"—express a world view that includes values and experiences particular to the culture that produces the art objects. The expression of these values is shaped by the social context, which defines who may produce the art, who may consume it, and how it may be displayed. When members of one culture consume the visual arts of another, the social and cultural context shifts. In the process, the tastes and expectations of the outside consumers may reshape and redefine the artist or culture that produced the art objects. Through their patronage, elite consumers may define the classification and characteristics of folk art.

Though they may seem to be static representations of immutable reality, the visual arts, like other aspects of expressive culture, are part of a dynamic process of defining cultural and social context.

PERFORMANCE ARTS:
STORY TELLING AND THEATER

Cultural values and the organization of social relationships are typically conveyed to us through **legends,** stories of heroic beings who have helped to shape our "history," and through **folktales,** stories that do not purport to report historical events but that do convey concepts important to a culture. These stories are a pleasurable form of moral instruction. Though their form and context are playful, the messages they convey are serious. Legends and folktales may be a secular adjunct to religious mythology. For example, Christian children in North America may be told both the story of Christ and the story of Cinderella.

Oral Traditions

We rarely get to hear the myths and legends of other societies. If we learn about them at all, it is through reading about them. This removes them from their social and cultural context. In oral traditions, folktales are meant to be acted out. They gain much of their power from the voice inflections and histrionic performances of the people who tell them. Oral traditions of people without a written language are flexible enough to allow for interpretation by the story-teller. Napoleon Chagnon observes that the Yanomamö have a rich system of beliefs about the nature of the cosmos, the human soul, and the plants and animals around them. This rich tradition is kept alive through the art of story telling:

> One fascinating dimension of their intellectual world is the extent to which individuals can manipulate and elaborate on the ideas and themes, but within a set of limits demanded by orthodoxy and local versions of "Truth." Not only can individuals "experiment" as artists and creators, but there is room for poets and verbal "essayists" as well. Despite lacking a written language, the Yanomamo have considerable freedom to turn a clever phrase or state something in a more sophisticated way than others are capable of doing. Some Yanomamo play with their rich language and work at being what we might call literary or learned. (Chagnon 1992:99)

Even in societies with a written language, the vigor of a particular concept may hinge on a turn of phrase, as in the famous soliloquy by Hamlet:

> To be, or not to be: that is the question:
> Whether 't is nobler in the mind to suffer
> The slings and arrows of outrageous fortune,
> Or to take arms against a sea of troubles,
> And by opposing end them. To die, to sleep—
> No more; and by a sleep to say we end
> The heart-ache and the thousand natural shocks
> That flesh is heir to: 't is a consummation
> Devoutly to be wish'd. To die; to sleep;—
> To sleep, perchance to dream; ay, there's the rub. . . .

Imagine how that eloquent sentiment would have been received if Shakespeare had chosen to write: "Should I suffer in silence or fight against my problems? Sometimes I just want to die and put an end to the whole business. But what if death is like sleep? Then I might not escape my problems; I would just experience them as a nightmare."

The convention is to portray Hamlet as an idealistic youth with high moral standards, but an actor playing Hamlet could put an entirely different spin on the story through the use of a gesture, posture, or inflection of the voice.

The Social Context

One barrier to understanding the folktales of other cultures is that we are unfamiliar with the context that makes them meaningful. Laura Bohannan describes her frustration in telling the story of Hamlet to a group of Tiv elders on a rainy day in West Africa. Story telling is a skilled art among the Tiv, and Bohannan was "aided" in her account of Hamlet's story by the interpretations provided by senior males. Bohannan's audience was fascinated by the story, which they interpreted as an example of filial disrespect and flouting of kinship rules by Hamlet. The Tiv practice the levirate, in which a woman marries the brother of her deceased husband, so they heartily approved the marriage of Hamlet's widowed mother to his uncle:

> "He did well," the old man beamed and announced to the others. "I told you that if we knew more about Europeans, we would find they really were very like us. In our country also," he added to me, "the younger brother marries the elder brother's widow and becomes the father of his children." (Bohannan [1966] 1990:81)

The Tiv rejected the idea that the ghost of Hamlet's father asked him to exact revenge on his brother and widow, because the Tiv do not have a concept of ghosts. As they put it, "Dead men don't walk." However, the Tiv do have a concept of witches, so they attributed Ophelia's death by drowning to witchcraft, since only witches can cause drowning. The Tiv also concluded that Ophelia's brother Laertes was the agent of witchcraft since he leaped into his sister's grave. The Tiv believed that the only possible motive for this strange act is that Laertes wanted to steal Ophelia's body and sell it to the witches.

Folktales and legends teach by the examples of the people in the story. For example, the story of Cinderella in Western culture conveys a wealth of information about social relationships and appropriate behavior for women. The stepmother's favoritism toward her biological daughters and her mistreatment of Cinderella reflect cultural views regarding the mother–child bond. Biological mothers can be trusted; stepmothers cannot. The stepmother and stepsisters are punished for their greed and for rising above their station. They are rejected by the prince because their large feet will not fit into Cinderella's tiny glass slipper.

Cinderella, in marrying the prince, is rewarded for her dedication to duty, her modesty, and her petite beauty. The dowry she brings to her marriage is her beauty and modesty; she does not have to be intelligent, witty, or well educated. On the other hand, the prince does not exhibit superior intellectual qualities, either. He is the hero by virtue of being handsome and occupying a high status; Cinderella is drawn to the ball by his wealth and social position.

The story also reflects the Western cultural concept that marriage can be based solely on physical attraction. Though his marriage to Cinderella will involve a transfer of wealth and social status, as well as succession to the throne, the prince knows nothing of the mother of his future children and heirs except that she is beautiful.

In many societies, folktales and religious myths are enacted on the stage by professional musicians or actors. Shakespeare's play *King Lear,* for example, retells the story of a legendary king of early Britain. In India, the *Mahabharata* is a Hindu epic poem describing the history of the Bharatas, people descended from a legendary hero of that name. Like the Judaic Bible, the *Mahabharata* was apparently compiled from a number of sources. Though compiled at least twenty-five hundred years ago, the *Mahabharata* is still acted out at Hindu festivals and forms the basis for some Hindu films. One part of the *Mahabharata* is the *Bhagavad Gita,* or *Song of God,* which imparts instruction on the importance of fulfilling one's duties as a member of a particular caste, on the nature of the god Krishna as the manifestation of Ultimate Reality, and on the various yogas, or spiritual paths.

The Human Dimension

Reading a legend, myth, or folktale to oneself can be a profoundly intimate experience that allows one to act out the story in one's mind. Telling the story or acting it out in a public context enhances the social content of the story. The personality of the storyteller and the visual drama of a play help to shape or enhance the meaning of the story. Watching the performance as a member of an audience also helps to shape our experience because we can draw on the reactions of others.

According to anthropologist Laurel Ashley Petersen: "In watching a comedy, we are able to laugh at human foibles, either satirically or sympathetically; a drama emphasizes the human dilemma" (pers. comm. 1996). The power of the theatrical performance rests on our ability to identify with the hero or central character. As Ashley Petersen puts it, "We can celebrate the hero and, by doing so, celebrate the human spirit. On the other hand we can lament the mysteries of the human condition" (pers. comm. 1996).

PERFORMANCE ARTS: MUSIC AND DANCE

As do other artistic forms, music and dance reflect culture and social organization. Cultural values can be conveyed in the words of a song, and the performance of a song or a dance is dependent on the social context. Rights to perform a song or dance nearly always reflect gender and other aspects of social organization. Though people in Western societies distinguish between musical performances and dance as well as between sacred and secular performances, in most societies performances of music and dance are inseparable, and there may be little or no dividing line between the sacred and the secular.

Colin Turnbull (1962) notes that BaMbuti foragers of the Ituri rain forest in Africa treat the *molimo,* a fifteen-foot-long musical instrument in the form of a pipe, as though it were alive. Women are not allowed to see the instrument, and male youths are not allowed to see it until they have proven themselves as hunters. When carrying the molimo through the forest, men immerse it in water whenever they stop at a stream to drink, saying, "The molimo likes to drink."

The molimo is played every night during the two-month "molimo festival." Each day, offerings of food and drink are collected from everyone in the camp, which is sealed off from the outside world. Turnbull writes of a festival he witnessed: "Before the men gathered together that evening I found that the path leading out of the camp toward the village had been closed. A fallen branch and some logs had been dragged across it, shutting out the profane outside world" (1962:80). Before the performance could begin, women and children shut themselves inside

Myths and folktales preserve many of the traditions of a society. Often they are acted out in some dramatic fashion, as in this scene performed at the Kyoto Theater in Japan. The formal staging by professional actors is characteristic of settled agricultural societies, which tend to be stratified.

their huts. Turnbull describes the performance:

> As the men sang in the camp, the voice of the molimo echoed their song, moving about continually so that it seemed to be everywhere at once. During a lull in the singing it started giving animal growls, and the men looked around to make sure that all the women were safely in their huts. Almost immediately Amabosu and Madyadya came running into the camp from the far end . . . , their feet up high in the air so that . . . they seemed to be floating above the ground they trod. (1962:81)

The two men were carrying the molimo. Madyadya balanced one end of it on his shoulder as Amabosu sang into the other end. Turnbull observes, "I noticed that the trumpet was still wet; it must have been given a 'drink' just before it was carried into the camp" (1962:81). The two men squatted down on either side of the campfire and engaged in a call-and-answer song with the men already gathered around the fire. Turnbull writes:

> Madyadya took the end of the trumpet in his hands and waved it up and down, passing it through the flames of the molimo fire and over the heads of all of us sitting there. Some of the men took up hot ashes and rubbed them over the trumpet, and some even put live coals in at the far end. As Amabosu sang harder and louder, sparks flew out over Madyadya's shoulder, disappearing into the night with the song. (1962:81)

In playing the molimo, the BaMbuti replicate the sounds of animals as well as the human voice. Turnbull describes one impromptu performance:

> Little more than a minute had passed when Amabosu, the great singer, appeared from the shadows below us. He looked at us without saying anything, without smiling or making any greeting. His eyes had the strange look they often took on when he was singing or playing the drums in a dance in the village. They seemed to be seeing something quite different from what was going on in front of them. He went up to Ausu and took the molimo from him and gently filled the forest with strange sounds—the rumblings and growls of buffaloes and leopards, the mighty call of the elephant, the plaintive cooing of the dove. Interspersed were snatches of song, transformed by the trumpet into a sound quite

DISCUSSIONS

The Story of "Being Indian"

Cultural knowledge is not rigid and unyielding. The various forms of expressive culture both reinforce tradition and provide a means for incorporating flexibility and changing circumstances into a society's world view and self-definition. In the following article, Joseph P. Gone, a cultural anthropologist and Gros Ventre Indian, explains how a story of his own family history links tradition with a changing cultural context.

"WE WERE THROUGH AS KEEPERS OF IT": THE "MISSING PIPE NARRATIVE" AND GROS VENTRE CULTURAL IDENTITY

Joseph P. Gone

In the summer of 1994, I inaugurated a journey that took me into the homes of many of my tribal elders on the Fort Belknap Indian reservation. I sought a better understanding of how contemporary Gros Ventres of my grandparents' generation make sense of being Gros Ventre, and detailed conversations with my tribal elders promised rich insight into modern Gros Ventre cultural identity. In one conversation with a respected elder, I was told that "being Indian" is "nothing but a story." Here, in the very words of this venerated elder, I heard a conviction shared by many proponents of narrative analysis (Mishler 1986, Somers 1994, Schiffrin 1996): identity and narrative are inextricably intertwined.

The narrative performance analyzed here is principally concerned with an account elicited from Mrs. Bertha Snow, my grandmother, in the spring of 1995. The historical events recounted in the "Missing Pipe Narrative" involve the traumatic discovery by an elderly Gros Ventre man that one of the sacred Pipes entrusted to his care by the Gros Ventre people was missing from its ceremonial bundle. The events described occurred in the southwestern area of the Fort Belknap Reservation near the Catholic mission within a decade of the close of World War II. The narrative consists primarily of quoted speech attributed to Bertha's father interspersed with commentary provided by her. The narrative begins with Grandma situating her father at home in his cabin:

He said, "I was sitting here reading and happened to glance up." He said, "In fact, I got up to get myself a cup of coffee." And he drank coffee all day long, a great big pot. He said, "Here this kid was running toward the house, and gee, I didn't know who he was really, until he got close and I recognized him." And he just come up on the porch, and the door was open all the time, you know, in the summer time. He was all out of breath and he said, "Fred, my dad wants you." He turned and ran all the way back home. He'd run and then he'd walk and he'd run. "And, boy, I grabbed my hat," he said, "and checked to see if I had enough matches and Durham. And I took off and I walked real fast over there. And I got there and I went in." He'd go visiting and talk about things and, you know, listen to (them). Talk about serious things that [happened] long ago. He made it his business to go talk to these old people.

And he said, "When I went in, his wife was in the kitchen, that little lean-to shed on a little log cabin, they used that for kitchen and dining area, and they slept in the log cabin. Usually, when I come to visit him he's sitting on his bed which is right in front of the door. His daughters has a bed over there. His sons have a bed. Two daughters and two sons."

"Here where I come in," he said, "that old man was sitting on the floor, and he had a plate of coals in front of him, and he was smudging. And he was crying. Tears were coming down his face. Geez, you know, scared me. For a while I thought maybe he had a heart attack or he got real sick and that's what I thought was wrong, you know." But he said, "After I saw him sitting like that, I just figured it was something else that was wrong (with him). So I sat down on a chair. They had a chair sitting right there waiting for me. I sat down and I didn't say a word. I figure in his own good time he's gonna tell me what he wants." So he got through with his smudge. He sat back, I guess. They sit like this you know, flat on the floor.

In the next segment of the narrative, the "he" in the story is the old man:

Then he took a deep breath I guess and he said, "Something unusual happened with that bundle this morning. When my wife got up to make fire, she happened to glance up there, and here she seen something laying on top of this bundle. So she goes closer and she looks at it and here it's a pelt. It's one of those pelts that belong inside this bundle." He said, "I'm scared and I don-no what happened. I don't know what to think. What's going on? I don't know. I don't know how to explain it."

"So I made her take it down," he said, "and bring it over to me, and sure enough, she took the whole bundle down she didn't touch that pelt. She took the whole bundle off of the nail." And see they'd tie it like this, with part of the string over this way, and

then they'd tie it around here so that it's got a handle. And that's hanging on a nail. So she brought it to him, and he—they—both looked at it really good to see if it had been tampered with, because right away I guess they thought maybe their kids got into it. But you know, in a way, they thought that people might think their kids got into it. But he knew his kids wouldn't get into it because he was an oldtimer and he knew he had his kids trained not to even consider touching that bundle, you know. And when the daughters got to that age, that bundle wasn't supposed to be in the house, when they have their menses. So they had to know. The mother told them to tell them when they did, they'd take the bundle and put it outside in the back of the house. So those four days—four, five days—that bundle would be outside.

Anyway he said, after they looked at it real good, and they said the knots and everything looked like they had never been tampered with. It was just the way it was—lord knows when was the last time they opened it you know. And so they-he opened it I guess to put this thing back in there. He said when he opened it, the Feathered Pipe itself was gone. He said, "And I'm responsible for this bundle. What are the people gonna say about me? How am I going to explain that pipe is gone? It's gone. What am I gonna do, you know?"

The significance of this cataclysmic event is narrated in terms of the consequences surrounding a pivotal existential crisis. The disappearance of the sacred Pipe that has been entrusted by the community to his care threatens not only to throw Gros Ventre belief and tradition into complete disarray but also to disrupt the old man's relationships with community members. The narrative voice then shifts to Grandma's father's response to the old man's predicament:

"Oh gee," he said, "I didn't know what to say. I really pitied this poor old man, because I know he's innocent. I know he would not ever consider letting anybody, or you know, his family wouldn't. I know his family wouldn't touch it. So I just said a prayer in the way I know how to the Blessed Virgin Mary, 'Please help me. Give me the right words to put this poor old man's mind at ease, so that he won't be blaming himself for something that he's not responsible for. If it be God's will, let me say the right words.'"

So I guess he started to talk. I don't know what all, but this is just what he told me: "I told him, 'This is, you know, we were all taught to respect and love this pipe, because all these years, far back as we could remember, our people have told us what this pipe has done for us. Down the years, it's been our father our grandfather our leader our protector. It's told us when to move. It's told us where to find buffalo to feed our families. It's told us everything. It has guided our lives all our lives. But today, they're teaching our children a different religion. Our children are learning things we never did learn.'" And he said, "Being as the Supreme Being gave us this pipe in a supernatural way, to protect, guide, and take care of us all these years since we got it, why shouldn't he take it back when he thinks we don't need it anymore?"

For Grandma, Gros Ventre spirituality is characterized by a radical *historical discontinuity* (Gone 1996) whereby ancestral Gros Ventre ceremonial tradition has been decisively and irre-versibly superseded by Catholicism, as a result of white domination and supernatural design. In the present narrative, the significance of the disappearance of the sacred Pipe is interpreted by her father in just this way. A second line of argument employed by Bertha's father pertains to the Pipe's status as an "orphan," given the drastic decline in ceremonial knowledge since the death of its greatest Keeper, Bull Lodge:

"You know yourself it's an orphan. It didn't leave a successor to Bull Lodge. Ever since Bull Lodge died, the pipe's been an orphan. His brothers took care of it. You know that yourself, you lived with it. You've been taking care of it, and you know your daughter isn't gonna be able to take care of it. So? It stands to reason that the Great Spirit came and got his child. That's all I could tell you. That's the way it looks to me. But I think that's what happened," he said.

The significance of orphan status in Gros Ventre life would be difficult to overemphasize, given the emphasis placed on *kinship obligations*. For example, my grandmother's esteem for this cultural ideal (Gone 1996) involves the expectation that Gros Ventres will provide materially for both their immediate and extended families (raising their sibling's children, if necessary) and generally support their "relations" in any significant family matter.

In this context, then, "orphan" status is seen to involve alienation from familial comfort and guidance as well as from shared material resources. As such, orphans are truly "pitiful" in Gros Ventre society, and Grandma quotes her father as portraying the Pipe as horribly alienated from the

(continued)

DISCUSSIONS

The Story of "Being Indian" (*continued*)

kinship relationships that it formerly enjoyed with its ceremonial Keepers. Recall that previously the old man cast his dilemma in terms of the potential for disrupted social relationships that might attend the inexplicable disappearance of the Pipe for which he cared. Grandma quotes her father as concluding his monologue in response to this concern:

> "Because you looked at that bundle. You say it hasn't been tampered with. I believe you, and I think everybody else would believe you too, because that's what people think of you. They think very highly of you. They would never accuse you of mishandling this pipe."

The old man's anxiety regarding the social consequences of his predicament emerges from the significance of social relationships for Gros Ventre personhood. For Gros Ventre people, personal status depends to a large degree on the relationships one maintains in the community. This intricate connection between individual status and social ties motivates my grandmother's esteem for the cultural ideal of *community-mindedness* (Gone 1996). Thus, to be severed from one's relationships in the community is a fate almost too horrible to contemplate. Grandma's father speaks to this angst by closing his monologue with comforting words designed to assuage the old man's fears.

The conclusion of the Missing Pipe Narrative centers on the old man's response to this explanation for the Pipe's disappearance:

> The old man listened and listened I guess and didn't say a word. He says, "Yeah," he says, "maybe you're right. It really shook me up." And dad says, "You know

what? Maybe I *am* right. Where did I get those words from? I got help from the Supreme Being."

This resolution is significant for two reasons. First, Grandma uses the present tense three times in quoting the words of first the old man and then her father. This switch to present tense may function to mark the interpretation ratified in the resolution as significant for Gros Ventre understanding today. Second, neither the old man nor Grandma's father is portrayed as dogmatically asserting the truth of these interpretations—both use the qualifier *maybe* in this segment of dialogue.

This caution in accepting interpretations of spiritual matters is reminiscent of two other features of my grandmother's world view. First, a moral universe saturated with spirituality raises the issue of *authority* for Grandma (Gone 1996), for the meanings of spiritual phenomena require considerable expertise and experience if they are to be discerned. The absence of such expertise in modern Gros Ventre life—given the abrupt discontinuation of Gros Ventre tradition—confronts my grandmother with the same crisis of authority that probably confronted (to a lesser degree) the narrative characters as well, given the significant decline of ceremonial tradition even at that time. Second, even if seasoned spiritual leaders existed then or today, there would be no guarantee that an authoritative interpretation of spiritual occurrences was always possible. For it is the nature of the numinous, according to Grandma (Gone 1996), to resist conclusive rational analysis—spiritual phenomena tend to retain their *mystery*.

Grandma herself offers an alternative explanation, in which she evalu-

ates the fact that photographs were taken of the sacred Pipe at a public opening of the bundle long after the precise details of the ritual had been forgotten:

> Well, maybe, maybe they shouldn't have done that. Because taking pictures of things like that is a taboo. And they took a lot of photographs that time. That's when that pipe had his nose twisted out of shape and so he pulled out.

In these words, Grandma Bertha recognizes the alternative explanation to the "divine plan" scenario, namely, that Gros Ventres themselves are responsible for the disappearance of the Pipe owing to *ritual malfeasance*. Each of these explanations has serious implications for the kind of cultural identity available to modern Gros Ventre people. If the Pipe is understood to have disappeared as a result of ritual negligence on the part of the Gros Ventres, the kinds of cultural identity available to modern tribal members emerge from the failure of *tenacity* (or effectual ambition) and the subsequent loss of *primacy* (cultural ideals important to my grandmother [Gone 1996]) to Catholicism and its Caucasian advocates. In contrast, if one understands that the Pipe was taken away by the Supreme Being because a Gros Ventre conversion to Catholicism was in the divine plan, then modern Gros Ventre identity may proceed with its cultural ideals intact and even reinforced (Fowler 1987).

Source: Adapted from Joseph P. Gone, "We Were Through as Keepers of It: The 'Missing Pipe Narrative' and Gros Ventre Cultural Identity," *Ethos* 27:4, December 1999.

unlike the song of men—richer, softer, more distant and unapproachable. (1962:78)

Dance, Trance, and Healing

As Turnbull implies, musical and dance performances are often associated with **trance,** an altered state of consciousness that can be induced by repetitive drumming, dancing, or by chemical means. !Kung foragers of the Kalahari Desert in Africa use trance dancing to heat up their *n/um,* or healing force. Marjorie Shostak describes the healing ceremony: "To the sound of undulating melodies sung by women, the healers dance around and around the fire, sometimes for hours. The music, the strenuous dancing, the smoke, the heat of the fire, and the healers' intense concentration cause their n/um to heat up. When it comes to a boil, trance is achieved" (1983:292).

When the n/um of the trance dancer has been fully heated, it becomes available as a powerful healing force. Shostak notes that it is then available to serve the entire community:

In trance, a healer lays hands on and ritually cures everyone sitting around the fire. His hands flutter lightly beside each person's head or chest or wherever illness is evident; his body trembles, his breathing becomes deep and coarse; and he becomes coated with a thick sweat—also considered to be embued with power. Whatever "badness" is discovered in the person is drawn into the healer's own body and met by the

n/um coursing up his spinal column. The healer gives a mounting cry that culminates in a soul-wrenching shriek as the illness is catapulted out of his body and into the air. (1983:292)

Shostak suggests that the concept of n/um is consistent with the "basically egalitarian nature of !Kung life. It is not reserved for a privileged few: nearly half the men and a third of the women have it. There is enough for everyone; it is infinitely divisible; and all can strive for it" (1983:294).

Dance and Society

Alan Lomax (1968) observes that musical rhythms and body movements in dance vary predictably cross-culturally depending on differences in social organization. For example, he notes that movement patterns of African dances are intermediate in complexity between those of Pacific Island groups and what he calls "Old High Cultures," which include areas of Asia and North Africa. Lomax adds that the body movements of dance are related to movements required in work:

In the Pacific an undulating movement spreads from the center of the torso, but in Africa the upper and lower body halves may be engaged in different activities and move in different directions, not only in the hip-swinging dances of Africa and Afro-America, but in work activity, as well. For instance, a Dogon woman [of Africa], planting seed in the fields, drops the millet grain into a furrow with her left hand and then, as she steps across

Before donning his lion mask for an appearance in a Chinese festival, this dancer "becomes" the lion in the movements of his body. Dances are part of festivals in many different societies. It is customary to dance on ritual occasions, such as weddings and initiation rites, as well as for enjoyment.

Sports, Gender, and Social Class

Gertrude Butterwick would have been proud the day the U.S. Women's Soccer Team won the women's World Cup and drew the United States into the world community of soccer fans, a feat that had long eluded the U.S. Men's Soccer Team. Gertrude Butterwick is the fictional heroine of P. G. Wodehouse's witty novels about upper-class England. Gertrude combines all the feminine graces with a fierce intensity honed by excelling at field hockey, an accomplishment believed to be incompatible with femininity in U.S. culture. Wodehouse describes a tense moment when Gertrude's cousin Reggie Tennyson urges her to reconcile with a suitor she has rejected:

> "One of these days you will wake up in the cold grey dawn kicking yourself because you were such a chump as to let Monty get away from you. What's the matter with Monty? Good-looking, amiable, kind to animals, wealthy to the bursting point—you couldn't have a better bet. And, in the friendliest spirit, may I inquire who the dickens you think you are? Greta Garbo, or somebody? Don't you be a goat, young Gertrude. You take my advice and run after him and give him a nice big kiss and tell him you're sorry that you were such a mug and that it's all on again."

An all-England centre-forward can be very terrible when roused, and the levin flash in Gertrude Butterwick's handsome eyes seemed to suggest that Reginald Tennyson was about to be snubbed with a ferocity which in his enfeebled state could not but

have the worst effects. That hard stare was back on her face. She looked at him as if he were a referee who had just penalized her for sticks in the game of the season.

Fortunately, before she could give utterance to her thoughts bells began to ring and whistles to blow, and the panic fear of being left behind by a departing train sank the hockey player in the woman. With a shrill and purely feminine squeak, Gertrude bounded off.[*]

In the proud tradition of Gertrude Butterwick, the U.S. Women's Soccer Team achieved yet another prize, greater acceptance of women in competitive team sports. North America has produced many sports champions in diving, tennis, and other individual sports. Women have competed in golf in both Canada and the United States since early in the twentieth century. In Canada, Marlene Streit dominated women's golf from 1953 to 1963. In the United States, "Babe" Didrikson Zaharias was an all-around athlete. She won gold medals in the 1932 Los Angeles Olympics for the javelin and 80-meter high hurdles and broke the record for the high jump. When she took up golf, Zaharias became the U.S. Ladies' Champion in 1947 and the first American British Ladies' Champion in 1947. She won the U.S. Women's Open in 1948, 1950, and 1954.

Tennis has been considered a suitable game for women from the beginnings of the sport, in the British Isles in the late nineteenth century. On a social level, the game seems to

have been viewed as a recreational activity similar to dancing, only more vigorous. The sport historian J. A. Cuddon writes "[Tennis] was extremely popular at house parties, not least because men and women could play together (hence 'mixed doubles'). Many a romance began (and ended) on the tennis court" (1979:498). Tennis also freed Victorian women from their "sartorial burdens of tight corsets and bodices, their bustles and long dresses (not to mention their cumbersome hats)," so that they "volleyed and spun their way into gentlemen's hearts" (Cuddon 1979:498).

Clearly, the vigorous sport of tennis was not perceived by nineteenth-century Victorians as being antithetical to gracious femininity. Still, the first Wimbledon match, held in 1877 as a fundraiser for the All-England Croquet Club, featured only one event: men's singles. The first competitive tennis match for women was held at the Fitzwilliam Club in Dublin in 1879, and women were allowed to compete at Wimbledon in 1884, little more than a dozen years after the inception of the prestigious championships.

Tennis quickly spread to the United States and the British commonwealth countries, where women contributed to the sport from the outset. Dominance of both men's and women's tennis shifted from Europe to the United States and Australia after World War II. Though U.S. men tennis players were somewhat eclipsed by the Australians in

---

[*]P. G. Wodehouse, *The Luck of the Bodkins* (Penguin Books, 1925), pp. 24–25.

the twenty years after the war, U.S. women virtually controlled the sport internationally.

British women were more successful than British men in challenging the drift of tennis titles from England to the former English colonies. Cuddon writes: "In the 1950s and 1960s British women made a fair showing in international tennis. They appeared somewhat more aggressive than the men, and needed to be to have a chance against the Americans and Australians" (1979:505).

The dominance of U.S. women was challenged between 1959 and 1966 by the Brazilian tennis star Maria Bueno. The fierce rivalry between the Brazilian and Margaret Court of the United States drew international attention to the sport. Maria Bueno "was regarded as a national heroine in her country. A postage stamp and a statue commemorated her feats" (Cuddon 1979:504).

The history of tennis challenges the prevailing North American view that the public is not interested in women's sports and that vigorous sports are not suitable for women. How can this seeming paradox be explained? For one thing, tennis from its beginnings has been an elitist sport. Having access to a tennis court and coach requires a tremendous financial investment, and training must begin in childhood. Tennis players typically make their mark in their late teens and early twenties. Thus, until recently, the sport has been dominated by athletes from the upper classes who can afford to invest in a pursuit that had little chance of financial return.

In many stratified societies, women of the upper classes or royal family have been able to participate in vigorous or competitive sports as part of their privileged social position. Queen Elizabeth I was an avid hunter.

Noblewomen of the ancient Persian Empire played polo, a game that developed on the Mongolian steppes as training for warfare. Historically, in Japan, samurai training was open to women of the samurai class. An essential criterion for becoming a samurai was being born into a warrior clan, or *uji*. Stephen Turnbull writes:

> A samurai band was organized like an extended family, with a nucleus of real kinsmen. Kinship terms were used to define relationships between members even though they were not true blood relatives. . . . The closest group to the clan leader, who was also the *shoen* [family land] owner, was his immediate family, *ichimon*. Branch families were called *ie no ko*, literally boys of the house, and nonkin samurai were *kenin*, or housemen. . . .The *kenin* received protection from the leader, to whom they owed loyalty in return for rights to a certain portion of the clan *shoen* lands. (1982:17)

Ultimately, the test of a samurai was the display of courage and skill on the battlefield. Twelfth-century Japan was the scene of a series of wars between the Minamoto and Taira clans, an era that marked the rise of the samurai heroine Tomoe Gozen, the wife of Minamoto Yoshinaka. The story of her last great battle is described in the thirteenth-century epic the *Heike Monogatari*. She and her husband had been defeated and surrounded, and her *naginata*, a long javelin-like sword, had been lost. She plunged into the midst of the enemy and "flung herself upon Onda and grappling with him dragged him from his horse, pressed him calmly against the pommel of her saddle, and cut off his head" (quoted in Turnbull 1990:28).

Such examples of women in sports and war historically and in the present undercut contemporary U.S. assumptions about female participation in sports, which are: (1) women are physically unsuited for participation in vigorous sports or aggressive activities; (2) participation in vigorous sports is incompatible with femininity; (3) women are not heroic material because they do not engage the public; (4) individual sports are more suitable for women than are team sports.

In the examples given above, it becomes clear that the first three assumptions are unfounded. (1) Women historically and cross-culturally have participated in vigorous sports and aggressive activities, and this participation is related to high social status. (2) Participation in the vigorous sport of tennis was not only viewed as feminine, even in the repressive Victorian era, but such participation was an important part of courtship among the nineteenth-century British elite. In Japan, participation of women in warfare was seen as consistent with their feminine role as partner and companion to their husbands. (3) The importance of women as heroic warriors is demonstrated in several cases noted above: the victory of the U.S. women's soccer team, the nationalistic pride in the Brazilian tennis player Maria Bueno, and the acclaim generated by the ferocity and courage of Tomoe Gozen.

It remains, then, to explain why participation in team sports is associated with masculinity in North America, whereas participation in certain individual sports is associated with femininity. This paradox can be explained as socialization into gender roles.

Girls in the United States, and in other countries as well, are encouraged to participate in the physically rigorous and dangerous

(*continued*)

Sports, Gender, and Social Class (*continued*)

sports of gymnastics and figure skating. They are also encouraged to envision themselves in the equally rigorous role of ballerina. The physical danger and rigor of the "feminine" pursuits are downplayed. A fall on a balance beam could be fatal or permanently disabling, and all three of these activities require great physical strength. A ballerina must develop the strength and muscular control to balance *en pointe*. A figure skater must be able to execute "balletic spirals, leaps, jumps, spins and linking movements," while displaying "poise, fluency, control, precision and agility" (Cuddon 1979:460). Cuddon describes the *axel*, "a jump in which one and a half turns are made in mid-air; in a double axel two and a half turns are made in mid-air; the take-off begins from an outside forward edge of one skate and the landing is on the back outside edge of the other" (1979: 460).

Prevailing cultural views deemphasize the great strength and agility required by these activities, not to mention the great discipline. The activities are seen as feminine because they are associated with grace and the aesthetic value of petite beauty. In U.S. culture, strength is associated with masculinity, whereas petite beauty is associated with femininity. Unacknowledged in this cultural view is the fact that all these activities—gymnastics, figure skating, and ballet—emphasize individual excellence and fierce competitiveness, the latter of which was repeatedly brought home to me by my coverage of Olympic

and international championships in gymnastics and figure skating.

"Masculine" team sports, on the other hand, emphasize cooperation and in-group solidarity. All athletes in my study (1982) emphasized the importance of "team spirit." Jack Ramsey, head coach for the Portland Trailblazers at the time of my study, told me, "We all work together to win. It's not the individual, but the team effort that counts." Athletes often described relations among team members as being "like brothers," and team sports were described as being "better" than individual sports. One sport psychologist described athletes in team sports as being "healthier" than those engaged in individual sports. Even athletes in individual sports emphasize the importance of "teamwork." The auto racer Jackie Stewart described his pit crew as his "team." Tennis players involved in the short-lived team tennis circuit—including such stars as Martina Navratilova and Chris Evert—said they preferred the team circuit to individual competition because of the opportunity to interact with teammates.

The prevailing cultural view in North America is that socialization of females emphasizes "embeddedness" or submergence in the social context, whereas socialization of males emphasizes individual excellence and competition. Values relating to participation in sports suggest just the opposite. Girls are encouraged to participate in sports emphasizing individual excellence and competition, whereas boys are encouraged to participate in sports emphasizing

cooperation and group competition against an out-group, the opposing team.

One traditional rationale for discouraging females from participating in contact team sports is that it may damage their reproductive capacity. Again, the evidence from sports medicine suggests just the opposite. In general, physical fitness associated with sports participation enhances female reproductive capacity; on the other hand, the extreme thinness important for success in gymnastics, figure skating, and ballet has been linked to amenorrhea, cessation of menses, and reduced fertility, which have been correlated with low body fat ratios.

This disjunction between cultural ideals of femininity and masculinity, which contrasts with prevailing norms of sports participation, is not as inexplicable as it seems. In fact, socialization through participation in sports is consistent with attributes considered important for female and male social roles. In the United States, a mythology of egalitarianism based in democratic ideals obscures social distinctions relating to class. Instead, a universalist view of "femininity" and "masculinity" prevails, in which women receive social rewards for beauty, whereas men are rewarded for their economic contribution, made possible by their ability to negotiate complex social relationships in the workplace. It remains to be seen whether success on the soccer field will be followed by a shift in prevailing cultural norms relating to femininity and masculinity.

the hole, pulls dirt across it with her right foot. (1968:256–257)

As noted earlier, many theorists—including Huizinga and Turner—consider expressive culture to be the creative wellspring of other aspects of culture and social organization. According to Lomax, folk music reflects dominant themes of a culture:

> Each song style we have studied thus portrays some level of human adaptation, some social style. Each performance is a symbolic reenactment of crucial behavior patterns upon which the continuity of a culture hangs, and is thus endowed with the emotional authority of the necessary and the familiar. (1968:8)

This statement evokes Turner's (1969) idea that ritual symbols convert the "necessary" into the "desirable." Turner and Lomax are also similar in their view that symbolic behavior gives rise to a dynamic process of cultural affirmation and renewal by uniting a range of themes to a single expression:

> Many levels of this symbolic behavior are brought into congruency with some main theme, so that a style comes to epitomize some singular and notable aspect of a culture, by which its members identify themselves and with which they endow many of their activities and their feelings. This is why an expressive style may become the focal point for cultural crystallization and renewal. (Lomax 1968:8)

Music and Masculinity

As noted in the discussion of the BaMbuti, access to performance of certain types of music or to the musical instruments may be controlled on the basis of gender and other aspects of social organization. Among many New Guinea groups, flutes are associated with secret rituals of masculinity. Male initiation rituals among the Sambia include an all-night and all-male songfest:

> There is the usual singing, smoking, and betel-nut chewing of all-male songfests. But the war songs and blowing of long bamboo flutes distinguish this songfest from ordinary ones. . . . Despite preparations and rumors, the actual day the rites will begin remains unknown to women and children. The urgent, mysterious power of the flutes announces the beginning of the ritual cycle that night. Initiates have told me how the flute sound alerted them of their inevitable initiation and made them worry about what was to come. (Herdt 1987:116–117).

The secrecy surrounding the flutes and starting date of the initiation reinforces the power of initiated men by giving them control over an event that will change the social relationships of everyone in the village. Boys will become men and move out of their mothers' house into the men's house; mothers must become distanced from their sons; married couples must refrain from sex; and the entire village becomes caught up in a round of festivities that will occupy most of their days and nights.

According to Gilbert Herdt (1987), the flutes have strong phallic associations, and initiates are said to be "married" to the instruments. As a boy learns the secrets of the flutes at initiation, he also takes on a series of changing sexual roles. The Sambia practice ritualized homosexuality during initiation, because they believe a boy needs both blood and semen to grow strong. Women provide the blood during pregnancy and childbirth; men provide the semen during initiation. A first-stage initiate is the object of homosexuality; older initiates inseminate the younger ones. The initiation cycle lasts more than ten years, culminating when the young men are in their early twenties. They then marry women and enter the period of heterosexual activity that will lead to establishment of families.

The sugar cane dance, performed by adult males on the first night of initiation, is blatantly sexual (Herdt 1987). The men hold the canes between their legs and thrust them up and down. They warn the initiates not to let their future wives cut their canes. In a dance later that night, women assert their power by dancing around a bonfire and beating the initiates with firewood. The dance evolves into a ritualized battle between the women and adult men, in which the men eventually drive away the women.

Dance and Sexuality

The role of musical and dance performances in society is far from escapist. These performances act out themes central to social relationships. Judith Lynne Hanna asserts that, by its very nature, dance is linked to sexuality. As a result, she suggests, it is associated with courtship and is an important means of conveying information about such issues as fertility and relations between women and men.

> The inherent sexuality of dance may be a reason why dance is a nearly universal activity and why gender is coterminous with sexuality in dance. Sexual intercourse

is seen to be life generating, an action with miraculous power and a magical sense of pleasure and relief. Courtship and foreplay arouse and anticipate. Signs of sexuality evoke these erotic images and sentiments. They also serve as symbolic references to other domains of power. (1988:46)

As Hanna suggests, gender is an important component of dance performances cross-culturally. In virtually all societies, male and female roles in dance are distinct. In many cases, male dance performances emphasize sexual potency, whereas female performances emphasize seduction or receptivity. Often, the association between dance and the importance of fertility is explicit, so that dancing is overtly erotic. In other cases, it is less explicit. For example, the minuet of nineteenth-century Europe was an extremely formal expression of relations between men and women, in which the central movements were bowing and toe pointing. In all cases, music and dance performances are linked to gender roles.

PLAY, SPORT, AND FESTIVALS

In his "Letter on Aesthetic Education," the eighteenth-century poet and dramatist J. C. Friedrich von Schiller wrote, "Man only plays when he is in the fullest sense of the word a human being, and he is only fully a human being when he plays." Earlier in this chapter we noted that Huizinga considered play to be the creative source of all other aspects of culture. Huizinga's definition of play, the basis of many contemporary studies of expressive culture, can be summarized according to three basic principles: (1) the play context is set apart from the "real" world, and this "apartness" is often reinforced by secrecy; (2) play is defined by a set of rules that are unique to the play context; and (3) the reward system of the "real" world is secondary to the reward system of the play world.

Play is bounded conceptually, linguistically, behaviorally, temporally, and spatially. Even a very young child can distinguish "play" from "real life" and can label it as such. For example, a child may say, "Let's play," or "Let's play 'house.'" With the assumption of the play mode, rules of the "real" world are suspended and "play" rules are assumed. When play ends, it is necessary for participants to signal a return to the "real" world; for example, they may say,

"I don't want to play anymore." In more formal systems of play, the onset of a game may be signaled by a referee's whistle, by throwing out the first ball, or by playing the national anthem. The physical boundaries are sometimes defined by permanent structures such as play houses, playgrounds, or golf courses. In other cases, the play arena may be temporary, using redefined articles of the ordinary world, as when children line up chairs and call them a "train" or a "school" (Womack 1982).

Because it is voluntary and "disinterested," play is ostensibly outside the system of reward and punishment that characterizes other aspects of society. In play, the system of reward and punishment is unique to the play context. For example, a player may be rewarded by winning or losing or by the satisfaction of outstanding performance. A good player may be esteemed outside the play context, but respect in the real world is not the primary object of play.

Play and Society

Even though play is deliberately set apart from the real world, the rules and forms of play are continuous with other aspects of society. In their cross-cultural study of children's play, Brian Sutton-Smith and John Roberts (1970) concluded that play provides an arena where behaviors can be practiced and tested before they are applied to real-life encounters. Sutton-Smith writes, "A game . . . is like a primitive school. . . . The game is an information model and gaming is a concretistic way of processing information" (1973:70).

In forager societies, boys learn to hunt by aiming child-sized arrows or spears at insects, frogs, or butterflies. In all societies, girls are given small-scale cooking utensils and dolls to prepare them for their roles as caretakers for the family. Sports, which involve some kind of physical contest, are used to prepare young men for such adult roles as hunting, war, and negotiation for status. For example, the game of polo developed among pastoralists in the Mongolian steppes, and it was used to prepare warriors to raid more settled groups by swooping in on horseback to grab booty without dismounting.

Huizinga and others stress the distinction among various play forms: (1) children's play; (2) games, which may include board games and children's games such as hopscotch, as well as such activities as tug-of-war; and (3) sports, which involve some form of physical contest. The forms of play correspond to

Children's play serves as a "dress rehearsal" for adult roles. Children learn parenting skills through playing with dolls or playing "house." Here, boys of Nepal learn competitive aspects of the male role under the approving gaze of their older peers.

the social organization of the groups in which they occur. Children's play occurs in all societies and is generally viewed as a way of practicing for adult roles. Games and sports vary according to social organization. Roberts and Sutton-Smith (1966) classify games according to whether they are based on physical skill, chance, or strategy. They note that some less complex or socially differentiated societies have no competitive games. Sutton-Smith suggests that, among these groups, "There appeared to be few distinctions in small group life around which ludic [playful] contest could profitably develop" (1968:136).

Sutton-Smith links games of physical skill with competition over hunting and fishing, and games of chance with nomadic groups faced with survival uncertainty. For example, gambling was an important pastime among Native American foragers. Sutton-Smith suggests that both gambling and divination, discussed in the previous chapter, were associated with decision making in hunting.

Games of strategy, which would include chess, are associated with both advanced technology and class stratification. Sutton-Smith writes, "The games appeared to have been a part of the learning of social diplomacy and military skills amongst the military or priestly elite groups. We saw the games as buffered models of power" (1968:137). In other words, games of strategy allow elites to practice status negotiation in a protected context.

In a highly stratified society, games are based on all three principles: physical skill, chance, and strategy. Sutton-Smith contends that "the game of today (particularly football) is that of a complex organization" (1968:145). In my cross-cultural study of athletic heroes, I noted that the various forms of ball games are associated with types of warfare practiced in the particular society in which they developed. For example, "snatch-and-grab" games on horseback, such as polo, are associated with the raid; games that marshal physical force, such as American football and rugby, parallel the maneuvers of armies; and one-on-one games, such as tennis, are closely related to the duel.

Play and the Flow Experience

Play may also be an attitude, taking an exuberant and spontaneous approach to activities that might otherwise be viewed as "work." The psychologist Mihaly Csikszentmihalyi studied what he called the "flow" experience among people engaged in such activities as rock climbing, dancing, chess, and basketball. He defines flow as "the holistic sensation that people feel when they act with total involvement" (1975:36). Csikszentmihalyi included in his study some people engaged in jobs they considered enjoyable—including composers of music, surgeons, and teachers—on the basis that "there is no unbridgeable gap between 'work' and 'leisure'" (1975:5). Csikszentmihalyi notes:

> Games are obvious flow activities, and play is the flow experience par excellence. Yet playing a game does not guarantee that one is experiencing flow, just as reciting the pledge of allegiance is no proof of patriotic feelings. Conversely, the flow experience can be found in activities other than games. One such activity is creativity in general, including art and science. (1975:36–37).

Csikszentmihalyi compares "flow" with an intense spiritual experience: "Besides play and creativity, experiences analogous to flow have been reported in contexts usually called 'transcendental' or 'religious'" (1975:37). The psychologist reports that engaging in "microflow" activities, small breaks in routine, such as gazing out of a window or greeting a colleague, contributes to one's sense of health and well-being. When Csikszentmihalyi induced his research subjects to stop "microflow" activities, a condition he calls "flow-deprivation," these individuals suffered from impaired ability to perform:

> Almost unanimously, our subjects reported being less relaxed, more tired, more sleepy, and less healthy after being deprived of microflow than they had been before the deprivation. Performance on creativity tests dropped sharply. Subjects rated themselves as more dull and in general perceived themselves in more negative terms. After just two days of deprivation, several had unusual minor accidents, and the general deterioration in mood was so advanced that prolonging the experiment would have been inadvisable. (1975:185)

Festivals

The various forms of expressive culture—including art, theater, music, dance, and sports—are enacted in festivals. A **festival** is a sacred or secular time of celebration—which may be associated with an important person, event, or the calendrical cycle—that includes a series of cultural performances. Alessandro Falassi notes:

> Both the social function and the symbolic meaning of the festival are closely related to a series of overt values that the community recognizes is essential to its ideology and worldview, to its social identity, its historical

continuity, and to its physical survival, which is ultimately what festival celebrates. (1987:2)

Festivals share a number of characteristics with religious ritual, and, in fact, many festivals are organized around a religious theme. Mardi Gras, for example, means "Fat Tuesday" and is held to commemorate the last day of feasting before the period of fasting and ritual purification of Lent, which begins on Ash Wednesday.

Festivals provide a forum for the enactment of antistructure, in which values and social relationships are taken apart ritually or symbolically, so that they can be reinforced or recreated. Festivals provide a context for the display or enactment of dominant symbols. Dominant symbols appear in many different contexts in a particular society and tend to occupy "center stage" in many of the ceremonies in which they appear (Turner 1967). In Fourth of July ceremonies in the United States, for example, the theme of triumphant patriotism appears in displays of the American flag and the colors red, white, and blue in parades and on front porches across the country. The flag may appear along with such other symbols as the American eagle. Both the flag and the eagle are dominant symbols. On the Fourth of July, the importance of the flag as a cultural symbol is emphasized by fireworks displays and the accompaniment of military marching bands playing such

For festivals and other ceremonial performances, individuals may take on the personnae of demons, gods, and cultural heroes, a transformation greatly aided by masking. This fanged entity from Sri Lanka is surmounted by stylized representations of cobras.

rousing songs as "Stars and Stripes Forever" and the national anthem. On the other hand, the theme of self-sacrifice for one's country is marked on Memorial Day, when the flag is displayed at half mast and military bands play "Taps" at cemeteries marked by crosses, another dominant symbol, over the graves of war veterans.

Festivals often include symbols that represent ritual inversion, when ordinary status and values are turned upside down and ultimately reaffirmed. Hilda Kuper (1963) describes the annual ceremony of kingship among the Swazi of southern Africa. During Incwala, a three-week festival held around the summer solstice, themes of power and regeneration, fertility, and the tension between darkness and light are acted out. The central figure and "owner" of the Incwala is the king. Performance of the ceremony by anyone other than the king is regarded as treason, punishable by death. The Incwala reflects the life cycle of the king, with simple ceremonies marking earlier phases of his life, and peaking in an elaborate series of ceremonies when he reaches full manhood and has acquired his first ritual wife.

Before the Incwala begins, "People of the Sea," or ritual specialists, are sent out to collect water and other ingredients for purification ceremonies. One group travels to the forests, another to the confluence of the main rivers of the country. Kuper writes, "They must draw 'the waters of all the world' and also dig potent sacred plants to strengthen and purify

the king" (1963:69). In the opening ceremonies, the king is reviled by his people in sacred songs:

> Jjiya oh o o King, alas for your fate
> Jjiya oh o o King, they reject thee
> Jjiya oh o o King, they hate thee.

This ritual inversion, which involves casting down the king, is followed by his triumphant emergence. Kuper writes: "Suddenly the chief councilor commands 'Silence,' and the singing ceases while the king spits powerful medicine, first to the east, then to the west, and the crowd is given the signal to shout, 'He stabs it!'" (1963:69). Kuper was told the significance of this ritual by her informants: "Our Bull (Our King) had produced the desired effect: he had triumphed and was strengthening the earth. He has broken off the old year and is preparing for the new" (1963:69).

Describing the king as a Bull is significant, because a black bull is sacrificed later in the Incwala. The king performs the sacrifice, and the animal is caught by ritually pure unmarried youths. Kuper writes: "The main event of the third day is the 'killing of the bull,' the symbol of potency. The king strikes a specially selected black bull with a rod doctored for fertility and 'awakening'" (1963:70). Kuper adds, "The 'Day of the Bull' fortifies the king for the 'Great Day' when he appears in his most terrifying image and symbolically overcomes the hostility of princely rivals" (1963:70). Throughout most of the Great Day, the king dances with

The ceremonial Central American ball game, the forerunner of soccer and basketball, was played for high stakes. Ball players were sacrificed to provide food for the gods, and the game itself represented the triumph of life over death. Points could be scored either by moving the hard rubber ball into goal zones or by putting it through stone rings in the center of the I-shaped court.

his people, preparing for the main event of the Incwala:

> Towards sunset the king leaves them; when he re-emerges he is unrecognizable—a mythical creature—clothed in a fantastic costume of sharp-edged green grass and skins of powerful wild animals, his body gleaming with black unguents. The princes approach and alternately drive him from them into the sanctuary and beseech him to return. Behind them the people sing and dance. (Kuper 1963:70)

Members of the royal clan and "foreigners" are ordered from the scene, as the king ritually battles his "enemies" in the company of his commoner subjects. Kuper notes: "The king remains and dances with his loyal supporters and common subjects. Tension mounts as he sways backwards and forwards. At the climax he appears holding in his hand a vivid-green gourd, known as the 'Gourd of Embo'" (1963:70).

The gourd is a symbol of the north, the place of origin of the royal clan. The king throws the gourd on the horizontally placed shield of a selected agemate, who must not let the gourd touch the ground.

The Swazi Incwala ceremony illustrates the mechanisms by which expressive culture challenges and reinforces the social and cultural order. As leader and protector of his people, the king must demonstrate his potency in all the important areas of social life: military, political, spiritual, and cultural. His association with fertility symbolizes the continuity of the group. The various ritual challenges to his leadership ultimately demonstrate his power over any forces that might oppose him. The dance at the culmination of the Incwala ceremony reinforces his solidarity with his people, but he is both with them and above them. He is a "mythical creature," with power to rule both the sacred and secular realms.

SUMMARY

Expressive culture—which includes the visual arts, theater, music, dance, and various forms of play—provides a context for reflecting upon cultural values and social institutions. The term *play* is often used inclusively to refer to the various forms of expressive culture. When used in this way, *play* refers to the creative component of culture. The "meaning" of our lives is told to us through those who live on the margins of society—artists, musicians, actors, and sports figures. The various art forms provide a cultural critique, whereas sports, a more conservative form of expressive culture, affirms the prevailing social order.

Play-forms derive much of their power from the fact that they are defined as "not real." They provide a safe arena in which conflicts and critiques can be explored and resolved. Culture is continually reinvented in the context of social interaction. Expressive culture provides a context in which values and relationships can be safely reexamined.

Still, expressive culture reflects its social context. In egalitarian forager societies, for example, all members of the group may participate in the various forms of expressive culture as both artists and consumers. In stratified societies, "appropriate" forms of expressive culture may be defined by a powerful elite who employ full-time specialists in the arts and as athletes. In these societies, the public participates primarily as spectators.

In virtually all societies, people adorn their bodies, their tools, their dwellings, and their ritual objects. Body adornment may include painting, scarification, tattooing, or piercing. In most cases, body adornment reflects gender and differences in social status. Pots and other objects are also decorated. David, Sterner, and Gavua suggest that pots are decorated because of their association with the human body. Projecting human traits onto nonhuman objects is anthropomorphism. People may also attribute "life" or "spirit" to the objects they decorate, or visual art may express religious themes.

Cultural values and important themes are transmitted through legends and folktales. Story telling is a dramatic art that enhances the content of the story through the voice inflection and histrionic performance of the storyteller. When introduced from one culture to another, legends and folktales lose their cultural and social context and are subject to reinterpretation. Legends and folktales teach cultural values and appropriate social behavior through the example of the characters in the story. In many societies, cultural themes expressed in legends and folktales are enacted in theatrical performances. Comedies teach by allowing us to laugh at human foibles; dramas allow us to celebrate the human spirit or lament the human condition.

Performances of music and dance reflect both cultural values and social organization. Among the BaMbuti of the Ituri rain forest in Africa, the right to see or perform on the molimo, a long, pipelike musical instrument, is restricted to men who have proven themselves as hunters. The instrument is viewed as having a life of its own, and it is often used in a ritual context. Through the expertise of the singer or musician, the instrument replicates the sounds of animals in the forest, as well as the human voice.

Music and dancing can also be associated with trance. Among the !Kung, trance dancing is used in healing. Shostak notes that access to the healing power of *n/um*, an essence within the healer, is egalitarian, as is !Kung social organization. Access to musical and dance performances may be restricted by one's position in the social organization. Among New Guinea groups, flutes are associated with secret initiation rituals of males and have explicitly sexual associations. Hanna argues that dance is linked to sexuality by its very nature. For this reason, she says, dance is associated with gender relations cross-culturally.

The various play forms—children's play, games, and sports—are set apart from ordinary reality conceptually, linguistically, behaviorally, temporally, and spatially. Children's play is universal and is generally viewed as preparation for adult social roles. Games and sports reflect the social organization of the society in which they occur. Sutton-Smith notes that games of chance and physical skill are associated with societies in which hunting is important; games of strategy are associated with stratified societies.

Festivals provide a context in which various forms of expressive culture—including art, theater, music, dance, and sports—can be enacted. Many festivals express religious themes, and all provide a context for antistructure, in which values and social roles are reexamined. The Swazi kingship ritual provides an example of ritual inversion; the potency and fertility of the king are reflected upon and reinforced through ritual inversion, in which the king is forced to prove himself before his subjects.

POWER WORDS

anthropomorphism	festival	icons	tattooing
artisans	folktales	legends	trance
expressive culture	iconography	scarification	

INTERNET EXERCISE

1. The term "tattoo" is from the Polynesian word *tatau*, introduced into the English language by European sailors exploring the Pacific Ocean. To learn more about Samoan tattoo designs and legends, visit the website **http://www.samoa.co.uk/tattoos.html**.

2. Kwakiutl masks are depicted and discussed on a website assembled by Laurie Close: **http://www.mala.bc.ca/www/discover/educate/posters/lauriec.htm**. The website is also linked to art of the Tsimshian of the region. Briefly compare and contrast the art of the Kwakiutl with their neighboring Tsimshian.

3. The website **http://www.festivals.com/** keeps track of festivals around the world. Choose a particular region and find out about the festivals of one of the groups studied by anthropologists and discussed in *Being Human*.

11
Foragers

In this chapter . . .

The forager way of life

For most of their history, humans have foraged for food. The forager lifestyle requires flexibility in the daily routine and in the organization of the household. Even today, foraging continues as a way of life, although most foragers have been displaced from the rich ecosystems they once inhabited. In this chapter, you will meet three forager groups, representing a range of adaptations—from the !Kung of Africa's Kalahari Desert to the Ainu of northern Japan and the Kwakiutl of the resource-rich western coast of Canada.

The San: Foragers of Africa's Kalahari Desert

You have already met the !Kung, a subgroup of the San foragers of the Kalahari Desert. For most anthropologists, the San illustrate the viability of foraging in the most extreme of conditions—a region with limited rainfall. Before the advent of colonialism, the San provided abundantly for their needs, gathering protein-rich plant life and hunting game animals. As a result of European colonialism, as well as the incursion of other African groups, the San have become an underclass in a region they once called their own.

The Ainu: Foragers of Japan

The Ainu may be the only modern foraging group representing a way of life common to northern Asia and Europe during prehistoric times. Their elaborate ceremonies honoring bears are similar to Celtic festivals of pre-Roman times. Until World War II, Ainu men hunted a variety of animals on their mountainous island in the north of Japan; women gathered berries and mushrooms as well as other edible plants and medicinal herbs and grasses. As is true for many other forager groups, the Ainu way of life is changing, and the behavior of modern young Ainu is virtually indistinguishable from that of other Japanese.

The Kwakiutl: Foragers of America's northwestern coast

Some Kwakiutl call themselves "probably the most highly anthropologized group of native people in the world." Before European colonialism, the Kwakiutl developed a stratified society with a sophisticated art complex by exploiting the abundant plant and animal resources of the western coast of Canada. Today, the Kwakiutl are trying to reclaim their cultural heritage by reinstituting ceremonies and feasts outlawed by colonial authorities and by bringing their treasured art objects home from museums.

Foraging—which includes hunting, gathering, and various types of fishing—has proved to be the most durable of human economic strategies. Humans evolved as foragers, and this form of subsistence is still practiced by groups that have been pushed to the ecological margins by more settled populations. Foraging also continues in the margins of stratified societies based on intensive agriculture. Homeless people in American cities forage for recyclable cans and food remains; farmers supplement their diet with small game and fish; and city dwellers hunt and fish for pleasure. On a larger scale, commercial fishermen supply large quantities of marine and fresh water products for growing international markets.

Anthropologists have long been fascinated by traditional foragers, who provide insight into small-scale societies and what may be the most nearly egalitarian forms of social organization. Foragers do not dramatically alter their environment because they do not produce food through domesticated plants and animals and because their populations are typically small and dispersed. In addition, the nomadic lifestyle of foragers has pervasive effects on all aspects of social life, from economics to the organization of family life and the allocation of power.

Many Native Americans were foragers, which means they did not have the same concept of land ownership as the Europeans who colonized them. For a forager, the best survival strategy is one that allows pursuit of game without the limitations of fixed boundaries or permanent land ownership concentrated in the hands of individuals. Instead, foragers acquire rights to utilize the resources of a particular territory through membership in a kin group. European colonizers came from an intensive agricultural society; their subsistence strategy was based on permanent land ownership by individuals. When Native Americans signed treaties transferring rights to land, they thought they were allowing Europeans access to the land; they did not realize they were surrendering their rights "in perpetuity."

Forager groups are usually organized around a loose association of related nuclear families, though some encampments consist of nuclear families related through the male or female line. An association of nuclear families is one of the more flexible kinship systems, allowing members to leave one kin group and affiliate with another in case of disputes or changing availability of resources. For example, brideservice among the !Kung extends a man's foraging rights to those held by his wife through her kin group while allowing him to maintain land rights in his own kin group. Kwakiutl households were typically occupied by patrilineal clan groups, but descent was ambilineal; that is, members could affiliate with either the wife's or the husband's kin group.

Foraging is generally associated with the band form of political organization, characterized by egalitarian, kin-based relations that promote household flexibility and extend rights to resources to all members of the group. As a rule, leaders of bands do not have formal authority, and their influence does not extend beyond the local group. Anthropologists consider the !Kung of Africa's Kalahari Desert, Australian aborigines (such as the Tiwi, described in Chapter 1), and the Inuit, who live above the Arctic Circle, to fit this model. However, forager social organization may vary depending on the abundance and availability of environmental resources, as illustrated by the three forager groups described in this chapter (see Figure 11.1).

Relatively few possessions and an easily transportable form of shelter facilitate the nomadic way of life characteristic of foragers. These Black Feet Indians of what is now Glacier National Park in Montana lived in teepees, which were easily dismantled and transported from one campsite to another.

The !Kung traditionally foraged in an arid region where resources were distributed over a broad geographic area. Leaders had little ability to impose their will upon others, and the system of bilateral descent gave rise to an extensive network of inherited foraging rights. The Ainu of northern Japan displayed differences in status and wealth based on the hunting ability of the household head. The Ainu leader could not pass on his position to his sons; instead, succession was decided by a somewhat formal panel of male elders. This more elaborate system of social organization appears to be related to the availability of abundant and varied environmental resources, which allowed the Ainu to establish semipermanent camps.

Like the Ainu, the Kwakiutl of Canada's western coast had access to a variety of abundant forest and marine resources. Their society apparently was more stratified, however, with a hereditary class of slaves. Kwakiutl leaders established and retained

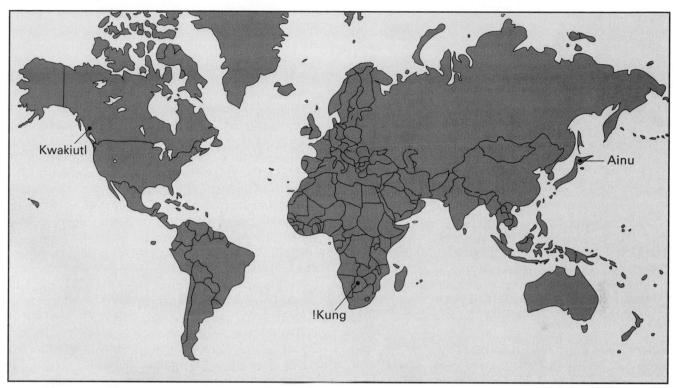

FIGURE 11.1 Foragers

The groups described in this chapter—the !Kung, the Ainu, and the Kwakiutl—represent three types of forager adaptation. The !Kung hunted animals and gathered plants in Africa's arid Kalahari Desert. The Ainu of northern Japan and the Kwakiutl of the western coast of Canada had access to varied and abundant resources, which allowed them to settle in semipermanent villages.

their position through the potlatch, an elaborate giveaway and display of wealth. Their use of the potlatch suggests that the Kwakiutl were organized into tribes, a regional, kin-based form of political organization in which leadership is based on demonstrated ability. In addition, however, Kwakiutl rank was based on inheritance of "titles" that ensured high-ranking leaders a prestigious "seat" at ceremonial feasts.

Most forager groups have been forced to abandon their traditional lifestyle, either because their land or natural resources have fallen under control of outsiders or because they have been drawn into a system of subsistence based on wages and taxation. The three forager societies described in this chapter illustrate a range of social organization and responses to colonialism and pressure from more stratified societies.

THE SAN OF AFRICA: TRADITIONAL FORAGERS OR A POSTCOLONIAL UNDERCLASS?

The San people of the Kalahari Desert in southern Africa belong to a linguistic family called Khoisan, which has many click sounds among its consonants. *Khoi* simply means "people," whereas the word *san* is a more specific designation meaning either "aboriginal people" or "people poor in livestock who must forage for food," depending on linguistic usage of the particular San group. There are three major subdivisions of this language family: northern (!Kung), central (Khoe), and southern (Twi). !Kung has five dialects, of

Since much of their land has been taken away from them, San foragers of Africa's Kalahari Desert have taken up new forms of subsistence, including cattle herding and horticulture. These San men are practicing a form of horticulture borrowed from their Herrero neighbors.

which the best known is Ju/"huansi. People who speak San languages are now found only in southern Angola, northern Namibia, and Botswana.

In the following essay, Edwin N. Wilmsen discusses San property rights in relation to other aspects of their social organization. Basing his analysis primarily on the Khoe and Ju/"huansi of Botswana, Wilmsen disputes claims of some other anthropologists that the San are egalitarian. If the Kalahari San appear classless, he notes, it is only because they are an underclass in comparison with other groups in the region. He adds that a romanticized view of foragers is detrimental to the San because it limits their ability to come to terms with present-day political and economic realities.

KALAHARI SUBSISTENCE FORAGING

Edwin N. Wilmsen*

Some anthropologists paint a very different picture of the Kalahari San than I portray here. These ethnographers believe that the Kalahari San had been relatively isolated from non-San people until the 1970s

*Adapted from Melvin Ember, Carol R. Ember, and David Levinson, *Portraits of Culture: Ethnographic Originals* (Upper Saddle River, NJ: Prentice Hall, 1995).

and that the San continue a long tradition of foraging that has provided a relatively abundant lifestyle. Others, of whom I am one, maintain that the San are not primal foragers at all, but instead are very poor rural people who forage on the fringes of the Kalahari economy because of their place in the unfolding of the history of the region.

The San have been subjected to incursions from other groups for millennia. Bantu people began moving down from central Africa shortly after the introduction of livestock over two thousand years ago. The Bantu brought with them goats and horticulture—sorghum, millet, cowpeas, and melons—as well as iron and copper metallurgy. Herero people began moving into the area around the sixteenth century. In the eighteenth and nineteenth centuries, Europeans and Americans opened trade routes to South Africa.

As the nineteenth century began, Khoe-speaking people continued to occupy by far the largest part of the Kalahari, as they had for millennia, but now they shared most of the region with others. Their relative social equality came to an end at this time. European goods were then filtering up in greater quantity to the southern margins of the Kalahari from South African trading ports. In addition, the Kalahari had become the major source of ivory and ostrich feathers, since European demand for these goods had resulted in the slaughter of elephants and ostriches almost to extinction farther south.

Batswana people, who are the ruling group of the modern nation-state of Botswana, were ideally situated to exploit the trade in ivory and ostrich feathers, since their lands lay between the European traders and Kalahari suppliers. A Tswana leader, Khama III, derived an annual income from this trade that would have made him a millionaire by modern standards. Almost all the ivory and feathers traded by the Batswana came from three groups of hunters: Khoe, Kgalagadi, and Tswana. After the ivory and ostrich feather trade collapsed in the late nineteenth century, many San people worked for the Tswana herding cattle and performing farm labor. This was the final step to San forager poverty.

Land Tenure

Security of **land tenure** is as important for men who hunt and women who gather as for those who herd cattle and grow crops. For this reason, Kalahari San peoples long ago developed rules of kinship that ensured that individuals would acquire such security at birth and retain it throughout life. San kinship provides for inheritance through descent and extension of land rights through marriage.

At birth, a San person inherits land rights from both parents. Each parent in turn had inherited these rights at birth, so a San acquires the right to the land of each grandparent. Since every person has four grandparents, every San acquires rights to four areas of land—two from the father's parents and two from the mother's parents. These four areas of land are the only ones a San person is entitled to use and pass on to his or her children. This kind of socially sanctioned security in land is called *tenure;* the Ju/"huansi word for an area of land held in tenure is *n!ore.*

A person's primary tenure is the place where he or she was born. Usually, this is the place the person will identify with and where the person will spend most of his or her life. For example, a Ju/"huansi person born at a waterhole called CaeCae will say, "My n!ore is CaeCae." This claim is validated by continuity through the generations. A Khoe man asserted, "This is my place—I was born here, and my father and my father's father were born here" (Cashdan 1980). Entitlements to inherited tenures from the other three grandparents may be retained by visiting and exchanging gifts with relatives in each n!ore. Upon marriage, a San person gains rights to use the spouse's tenures, but entitlement to this land is passed to the couple's children only through the spouse.

It should be apparent that a San person gains entitlement to land only through a network of social relations with other people in the same group. Land itself is not inherited, but rights to its use are acquired by being born into a specific social group. This means that no San "owns" land in the sense of being able to give or sell it to someone else. Rather, the group is the corporate owner of its land; entitlement to use the land is vested in all members of the group.

This corporate relation to land is marked in the G!wi San girl's puberty ceremony, when the young woman's mother says to her, "This is the country of all of us, and of you; you will always find food here" (Silberbauer 1981:151). Among the Ju/"huansi, members of such a group are called *n!ore kausi,* "owners of a country." These people refer to themselves as "those who have each other," while members of a Khoe group, the Naro, say they are "owned" by their grandparents (Wilmsen 1989b).

Kinship and Marriage

Though Khoe and !Kung peoples have similar land tenure institutions, they have different kinship sys-

The !Kung, or Ju/"huansi, live in camps, usually consisting of fewer than fifty people. Members of a camp gain rights to forage in that territory through bilateral descent, but rights to tenure in land are reinforced by residence in a particular camp. A person's primary *n!ore,* or place of tenure in land, is the place where he or she was born.

tems. The differences lie mainly in terminology (what a person calls a specific kind of relative—for example, a cousin) and the way in which kinship is extended to persons who were born into a different group. However, these differences are used to achieve similar results with regard to land and its use.

All !Kung-speaking people separate **lineal kin** (those descended from the same set of great-grandparents) from **collaterals** (kin descended from siblings of those great-grandparents). They also use one term for all cousins of the same sex and another term for cousins of the opposite sex. Thus, a Ju/"huansi woman calls all her female cousins *!u!naa* and all her male cousins *txu,* while a man calls his female cousins *txu* and his male cousins *!u!naa.* Note that both use the same terms, but they apply them reciprocally, according to the sex of the individuals. Because opposite-sex cousins are preferred marriage partners, *txu* can be said to mean "marriageable person."

The term *!u!naa* (literally, "big name") is also applied to same-sex grandparents (by a woman to her grandmother and by a man to his grandfather). When applied to a grandparent it means "name-giver," and when applied to a cousin it means "name-sharer." This is because a Ju/"huansi person receives the name of a same-sex grandparent or someone socially equivalent, and the same set of names is passed through many generations of a family line; these are the people who "have each other."

Property rights transfers that occur when people marry are largely a matter of reshuffling priorities among latent claims by members of a descent consort. The new married pair will already, as children of their related parents, hold a set of entitlements in common, because they have a grandparental or great-grandparental sibling pair in common. Any proper marriage will unite entitlement strands through one parent of the bride and one of the groom; a more desirable marriage will unite strands through each parent of the couple. Marriage strategy is directed toward bringing about this more desirable condition, which strengthens individual security of tenure and consequently contributes to local descent group solidarity. If this strategy is successfully employed by sibling sets from generation to generation, kinship ties are strengthened for individuals, and group solidarity is passed on from grandparental to current sibling sets.

San brideservice, in which the man lives with his wife's family and contributes to its economy for a period of years, is crucial to the operation of this system. It can be seen as a form of marriage payment that mediates the conflicts over land that inevitably occur among mutually interdependent groups.

Property and Exchange Networks

The transfer of property at marriage begins with negotiations and gift giving between principals to the marriage, primarily the parents of the bride and groom, who will be future coparents-in-law. This process may extend over a period of many years. It begins to take more concrete form with the establishment of a new household located close to the woman's parents. This marks the beginning of brideservice. The period of brideservice is answered in terms of offspring, its conditions being satisfied when two or more children have been born to the union. Among Ju/"huansi, children born during this period in the woman's n!ore will have that locality as their primary place of land tenure. This practice confers lifelong mutual obligations between persons in the woman's family and her children and on the descendants of those children as long as kinship obligations are met.

During the period of service in the Ju/"huansi wife's home n!ore, rights in the husband's n!ore are kept open by visiting his primary kin who reside there and participating with them in foraging from their mutually possessed land. These visits revalidate entitlements through production relations; visitors who stay for longer than a couple of days are expected to contribute to the food supply. After the period of brideservice, if household residence changes to the husband's n!ore, rights in the wife's n!ore are kept open by visiting her kin who remain there. Such visiting is undertaken not only to enjoy the others' company but also to ensure the n!ore inheritance by children during the lifetime of the parents.

Frequent visits are necessary because there are conflicts over rights, and rights to a n!ore may be withdrawn if the individual fails to participate in production. Thus, fights are common during visits; nearly 70 percent of all homicides occur when families are together, and a high proportion of the fights and murders occur between in-laws. These risks are counterbalanced by the need to keep options open through fulfillment of obligations to participate actively in social relations to land.

In addition, the Ju/"huansi have developed formal exchange systems, called *haro*, which involve a kind of linked-partner exchange. Sixty-two percent of haro partners trace descent from the same grandparents, and 82 percent from the same great-grandparents (Weissner 1977:119). Given the marriage preference, these people will be consanguineal relatives among whom are potential as well as actual marriage partners. It is this group of people who form the stable set of descendant tenure holders; they are the *n!ore kausi*, those who have continuous entitlement of tenure in their land through the generations. Much of the exchange they engage in is associated with marriage negotiations designed to ensure continuity into the future.

The Politics of Production

Relations of production are created through the politics of implementing this strategy. Negotiations for marriage ties occupy much of the time and energy of descent group elders. Elders are hierarchically dominant—particularly fathers and parents-in-law—and have a defined right to an extra portion of the production of their descent group. Part of that extra portion is the right to arrange marriages, a right that carries with it increased access to material and social resources. This is the reason Ju/"huansi parents strive diligently to reserve for themselves this potentially onerous right, which leads to the fights and homicides just noted.

No local descent group can independently reproduce itself within the limits of a single n!ore. For this reason a significant number of marriage ties are negotiated with strategically placed collateral in-laws in adjacent and nearby n!oresi. Adults with mature children choose to gain strength through intensified haro and other forms of cooperation in specific n!ore areas. The person with the broadest social influence is likely to be the most effective in arranging marriages for his or her children to spouses in other n!oresi.

Cooperation is facilitated and influence strengthened by passing on productive partnerships between first cousins from parents to children. Such inheritance accounts for 45 percent of the haro links of Ju/"huansi individuals, and these links are the most secure and long-lasting of all partnerships, some of them spanning many generations. Since first cousins of one's parents are the parents of one's preferred marriage partner, maintaining good relations with them increases the chances of obtaining a desirable marriage partner from them.

Haro exchanges between parties in these partnerships begin in childhood. They intensify in the parental generation during the period of marriage negotiations, solidify during the period of brideservice, and devolve incrementally upon the next generation. Thus, haro partnerships are inheritances that provide a person with working keys to the future.

Wealth, Status, and Leadership

Because all members of a descent group may participate in land tenure, the negotiation of proper marriages protects the undivided inheritance of that land. Marriage negotiations, therefore, are not the simple prerogative of single families, but instead involve numbers of senior members of an entire group. Without strong control of marriage, descent group land inheritance could not be perpetuated.

Some kin units are able to retain or expand family land at the expense of politically weaker factions of the social formation because a concept of unequal possession is inherent in Ju/"huansi ideology. This is expressed in their linguistic contrast between a "wealthy person" (*xaiha*) and a "poor person" (*gaakhoe*). Xaiha is also the term for "chief" or "leader of a group." Inequality between the status of wealthy and poor persons tends to be enhanced because those who can regularly produce a surplus have a broader sphere of haro (Wiessner 1977). As we have seen, a broader sphere of exchange partners is associated with enhanced political influence, or power.

The basis of wealth resides in n!ore entitlements and the productive benefits they entail. These entitlements are inherited by all members of a descent group, but it is apparent that leadership positions are passed through a smaller subset of families within the n!ore entitlement group. For example, all leaders at CaeCae are descendants of several generations of the same families. Richard Borshay Lee describes the basis of power of these leaders: "Because his kin ties to past n!ore owners gave Tsau a strong claim to legitimacy, he did not elicit from his own people the same degree of hostility and criticism that other !Kung leaders suffered when they tried to deal with outsiders" (Lee 1979).

Also, clearly, xaihasi are able to mobilize labor and extract a surplus. The CaeCae leader and his extended family were the beneficiaries of the ivory and feather trade in the nineteenth century, and it is these families who recall the prosperity of that heyday of the hunters with affection. These same families were able to appropriate for themselves the cattle post positions that became available after hunting prosperity collapsed. Their advantageous position is visible today in the economy of CaeCae: although they are only 45 percent of the population, these families own 90 percent of the cattle kept by Ju/"huansi there, receive 88 percent of the wages paid there, and kill and consume 60 percent of the animals hunted in the area. Their success in hunting is due primarily to their ability to invest in horses, which allow them to range widely after the few large animals remaining from nineteenth-century depletion. Poor people are forced to hunt small animals on foot, and people displaced from other n!oresi have no rights to the land and are not allowed to hunt at all.

These differences in wealth and access to land tenure have led to conflicting perceptions among the Ju/"huansi over what now constitutes a "proper" marriage. On the one hand, the wealthy say that to marry properly is to marry as was proper in the past. These people have secure entitlement in place. Their strategy is aimed at retaining the advantage accruing in entitlement; the old way results in protection of the undivided inheritance of descent group land. On the other hand, the poor insist that one should marry anyone other than kin. These people have lost entitlement to any land. Their strategy is to seek alliances with a large productive group so as to acquire a stronger base for developing reciprocal obligations.

These conflicting perceptions are rooted in divergent interests of persons who find themselves in contrasting circumstances. The relations between them have been defined in a particular history of political struggle over access to land resources and their products. This structure is inherent in Ju/"huansi social relations and has not been imposed by external forces in recent decades.

Present conditions of political and economic asymmetry visible at CaeCae are, of course, a result of the colonial era and its aftermath, that is, of the particular modern history of the region. But particular histories engage underlying structures to produce visible results. These structures may not be deterministic in the sense that the conjunction of certain variable events has a fixed outcome, but they do shape the outcome in terms of their own logic. For example, if Ju/"huansi ideology were in fact egalitarian, its structural logic would distribute entitlements and leadership positions among individuals on an unbiased, perhaps random, basis. Yet the evidence demonstrates that quite the opposite is the case. Clearly, n!orekausi homesteads reproduce the conditions of their exclusive entitlements, and those families from which the leader is drawn reproduce the conditions of their dominance. These fundamental conditions of class reproduction are endemic in Ju/"huansi social relations.

If, nonetheless, to even careful observers, Ju/"huansi, along with all Kalahari San, appear to be superficially classless today, it is because they are incorporated as an underclass in a wider social formation that includes the Tswana, the Herero, and the other peoples of the region.

Current Rural Poverty

A pattern of San cattle ownership similar to that of rural Botswana as a whole has emerged. Fewer than a third of the families in a language group own any cattle at all, and in 1981, cattle-owning San families had on average five head, as compared with twenty for all rural Botswana. Typically, less than 10 percent of these families own more than half of all animals

held by their group; among these, a very few have entered the middle-class ranks of rural Botswana.

Most San families with wage earners fell within the lowest 10 percent of income level and did not reach the minimum considered necessary for the bare essentials of life. Since this bare existence was available only to those with cattle or a wage-paying job, or both, some people were forced into subsistence foraging. Those without such assets foraged and scavenged and had no disposable income at all. Many have left their home tenures to seek employment on the fringes of towns.

These inequities in the overall political economy are shared by all the rural poor of Botswana regardless of their group identification. The inequities reproduce the structural deprivation of a rural underclass deprived of a market for its labor. They are the modern legacy of the history of progressive deprivation buttressed by a prejudice that describes the San as bewildered by the present. In the 1990s, San peoples began to organize to overcome this legacy. A first step toward the realization of their aspirations leads away from a fascination with a fixed forager image, a fascination that obscures the image of the people in the present and circumscribes any vision of their future.

THE AINU: FORAGING AMONG THE DEITIES IN NORTHERN JAPAN[*]

The origins of the Ainu are a mystery. Though they live on the northern islands of Japan, the Ainu look distinctly different from the Chinese, Koreans, and Japanese who are their neighbors. Emiko Ohnuki-Tierney writes, "These striking people with deep-set eyes and abundant body hair fascinated both scholars and laymen" (1974:1). Ohnuki-Tierney adds that much of the fascination with the Ainu stems, not only from their mysterious origins, but also from the richness of their cultural traditions:

---

[*]Adapted from Emiko Ohnuki-Tierney, *The Ainu of the Northwest Coast of Southern Sakhalin* (New York: Holt, Rinehart and Winston, 1974).

Fearless hunters on land and sea, the Ainu nevertheless maintained a tradition of aesthetic sensitivity. They produced beautiful and highly stylized epic poems, whose superb literary quality is considered comparable to those of the Greeks. Their oral tradition was indeed rich and well developed. . . . The sensitivity of the Ainu to beauty in life was also expressed in skillful woodcarvings by men and appliqué, embroidery, and weaving by women, who in addition were almost comparable to trained botanists in their knowledge of local vegetation. (1974:2)

The Ainu once occupied the islands of Hokkaido, southern Sakhalin, and the Kuril Islands, and their territory once included Kamchatka in Russia and the northern part of the main Japanese island Honshu. After World War II, when the former Soviet Union gained control of Sakhalin, the Ainu who inhabited that area were relocated to Hokkaido. Most of those who left Sakhalin settled in the coastal areas of Hokkaido, hoping to make fishing their occupation. However, depletion of fish in the region forced many young men to seek jobs at more prosperous fishing ports as lumberjacks or as crew members on ocean fishing boats. Ainu women sought employment in cities of the region, since their small fishing communities had no jobs for them.

The Seasonal Cycle: Subsistence Activities

On Sakhalin, the mountain chain runs north and south in the center of the island. Ainu settlements—from a few houses to about twenty—were sandwiched between the mountains and the sea. Ainu economic life was organized around the long cold season and the short warm season. During the long, snowbound winters, Ainu males hunted land and sea mammals, while the women concentrated on making a year's supply of clothing for the family. Summers are short in this northern zone, and the men made maximum use of it by fishing as much as possible, both for immediate use and to store as a winter supply of food for both humans and dogs. Women helped dry and smoke fish as well as collect plants, many of which were also dried for winter use.

The Cold Season   The cold season started in mid to late October, when men went to the mountains to trap marten, fur-bearing mammals similar to weasels. The Ainu also hunted bear, musk deer, reindeer, fox, otter, hare, and squirrel. They hunted primarily for

meat, but they also used animal fat for cooking, as well as an ointment for burns and other skin ailments. They made relatively little use of the fur of land animals, but they made extensive use of sea mammal and dog skins, as well as fish skins.

The Ainu relied primarily on various kinds of traps, but they also hunted with bow and arrow. Ohnuki-Tierney writes, "The Ainu may be the only people who use bow and arrow to hunt such formidable game as bears" (1974:19). Bears were particularly important, hunted both for their meat and for ceremonial purposes. When a bear was killed, it was given a ceremony similar to a funeral for a human.

The Ainu regarded hunting and trapping as religious activities. As Ohnuki-Tierney puts it, "Even more precisely from the Ainu point of view, there is no demarcation between activities relating to the obtaining of animal meat and those dealing with the deities" (1974:20). Hunting and trapping were regulated by religious rules, which included many taboos, or rules of avoidance. Women were barred from hunting or trapping deified animals, in the belief that the smell of menstrual and parturient blood—the blood that accompanies childbirth—is offensive to the deities. Since the smell of blood was believed to pervade women's clothing, they were forbidden to participate in all matters dealing with deities. Women could trap nondeified animals, such as hares, however.

A man who came into contact with a woman who had just given birth was required to abstain from hunting for several days, since he was believed to be contaminated by the parturient blood. Every man at all times was required to go through a special purification rite when he went into the mountains for hunting, because the mountains were considered the habitat of all the deified land mammals and were, therefore, the most sacred part of the Ainu universe.

The bear was the supreme deity in Ainu cosmology. A hunter injured by a bear was treated respectfully as a bear deity until the injury healed. Physical contact with a deity, the bear, temporarily transformed the hunter into a deity. An injured hunter could not be placed in his home. His family had to build a temporary hut near the house, much as they would build a separate home for a bear awaiting the bear ceremony. An injured hunter was kept separate from menstrual women or "unclean" firewood—firewood that had been lying outside and might have been contaminated by urine and other things offensive to the deities. If an elderly woman were in the

The Ainu of Sakhalin were driven from their traditional territory after World War II, when their island homeland became property of the Soviet Union, now Russia. These Ainu of the Japanese island of Hokkaido try to keep their culture alive by performing their traditional ceremonies.

family, she would be in charge of the patient, ensuring that only clean, freshly cut firewood would be used for cooking.

When available, sea mammals were caught year around, but the most intensive hunting of sea mammals took place at the end of the cold season. The Ainu used virtually every part of sea mammals, including meat, skin, and oil. They cooked the meat and brain in sea water for immediate consumption and preserved some of the meat for winter by drying and smoking it. They extracted oil by boiling sea lion and seal blubber in a large pan. Women pounded and dried sealskins for garments and shoes, as well as for bags and knife sheaths. Baby sealskin was used for the soles of sealskin shoes.

Sea mammal hunting was also a religious activity, since the ocean was viewed as the sacred residence of the sea deities. Women were forbidden to participate in sea mammal hunting and sea fishing, though this taboo was not enforced in all settlements. In some settlements, women did go to sea and help men in rowing boats. The Ainu also ice-fished on rivers and lakes. Though ice-fishing was considered a male job, it was often carried out by women and children because the men were too busy hunting.

The Warm Season The beginning of the warm season in May was signaled by the herring run, which precipitated the move from winter settlements near the mountains to summer settlements near the shore. The Ainu spear-fished for trout and salmon.

Both men and women participated in drying fish on wooden racks in a specially designed hut. Major responsibility for the task often fell to the women; the men were usually busy fishing.

Smoking fish provided a holiday for adults of both sexes. From mid-August until mid-September, men and women from several adjacent settlements would leave the children and aged behind and gather in a wooded area near the upstream of a river to catch trout. They built one hut for themselves and another, without walls, for smoking the fish. The fire for smoking was kept going day and night, and someone had to tend it, but the rest of the people delighted in taking off to nearby woods to gather various kinds of berries. Romances often started in this pleasant holiday atmosphere.

Gathering Plants The Ainu depended as much on plants as they did on animals. Gathering was done primarily by women, though gathering was not taboo for men. Plants were especially important to settlements located in poor fishing areas and to households having no adult male to hunt or fish. Gathering of plants began as soon as the snow melted, and women spent every spring day digging bulbs, including leeks. Minced leek was indispensable for most Ainu dishes, and dried leeks were required in shamanistic rites. Leeks were also used to cure gynecological diseases. The Ainu had to perform an offering of leeks to the deities at the end of a day of gathering.

The Ainu used about sixteen species of berries, which they picked from August until after the first snowfall. They used the berries in cooking, and most were dried for use during winter. Around the time of the first snowfall, the Ainu also gathered nettle, which was used to make threads for clothing. They also collected mushrooms and marine plants, as well as about one hundred species of edible and medicinal grasses and shrubs. Despite their heavy dependence on plants, the Sakhalin Ainu considered these valuable sources of food and medicine to be immobile and powerless. Therefore, plants were not deified.

Domestic Activities

Just as Ainu subsistence activities were oriented toward the sacred beings in the mountains and sea, their homes were organized around more and less sacred areas (Figure 11.2). The Ainu pictured a

house as a human body lying on its back with its head in the direction of the mountains and its right hand toward the north. The most sacred area of the one-room Ainu home was the side facing the mountains, the head, because that is where mountain deities—including bears—reside. A sacred window was made on this wall, toward the east for western coast Ainu. All the deified animals were brought into the house through this window and were seated or "enshrined" on this side between the hearth and the

Even in societies based primarily on agriculture, foraging continues to contribute to the economy. In North America, for example, farmers may supplement agriculture with hunting game animals, foraging for wild berries and nuts, and fishing in streams or lakes. In southern Thailand, this fisherman exploits the nutritional resources of a swamp lake.

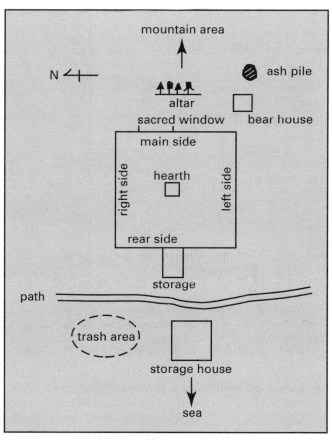

FIGURE 11.2   Ainu Household

The most sacred area of the Ainu home was the side nearest the mountains. Rituals and bear ceremonies were held between the house and the mountains. On the inside, only visiting male elders could be seated along the side closest to the mountains. The "right side"—which corresponds to the right side of the human body—was the second most important area, where the head of the house and his wife were seated. Young males were seated on the "left side," the third most important area; young females were seated in the place of lowest importance, the side opposite the mountains.
Source: Adapted from Emiko Ohnuki-Tierney, *The Ainu of the Northwest Coast of Southern Sakhalin* (New York: Holt, Rinehart and Winston, 1974).

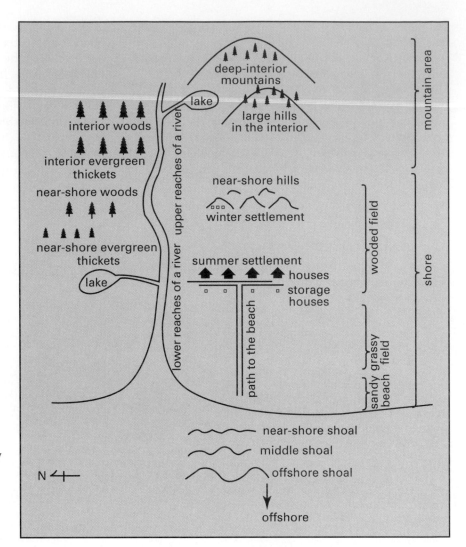

FIGURE 11.3 Ainu Settlement

Like Ainu homes, Ainu settlements oriented toward the mountains, considered the most sacred part of their territory. As this drawing illustrates, the Ainu had access to abundant resources from a variety of ecological zones, from the mountains to the sea.

Source: Adapted from Emiko Ohnuki-Tierney, *The Ainu of the Northwest Coast of Southern Sakhalin* (New York: Holt, Rinehart and Winston, 1974).

wall. Among humans, only visiting male elders could be seated in this area.

The second most important area was the side toward the north, the right hand, where the master of the house and his wife were seated. The Ainu considered the right hand superior to the left. As in English, the Ainu word for "right" also means "true." The northeast corner of the Ainu house lay between the most sacred, or east side, and north, or "true" side. In keeping with the sacredness of this corner, ritual sticks for the God of the House were erected at this point. Ritual sticks for Grandmother Hearth (the Fire Goddess) were placed at the northeast corner of the hearth. Young males were seated on the south side of the house, and young females were seated on the west side—opposite the most sacred, or east, side.

The sacred directions extended to the area surrounding the house. An altar was erected between the house and the mountains (Figure 11.3), and this is where all group rituals were performed. Women were not allowed in this area, and men were expected to walk quietly and speak softly. The bear cage and pile for ashes from the hearth were located in the northeast area. The ash pile was viewed as the graveyard for Grandmother Hearth, and the Ainu renewed the life of the goddess by ritually depositing ashes from the hearth on the ash pile. The region south and west of the house was used for more mundane purposes. This is where the trash pile, the storage area, and the toilet were located.

Daily Routine Just as the house was organized into sacred and profane areas, the day was divided into two periods: the "light-day" (daytime) was allocated to humans, and the "dark-day" (night) to deities and demons. Ritual activities were held in the morning, when the Goddess of Sun and Moon was in good spirits and able to deliver messages to other deities.

Men's Jobs   When the weather was unsuitable for hunting, men gathered firewood and did various kinds of woodwork. The Ainu were accomplished carvers and made a variety of objects from wood, from the largest boats to the smallest utensils. Only men could carve ritual objects, such as the ritual sticks used in all sacred ceremonies, and these had to be carved in the morning. Men also carved five-stringed musical instruments called *tonkori,* which were referred to as deities. When a tonkori was completed, the maker placed a pebble in the hollow part, which was considered the soul of the instrument. He then adorned the tonkori with pieces of colored material and placed bells around its "neck."

Historically, the Ainu did not carve bear figures, because all objects associated with bears were sacred and attended by taboos. The only exception was a small bear head used during the bear ceremony and handed down from one generation to the next. In recent years, men have been carving bears and selling them to tourists.

Men also cared for sled dogs, the Ainu's only domesticated animal. Dog-drawn sleds provided the only means of transportation for Sakhalin Ainu during the snowbound winter. Sleds were drawn by male dogs, and female dogs were used for food and clothing. Dogs were also sacrificed whenever a bear was killed.

Women's Jobs   During the cold season, women made clothing for the entire year, producing thread and fabric from a variety of plants and animal skins. Men, women, and children wore much the same style clothing, a collarless coatlike garment with wide sleeves. Sex and status differences were indicated by fabric and design. Only women wore sealskin, and nettle fibers were worn only by male elders. Garments worn by male elders were decorated with many elaborate designs using the color red, produced by soaking the bark of alder in water. Women's garments had only a small number of designs, and no red was used.

Women also wove grass mats for a variety of purposes. The mats could be spread for sitting or sleeping, rolled up for pillows, or hung at the door or on the walls to prevent drafts. Mats used for decoration or ritual purposes were decorated with colored designs in intricate patterns. Dyes for these designs were obtained from berries and tree bark.

Games, Music, Dancing, and Story Telling   Ainu daily life was enriched by various types of games and creative activities. Games could arise spontaneously and were engaged in by a few individuals or the whole settlement. One indoor game consisted of throwing sticks in the air and catching an odd number, such as three, five, seven, or more. The person catching the largest odd number of sticks won and was rewarded, often with dried fish. The loser was penalized by being slapped, marked with soot, or sent on various kinds of errands.

Tug-of-war was played whenever there was leisure time. A group of people would decide to play this game and announce it to others, who would begin preparing food for treats. The organizers would string heads of dried cod or herring at one end of a strip of sealskin and go around throwing it into each house of the settlement. Those inside the house would grab the end and start a tug-of-war with those outside. When the game was over, the visitors were invited in for treats.

Pastimes engaged in exclusively by males usually involved a contest of skill and courage, and the reward was esteem. In the most daring contest, young men charged a bear being raised in the settlement and grabbed it by the ears. If they failed, the bear would grab them and seriously injure them. If a man successfully grabbed the bear by the ears, it was said he would become a great leader.

The Ainu were also fond of riddles, dancing, music, and singing. One song tells of a woman searching for her lost child in the snow. Another recites the tale of lovers who planned to elope, but when the man arrived at their meeting place, the woman was not there. Ainu were accomplished storytellers, recounting epic poems and legends. An Ainu story about a bear reflects the interdependency of humans and animals, an interdependency characteristic of forager societies:

Once a hunter lost his way and went by mistake into a bear's den. The bear welcomed the hunter and taught him how to lick his palms in order to quench his thirst and hunger. It explained that as the bears go up a river toward their dens, they eat and drink as much as they can. Then they can survive winter by sucking their paws. The hunter stayed in the den with the bear until spring, when the bear led the way out of the den. The mountain snow was still deep, and every now and then the bear put the hunter on its back when the snow was too deep for him to walk. The two traveled for a long time until they came near the shore where the man's settlement was located. The hunter thanked the bear and told it to go back to the mountains before his fellow men came to attack the bear. (Ohnuki-Tierney 1974:22)

Some epic poems took two or three nights to recite, providing entertainment during long winter evenings and imparting important cultural values to younger generations.

Kinship, Marriage, and Social Status

The preferred residence was patrilocal, and a household typically consisted of a patrilineal extended family. However, this was not a strict rule. A wife's relatives could reside with the family, and a man could choose to live with his wife's relatives. As a result, households typically consisted of closely related nuclear families. This pattern of residence produced a flexibility in household size and composition that is important in forager societies.

Ainu settlements were linked by ties of kinship and marriage. Ideally, marriages were arranged by the parents or other kinsmen at the time of a child's birth or before its fifth year. Such engagements could be broken if one party fell in love with someone else. Women married during their mid-teens, men in their early to mid-twenties. Some time before the wedding, the groom began brideservice with the bride's family. During brideservice, the groom could back out of the marriage, but the bride had no such option. Dowry was given only by chiefs or extremely wealthy families.

The Ainu practiced polygyny, and prominent males typically had two wives. Usually, a man acquired his first wife (called "old wife") through a marriage arranged by his parents and then married a co-wife ("little wife") from romantic inclination. In most cases, the co-wife maintained a separate household in her own settlement. Polygyny was considered advantageous for a man because it enhanced his status and produced more children to care for him in his old age. The custom was also believed advantageous for the children, since half siblings were considered better allies than strangers in times of need.

Descent was traced bilaterally, but a man's possessions were divided among the sons of all his wives. Daughters did not inherit from their fathers. The major share of possessions and responsibility for the household typically passed to the eldest son of the first wife. As is true of many forager societies, an Ainu male could not inherit his father's position of leadership in the community, though he would be in the preferred line of succession.

Leadership in larger settlements usually resided in three official positions: chief, vice-chief, and official messenger. The messenger was charged with the responsibility of announcing significant events such as weddings and funerals. When a chief died or retired, his successor was elected by male elders on the basis of qualifications. A chief was expected to be wise, well versed in Ainu custom, generous, and usually wealthy.

A wealthy man was one who could afford more than one wife or who could almost annually host a bear ceremony, an expensive undertaking. Wealth was also indicated by possession of a boat, sled, sled dogs, and, in some cases, servants. To be wealthy, a man had to be a good hunter and fisherman who could obtain a surplus of fur, fish oil, or other resources to exchange for trade goods. A good hunter could also capture bear cubs for the bear ceremony. An important indicator of wealth was a house with two hearths, which meant it was a sacred house with two seats for the Goddess of the Hearth. It was also a house where many offerings were enshrined, since trade goods were primarily used as offerings to the deities.

Ohnuki-Tierney notes, "The primary role of a chief is to preside over war without and peace within" (1974:75). Though the Ainu have not engaged in warfare for over a century, their oral tradition includes accounts of raids conducted in the historic past. As a peacekeeper within the group, the chief presided over meetings held to resolve conflicts when individuals could not reach agreement themselves. Usually, participants in the meeting were male elders, but female elders might be present at meetings involving some types of infractions, such as an affair between a woman and a married man.

To the Ainu, the most serious offense was homicide, but other crimes included adultery, theft, and falsehood. Most cases were resolved by payment of fines. Capital punishment was meted out only to murderers, who were buried beneath their victims. The same punishment was imposed on a bear who killed a man, stressing the equivalence of bears and humans. In this case, if the bear could be caught, an incision was made in its stomach to allow the man's soul to escape. The dead bear was "punished" by placing a stick in its mouth so that it could not eat in the world of dead bears. A deep hole was dug in the place where the "murder" had occurred. The bear was placed at the bottom of the hole, and the man was placed on top of the bear. Dirt was placed over the hole, and an altar of ritual sticks was built at the spot.

Beliefs, Rituals, and World View

In traditional Ainu belief, most beings of the universe are soul owners. Every Ainu, plant, and animal has a soul, as do most man-made objects, including tools, kitchen utensils, and grass mats. The behavior of the soul and not the appearance of its form was of primary importance to the Ainu. When inside a person, the soul is invisible; it manifests its presence in strong emotions such as anger, hatred, and deep sorrow.

The soul is most clearly perceived when outside its owner's body. When a person dreams, the soul frees itself from the body and travels to places distant in time and space. The Ainu believed that dead people could appear in dreams, since the souls of the dead can travel from the world of the dead at this time. During fainting, or "temporary death," one's soul visits the world of dead Ainu.

Death takes place when the soul departs permanently from the body. At this time it was necessary to hold a funeral to transfer the dead person's soul to the world of the dead so that its life could continue. Not only humans, but every soul-owning being had to have a proper funeral at its death. The Ainu maintained separate bone piles for bears and other animals of the mountain, for sea mammals, for sea gulls, and for fish. Even kitchen and eating utensils had a place outside the house where broken pieces—the corpses—were placed.

If no proper funeral took place, the soul of a dead being could trouble the living Ainu, usually in the form of illness that did not respond to treatment with herbs or other medicine. It was then necessary to call a shaman to determine what soul had possessed the sick person and what must be offered to the possessing spirit so it would leave the sick person's body.

A shamanistic rite could be held at any time of the year, but it always took place after sunset, with embers from the hearth providing the only light. The rite was always held inside beside the hearth, with no menstruating women present, either as shaman or as spectator. The ritual began with drumming. The shamanic drum functioned both as a charm against evil spirits and as a means of summoning spirit helpers and attracting the attention of the deities.

The shaman began the rite by asking Grandmother Hearth and other deities for help. He or she then presented the specific case for which the rite was being performed, for example, by describing the client's symptoms. The shaman then became possessed by his or her spirit helper and entered a semitrance. Throughout the rite, the shaman drank sea water in which spruce, larch, and a piece of kelp had been soaked. Normally, the Ainu considered the solution too salty for human consumption, but they believed that the saltwater mixture was drunk by the shaman's possessing spirit helper, not by the shaman. At the beginning and end of a rite, the shaman exorcised evil spirits by spraying sea water from his or her mouth. At the peak of the rite, the spirit helper related, through the shaman, a message received from a deity describing the cause of the disorder and prescribing a mode of treatment.

Deities Among the soul owners of the universe, some beings were deities. Most of the important deities were classified into four groups based on the area of their habitats. Shore deities included Grandmother Hearth, God of the House, and God of the Ground. Mountain deities included bears, wolves, foxes, and owls, who were collectively known as the "mountain people." The two most important sea deities were Creator of Fish and a general protector known as *Co:haykuh*. The fourth group contained the sky dwellers, among whom the Goddess of Sun and Moon and the Dragon Deities were of greatest importance.

Grandmother Hearth, also known as "Fire Grandmother," was foremost among the shore deities, second only to the bear deities in the Ainu pantheon. In shamanic rites, she had to be addressed and asked to deliver messages to other deities. Without her help, the Ainu had no way of communicating with any other deities. Grandmother Hearth was a powerful protector, able to stop a storm at sea, bring a hunter home safely, or intercede when the soul of a person was chased by a demon while dreaming.

Bears were the supreme deities, providing food and looking after the general welfare of the people. Ainu dependency on the bear was expressed both in rites that had to be performed when a bear was killed in the mountains and the much more elaborate bear ceremony, performed at least every two years.

DISCUSSIONS

Is There an Ecologically Noble Savage?

In Chapter 3 we noted that some seventeenth and eighteenth-century scholars romanticized the lifestyle of people living in forager bands and suggested that this represents a distorted view of the way traditional foragers actually lived. The human animal, *Homo sapiens,* is essentially the same everywhere, with similar biological and social requirements for survival. Variations in human behavior can be traced to social and cultural differences, which may become distorted when observed through our own cultural lens.

Romanticizing the behavior of people whose lifestyles differ from ours is as much a form of ethnocentrism as making negative value judgments about their behavior. One pervasive romantic bias in U.S. popular culture is the idea that forager societies did not overexploit their environment, as did Europeans and North Americans. In the following article, Peter Gray discusses factors that shape the relationship of traditional hunters to their environment.

DO TRADITIONAL HUNTERS CONSERVE GAME?
Peter Gray

Native Americans in particular and traditional people in general are commonly depicted as living in harmony with their environments. The idea that traditional people apply an intimate knowledge of their environment to conserve the resources on which their livelihood depends is prevalent in American popular culture, as evidenced in such films as *Pocahontas.* The theme also emerges in anthropological literature. However, the view of traditional people as natural conservationists may present a false picture. K. Redford (1991) suggests this may be a reformulation of Rousseau's concept of the noble savage in contemporary terms, as the "ecologically noble savage."

Some anthropologists argue that the apparent equilibrium of traditional people with their environments results from other factors. Limited technology, low population density, an absence of markets (Alvard 1993) and high mobility (Winterhalder 1981) may have produced the illusion of conservation. Because foragers move regularly in small groups and exploit resources with simple technology, their impact on the environment is dispersed. Where markets are unavailable, trade incentives for overexploitation may not be present.

Conservation generally refers to maintenance of biological diversity. Archaeological evidence demonstrates that traditional hunting societies have not always conserved game, and in fact some groups overexploited game to the point of extinction. P. Martin (1984) argues convincingly that North American big-game hunters were partly responsible for the extinction of such large mammals as the woolly mammoth and mastodon. In New Zealand, moas and other flightless birds were hunted to extinction within a thousand years after Polynesians arrived on the island (Cassels 1984).

Some ethnographic examples support the idea that traditional people are game conservationists. The Yukaghir of northeastern Asia preserved a breeding pair of reindeer from each hunt (Heizer 1955). Yurok hunters of northwestern California preferentially hunted male deer; they took females only when food was extremely scarce. In practical terms, this pattern preserves females for production of offspring. To the people involved, the practice may be embedded in religious beliefs. For example, it was believed that Yurok who violated game laws would lose their good fortune in hunting (Heizer 1955).

In other groups, the conservation picture is less clear. For the Machiguenga of Peru, populations of favored game such as peccary and spider monkey have been depleted

The Bear Ceremony   The bear ceremony began in spring, when men went to catch a newborn cub in the den or a cub strolling with its mother after coming out of hibernation. The cub was called "deity grandchild" and was raised as a member of the host family—the family of the man who captured the bear. If the cub was a newborn and required nursing, any woman in the settlement who was nursing her baby would nurse the cub at the same time. When the cub became too dangerous to keep in the house, it was transferred to a "bear house," a specially built cage outside the house of the host family. The oldest woman of the host family was officially in charge of caring for the bear, but all members of the settlement participated in feeding the bear, cleaning its cage, taking it for a walk, and bathing it along the shore.

within a one- or two-hour walking distance of the settlement (Johnson 1989). Hunting by members of a Siona-Secoya community in northeastern Ecuador has reduced populations of three prey species but has had negligible effects on other species (Vickers 1988).

My comparison of data from seventeen foraging societies does not support the idea that traditional hunters practice techniques that conserve game, based on the following criteria: harvesting animals of an age or sex that would maximize sustainable yields; avoiding pursuing prey in depleted areas or hunting prey to extinction; harvesting game near maximum sustainable yield even when new technology is made available; and having rules or taboos that prevent overexploitation of game, with harsher sanctions against overhunting prey species that take a long time to replenish their populations. Game conservationists would selectively prefer killing of males over females since larger numbers of females are needed to replenish the species. In addition, game kills would be biased toward the less reproductively valuable young and old age classes, leaving breeding pairs to reproduce the species.

Most groups do not preferentially hunt males; rather, they take whatever game is available. In some cases, females and their young are preferentially hunted. The Efe of Zaire imitated the call of a baby antelope and shot its mother when she approached (Schebesta 1936). The Agta of the Philippines used dogs to sniff out female wild pigs giving birth and their litters (Rai 1982).

Traditional hunters do show a preference for highly productive areas where game is plentiful, but this appears to be related to maximizing rates of return rather than conserving game in depleted areas. They are not averse to killing animals wherever they are found, and there are examples of traditional groups hunting game to extinction. In general, however, hunters do not increase their kills with the introduction of new and more efficient technology, such as guns, unless an incentive is provided in the form of a market. For example, with the development of an international market for sea turtles, the Miskito of the eastern coast of Nicaragua used nets and canoes to overexploit this environmental resource (Nietschmann 1974).

Though a number of groups have religious beliefs or supernatural sanctions that would appear to discourage overexploitation of certain game, these beliefs appear to have little effect when the game is desirable. For example, among the Piro of Peru, deer are thought to be the spirits of dead relatives, "and killing one in certain situations can lead to harm" (Alvard 1993:94). However, this belief did not deter hunters. Some tabooed animals—including anteaters, bushdogs, puma, and sloth—are not hunted simply because the Piro think the meat is poor.

Cross-culturally, few rules prevent overexploitation of game. When kills are biased toward those age and sex classes that would increase the sustainable harvest, the bias is due to factors unrelated to conservation. Potentially overexploitable prey are not avoided, and hunters are not averse to killing game in depleted patches. When more efficient hunting technologies are introduced, they sometimes lead to higher rates of exploitation. In cases when they do not, ethnographers suggest that the hunters' restraint is due to a limited need for game not to a conservation ethic.

Source: Based upon a student paper written for *Being Human*.

At the beginning of the cold season of the year following the capture of the cub, which would now be a year and a half old, the elder male of the host family would hold a ceremony for the bear. The ceremony had to be held when the new moon first appeared, that is, when the Goddess of Sun and Moon was in her best mood. Whereas all other Ainu rituals were held by an individual family or an individual shaman, the bear ceremony involved all members of the settlement and drew friends and relatives from numerous other settlements. It was one of the few occasions on which people from distant settlements could visit with each other.

On the evening preceding the ceremony, a shamanistic rite was held to ask Grandmother Hearth to deliver the messages of the Ainu to the bear

Forager Societies

Foragers are of great interest to anthropologists for two reasons: (1) They may provide a glimpse into the lifestyle that characterized human groups for more than four million years. Evaluating this information is difficult, however, since modern foragers occupy marginal ecological areas, whereas prehistoric foragers could gravitate to areas that offered the most abundant environmental resources. (2) The social organization of foragers provides an instructive alternative to the complex, stratified, densely populated, and industrialized societies that developed from the western European model.

Foragers are generally organized into egalitarian bands, with informal leadership based on the local group. Forager groups are small, usually from fifty to one hundred people, and population density is low. Local groups are usually composed of related nuclear families, and their kinship system reflects the need for flexibility and mobility, since most forager groups are nomadic. The degree of mobility is related to the type of resources available: foragers who subsist primarily by fishing may be more settled than those who rely primarily on hunting animals and gathering plants.

There is a division of labor by age and gender among foragers. Typically, women gather and men hunt, though women "gather" small animals and in some groups, such as among the Agta of the Philippines, hunt large animals. Among the Inupiat (often known as Eskimos) women and children join men in clubbing seals during the spring when the animals are most abundant. Both men and women may engage in fishing, depending on the means employed. Net fishing in rivers and streams may engage the labor of both women and men, children and adults. Fishing on the open sea, in canoes or other craft, typically is the work of men.

The three groups discussed in this chapter represent a range of forager adaptation. The following is a comparison of different aspects of their lifestyles:

The San of Africa's Kalahari Desert

Ecology	Arid; uniform annual temperature; wet and dry seasons.
Group Formation and Residence	Temporary camps organized around bilaterally related nuclear families.
Subsistence Base	Plant resources, small and large game animals.
Division of Labor	Men hunt large animals; women gather most plant foods; but both men and women "gather" small animals, and men gather plant foods while hunting.
Exchange Systems	Generalized reciprocity and balanced reciprocity.
Kinship	Bilateral descent; neolocal residence; cross-cousin and parallel-cousin marriage preferred; arranged marriages; brideservice.
Status and Leadership	Little difference in status; "wealth" based on bilaterally inherited land entitlements; leadership based on status as "elder" and ability to influence.
Religion	Belief in a major god and a number of lesser deities; healing by trance; shamanism open to all.
Expressive Culture	Story telling, dancing.
Cultural Change	Hunted ivory and ostrich feathers for sale to Europeans during colonial times; traditional hunting lands divided by national boundaries, much of it taken for Western farms, a game preserve, and distribution to other groups.

The Ainu of northern Japan

Ecology	Varied; island includes both mountains and sea; cold and warm seasons.
Group Formation and Residence	Semipermanent settlements; nuclear families with patrilocal residence preferred, sometimes extended families based on males who trace descent from a common male ancestor.

Subsistence Base	Bear, wolf, and other game animals; freshwater fish and river resources; sea mammals and fish; varied plant resources.
Division of Labor	Men hunt game and marine animals; women gather plants; men carve; women sew clothing; both males and females process meat; women cook for family; men cook for ceremonies.
Exchange Systems	Generalized reciprocity; redistribution in the form of the annual bear ceremony hosted by leader.
Kinship	Bilateral descent; patrilineal inheritance based on male primogeniture; polygyny preferred; arranged marriages; brideservice.
Status and Leadership	Wealth based on hunting skill; official elected positions of leadership include chief, vice-chief, and messenger; conflicts resolved at meetings presided over by male elders with females sometimes in attendance.
Religion	Male control of hunting enforced by taboos regarding female "pollution"; game animals and natural features deified; bear ritual blurs distinction between animals and humans and between deities and material beings; male and female shamanic specialists heal through trance.
Expressive Culture	Story telling, epic poems, and legends; games, including male games involving tests of skill and courage; riddles, dancing, music, and singing; fine woodcarving and needlework.
Cultural Change	Displaced from traditional island after World War II; settled in coastal regions of Japan; men take wage labor jobs as fishermen or lumberjacks; women seek employment in cities.

The Nimpkish of western Canada

Ecology	Varied marine resources; rivers where salmon spawn; thick forests with game animals and plant resources; mild, wet climate with winter and summer seasons.
Group Formation and Residence	Semipermanent settlements; four to six households occupy large winter dwellings organized around cognatic descent groups.
Subsistence Base	Abundant salmon and berries available seasonally; deer and other large game animals; smaller animals; sea mammals and fish; abundant bird life; clams and other mollusks harvested along the seashore.
Division of Labor	Fishing from boats by males with spears and hooks; females, children, and elderly process fish; men hunt game animals; women and children gather berries.
Exchange Systems	Generalized reciprocity; redistribution organized by titled leaders.
Kinship	Ambilineal descent; exogamous cognatic descent groups; arranged marriages; bridewealth and dowry.
Status and Leadership	Ranked cognatic descent groups associated with titles inherited through male primogeniture or acquired as dowry or through warfare; leaders were men with titles; slavery hereditary or resulting from capture in war.
Religion	Cosmology of four spirit worlds: sky, bottom of the sea, the western horizon, and beneath the earth; belief that plants and animals have supernatural power; shamans obtain power to heal from spirits; spectacular performances staged during winter ceremonies.
Expressive Culture	Hereditary rights to dance performances involving masks, songs, and costumes; carved masks.
Cultural Change	Traditional potlatch and winter ceremonies outlawed by Canadian government; ocean fishing from power boats regulated by commercial fishing laws; Nimpkish insist on reclaiming their heritage.

deities. This was followed by a night of dancing and feasting. At sunrise on the day of the ceremony, the celebrants danced around the bear cage, with a single line of men preceding the line of women. The bear was taken out of its cage and tied to a tree, which was bifurcated at the top and had been fashioned into a ritual stick. The bear was decorated with presents, which it would take back to its home in the mountains.

Women then went back to their homes, and the elder of the host family recited a prayer to the bear deities, emphasizing the care given to the bear, the family's gratitude for the bear's stay among them, and hopes for more visits by the bear in the future. The elder purified the bear by waving a ritual stick over it, and a specially chosen marksman—not a member of the host's family—shot the bear with two metal-tipped arrows. Killing the bear was believed to release its soul so that it could go back to the mountains and renew its life there. Two choice male dogs were then sacrificed as offerings to the bear deities, since dogs were considered to be servant-messengers of the bear deities.

After preliminary feasting in front of the altar, in which both men and women participated, the cut-up meat and hide attached to the skulls of the sacrificed animals were brought into the house of the host through the sacred window. The hides were placed on the sacred side of the house toward the east, and the meat was cooked in the hearth. Despite the Ainu aversion toward raw food, some men ritually consumed the bear's brain raw and drank its blood on this special occasion. Women were forbidden to eat any part of the bear's head, and members of the host family had to abstain from eating the meat, since they had raised the bear as their own grandchild. However, the bear's meat was meticulously distributed to all other participants, including infants.

When the celebration was completed after several days, at dusk the elders carried the skulls stuffed with sacred wood shavings, along with the bones of the bear and the dogs to the special bone pile of the bears. The skulls were individually placed on bifurcated poles, the bear in the center with a dog on each side. The Ainu believed the bear would be reborn in the mountains. As proof of its rebirth, they tell the story of a man who killed a bear in the mountains and, upon opening its skull, found the ritual shavings he had stuffed into the brain cavity of a bear during the previous year's ceremony.

The Reign of the Ainu Deities Comes to an End

Emiko Ohnuki-Tierney conducted her classic study of the Ainu in the 1960s. Even at that time Ainu culture had been greatly disrupted by the transfer of much of their traditional territory to what was then the Soviet Union and by economic competition with the dominant Japanese culture. Ohnuki-Tierney wrote in 1974: "The Ainu way of life as described in this book has almost disappeared; some might say that it has already gone" (1974:117).

Ohnuki-Tierney gained much of her data about the traditional Ainu way of life by talking to older members of the community who remembered pre–World War II days. One of her most informative subjects was Husko, a shaman who was born in Sakhalin in 1900. Ohnuki-Tierney notes that, even among the elders, few fully believed in the Ainu way of life. She adds, "There is little difference between younger generations of Ainu and Japanese in terms of overt behavior" (1974:117). Today, Ainu stage dances and religious ceremonies for tourists and interested scholars, but these no longer form the basis for Ainu social life, and some Ainus object to the consumption and distortion of their culture by outsiders.

With the end of their forager lifestyle, the Ainu can no longer sustain their sacred tie with the deities of the shore, mountain, sea, and sky. And, with the end of the bear ceremony, there is no one to carry their presents and prayers back to the deities in the mountains.

THE KWAKIUTL: ORGANIZING ABUNDANCE ON CANADA'S WESTERN COAST

The abundant natural resources on the western coast of Canada from Vancouver to southern Alaska supported a somewhat stratified lifestyle considered to be atypical among forager groups. Haida, Tsimshian, Tlingit, and Kwakiutl, among others, developed rich art complexes supported by ritual and dance. They participated in elaborate exchanges organized around a system of ranked political leadership. In the following article, Donald Mitchell describes the annual cycle of subsistence and ceremonies among the Nimpkish Kwakiutl of what is now British Columbia.

NIMPKISH: COMPLEX FORAGERS OF NORTH AMERICA

Donald Mitchell*

Through the lower reaches of the Nimpkish River pass some of the largest runs of Pacific salmon on the central British Columbia coast. Upward of 250,000 fish annually enter these waters now, and it is likely their numbers in earlier times were even greater. Some, like the pink, chum, and coho salmons, spawn in gravel on the river's floor; others, like the sockeye and spring salmons, move on through the lake to ascend and deposit their eggs in its feeder streams.

No one lives here now, but in the thick forest that lines the riverbanks and on a grassy bluff near its mouth lie the remains of settlements belonging to the Nimpkish people. Nimpkish people now dwell nearby, on Cormorant Island, but a few generations ago Nimpkish existence centered on this river, and it was here they lived for much of the year.

Between late-eighteenth-century contact with Europeans and late-nineteenth-century resettlement at Alert Bay, the Nimpkish were but one of some twenty-five politically autonomous local groups whose territories lay on northern Vancouver Island and the adjacent mainland. Anthropologists have long referred to this set of local groups collectively as the Kwakiutl. More recently, the Kwakiutl have encouraged use of the name *Kwakwaka'wakw,* meaning "those who speak Kwakwala," the language shared by all twenty-five local groups.

Environment and Population

The principal land area occupied and used by the Nimpkish is a narrow coastal plain lying between the mountains of northern Vancouver Island and the protected waters at the head of Queen Charlotte Strait. Dense forests of hemlock, Douglas fir, and cedar clothe the land from shore's edge to high on the mountain slopes. The canopy of mature evergreen forests blocks light and curbs undergrowth, with the result that the woods themselves, though carpeted in mosses and ferns, are largely devoid of wildlife. However, summer fires periodically

---

*Adapted from Melvin Ember, Carol R. Ember, and David Levinson, *Portraits of Culture: Ethnographic Originals* (Upper Saddle River, NJ: Prentice Hall, 1995).

sweep through the timber, forming large tracts of brushland over which deer, elk, and black bear forage. In such areas and along the margins of streams and lakes, trailing blackberries and shrubs like salal, huckleberry, cranberry, and salmonberry thrive.

A century ago, large land mammals in the area included deer, elk, bear, cougar, and wolf. Near those mainland locations to which the Nimpkish seasonally traveled were grizzly bear and mountain goat. Along the shore or in the woods were smaller mammals like river otter, raccoon, mink, and marten. Sea mammals in their territory included harbor seal, sea lion, porpoise, killer whale, and the occasional gray whale. Bird life is still plentiful. There are summer-resident ducks, geese, and swans and a wide range of migrating shorebirds and waterfowl in both spring and fall. A small population of diving birds winters in Broughton Strait.

Unquestionably, the most important Nimpkish resources were to be found in the sea, on its beaches, and seasonally in its tributary rivers. The sea held such fish as halibut, herring, lingcod, rock cod, perch, and sculpin. To the rivers came five species of salmon as well as steelhead trout, and to selected mainland rivers, eulachon, a smelt with an exceptionally high oil content. Since the eulachon's high oil content made it a desirable source for lamp oil, it is often called candlefish. On or in the beaches were three species of clams as well as cockles, mussels, snails, barnacles, sea urchins, sea cucumbers, and crabs.

The Kwakwaka'wakw subsistence cycle and social life were organized around the seasonal availability and geographically specific distribution of environmental resources. Because of the need to harvest resources as they became available, the Nimpkish adopted preservation and storage techniques that permitted stockpiling for lean seasons. The unpredictability of certain environmental resources was accommodated partly by preservation technology, partly by trade, and partly by the common practice of intergroup feasting.

The Annual Subsistence Round

Kwakwaka'wakw local groups each consisted of a number of extended house groups that traditionally gathered in winter at a common village. During the rest of the year, these house groups might be found at any of several settlements within or beyond the home territory. The winter season was brought to a close with the appearance of the year's first abundant and important resource: the herring. As early as February or March, vast schools of Pacific herring approach the beaches to spawn, and Nimpkish who had the right to exploit this resource would move their house groups to these beaches.

A household group would dismantle their house at the winter village, leaving only the heavy posts and beams of its framework. The large split-cedar planks forming the roof and walls were loaded and lashed crossways on pairs of big cedar dugout canoes to form platforms for passengers and possessions. Up to four pairs of canoes, accompanied by smaller canoes, would be required for each house group. On a favorable tide, these were paddled across the strait and through the islands to Ksuiladas, where the house groups held foraging rights. The cargo was unloaded onto the beach, and planks were set up on a log framework similar to that at the winter village.

From this base, parties traveled out each day in the small canoes to search for and observe herring. Once the probable spawning beaches had been determined (ones where the water is whitened by discharged milt, the secretion of male reproductive glands), preparations were made for the harvest. Evergreen boughs were thrust into the beach at low tide to form a miniature temporary forest. When the herring came inshore with the rising tide, they deposited many of their eggs on these branches, and the Nimpkish harvested the spawn simply by gathering the heavily laden branches. Herring were taken by paired fishermen in small canoes, one at the stern paddling the canoe through the schools of fish, the other at the bow plying a "herring rake," a narrow strip of wood with prongs at one end. Herring and eggs were taken back to Ksuiladas, where they were dried by wind and sun on a pole framework or by heat and smoke high in the rafters of the houses.

Some Nimpkish house groups stayed in this settlement at the end of the brief herring season; others moved on to exercise their rights to fish for eulachon. Those who remained at Ksuiladas took halibut from the banks of nearby Queen Charlotte Strait and hunted for porpoise or seal in the same waters. Halibut are big fish and were processed by filleting them into thin strips of flesh and hanging the pieces over pole frames in places where wind and sun could combine to dry them.

House groups with rights to fish for eulachon moved to a stretch of the Klinaklini River estuary, where they set up residence in closely neighboring villages. The spawning eulachon were taken in large fine-meshed, nettle-twine bag nets or were captured in baskets at the apex of wicker V-shaped fences set in the river shallows. Oil was extracted from the eulachon by a process that combined putrefaction and boiling. Large wooden vats filled with water and partially rotted fish were brought to the boiling point by the addition of hot stones. Oil was skimmed from the surface and stored in tightly fitted containers. By the end of the eulachon season in May, the households would return to the Nimpkish River. Some of the oil was traded to groups on Vancouver Island, where no eulachon ran.

After the eulachon season, the Nimpkish took up residence at their winter village or some other location and exploited a variety of summer resources. Nearby beaches were dug for clams, and seaweed was gathered along the shore. Seaweed and berries were dried for later use.

From midsummer until late fall, however, the main activity was catching and processing salmon. This was a period of intensive work for all, and each segment of the household group had its designated tasks. In general, men attended to fish traps and speared or netted fish, while women processed the fish for storage, a far more time-consuming task. Children helped, and slaves could be pressed into service. Given the size of the Nimpkish River fish runs and the effectiveness of the traps, producing dried salmon for storage must have been limited not by "catching" labor but by "processing" labor.

Each fish had to be gutted, its head and backbone removed, and its body split lengthwise to the tail. The flesh on each side was then scored with a sharp knife to permit easy penetration of air and smoke. The paired body pieces were hung on pole frames and allowed to dry. As the season advanced and rainy days grew more frequent, the drying process moved indoors. The prepared fish were hung high in the rafters, where hot air and smoke could finish the process. When ready, the fish were packed in boxes for winter storage (Curtis [1915] 1970:19).

At the beginning of fall, some attention was turned to trapping deer and elk. Deer, it was said, were so bold and plentiful that they came right into the villages among the houses. Along the game trails, the Nimpkish constructed deadfalls, traps in which a log would fall on the animal and kill or disable it. This permitted taking of game without interrupting the catching and processing of salmon. During the fall season, some Nimpkish traveled to lakeside camps,

Material Culture

The mild but wet climate of southwestern Canada is reflected in Nimpkish clothing and dwellings. For much of the year, men wore nothing; women wore a simple apron. Either might don a loose-fitting robe or blanket when it grew cool and a woven cape and conical hat if they wished to keep off the rain. They went barefoot year round (Boas 1909:431–434; Curtis [1915] 1970:4–5).

Nimpkish dwellings were large and airy, with upright supports and beams of heavy cedar logs and walls of split-cedar planks. A raised earthen platform around the perimeter bore the sleeping and storage chambers, and a central sunken court served as the work area. There were no windows, and light entered through cracks between the wall planks and openings in the roof through which smoke could escape. The houses were usually about nine meters square, though in later years, some were fifteen to eighteen meters square.

Household furnishings included floor-level backrests near the fire and woven cedar bark mats for the sleeping areas. Household possessions—animal hides, woven blankets, wood or mountain goat horn spoons, wooden dishes, and fishing equipment—were stored on the platform between the sleeping areas, often in distinctive decorated wooden chests. During the nineteenth century, free-standing carved poles—known to Europeans as totem poles—became fashionable (Vancouver 1798, Boas 1909, Curtis [1915] 1970).

Residential and Kin Groupings

The large winter dwelling accommodated up to thirty people, with around fifteen people on average. From four to six households, each with its own cooking fire and sleeping and storage platform, made up the house group. A group of closely related males, commonly brothers, with their wives and children formed the core. Also in the house would be assorted elderly relatives and slaves belonging to the occupants.

Nimpkish house groups were linked as members of one of four major social divisions, each consisting of a cognatic descent group, or *numaym*, with associated spouses. In a cognatic descent group (sometimes called an ambilineal descent group), links back to a common ancestor are traced either through males or females. Nimpkish individuals had the right to

During the summer, the Kwakiutl of Canada's western coast dried berries and fish to carry them through the winter. This fish-drying rack is from Kotzebue, Alaska. The Kwakiutl shared their rich territory with other foraging groups, including the Haida, Tsimshian, and Tlingit.

from which men set out to hunt deer and elk with spears, bows and arrows, and, later, guns (Vancouver 1798:627). Women would gather and dry the last of the season's berries.

For much of the period before the historic move to Alert Bay, when the fall's work was done, all would settle in their large plank houses at the winter camp. The plank dwellings served as shelter for their inhabitants and as storage places for the house group's supply of food. Some hunting and fishing continued through the winter, but the focus of attention was on ceremonial activities within the houses. The great feasts accompanying these affairs drew, not on the little fresh food that could be gathered in the cold wet season's few hours of daylight, but on those dried and smoked provisions the people had earlier worked so hard to assemble.

membership in the numaym of either the father or the mother; most often the father's group was chosen. The numaym was a generally exogamous unit and a corporate group that was certainly the most important Nimpkish social division. As noted in Chapter 6, a corporate group can hold property and make decisions in common.

With the numaym were identified village residential areas, rights to locations of certain resources, and a host of other properties, including ranked titles or "seats," songs, performances, myths, and names for people, dogs, houses, feast bowls, and canoes. The most important of these properties, such as the ranked titles, remained with families in the numaym, usually passed down through the generations along lines of male primogeniture, preferred inheritance by firstborn males. On occasion, these properties could descend in trust to a female for her eldest male child (Boas 1966). Properties of a lesser value might be transferred to another group as part of a bride's dowry.

Unlike most other forager groups, the Kwakiutl were relatively sedentary because of their abundant environment, which included forest, river, and marine resources. They were able to develop a degree of stratification and an elaborate art and ceremonial complex, as evidenced by this totem pole from the area inhabited by the Nimpkish. Totem poles reflect clan affiliation and in some cases tell a story about the history of the kin group.

Rank and Social Stratification

Ranked positions—"names," "titles," or "seats"—held by the numaym were of paramount importance. These "names" or "titles" gave the holder a "seat" when attending a feast. The origins and ranking of the titles lay in the distant, mythic past. Titles inherited within the numaym were ranked with respect to one another, but when Nimpkish met at feasts, precedence was based only on the relative position of each numaym's highest-ranking title holder (Drucker and Heizer 1967). In practice, internumaym ranking was only of consequence when two or more title holders were together at a feast or when marriages were being arranged. At feasts, rank was expressed in a variety of ways. For marriage, care was taken to arrange unions that would involve families with title holders of similar status.

Although each numaym included several title holders, the highest-ranking title reflected on the position of all. In return, the holder of the top rank in each numaym could count on other members for assistance in upholding the worth of the title. The title's merit was imperiled if the holder did not mount feasts and distributions of scale appropriate to rank, and this required cooperation among all members of the numaym.

Rank and Resources   The system of rank seems to have structured leadership within the local group. The holder of the highest title in each house led the house group, and the highest in the numaym was its leader, or "chief." With four numayms, the Nimpkish had four such "chiefs," who were graded by rank with respect to one another. Numaym leaders were primarily active in guiding and coordinating the ceremonial activities of their groups. They also decided when villagers should dismantle their houses and move on to the next seasonal settlement. Leaders were the nominal "owners" or "caretakers" of such numaym or house group resources as salmon streams, fishing stations, clam beaches, and berry patches.

Social Class   At the top of the system of social ranking was the title holder class. This included all those who currently possessed ranked names or seats, who had occupied such a seat in the past, or who could expect to succeed to a ranked position. Members of the title holder class married other members of that class. There was no advantage to arranging marriages with any other category, as those outside the titled class had no seats or other prerogatives to convey to the partner or to the children.

Those who did not have and could never reasonably aspire to ranked positions within their numaym formed a second stratum of free society. These were the commoners, numaym members far removed from the primogenitural line of succession or persons in lines of descent that carried no privileges (Boas 1966). As population declined through the nineteenth century, this class essentially disappeared.

At the bottom of the status hierarchy were slaves. They constituted a hereditary class or caste and were, in theory, self-perpetuating in that children of slaves were raised as slaves. However, a more important source of slaves was provided by captives taken in raids. Adult male captives were sometimes killed; adult females and children were more commonly kept as slaves. The lives of slaves were controlled absolutely by members of the free classes. Slaves might be traded, given away as feast gifts, or even killed on ceremonial occasions. Owners reaped full benefit of their labor, which was directed to tedious tasks such as fetching water and firewood, paddling canoes, and preparing fish for winter storage.

Marriage

Arranging advantageous marriages was a perpetual concern of the title holder class. Because the numaym was commonly exogamous, partners were usually sought among the other Nimpkish numayms. To some extent, such matches served to tie numayms or local groups together, but of even greater importance to the Nimpkish seems to have been the transfer of property that indispensably accompanied a marriage (Curtis [1915] 1970, Boas 1966).

The initiative was taken by the groom's family or the groom himself if he was an adult. A spokesman secretly contacted the father of the desired bride to determine if a proposal would be accepted. If the response was favorable, emissaries of the groom's numaym were sent to the bride's house to announce, loudly and publicly, the intended marriage. Subsequently, a solitary representative of the groom visited the prospective bride's father to work out details of the brideprice and dowry and when the event was to take place. Once mutually acceptable terms had been negotiated, a token gift of animal pelts or woven blankets was delivered to the bride's father as an initial payment of the brideprice.

Up to a year elapsed while the groom's family assembled goods to be given to the father of the bride. On the appointed day, the groom's party arrived in canoes at the beach before the bride's house, a custom followed even if the marriage was between residents of the same village. A mock battle might ensue when the party tried to make its way across the beach and into the house, a form of symbolic bride capture. The Kwakwala words for "war" and "marriage" are identical.

Once inside the house, and after speakers for each side had proclaimed the greatness of the numayms or local groups, the brideprice goods were piled before the bride's father. He, through his speaker, announced the amount of the dowry and produced an initial installment composed largely of the boxes, spoons, mats, and blankets necessary to establish the new household. The groom was then led forward and seated beside his bride, concluding the ceremony.

Most commonly, the new couple took up residence with the groom's house group. After the birth of the first child, there was a further ceremony at which more of the dowry was conveyed to the groom. Most valued as dowry were rights to winter ceremony performances. Also prized were "coppers," large metal shields.

Feasts and Property Distributions

One important duty of top-ranking title holders was to invite other title holders to elaborate feasts to mark significant events in the life of the host or the host group. At the feast, the host would distribute valuable property to the assembled guests. Anthropologists refer to these events as *potlatches*, a term adopted by the Nimpkish themselves.

A feast and distribution might be held as a memorial for a previous holder of the title or to celebrate such events as the naming of a child, a marriage, construction of a new house, or the launching of a canoe. The affair might be small, involving only the numayms of a single local group, or of a grander scale, with the title holder and his numaym serving as hosts to title holders from other groups.

Years of preparation might be involved in hosting a particularly elaborate feast, and the feast itself could last for several days. In preparation, food was stockpiled, and gifts were manufactured or acquired. The usual gift was a hide or woven blanket, but canoes, household utensils, and even slaves could be presented. Suitable items were amassed through the labor of the title holder's house group, by calling in loans previously made at interest to other title holders and by borrowing from relatives and friends.

Feasts centered on speeches, meals, and property distributions. Orators, each acting on behalf of the host title holder or a guest title holder, in turn recited the accomplishments of the assembled title holders and their predecessors and listed the important prerogatives and possessions of each numaym present. Throughout the proceedings, rank was evident in such conventions as the order in which title holders' presence was acknowledged during speeches. The seating arrangement for title holders reflected their rank. Generous amounts of food were served to guests in order of their rank, and gifts were distributed according to standing. A high-ranking guest might receive a canoe or a slave; one of lower status, some carved spoons. When blankets were distributed, rank was reflected in the height of the pile

before each guest. These feasts publicly proclaimed the worth and rightful position of the host and his numaym and in addition acknowledged the relative status of the guests.

Winter Ceremonies

The ceremonial period was a special time when spirit beings returned after long months spent circling the earth. Cedar bark dyed a conspicuous shade of red was charged with supernatural power and figured prominently in the costumes of dance officials and of many performers and their attendants. Titles and names employed by men and women during the rest of the year were replaced by special ones used only at this time. Such names might be humorous or sexually suggestive, reflecting a purposeful relaxing of moral standards (Boas 1897, Curtis [1915] 1970).

The dance performances that formed the core of each ceremony formed yet another system of rank.

Northwest Coast Indians staged elaborate ceremonies during the winter, when they lived off food dried and stored during the summer. Central to these ceremonies were performances by ranked groups of dancers who owned rights to specific dances and the dramatic costumes associated with them. These Chilkat dancers from southern Alaska illustrate the theatrical staging of the winter ceremonies.

Whereas titles were ordered individually, dancers were ranked by category, in terms of their right to perform a particular dance. Most dance categories were the province of either males or females, while a few could belong to both. The rights to perform a particular dance and to use the mask and costume associated with it were valuable property passed down through the generations. The right to perform a particular male dance, for example, might be transmitted from father to son or, more commonly, from father-in-law to son-in-law as part of the bride's dowry (Boas 1966). Other inherited positions included master of ceremonies and his speaker and a number of individuals responsible for the rituals associated with different stages of the ceremony (Curtis [1915] 1970).

Before performing a dance for the first time, participants were required to undergo initiation, lasting for a few days or several months, depending on the dance. However elaborate, the initiation involved the same basic process: a guiding spirit abducts the novice and carries him or her off for instruction (Curtis [1915] 1970). In time, the novice reemerges and, with the help of attendants, dances for the first time in a ceremony in one of the houses. Each winter ceremony had a different host marking the initiation of one or more dancers with a distribution of food and gifts. The novice's sponsor hired songwriters (one for the music, one for the lyrics) to assist the new dancer in developing a unique set of songs.

Each host's residence served as a dance house, fitted with a secret chamber at the back, behind a painted screen that provided the backdrop for most performances. The presentation of a dance was an elaborate affair, with rich costuming, often including a large wooden head or face mask, designed to depict the essence of the animal spirit that was the dancer's inspiration and protector. Much use was also made of clever theatrical devices. For example, the audience might see a dancer, usually a female, placed in a wooden burial box, with the lid then tightly lashed in place. The box is placed on the fire, and the woman's singing voice is heard issuing from the box. The voice ceases, and attendants pick the dancer's charred remains from the fire and deposit them in a box. In a short time, the dancer arises from the box, apparently unscathed and whole. The entire performance was skillfully staged through the use of a tunnel with hidden entryways, a speaking tube made of kelp, and a genuine corpse stolen from its burial place.

Similarly "miraculous" resurrections were staged by dancers who had been "beheaded" or "stabbed." Others caused thunder to sound or caused animals, people, or objects to fly through the air (Boas 1897, Curtis [1915] 1970).

Over four successive evenings, new initiates emerged from behind the screen, performed, and then withdrew behind the barrier. Each evening, dancers who had performed in previous seasons might be moved to perform, coming forward from a corner of the house where they had been guarded by attendants. On the fourth evening, the dancers were generally subdued, or "tamed," evidence that the guiding spirit's control was weakening and the dancer would soon return to normal. The host's numaym distributed more property and food, then attention shifted to another host, who provided villagers with food and entertainment over the next few days.

In this manner, the winter season was spent, until the final host numaym had distributed the last of its food, the performers had all been tamed, and the spirits had set off on the return journey to their distant world. With the close of the ceremonies, "summer" names came back into effect and the usual rules of moral conduct were once more in force.

The Nimpkish Today

The Nimpkish live now at Alert Bay, on Cormorant Island, within sight of their river. Fishing is still a major occupation, but it now employs a vastly different technology, involving boats equipped with electronic aids such as radiotelephones, radar, long-range navigation, global positioning, and fish-finding sounders. The potlatch was banned in the early twentieth century by Canadian authorities, and for several decades the winter ceremonies and potlatch customs were banned as well. Masks were confiscated, and a few leaders were jailed. A revision of the Indian Act in 1951 dropped these prohibitions, and since then Nimpkish people have been at the forefront in reaffirming the importance of feasts and ceremonies in their lives. They have also been actively renegotiating their relationship with the government of Canada and the province of British Columbia in an attempt to regain greater control over the traditional resources of their territory.

SUMMARY

Anthropologists have traditionally looked to foragers for clues regarding what life might be like in small-scale egalitarian societies, where people are unburdened by mortgage payments, time clocks, and freeway traffic jams. The anthropological view of such societies has been somewhat romanticized, but even when seen through rose-colored glasses, foragers provide an important perspective on a lifestyle characteristic of humans for over four million years.

Modern forager groups occupy the most marginal econiches, and most have been forced to settle down, to support themselves through small-scale farming, herding, commercial fishing, or wage labor. The San of Africa's Kalahari Desert have survived incursions by neighboring pastoral groups, European colonialists, and traders in ivory and ostrich feathers. Their foraging lifestyle succumbed at last to partition of their land among competing nation-states, but their traditional way of life continues to be part of the ethnographic record.

San people inherit rights to forage on certain territories from their parents, who in turn had inherited those rights from their parents. Land tenure has a degree of flexibility, as is appropriate for people who forage for food. A San person can ensure rights to land by visiting relatives and exchanging gifts. Land tenure is extended through kinship ties, both consanguineal and affinal. Bilateral descent, marriage to a cousin, and brideservice strengthen the rights of individuals to land and promote group solidarity. Ju/"huansi San enhance these rights through formal exchange systems linking kin of the marrying couple.

The Ainu of northern Japan illustrate the close relationship of forager people with the animals and plants that provide them with the basic necessities of life. The Ainu subsisted on the abundant forest and marine resources of a mountainous island. The Ainu lived in semipermanent settlements, moving close to the mountains to hunt bears and other animals in the winter and settling near the coast to fish and hunt sea mammals in summer. The Ainu depended as much on plants as they did on animals. In summer, women gathered a variety of plants for food and medicinal purposes.

The Ainu world was organized around sacred spaces and beings. Animals hunted in the mountains were mountain deities; there were also sea deities, shore deities, and sky dwellers. The Ainu believed that all beings—humans, animals, plants, and certain household objects—were soul owners. When these beings "died" their remains were accorded the respect due a dead person. Relations between humans and deities were maintained through ritual practices, including the all-important bear ceremony, and by shamans who restored harmony when it was disrupted by illness or misfortune.

Unusual among foragers, the Kwakiutl of Canada's western coast supported a complex, stratified society utilizing the abundant resources available in the area. Kwakiutl subsistence centered on the sea, where they made use of a variety of fish, including halibut, herring, and cod. The rivers yielded several species of salmon, and beaches were the source of shellfish and crabs, among other resources. The area was also home to a large number of land and sea mammals, including deer, elk, bear, seal, and sea lion.

In summer, the Nimpkish Kwakiutl of what is now British Columbia harvested and preserved large numbers of fish and berries for consumption during the winter. In winter, Nimpkish lived primarily off food stored from the summer and occupied themselves with an elaborate round of ceremonies. Kwakiutl society was organized around cognatic descent groups, whose importance was determined by ranked titles, or "seats." Rank was negotiated through feasts, marriage arrangements, rights to dance performances, and potlatches. Unlike most other forager groups, the Kwakiutl had slaves, who were either captives of war or were born into the position of slave.

The San, Ainu, and Kwakiutl represent three variations on the foraging lifestyle. Many anthropologists believe the differences among them are related to variations in their environment, affecting the amount, type, and variability of resources available to them. The San have long been viewed as relatively egalitarian. The Ainu exhibit status differences associated with wealth, which is directly dependent on a man's ability to hunt and host the elaborate bear ceremony. Kwakiutl society is the most stratified of the three, organized around inherited status.

In all cases, the traditional lifestyles of these forager groups have changed as a result of contact with outsiders. Many San have become members of an impoverished fringe group; the Ainu have blended into Japanese society; the Nimpkish Kwakiutl still fish in their traditional territory but are now commercial fishermen, making use of large boats, radar, and long-range navigational equipment.

POWER WORDS

collaterals   land tenure   lineal kin

INTERNET EXERCISE

1. For more information on the !Kung of Africa's Kalahari Desert, check out the website **http://www.ucc.uconn.edu/~epsadm03/kung.html**. The site also has a link to Harvard's Peabody Museum that provides more information on the !Kung. Does the information at this site support Edwin N. Wilmsen's view provided in this chapter, that !Kung foragers are not egalitarian as previously assumed?

2. The website **http://www.japan-guide/com/e/e2244.html** briefly discusses historical discrimination against the Ainu and provides a link to the Ainu Museum. What effect might tourism and the changing lifestyle of the Ainu have on their traditional arts and culture?

3. A traditional Kwakiutl House is depicted at **http://www.tbc.gov.bc.ca/culture/schoolnet/carr/gallery/gallvag/42333a.htm**, courtesy of the Vancouver Art Gallery. Briefly discuss whether a house of this type could be maintained by foragers in a less abundant environment.

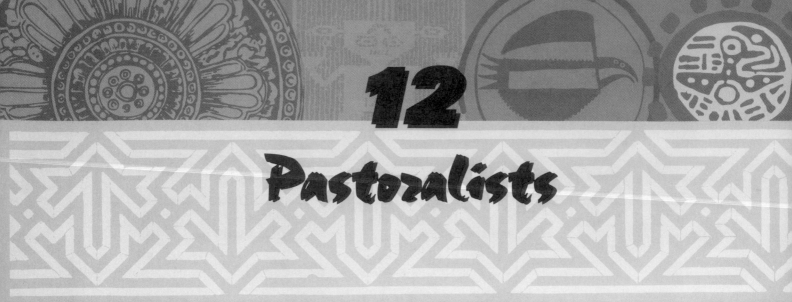

12

Pastoralists

In this chapter . . .

The pastoral way of life

The social organization of pastoral societies defies easy classification because it depends to a great extent on the type of animals herded and on the resources available in the environment. In general, pastoralists practice a form of seasonal migration known as transhumance. They live in extended-family groups, which provide labor to care for the animals, and rights to animals and migration routes are usually held by descent groups rather than individuals.

The Nandi: Eastern African cattleherders

As do other African pastoral groups, the Nandi of Kenya herd sheep and goats, but they identify themselves primarily with cattle. Nandi circumcise both males and females at puberty, at which time Nandi males acquire membership in an age set, which provides them with a social identity for the rest of their lives. Nandi also practice female–female marriage, which allows women to assume the status of males. Like other traditional groups, the Nandi have felt the effects of Christianity and have taken on many characteristics of settled agriculturalists.

The Basseri: Pastoralists of southern Iran

Among Basseri sheep herders of the mountains of southern Iran, households consist of nuclear families typically banded together in patrilineal descent groups. However, members of the wife's family can join the group, which in practice may result in some bilateral camps. Local groups are linked as regional groups under the leadership of a chief, who has the authority to command obedience. Within the group, leadership is based both on the appointment of the regional chief and on wealth, figured in terms of livestock.

The Yolmo: Zomo herders of the Nepal Himalayas

In the Yolmo Valley of the Himalaya Mountains, social life centers on temple-villages founded by Tibetan Buddhist monks or priests. The economy is based on herding of zomo, the hybrid offspring of a yak and a cow, one of the few bovines able to survive at altitudes between seven thousand and fourteen thousand feet. Zomo produce butter, important for both food and rituals. Though zomo herders spend most of their time in camps with their animals, they usually maintain permanent houses in the village of Melemchi, so they can participate in the rich ritual life and gain status as talpa, taxpayers to the temple that provides the focus for village life.

In their songs, Masai herders of Kenya lovingly recount the assets of each cow—its horns, its coloring, its personality. Like people in other pastoral societies, the Masai are expressing their interdependency with their animals. Pastoralists rely on their animals for subsistence, and the animals rely on the people for their very existence. In another tradition, Christ compares his relationship with his followers to that of the shepherd with his sheep: "I am the good shepherd: the good shepherd giveth his life for the sheep" (John 10:11). And King David of Judaic tradition sings, "The Lord is my shepherd; I shall not want" (Ps. 23:1).

Because of the interdependence of pastoralists and the animals they herd, it is difficult to generalize about pastoral societies. Their social organization depends to a great extent on the types of animals being herded and on the environment. Like foragers, pastoralists are nomadic; however, since pastoralists carry their food supply with them, their movements depend more on the needs of the animals than their own. In most cases, pastoralists are transhumant, which means they migrate on a seasonal basis.

Large grass-eating mammals consume many calories, and they would very quickly overgraze a limited pasture. Some cattleherding pastoralists supplement environmental sources of fodder with hay or other cultivated fodder. This type of pastoralism can support a somewhat sedentary way of life. Cows can also be raised in large feed lots, as in the United States. In general, herders of cattle tend to be somewhat more sedentary than pastoralists who herd sheep or goats. Sheep are more efficiently managed in large herds, they must be constantly watched, and they require a larger grazing area. Thus, sheepherders must spend more time in dispersed groups with their animals.

Many pastoralists are organized into unilineal extended families, as in the case of the Masai. Since unilineal descent groups can be corporate, making decisions and owning property as a unit, this type of family organization provides common access to grazing grounds and labor to tend the animals. In many cases, the descent group owns the animals in common. The Basseri of southern Iran own animals in nuclear family units but travel as an extended family group. Neolocal residence is the preferred pattern for zomo herders of Nepal.

In the discussions of the Basseri and Yolmo herders in this chapter, note that neolocal residence—which produces the nuclear family—produces a shortage of labor needed for herding at key points in the life cycle of the family: before children are old enough to tend the herds and after they have left to establish families of their own. At these times, neolocal pastoralists compensate for the labor shortage in the household by forming some type of cooperative herding unit, by hiring herders, or by a temporary extended-family arrangement.

Many pastoralists are nomadic or seminomadic, and the organization of kinship into associations of nuclear families permits a more flexible form of

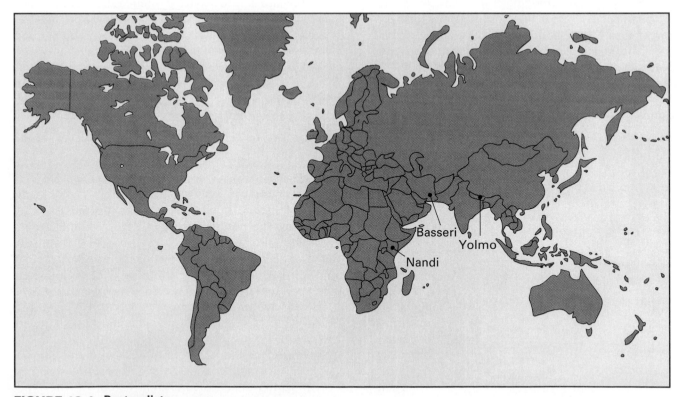

FIGURE 12.1   Pastoralists

The three pastoralist groups described in this chapter—the Nandi of eastern Africa, the Basseri of southern Iran, and the Yolmo of the Himalayas in Nepal—represent a variety of adaptations based on the types of animals herded and on their environment. The Nandi are a classic example of African cattleherders; the Basseri herd sheep and goats on diverse terrain ranging from mountains to plains; the Yolmo herd the zomo, a hybrid animal especially adapted to the high altitudes of the Himalayas.

residence and affiliation than would the extended family, in which subsistence assets are shared. Many pastoralists, like foragers, tend to have a more flexible household organization than do horticulturalists or intensive agriculturalists. The Nandi of Kenya are patrilocal, but families are not restricted in residence by affiliation with a descent group. The three groups described in this chapter (see Figure 12.1) are all patrilineal. However, the Navajo, sheepherders of the U.S. Southwest, are matrilineal.

Political organization also varies, but the most common form appears to be the tribe, an informal system that links together several local groups. The Nuer and some other African cattleherders are linked together by their **segmentary lineage** system (Figure 12.2). In this system, several local groups trace descent patrilineally to a founding male ancestor. As local groups grow, they fission along patrilineal lines. That is, when

a village begins to number about two hundred people, brothers split the group and, taking their own descendants, establish new settlements. Over many generations, this process produces a settlement pattern in which some groups are closely linked by descent, whereas others are more distantly related. The entire descent group is allied militarily and politically by varying degrees of patrilineal kinship.

Chiefdoms are also found among pastoralists, as appears to have been the case with Semitic tribes of

Among the Nuer of Africa, disputes between members of different lineages were often mediated by a leopard skin chief, so called because of his right to wear the leopard skin, a badge of informal authority.

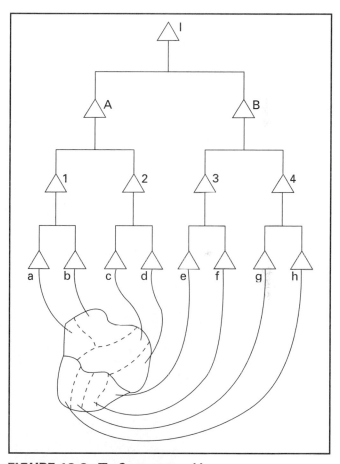

FIGURE 12.2 Tiv Segmentary Lineage

The segmentary lineage of the Tiv and the Nuer, African cattleherders, is an example of tribal organization based on a unilineal kinship system. In the case of the Tiv, members trace descent from a founding ancestor (I at the top of the diagram). Members of the fourth generation (a through h) are household heads who occupy a territory with their wives and children. The households and territories are allied through descent from members of the third generation (1 through 4) and more distantly by descent from the second generation (A and B). Ultimately, eight hundred thousand Tiv of northern Nigeria are allied to each other through a series of segmentary lineages.
Source: Adapted from Paul Bohannan, "The Migration and Expansion of the Tiv," *Africa* (1954) 24: 3.

the Bible. King David had absolute authority over his followers, as indicated in the story of David and Bathsheba, the wife of one of his generals. David sent Bathsheba's husband into a fatal battle so he could acquire her as one of his wives.

Though such systems of formal leadership are unusual among pastoralists, a chiefdom may offer an advantage when the group comes into conflict with neighboring societies. Biblical people frequently interacted with settled agricultural societies that were able to field large armies headed by a commander with absolute power. The absolute authority of a chief, who is able to order troops into battle, provides a military advantage over leaders who must rely on informal systems of persuasion. Among the Basseri, local groups are headed by a leader without formal authority, but these are united under the authority of a hereditary chief with formal authority.

As do most other pastoral societies, the three groups represented in this chapter rely to some degree on the cultivation of crops. The Nandi of Kenya cultivate millet and maize, or corn. The Basseri cultivate several cereals and grains, though their cultivation of these crops may be a relatively recent phenomenon. Yolmo herders plant wheat and a variety of barley suitable for high altitudes.

Cattle were first domesticated in Africa, and African cattleherders provide the classical example of pastoralism. The Nandi are characteristic of such groups, in that they are patrilineal and polygynous. Both males and females are circumcised in puberty rituals, at which time males acquire membership in an age set. An age set consists of a group of males who move through all of life's stages together. Among the Nandi, the age sets include four sets of elders, "senior warriors," initiates, and a group of boys who have not yet been initiated.

The Basseri are characteristic of Middle Eastern pastoralists. They live in a mountainous region of southern Iran and herd sheep and goats. Though the Basseri are neolocal, in that a couple occupies a separate tent upon marriage, descent is reckoned patrilineally, and the group travels as an extended patrilineal family unit.

The economy of Yolmo herders centers on a hybrid animal, the zomo, offspring of a yak and a cow. Only the zomo can survive and produce milk at altitudes of between seven thousand and fourteen thousand feet. Residence is neolocal, but the husband's parents may move in with a young couple, providing needed labor for herding until the couple's children are old enough to help with subsistence chores.

When the traditional foraging way of life of Navajos of the U.S. Southwest was disrupted first by the Spanish and later by U.S. soldiers and settlers pushing westward, they changed their pattern of subsistence to herding sheep. According to James F. Downs, "The social and cultural life of a family owning even four or five sheep is largely determined by this ownership" (1984 [1972]:57). These Navajo are tending sheep on Marble Canyon reservation in Arizona.

These pastoral groups all occupy mountainous econiches, regions unsuitable for intensive agriculture. The Nandi live in extended family compounds; the Basseri carry their tents with them in their seasonal migrations; the Yolmo live in permanent villages carved out of the steep mountainside. Their cultures are very different, but all three groups share common problems in adapting to the demands of herding at high altitudes.

THE NANDI: FROM WARRIORS TO STUDENTS

The Nandi were among the most feared warriors of East Africa during the nineteenth century. *Nandi* is said to be a name of recent origin derived from the Swahili word for "cormorant," *mnandi*. To the Swahili inland traders, eastern African coastal people of mixed African and Arab ancestry, this fish-eating, diving bird was a metaphor for Nandi warriors. Like the cormorant, the Nandi swept down from the heights to strike suddenly at their prey, the people of the plains. In the late 1800s, the Nandi were the bane of British colonial attempts to lay rail and telegraph lines, as Nandi warriors repeatedly swooped down the Southern Nandi Escarpment to steal iron and wires. The Nandi became famous among Africans for the tenacity of their resistance to British rule; they were subdued only after a massive "punitive expedition" against them in 1905. In the following essay, Regina Smith Oboler describes the changing lifestyle of the Nandi.

THE NANDI OF EAST AFRICA

Regina Smith Oboler*

As one travels northwest from Nairobi, Kenya, through lush farmland dotted with herds of dairy cattle, the terrain slopes gradually upward to the edge of the Great Rift Valley. Here the view stretches off seem-ingly to the ends of the earth. Winding down to the valley floor, the road continues across

---

*Adapted from Melvin Ember, Carol R. Ember, and David Levinson, *Portraits of Culture: Ethnographic Originals* (Upper Saddle River, NJ: Prentice Hall, 1995).

arid plains and finally descends toward Lake Nakuru—pink around the edge with thousands of flamingos—and Nakuru town. Climbing the other side of the Rift Valley, the road levels off slightly but keeps ascending through the Tinderet Forest, crossing the equator near Timboroa Summit at an altitude of over 10,000 feet. Here begins a gradual descent across the Uasin Gishu Plateau—bleak, windy, chilly, and often overcast—to the town of Eldoret, and the home territory of the Nandi. The road into Nandi District descends gently from an altitude of over seven thousand feet through rolling grasslands, crossing marshes filled with crested cranes before reaching Kapsabet, the district center.

It is lush and green here, unlike the arid plains of the Rift Valley. It rains here every month, though during the main dry season in January and February as many as two weeks can pass with no rain. During the height of the rainy season in July, however, it can stay overcast and drizzly for days at a time. During most of the year, the day dawns bright and sunny, but rain clouds roll in predictably during the midafternoon. After a downpour, it clears again for the last few hours of daylight.

South and west of Kapsabet, the countryside becomes broken into more distinct and frequent hills and valleys with rocky outcroppings, until one reaches the Mau Escarpment in the west and the Southern Nandi Escarpment in the south. It is hard not to be affected by the grandeur of the physical environment, and to expect that the inhabitants will match it. And the Nandi are impressive: physically tall and fit, dignified in demeanor, and, though friendly, exuding self-confidence and fierce pride in their warrior heritage. The international track-and-field community knows these people well, since they produce a disproportionate number of world-class distance runners, the best known of whom is Kipchoge ("Kip") Keino.

East Africa is known for aggressive cattle raiding. A popular myth among the Nandi is also found among the Masai and other African pastoralist warrior people: "At the beginning of the world, God created cattle and gave them to our people. However, as time went on, many cattle wandered into the wrong hands. Though it is a serious crime to steal a cow from one of our own people, raiding others for cattle is simply restoring them to the ownership that God intended." Modern East African countries no longer permit cattle raids, but this ethos is still alive symbolically. A young man, leaving home on a track scholarship to an American university, was presented with a spear and shield by his father's older brother and told: "In the past our young men raided with spears and shields; today you raid with pens and papers, but with the same goal—to bring wealth to our people."

Economy

Cattle have been central to Nandi life and economy for as long as anyone remembers. Fresh and preserved milk (*mursik*) were dietary staples. Nandi slaughtered sheep and goats, particularly on special occasions, but like other African pastoralists, they rarely slaughtered cattle. They added animal protein to their diet by bleeding cattle and mixing the blood with milk. Bleeding was done by tying a strap around the animal's neck so a large vein stood out, shooting an arrow partway into the vein, then withdrawing the arrow and allowing the blood to flow into a container. The animal was little damaged and could "give blood" again in a month to six weeks. This practice has now been all but abandoned. With limited pasture, people keep only plow oxen and dairy cattle and cannot afford to weaken animals whose productivity has clear economic value.

The traditional economy did not depend entirely on cattle. Because of rich topsoil and plentiful rainfall, Nandi District is excellent farmland, and the Nandi have always been farmers. Before the colonial period, the staple crop was eleusine (finger millet), cooked into a hard porridge and eaten with a variety of green leafy vegetables. Crops were cultivated near homesteads, and most cattle were taken by young men to graze in distant pastures. Women took sheep and goats to the lowland villages of other ethnic groups to trade them for grain.

During the colonial era, hybrid maize, which produces well at high altitudes and with heavy rainfall, replaced eleusine as the staple. Eleusine is still grown for dietary variety and as a component of local beer. Because the colonial government believed privatization of resources was the best route to economic development, land was divided into individual holdings beginning in 1954. Today, Nandi live on small individual farms. Each family grows crops and grazes cattle on its own land. Most families produce a surplus of maize for the market, and tea is a common cash crop.

Cattle continue to be important. The Nandi have a rich vocabulary describing cattle—anatomy, physical features, variations in color, and so on. Much conversation time was devoted to cows and their merits. This is still a popular topic, but the emphasis is now differ-

Among the Masai, as among other African pastoralists, a man's wealth and social identity are linked to the number and quality of his cattle. Like other African cattleherders, the Nandi do not kill cattle for food, although they slaughter sheep and goats. Instead, protein is obtained from cattle by milking and bleeding them.

ent. People no longer try to maximize the size of their herds; instead, they try to maximize milk production. Kenya Cooperative Creameries, the government-sponsored dairy, buys milk daily and processes it into a wide variety of products including ultrapasteurized "shelf milk" and tinned butter and cheese. These products are exported to other African countries. Most Nandi families' major source of income is production and sale of maize, milk, and tea in varying combinations. Few traditional zebu cattle remain in Nandi; they have been replaced by "upgraded" cattle, a mix of traditional and European strains valued for resistance to disease, or Holstein-Friesian dairy cattle, valued for high milk production. Bulls have largely been replaced by artificial insemination.

Male and Female in Nandi Culture

I first arrived in Nandi in 1976 as a young doctoral candidate in anthropology, armed with research fellowships from the National Science Foundation, the National Institute of Mental Health, and the Woodrow Wilson Foundation. My husband, Leon, then a graduate student in film and photography, accompanied me. Our goal was to study social change and gender roles.

We chose as our research site a location on the edge of a forest. This was a recently settled area, typical of other Nandi communities in many ways. Our host family was headed by Jacob (a pseudonym, as are all African names used here). We lived in Jacob's compound, a collection of houses, some close together, some farther apart, that face each other across an open space and are connected by a network of pathways. The house belonging to Jacob, his wife, Rael, and their children, with their kitchen shed and granary, was the center of our compound.

The group of men who first recruited us to the community became Leon's "agemates" and close associates. The first day we settled in, they came in the late afternoon to invite him to go to the river to bathe. A huge group of neighborhood boys trooped along after them. The next day I heard from Rael that Leon had neighborhood approval on two important counts: he was circumcised (the mark of male adulthood among the Nandi, who practice adolescent circumcision), and he didn't shiver in the cold water. Throughout the day, other women congratulated me on my husband's ability to tolerate cold water.

In time, I learned that the house and hearth are women's domain; the shade tree (*kok*) where gatherings take place is men's domain. It is considered effeminate to hang around the hearth too much; it is manly (in a climate where it rains a lot and can get quite cold owing to the altitude) not to mind exposure to the elements. Therefore, real men don't shiver. The Nandi believe that a woman can make her husband weak-willed and subject to her control by feeding him polluting bodily substances (*kerek*) or ground-up grass crabs. Inability to stand cold and frequent shivering are the outward signs of such poisoning.

As in many cultures, males are the preferred sex at birth. However, the preference is only slight. The ideal family includes both sons and daughters. Since the Nandi are patrilineal, sons continue the line of descent, but the bridewealth received when daughters marry enables their brothers to marry in turn.

Parents have different expectations of sons and daughters. Both sexes have major work responsibilities, but the tasks they are assigned are usually different. Girls are expected to care for younger children and help with weeding the fields and doing domestic chores, such as fetching water and firewood. Boys herd cattle, help with plowing, and perform miscellaneous errands and tasks. Boys' chores take them farther from the compound and give them more scope for independent action. Boys may care for children, and girls may herd cattle, if no child of the ideal age and sex is available. Nevertheless, families try to arrange things so that a child of the appropriate sex is available, and this effort in part accounts for the widespread custom of fostering.

Every household needs a *cheplakwet* (child nurse) and a *mestowot* (herdboy). So essential are these roles that a newly married couple not living in an extended family will "borrow" children from other relatives or friends to fill them. Many Nandi adults I interviewed had spent time as foster children. The fostering family is responsible for feeding and clothing the child and, in the modern setting, paying school fees.

Until recently, boys were much more likely than girls to attend school. A daughter leaves her family for another at marriage; a son remains and the family benefits from any increased earning potential he gains through education. Now, with primary education free, boys and girls are educated at the primary level in equal numbers. Boys are still more likely to pursue secondary school and higher education, though the gender gap in education is narrowing.

Nandi mothers believe that male and female babies are inherently the same at birth, but they consider adult males and females to be greatly different in basic character traits. Men are said to have greater physical endurance: to be *korom*, "fierce" (courageous in confronting enemies or wild animals—women must also be courageous and stoic, in childbirth and in coping with injury or grief). Men are also thought to be more intelligent, foresightful, and decisive and to be more inclined than women to forgive without holding a grudge. Women are seen as more empathic than men, more capable of feeling "pity" (*rirgei*, "cry together"). These differences are believed to be learned, but they are also thought to be set in place and reinforced by initiation.

Adolescent Initiation

Adolescent initiation, especially of boys, is a central Nandi institution. Boys and girls are initiated between the ages of twelve and eighteen. The central feature of the process is male circumcision or female clitoridectomy. The initiates are expected to be brave, quiet, and unemotional throughout. Initiation is thought of consciously as a test of the courage and toughness needed for childbirth or warfare, though warfare is now a thing of the past. **Clitoridectomy** is genital surgery performed on females and involves the excision of all or part of the clitoris and sometimes part of the external labia as well. This is a customary operation in many sub-Saharan African societies, not to be confused with **infibulation** (practiced in northern Sudan), the partial sewing shut of the vaginal opening.

Girls' initiation takes place individually or in groups of two to four in the family compound. The girls are outfitted in a standard costume for the occasion: a red skirt, men's white dress shirt, tie, a tall helmet, crossed bandoliers trimmed with colobus monkey fur and beads, knee socks, and athletic shoes. Many of these elements are associated either with the traditional dress of warriors or with contemporary male roles (e.g., the military, athletics, business). Though women direct the ceremony, costuming is in the hands of male specialists. Gender role reversals occur in both female and male initiation and include aspects of cross-dressing, men carrying water for women, and, during girls' initiation, women attacking men physically with sticks.

The initiation ritual begins in the late afternoon. The girls dance all night, accompanied by a group of younger girls. Guests visit throughout the night, and a crowd assembles in the morning, after dawn. The initiates distribute small gifts (candy, cigarettes, and so on) to the guests, and then a group of initiated women moves away from the main crowd and forms a circle in which the operation is performed. If the girl shows courage, the older women break from the circle and dash toward the crowd, whooping and ululating (wailing or chanting produced with the tongue and throat), to congratulate the male members of the families and drape them with sinendet, a ritually important plant. Singing, dancing, and celebrating continue all day. The initiates are secluded in neighboring compounds for several weeks, not to be seen again until their marriages are arranged.

Male circumcision is an important mark of both adult status and ethnic identity. The Nandi ridicule ethnic groups whose men are uncircumcised. Male initiation is a communitywide event with larger numbers of initiates (ten to fifteen) than in female initiation. Men of the next older age set supervise the process. Beginning in the morning, the boys have their heads shaved, are forced to behave submissively, are harangued and verbally abused, are made to perform "women's work," such as carrying water and firewood, and are made to sing and dance before the assembled crowd. At intervals, they are taken into a secluded grove for "secret instruction."

As sunset approaches, the boys appear for the last time, and female friends and family members tie scarves around their necks as tokens of moral support, since women are forbidden to be present at the actual circumcision. During the night, the boys undergo minor tortures and physical hazing, building up to the operation itself in the predawn hour.

The women of their families sit up all night waiting around bonfires in the public ceremonial space. Just before dawn, some of the circumcision "instructors" reappear to return the headscarves and drape the women in sinendet. At a ceremony I attended, some women refused to accept the tokens until they

The Nandi follow a number of customs associated with some other African cattleherders, including woman–woman marriages and circumcision of males and females at puberty. This Masai woman is taking her first "feast" after having been circumcised.

were assured that their sons had been as brave as they could possibly have been. Moments later, as the first rays of the sun appeared above the horizon, all those assembled dropped to their knees facing the sun and sang a traditional Nandi hymn. The boys—now young men—remained together in seclusion until their wounds had healed, during that time receiving instruction in traditional lore.

For young men, initiation marks the onset of a period of social freedom and intense sexual activity. Traditionally, this would also have been a time of high risk taking as the new warriors went on cattle raids to prove their mettle and began to amass their own herds. Today, very often initiates are students and are exempt from adult responsibilities.

In the late nineteenth century, the young men of each neighborhood slept in a communal barracks, often accompanied by their lovers, girls not yet old enough for initiation. These couples were free to engage in all forms of sex play, except actual penetration, without social stigma—girls were expected to be technically virgin at the time of their initiation. At present, young men have their own huts in their parents' compounds, and there is no disapproval of young uninitiated women spending nights in their boyfriends' huts.

Social and Political Organization

For men, initiation marks the entry into one of seven age sets (*ibinda*; plural, *ibinwek*). The age set members move as a unit through the life cycle. The names of the age sets are always the same, and they rotate through time: Kaplelach, Kipkoimet, Sawe, Chuma, Maina, Nyongi, and Kimnyigei. At any time there are four sets of elders, the "senior warriors," the initiates, and a set of boys. When all in the oldest age set have died, its name comes back into use as the name of the set of the new initiates.

All men who are circumcised within a certain period of time belong to the same age set and are viewed as **agemates.** Because age at circumcision varies, there may be some overlap of ages at the margins of an age set, with the oldest members of a junior set being older than the youngest members of the next-senior set.

There is a strong sense of solidarity within age sets and a tendency for the members to act as a unit in taking on activities, such as community improvement projects. The idea of unity is especially strong among those men who were initiated together in the same ceremony (called a *mat*, or "fire"). They are likely to have strong bonds of friendship for their whole lives and provide mutual aid and support. I once went with a young Nandi man to visit another young man. When we arrived, the man was not at home and his door was closed. My friend walked in and traded his dirty shirt for a clean one he found inside. When I expressed surprise, he responded, "Why should I not take anything I need? He's my agemate. I am free to take whatever he has."

Relations among members of different age sets are controlled by definite rules of etiquette. Men of younger sets defer to men of older sets. Sons should belong not to the age set adjacent to that of their father but to the next lower one. Familiarity between members of these age sets is avoided. A man may not marry his agemate's daughter, nor a woman her father's agemate. There are no age sets for women. Groups of women around the same age are often referred to as "wives of . . . " with the name of a men's age set.

The Nandi have extended families and clans with animal totems. Descent is traced patrilineally. The clans' only function is the regulation of marriage. Certain clans do not marry members of certain other clans, though ritual elders told me that the pattern of marriage rules is continually shifting, depending on what interclan marriages have been successful in the recent past. Marital residence is patrilocal, but communities are not based on kinship. Traditionally, families could move into any locality where they would be sponsored by people already living there—relatives, in-laws, agemates, or others. Now with private land ownership, people move into communities where they can buy land.

Traditionally, the local community (*koret*), consisting of several hundred people, was the most important unit of day-to-day life, the site of ceremonial and economic cooperation and dispute settlement. The term for the community's council of elders, *kokwet*, is used both for the council and the territorial unit, which might be called a "neighborhood." The unit immediately larger than the kokwet was the *pororiet*, called a "regimental area" because its warriors formed a single fighting unit. The pororiet council made decisions about matters of concern to the local communities—such as warfare, circumcision, and planting. It was made up of representatives from each kokwet council and two representatives each from the warriors and the Orkoiyot (Huntingford 1953).

The Orkoiyot was a religious-political figure, a kind of chief, though his power was more ritual than political. This hereditary office created some political centralization for all the Nandi for a short time, from the mid-nineteenth century to the British conquest. The main functions of the Orkoiyot were to coordinate military activities and to sanction cattle raids. Warriors planning a raid would ask the Orkoiyot (who was believed to foresee the future) to predict its outcome. They would stage the raid only if he predicted success and would thank him with a gift of captured cattle if the raid was successful.

According to Nandi mythical tradition, the family of the Orkoiyot descended from powerful Masai *ilai-bonik,* ritual experts with paranormal powers, who immigrated to Nandi and were absorbed into the Talai clan. The Masai, however, believe that their ilai-bonik came from elsewhere, perhaps from Nandi, so the Nandi story may reflect symbolic relationships between groups rather than history.

Marriage

For women, marriage took place shortly after initiation and for the most part still does. The average age at marriage for women in my census was 17.8 years old. Young men, after initiation, spent about twelve to fifteen years as warriors and did not marry until most of this time had elapsed. Today, with peace, men marry younger; the average age at marriage is in the early twenties.

Ideally, a girl in seclusion after initiation waits for a group to come seeking her as a bride on behalf of a young man. This is known as coming for "engagement" (*koito*). This group, the "engagement party," contains both women and men, including the prospective groom's parents, uncles, aunts, older siblings, and close friends and relatives, at least some of whom know both families well. On the second visit, the girl's family makes sure to also have relatives and friends assembled, and the two groups begin negotiating details of the proposal. There is no formal marriage contract, but information is sought on such matters as how many cattle the groom has or stands to inherit, where the couple will live, and so on. The exact amount of the bridewealth—in cattle, sheep, goats, and money—is also negotiated. Women in the two groups negotiate almost as actively as the men.

The bride must observe the prospective groom from behind a screen, and it is the responsibility of the bride's father's sister to ensure that she finds the man acceptable. If she really dislikes him, she can hold out against the arrangement. Girls are sometimes pressured into accepting less-than-ideal matches, however. In reality, by the time a girl is initiated her marriage may already have been arranged, at least informally, through talks between the two mothers. Romantically involved couples can arrange in this way to be married, and this practice is becoming more popular.

Marriages between people whose families live in the same community are common. Sisters, in particular, try to marry men who live near each other, so they will be able to turn to each other for assistance. The term *lemenyi* refers to men married to sisters, and this relationship is supposed to be close and supportive. Friends and agemates sometimes try to arrange to marry sisters and thus become lemenyi.

Nandi men and women expect that the husband will be the dominant partner. In public, wives behave submissively toward their husbands, though private behavior is often more egalitarian. The husband has the right to punish the wife physically for "misbehavior," in particular for public disrespect. A Nandi college student told me that he did not like this aspect of his culture, but admitted to being governed by it: "It depends on what she does. If she does certain things, I will have to beat her or people will lose respect for me." Both men and women spend more social time with same-sex friends than with their spouses, but socializing as couples is becoming more common among younger, educated people.

The payment of bridewealth is the central act that creates a marriage among eastern African pastoralists. Nandi bridewealth is lower than most, at five to seven cattle, one or a few sheep and goats, varying amounts of cowrie shells, and cash generally equal to the value of a cow. When families negotiate bridewealth, specific animals are indicated by name, and attention is paid to the exchange history of the animals. It is important to include at least one cow, or its progeny, from the bridewealth given for the groom's father's sister. If the groom's full sister is married, an animal received as her bridewealth is given. A full sister is one who shares both a father and mother. The daughter of one's mother's co-wife is a half sister.

The cattle given as bridewealth for a daughter should be used for the marriages of, or inherited by, only her full brothers. Each of a man's wives is the founder of a separate genealogical unit called a "house" and holds cattle separately from any other wives. At her marriage, a woman is given some of her husband's cattle to serve as the basis of her "house property" herd, which also includes animals her relatives give her as wedding gifts. The herd grows through natural increase, further allocations from her husband, the addition of cattle she can sometimes acquire herself, and bridewealth given for daughters.

In any decisions concerning house property cattle, a wife must consult her husband; he also is not supposed to sell, give away, or do anything with the cattle without consulting her. A husband, however, usually has cattle that have not been allotted to the house of any of his wives, and these are his to do with as he pleases. While husbands therefore have greater property rights than wives do, they do not have complete control of family property. Nandi women told me that wives have the right to go to any lengths to prevent their husbands from taking their house property cattle. In one instance, the wife took her complaint to the community elders and stopped the sale of her cow.

As in most African societies, marrying more than one wife was a mark of status for a Nandi man. Wives have no right to object to their husbands' marrying other wives, and some desire it. Although many men now claim that as Christians they have no intention of marrying second wives, analysis of census data shows that, with age controlled, Christians are only slightly less likely to be polygynous than are Nandi traditionalists. With private land ownership, however, it is becoming difficult for a man to provide adequate land inheritance for the family of more than one wife.

Traditionally a marriage was considered revocable until after the birth of a first child. After that point, divorce was considered to be impossible. Once married, a Nandi woman is forever the wife of the man she first married, and all children she bears are considered to be his children, even if she has not seen him for years. A widow is prohibited from remarrying; if she has further children, the father is considered to be her original husband, and it is his property that her sons inherit. A young widow is expected to practice the levirate, cohabiting with a kinsman of her husband, who begets children regarded as those of her dead husband. Though this is the "respectable" thing to do, it is not required. A widow may instead take lovers of her own choice.

Woman–Woman Marriage

The Nandi practice woman–woman marriage, which makes up about 3 percent of all marriages, a rate that seems to be remaining steady. Woman–woman marriage is related to patrilineal inheritance. Though each married woman holds a separate fund of property and is expected to become the founder of a "house," only sons may inherit property. If the house has no male heir, its property will go to the sons of co-wives or of the husband's brother. The Nandi solution is for the heirless woman to become the "female husband" of a younger woman and "father" to her children. One young man describes his female father: "The woman who married my mother was my father. She acted just like any other father."

The female husband "becomes" a man, and she must discontinue sexual relations with men. Though she has no sexual relationship with her wife, she has all the other rights of a husband. Her wife should cook for her and do all the domestic work. Outside the home, there is considerable ambiguity about whether female husbands in fact act like men in ways they claim are permitted to them, such as participating in political meetings and attending male initiation. It might be more accurate to see female husbands as occupying an ambiguous gender status, while they and others go to great rhetorical lengths to argue that they are in fact men.

Another alternative when there is no heir for house property is for a daughter of the house to "marry the center post." She thus becomes like a daughter-in-law rather than a daughter. She remains at home and takes lovers, and her sons are the heirs.

Childbirth, Mothers, and Fathers

Childbirth usually takes place at home, attended by local midwives, though some women now go to the hospital in the district center. Women in labor are expected to be stoic. I watched a young woman give birth without a whimper, though pain was etched on her face. In another instance, a woman behaved in a "cowardly" way during labor and thus became the subject of amused gossip and teasing for a long time afterward.

Childbirth is "women's business," and men are expected to stay away from the house at this time, waiting with other men nearby for news of the birth. In the nineteenth and early twentieth centuries, it was months before the father would resume living in the house, and he would not touch the child or resume sexual relations with the mother until the child had been weaned and could walk. Such **postpartum sex taboos** are used by many people for birth spacing.

Among the Nandi, postpartum sex taboos were enforced by the belief in *kerek*, a substance that was thought to emanate from infants and nursing women and was believed to be ritually polluting to men. Close contact with either the mother or the child could make the father (and perhaps his male associates) lose skill with weapons, become weak-willed and indecisive, and shiver in the cold.

Nursing wives could cook for their husbands only after going through a lengthy ritual of washing with river sand and cow dung and returning home without touching their body or clothes. The *cheplakwet* (child nurse) held the baby until after the mother cooked. If an unweaned child touched an object in the house, the object was traded to a childless neighbor for a similar object. Some people now claim this was only superstition; others say kerek became a matter of less concern with the introduction of soap, which dissipates the polluting substance very effectively. In any case, men now rarely hesitate to have contact with babies, and most people say this is a positive change. It is also true that births are now spaced much more closely and families are larger.

The Modern Division of Labor

All family members participate in production. Men clear ground for planting and initially break it, in the past, with iron-bladed hoes, today with an ox-drawn plow. It takes a team of two men to plow, one to drive the oxen with a whip, and one to hold the plow. The only instance of a woman plowing that I ever saw was when Rael helped a man she hired to plow a field for vegetables she was growing to sell. All ages and sexes plant and harvest, usually in cooperative work groups larger than one household. Cultivation during the growing cycle is done by both sexes, and women spend slightly more time at agricultural activities than do men. Cattle herding is done mostly by children, but women more than men participate. Women and children do most of the milking.

Most men try to find some sort of full-time or part-time employment, but jobs are scarce in rural areas. Many men who are not formally employed engage in some kind of entrepreneurial activity: agricultural contract labor for large landholders, cattle trading, charcoal making, dredging sand from rivers to sell for making concrete, and so on. There are also some skilled artisans with shops in the local center—for example, a tailor and a bicycle repairman. Only a few women engage in such activities or have jobs. Profit from sale of cash crops—maize, tea, and milk—goes to male household heads, who are supposed to use it for the benefit of the household. Women often grow vegetables for sale or sell chickens and eggs. Women are said to "own" chickens (sometimes called "the cattle of women"), vegetables, and the afternoon milk, which is for family consumption. Morning milk, which belongs to men, is marketed through the Kenya Cooperative Creameries. Women's biggest source of cash in 1975–1977 was from brewing and selling maize beer. In the 1980s, a ban on selling beer cut off this income source.

THE BASSERI OF SOUTHERN IRAN*

The Basseri are pastoral nomads, numbering about sixteen thousand people in all, who migrate across mountains and steppes in a territory of southern Iran spanning about three hundred miles long and fifty miles wide. Basseri territory is diverse, ranging from desert to mountain. Throughout their range, rain is scarce, falling primarily in winter. Because of snowfall in the mountains, there is more vegetation and forested land in these areas. Where the land is flat and low, there is very little vegetation, limited to a thin cover of grass during winter and early spring. Sedentary people surrounding the Basseri subsist primarily by agriculture, made possible by irrigation.

Ecology

Because Basseri pastures are seasonal, these sheep and goat herders must have access to an extensive amount of grazing area. In the winter, the northern areas are covered with snow, but there is still usable pasture land in the south. In the spring, areas of low and middle altitude have plentiful grazing areas. As

---

*Based on Fredrik Barth, *Nomads of South Persia* (Oslo, Norway: Scandinavian University Press, 1961).

these start to dry out, better areas are available at higher altitudes. Although fall is the most tenuous time, the Basseri graze their flocks on land owned by agriculturalists once fields have been harvested, a mutually beneficial arrangement since manure from the animals makes excellent fertilizer.

As do other nomadic groups, the Basseri follow an annual migration route. The route, including a schedule of arrival times at each location, is their *il-rah*, the "tribal road," and each il-rah is considered the property of a particular tribe. Il-rah customs grant the Basseri recognized rights to particular land at a specific time. As the group moves north, alternative routes within the il-rah allow some dispersal of the tribe. Breaking camp and moving are usually done daily in the spring and fall, as the Basseri move between summer and winter camps. The groups become more stationary when they occupy the seasonal camps.

Subsistence

Sheep and goats provide the bulk of subsistence products, including milk. Donkeys are used as pack animals and are ridden by women and children. Men ride horses, which carry no other load. Camels carry the heaviest items. The Basseri herd no cattle because the terrain is too rocky for cattle to negotiate (Barth 1961). Each shepherd is responsible for a mixed flock of three hundred or four hundred sheep and goats.

Milk and milk products are the staples of the Basseri diet. Sheep's and goat's milk, mixed together, are never consumed without being heated. Fresh milk is soured by adding a bit of sour milk or the acidic contents of a lamb's stomach. Cheese is made from junket, a sour-milk product, during the more sedentary summer encampment periods. Sour milk is also stored by separating the curds from the whey. The solid curds are shaped into dumplinglike balls and preserved through the winter by drying them in the sun. The liquid whey can be fed to watchdogs; the sour milk is churned into buttermilk or butter. Buttermilk is usually consumed immediately and butter is eaten fresh, but quantities of butter are also stored for sale.

Young animals, usually male, not needed to supplement the adult herd are slaughtered for meat and their hides are sold. Lambskin is a much-sought-after product at market, and hides provide containers for storage and transport. Sheep also provide wool both for sale and for the tribe's own use. Wool may be spun and woven or processed into rope. Spinning and weaving require great skill and consume much of Basseri women's time. Women fashion all the saddlebags and cloth packs that carry the tribe's belongings, as well as carpets and rugs for sleeping. Tents are made of woven goat hair, which is impermeable to rain and provides insulation, so that heat is retained in cooler months and dissipated in the summertime.

The Basseri milk-based diet is supplemented by cultivating cereals and grains, a relatively recent phenomenon. Wheat and other cereals can be planted upon arrival at summer camps and harvested before camp is broken in the fall. Often, the Basseri contract with settled local residents to plant the crops before they arrive to do the harvesting. This agricultural work is not highly valued; many nomads refuse to participate and look down on those who do (Barth 1961). Some Basseri solve this difficulty by becoming landowners. Though they do not settle on the land, ownership allows them to avoid agricultural work by leasing the land to others in return for a portion of the yield.

The Basseri secure many necessities through trade. The most important of these is flour, since unleavened bread is part of every meal. The Basseri trade butter, wool, hides, and occasionally animals for sugar, tea, and fruits and vegetables. Through trade, they also obtain clothing, cooking utensils, saddles, and luxury items, which may include jewelry, narcotics, and portable radios (Barth 1961).

Kinship and Household Organization

As do other Middle Eastern pastoralists, the Basseri reckon descent patrilineally. Inheritance is usually from father to son, and more distant **patrikin**— relatives in the same patrilineal descent group— supplant daughters in inheriting land rights and other goods. A woman bestows on her offspring no membership rights to her own group; the son of a Basseri male is a Basseri regardless of the affiliation of his mother. Local groups are often formed by brothers.

Most Basseri households consist of a nuclear family living in a single tent, possibly with a widowed or single relative. Camps are generally made up of thirty or forty tents, which constitute the basic unit of production and consumption, as well as of ownership of cattle.

Although some goods may be owned by individual family members, the household is regarded as the property-owning unit. Within the household, there is a clear line of labor and authority. The household is represented in tribal matters and dealings with outsiders by the head, who is invariably male. If the tent consists of a nuclear family, the husband-father is head. If not, the senior male assumes this role. If no adult male resides within the household, a woman may be regarded as the head, but she will be represented by a male relative in formal matters.

Within the domestic unit, there is much more egalitarianism. Decisions concerning family, children, marriage, and kinship, as well as the wider realm of social and group relations, are made by adults in consultation with one another. The household's most assertive or wisest member predominates, regardless of gender (Barth [1961] 1986).

Marriage Alliances between households are most often reinforced by affinal (marriage) ties. Marriages are arranged by household heads, who are usually the fathers of the prospective bride and groom. Bridewealth among the Basseri is called "milk-price," and it pays for the woman's labor and fertility as well as the household items she will bring along with her. There is also an "insurance" fee promised, which will be the woman's compensation should the marriage end in divorce. Before the wedding, the prospective groom gives minor tokens to the bride and her family, as well as some brideservice in the form of small favors to her parents.

Sister exchange (in which a groom's sister is given to the bride's family in compensation for the bride) is common, and the Basseri conform to the rules of the levirate and sororate (replacing a deceased spouse with an analogous family member), even in the face of protest by the individuals involved. Families also seek to perpetuate affinal ties in subsequent generations of marriage arrangements.

Fredrik Barth (1961) suggests that the active pursuit of continuing affinal ties derives from the political and economic independence of the Basseri nuclear family unit. The only way to ensure the continuity of the community of these autonomous units is to knit households together by marriage. Marital ties, especially if siblings marry into the same family, can keep tents allied with one another, thus preserving the nomadic community. The desire to maintain ties that will generate good-will in a local camp and thus foster consensus in daily migratory decisions and solidarity in general results in a high number of marriages between close kin.

A Basseri woman is important economically. There is a high level of mutual dependence between husband and wife, and women possess tremendous authority within the domestic sphere, which among migratory peoples is the one unchanging portion of their environment. Upon marriage, a woman joins her husband in his family's tent, but this is only a temporary arrangement. As soon as they can acquire enough animals to become economically self-sufficient, a new couple establishes an independent household, since the preferred residence pattern is neolocal.

Fathers may give several animals to their sons in times of plenty, when the family can afford to do so. This practice teaches the boy to care for the animals, which can later be taken to his own household. Boys may also work as shepherds for other households and receive payment in lambs. A diligent worker may be able to build up a small herd of his own. The accumulation of a herd is further ensured by the practice of "anticipatory inheritance," in which a son receives upon his marriage that portion of his father's flock to which he would be the rightful heir at his father's death (Barth 1961).

The ideal household has, at minimum, an adult male who performs the labor associated with his role and takes his place in the leadership of the migration, an adult female who accomplishes the numerous and difficult domestic tasks, and at least one individual who acts as shepherd. For the nuclear family, there are long periods of time before the children are of shepherding age and after the children have grown and established their own households. At these periods in the household life cycle, additional labor must be contracted for by hiring a shepherd or adopting a close relative, but more often families band together to form small cooperative units to share herding tasks.

Usually, several households combine their flocks under the care of one shepherd, with adults of each household milking their own animals. Families who have entered into a cooperative arrangement generally pitch their tents together at night and regard each other as equal partners. A family may end its participation in the cooperative at any time, and as families shift alliances, the clusters of households change over time.

Camps

During the spring and summer, when fodder is plentiful, larger camps can be supported, and Basseri camps may then number as many as forty tents. During the winter, dispersing over a wide range is the best way to use the depleted environment, and a camp may consist of only a few tents.

Maintaining a sense of community is a challenge among nomads. For settled peoples, alliances are reinforced by ongoing interactions during the daily routine. For nomadic tribes, however, the decision to remain a community is an active one, not simply a consequence of the inertia of routine. Each day, residents of a local camp must convene and assess their surroundings to make the crucial decision of whether to move on. This decision cannot be made lightly, since the health of their herds and the economic base of their existence are at stake. The wisdom of each household head will determine his family's fate, and there must be agreement among tents to proceed. In some cases, failure to reach consensus about daily migration has resulted in a change in the composition of the community. Barth notes:

> Every household head has an opinion, and the prosperity of his household is dependent on the wisdom of his decision. Yet a single disagreement on this question between members of the camp leads to fission of the camp as a group—by next evening they will be separated by perhaps 20 km of open steppe and by numerous other camps, and it will have become quite complicated to arrange for a reunion. The maintenance of a camp as a social unit thus requires the daily unanimous agreement by all members on economically vital questions. (1961:26)

Reaching consensus about daily movement is greatly facilitated by recognizing a single leader in each camp. This individual both influences decision making within his group and represents his group in dealings with other camps. The status of leader is typically inherited, usually passing from a man to his next most senior male relative. Local Basseri groups are united under the authority of a single hereditary chief, who has the right to formally recognize local leaders. However, camp members may select the person they consider most deserving of

the position; they may also unseat one they deem unfit. Traditionally, a leader who had been formally recognized by the chief was known as *katkhoda*, or "headman." A leader who had not been recognized by the chief was known as *riz safid*, literally, "whitebeard." However, this traditional distinction has been eroded through the authority of the Iranian government.

The requirements for being headman depend in part on a man's economic position within the group, but the importance of wealth is somewhat tenuous. Wealth is, by and large, livestock, and all Basseri are subject to loss of animals through circumstances beyond their control. Thus, no one can depend on wealth to support his position. Barth (1961) reports that some headmen have suffered serious reduction of their herds without loss of status.

Political Organization

The position of chief among the Basseri is typical of Middle Eastern centralized leadership, in that it is believed that power emanates from him, rather than having been vested in him by those he leads (Barth 1961). The chief and his close kin are set apart from other Basseri through kinship, residence, and wealth. Chiefs are viewed as being descended from a noble lineage, a view that forms a basis for their authority and the respect due them. Furthermore, chiefs are removed from the nomadic life; they own land, houses, villages, and herds numbering in the thousands. The chief is expected to conduct himself in a manner befitting a man of power and privilege. He is expected to live lavishly and bestow gifts generously. Taxes, payable in sheep, are imposed on tribe members. Annual taxes of butter are also paid, and the chief expects gifts from anyone who comes before him.

The chief is responsible for allotting pastures and organizing migratory patterns, settling disputes, and representing the tribe to outside authorities. Organizing travel and use of grazing land among a large nomadic population is a monumental feat. The chief must coordinate a schedule that avoids overuse of land and prevents a logjam of people moving along a particular road. Without this tightly orchestrated direction, a nomadic lifestyle would be unworkable (Salzman 1974). Among other nomadic peoples in Iran, allotment of pastures is often used as a method of **sanction,** or punishment, and it has been

DISCUSSIONS

The Killing of Cattle:
Sacred and Secular Forms of Sacrifice

Wherever they are herded, cattle occupy a special place among domesticated animals. African cattle herders kill sheep and goats for food, but cows are killed only for sacrifice. Cow killing is banned by modern Hindus, but their forebears practiced cow sacrifice.

The bull as a symbol of death and rebirth was prevalent throughout the ancient Middle East, and the bullfight in Spain continues to provide an arena for enacting themes of courage and sacrifice. The association of cattle with the invention of culture also appears to be pervasive, not only in the ancient Middle East but among the Celts of Europe as well. Among the Welsh, bulls were linked with the god Hu Gadam, who divided the Cymry, or Welsh Celts, into clans, taught them to plow, and invented music and song.

The Gilgamesh epic, carved in stone by a Sumerian scribe, may symbolically represent a bullfight. Composed in the third millennium B.C., the epic delineates motifs that consistently underlie bull sacrifice: fertility, nature transformed into culture, the certainty of death, and the quest for immortality. The epic hero is himself often compared to the bull in strength and vitality. Gilgamesh's close companion is Enkidu, a wild man whose body is covered with matted hair "like Samugan's, the god of cattle." Enkidu roams the hills eating grass, until he is tamed by sexual intercourse with a harlot sent by Gilgamesh. The woman teaches Enkidu to eat bread instead of grass, to drink wine, and to wear clothes. In short, she domesticates the wild man.

Gilgamesh and Enkidu are drawn into battle with the Bull of Heaven when Gilgamesh rejects the advances of Ishtar, the goddess of love. Although Gilgamesh strikes the killing blow, Enkidu prepared the animal for the coup de grâce when he "dodged aside and leapt on the Bull and seized it by its horns." Gilgamesh kills the Bull by thrusting his sword into the back of the animal's neck. He and Enkidu then cut out the animal's heart and give it to Shamash, the sun god. Enkidu's vault over the animal anticipates later Cretan ritual, while the method of killing the bull is similar to that practiced in early bull sacrifice and in the modern bullfight.

In punishment for the cosmic misdeed, the gods decree that Enkidu must die. Gilgamesh's grief over the death of his friend compels him to set off on a great journey to find the secret of immortality. As he travels, Gilgamesh puts off his kingly robes and begins wearing the skins of animals. Symbolic transformation is evident here. Enkidu leaves the wilds and enters the world of civilization, where he dies. Gilgamesh leaves the world of civilization and ventures into the wilds seeking immortality. On his journey, Gilgamesh meets Siduri, the woman of the vine, who says:

> Gilgamesh, where are you hurrying to? You will never find that for which you are looking. When the gods created man they allotted him death, but life they retained in their own keeping. As for you, Gilgamesh, fill your belly with good things, day and night, night and day, dance and be merry, feast and rejoice. Let your clothes be fresh, bathe yourself in water, cherish the little child that holds your hand,

and make your wife happy in your embrace; for this too is the lot of man.

It is significant that Gilgamesh, repeatedly compared with a bull, is instructed in culture by the woman of the vine. The association of the blood of the bull with wine is repeated in Mithraism, in the Dionysian cult of Greece, and later in the symbolism of the bullfight. Cultivation of the vine and the conversion of grapes into wine are also associated with the invention of culture.

Bull and cow symbolism permeate the Rig-Veda. Composed between 1500 and 1000 B.C.E., according to some estimates, the Rig-Veda is the earliest of the Vedic sacred writings that form the nucleus of Hindu belief. The Rig-Veda traces the origin of religious ritual to the bull sacrifice: "The heroes roasted the dappled bull. These were the first ritual laws."

In the Rig-Veda, the bull symbolizes strength and fertility; the milk of the cow represents immortality, the "prize to be won." Together, the cow and bull make up "sky-and-earth," a kind of entity that encircles the sun. "Sky-and-earth" are seen as the "two world-halves." The sky is represented by the bull, who fertilizes the earth, represented by the cow, who gives birth to the sun, depicted as a charioteer. The semen of the bull is often equated with rain, that precious liquid that allows the earth to bring forth sustenance.

Mithra, the Persian god associated with ritual bull sacrifice, was known in India, where other forms of cattle sacrifice were also practiced. By about two thousand years ago, a ban on cow slaughter had become

widespread, and the penalties for killing a cow were about the same as for killing a person of a high caste. Ironically, the modern Hindu concept of the sacred cow and the ban on killing of cattle originated in the early veneration of the animal expressed in sacrifice.

In Mithraism, developed in Persia, Mithra was viewed as the chief warrior in the struggle between Good and Evil, leading the fight against the Prince of Darkness. Mithra appears to have been a sun god who drove across the skies in his chariot. The central act of worship in Mithraism was the sacrifice of the bull. As commander of the cosmic army of Good, Mithra later became a favorite deity of Roman soldiers.

In the cosmology of Zoroastrianism, the leading religion of Persia, the bull was the first creation of Ahura Mazda, the supreme being. The bull was slain by the Prince of Darkness, but through its death gave birth to vegetable life on the earth. From its spinal marrow "grain grew of 55 species, and 12 species of medicinal herbs." The bull's semen was "carried up to the moon," where it was purified and produced the various species of animals. From the bull's blood came "the grapevine from which they make the wine." This legend expresses the idea that the death of the bull was the source of life, a recurring theme in bull sacrifice.

Bull worship was a well-developed institution in Egypt. As an incarnation of divine procreativity, the Apis Bull was worshiped at Memphis from early times. When it died, the bull was given full funeral rites. Egyptians believed the Apis Bull was immediately reborn, and priests searched for a bull calf showing special marks. The

animal was viewed as a savior and god associated with the afterlife, fertility, and oracles.

The golden calf is believed to have been a central object of worship for the Canaanites for about one thousand years. The calf may not itself have been revered as a deity, but as a mount for the gods. The chief god of the Canaanites was El (which means "god"), who was described as the "Father of Men." He is usually shown seated, wearing bull's horns signifying strength.

Bull sacrifice at the height of Cretan culture, between 3000 and 1470 B.C.E., combined religious ritual with secular display. Bulls were sacrificed in Crete both by stabbing them and as part of an acrobatic performance that may have been associated with a fertility rite or an initiation ceremony. Young men and women seized the horns of a charging bull and somersaulted over the back of the animal, either landing on its back or on the ground behind it. Significantly, the vault was performed in front of an audience, perhaps marking the transition from ritual to sport.

Various forms of ritual encounters with bulls were widespread in the Mediterranean area. In religious ceremonies known as *taurokathapsia*, Thessalonians fought bulls that were roused to fury with red cloths. The bullfighters leaped onto the animal's back, caught it by the horns, and brought it to the ground before killing it.

All the religions involving bull sacrifice eventually gave way before the might and power of the Roman Empire after it embraced Christianity and the later Arab sweep across the Middle East and Africa under the banner of Islam. Only the bullfight, which

bridges the gap between sacred and secular, has survived and flourished, uniting the various concepts of death and rebirth associated with bull sacrifice.

Before the rise of Christianity, imperial Romans fought a variety of animals in their amphitheaters, bulls among them, and it is probable that they introduced a form of the bullfight into the Iberian Peninsula, which includes Spain and Portugal. The bull sacrifice of Mithraism never flourished in Iberia as it did in other parts of Europe, but the bullfight in amphitheaters certainly did. Iberia was a fertile ground for the bullfight, since the Celtiberians hunted ferocious cattle in their forests and contended with them in a contest using an animal skin or cloak to baffle and distract charging bulls.

As in the Middle Eastern bull sacrifice, in Iberian custom and folklore, bullfighting is associated with virility and fertility. During the thirteenth century, in what is now Portugal, marriage ceremonies included the ritual killing of a bull. The bridegroom and his friends obtained a bull from the slaughterhouse. They then ran the animal through the village, agitating it with jackets and wounding it to ensure a flow of blood. Symbolically, this wound may be associated with the concept of opening the womb through piercing the hymen. The flow of blood from the bull may also symbolize the menstrual flow, which signifies the ability to conceive.

The modern bullfight continues the symbolic association linking the bull, men, and wine, as indicated in a poem by Ignacio Aldecoa:

Blood of the toro,
Fire of the rockets
Power of men's muscles,

(continued)

The Killing of Cattle:
Sacred and Secular Forms of Sacrifice (*continued*)

Rhythm of the dance.
Blood of men,
Fire of the banderillas.
Power of the toro,
Rhythm of the veronica.
Blood of wine,
Fire of the sun,
Power of fire,
Rhythm of the blood.

The poem also associates the strength of men and bulls with fire and the sun, as in early rituals involving bull sacrifice. Whether by chance or design, Ernest Hemingway's novel *The Sun Also Rises* reiterates the long association of bull sacrifice, fertility, the course of the sun god through the sky, death and rebirth, and the transformative powers of the grape. The book's title is taken from Ecclesiastes (10:20): "One generation passeth away, and another generation cometh but the earth abideth forever. . . . The sun also ariseth, and the sun goeth down, and hasteneth to the place where he arose." Those

sentiments could have come straight from Gilgamesh, whose quest for immortality was initiated by killing the Bull of Heaven.

Jake, the male hero of Hemingway's novel, is unable to physically consummate his love for Brett, the female hero, because of a war injury. Brett, on the other hand, evinces a fascination with virility of all forms. On a trip to Spain to see the bullfights, Jake, who seems to know everything that matters, gives Brett her first look at fighting bulls. Hemingway describes that initial encounter from Jake's perspective:

I saw a dark muzzle and the shadow of horns, and then, with a clattering on the wood in the hollow box, the bull charged and came out into the corral, skidding with his forefeet in the straw as he stopped, his head up, the great hump of muscle on his neck swollen tight, his body muscles

quivering as he looked up at the crowd on the stone walls.

The bull charges two steer, who seem to serve little purpose but to draw the thrusts of the bull. Like Jake, the steer are sexually impotent. After the religious procession and the running of the bulls through the streets of Pamplona, Brett is seated on a wine cask in a wine shop and the people of the town cluster around her, singing and drinking wine. Hemingway seems to suggest that Brett is the object of a ritual that symbolically links wine with fertility, virility, death, and rebirth, recurring associations since the time of Gilgamesh.

Today, bullfighting is variously viewed as spectacle, theater, barbaric butchery, sport, and art. Along with reverence for the cow in India, it may represent the last vestige of cattle cults that were once widespread from India throughout the Middle East.

suggested that this is practiced among the Basseri as well (Salzman 1974).

The Basseri are part of a **plural society,** which means they must interact with people unlike themselves, who do not share their expectations of social conduct. The chief's role as representative to the Iranian government and non-Basseri groups is crucial. In times of conflict between a Basseri and a sedentary individual, the Basseri is at a disadvantage because of his nomadism. He must move on or his herds cannot graze, and he will be effectively cut off from his entire community, which will move on without him. A farmer can go to court and wait for his case to be heard; a nomad cannot.

The fact that the chief does not maintain a nomadic lifestyle is of paramount importance. He is not a stranger passing through; he is not a man of lowly means. As the powerful representative of any individual in the tribe, he is invaluable to each and every member. He mediates the nomads' congress with the sedentary society that surrounds them and can develop the friendly relations and alliances that the mobile group cannot.

Economic Organization

The complete attention of the Basseri people is focused on the most important feature of their economy: the herds. Their daily concerns are to foster the health and well-being of the animals, to ensure that the animals grow and reproduce, and to avoid risks that place them in jeopardy. Drought, frosts, insects, and diseases afflicting the herd all threaten herders, whose economic survival is invested in the animals.

This ongoing focus leaves little time to manipulate other features of the environment. For example, in the southern part of Basseri territory are several areas of pasture that are never used. The Basseri admit that

Pastoralists of Iran must herd their sheep and goats across rugged and often dangerous terrain. The Basseri migrate seasonally, pasturing their flocks in the mountains during the summer and driving the animals to low lands farther south when the snow begins to fall in the mountains.

this land would be superlative for pasturing were there only a water source. These pasture lands could be made usable by digging a well, but this is not a project for small, autonomous households; rather, doing so requires organized communal effort. Barth asks: "Who would tend their flocks while they were engaged in the work, and why should one particular camp do it, when the fruits of the labour would be reaped by dozens of other camps as well?" (1961:102).

As an individual herd grows and the wealth of the owner increases, there comes a point at which his capital is less secure. Barth writes: "It is a characteristic feature of wealth in herds that the net productivity rate for the owner declines as the size of the herds increases" (1961:103). The owner of a larger herd cannot personally oversee his animals, and a shepherd under contract will not watch a flock with the same vigilance he gives to his own. A hired shepherd can appropriate several animals and say they were lost, or he can keep or sell dairy products without the owner's knowledge. Therefore, it is to the wealthy herd owner's advantage to convert his wealth in livestock to other, less risky forms of wealth. He may purchase jewelry or carpets or, in ideal circumstances, land.

Along their migratory route, nomads can purchase plots that they then lease to sedentary villagers living in the area. The advantages of this system are twofold: it gives the Basseri herder a more secure form of wealth, and it affords him great social status in the sedentary society outside the tribe. Basseri purchase land without any intent of settling on it; they are more interested in gaining a portion of the agricultural yield, which they would otherwise have to purchase.

Inevitably, however, there are some Basseri whose wealth becomes more and more invested in land and who grow less interested in their herds and traditional lifestyle. These individuals compromise by settling on their land for half the year and spending the other half camping in tents near their former il-rah.

When men have sons, much of the fathers' capital is drained off through the custom of anticipated inheritance. Therefore, cumulative growth over a lifespan can really accrue only to fathers of daughters or men with no children at all. In this way, lack of male heirs can lead to wealth-induced sedentarization for some households. On the other end of the

A Closer View

Pastoral Societies

Few patterns are characteristic of all pastoralists. Generally, pastoralists are transhumant, but even this depends on the environment and the type of animals being herded. Cattle herders of Tirol in the European Alps, and the Besseri, who herd sheep and goats in the mountainous regions of southern Iran, both practice transhumance on a winter–summer cycle. The Tiroleans, however, are more sedentary because they feed their cattle during winter on fodder from crops.

Many pastoralists are organized into unilineal kin groups that provide common access to migratory routes and in some cases ownership of animals. The kin group typically forms the basis for allocation of political roles, as in the case of the segmentary lineage found among the Nuer and some other African cattle herders. The most common form of political organization is the tribe, in which leadership is informal and local groups are linked by some type of overarching structure. Many pastoralists engage in warfare when their grazing needs bring them into conflict with other groups.

The three pastoral groups described in this chapter illustrate a range of adaptations to the diverse ecology of mountainous regions.

The Nandi of East Africa

Ecology	Varied; mountains and low hills, rainy and dry seasons.
Group Formation and Residence	Patrilineal extended-family compounds.
Subsistence Base	Sheep and goats herded for meat and milk; cattle herded for milk and blood; cultivation of millet and maize.
Division of Labor	Boys herd and help with plowing; girls care for children and help with domestic chores; men clear fields and plow; all ages and both sexes plant and harvest in cooperative work groups; women and children milk; women grow vegetables and produce chicken and eggs for sale; men market produce and work at full- or part-time wage jobs.
Exchange Systems	Generalized reciprocity; market.
Kinship	Patrilineal descent; patrilocal residence replaced by residence based on buying land; arranged marriages; males try to marry sisters; bridewealth, polygyny; woman–woman marriage.
Status and Leadership	Males ranked according to age sets; hereditary leadership based on belief in magical powers.
Religion	Male fear of female and infant pollution, accompanied by taboos associated with menstruation, parturition, and nursing.
Expressive Culture	Dancing and singing at adolescent initiation rites.
Cultural Change	Warrior lifestyle ended by British colonial rule; after initiation, boys attend school rather than become warriors; introduction of maize replaces millet as dietary staple.

The Basseri of Iran

Ecology	Arid but diverse, ranging from desert to mountain; winter and summer seasons.
Group Formation and Residence	Transhumant; loose organization of patrilineal nuclear families sharing an il-rah, a tribal road or migration route.
Subsistence Base	Sheep and goats herded for milk, meat, wool, and other products; horses, donkeys, and camels for transport; diet supplemented by cultivating grains or obtaining them through trade.
Division of Labor	Both men and women herd and milk; women weave and fashion clothing, packs, and tents.
Exchange Systems	Generalized reciprocity; balanced reciprocity; market.
Kinship	Patrilineal descent; local groups of nuclear families formed around brothers; arranged marriage; sister exchange; bridewealth and brideservice; levirate and sororate.
Status and Leadership	Households represented by male heads; groups headed by informal leaders; local groups linked by hereditary chief.
Religion	Shi'a Islam; little observance of Islamic feast days; ritual observances organized around life cycle; belief in the "evil eye."
Cultural Change	Forced to settle down early in the twentieth century, most have returned to nomadism; some settle down owing to wealth or to poverty resulting from loss of herd.

The Yolmo of Himalayan Nepal

Ecology	Varied; rich valley at the middle ranges of the world's highest mountains.
Group Formation and Residence	Permanent temple-villages and semipermanent camps.
Subsistence Base	Herd zomo, hybrid offspring of cow and yak; butter consumed and used in rituals; herd sheep and keep chickens; villagers grow grain and produce.
Division of Labor	Men cut wood and fodder, buy, sell, and breed animals; women milk, process milk, do domestic work including child care.
Exchange Systems	Generalized reciprocity; balanced reciprocity; redistribution; markets.
Kinship	Patrilineal; patrilocal; clan exogamy and cross-cousin marriage.
Status and Leadership	Villages organized around Buddhist temples, headed by lineage lamas; village membership open to taxpayers, who choose leaders to oversee affairs and manage resources.
Religion	Tibetan Buddhism, with calendar organized around six festivals; Buddhist lama, with status both ascribed and achieved; spirit mediums (shamans) heal by trance possession.
Expressive Culture	Elaborate torma or spirit houses, made of dough and colored butter; writing and art associated with Buddhism.
Cultural Change	Political changes opened region to outsiders and closed off trade to Tibet; villagers formerly paid tribute to Buddhist lama, now pay taxes to village; circular migration to other parts of Asia; national park and tourism; education and literacy; television.

scale, sedentarization can result from impoverishment through loss of one's herd.

Religion and Expressive Culture

The Basseri are Shi'a Moslems, though they practice Islam in a less formal manner than some. They are, according to Barth, "uninterested in religion as preached by Persian mullahs, and indifferent to metaphysical problems" (1961:135). He adds, "The Il-e-Khas, who recently rejoined the tribe after having resided in the Isfahan area for 100 years, are a partial exception to this rule, and are today criticized and somewhat despised by other Basseri as being rigidly orthodox, miserly, and humourless" (1961:135–136). For the Basseri, the needs of their animals are more important in their daily lives than the pronouncements of religious authorities.

In keeping with the importance of animals, much Basseri belief and practice is designed to promote good luck and avoid misfortune. Most beliefs about good and bad luck pertain to animals: which ones should not be together during shearing, what practices should be avoided during milking.

The difficulty in mediating social relationships is reflected in beliefs about the evil eye, which derives from envy. Envious thoughts on the part of any individual may result in the illness or death of the individual envied. There is no cure for the ills brought by the evil eye, and it acts beyond the awareness of the person in whom it resides. Since spontaneous thoughts of envy may come unbidden into anyone's mind, precautions are taken to protect potential objects of envy, usually a child or an animal, by decorating them with strings of blue beads, rags, or broken pottery.

The Basseri annual cycle is governed by three considerations: (1) the Islamic calendar, (2) the Persian solar year, and (3) "the yearly cycle of their own migrations, which brings them past the same series of localities in regular succession. Each of these cycles is marked by a few ceremonies" (Barth 1961:136). The Islamic calendar is less important than the Persian solar year, since the chief organizes and directs the migrations by the Persian calendar. The Persian calendar also defines the one universally observed feast day: Nowruz, the Persian New Year, which coincides with the spring equinox. Barth writes:

> On this day everyone wears new clothes, or at least an item of new clothing; the women and girls colour their hair and hands with henna; friends and acquaintances greet each other formally, exchanging good wishes for the coming year; and there is much intervisiting and serving of food and tea in the tents of a camp, and between related and adjacent camps, and nomads and village friends. (1961:137)

As Barth suggests, Nowruz provides an opportunity to renew ties within the camp, between camps, and between camps and outsiders. Nowruz also falls at the beginning of the main spring migration and thus coincides with the far more significant annual migratory cycle.

Most Basseri ritual observances are associated with the human life cycle. The birth of a child (especially a firstborn) is an occasion for great celebration, when sweets are passed out and rifles are fired into the air. For the first three days of life, and weekly for more than a month, an infant is cut with razor blades on the nose, neck, and chest to prevent the child's blood from becoming polluted. Adolescent pimples are a symptom that a child's blood is polluted. Boys are circumcised in infancy by village physicians or barbers if the travel schedule permits. No analogous ritual is performed for girls.

Marriage is perhaps the most elaborate of all rites, with ceremonial feasting, ritual bathing of the bride and groom, and participation of neighboring camps. The event is marked by music and dancing and by stick fights and horse racing by the men. The bride and groom are each prepared in separate ritual tents, where they are shaved, bathed, and oiled. A bridal tent is prepared, where the groom waits for his bride. She is led on horseback to the tent by her father. At the entrance to the tent, the father and the groom engage in ritual battle for possession of the bride. The groom then lifts the bride down from the horse and carries her into the tent. The women in attendance then enter the tent and drive him out. At sunset, the groom reenters the tent and consummates the marriage. A male relative of the groom stands outside the tent, rifle in hand, ready to fire a round of shots to alert the community that the marriage has been consummated. In the morning, the families of both bride and groom examine the white bridal sheets together, looking for the blood believed to signal that the bride was a virgin. If blood is not in evidence, the marriage may be immediately dissolved, with the groom under no obligation to give back the dowry (and, often, with the bridewealth returned to the groom's family).

Death and burial are attended by minimal ceremony. Household members spend several hours in their tent grieving, and the body is immediately buried in a village cemetery. Before burial, the body is washed, and words from the Koran are chanted if a relative of the deceased knows the appropriate section. Subsequent treks may allow the Basseri to visit the gravesite of the deceased, and family members often approach the grave weeping and chanting.

As nomads, the Basseri have little need for monumental religious structures and little use for elaborate religious rituals that might distract them from the vigilance necessary to protect their flocks. Holly Peters-Golden notes: "For the Basseri, their movement is their ceremony. As their il-rah unfolds before them and they journey through the seasons and through their year, they are in effect celebrating their very existence" (1994:39).

YOLMO: ZOMO HERDERS OF THE NEPAL HIMALAYAS

Few places lure people with such promises of mystery and adventure as the Himalayas. Fact and imagination intermingle in the world's highest mountains; the mythic Shangri-La is comfortable amidst the real cultures of Tibet, Bhutan, and Nepal. Red pandas, blue bears, and wild yaks are almost as elusive as the legendary yeti. The dangers of rockslide, avalanche, and flooded rivers are personified by the deities who reside in the mountains, and in the high thin air the whistling wind could be their conversation. (Bishop 1978:11–12)

In this setting, described by John Melville Bishop in his book *An Ever-Changing Place,* the people of the Yolmo Valley in Nepal herd an exotic beast, the zomo, the hybrid offspring of a yak and a cow. The village of Melemchi, in the Yolmo Valley, appears remote from the capital city of Kathmandu despite its geographic proximity, because Nepal has few roads and none in the mountains where Melemchi is located. As Bishop puts it: "Melemchi is on the road to nowhere. No trade routes or paths of pilgrimage pass through, and the only contact with the world outside results from excursions from the village" (1978:23).

Bishop, a filmmaker, and his wife, Naomi, a physical anthropologist, journeyed to the village of Melemchi to observe the behavior of langur monkeys. But their quest led them to form a long-term association with the people of Melemchi. In the following essay, Naomi Bishop describes the challenges of herding zomo in this remote region of the Himalayas.

HIMALAYAN HERDERS OF NEPAL
Naomi Bishop

When we first came to Melemchi in 1971, it seemed a timeless place, existing as it had for centuries. Only a few families lived in the village year round; the rest lived out with their herds, moving up and down the mountainsides, or were away in "Burma." Our neighbors were barefoot and produced, bartered, or gathered most of their food. They spoke only their local Yolmo language and lived in a feudal relationship to the Chini Lama, the head lama at the Boudhnath stupa in the Kathmandu Valley.

Our interest was in the socioecology of langur monkeys, and we came to Melemchi because we wanted to work in an isolated area. Although we spent most days climbing the mountains with the monkeys, we returned each night to the village, and over the year got to know the year-round residents well. In fact, Melemchi was not a timeless place.

Before 1950, Nepal had been relatively isolated. The Himalayas on the northern border and the malarial Tarai jungle on the southern border were geographic barriers to Tibet and British India, and the Nepalese government enforced political isolation by curtailing travel both in and out of the country. Nepal underwent a major transformation during the twenty years following a palace coup that overturned the hundred-year regime of the Ranas in 1950. During this period the country was opened to the rest of the world, and numerous international aid, development, and research projects got under way.

Melemchi seemed separated from these forces, though this perception was mostly due to our lack of perspective. As new residents, we tended to see each fragment of information about how people live in that environment as a permanent feature of Melemchi culture and society. In retrospect, it is obvious that things were changing even as we were there. Over the next twenty-five years, as our informants aged with us and their children grew up, those changes accelerated. It was this process of change that became the focus of research on subsequent visits continuing into the present. The langurs remain in the forests above the village, but our interests shifted to understanding the ways in which Melemchi was affected by and participated in events at both the local and national levels between 1971 and the present.

Melemchi is the northernmost village in the Yolmo Valley, at an altitude of eight thousand five hundred feet. A few miles to the north, over an eighteen-thousand-foot pass, are the Langtang Valley and the snow mountains of the Tibetan border. To the south, the Yolmo Valley flanks the Melemchi River. Buddhist temple-villages occupy the ridgetops and the upper slopes; Tamang villages with their terraces of corn and millet lie in the middle, and along the river bottom sit the villages and rice fields of the Chhetri Bahuns. The Kathmandu Valley is a three-day walk to the south.

The houses and fields of Melemchi occupy a flat shelf on a mountainside where once meditated Guru Rinpoche, the eighth-century yogi venerated as Padmasambhava who brought Buddhism to Tibet. Since that time, the Guru Rinpoche cave in Melemchi has been a place of pilgrimage and meditation. The village *gompa,* or temple, is believed to have been there before the families who constitute the four major clans migrated from Kyirong, Tibet, in the mid-nineteenth century.

Subsistence

The steep valleys and sharp ridges of the Himalayas present challenges to human subsistence. Within a few square miles, as laid out on a map, the mountains rise from a four-thousand-foot river bed to over twenty thousand feet, with each bend and fold differing in exposure to the sun, altitude, drainage, and vegetation. This terrain provides a variety of niches for human populations, and the people of the Nepal Himalayas amply demonstrate the diversity and complexity of human responses. The people of Melemchi exploit the part of the mountain to which they have claim, the middle-altitude zone between seven thousand and fourteen thousand feet.

Melemchi people are agropastoralists; they grow crops around their houses on terraces cut into the slopes between eight thousand and nine thousand feet, and they herd zomo, the hybrid offspring of a yak and a cow. Zomo herding is a dairy adaptation; the zomo are kept to produce butter, which is consumed and used locally in diet and ritual and is sold to those who do not keep herds.

Herding   Like their yak father, zomo are stocky and have short legs. They have large horns with a unique shape, and their tail is bushy. In other respects, zomo look like their cow mothers, rangier than yak and without the belly hair. As hybrids, they show enhanced vigor over their parents, in the quantity of milk they produce, their duration of lactation, and their ability to produce offspring each year. Most important, they thrive in the middle-altitude zone between seven thousand and fourteen thousand feet. Cows can't be taken much above seven thousand feet without suffering illness, especially in winter. Yak are unable to live below twelve thousand feet without becoming weak and succumbing to disease. The hybrid zomo fits in between the parent stock.

Transhumance   Herding requires pasture. It is possible to keep a few large bovids (cows or buffalo) in the village, where they are fed with fodder in their stalls, but large animals have large appetites, and pasture is necessary to maintain a herd. In Melemchi, where crops are grown within the village at least nine months of the year, it would be impossible to have herds of animals present during the growing season. Therefore, these Himalayan agropastoralists are transhumant: they move with their herds over an annual cycle. They are not nomadic; nomads have no fixed abode, whereas Melemchi herders are village taxpayers, whether or not they actually own a house.

Melemchi herders take the animals up to high pastures (as high as thirteen thousand feet) in summer and bring them low in winter to escape the snowline, which is around ten thousand feet in winter. Each herding family owns or rents access to a series of pastures, which are used in sequence as the grass runs out.

Domestic Organization   Families who live on the move must carry everything with them. In this part of Nepal, animals don't carry loads; people do. Each move involves at least nine adult loads, carried in baskets on the back with the help of a head strap (*namlo*). Most pastures have stone houses, or *kharkes,* which are owned by a herder along with the pasture. The kharkes usually have one room, with fresh ferns

In the Himalaya Mountains of Nepal, zomo herding requires the labor of the entire family. When migrating to summer pastures in the mountains, people carry their belongings in large baskets. Before a couple has children old enough to help with herding, milking, and churning butter, the husband's parents may live with them to help with the work.

for flooring, a fireplace for cooking and warmth, and a corner for baby animals, chickens, and the Tibetan mastiff dog who barks to warn the family of intruders. The roof may be a permanent one made of planks, or it may be constructed of bamboo mats. In pastures without kharkes, bamboo mats are stretched over a structure of poles to serve as a dwelling.

Equipment for dairying includes a large wooden churn two feet across and three feet high for making butter, as well as a variety of wooden buckets and dippers. The family carries with them salt, tsampa flour (flour made from a type of high-altitude barley called *changda*), tea, and a few staples, which they replenish on frequent trips to the village. Most herding families eventually build a village house that they use for storage or as a place to stay when in the village tending crops and carrying out other business. When parents finally turn over all their livestock to their children or sell off their herd, they retire to live in their village house.

Herding is a family activity. The common pattern is for a young man to receive zomo and a bull from his parents when he marries. The early years with the herd are difficult for the young couple, and the husband's parents often live with them for periods of time to help out. The standard division of labor within the family is that men cut wood and fodder; manage the buying, selling, and breeding of animals; and do all the travel away from the pasture to resupply the family. Women are responsible for milking

the zomo, processing the milk, doing all the domestic work including child care, and maintaining the entire operation in the absence of the husband.

In the early years of a family, before the children are old enough to help, both husband and wife work tremendously hard. Melemchi herders typically have large families, which eventually provide helpers, freeing women especially from the heavy domestic workload. Teenaged sons and daughters can be left for a few days completely on their own, making it possible for the parents to diversify their activities.

Economic Challenges As a hybrid animal, zomo provide some challenges for dairy farmers. First, calves are necessary but unwanted. To produce milk, zomo must be bred and give birth. Unlike some hybrids, female zomo are not sterile, but males are. Therefore, the herd consists of a number of female zomo and a bull for breeding. Tibetan bulls, a dwarf species well adapted to higher altitudes, are preferred. Calves from Tibetan bulls are smaller, which means there are fewer birth complications, and they are weaker, which means they are more likely to die. Their dying is desirable, because calves compete with humans for milk. Once the mother gives birth, she begins to produce milk.

The herder wants all the milk for butter production. Since the calf is an F2 hybrid (the hybrid offspring of a hybrid), it is weak and shows none of the vigor of its mother. It will not be a good milk producer itself and will be a drain on the pasturage. The herder can't kill the calf, because in Hindu Nepal it is illegal to kill a cow or a cow hybrid. Furthermore, as Buddhists, Melemchi avoid killing animals of any kind. The solution to this dilemma is to let the calf kill itself. The calves are given minimal access to the mother for several days and then are put out to eat grass. The ensuing colic kills them.

Zomo females display individual temperaments. Occasionally, a zomo mother needs her calf to stimulate the lactation response, so the calf is retained either for a few months or into adulthood. Some zomo can be stimulated to let down milk by just the sight or smell of the hide of their dead calf. Each animal is known and treated as an individual in all aspects of its management, making it difficult for women, who do the daily milking, to get away at all.

A second economic problem comes from the fact that, as hybrids, zomo do not replenish themselves, and herders are dependent on suppliers in other regions. Herders must travel to areas where zomo are bred and buy new animals. This trip requires major expenditures of cash. Beginning in the mid-1980s, several men in Melemchi decided to try to breed zomo themselves. These families used many of the same pastures that they use for their zomo herds, but instead they herded cows with a breeding yak.

Those who tried this new type of herding were all older men with a lifetime of experience managing zomo. They hoped this would be a good way to make cash from the sales of the zomo calves, without the daily dairying chores. Herding cows would permit them to live at lower altitudes for more of the year and be close to the village. They, and especially their wives, were tired of the isolation and hard daily work of tending a zomo herd. In the winter, when the herd was on the lowest pasture, the yak could be "boarded" with a zomo herd higher up and the cows kept near the village.

It was not a uniform success. Managing a yak, as well as maintaining two species of animals with widely differing ecological tolerances, proved difficult for these herders, whose expertise lay in zomo husbandry. Yak are expensive to buy and fragile to keep in the altitudes around Melemchi. The cows often died in the winter, many cows did not conceive, and there is a long maturation period before the babies can be sold. Eventually, some men sold out and retired to the village; others switched back to zomo herding. A few men continue the experiment, invigorated by the challenge of something new.

Butter Melemchi pastoralism is geared toward the production of butter. When the zomo are lactating, milk is collected twice every day. Every other day, the accumulated milk is churned into butter. The leftover buttermilk is boiled until it separates into curds and whey. The curds are eaten fresh or, more often, are squeezed out into strips and dried over the fire to produce a hard, smoky, sour-tasting dry cheese called *chiurpi*. Herding families sell both butter and chiurpi. In the old days when almost everyone had herds, the butter was carried down to lower elevations, including to Kathmandu, for sale. Now more families have given up herding for village life or are away in India, and butter is in short supply.

Butter is an essential component of the Melemchi household. Every household produces a continuous supply of "butter tea," which is tea, butter, and salt churned together. It is drunk plain or combined with tsampa flour to form a paste. Eggs are fried in butter, and many people in Melemchi enjoy their home-distilled liquor heated with melted butter. Tibetan Buddhists use butter in their rituals: there are butter lamps; dough statues made of flour, butter, and water decorated with butter medallions called *torma;* and blessings of butter daubed onto prayer flag poles, ritual plates of food, and even foreheads.

Agriculture

Residents today in their seventies and eighties say that in their youth only a dozen houses were in the village. In those days people planted potatoes near some of their pastures and tended them during the spring and summer when they were there with the zomo. In the village, a few people planted wheat and changda. Today, wheat and changda fields occupy nearly all of the prime village agricultural land, with potato fields on the periphery.

Melemchi is unique among the Yolmo temple-villages in its gently sloping shelf, making it possible to cluster sizable fields together. Today, wheat, changda, and potatoes are all grown around the houses of Melemchi. In some years, corn is planted on the fallow wheat-changda fields in summer, but generally the fields are rested and corn is planted on

Men of the Yolmo Valley in Nepal make torma, formed from barley flour and decorated with brightly colored butter designs. Spirits reside in the torma during rituals. In Melemchi, an elaborate Buddhist festival can draw on the labor of the entire temple-village.

the steeply sloped terraces of Tarke Tho, about one thousand feet below Melemchi.

Grain is used for food. Wheat flour is made into ceremonial bread at two of the annual festivals; changda is toasted and ground into tsampa flour, then mixed with liquid and eaten as a dough; and corn is cooked into mush and eaten with curry. Grain is also made into alcohol, both fermented into beer and distilled into liquor. Taxes are paid in grain, and changda and wheat are sold or bartered for lowland grains such as millet or rice.

In mountainous terrain, microclimates vary with altitude and, just as with cattle, plants are vertically stratified. Rice grows up to five thousand feet, millet up to seven thousand feet; corn grows between six thousand and eight thousand feet, while wheat and changda need the cold winter and cool spring of Melemchi's altitude for optimal growth. People grow what they can where they live and barter for other grains with neighbors.

Combining herding with agriculture requires coordinated time management. The agricultural cycle is fixed; planting and harvesting are adjusted to the climate and rainfall and vary only slightly from year to year. Herders must make the appropriate labor available for agriculture at the right time in the planting and harvesting cycle. In some herding families, a few family members go down to the village to tend to agricultural chores, while others stay with the herd. Extended families cooperate in informal labor exchanges within the family or clan and assist herding family members with agricultural tasks as necessary.

Social Organization

The temple-villages of the Yolmo Valley were founded by nonmonastic lamas, or priests, who emigrated from Tibet, most likely from the region around Kyirong, just northwest of Yolmo. These founders represented several sects of Tibetan Buddhism; the founding lineage for Melemchi's temple, or *gompa*, is believed to be members of the Hlalungba clan, who came from the Nyingma sect. These founding lamas were a married priesthood who established lineages of succession for the gompas based on male primogeniture. New gompas, and villages, were founded by sons who didn't inherit the paternal gompa. These lineage lamas, as they are called, controlled each gompa and their surrounding territories.

Hlalungba men in Melemchi today do not own herds, nor did their fathers. They do have fields in the village and preside over all major rituals. They have learned to read Tibetan, and they have studied with family members and spent time with visiting lamas learning the texts and rituals. Otherwise, they are just like other Melemchi families.

These founders intermarried with the Tibeto-Burman–speaking Tamang from the lower elevations, so that today Yolmo culture resembles both the Tibetan and Tamang cultures. Like the Tamang, the Melemchi people are a patrilineal, patrilocal society, organized around clans. They prefer cross-cousin marriage and practice clan exogamy, whereas surrounding groups—Tibetans in general and Sherpas from the Khumbu region around Mount Everest—look upon cross-cousin marriage as incestuous.

Village membership is open to those who own fields or houses or who request membership. Some herding families are village taxpayers (*talpa*), even though they do not own a house. Village membership entails certain obligations, including contributions of labor, grain, and cash to the village gompa. The village chooses five men to oversee affairs, collect taxes, and manage local disputes. An additional three men are selected to manage the village forest resources.

Ritual Life

Without monasteries nearby to supply lamas, the temple-villages of Yolmo depend on their members to conduct Buddhist rituals. Yolmo people are called "lama people" because of their membership in a temple-village. As such, all men are considered eligible to assist with Buddhist rituals. The members of the lineage lamas in each village use the term *lama* in their names, which reflects their position in the village.

At any gompa ritual, the highest-ranking lama presides, with a descending hierarchy of helpers based on their training and monastic education. In Melemchi, the presiding ritual specialist may be a temporary resident Tibetan lama. If none is available, the honor falls to the highest-ranking member of the lineage lamas of Melemchi, the Hlalungba clan. Below the Hlalungbas sit villagers who have some Buddhist training; then come the villagers who can read Tibetan. (Until the opening of the government school, this was the only form of literacy training available in Melemchi.) The resident Tibetan refugees who care for the gompa are very much involved in organizing the rituals. They read the books, but they do not preside.

Not only do village men participate in the ritual book reading; they also make the bread for the Nara festival, prepare all the ritual torma, and conduct all the ceremonies. Such lay participation in Tibetan Buddhist rituals is unusual and results from the particular history of the development of temple-villages in Yolmo.

The Ritual Calendar The Melemchi ritual calendar is organized around six major festivals: (1) *Loshar,* the Tibetan New Year, celebrated by each family in late January or February; (2) *Yum,* a festival held on Buddha's birthday, in which the Tibetan Buddhist texts are taken out of the gompa and carried around the village boundaries; (3) *Dabla Pangdi,* held in early spring to ensure a good harvest; (4) *Tupu Sezchu,* a one-day festival held at the Guru Rinpoche cave at the top of the village; (5) *Nara,* a five-day festival in midsummer, honoring the founders of the gompa; and (6) *Nyungne,* held in September, a ritual of atonement participated in by lamas and elderly men and women.

All talpa take a turn as host for four of these festivals in a single year: Dabla Pangdi, Yum, Tupu Sezchu, and Nara. This is a huge undertaking, requiring the assistance of many relatives during that year. The host collects donations of money and foodstuff from all villagers, and even from relatives of villagers throughout Yolmo. The host's family must arrange for all supplies to be ready and prepared for each festival. He also cooks and serves the entire village two meals a day for each day of the festival and fulfills all roles as host.

Hosts have been known to sell their herds and return to live in the village when their turn comes around. One host built an addition onto his house for cooking the liquor and preparing the meals. The rotation is fixed and known well in advance, and given the number of talpa in the village, it is understood that this is a once-in-a-lifetime obligation. A separate host is designated for Nyungne, and that duty also rotates among the talpa. When the festivals are a success, the host is praised, but when there are problems, such as sour beer or torma that fall down and crack, the host is held responsible.

Spirit Mediums (Bombos) When people are ill, if a lama is available, they may call on him to divine the cause and suggest a cure. More often, people call the *bombo*, a shaman who uses his powers of divination and trance to seek the cause of the illness and to cure it. Bombos set up ritual altars that include dough torma who represent temporary homes and bodies for the gods that are called.

Beating a drum and shaking their harnesses of bells, bombos go into trance and are entered by the spirits, who help them divine the cause of the problem. The spirits also enter the torma and can then be dispatched or treated in that form. Bombos are called for a variety of problems, ranging from physical illness to psychological and social stress, to bad luck. They are also consulted when members of a herd are sick.

Bombos are village men who have felt the calling and who are successful in situating themselves in the world of spirits during their training. They are trained by other villagers; in Melemchi, three men were said to have these powers. Since their rituals may involve killing animals and feeding their blood to the spirits, an act forbidden to Buddhists, bombos are quite separate from lamas, but villagers freely use both sources of divination and healing.

The World beyond Yolmo

In general, people in Melemchi are self-sufficient. They can produce most of the food they eat; their houses are built from mud and stone hacked out of the geological shelf they stand on. They use wooden implements made from the forests on the slopes above and beyond the village; they make mats and baskets from bamboo growing above them and paper from the *Daphnia* shrubs growing all around the village.

People of Melemchi barter with people at other altitudes and in other villages for things they can't grow or don't make. Bartering relationships are long-standing and specific. The villager who grinds everyone's flour at the water-driven mill in Melemchi trades with a man in a village one day's walk away for the special brush he uses to sweep the flour together after it is ground. Marriage links Melemchi families to others throughout the Yolmo Valley, and these become an economic and social support network. Despite the potential for self-sufficiency in Melemchi, there is always a need for cash to buy things such as salt, cloth, or tea and for large expenditures such as buying zomo.

Tibet Before the Chinese takeover of Tibet in 1950, a few Yolmo villagers engaged in a sheep-brokering business between the herders in Tibet and Hindus in the Kathmandu Valley. Prior to the autumn Hindu festival of Dassai, celebrated in Kathmandu with massive animal sacrifice, people from Yolmo walked to Tibet, purchased several hundred sheep, and together drove them south to the Kathmandu Valley to sell as sacrificial animals. These were large parties that included several Yolmo buyers, each of whom had as many as eight porters to carry the metal coins that were used as cash, as well as blankets, cigarettes, and other items to sell along the way. The three-week trips were long remembered for their adventure and fun.

In 1950, the Chinese took over Tibet and closed the border, stopping the trade in sheep as well as easy access to Tibetan bulls and other livestock. At the same time, Nepal, which had been relatively inaccessible, underwent a revolution that opened its borders to the West and made it easier for Nepalese people to travel abroad, especially to India. Though Melemchi was geographically and culturally isolated from these changes in the nation's capital, the effects became increasingly important.

Circular Migration Since 1950, an ever-increasing number of villagers have traveled to India, Sikkim, Bhutan, and Assam to work as laborers in high-altitude regions, building roads and military installations. In Melemchi, these travels are referred to as going to "Burma," since that was where the first migrants went. Initially, men went with friends to areas where there were networks of Yolmo people.

Soon, whole families were going and coming back in a pattern of circular migration that has continued in increasing numbers through the present. Some never returned; others came back every year or every few years bringing money and new experiences. Some left their families behind in the village or took the older children who could work. It was tough to manage in India with a family, and at least two incomes were usually needed there to produce enough extra cash to bring home to Melemchi.

There were many pitfalls for these migrants: exposure to new diseases, the possibility of incurring gambling or other debts, unscrupulous employers who took advantage of them because they were illiterate or foreigners, and backbreaking labor in risky situations such as dynamite blasting. Most families have some members who died in "Burma" or who disappeared without a trace.

But many have taken advantage of opportunities to alternate time in "Burma" with herding zomo in Melemchi. In recent years, money from work abroad has been used to build new houses with tin roofs and airtight stoves in Melemchi, to buy rice fields down the valley to be farmed by tenants, and to buy property in the Kathmandu Valley.

Migration has become increasingly common in the past few decades. Circular migrants now rarely do backbreaking work; they have built up networks and skills to enable them to become labor contractors in their own right and to supervise the work of others, especially in building construction. Many young people now live "permanently" in India. The areas in which they have settled usually have a large Tibetan Buddhist presence, such as Kashmir in the western Himalayas or Bamdilla in Arunachal Pradesh, with access to gompas and lamas for important life cycle events.

These young people return to Melemchi for visits, and their families continue to maintain their houses in the village and pay the annual taxes to maintain their talpa status. The young people say they are coming back, but in fact their children are growing up in India with access to English schools and popular culture of the world through satellite television. They also speak Hindi.

Living in a National Park Another factor for change was introduced in the mid-1980s, when Melemchi was incorporated into the Langtang National Park. This change brought Melemchi into close contact with national park officials, who regulate all activities in the park, and with the Nepalese army, which enforces park regulations. The early years were marked by numerous misunderstandings, abrogation of residents' rights and privileges, and loss of control over resources and livelihoods.

Melemchi people were pressed by new regulations ranging from "no loud noises in the national park" to curtailment of pasture rights. The park attempted to regulate cutting of trees and fodder, tourist facilities such as lodges and restaurants serving the many foreign trekkers in the region, and hunting of animals, including wild pigs, that destroy crops and endanger people. The army caused many problems for the residents, appropriating food, livestock, and even women.

Several herding families sold out during this period, claiming that the national park made it impossible to manage the herds. Despite these problems, most Melemchi residents today view the park as a benefit. Park personnel helped them learn how to manage a tourist business by training lodge owners in hygiene and cooking. The regulation of lodge licenses helped control the competition for the trekking business, which was threatening to divide the village.

National park personnel were the first contact most villagers had with the national government and its policies. They could seek out this authority for assistance with problems or complaints. Park personnel encouraged them to pay their taxes to the village gompa instead of following their traditional policy of paying them to the Chini Lama. Park personnel also encouraged them to obtain land ownership papers from the district headquarters.

Essentially, through their interactions with the national park, the people of Melemchi began to see themselves as citizens of Nepal connected to the national government. In recent years, the excesses of the early days have passed, and restrictions have been relaxed; the park and residents of Melemchi enjoy a cooperative relationship.

Education In 1985, a Nepali schoolteacher arrived in Melemchi to set up the first government-sponsored school. A school building constructed by the villagers in 1989 houses a primary school, grades one through five. Children learn the Nepali language, reading, health, science, math, Sanskrit, and "morals." Adult literacy classes have begun, so that now both children and parents can manage the paperwork necessary to secure title to their land or to prove their citizenship.

Literacy has also spawned graffiti, which is appearing on buildings and boulders. It has even been carved into the window frames of the stone kharkes at high altitudes. As is true of graffiti everywhere, Melemchi scrawls deal with matters near the heart. One might see a heart with an arrow through it and the words "CHHULTIM LOVES MAYA" written in English. Hindi film stars are popular objects of affection in Melemchi graffiti.

The Future

Where once Melemchi people traveled by bus to their destinations in Assam and Ladakh, they now make airline reservations in Kathmandu and fly from New Delhi. Since 1992, a small hydroelectric plant on the Melemchi River supplies electricity for several hours every evening, and the village has several television sets, giving Melemchi access to the world, if not the world access to Melemchi.

Some people have traveled as far as Taiwan to work in clothing factories, returning with enough money to buy houses in Kathmandu. And in 1996, the central government began building a dam on the river below Melemchi to bring water to the Kathmandu Valley, a project that will bring a motor road to within a few hours' walk of the village.

SUMMARY

The life of pastoralists is shaped by their interdependency with their animals. This interdependency is reflected in forms of migration as well as in family and political organization. The pastoral pattern of seasonal migration known as transhumance varies depending on the type of animals herded. Dairying can be somewhat sedentary since the fodder of cattle can be supplemented with cultivated crops. Sheepherding, which requires more intense supervision of animals and long stays away from home, increases the division of labor by gender and age and emphasizes the economic and political importance of males. Most pastoralists are organized into unilineal extended families and, as among nomadic foragers, family organization among transhumant pastoralists tends to emphasize flexibility.

As do many other pastoralists, the three groups represented in this chapter rely to some degree on cultivation of crops. The Nandi, cattleherders of Kenya, cultivate millet and maize, or corn. The Basseri of Iran cultivate a number of cereals and grain but subsist primarily by herding sheep and goats. The Yolmo of Himalayan Nepal herd zomos, a hybrid animal produced by breeding a cow with a yak, and supplement their diet with wheat and other grains.

The Nandi illustrate the importance of kinship relations and strong gender role divisions characteristic of African cattleherders. House and hearth are women's domain; men gather around a shade tree in the "public" domain. Both boys and girls are initiated at adolescence. Males are circumcised, and females undergo clitoridectomy. Traditionally, initiated males went out on cattle raids to prove their mettle and begin to amass their own herds. Now, young initiated males are often students. Males initiated together form an age set, a group identified by a name and expected to show solidarity.

For women, marriage takes place shortly after initiation. Marriages are arranged by the families, and men try to marry sisters, since this is considered an especially close and supportive relationship between males. Once married, a Nandi woman is forever the wife of the man who first married her, and all her children are considered to be his. A widow is expected to cohabit with a kinsman of her dead husband, a practice known as the levirate. The Nandi also practice woman–woman marriage. If a household has no male heir, a woman can retain property rights in the lineage by taking wives and assuming the social role of a male.

The Basseri herd sheep and goats in the mountainous regions of southern Iran, practicing a form of transhumance that involves spending winters on low pasture land and summers in the mountains. In fall, Basseri graze their flocks on harvested fields of agriculturalists, providing fodder for the animals and fertilizer in the form of manure for the fields. The annual migration route—called the il-rah, or "tribal road"—is considered the property of a particular tribe.

The Basseri figure descent patrilineally, and local groups are often formed by brothers. Most Basseri households consist of a nuclear family living in a single tent, and camps are generally made up of thirty or forty tents. The household is represented in tribal matters by its head, who is invariably male. Alliances between households are reinforced by affinal ties, and marriages are arranged by male household heads. Bridewealth compensates a woman's kin group for her labor and fertility, as well as for the household items she will bring with her. Sister exchange is common, and the Basseri practice the levirate and sororate.

Basseri camps are large in summer when fodder is plentiful, but the groups disperse in winter, when the environment is depleted. Decisions about when to migrate are arrived at by consensus of the household heads, under the influence of a camp leader, who may be appointed by the Basseri chief. Though local leadership is informal, the position of chief is hereditary and powerful in its own right. The chief allocates migratory routes within the group and acts as the Basseri representative to outsiders.

Yolmo herders of Nepal live in a remote region that has achieved almost mythical proportions through the legend of Shangri-la and the romance of the Himalaya Mountains. Nepal was long isolated from political forces that appeared to govern the people around them until the national government was overturned in a palace coup.

The Yolmo tend an animal that never existed in nature: the zomo is the hybrid offspring of a cow and a yak. Because zomo are hybrid, males are sterile and offspring of females are weak. Yolmo must continually acquire new animals for their stock. Zomo cows are also temperamental, and each one requires knowledge of her special needs for milking. Milk is used in producing curds and whey, cheese, and butter. Butter is used in tea, in liquor, and in Buddhist rituals. Melemchi villagers also grow grain and vegetables.

The temple-villages of the Yolmo Valley were founded by Buddhist lamas from Tibet. Their descendants form a patrilineal, patrilocal society, and village membership is open to taxpayers who support the complex ritual life of the community. Guru Rinpoche, who is credited with introducing Buddhism to Tibet, figures prominently in local legend. The Yolmo are called "lama people" because of their membership in a temple-village. The Melemchi calendar is organized around six major festivals. In addition, spirit mediums, or bombos, use their powers of divination and trance to diagnose and cure illness.

Together, the Nandi, Basseri, and Yolmo represent variations on the pastoral way of life shaped by the environment and the type of animals being herded. They also illustrate the importance of kinship and household organization, as well as the division of labor by age and gender, in providing durable social bonds combined with the flexibility needed to care for herd animals under varying climatic conditions.

POWER WORDS

agemates	**plural**	**sanction**
clitoridectomy	**society**	**segmentary**
infibulation	**postpartum**	**lineage**
patrikin	**sex taboo**	

INTERNET EXERCISE

1. The Nuer and Dinka, neighboring African cattle-herders of southern Sudan, have had a long history of conflict resulting from raiding each other's herds. The website **http://members.tripod.com/~SudanInfonet/Nuer-Dinka.html** provides information on efforts to make peace between the two groups. The website **http://www.fas.harvard.edu/~fsc/NUE.html** provides information on Nuer self-identity. Where did the name *Nuer* come from? Do the Nuer use it to describe themselves?

2. Traditional Persian weaving designs, including a medallion design characteristic of the Basseri, are displayed at **http://www.turkotek.com/salon_00013/rug3.htm**. Based on their subsistence pattern, why is Basseri art expressed in weaving?

3. The Yolmo described in the article by Naomi Bishop in this chapter are facing dramatic changes in their lives as a result of tourism and national politics. The online news source *Explore Nepal Weekly* at **http://www.catmando.com/news/explore-nepal/explrnpl.htm** describes issues and debates facing Nepal. What kinds of events does this news source consider sufficiently important to report?

13
Horticulturalists

In this chapter . . .

The horticultural way of life

Because their subsistence centers on cultivating gardens, horticulturalists do not follow the migratory patterns of foragers and pastoralists. Because horticulturalists do not produce a significant food surplus, they do not develop the stratification characteristic of agriculturalists. The three groups discussed in this chapter represent a range of adaptation based on horticulture, from the Yanomamö, who are sometimes mistaken for foragers, to the Yapese, who have been greatly influenced by American colonial governance. In between, the Mundugumor represent a way of life organized around the Big Man, a leader who is able to extend his range of influence through marriage and ceremonial exchange.

The Yanomamö of Brazil and Venezuela

The Yanomamö grow plantain, a type of banana, and several starchy root crops. They supplement their diet by foraging and hunting for plants and animals, which are abundant in the tropical rain forest in which they live. The Yanomamö maintain alliances between villages through economic exchanges, hosting feasts, and marriage. Though the village headman has little power, his influence is important in settling disputes within the village and maintaining alliances with other groups.

The Mundugumor of New Guinea

The Mundugumor, known to U.S. audiences through the writings of Margaret Mead, are horticulturalists who live along the Sepik River in New Guinea. The Mundugumor world is based on the principle of exchange. In the Big Man complex, a man gains a position of leadership through a system of marriages and economic exchanges. The Mundugumor extend the concept of reciprocity to the spirit world, so that making an offering to a spirit being obligates that being to come to one's aid.

The Yap Islanders of the Western Pacific

U.S. military occupation of Yap since World War II has transformed most of these horticulturalists into government laborers and, for the most part, educated bureaucrats. Under the traditional division of labor, women gardened and men fished, and these economic roles influenced patterns of courtship and marriage. American political authority, wage work, and popular culture have transformed relations between the sexes, allowing women to move out of their traditional domestic roles and bringing the younger generation into conflict with traditional ideas of gender and status.

Horticulturalists are food producers who live by small-scale gardening, without the use of plows or irrigation. They commonly practice slash-and-burn agriculture, also known as shifting or swidden agriculture, as described in Chapter 5. Horticulturalists are more settled than foragers or pastoralists; they live in permanent or semipermanent villages close to their gardens. Many horticultural groups have domesticated animals, such as dogs or pigs, but these are not the primary means of subsistence.

Horticulturalists typically do not produce a food surplus sufficient to support the stratification or urbanization characteristic of intensive agriculturalists. The political organization of most horticultural groups is the tribe. Leadership is informal, based on an individual's demonstrated ability, as expressed in oratory skills, military prowess, ritual knowledge, or capacity for forming alliances through marriage or economic exchange.

The New Guinea Big Man complex is the classic example of tribal leadership among horticulturalists. A Big Man gains status throughout a region by his ability to control redistribution of pigs and yams through an elaborate network of consanguineal and affinal kin. A man cannot hope to become a Big Man without being married, since women tend gardens and raise pigs. Women also add to a man's ability to control economic resources through their own extensive kin networks. In addition, alliances between kin groups and villages are created and reinforced through marriage.

As is true of most horticultural societies, New Guinea political and economic alliances center on unilineal kin groups, traced either through the male or the female line. Because unilineal kin groups are corporate, having clearly defined boundaries, this form of descent system forms the basis for allocating access to gardens. The backbone of a horticultural village is typically the lineage, traced matrilineally or patrilineally depending on the prevailing customs of the group. Individuals acquire rights to gardens through their unilineal kin group, and ceremonial events that allow a Big Man to gain status are organized around the clan, which traces descent to a common ancestor.

The three groups discussed in this chapter (Figure 13.1) represent variations on a common horticultural theme. The Yanomamö live in widely dispersed patrilineal villages linked to each other by marriage and economic exchange. The Yanomamö have remained relatively isolated until recently, when their traditional way of life was disrupted by gold miners in Brazil and by missionaries in both Venezuela and Brazil.

The Mundugumor of New Guinea exhibit both the Big Man complex and patrilineal clan alliances formed through marriage. Principles of exchange are expressed not only in politics, kinship, and economics but also in the relationship of the Mundugumor to the spirit world, so that spirit beings must reciprocate the

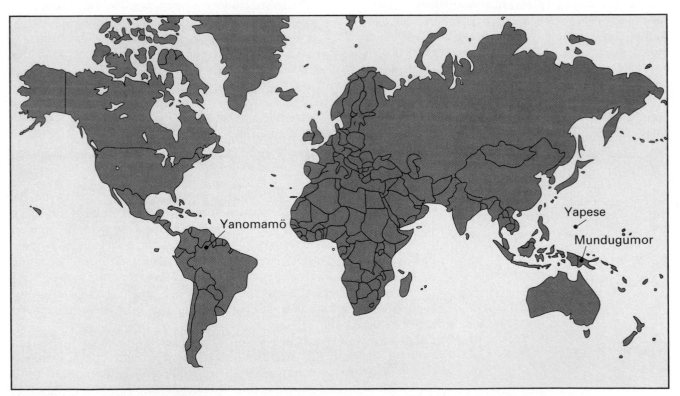

FIGURE 13.1   Horticulturalists

The three groups described in this chapter—the Yanomamö of Venezuela and Brazil, the Mundugumor of New Guinea, and the Yapese of the western Pacific—represent variations on horticultural adaptation. The Yanomamö supplement small-scale cultivation with foraging; the Mundugumor are an example of the New Guinea yam-and-pig complex, and the Yapese are Pacific Islanders whose traditional way of life has been dramatically changed by U.S. occupation since World War II.

favors provided for them. The Mundugumor are known to U.S. audiences through the writings of Margaret Mead, who used them as an example of gender behavior that refutes the American views that masculinity and femininity are biologically determined.

Among the Yap Islanders of the western Pacific, descent and access to land are traced matrilineally, so that people of the same clan are said to be "people of one land" or "people of one belly," in that they "come from the same womb." Since World War II, Yap culture has changed dramatically in response to U.S. military and political occupation. These changes have had an impact on both kin and gender relationships. In the following pages, we will consider these three variations in the horticultural way of life.

FROM THE BLOOD OF THE MOON: THE YANOMAMÖ OF VENEZUELA AND BRAZIL*

The French anthropologist Jacques Lizot describes a torpid afternoon spent among Yanomamö villagers, horticulturalists of Venezuela and Brazil:

> The heat is unbearable. The hammocks, swollen with prostrate bodies, sway imperceptibly. All around the shelter a multitude of banana trees of all species make up the garden. One can recognize the plantains with their beautiful leaves delicately fringed and stained blood red, the *tabitabirimi* with their light and fragile leaves that flutter in the wind, and the *baushimi* with vaguely yellowish leaf stems. One can also recognize the sturdy and violet-tinged stems of the *rokomi*. New leaves are unrolling their scrolls. Next to the shelter, where the roof ends almost at ground level, rise a few *rasha* palms with their thorny trunks and their beautiful, shiny green fruits hanging down in thick clusters. The rustling of the palms in the light but warm and moist breeze spreads like a light shudder over the surrounding vegetation. Nearby the edge of the forest raises its thick curtain, beyond which rings out the ear-filling chirping of the cicadas. Remaema [a Yanomamö woman] listens to their singing and, modulating her voice to theirs in

---

*Adapted from Napoleon Chagnon, *Yanomamö,* 4th ed. (Fort Worth, TX: Harcourt Brace, 1992).

order to hasten the ripening of the *rasha,* of which she is fond, she murmurs: "Red-redden, red-redden!" For it is said that the cicadas announce the imminent ripening of the *rasha,* which they thus celebrate in their own way. (1991:60)

Early reports about the Yanomamö erroneously described them as foragers. In fact, the abundant rain forest in which the Yanomamö live could easily provide for the complete diet characteristic of foraging groups. The forest is dense and green, with varied growth. Its thick floor of vines and scrub make traversing it difficult; on cloudy days its impenetrable canopy keeps out most light. The Yanomamö exploit the plentiful wild foods found in their environment, but more than 80 percent of their food comes from their village gardens, which are prepared by slash-and-burn techniques.

Gardening and Foraging

Plantain, a type of banana, is the most important crop for the Yanomamö, but manioc, taro, and sweet potato are also cultivated. Cane used in arrow manufacture is grown in village gardens, as is tobacco, a crop of central importance. All Yanomamö chew tobacco daily and guard it jealously. The value of tobacco is evidenced by the fact that the local word for being "poor" is literally "without tobacco" (Chagnon 1992).

Cotton grown in village gardens is used predominantly for the construction of hammocks, an item owned by everyone. Cotton is also used to make what little clothing the Yanomamö wear. Men typically wear little more than a string around the waist, whereas women wear more ornate belts. Single strands of cotton string are also tied around wrists and ankles.

When fruits and vegetables in the rain forest are ripe, the Yanomamö break into small groups to go off on collecting expeditions that may last for several weeks. Honey is the ultimate wild prize, and honeycombs are often consumed with the larvae still inside.

The Yanomamö commonly hunt wild pigs, large and small birds, monkeys, deer, rodents, and anteaters and collect insects and shellfish. Monkeys are hunted with arrow points made of palm wood tipped with curare, a poison extracted from a local vine. The arrow point is dipped in curare and shaved to ensure that it will break off beneath the skin, preventing the victim from removing it. Napoleon

Chagnon observes: "A monkey can pull an ordinary arrow out, but it cannot pull out a point that is broken off deep in its body. The curare gradually relaxes the monkey, and it falls to the ground instead of dying high in the tree, clinging to a branch" (1992:49). Curare is also used in warfare, and poisoned arrow tips are among the most popular items of trade between villages. Lizot describes the return of a Yanomamö hunter to the village:

> A hunter comes home, walking with hurried steps under the oppressive sun, a curassow [game bird] swinging on his back, the bird's white down stuck into his earlobe plugs. Some young people squabble, overflowing with magnificent insolence. Near Remaema, a young mother is carrying a newborn in her arms, a faint smile revealing her regular, even teeth; she playfully rubs her index [finger] on the infant's vulva, sticks a tuft of hair on her pubis, and says: "That's how she'll be when she is grown."(1991:60)

Yanomamö take armadillos, who live in underground burrows and cannot be hunted with bow and arrow, by smoking them out. Once an entry to a burrow has been located, a slow, smoky fire is lit. Smoke escaping from other burrows indicates exits to be dammed up. Once all escape routes have been blocked, hunters listen with an ear to the ground for the scurrying of the animal and dig straight down to retrieve it.

Fishing is an occupation of women. Lizot describes a fishing expedition undertaken by Yanomamö women:

They walk in single file, without hurrying; the carrying baskets on their backs rock in rhythm with their steps, and fat, whimpering infants ride on their hips. . . . They reach the bank of a rivulet, where they sit down to chat at their ease. One of them takes her seat on the lower branches of a tree leaning over the water, unwinds a fishing line, and casts it with a casual yet precise movement. . . . The fisherwoman catches a few small fish that she throws on the bank where they thrash about a long time before suffocating. (1991:64)

Yanomamö women also take fish from nearly dried-up water holes by using improvised nets or traps. Lizot describes this type of fishing:

> They wade into the mud up to their bellies, pushing before them a long screen of vegetable fibers in which they ensnare the fish. As soon as a fish comes to the surface of the dirty water, they stun it with a stick, catch it, and break its backbone. Some fish, long as eels and with narrow heads, disappear into the liquid mud, where they cannot be found. The women methodically cover the whole pond in this manner, without ceasing their merry chatter. Then they clean the catch piled up at the water's edge and make neat bundles with leaves and vines. (1991:64)

Village Construction and Fission

Houses are constructed from readily available local materials: saplings for support posts, vines and leaves for thatching. Houses are not very durable, despite the substantial labor that goes into their construction.

The Yanomamö of Venezuela and Brazil live in villages organized around patrilineages. Nuclear families occupy individual homes linked by a thatched roof, so that households look out onto a central clearing.

The *shabono,* or living space, consists of a series of individual homes, sheltered under a common roof and surrounding an open central plaza. Men sink the four main posts into the ground, and women and children gather the vines and leaves used for thatching. Thousands of leaves are needed to cover the structure. A village may house as few as forty people or as many as three hundred.

When villages grow too large and unwieldy, they may split apart, or fission. Lizot notes that the cohesion of a Yanomamö village is weak and disagreements are common: "The entire political interplay within the settlement is a fragile and subtle balance between the different lineages that make up the group, the factions, and the maneuvers of individual leaders" (1991:61). Lizot describes a process of fissioning brought about on the basis of access to resources:

> One day, Kaomawë and his brothers decided to clear a new garden on the very bank of the "river of rains." The first harvests from that garden were excellent, and since the place was attractive, they decided to move there. But the others refused to join them and preferred to remain in their old site, which they found comfortable. They separated without any quarrel—which is not always the case when a community divides—and continued to maintain good neighborly relations. (1991:61)

Marriage, Exchange, and Leadership Roles

Yanomamö village life centers on a tribal form of political organization. As is characteristic of this form of political organization, the Yanomamö village leader, or headman, must rely on his personal attributes, rather than formal authority, to ensure conformity to his wishes. The headman plays an important role in maintaining order within the group and through his alliances with other villages. Trading and feasting provide channels for creating ties between villages, but the most secure alliances are formed by marriage.

Leadership Each Yanomamö village has a headman, a man who usually belongs to the largest kin group represented in the village. He serves more as a representative in dealings with other villages than as an authoritarian figure within his own village. Leaders act as hosts and negotiators, and their opinions carry somewhat more weight than do the opinions of other villagers. However, headmen lead by example rather than by decree. Lizot writes:

> When the leader of a faction makes a decision, he commits only himself and those who are closely tied to him. The others do as they please. Yanomami [leaders] exercise only moral authority; they can rely only on their prestige and on the possibility of rallying others through persuasion. They cannot use coercion, nor can they compel would-be rebels. Even in warlike expeditions, participation is optional and depends only on the prevailing moral code: the obligation to display one's courage or to avenge a relative. (1991:61)

If there is trouble within the village, it is the headman's responsibility to attempt to restore order. He exhibits the bravery, self-control, and industriousness that he expects others to display. Chagnon notes that there are different styles of leadership among the Yanomamö:

> Some leaders are mild, quiet, inconspicuous most of the time, but intensely competent. They act parsimoniously, but when they do, people listen and conform. Other men are more tyrannical, despotic, pushy, flamboyant, and unpleasant to all around them. They shout orders frequently, are prone to beat their wives, or pick on weaker men. Some are very violent. (1992:27)

The headman Kaobawä, headman of the village where Chagnon conducted much of his fieldwork, represented the quiet and unobtrusive end of the spectrum. Chagnon writes: "He can afford to be this way at his age, for he established his reputation for being forthright and as fierce as the situation required when he was younger, and the other men respect him" (1993:28–29). In addition, Kaobawä had strong kinship alliances that maintained his position, including both consanguineal kin in the form of biological and classificatory brothers and affinal kin because of his own polygynous marriages and as a result of giving sisters and daughters in marriage. Classificatory kin are those who are considered the social equivalent to certain types of biological kin. For example, Kaobawä's male parallel cousins are referred to as his "brothers," in addition to his brothers, who are related to him through both his father and his mother, and his half-brothers, who are related to him as children of his mother's co-wives.

Trading Trade in the form of balanced reciprocity between Yanomamö villages is self-perpetuating, so that each exchange leads to more trade later. All items in a trade must be reciprocated with an item of a different sort, usually representing the village specialty. Yanomamö villages don't usually have a unique resource or skill; instead, the "specialty" helps maintain alliances between villages by requiring traders to visit a particular village repeatedly for a specialty item.

Generalized reciprocity in the form of gifts also reinforces ties between villages. A gift cannot be repaid immediately; it must be presented at an appropriate later time. Thus, the "debt" serves as an excuse to continue trading with a particular village. Both the idea of a village specialty and perpetual indebtedness produce an ongoing relationship, since one village always owes payment to another.

Feasting   Feasts among the Yanomamö are much anticipated by both hosts and guests. They are an opportunity to eat, drink, and flirt; to display oneself; and to affirm and deepen ties of mutual interdependence. Men take responsibility for preparing food for guests, who may number one hundred or more. Preparation for the feast begins long before the occasion, although a messenger is sent to the guest village on the day of the feast.

Game meat and plantain are the main foodstuffs served, and, in anticipation, large quantities of plantain are harvested and hung to ripen. Much of the plantain is used to make soup, cooked in large strips of bark fashioned into containers large enough to hold up to one hundred gallons of soup. A hunting party is organized, and as the hunters set off, the excitement begins to build. When the hunters return

with game, the meat is presented to the headman, smoked at his fire, and wrapped for later presentation, thus affirming the important role of the headman as host of the feast.

Both village and villagers are groomed for the festivities. The central clearing is weeded and swept to prepare it for dancing. On the day of the feast, both men and women paint their faces and bodies and decorate themselves with bright feathers. Men also ingest hallucinogenic drugs. The Yanomamö prepare a number of hallucinogens from both domesticated and wild plants. All these hallucinogens are referred to as *ebene*.

Guests also prepare themselves for the feast by decorating their bodies and ingesting ebene. Guests are responsible for staging the formal beginning of the feast. Chagnon describes the dramatic entrance of the guests at a feast hosted by Kaobawä:

Asiawa [the son of the headman of the visiting village] entered the clearing, touching off an explosion of wild cheering that marked the opening of the dance. He was spectacular in his bright new loincloth, long red parrot feathers streaming from his armbands, and black monkey-tail headband covered with white buzzard down. He marched dramatically to the center of the village clearing, while all of Kaobawä's followers cheered, and struck the visitor's pose: motionless, head upward, and weapons held vertically next to his face. He stood there two or three minutes so his hosts could

The Yanomamö create alliances with other villages through marriage, balanced reciprocity, and ceremonial feasting. These Yanomamö Indians of Brazil are loading baskets with cassava, a starchy root, in preparation for feeding feast guests.

admire him. This gesture signified that he had come in peace and was announcing his benevolent intentions by standing where all could see him. If they bore him malice, they had to shoot him then or not at all. (1992:174)

The leader of the guest delegation then approaches the designated host (the village headman or his representative), and the two begin a chant that signifies acceptance of the invitation by the guests and officially initiates the feast. The two men dance and chant for a few minutes, and the guest is then fed. After being laden with food, the guest departs to arrange the formal entry of the members of his village. Guests assemble at the entryway, with the men in front, and women and children holding gifts behind the front ranks. At their headman's signal, visiting males spring into the village in dancing pairs, whirling and chanting along the edge of the central plaza, and then returning to the rest of the group, still outside the village walls. Each man enters the village in this manner, displaying his unique body painting, chant, and aggressive facial expression. When all the males have had a chance to do this, attended by the enthusiastic cheers and whoops of the hosts, all the guests enter, one by one, dancing along the rim of the clearing and coming to a halt in the center of the plaza, where they stand for silent inspection.

One by one, the hosts approach the throng of guests and lead each family unit off to their own houses. From dusk to dawn, all are engaged in chanting and trading. Visitors tell their headman which items they want; these requests are relayed to the host headman, who entreats one of his villagers to provide it. Once presented, a gift is inspected by the recipient and his friends, who praise it even as the donor apologizes for its inadequacies.

Marriage The Yanomamö call everyone in their society by a term that indicates consanguineal kinship, thus extending kinship terms to people unrelated by blood. Chagnon was called "sister's son" by one Yanomamö man and "elder brother" by another. As noted in Chapter 6, people who are not blood relatives but are referred to in these terms are fictive kin. Fictive kin include relatives by adoption or people who stand in a close kinlike relationship, such as godparents in Mexican societies. For the Yanomamö, Chagnon says, addressing a nonrelative by a kin term establishes a basis for proper and expected behavior. "To be outside the kinship system is, in a very real

sense, to be inhuman or nonhuman: real humans are some sort of kin" (Chagnon 1992:139).

The preferred Yanomamö marriage is with bilateral cross-cousins, and men refer both to their wives and to their female cross-cousins as *suaboya*. Males establish warm, affectionate ties with their male cross-cousins, who are either their wife's brother or the brother of women they could marry. Ideally, male cross-cousins marry each other's sisters.

Descent is patrilineal, and the cross-cousin marriage rule means that, by definition, a man must marry outside his own lineage, or exogamously. Through the generations, cross-cousin marriage creates ongoing alliances among several closely related lineages, since a man marries his father's sister's daughter (FZD) or his mother's brother's daughter (MBD). In practice, a man's FZD is also likely to be his MBD. Figure 13.2 illustrates the genealogy of a Yanomamö man's relationships to his two wives. Wife number 1 is his FZD and wife number 2 is his

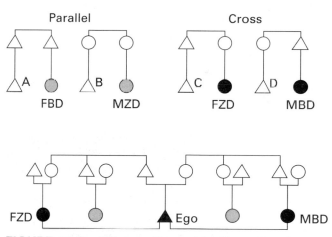

FIGURE 13.2   Alliances Formed by Cross-Cousin Marriage

Yanomamö men may marry their female cross-cousins, either their father's sister's daughter (FZD) or their mother's brother's daughter (MBD). As illustrated in the diagram at upper right, males C and D are related to their potential marriage partners through a cross-sex parental link. Parallel cousins may not marry. As shown in the diagram at upper left, males A and B are related to their father's brother's daughter (FBD) or their mother's sister's daughter (MZD) through a same-sex parental link. As illustrated in the diagram at bottom, the practice of polygyny allows a man to ally himself with two closely related lineages by marrying both his FZD and his MBD.

Source: Adapted from Napoleon Chagnon, *Yanomamö*, 4th ed. (Fort Worth, TX: Harcourt Brace, 1993).

MBD. As this example illustrates, the Yanomamö are also polygynous, an advantage for a man who wishes to strengthen his political position, since more wives can produce more children. A man who has more than one wife not only generates alliances through his own marriages but can also promote alliances by arranging the marriages of his children. Headmen often gain their position through kinship and marriage (Chagnon 1992:7).

Religion and Expressive Culture

The Yanomamö envision the universe as being constructed of four layers, with a thin slice of space between each layer (Figure 13.3). The top layer now lies fallow, though things may have come from there long ago. The next lower layer is the sky. People can see only its underside, onto which stars are stuck, but the surface of the sky is believed to look much as the earth does, with trees and other plants and animals. Souls of the dead live there much as they had on the earth.

The third layer down, on which the Yanomamö live, was created when a section of the "sky" layer cracked off and toppled down. The fourth layer, which now lies under the earth, was formed when sky fell to earth on top of a settlement and pushed it down through the earth to the underside. It is still inhabited by the people, who have their homes and gardens but not their hunting grounds. Having no forest in which to hunt game led the people of this layer to seek meat through cannibalism, and they especially like to prey on the souls of Yanomamö children.

Humans and Hekura The Yanomamö creation myth states that people originated from the blood that fell on the ground when Moon was shot in the

FIGURE 13.3 The Yanomamö Cosmos

The Yanomamö cosmos consists of four layers. The top layer is empty but was the source of many things that now exist in the other three layers. The next-lower layer, the "sky," is similar to the earth on its topmost side. Populated by the souls of the dead, it has trees, gardens, villages, animals, and plants. Humans live on the third layer, which was formed when a chunk of sky layer broke off and fell downward, carrying the people, their homes, and their gardens with it. The fourth layer, which lies under the earth, is inhabited by people who have homes and gardens but no forest. Since these people have no forests for hunting, they have become cannibals, preying on the souls of Yanomamö children.

Source: Adapted from Napoleon Chagnon, *Yanomamö*, 4th ed. (Fort Worth, TX: Harcourt Brace, 1993).

belly. Some Yanomamö believe that these early humans were all males and that women developed from the fruit of a vine the early men were collecting. The original human beings were different from people today in that they were part human, part animal, and part spirit. When they died, they became all spirit—the *hekura*, who can cause illness or be called on by shamans for healing. Many Yanomamö myths are built around these original humans, called "those who are now dead." They are considered responsible for creating many plants and animals and are believed to be the spirits of those living things that bear their names.

Stories about these early humans are a source of diversion and instruction for the Yanomamö. Men are generally the storytellers, and elegant orators are greatly respected. A myth is "performed" rather than "told," and the histrionic gifts of the storyteller are often enhanced by hallucinogenic drugs.

The jaguar plays a prominent role in many of these stories. Chagnon (1992) suggests that the jaguar exemplifies the fundamental distinction between "nature" and "culture" in Yanomamö society. Among the Yanomamö, Chagnon notes, Jaguar is a figure in which nature and culture overlap. The Yanomamö are proud that humans have culture and animals do not; yet Jaguar is as skilled in the hunt as the Yanomamö. Jaguar hunts not only animals but people, as the Yanomamö do. Jaguar is an animal, a creature of nature, who shares traits with humans, bearers of culture. As a marginal symbol who combines nature and culture, Jaguar is both feared and respected. In many stories, the fierce and powerful Jaguar is reduced to a clumsy and inefficient beast. In these stories, culture triumphs over nature.

The Yanomamö Soul The Yanomamö soul consists of four parts, each of which has a function in both life and death. The part that conforms to the "will" in English terminology makes the journey to the afterlife. At death, it climbs up the ropes of the dead person's hammock, entering the layer of the universe above the earth and beginning a journey down a road that divides into two paths. The fork in the road is guarded by a spirit who is charged with assessing the generosity shown by the soul's owner during its earthly life. Generous souls are directed down the path to the comfortable earthlike place; stingy ones are shepherded down the fork to a fiery place.

Another part of the soul is freed when the body is cremated after death. This portion lives on in the jungle, where it has the potential for evil, clubbing people who visit the jungle at night. The most crucial part of the Yanomamö soul resides within the chest or flank, and it is most vulnerable to attack. This portion of the soul can be stolen and subjected to supernatural attack. If it is stolen or attacked, the individual sickens and will likely die unless this part of the soul is restored.

The last aspect of the soul lives both inside and outside the individual. Inside, it is a part of the individual spirit (the part captured by the camera when a person is photographed); outside, it is a person's animal counterpart, which leads a parallel life. When the person eats, his or her animal-self does the same; when the person sleeps, so does the animal. Ordinarily, one never meets the animal alter ego, but if by some twist of fate one were to hunt and kill it, one's own death would follow, as it does when another hunter kills "your animal."

Illness and Healing Illness is caused by the hekura spirits, which harm a person by consuming a portion of their soul, usually at the behest of someone from an enemy village. A shaman calls upon his own powerful hekura to counterattack, thus curing the sick villager. Only Yanomamö men can become shamans, but there are no other restrictions by birth or special characteristics. Older shamans guide novices in learning the ways to call their own hekura spirits to them. Any male who wishes may undertake the training, if he is willing to undergo the rigors entailed. These include a fast that may last up to a year, during which time the initiate becomes emaciated.

Initiates must learn the likes and dislikes of the hekura to lure them into their chests. This feat is not easy, since hekura are difficult to seduce. Hekura are also fickle and likely to leave abruptly. An aspiring shaman must make the interior of his body an attractive terrain in which the hekura may dwell in comfort. If the hekura find verdant mountains and cool streams in the shaman's chest, they may stay. Older, more proficient shamans may have succeeded in attracting many hekura spirits to live within them, yet they are always striving to keep them happy. Because hekura are repelled by sexual activities, novices must be celibate. Once a shaman has established a stable relationship with the hekura, he may engage in sex without fear that his spiritual powers will abandon him.

Hekura, who dwell among the Yanomamö in the thousands, are both male and female, and all are exceedingly beautiful. Different ones have different temperaments. The most fearsome are the "hot and meat-hungry" hekura; these are the ones who devour the souls of enemies. Because the hekura are themselves beautiful, they require attractiveness of the shamans, who wear feathers and paint themselves in elaborate designs. Once the hekura have danced down their trails and into the chests of their hosts, they can aid a shaman in curing. They can also be sent to enemy villages to avenge the sickness brought on local villagers.

Shamans have access to the hekura only while under the influence of hallucinogens. These drugs are used on a daily basis, and their preparation is ongoing. Hallucinogens are ingested in powder form, blown into the shaman's nose through a long, hollow pipe by another man. The initial effects are painful, causing coughing, choking, watery eyes, and retching. The drug's power takes effect almost immediately. As the shaman begins to feel intoxicated, he begins to chant to call his hekura to him.

Death and Mourning When a Yanomamö dies, the body is cremated. Chagnon notes that smoke from the cremation fire is considered contaminating:

> The children and those who might be sick are asked to leave the village, for the smoke from a burning corpse can contaminate the vulnerable and ill. [The Yanomamö] often wash their bows and arrows after a cremation, for the smoke of a burning corpse can contaminate such possessions. On one occasion I also saw them wash all the smoked meat the hunters had brought back for a feast, for it, too, had been contaminated by the smoke of a cremated corpse. (1992:115)

One person is designated to watch the fire, making sure the entire corpse is consumed, leaving only the ash and bone. A log is hollowed out to hold the teeth and bones, which are ground up by a close kinsman. Chagnon describes the mourning ritual:

> When the bones are all pulverized, they are carefully poured onto a leaf, and then transferred to several small gourds, each with a small opening in it. The dust and ash that remain in the hollow log is rinsed out with boiled ripe plantain soup and solemnly drunk as the assembled, squatting relatives and friends moan loudly and frantically, rending their hair with their hands and weeping profusely. The log is then burned. . . . The gourds are carefully and tenderly stored in the roof of the kin's house, plugged shut with white down, and

kept for a future and more elaborate ash-drinking ceremony that might be attended by kin who live in distant villages. (1992:115)

Cultural Change

Life for the Yanomamö is changing. Contact with Catholic missionaries began many years ago in some villages. The missionaries have started schools and economic cooperatives in some villages, leading the Yanomamö to become dependent on the missions. Missionaries also encourage the Yanomamö to work for wage labor at the missions, which gives them money to buy material goods, such as shotguns. Missionaries believe the guns are used in hunting; however, Chagnon notes that they are also used in warfare:

> Significant numbers of Yanomamö in the remote villages are being shot and killed by raiders from mission villages who, now that they have an arms advantage, invent reasons to get "revenge" on distant groups, some of which have had no historical relationship with them. (1992:220)

Some of the most dramatic changes for the Yanomamö have resulted from the 1987 gold rush in Brazil, which brought not only miners with guns and heavy machinery but also previously unencountered diseases, which the indigenous people could not withstand. Airplanes and heavy machinery used by the miners drove away the game, and miners processed the gold by diverting rivers and streams into sluices and using mercury to separate the gold ore from the mud. The mercury-contaminated water was then allowed to flow back into the rivers, killing the fish and making the water unfit for humans and other forms of life.

Many anthropologists fear that the Yanomamö—like many other people facing incursions from outsiders—may be doomed to join the millions of displaced people who crowd the slums of the world's cities. Chagnon notes that in Venezuela, where he studied, the government is taking steps to avert this crisis. Still, he notes that the Yanomamö face serious difficulties. Chagnon says:

> What the remaining native peoples of the world most need for their survival—and by survival I mean not only cultural survival but their biological survival—is guaranteed rights to their land and some kind of health program that will attend to diseases that were introduced as a consequence of contact with the outside world. (pers. comm. 1994)

MEAD'S "NATURAL LABORATORY": THE MUNDUGUMOR OF NEW GUINEA

The Mundugumor are well known to anthropologists through the writings of Margaret Mead. Mead traveled to New Guinea in 1932 to investigate a particular problem: Are men and women temperamentally different? And, if they are, is the difference due to biology or to culture? At the time, very little was known about the many societies of New Guinea (there are over one thousand separate language groups on the large island of New Guinea and the surrounding islands). Mead hoped to use what she considered a "natural laboratory" to study the relationship between biology and human temperament. The results of Mead's study were published in a classic book, *Sex and Temperament in Three Primitive Societies.* She argued that each individual is born with a biologically given temperament that society can mold to a desired shape through socialization.

Mead studied individual variation in three societies in the Sepik River region of New Guinea. She compared the mountain-dwelling Arapesh, the river-dwelling Mundugumor, and the lake-dwelling Tchambuli (now known as the Chambri). Although the Arapesh lived in a harsh environment, both men and women were gentle and nurturing. Among the Mundugumor, both women and men were expected to be histrionic, volatile, and quick to assert themselves. The Tchambuli exhibited gender characteristics that were, according to Mead, the reverse of those in American society. Men were gentle, passive, and "feminine," while women were assertive, active, and "masculine." All three groups exhibited individual variation, what Mead called "deviance," but she felt these examples confirmed her view that biology does not determine male and female personality.

Mead's study has been criticized by some anthropologists, who note that the three examples form a pattern that is "too perfect," since fieldwork data do not usually conform so exactly to a researcher's expectations. They suggest that she may have overlooked some data and exaggerated the importance of other findings to bolster her results. However, the importance of Mead's work is indicated by the fact that *Sex and Temperament* is still read, studied, and debated by scholars and laypeople alike.

Mead died before she could realize her ambition of writing up all the materials she had gathered on the Mundugumor. She asked Nancy A. McDowell to publish a work on the Mundugumor, based on Mead's field notes and McDowell's fieldwork along the Sepik. McDowell conducted fieldwork in a village upriver from Mead's Mundugumor, who now prefer to be known as the "Biwat," after the river that runs through their land. McDowell notes that the group she studied and Mead's "Mundugumor" are "culturally and linguistically very similar but consider themselves to be different groups and indeed are described as speaking two separate languages."

In the following essay, McDowell discusses the Mundugumor on the basis of Mead's field notes and her own visits to the village where Mead and her husband, Reo Fortune, conducted their fieldwork.

MUNDUGUMOR: SEX AND TEMPERAMENT REVISITED

Nancy A. McDowell*

The Sepik is a broad and meandering river that slowly makes its way north to the Pacific Ocean while flowing through lowland swamps and grasslands. It has several tributaries that begin at higher elevations and join the Sepik at various points. The Yuat River is one of those tributaries; it is fed by several highland rivers and is noted for being turbulent and dangerous in its higher elevations. Most of the Sepik River region is flat, swampy lowland. However, at the upper reaches of the Yuat, where the Mundugumor live, the ground is higher and drier than the neighboring lands. Margaret Mead believed this ecological situation helped produce the strength and power of the Mundugumor people. They lived on the only high and dry ground in the area, so they had ample land for gardening and hunting and access to a variety of ecological niches. Because of this advantageous locale, they could dominate their neighbors.

There is no way of knowing for how long the Mundugumor held this position; their creation myths assert that after they moved into the area, the course of the river changed and turned these land-loving

*Adapted from Melvin Ember, Carol R. Ember, and David Levinson, *Portraits of Culture: Ethnographic Originals* (Upper Saddle River, NJ: Prentice Hall, 1995).

people into river dwellers. We do know that when explorers first encountered them, probably in the late nineteenth or early twentieth century, they were a warlike people who were difficult to pacify. It was not until colonial authorities jailed leaders that the warfare and raiding ceased.

Subsistence

The staple food of the Mundugumor was sago. This is a carbohydrate leached from the interior pith of the sago palm. Men felled the large tree and cut open the trunk; women beat the interior into slivers and shreds, which were washed to leach out the sago paste. The paste was usually reconstituted as pudding by adding boiling water; sometimes it was fried or used in other ways. Sago was eaten daily by almost everyone.

Sago was usually supplemented by some protein source: fish caught in the rivers or swamps, pig or smaller game hunted in the forest, grubs gathered from downed trees, some leafy green vegetables grown in gardens or gathered in the forest. The basic diet was supplemented substantially by items produced in slash-and-burn gardens: yams, taro, sweet potatoes, greens, coconuts, bananas, and a few other crops. Tobacco was an especially important crop. The fertile, high, dry ground along the river was perfect for growing tobacco, and the Mundugumor made much of this. They were inveterate smokers themselves, but they also traded this crop to their neighbors for a variety of products, such as clay pots and woven baskets. Betel nut was also an important item, consumed locally and traded with neighbors for crafted items.

Trade   The Mundugumor participated in two general trading networks. The first was with bush, or nonriver, villages in the area. Especially important were the three villages located in the nearby swamps: Yaul, Dimiri, and Maravat. These villagers produced pottery and were given garden products in exchange. With other "inland" villages the Mundugumor traded for mosquito baskets (large baskets in which people slept to escape the mosquitoes) and other crafted products. The second trading network linked a series of villages along the waterways with other villages up in the mountains. Down from the mountains came stones and bird plumes, which were traded for shells and other sea and river products. The Mundugumor acted as middlemen in this system, adding pottery obtained from nearby nonriver villages, as well as tobacco and betel nut to the flow of goods. Their role as middlemen provided a politico-economic advantage in the region. All trading, whether with bush villages or on the river system, was conducted by way of balanced reciprocity between individual inherited partners.

The Sexual Division of Labor   Men hunted while women did most of the fishing. Both sexes helped in the processing of sago; men cut the trees, while women leached the starch. Men felled trees and did heavy clearing work in the gardens; women did most of the planting, weeding, and harvesting. The only exception to this rule was a special kind of yam garden; because of their association with certain rituals, these gardens were the exclusive province of men, and women were not allowed to help. Both sexes gathered products from the environment on occasion. Women did most domestic chores and child care, while men constructed houses and canoes. Women made the essential fishing nets and woven bags used for carrying all sorts of items; men devoted considerable time and energy to political activities and warfare.

Mead did not record whether the people conceived the sexual division of labor as a reciprocal exchange of male and female goods and services.

New Guinea subsistence is based on yams, sweet potatoes, and a variety of other vegetables. Using slash-and-burn techniques, men clear the gardens and women tend them. Because of the important economic role of women, a man cannot enhance his status without one or more wives.

However, the pattern of complementarity between male and female roles does conform to the principle of reciprocity that appears to govern much of Mundugumor social interaction.

Demography

The people identified as the Mundugumor lived in six villages: Biwat, Branda, Kinakatem, Akuran, Dowaning, and Andafugan. The first four were located on the Yuat, or Biwat, River; the latter two were inland from the river. Together, the population of the four river communities could not have totaled much more than 750 people. The village of Kinakatem, the place where Mead and Reo Fortune actually lived and made their base of operations, contained only 183 people.

Biwat, Branda, Akuran, and Kinakatem were not separate villages with definite boundaries. Rather, each locality was a dispersed settlement. People lived with family members in hamlets scattered throughout the bush area. One reason for dispersed living is that it was easier to keep a particular hamlet's location secret from enemies; in fact, some paths were secret. In addition, fewer people meant fewer arguments, and with individuals scattered throughout the bush, conflict was less of a problem.

Some hamlets contained only one household, but others consisted of more than one. A household was a recognized residential and social unit headed by an adult male. The head of household might have more than one wife, and each wife ideally had a separate dwelling for herself and her children. Other relatives and supporters in the household might include the head's dependent brother, an ambitious nephew, or a widowed mother.

The size of the household varied, usually depending on the number of wives. The ideal for a man was to head a household composed of many wives, many children, and many other dependents. However, few men managed to achieve this goal. Of the twenty households in Kinakatem in 1932, only two conformed to this ideal. Most households had between five and twelve members; two had only three members; and one man lived alone.

Political Organization and Leadership

Among the Mundugumor, a man achieved some measure of power and renown by his own actions and force of character, as evidenced by his role in exchange. By strategically investing in others and thereby indebting them to him, a man gained fame and power, and thus became a Big Man.

Big Men were rarely rich, at least in material terms. If they acquired many pigs, they gave away many pigs. By giving a relative a pig, the Big Man indebted the recipient to him and made him a political subordinate. Shrewd investing in others was necessary to achieve influence, a pattern common throughout Melanesia. Political leaders are rarely the richest men because they do not hold on to wealth; rather, they distribute it to others.

Among most New Guinea groups, a man's status is based on his ability to produce ceremonial yams and pigs, which are distributed in giveaways at pig feasts. One of the most elaborate systems of male prestige is found on the Trobriand Islands, where these yams are stacked for display.

The more wives a man had, the more pigs he had and the more tobacco he could raise. These activities gave him an important place in external as well as internal trading transactions. If a man had many wives, he also had many in-laws, who also helped him achieve renown. The two men who headed the largest households in Kinakatem had married many women, had many people dependent on them, and were respected and feared both within and outside the village.

Prowess in warfare was another way in which a man could achieve fame and renown, because success in warfare attracted adherents and supporters. People who feared enemy raids took shelter with strong, violent men and thereby became indebted to them. The Mundugumor leader, then, was a man of forceful personality, given to violence and self-assertion, one who took wives when he could and defended himself and his household against all others. He would take the initiative in organizing and leading raids on other villages and would never let someone take advantage of him.

Relationships with other villages varied. Although there was tension even among Mundugumor villages, there was usually a limit to the violence that took place. Relations with non-Mundugumor villages were different. Although some villages could be called enemies and others were trade partners, there was no firm line between the two categories. A village could be a trade partner one moment but become an enemy the next. Trading expeditions were often carried out in an atmosphere of mutual hostility, fear, and mistrust. On occasion, to ensure safe exchanges with potentially hostile villages, child hostages could be taken: if the enemy villagers harmed anyone from the Mundugumor village, the hostage was killed.

Preparations for warfare, the conduct of warfare, and defense in warfare shaped much of Mundugumor society. Because most warfare was conducted in stealth, by surprise raids rather than openly confrontational battles, hamlets were scattered and hidden, making it more difficult for enemies to find and surprise inhabitants. Raids were carried out by young and adult men. Target villages were surrounded, and the ideal was to kill as many people, including children, as possible. Sometimes, women were taken as wives for the most influential men. Cannibalism was practiced, and skulls were kept as war trophies. Mead's impression was that the Mundugumor of 1932 were dominant in the region and that their reputation for fierceness extended far.

Marriage and Kinship

There was an intimate connection between political organization and the ideal of polygyny. Men acquired power by acquiring wives, and men with power acquired more wives. How did men acquire wives to begin with? There were four possible ways: the levirate, bridewealth or brideprice, raids on enemy villages, and brother–sister exchange.

A man could acquire a wife through the death of a male relative, such as a brother or father's brother. Known as the levirate, this system allowed the man's kin group to retain control of a woman's labor and rights to any children produced in the marriage. A man could also obtain a wife through providing her kin group with bridewealth. In practice, few younger men could control the valuables necessary to acquire a wife through this means. Men could also acquire women by stealing them from enemy villages through warfare and raids. Older, more powerful men were more likely than younger men to use all three of these means of marrying.

The ideal way to acquire a wife was through brother–sister exchange. Men would try to arrange marriages for their children (with the advice of wives and mothers). Sons were often glad to have marriages arranged for them; they rightly feared that their fathers might use their sisters to acquire more wives for themselves, rather than for the sons. A man without a sister was in an unfortunate position. No men would want their sisters to develop an interest in him, since he had no way of reciprocating. Sometimes a sisterless man was able to make a payment in bridewealth in lieu of a sister, especially to men who already had enough wives of their own. Or he might be able to convince relatives in his clan to use a distant "clan sister" in place of a biological sister.

The ideal was that all marriages took place as part of an exchange, and arranging such exchanges could be difficult. Men had to have "marked sisters" of the right age, and the man to whom the marked sister was to go had to want a wife of the appropriate age. The women involved had to agree to the transaction, or at least be talked into giving it a try. Brothers had to agree which of their sisters would be used in the exchange. Fathers had to be prevented or discouraged from using their daughters to acquire additional wives for themselves.

It is easy to see why marriages were difficult to arrange and often caused conflicts. Tensions could arise between the two sets of in-laws; for example, a man might not want the sister offered in exchange for the sister he had provided. Tensions could also arise between male relatives—brothers or sons and fathers. The ideal was that brothers used their marked sisters for exchange, but the reality was that men used any female relatives they were strong enough to take. One of the main reasons brothers split apart and did not constitute one large household together was that tensions almost inevitably developed out of the marriage system. This system was one of the main causes of conflict both within and between villages. If a man from Kinakatem married a woman from Branda but his sister did not marry the appropriate man from that village, there would be bad feelings in both the families and the villages.

It is not surprising that Mundugumor marriages tended to be stormy. Spouses frequently fought; women went home to their natal families; physical violence between spouses was common; and divorce, especially in the first year or so of marriage, was also common. Once a couple settled down and had one or two children, the marriage calmed down and was more likely to last. If a man acquired additional wives, he did so only after quelling the protests of his current wife or wives. Jealousy and physical attack were common between co-wives, each of whom protected what she perceived as her rights and the rights of her children. A smart polygynist, it was agreed, built a separate domicile for each wife and her children. Each adult woman would cook at her own hearth for her husband and the others of her domicile. Children who were unhappy with the way they were treated in one place could attempt to attach themselves to another.

In most New Guinea societies, political and economic life centers on the clan or unilineal descent group, but this pattern was not so pronounced for the Mundugumor. Individuals gained primary access to land through the clan, but land was plentiful and rights to it could be acquired through another source. Clans were exogamous. One could not marry a member of one's own patrilineal clan or the patrilineal clan of one's mother. Individuals took their primary identity from the clan. Each clan had a different origin myth, as well as a different signal call on the *slit-gong* drum, an instrument of ritual importance. First, one's own clan signal would be struck on the drum, then the signal for one's mother's clan, then further relatives until there could be no doubt which individual was being summoned.

For the Mundugumor, it was not the descent group but ongoing alliances established through marriage and other types of economic exchanges that held the society together. For example, if one brother–sister pair married another brother–sister pair, they had obligations to one another for life, and their obligations continued into the next generation. A man had ritual obligations to his sister's children, including sponsoring his sister's son at his initiation into one of the Mundugumor secret societies. The ideal was that the descendants of the first intermarrying pair would themselves marry in the fifth generation. These exchanges thereby united individuals into an interconnected network of obligation and reciprocity. This overlapping network of exchange obligations knitted Mundugumor society together.

World View and Religion

Mundugumor world view was based on the principle of exchange and reciprocity. Much as Westerners assume that gravity will work when they get out of bed in the morning, the Mundugumor assumed that the world operates according to the principle of reciprocity. Exchange and reciprocity were dominant in Mundugumor religion, just as they were central to the economic and political systems. The universe and all beings and forces within it adhered to the principle of reciprocity. If one broke a taboo imposed by a water spirit, then one became ill; if one then made the proper offering to that spirit, one would recover. The world was populated with spirits of various sorts, but there were rules by which one could control or at least counteract their effects. Most control came through exchange and the giving of gifts. For example, if a spirit accepted a particular offering, then the spirit had no choice but to make the donor well— that's the way the world works.

The Mundugumor would not have described the various spirits who populated their world as supernatural, because these beings were, to the Mundugumor, a part of the natural world. Spirits lived in known, defined territories and could manifest their existence to people. Most frequently encountered were water and bush spirits. Spirits could even interact with people by assuming some material form. For example, water spirits frequently appeared as crocodiles; bush spirits could appear as human beings and interact with real people. Sexual intercourse with a bush spirit was considered a possible cause of death. People avoided breaking taboos related to these spirits and sometimes asked their assistance in some human endeavor, such as warfare or pig hunting. These spirits were often the cause of illness but rarely the cause of death.

Spirits of dead human beings, or ghosts, were also sometimes encountered. Elaborate funerals were held to ensure that ghosts were properly dealt with and therefore unlikely to cause harm. People believed that if they performed the rituals properly, the ghosts had no choice but to leave living kin in peace. People did not worship ghosts and rarely appealed to them.

The very old could die natural deaths, and obvious accidents and deaths in warfare were not necessarily sorcery-related, but most other deaths were attributed to the work of sorcery or harmful magic. There were several kinds of sorcery, but most relied on two important elements: knowing the proper technique or ritual and possessing some part of the victim. The Mundugumor hired sorcerers from other places who knew the techniques, but they had to supply the victim's "dirt" (nail clippings, hair, or a piece of half-eaten food). People were therefore careful about what they left behind and who had access to their dirt. Any enemy or person with resentment could get hold of a piece of dirt and hire the services of a sorcerer. People were thus naturally suspicious of those they had offended. It was not uncommon for wives to procure the services of a sorcerer to murder their husband, and semen for use in sorcery was easily acquired by a seemingly respectful wife. The motivation for hiring a sorcerer to harm someone varied, but it usually involved a slight, an insult, or anger over an exchange or transaction.

The Mundugumor Today

A great deal has changed in Kinakatem since 1932, but much has remained the same. Photographs I took in 1981 are sometimes difficult to distinguish from those Mead took almost fifty years earlier. The village looks very much the same; houses are still built out of bush materials and the canoes are dugouts. But if one looks closely, one can see dramatic evidence of change. In the village of Biwat stands a large Catholic church, staffed by a resident priest, that is well attended every Sunday. Many of the dugout canoes have powerful outboard motors attached to them.

Sago remains the staple crop despite the purchase of rice in the local stores. Tobacco and betel nut are still significant items of trade, but they are taken to market now in locally owned power canoes and trucks, sometimes even in chartered airplanes. People are quick to show photographs of their children, most of whom have gone to the local school and some of whom have gone to colleges and universities outside the area.

Mead would probably still be able to find much that is familiar in Kinakatem, but descendants of the women and men she knew in 1932 are no longer isolated from the outside world. Her "natural laboratory" has now become part of the global economy.

GENDER AND CHANGE: YAP ISLANDERS OF THE WESTERN PACIFIC

Located east of the Philippine Islands in the western Pacific, Yap comprises four major high islands surrounded by a fringing coral reef. People live in nearly one hundred villages, which occupy all the viable agricultural land and fishing reef on Yap. The villagers are farmers and fishermen. Women work on the land to produce vegetable foods, and men work on the reef to provide fish. About two thousand people live in the port town of Colonia, created by U.S. government officials after World War II. About half of the adult population of Yap works for wages in the small government town, and they buy canned fish, rice, and other imported goods to contribute to the household economy.

Sherwood G. Lingenfelter first conducted research in Yap from 1967 to 1969, when the islands were an administrative district of the U.S. trust territory of the Pacific Islands. He returned to Yap in 1979 to study the impact of twenty-five years of American administration and education on marriage and family relationships.

Today, these islands are part of Yap State in the Federated States of Micronesia. They are politically independent but are still under a "free-association" agreement with the United States. In the following essay, Lingenfelter describes the impact of American colonialism on traditional Yapese gender roles.

YAP: CHANGING ROLES OF MEN AND WOMEN

*Sherwood G. Lingenfelter**

From 1950 to 1990 the Yap Islands were a minor outpost in America's strategic defense against Communism. Militarily, the islands were insignificant, since they have little land and poor anchorage. Politically, they constituted part of the United States trust territory of the Pacific Islands, wrenched from the Japanese at the close of World War II and retained as a strategic trust.

The political significance to Americans of these and other islands in Micronesia after World War II lies at the heart of much that has happened there since 1945. American officials have evangelized, cajoled, and coerced Yapese to adopt their form of democratic government. American educators have taught Yapese children the English language, science, math, and even American history. American doctors have delivered babies, operated on appendixes, treated injuries, and brought new standards of health to the islanders.

With the establishment of a permanent administrative center on Yap after World War II, American officials demanded the same conveniences they had at home and created a port town, aptly named Colonia, to furnish the means to satisfy their wants. Using Yapese labor, they built a diesel-powered plant to furnish electricity. They constructed a reservoir to supply fresh water. They cleared the shipping channel and remodeled a dock to receive ships and goods from the United States. They created warehouses to store goods and installed freezers for meats and other perishable goods. They remodeled Japanese houses and added new ones to duplicate a way of life familiar in any American town.

---

*Adapted from Melvin Ember, Carol R. Ember, and David Levinson, *Portraits of Culture: Ethnographic Originals* (Upper Saddle River, NJ: Prentice Hall, 1995).

Yapese labored and learned on the construction projects. They used their wages to buy kerosene, cigarettes, beer, and canned foods in the local general store. They drove the jeeps, sat on the porcelain toilets, and drank coffee from the electric coffee makers. They evaluated all of these things and only gradually adopted some of them as their own. Yapese reluctance to jump on the American bandwagon was not so much a rejection, as interpreted by some observers, as the desire to retain, and remain in control of, their own way of life.

Colonia As Crossroads and Marketplace

If you were to conduct a survey of small tropical port towns, Colonia would fall very low on your list of exotic places to visit. The most fundamental characteristic of Colonia is its position as a crossroad between Yap and the outside world. Three mornings a week a Boeing 737 screams to a halt seven miles out of Colonia, bringing passengers, cargo, and mail from Guam, Japan, the Far East, and the United States. The new dock, opened in March 1980, can service the most modern container cargo ships, which come directly from the United States and Japan.

What does it mean to have a shipping port? Ordinarily it means cars, clothing, canned fish, cookies, and ship biscuits from Japan; rice, beef, and corrugated iron from Australia; and beer, canned goods, coffee, chickens, cigarettes, cement, nails, flour, and sugar from the United States. On special occasions it may mean lanterns from England, canned hams from Denmark, kerosene refrigerators from Sweden, gasoline and kerosene from the Philippines, and shoes from Taiwan. In the summer of 1970 I watched one ship unload thirty-three cars for Yapese buyers to be used on a total of forty-five miles of road. Ships are the Yap's link to the products of the world, and the more frequently they come, the more important these products become in the lives of the Yapese.

The town as crossroads exerts significant forces in the lives of the Yapese people. It creates a situation of mobility, in which people can go places, meet people, and do things they have never done before. Before roads, most Yapese women and children never visited villages outside their immediate locality. A seventy-year-old Yapese woman told me she had never been south of Colonia until she went in a car, and she had been to Colonia only three or four times in her life until they built the roads. Today people drive to the airport to watch the planes land and see the people who come and go. Others, especially older people, make weekly trips to the farmers' market, where they socialize with others of their age group from all over Yap. Some come to town for Sunday worship at the Catholic or Protestant mission center. All of these activities greatly expand the network of social interaction in a way not possible before the completion of roads.

The Yapese have little to offer the outside world to balance their shopping desires. Copra, the dried meat of the coconut, has been the major export from Yap for many years. The labor required to produce it is tedious, profit is low, and most Yapese consider it a waste of time. Some Yapese produce food for the farmers' market, selling to Yapese,

The traditional horticultural lifestyle of many Pacific Island groups has been disrupted by various forms of colonialism. This man on the island of Bora Bora in Polynesia is opening coconuts for copra, dried coconut meat, to be sold on the international market. Yapese produce a small amount of copra, but their primary source of cash is from government jobs resulting from the U.S. military occupation of the Yap Islands since World War II.

Palauans, and Americans who live in Colonia. Income from marketing garden products requires less work than copra production, and marketing garden products yields more profit. However, the demand is limited, and only a few Yapese produce regularly for the market.

The major commodities the Yapese have to offer are their labor, land, and culture. Labor for the government, or in support of facilities for American officials, has furnished the major source of income for the Yapese. In the 1980s, tourism provided a small but increasing source of income. A few Yapese and Palauans have built small hotels and restaurants to cater to a predominantly Japanese tourist industry.

The Colonia Workplace: Government, Business, and Education

Colonia is the workplace for a majority of Yapese. Office staff are required for all branches of government, including education, public health, resources and development, and public affairs. Outside the government, private businesses provide numerous other office positions. Yapese compete for office jobs, but they are not interested in less prestigious labor. Public works, employing carpenters, mechanics, road maintenance, and other laborers, has a difficult time keeping a permanent core of labor. About 25 percent of these jobs were held by Palauans or non-Yapese.

As in the United States, the key to prestige is the amount of educational training required for the job and the degree of administrative responsibility assigned to the title. The implications of such a system of job stratification are that few people strive to fill the manual and service occupations. The reward system, then, totally disregards the essential needs of the social and economic structure in favor of a set of values imported from the United States and slanted toward education ideals, impractical for their long-term advantages to Yapese. As a consequence, very few young Yapese are interested in cultivating service skills and occupations. The only route to success is high school, college, and an office job.

Education and Change Education, formal and informal, is one of the most fundamental forces for change. In 1962, the government began a program of hiring American schoolteachers on two-year contracts to come to Yap and other Micronesian islands and work full-time to upgrade the educational program. Any Yapese born after 1950 was required to have an eighth-grade education and was encouraged to graduate from high school. In 1956 over seventy Peace Corps volunteers were invited to Yap. Most of these volunteers were trained to teach English in the elementary grades. By 1974 all Yapese children entering high school had seven years of intensive English language instruction.

The informal education of movies, radio, television, and public events may have had even greater impact on the Yapese than schooling. In 1974 Colonia had an outdoor theater that showed two movies every night and an indoor theater that offered single and double features. In 1980 the new television station and the extension of electricity south beyond the town cut drastically into the moviegoing audience. The indoor theater closed, and business at the other was marginal. By March 1980, 124 of about 1,000 households had television sets, presenting a daily fare of American sports, advertisements, sitcoms, and movies for these families and their neighbors. For older Yapese and children, these pictures create an image of life based on cowboys and Indians, cops, gangsters, and sex sirens. Many movies and programs convey images of fantastic wealth and a lifestyle of violence and sex. Although most Yapese know television is not true to life, only those who have traveled extensively outside of Yap have the experience to evaluate with any degree of accuracy what is real and what is imaginative entertainment.

Politics and Change The political scene is the most overt area of contrast on Yap. For more than thirty years, Americans and Yapese have engaged in a struggle for political power and control. The Americans, by force of their occupation, held ultimate authority and power. However, they were limited in the application of that power by their own ideals of democracy and their cultural need to be "loved" by the people they dominated. In addition, the Yapese retained some measure of autonomy and control because Americans never understood their language or their political system.

For example, in 1946 Americans demanded that Yapese elect their chiefs. The Yapese promptly elected the traditional hereditary leaders as chiefs. In 1952, Americans changed the title to magistrate and scheduled regular elections each year. Each year Yapese elected traditional leaders as their magistrates. In 1955, Americans demanded that the magistrates separate executive and legislative powers and form a new legislature. This demand created greater problems for the Yapese, but in 1959 they formed a legislature, and the traditional leaders retained control by telling the legislators what they should do.

Gradually, the younger, better-educated legislators achieved power, based on their new knowledge and skills and advantages gained from American-introduced processes, but they, too, sought to retain Yapese control of their affairs and continue to do so today. Over several years, from 1978 to 1986, the United States granted independence to the six island districts of the U.S. Trust Territory, and Yap State was officially formed with its own government. Since that time, Yapese have had relative autonomy in the governance of the matters of their state.

The Yap State Court is another American innovation, centered in Colonia, that provides alternative ways for Yapese to address economic and social conflicts. When people are unable to settle their differences peaceably in their communities, many bring them to the court. Some people haul neighbors and acquaintances to court to extract payment for debts or for property damage. Yap judges preside over the state court and adjudicate most civil and criminal actions. The court resolves most differences by levying fines, reparations, or jail sentences, depending on the nature of the crime.

Traditional Courtship and Marriage

Old Yapese define the relationship between people in two significant ways: *girdien e tabinaw,* "people of one land," and *girdien e genung,* "people of one belly." Descent was matrilineal. People who were of the same genung came from the same womb or were related through women who had come from the same womb. Yapese genung were named groups that traced ancestry through women to a mythical common female ancestor. Anthropologists have generally referred to this type of group as a **sib,** or clan. People who were of the same tabinaw shared names belonging to particular parcels of land (an estate) and the right to partial inheritance from the lands on that estate. All individuals held membership in two groups, the sib of their mother and the estate of their father.

Marriage Rules Traditionally, the genung and tabinaw were exogamous. The elders said if two people from an estate had intercourse or married, the ancestors of the estate would punish the whole group

DISCUSSIONS

Rituals of Manhood:
Male Initiation in New Guinea

Male initiation rites among New Guinea horticulturalists have long attracted the attention of anthropologists because of their harshness and because of their complex cultural and social context. In many New Guinea societies, there is strict separation between men and women; women are viewed as ritually polluting, and males live apart from their wives in ceremonial men's houses. Males possess "secret" knowledge that is strictly taboo to women and children.

At puberty, males are separated from their mothers and subjected to an intense period of initiation in which they may be ritually beaten, bled from the nose, subjected to periods of fasting without food or water, deprived of sleep, buried, and rubbed with stinging nettles. They also undergo circumcision and subincision. *Subincision* involves slitting the penis from the glans to the scrotum. Among some groups, boys are the objects of ritualized homosexuality, in the belief that it takes both blood and semen to grow a man. The blood is supplied by the mother; the semen, by males who conduct the initiation.

Nancy Chodorow (1974) suggests that male puberty rites such as these offer a means of separating boys from their mothers, which would explain why boys are more often subjected to harsh initiation rites than girls are. Chodorow notes that women are the primary caretakers in all societies, so they provide both boys and girls with their earliest role model. The female role model is appropriate for girls but inappropriate for boys. Adolescent initiation rites

allow boys to become masculinized by enforced separation from their mothers and dramatic identification with initiators who provide the necessary male role models.

Melford Spiro argues that male initiation rites are aimed at resolving the Oedipal complex by "containing" the Oedipal desires of the boys and by gratifying the "complementary Oedipal complex of the men" (1982:170). According to this model, the initiation severs the mother–son bond and allows fathers to punish the boys for their Oedipal desires.

In his book *Symbolic Wounds* (1954), Bruno Bettelheim argues that male puberty rites that involve circumcision and subincision express male envy of the female reproductive function. Ian Hogbin, in *The Island of Menstruating Men* ([1970] 1996), equates the blood associated with incising the penis in New Guinea male puberty rites with blood of females during menstruation.

The purpose for harsh male initiation rites among New Guinea horticulturalists is still subject to debate. The Sambia, studied by Gilbert Herdt, say that initiation makes boys big and strong and turns them into aggressive warriors by transmitting to them the power called *jerungdu*. Herdt writes:

Sambia men associate this power with homosexual intercourse and the use of phallic symbols, especially the ritual flutes that represent the cult and masculinity. The men's club honors the old men and denigrates women, so we may refer to it also as a phallic cult. Much of its power derives from its secrecy; or,

to be more precise, from the way the men use secrecy to accomplish military, ritual, and sexual aims. (1987:101)

In the following article, taken from his ethnographic account of the Sambia, Herdt follows Chodorow in suggesting that male puberty rites forcibly separate boys from their mothers.

INITIATION FOR STRENGTH
Gilbert Herdt

The main goal of initiation is to make boys big and strong, to make them aggressive warriors. This requires changing them: where they sleep and eat, how they act, whom they interact with, look up to, and obey. This is no easy change. They must be removed, by force if necessary, from the women's domain and placed in the culthouse [of the men]. This changes them dramatically, for they lose their childhood freedom and must conform to rigid roles. Pre-initiates are seen as boys, not men, for they show feminine traits such as shyness and crying, and they engage in female tasks and routines such as babysitting and weeding. In this sense they belong to the female world, though they are not female. Though they must become participants in the men's secret society, they are too "feminine" in the above ways to be admitted without change—radical change. They must learn new things, but they must also unlearn old traits and ideas, so that they can truly feel in their gender identity: "I am *not* feminine; I *am* masculine." Such

marked change we call *radical resocialization.*

The change from boyhood to manhood is tough, and men do not spare boys the ordeals of initiation. To the elders, this is necessary. Warfare was the number-one reality to be reckoned with, and the men still prepare for it. *A war is going on;* this is the old idea that underlies initiation. The whole secret society is oriented toward the constant struggle to survive war.

How are boys to acquire the strength to be warriors? Here the dilemma in Sambia thinking about *jerungdu* [male strength and virility] is twofold. First, the male body is believed incapable of manufacturing semen, so it must be externally acquired. This means that *jerungdu* itself is not an intrinsic capacity of male functioning but must be artificially created. . . . Second, semen can be "lost" (ejaculated), and, along with it, the *jerungdu* that it sustains. Therefore, ritual measures must be taken to artificially replace what essence is lost in order to prevent weakness and death. No semen, no *jerungdu,* no masculinity. Overcoming these masculine challenges is the long-term goal of Sambia secret initiations. This entire process I call *ritualized masculinization.* Oral ingestion of semen— ritualized fellatio—is critical to the development of *jerungdu* in boys. Only after years of ritualized homosexuality and body treatment do the key sexual signs of strength take physical form. Initiation is thus a means of simulating maleness and masculinity. Be clear about what this means: *jerungdu* is felt to be a real force, not a metaphor or symbol. Fellatio behavior is a concrete means of attaining it. Men are absolutely convinced of their innate lack of semen and the need for their rituals, and they transmit their convictions to boys in ritual teaching.

Men likewise stress the cultural values of strength, equivalence, and weakness, which are vague in childhood but made explicit in ritual initiation. *Jerungdu* motivates aggressiveness and assertive protests. Equivalence places initiates in age-mate relationships that require them to match their peers' achievements. The unmanly label *wogaanyu* [weakness] makes boys conform to masculine standards that despise weakness and passivity in all actions. And females—the softness of femininity—represent a lower and weaker condition. Through initiation boys are radically resocialized to change their cultural orientations, like a sort of brain-washing that traumatically modifies their thought. The effect is to end their attachments to their mothers and to create new aggressive and sexual impulses, thereby directing boys along the lines of culturally standardized male gender role and identity.

Initiation is the true funnel into the warriorhood. It has the pomp and ceremony of a festival and is also sacred, so its secret parts are solemn and dramatic. Initiation occurs at the harvest season, when men recognize the bounty of nature's fertility. Organized by one's fathers, brothers, and clan elders, the ritual is done by the most loved and admired people in society. Even one's mother takes pride in the event and in her son's accomplishment. For, despite her husband's demands, her workload, the heavy gardening responsibilities expected to ensure the success of the event, her other babies' needs and her own—and notwithstanding her ambivalence in losing a son's companionship and help, or her occasional opposition to the idea of initiation, which sometimes provokes nasty quarrels with her husband—a mother surely recognizes that this is the course a son must take, that the hamlet needs her boy as a defender. Where mother loses a son, father gains a comrade. This is so for all of one's playmates, too, the lads who become age-mates, members of the village warrior class.

The pre-initiated boy, then, is seen as a small person with a penis who is polluted, weak, and not yet manly. He is still polluted from the womb, and has taken in mother's food and saliva. He has been constantly in touch with the contaminated skin of her breasts and body. He is entirely too dependent on her for protection and warmth; her body remains too much of a haven for him. There is more than a hint of femininity about him; he even wears the same type of grass apron as females. He is undisciplined and bawls and throws tantrums when unable to get what he wants. At such times men are openly hostile to boys, taunting them till they cry, saying "Go back to your mother where you belong!" The boy sometimes disobeys his parents and talks back to them. Men cannot forget that their sons are carriers of feminine pollution, so they watch them lest they pollute men, their weapons, or their food. Boys are, of course, kept ignorant of ritual secrets and chased away when these are discussed.

(continued)

DISCUSSIONS

Rituals of Manhood:
Male Initiation in New Guinea (*continued*)

Such considerations come to mind when men discuss the need to initiate their maturing sons.

Another urgent thought is that masculinization is literally a matter of life and death. A boy's body has female contaminants inside it that retard masculine development. His body is male: he has male genitals and his *tingu* [penis] contains no blood, nor will it activate. Yet for boys to reach puberty requires semen. Milk "nurtures the boy"; sweet potatoes and other "female" foods provide "stomach nourish-ment" and become only feces, not semen. Women's own bodies internally produce menstruation, the hallmark of reproductive maturity. No comparable mechanism is active in boys to stimulate their biological secondary sex traits. Only semen can do that, and only men have semen—boys have none.

What is left to do, then, but initiate boys and thereby masculinize them? Only through initiation can men collectively and immediately put a halt to what they perceive as the stultifying effects of mothering upon their sons. The mother's blood and womb and care, which gave life to and nourished the lad, are finally seen by the secret society [of men] as symbols of anti-life. To undo these feminizing effects, boys must be drastically detached from women and then ritually treated. Thereafter boys avoid women until marriage, by which time the idealized masculine behaviors of initiation have remade the boy into the image of a warrior.

Source: Gilbert Herdt, *The Samba Ritual and Gender in New Guinea* (Fort Worth: Harcourt Brace, 1987).

---

by causing someone to get sick and die. If two people from the same sib married, they would not have any female children, and thus the woman's biological line would die out.

Yapese society was further divided into two major classes: landowners called *pilung,* "those who give the word," and landless serfs called *pimilngay,* "those who run to do it." These two divisions of society formed endogamous castes of landowners and serfs. Marriages of high-caste men to low-caste women have occurred, but only rarely and against great social pressure. Marriages of high-caste women to low-caste men were completely prohibited, and few have ever desired or dared to break this rule.

Yapese also preferred that their children marry someone who lived close by. Parents discouraged their daughters from courting men from villages other than their own unless the man came from a village or estate of high rank and title. The prize for a Yapese girl was to marry a son of a chief or to marry into a higher-ranking village than her own.

Courtship and Exchange   The Yapese viewed the relationship between a man and a woman as a contest of reciprocal exchanges that began with courting and continued until the relationship was dissolved. A man who wanted to establish a relationship with a woman knew he must begin with gifts. However, the Yapese frowned upon any public show of interest or affection. Therefore, a man had to be discreet in how he conveyed his interest. Sharing betel nut was often the first step in initiating the courting relationship.

Betel nut was and is a necessary prerequisite for all social conversation on Yap. For the betel chew, Yapese collect the green nuts of the areca palm, leaves from the pepper vine, and lime made from burnt coral. To make the chew, an individual splits the nut with her teeth, sprinkles lime in its center and wraps it in the pepper leaf. She then places the wad in her mouth and chews it very rapidly and vigorously to mix the lime with the various juices and create the proper chemical reaction. The juice produced by the chemical is bright red and has a mild narcotic effect similar to that produced by cigarette smoking. This juice gradually blackens the teeth if they are not cleaned, and many older Yapese saw betel-blackened teeth as a mark of beauty.

Yapese men and women both carry handbaskets in which they keep all the elements for betel chewing and other personal items, such as combs, wallets, and knives. Each person tries to keep a supply in his or her basket, but everyone depletes one or more of the elements of the betel chew frequently. A common social interaction is to request lime, areca nuts, or pepper leaves from a friend or passerby. This custom provided an opportunity for exploratory courting contacts.

These "casual" encounters allowed the couple to conduct brief conversations to discover whether there was mutual interest. If the girl was receptive, the boy followed with any number of steps. He sometimes sent love notes through a friend or small child, or he conveyed his own message of interest in the few quick moments as they exchanged betel supplies and chewed together. Long public encounters were socially unacceptable, and if a couple lingered too long, their peers taunted them.

When a couple finally agreed upon a "date," they met after dark in a predetermined private place. Bathed and adorned with flowers in their hair and sweet-smelling garlands of leaves around their head or neck, they came ready to exchange their gifts and to sit and talk and chew betel until early morning. The young man usually carried a basketful of betel and other personal gifts such as candy, fragrant soap, or perfume. The young woman brought garlands of flowers or something else she had made. On the first date, the emphasis was on satisfying conversation.

If the first encounter was mutually satisfactory, the frequency of their "chance" public encounters would increase. Through an intermediary they would exchange love messages or notes and plan a second and third meeting. At these later meetings the man again brought gifts, more lavish and generous than before. Men usually also pressed their amour with more fervor, while women generally resisted their advances, testing their commitment.

If a couple was in love, the sharing of sex was the next major test of the relationship. If the sexual encounter was satisfying to both, they continued their affair. However, their relationship remained conditional upon the man's consistent presentation of small gifts and the mutual satisfaction of being together. Elder Yapese often report they had several affairs before they found a satisfying relationship. When the excitement of a new love grew cold, each looked to other partners for the elusive ecstasy of love. Much of the joy was found in the process of courtship, and young people were reluctant to marry until they were in their mid-twenties or even thirties.

Marriage   Marriage was precipitated by two major concerns: weariness of clandestine encounters and pregnancy. Once a couple had established a more or less permanent commitment to each other, they began to talk about marriage. Women were sometimes more reluctant than men to marry because of the added work and responsibility. Once the couple agreed, however, the marriage became public when the man brought his lover home and announced to his father that they wanted to marry. Fathers rarely refused such a request. The typical response was for a man to go with his son to the house of the woman's father to offer a piece of shell money to obtain approval of the marriage. When her father accepted the shell, the marriage was recognized and the couple established their own household at the home of the young man.

Pregnancy created different options. Sometimes pregnancy occurred after a couple had engaged in a fairly long-term relationship. When the pregnancy was obvious, they merely notified their parents. The parents met formally to complete the shell money transaction, and the couple established a household with the husband's family. In some cases, however, the couple may have severed ties, only later to discover the pregnancy. In such a case, the woman's father visited the family of the responsible man to seek a marriage arrangement. If the young man refused to marry the woman, the child was often adopted by her parents. The man might also marry the woman for a short period until the child was born and given a name from his family. By conveying the child's name, the man's family claimed the child as its own and entitled the child to inherit rights to land from the father's estate.

Cars, Beer, and Rock Guitars: Changing Expectations

To the outside observer the most obvious changes on Yap have occurred in the area of courting. Dating between Yapese girls and members of the U.S. military and Peace Corps volunteers has introduced new standards of public behavior. Because Peace Corps volunteers spoke some Yapese and lived in the villages, they influenced village young people who would not otherwise have socialized with Americans. Single Peace Corps volunteers introduced Yapese

Horticultural Societies

Horticulturalists tend to be more settled than either foragers or pastoralists, because they must remain close to their gardens. Most horticulturalists practice slash-and-burn agriculture and do not produce a food surplus or develop stratification. Access to gardens is typically based on membership in a unilineal kin group, and the political organization is typically that of a tribe. However, some horticultural groups, such as the Trobriand Islanders studied by Bronislaw Malinowski, support chiefs, while the lifestyle of other horticultural groups, such as the Yanomamö of Venezuela and Brazil, appears similar to that of foragers.

The Yanomamö of Venezuela and Brazil

Ecology — Rain forest with abundant and varied game and plants.

Group Formation and Residence — Semipermanent villages organized around patrilineal nuclear families, usually brothers; individual homes under a common roof.

Subsistence Base — Slash-and-burn horticulture of plantains, manioc, taro, sweet potato, cane, cotton, and tobacco; foraging for fruits, vegetables, and honey; hunting wild pigs, birds, monkeys, deer, rodents, anteaters, and armadillos; collecting insects, shellfish, and fish.

Division of Labor — Men hunt; women collect plants and fish; women cook and collect firewood; men clear gardens; women tend them.

Exchange Systems — Generalized reciprocity; balanced reciprocity; redistribution through hosting feasts.

Kinship — Patrilineal descent; patrilocal residence; arranged marriages; polygyny; bilateral cross-cousin marriage; sister exchange.

Status and Leadership — Position of village headman based on personal attributes, hosting feasts, and kinship network; villages linked by marriage, feasting, and trading.

Religion — World consists of four layers: originating top layer, second layer where the dead live, third layer where people live, and bottom layer where cannibals live; people developed from blood of the moon; human soul has four parts; illness caused by hekura spirits of early humans; male shamans cure by winning support of hekura, contacted through ingesting hallucinogens.

Expressive Culture — Dramatic storytelling by men.

Cultural Change — Missionaries have introduced guns, diseases, and wage labor; gold miners have polluted streams, driven away game, introduced diseases, and encouraged economic dependence among Yanomamö.

The Mundugumor of New Guinea

Ecology — Varied ecological niches with both forest and river resources; Mundugumor live on high, dry area on the Sepik River between groups occupying mountains and those in low-lying swampy areas, giving Mundugumor a trade advantage.

Group Formation and Residence — Dispersed villages loosely organized around a family composed of a man, his wives and children, as well as dependent relatives.

Subsistence Base	Cut down sago palm for starchy pith; hunt pig or smaller game; cultivate yams, taro, sweet potatoes, greens, coconuts, bananas, and a few other crops; gather tree grubs and vegetables; produce tobacco for trade; also trade betel nut.
Division of Labor	Men fell sago palm, women prepare pitch; men hunt, women fish; both gather; men clear gardens, women tend them; women perform domestic chores and tend children, men construct houses and canoes; women make fishing nets and woven carrying bags, men conduct political activities and warfare.
Exchange Systems	Generalized reciprocity; balanced reciprocity; redistribution.
Kinship	Patrilineal clans; clan exogamy; polygyny; bridewealth; brother–sister exchange; levirate.
Status and Leadership	Big Man complex based on exchange and kinship; relations between villages based on trade and marriage, occasional taking of child hostages to prevent raids.
Religion	World populated by spirits who operate on the principle of exchange; illness or misfortune caused by breaking taboos; spirits placated by observing taboos and making offerings; ghosts of people who had not been buried properly cause harm; shamans and sorcerers.
Cultural Change	Subsistence pattern much the same; introduction of power boats, Catholicism, marketing of tobacco and betel nut; children now leave the village to attend colleges and universities.

The Yap Islanders of the Western Pacific

Ecology	Four high islands surrounded by coral reef; lagoon.
Group Formation and Residence	Permanent villages and a port town.
Subsistence Base	Cultivation of taro, sweet potatoes, yams; fishing for marine resources; production of copra for international market; since 1980s, tourism and American government office work, building of roads and other facilities.
Division of Labor	Men fish, build and repair homes and canoes, clear gardens; women garden, cook, care for children, tend to household needs; since arrival of Americans, both men and women work for wages.
Exchange Systems	Generalized reciprocity; balanced reciprocity, market exchange.
Kinship	Matrilineal descent group or clan; rights to land inherited patrilaterally; patrilocal residence; clan exogamy; caste endogamy; marriage initiated by bride and groom.
Status and Leadership	Traditional ranked leadership vested in elders, based on inheritance rights to lands; since arrival of Americans, elected leaders, formal court system and government; status based on education, wages earned from government jobs.
Religion	Menstrual taboos.
Expressive Culture	Traditional male oratory and weaving of flower garlands by females coexist alongside American movies, television, rock-and-roll bars, guitar playing, singing, dancing, and drinking beer.
Cultural Change	American government and military occupation have effected changes in all aspects of life, including gender relations, the economic and political system, and the expressive culture.

men and women to public dancing in a local bar. Dancing then furnished a new male-female activity in which public personal contact was not only accepted, but expected.

The tactics of courting have also been significantly influenced by the economic and educational changes of the past twenty years. The expectations of transaction between men and women in courtship have not changed, but the materials transacted have. Men in groups of two or three now combine funds to rent a car and then persuade young women to join them for a weekend of guitar playing, singing, and drinking beer in some rural location. To be successful in attracting young women, the men not only have to rent a car, they also have to purchase large quantities of Budweiser beer and other refreshments.

With these significant economic and social changes in courting came attitude changes. Because men spend substantial sums of money for a car and beer, many feel that women are required to reciprocate with sex. Women in turn reject the traditional norm to refrain from drinking in the company of men. This new drinking behavior places them in deeper obligation to men and less able to resist sexual advances.

A few women have developed alternative strategies for courting. On several Friday evenings, I observed two or three young women renting their own car and buying their own cases of beer for the weekend entertainment. Having their own car freed them from economic obligation to young men, and buying their own beer established a basis for balanced exchange. Only employed young women have the financial resources for this style of courtship, however. Unemployed women are at a disadvantage, able only to go out for the weekend as the guest of other women or men and thereby becoming indebted to them.

The Ideal Man, the Ideal Woman, and Marriage

During a conversation with an old Yapese man, Tamag, and his wife, Rungun, she began to complain about her son's wife. She said the girl was frivolous and lazy. All she ever did was comb her hair, make sweet-smelling garlands, and drive around in her husband's car. Rungun added that any girl who drove around in a car and never stayed home could not be good. She was probably flirting with other men when she should be working with her mother-in-law developing her garden. Rungun complained that modern Yapese girls were not learning the proper way of

life. Most of them did not know anything about gardening or preparing food. How could they ever have children and take care of them the way a Yapese woman should?

At this point, Tamag interrupted to say that he had been like his son when he was a young man. He had liked beautiful girls and chased after every pretty grass skirt he saw. He even married a few of those girls, but he did not stay married very long. Then, as he got older, he began to realize that he needed a hard-working wife to feed him and raise heirs for his estate. He began to look around for the right kind of woman who could provide for him in his old age, and that was why he had married Rungun.

Rungun nodded her head with approval and then elaborated further on the ideal Yapese woman. A woman should go to her taro patch and garden early every morning to weed, plant, cultivate, and obtain food for that day. Her garden should be well tended and free of weeds, and she should provide a variety of yams, sweet potatoes, and other vegetable crops to add interest to her family's diet. She should cook each morning and evening, with one pot of food especially for her husband and a separate pot for herself and her children. She should be generous and offer food to her husband's visitors or others who have occasion to stop at the household. Rungun concluded that a good wife should be submissive to her husband and to her mother-in-law.

People in other parts of Yap emphasize these same attributes in the ideal woman. They also express certain expectations for the ideal man. Productive and successful men are as much admired as hard-working women. A poor fisherman makes a poor husband. Fishing is a man's primary occupation, and any meal without fish means a man is not doing an adequate job. If a man is a good fisherman, he will not only get enough for his wife and children, he will be able to share with others as well. Yapese also speak highly of men whose homes are kept in good repair and whose boat or canoe is always ready for use.

Yapese esteem men who are skilled in public speaking and articulate in conversation, and men who can speak with facility and eloquence in public have great potential for political success. Through oratory, they may increase the prestige and influence of their family in the community or obtain lesser punishments for members who have broken community rules. In addition, men who master a body of knowledge and apply it with intelligence for the good of the community earn public renown.

Yapese describe marriage as something of a contest of exchanges between a man and a woman. A man brings the land from his father to his marriage and the woman brings her fertility. The woman works on the man's land and produces food. The man works on the woman's fertility and produces children. The woman nurtures the children with food from her labors, while the man names them with names from his estate and ultimately confers the estate upon them as his heirs.

The Yapese liken a woman to the large stone disks, traditional valuables that are propped against the stone foundations of their houses. The woman stays close to the children and to the land, cultivating both to be productive resources for the larger family and society. She is also a stranger, brought from another place and another family to her husband's home, and, like a piece of stone, is liable to theft by other unscrupulous men. Her mother-in-law thus keeps a careful eye on her to prevent casual encounters with men who might steal her away.

Men, on the other hand, are likened to shell valuables, which they exchange at political events between estates and between villages. A man conducts the public affairs of the family. He represents his family in meetings of his local community and goes with other men of the community to participate in events and affairs outside the community.

Marriage Exchange Because of the fragile nature of Yapese marriage, families generally do not celebrate the event with public ceremony until sometime after the first or second child is born. If the couple has been married for several years, if they have a child or children, and if it looks as though they may have an enduring relationship, the families of the couple may plan a "marriage exchange."

The exchange between the two families symbolizes the daily exchange between the man and woman as they contribute their diverse productive activities to the welfare and survival of the family. The woman's family gives stone valuables, symbolizing both the woman's role as the foundation of the family and their desire to anchor her and her children to the land of her husband's estate. In addition, the woman's family contributes large quantities of the products of a woman's labor, including taro and baskets of yams and other vegetable foods, which the wife and her female relatives have produced in their gardens.

The husband's family reciprocates with the products of a man's labor. The men of the husband's family attempt to bring baskets of fish and coconuts equivalent to the baskets of vegetable food they receive from the wife's family. In addition, they may contribute shell valuables equivalent to the stone valuables they will receive. In these exchanges, as in the routine of daily life, the wife's side often wins the contest, because a woman's diligent work ensures a stable supply of vegetable crops, whereas fishing is a more uncertain enterprise, subject to the vagaries of weather, tides, and luck.

Wage Work and Power: Relations between Men and Women

Wage work and the money economy introduced new variables and potentials into the marriage exchange, upsetting the traditional economic balance and threatening the very structure of marriage relations. A man's work in town cut sharply into his available time for the domestic labor traditionally required of him. Weekdays are spent working; weekends are spent celebrating.

Money, however, allows a man to maintain his economic responsibilities. He can purchase canned fish, beef, and other meats to fulfill his subsistence obligations. He can buy nails, sheet metal, and corrugated iron roofing to eliminate most of the house maintenance required for traditional thatch and bamboo. He can substitute coffee, tea, and chocolate for coconuts and can summon sons or younger brothers to pick breadfruit when it is in season. The only task for which he cannot find a functional equivalent is clearing forest land for new yam gardens.

Wage labor provides a man with other economic advantages, however. His cash income allows the purchase of clothing for himself, his wife, and their children, effectively eliminating one of his wife's traditional contributions to the relationship. Weaving loincloths and making grass skirts have become peripheral activities. The husband's income also permits the purchase of rice, eliminating the necessity for his wife to garden. As a result, cash shifts the traditional economic advantage and power from a woman to a man.

In the traditional marriage, the woman's vegetable products sustained the Yapese household. Without them, the family could not survive. Today, her garden can be replaced with purchased bags of rice. Her power as producer of Yapese staple crops has been undercut by her husband's power through money. The symbolic exchange between a man's family and a woman's family no longer expresses the structural facts of the marriage relationship. A man now holds all the trump cards in the contest, and the balance of transactions has shifted in his favor.

Many Yapese women are unwilling to let their power pass easily, and they continue to produce the majority of the vegetables consumed by their family. Others accept freedom from garden labor as the price of increased dependence on their husbands. To these women, the duties of cooking and child care are demanding enough. They readily relinquish the heavy labor of gardening.

Education and experience with outsiders have also altered the expectations of many men with regard to the social skills of a wife. Some men now demand that their wives accompany them to public functions and interact with American officials and their wives. A traditional Yapese woman is totally unprepared for such encounters and can offer little public support for an upwardly mobile husband. He may begin to feel cheated in the relationship because his wife demands more goods and entertainment but cannot reciprocate by fulfilling his social and political needs. He may look elsewhere for a better-educated woman with the social skills to enter these new experiences with ease.

Both men and women expect warm companionship and sexual satisfaction in marriage, and if they do not find them they may begin to search elsewhere. Men who work in town and live in the village have limited interaction with their spouses and children. In addition, some men who work in government and business find the conversations and gossip of village life less and less interesting. Some who have had college training find their uneducated wives unable to understand some of their feelings and experiences. At the same time, these men interact daily with educated Yapese women or more cosmopolitan town women who frequent the businesses and bars. Many Yapese marriages today suffer from the stresses emerging from the new town-oriented lifestyle.

New Ideals for Men and Women

Changing ideals for women most graphically illustrate the generational conflict between Yapese elders and youth. Education was the first radical step. The American government required both boys and girls to attend elementary school, and Yapese parents generally supported this rule. At first, girls who began to menstruate followed the traditional custom of living in menstrual houses, where they were isolated from community life for one year. At that time, most Yapese women went to menstrual houses during their monthly period, so girls always had some adult female company. Older women instructed the girls in taboos and restrictions governing menstruation and, by word and example, taught them the standards for an ideal Yapese woman.

As the American program of education improved, many communities began to allow girls to remain in school even after they began their menses, therefore missing much of the instruction in traditional beliefs and rules disseminated in the menstrual houses. This radical change in a woman's education altered Yapese ideals of what a woman is and ought to be.

In the late 1950s and early 1960s, some young women were educated abroad and returned to serve in important positions in education, administration, and public health, furnishing new models of femininity. These educated women represent the antithesis of the traditional, homebound woman, surrounded by her children and subservient to her husband and mother-in-law.

Educated women often earn a substantial income, making them economically self-sufficient and independent. Most have married Yapese men who are well educated and occupy contemporary positions of authority and prestige. All these women are articulate in English and have cultivated an ability to move in the public eye with assurance and ease. At the same time they are capable Yapese. Most still cultivate some village gardens and meet kinship and village social obligations. They are mobile, moving easily from town to village and back to town, driving by themselves or with their husbands.

Ideals for men have also changed, but not nearly so radically. Education is also the key to prestige for men, and a college degree is a must for the politically ambitious. Public professionalism is not new for Yapese men, however. In the traditional culture, many men were experts in building, fishing, magic, or other skills; now they are experts as legislators, administrators, educators, craftsmen, or technical specialists. Yapese men have always been mobile; today that mobility has expanded—many leaders have traveled extensively abroad, and some have even been around the world. It is still important that men be articulate, and the most prominent men speak at least two languages fluently.

Two significant masculine models emerge in this new setting: (1) the traditional Yapese man who derives power and authority from land and who has successfully adapted to the changing times and (2) the new college-educated man who has become successful in contemporary politics. The traditional men have earned fame by business acumen and increasing wealth. The educated men have earned fame by political acumen and increasing prestige. Both have exhibited a marked degree of individualism and personal independence not ordinarily sought or considered desirable in the traditional context.

SUMMARY

Horticulturalists subsist by gardening without the use of plows or irrigation. They do not produce a food surplus as do intensive agriculturalists, and they do not exhibit stratification or the development of cities. Instead, horticulturalists live in villages that allow them to settle close to their gardens. Leadership is based on ability rather than office.

The Yanomamö supplement their diet—which centers on cultivating plantain, manioc, taro, and sweet potato—by hunting game animals, gathering wild fruits and honey, and a limited amount of fishing. They live in villages of from forty to more than a hundred people. The Yanomamö leader has no official authority. Instead, he influences the behavior of others through his example.

Alliances between villages are established through exchange, ceremonial feasting, and marriage. Trade alliances are formed along the lines of balanced reciprocity, and gift exchanges in the form of generalized reciprocity ensure continued interaction between members of different villages. Similarly, ceremonial feasting promotes exchange between groups. Polygyny and cross-cousin marriage link different villages together and allow Yanomamö leaders to extend their base of support beyond their own local group.

The Yanomamö believe the universe consists of four layers and that humans were created from the blood of Moon when he was shot in the belly. These early humans continue to exist in spirit form as hekura. Just as there are four parts to the universe, there are four parts to the Yanomamö soul. Illness is caused when hekura eat a portion of a person's soul. Healing can take place only at the behest of a shaman, who has undergone a long period of training and purification to attract hekura to live in his own chest. Shamans have access to the hekura only when under the influence of hallucinogenic drugs. When a Yanomamö person dies, his body is cremated and the ashes are ritually consumed by grieving relatives.

The Mundugumor of New Guinea are known to people in the United States through the writings of Margaret Mead. The Mundugumor supplemented their staple food, sago, with fish, tree grubs, and wild pigs, as well as leafy green vegetables grown in gardens or gathered in the forest. Trade was an important economic and political activity for the Mundugumor, who acquired pottery and other important goods from river-dwelling people and acted as middlemen in a system of exchange that linked mountain areas with the sea.

As in other New Guinea groups, Mundugumor leaders were Big Men, men who extended their influence by negotiating favorable marriages and conducting shrewd investments of valued goods, especially pigs. Men also gained status through warfare, and much effort was centered around this activity. Men acquired wives through the levirate, paying bridewealth, raiding enemy villages, and brother–sister exchange. As were gender roles, economic activities, and political activities, marriage was based on the principle of reciprocity. Mead suggested that marriage exchanges were more important than descent groups in binding Mundugumor society together.

The principle of reciprocity was also extended to the spirit world. The Mundugumor believed that breaking a taboo invited punitive retaliation from a water or bush spirit. On the other hand, making an offering obligated a spirit to reciprocate in some way, such as healing an illness. Spirits of the dead, or ghosts, could harm living humans if they were not placated by the appropriate funeral rituals.

The village studied by Margaret Mead in 1932 looks much the same today. The economy is still based on exchange, and sago remains the dietary staple. But people of the village now attend the Catholic church; take goods to market in power canoes, trucks, or airplanes; and send their children away to study at colleges and universities.

Yap Islanders of the western Pacific traditionally cultivated taro and yams in their gardens and fished on the reef along the island. Now, however, half the adult population of the main port town work at jobs created by U.S. military and administrative operations. These wage earners buy canned fish, rice, and other goods.

Since World War II, Yapese have been exhorted to attend American schools, seek treatment from American doctors, and work to supply American officials with electricity, abundant fresh water, shipping facilities, and American-style homes and roads. The port town of Colonia serves as a crossroads, bringing goods to Yap from the rest of the world, but the Yapese have little but their labor to offer the world in exchange.

Yapese seek college educations to compete for office jobs in government or private businesses. Informal education is provided by American movies, radio, and television. American values are transmitted to Yapese by government officials, who insist that Yapese elect their leaders, rather than follow the guidance of traditional leaders, who were esteemed for their oratory skills and their land rights acquired through clan membership.

American influence has also altered the traditional system of courtship and marriage. Courtship was formerly carried out in secret, since the Yapese frown on public displays of affection, and young people of both sexes could engage in a series of relationships. Because of American influence, young Yapese now show affection in public and dance to rock-and-roll music in Colonia bars. Because courting now costs more, young men often expect sexual favors from the women. Some employed Yapese women free themselves from economic obligations to the men by underwriting the cost of entertainment.

The Yapese view marriage as an exchange. In the traditional marriage, a woman tends gardens and prepares food for her husband and children. A woman is submissive to her husband and mother-in-law. The ideal man is a good fisherman and keeps his home and boat in good repair. The Yapese compare a woman to the traditional stone disk that is propped against the foundation of their homes; a man is like the shell valuables exchanged at political events. Women secure the home; men conduct public affairs of the family.

The introduction of wage work has upset the traditional exchange system and has tipped the balance of marriage relations in favor of males. The husband's wages allow the purchase of food and goods traditionally produced by women. As a result, the traditional woman's power of providing for her family has been preempted by the man's power to earn money.

The American influence has also increased the gap between the generations, a change that is especially apparent for women. When American education was introduced, some girls left the islands for further schooling in Hawaii or the Philippines. These women now occupy positions of importance, furnishing new role models for Yapese women. They often earn a substantial income, making them economically independent.

Ideals for men have also changed, but not so radically, since men have always occupied positions of public prominence. Traditionally, prestige accrued to men who had skill in fishing, oratory, and inheritance of ancestral lands. Now men can increase their status through earning a college degree and becoming an expert administrator, teacher, or public official.

The Yanomamö, the Mundugumor, and the Yapese represent a range of adaptations based on horticulture. The Yanomamö are more dependent on foraging than are the other two groups, and their social organization reflects the importance of warfare and alliances generated and reinforced through kinship and various types of exchange. The Mundugumor are an example of the New Guinea Big Man complex. The extension of U.S. political control over the Yap Islands has disrupted their traditional social organization, based on matrilineal descent and reciprocity in marriage. The introduction of education based on the U.S. model has also altered relations between the generations.

POWER WORDS

sib   subincision

INTERNET EXERCISE

1. A two-minute version of the film *The Ax Fight*, produced by Napoleon A. Chagnon and Timothy Asch, can be viewed at **http://www.anth.ucsb.edu/projects/axfight/**. Based on this brief look at conflict among the Yanomamö, out of the context of other aspects of their lives, is it fair to call them "the fierce people"?

2. Learn more about the people, arts, and culture of New Guinea at **http://www.niugini.com/**, a website maintained by the government of Papua New Guinea.

3. The article by Sherwood G. Lingenfelter in this chapter suggests that the traditional way of life of Yap Islanders has been dramatically changed as a result of U.S. influence. The website **http://www.destmic.com/yap.html** is designed to lure tourists, especially those interested in diving. Compare the description of the lives of Yap Islanders on the website to that of the anthropologist given in this chapter.

14

Agriculturalists

In this chapter...

The agricultural way of life

Agricultural societies produce a food surplus through the use of the plow, irrigation, and often fertilizer. The food surplus allows the development of stratification and the accumulation of great stores of wealth. It also results in increased population and task specialization, including artisans who can produce a variety of utilitarian and luxury goods. Protecting these resources requires a standing army, typically under the command of a ruler who has power of life and death over his subjects.

The Aztecs of central Mexico

Aztec society was at its peak in the sixteenth century. Rulers of the city-state of Tenochtitlán lived in exquisitely designed palaces, wore richly decorated garments, and presided over a stratified society. Elaborate temples were maintained by a hierarchy of priests. Through their military prowess, Aztec rulers maintained political dominance over a number of city-states. The arts—literature, sculpture, oratory, and music—flourished. With the arrival of the Spanish, this rich society was reduced to ruins, most of the literature was lost, and the stones of the razed city were used to construct the new Spanish capital of Mexico City.

The Nayar of southern India

The Nayar, a warrior subcaste, have long fascinated anthropologists because of their unique system of marriage and family organization centering on matrilineages. Because women produced children for their own kin group, they were not required to form exclusive alliances with one man; instead, they and their children resided in a household with their matrilineal kin. As a result of British occupation, economic pressures, and internal political changes, the traditional matrilineal system is being replaced by a more male-dominated system characteristic of other parts of India.

The Han of northern China

The Han illustrate four important conflicts that arise in complex societies: they occupy a disputed territory on the border of two competing nation-states; farmers and pastoralists exist side by side with differing subsistence needs and social organization; the Han must contend with ethnic tensions arising from their migration into Mongol lands; and they must mediate between the demands of national policy and local traditions. The Han provide a picture of differences in subsistence adaptations that permeate every aspect of life, from the organization of labor to relations between women and men.

Agricultural societies can be distinguished from groups who practice other methods of subsistence by several characteristics: large populations, concentrated mostly in cities; stratification and accumulation of vast wealth by a nobility; and the dominance of a ruling class extended over a broad region through trade or warfare.

In general, intensive agricultural societies are associated with the state form of political organization; that is, they are hierarchical and organized around bureaucracy rather than kinship. States exercise control over a regional territory, and leadership is based on office rather than demonstrated ability. Heads of states generally have power of life and death over their subjects, can exact tribute or taxes, command the labor and resources of others, and maintain a standing army.

The food surplus generated by intensive agriculture permits a high degree of task specialization. Artisans flourish, and their crafts are eagerly sought by the nobility and wealthy merchants. Large-scale ceremonies and festivals entertain the public and enhance the power of the rulers. In most cases, religious leaders gain high status and preside over important ritual complexes, while shamans may continue to

Intensive agriculture produces a food surplus sufficient to support task specialization, stratification, and a large settled population. These corn and wheat fields in the St. Lawrence River basin of Canada illustrate a rural settlement pattern characteristic of North American agricultural societies.

serve as healers and informal counselors to the less affluent.

Some anthropologists suggest that, whereas forager and horticultural groups remain stable through time, societies based on intensive agriculture follow a cycle of florescence and collapse. Forager and horticultural societies may be more stable because their population remains small, and their more egalitarian form of social organization precludes the accumulation of wealth that attracts invaders. According to this theory, stratified societies based on intensive agriculture eventually collapse, either because of overexploitation of the environment to meet the demands of their large populations or as a result of being conquered from outside.

Since the rise of food production around ten thousand years ago, world history has been littered with the rubble of intensive agricultural societies that have risen to regional prominence, built great cities, and then collapsed. In the Mediterranean area, Sumer, Babylon, Egypt, and classical Greece and Rome have all "danced their hour upon the stage," to paraphrase William Shakespeare. In Southeast Asia, the ancient ruins of Angkor Wat stand as grim sentinels to the dangers of dynasty.

The three intensive agricultural societies described in this chapter (see Figure 14.1) have all undergone reversals of fortune as the result of incursions from outside or armed conflict within. The Aztecs of Central America were at the peak of their civilization when they were overrun by the Spanish in the sixteenth century. We will never know whether they would inevitably have gone through a period of decline, as the Mayans farther south did. The Mayans had abandoned their great cities by the time the Spanish arrived.

The Nayars still occupy the state of Kerala in southern India, but their traditional way of life was dramatically altered by British colonial powers. The Nayars were a warrior subcaste at the pinnacle of southern India's elaborate system of class and caste. They have long fascinated anthropologists because of their extreme matrilineal, matrilocal, extended-family form of social organization. The essay in this chapter describes the shift to a more male-oriented system—a result of economic, political, and legal challenges to the traditional way of life.

In modern times, China has been beset by political incursions by the British and Japanese, internal political upheaval, and a potentially devastating problem of overpopulation. The Han are a unique case that represents classic themes of complex agricultural societies. They live near the Great Wall on China's northern frontier bordering Russia, a traditionally disputed territory. Thus, in their daily lives they continuously enact the brinkmanship of competition between nation-states. Han farmers share their rugged environment with pastoralists, who have different subsistence needs, organization of labor, and family structure. In addition, the Han have undergone a period of social experimentation instituted by Chinese communist leaders, who emphasized collective farming and a form of social organization oriented toward the state. This system is in direct conflict with the traditional Chinese system centering on the family and village.

These three groups—Aztecs, Nayars, and Han—represent very different cultural traditions. Because of their shared dependence on agriculture, however, they together illustrate the effects of stratification and the state form of political organization on the ordering of daily life.

THE AZTECS OF CENTRAL MEXICO*

No one knows the origins of the Aztecs, only that they migrated into the Valley of Mexico from some place farther north, called Aztlan ("Place of the Heroes").

---

*This section owes much to Frances F. Berdan's account of the Aztecs, *The Aztecs of Central Mexico: An Imperial Society* (Fort Worth, TX: Holt, Rinehart and Winston, 1982), supplemented by other sources.

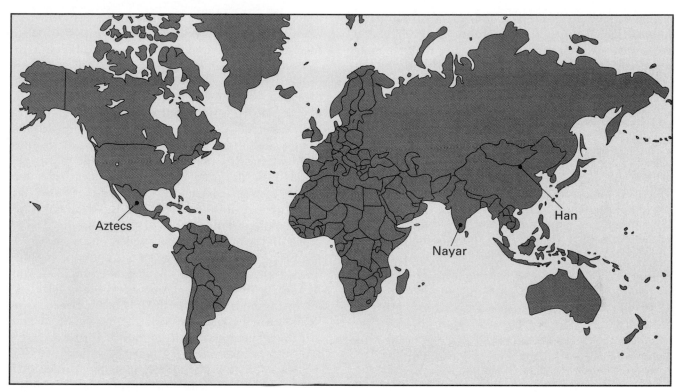

FIGURE 14.1 Agriculturalists

Though they inhabit geographically disparate regions of the world, the groups described in this chapter—the Aztecs of central Mexico, the Nayar of southern India, and the Han of northern China—display the common characteristics of stratification that are associated with intensive agriculture. The Aztecs developed a priestly complex based on maize (corn) production and conquest; the Nayar were an upper-caste warrior group organized around matrilineal descent; Han farmers have established an agricultural stronghold along China's northern border, displacing Mongolian pastoralists.

The exact location of their original home is now shrouded in speculation and myth. It could have been as close as seventy miles northwest of Mexico City or as far away as the American Southwest. An anonymous sixteenth-century Spanish conqueror describes the Aztecs, who called themselves the Mexica:

> The people of this province are well proportioned, tending to be tall rather than short; they are swarthy or brownish, of good features and mien. For the most part they are very skillful, stalwart and tireless, yet they sustain themselves with less food than any other people. They are very warlike and fearless of death. (cited in De Fuentes 1963:168)

Another sixteenth-century Spaniard notes: "Their understanding is keen, modest, and quiet, not proud or showy as in other nations" (Motolinía [1536–1543] 1950:168).

In 1325, the Aztecs established their capital at Tenochtitlan, near the heart of what is now Mexico City. The Valley of Mexico covers two thousand five hundred square miles and lies at an elevation of over seven thousand feet. It is surrounded by low hills to the north and mountains to the west, south, and east. Some mountains have perpetually snowcapped peaks reaching elevations of more than seventeen thousand feet. This diverse terrain presented the Aztecs with a variety of ecological niches, each offering different potentials for human use.

A series of connected lakes added to the ecological variety. During the fifteenth century, the Aztecs undertook massive feats of engineering to control flooding and improve water quality. They built dikes, aqueducts, canals, and causeways, or raised roads. The lakes provided an effective means of transportation and were laden with canoe traffic supporting commerce throughout the valley. The lakes also supplied varied and abundant aquatic resources, including fish, birds, reptiles, and amphibians. The Spanish conqueror Bernal Díaz del Castillo describes the scene:

> When we saw so many cities and villages built on the water and other great towns on dry land and that straight and level Causeway going towards Mexico [Tenochtitlan], we were amazed and said that it was like the enchantments they tell of in the legend of Amadis, on account of the great towers and cues [temples] and buildings rising from the water, and all built of masonry. And some of our soldiers even asked whether the things that we saw were not a dream. ([1560s] 1956:190–191)

By the time the Spanish arrived in 1519, the Aztecs had forged alliances with their neighbors to the east and west, the Acolhuacans of Texcoco and the Tepanecas of Tlacopan. Together, these three groups forged a vast empire in Mesoamerica, called the Triple Alliance or the Aztec Empire (Berdan 1982:2).

Economic Organization

Maize, or corn, was at the heart of Aztec agriculture and the mainstay of the Aztec diet. Aztecs also cultivated beans, chiles, squashes, prickly pear cactus, maguey, and a multitude of other fruits and vegetables. Many deities were dedicated to fertility, and some looked specifically after corn. During May, the Aztecs venerated the corn goddess Chicomecoatl ("Seven Serpent") and carried out rituals to ensure the arrival of sufficient rain and a bountiful crop.

Domesticated animals were few, but important in the diet. Turkeys were raised for meat and eggs; dogs provided companionship and meat. The versatile maguey plant, a succulent of the agave family, was used for medicine and for producing an alcoholic drink called *pulque*. Its fibers were used for clothing and its thorns, for sewing needles. Maguey was personified as Mayahuel, a fertility goddess with four hundred (i.e., innumerable) breasts. Cotton and cacao—both considered elite goods—were cultivated in the more distant reaches of the empire.

Central American farmers relied on two means of producing crops: fallowing and irrigation. In some cases, these techniques may have been supplemented by the use of terracing, crop rotation, and fertilizers. Fallowing involved cultivating land for two or three years, allowing it to rest for an equal period of time, and then recultivating it. Floodwater irrigation systems were constructed in some shallow lake beds, but *chinampas*, highly productive plots of land claimed from the shallow beds of freshwater lakes, were the most intensive form of irrigation. Misnamed "floating gardens," chinampas are still cultivated in and around Xochimilco, in the southern part of the Valley of Mexico, and are a popular tourist attraction.

Foraging Farmers supplemented agriculture by gathering wild plants, hunting, fishing, and fowling.

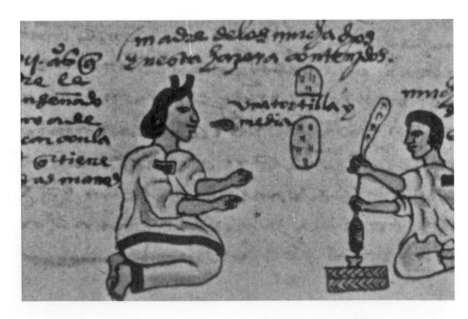

The wealth of Aztec society sustained a wide variety of artisans, who produced objects of great artistic value from gold, various types of stone, and feathers. However, women of all social classes were expected to spin and weave. Here, in a drawing from the *Codex Mendoza* of about 1550, an Aztec woman teaches her daughter to spin.

Herbs, fruits, wood products, and salt were especially sought, and medicinal herbs were in high demand. The hallucinogens peyote and a species of mushroom were also used for medicinal purposes. Aztecs hunted land and water animals for food and skins, but some animals were also captured for the rulers' zoos and as pets. Deer, rabbits, hares, opossum, armadillos, pocket gophers, wild boars, and tapirs were all eaten. The skins of jaguars and deer were prized; rabbit fur was spun, dyed, and applied to expensive capes.

The lakes and lake shores teemed with animals, fish, and waterfowl. Turtles, salamanders, frogs, tadpoles, mollusks, and crustaceans were abundant and were prized as food. Many varieties of large and small fish were caught in the lakes and streams with the aid of nets and spears. Ducks were especially abundant in the lake areas, but geese, cranes, pelican, and a number of other birds were also plentiful and popular. The nobility dined on other wild birds, including quail, pheasants, partridges, and pigeons. Birds were sought for both meat and feathers; featherworking was valued by the Aztecs as one of their finest artistic skills.

A great many other foods were gleaned from the environment. These included locusts, grubs, fish eggs, lizards, honey, and *tecuitlatl*, a green lake scum formed by water fly eggs; tecuitlatl was made into bread with a cheeselike flavor (Díaz del Castillo [1560s] 1956:217).

Craft Production Craft manufacture was highly specialized in central Mexico. Entire neighborhoods of Tenochtitlan and other major urban centers were populated by full-time artisans and merchants. In Texcoco, for example, each of more than thirty occupations, including goldworkers, silverworkers, painters, lapidaries, and featherworkers, had its own residential section in the city. These artisans were organized into guilds, each with its own neighborhood; control over membership, education, and ranking; ethnic origins; and patron deities and religious ceremonies.

Trade and Professional Merchants Virtually everyone in central Mexico could engage in trade. At the simplest level, any family could sell the household surplus in the marketplace. Professional merchants dealt in relatively large lots of goods and traded in luxury items that were the prerogative of the nobility. Professional merchants conducted exchanges both in marketplaces and in ports of trade beyond the boundaries of the empire.

Almost all communities had a marketplace, but those of the major cities displayed an enormous array of goods. Utilitarian goods ranged from many varieties of corn and chiles to pottery, firewood, mats, lumber, and clothing. Numerous vendors sold cooked food. Luxury wares included ornate clothing, tropical feathers, precious gems, gold ornaments, and cacao beans. Services were also for hire: barbers, porters, carpenters, artisans, and prostitutes plied their trades in the marketplace.

Kinship and Social Organization

As in other complex, stratified societies, Aztec social organization provided for differential allocation of power, privilege, prestige, and property. Aztec positions were both ascribed and achieved. **Ascribed status** is assigned at birth; **achieved status** is attained by an individual on the basis of skills or qualities.

Class The fundamental social division in Aztec society was between the nobility and the commoners, with intermediate positions occupied by certain specialists, largely merchants and artisans of luxury goods. The distinction between nobility and commoners was theoretically established by birth. To be considered of noble birth, Aztecs had to be able to trace descent from the first ruler, Acamapichtli. This was probably not an exclusive company, since many nobles practiced polygyny, and the Aztec descent system was bilateral. The lineage of nobles was figured along sacred as well as secular lines of descent. Their founding ancestor was believed to be the god Quetzalcoatl, creator of human beings and the deity who first supplied humans with the staple crop maize.

Only rulers could wear the most expensive decorated cotton cloaks, and the relative ranking of nobles was indicated by the quality of their cloaks. Commoners were allowed to wear only the simplest clothing made of maguey or palm fiber. The cloak of a commoner could not reach below his knee, unless he had been wounded as a warrior:

> And so it was that when one encountered a person who wore his mantle [cloak] longer than the laws permitted, one immediately looked at his legs. If he had wounds acquired in war he would be left in peace, and if he did not, he would be killed. They would say, "Since that leg

did not flee from the sword, it is just that it be rewarded and honored." (Durán [1581] 1964:132).

Only the ruler and other nobles could wear gold headbands with feathers, gold armbands, lip plugs, ear plugs, and nose plugs fashioned of gold and precious stones. Only the ruler and his second-in-command could wear sandals in the ruler's palace. Only certain nobles were granted permission to wear sandals at all. Warriors who had performed great feats in battle could wear sandals and certain adornments, but these must be "cheap and common" in materials and design. Only nobles could construct houses with two stories.

Commoners and nobles were judged in separate courts and had different access to resources. Nobles were judged by a stricter moral code. For example, public drunkenness was a serious offense for all but the elderly. A commoner discovered drunk in public would be shamed by having his head shaved, but a noble would be put to death. The nobility controlled most of the strategic economic resources of the empire, especially land. Commoners, through their tribute obligations, worked the land and provided the nobility with clothing, status-linked ornaments and paraphernalia, and such daily household requirements as firewood and water.

The Noble Ranks The nobility was made up of three subclasses: (1) *tlatoque*, or "rulers," (2) *tetecutin*, or "chiefs," and (3) *pipiltin*, or "sons of nobility." A *tlatoani* (singular form of *tlatoque*) was ruler of a region or town or, in some cases, a section of a town or city. The tlatoque controlled tribute paid by commoners in their jurisdiction, controlled privately owned lands, and managed the labor and tribute of their rural tenants. Tlatoque were responsible for organizing military activities, sponsoring certain religious celebrations, and adjudicating disputes not resolved at a lower level.

Tlatoque of conquered areas paid tribute to the more powerful tlatoque of the Triple Alliance capitals, who were at the apex of the imperial political system. These rulers controlled extensive private lands by virtue of their noble birth and exacted tribute from conquered areas. The tlatoani at Tenochtitlan presided over a regal household:

> His dress was rich and elegant, his dwelling pleasant and extensive, his servants and slaves numerous, and his recreations varied. He particularly was amused by jugglers, acrobats, and jesters kept in his household; he wagered heavily in the ball game . . . ; he hunted

game and birds; he sang, and was told proverbs and tales for his enjoyment. He also ate well. (Berdan 1982:51)

The next lower rank of nobility was made up of the numerous *tetecutin*, who attained their impressive titles primarily through military successes. However, it was usually mandatory that the tetecutin be nobles by birth. The Aztec ruler could bestow or create titles as he wished, and in many cases these titles would be distributed among his own kin group. The pipiltin, children of rulers and chiefs, were attached to the household in which they were born. Some pipiltin succeeded to the rank of ruler or chief, while many others served as administrators in the far-flung realms of the Triple Alliance. Only nobles could attend the *calmecac*, a school providing instruction in the martial arts, religion, politics, history, law, astrology, and other subjects considered essential to administering the empire.

Commoners Most people of central Mexico were commoners. They tilled the soil, fished, and practiced various types of crafts, and all paid tribute to some member of the nobility. In addition, commoners formed the rank and file of the military. The lifestyle of commoners varied according to their ability to control resources, but none could wear or display ornaments or insignia of the nobility.

Most commoners were grouped into *calpulli*, wards or neighborhoods of a city with rights to the use of certain lands. A member of a calpulli was allocated rights to work a particular parcel of land and could pass on these rights to his heirs. If a landholder failed to work his land, went to live in another calpulli, or committed a crime, the land reverted to the calpulli and was reallocated. Each calpulli had its own *telpochcalli* ("young men's house"), a school that focused on training for war.

Mayeque, or rural tenants, occupied a position much like that of serfs in medieval Europe, in that they were attached to the lands of the nobility:

> These mayeques could not leave the land to which they were attached. . . . The sons and heirs of the lords of such lands succeeded to them, and the land passed together with the mayeques who lived on it. . . . The rent consisted in payment of a part of the mayeque's harvest to the lord, or in working a piece of land for the lord, and varied according to the number of mayeques and their agreement with the lord. (Zorita [1570s or 1580s] 1963:182–183)

Slaves *Tlacotin*, or slaves, generally consisted of two categories. Those captured in warfare were usually sacrificed to the gods and, as a result, became heroes in the afterlife. In other cases, people became slaves because of gambling, poverty, failing to pay tribute, or for committing a crime. A person could sell himself or a member of his family into slavery. If someone died without paying a debt, the wife or son might become a slave in payment of the debt. Aside from the obligation of rendering service to his owner, the tlacotli retained most of his personal freedoms, including rights to marriage and property. In some cases, tlacotin amassed considerable amounts of property, even owning slaves themselves.

Kinship Aztec kinship was traced bilaterally, with patrilineal inheritance of titles and position and bilateral inheritance of property. Daughters could not inherit titles directly, but they could transmit their father's position on to their sons. Marriages of nobles were usually arranged to establish or reinforce political alliances. For example, through the fifteenth and sixteenth centuries, the royal families of Texcoco and Teotihuacan maintained close political ties through cross-cousin marriage. Typically, a ruler of Teotihuacan married his mother's brother's daughter, a royal female cross-cousin from Texcoco. There were no fixed rules of exogamy beyond a prohibition against marrying within the nuclear family. Nobles practiced polygyny, but commoners apparently did not. The oldest son of the principal wife of a noble was considered the legitimate heir, but children of other wives were also considered noble and inherited property rights if their mothers were of the nobility.

Imperial Politics and Warfare

At the center of Aztec political institutions was the city-state, a large community that served as the political, economic, and religious center of its surrounding dependent areas. Typically, the dependent districts were politically and militarily subject to the center, providing considerable amounts of tribute in goods and services. During the brief history of the Aztec empire, power was increasingly consolidated at Tenochtitlan, but the empire remained loosely organized.

Government Each city-state was the domain of a ruler, or tlatoani. Some of these rulers were autonomous; others were under the domination of powerful imperial rulers, such as those of the Triple Alliance. The tlatoani conducted wars, meted out justice, and supervised major rituals. He was at the same time the advocate of the rights of the nobility, defender of the commoners, and benefactor to the poor. The tlatoani of Tenochtitlan was considered the earthly counterpart of a god. Upon his coronation, the ruler was told:

> Now thou art deified. Although thou art human, as are we, although thou art our friend, although thou art our son . . . no more art thou human, as are we; we do not look to thee as human. . . . He [the god] is within thee, he speaketh forth from thy mouth. Thou art his lips, thou art his jaw, thou art his tongue, thou art his eyes, thou art his ears. (Sahagún [1569] 1950–1969: 52–53)

The Tenochtitlan tlatoani had to be both warrior and diplomat, tried in battle and elegant in speech. He was chosen by the supreme council of four advisers, all of whom were from the same family as the ruler. A ruler began coronation ceremonies by paying homage to the Aztec patron god Huitzilopochtli at his temple, fasting, and offering a sacrifice of his own blood to the god. The new ruler then departed on a war of conquest to prove his mettle on the battlefield and to provide prisoners for the human sacrifices that would honor his inauguration.

Warfare and Conquest Warfare touched virtually all aspects of Aztec life: social, political, economic, and religious. At birth, a boy was dedicated to the battlefield, and a mother who died in childbirth was likened to a warrior. A man slain on the battlefield, an individual sacrificed to the gods, and a woman who died in childbirth were granted a glorious afterlife. Successful warriors were rewarded with food and luxury goods acquired as tribute.

Since Tenochtitlan was not economically self-sufficient, it required external material support in the form of tribute from conquered provinces. Warfare was justified by their patron deity Huitzilopochtli, and captured enemy warriors would be sacrificed to provide food for the gods to keep the universe intact. Thus, for political, economic, and religious reasons, it was essential that warfare be fairly continuous.

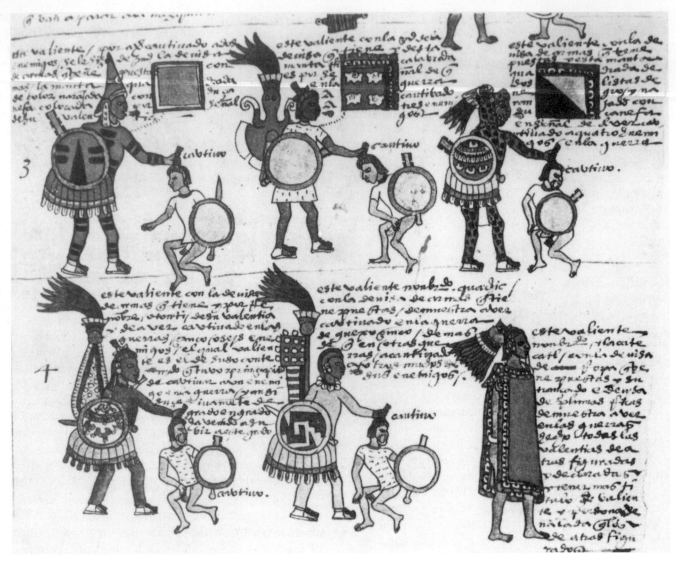

The Aztecs developed a stratified society based on cultivation of maize and other crops. However, their economy and political organization centered on conquest, which yielded tribute in the form of food, consumer goods, and precious metals. Aztec warfare also produced captives for use in human sacrifice.

The Aztecs were brilliant military strategists, and a great number of cities and city-states fell to their armies, which included warriors from Tenochtitlan, Texcoco, and Tlacopan, as well as soldiers from previously conquered cities. Immediately upon capturing a city, the Aztecs burned the major temple, thus asserting the supremacy of Huitzilopochtli over the local patron deity. The next order of business was to arrange the amount of tribute the conquered city would pay. The Aztecs rarely razed cities or destroyed populations because doing so would have been counterproductive to the goal of ensuring a continuous source of tribute.

Religious Belief and Ritual

Religious themes permeated every aspect of Aztec life, from planting crops to conducting warfare to the daily cycle of the sun. The sun was believed to be the god Huitzilopochtli, and other gods governed other forces of nature. Human sacrifice held a prominent place in Aztec ritual because it was believed that the deified sun needed to be fed human blood to maintain his dominion over the moon and stars. Theoretically, all sacrifices were to the sun god, but other gods, such as Tlaloc, the rain god, also demanded their share of blood.

Human Sacrifice Many sacrificial victims were enemy soldiers captured in war. When Hernán Cortés attempted to invade Tenochtitlan in 1521, sixty-two of his soldiers were captured and sacrificed. Among the horrified Spanish onlookers was Díaz del Castillo, who described the scene:

> The dismal drum of Huichilobos [Huitzilopochtli] sounded again, accompanied by conches, horns, and trumpetlike instruments. It was a terrifying sound, and when we looked at the tall cue [temple-pyramid] from which it came we saw our comrades who had been captured in Cortés' defeat being dragged up the steps to be sacrificed. When they had hauled them up to a small platform in front of the shrine where they kept their accursed idols we saw them put plumes on the heads of many of them; and then they made them dance with a sort of fan in front of Huichilobos. Then after they had danced the papas [Aztec priests] laid them down on their backs on some narrow stones of sacrifice and, cutting open their chests, drew out their palpitating hearts, which they offered to the idols before them. (cited in Harner 1980:209)

The Aztec calendar had eighteen months, each of which was dedicated to a religious theme and required a particular type of sacrifice. A common feature at the monthly religious rituals was the sacrifice of one or more deity impersonators. For example, a handsome young man free from physical flaws was chosen to represent the god Tezcatlipoca, one of the creator gods. The young man assumed the identity of Tezcatlipoca for a full year before the sacrifice was to take place. One month before he was to be sacrificed, he was married to four women who represented goddesses. He and his wives journeyed from place to place, singing and dancing. When he arrived at his designated temple, he voluntarily ascended the steps alone. The priests threw him onto the sacrificial stone and cut out his heart, offering it to the sun. As were virtually all those sacrificed, he was then decapitated, and his head was taken for display on the skull rack.

The person being sacrificed was a sacred offering, a messenger to the gods. Frances F. Berdan writes, "It was considered an honor to provide sacred nourishment for the gods and keep the sun strong, the rains

sufficient, the maize plentiful, and the wars successful. . . . Those who were sacrificed became divine, those who consumed the flesh of a sacrificed person were consuming the flesh of a sacred entity" (1982:115–116).

The most common form of sacrifice involved drawing blood from one's own body by puncturing one's earlobes, tongue, thighs, upper arms, chest, or genitals with a sharp thorn from a maguey plant. Priests often drew blood from their own bodies, but at some rituals virtually everyone, including children, was required to offer blood to demonstrate religious devotion.

Cosmology The Aztecs believed that creation began with two deities, Ometicutli ("Lord of Duality") and Omecihuatl ("Lady of Duality"), who became the parents of four sons, all of whom went by the name Tezcatlipoca. Each of the sons was associated with a different cardinal direction, color, tree, animal, and other natural and cultural phenomena. The Blue Tezcatlipoca was Huitzilopochtli, the patron deity of the Aztecs. The Red Tezcatlipoca, or Xipa Totec ("Our Lord the Flayed One"), was a fertility god. His rituals, which took place in the second Aztec month (corresponding to March 5–25), signaled the beginning of the spring planting season. Individuals sacrificed in his honor were flayed, and their skins were worn by the priests.

The Aztecs believed the gods tried five times to create humanity. The first world, presided over by Tezcatlipoca, was peopled by giants who subsisted on acorns. The world ended when the giants were eaten by jaguars. The second world, presided over by Quetzalcoatl and inhabited by humans subsisting on piñon nuts, ended when the people were transformed into monkeys and hurricanes destroyed the earth. The third world, presided over by Tlaloc, the rain god, and inhabited by humans subsisting on an aquatic seed, ended when the people were transformed into dogs, turkeys, and butterflies, and the earth was destroyed by fiery rain. The fourth world was presided over by Chalchiuhtlicue, Tlaloc's consort or female counterpart, and was inhabited by humans who subsisted on wild seeds. It ended when the people were transformed into fish and the earth was destroyed by a giant flood.

The Aztecs believed that the present world, the fifth attempt by the gods to create humanity, would meet a similar fate, and that there would be no sixth world. Instead, the world would fall into deep darkness at the end of the fifth sun. This world is presided over by Tonatiuh, a sun god, and is inhabited by humans subsisting on maize. The Aztecs believe it will end when the people are devoured by celestial monsters and the earth is destroyed by earthquakes.

Priests   The Aztec pantheon was richly populated with an abundance of gods, both male and female. Each deity was housed in its own temples, surrounded by its characteristic paraphernalia, honored by its own rituals, and served by its own cadre of full-time priests. Some deities were also attended by female priests, individuals who had made special vows to serve the deity for a specific period of time, or laypersons who felt a special affinity for that god.

A priest was in the service of one god and spent most of his time attending that deity: sweeping the temple; caring for the god; manufacturing and caring for the deity's sacred paraphernalia; keeping the temple fires lit; and offering penance, prayers, and gifts of incense throughout the day and night. The bodies of priests were usually dyed black; their hair was long and bound; and they exhibited the marks of numerous piercings from offering their own blood to the gods. H. B. Nicholson notes that a "permanent red smear of blood on each temple [cheek] was an important badge of their profession" (1971:437).

Female priests engaged in similar day-to-day activities, especially sweeping and offering incense, but their range of duties seems to have been narrower than that of male priests. They helped organize and participated in some of the major religious ceremonies, but much of their time was spent weaving and embroidering the fine cloths used to decorate the god and the temple.

Shamans and Sorcerers   Whereas the priestly hierarchy tended to the needs of the state and society, an assortment of shamans and sorcerers ministered to the needs of individuals. Shamans could be either males or females, and anyone born on the evil days of One Rain or One Wind was presumed to be inclined to be a sorcerer, whether male or female, noble or commoner. A person born on the day of One Rain was likely to become a "human owl" who could transform him- or herself into an animal to cause illness or to kill.

Intellectual and Artistic Accomplishments

Aztec intellectual achievements were impressive. Their complex calendar system, based on long-term astronomical observations, took into account the movements of the sun, Venus, and Mars. The solar year was grouped into eighteen months of 20 days each. The 365-day year was rounded out with an additional five days that were viewed as unlucky. The solar calendar was linked to a ritual calendar based on a 260-day cycle. Combining the solar calendar with the ritual calendar resulted in a 52-year cycle, after which time the calendar round would begin anew.

This dangerous time at the end of the 52-year cycle was observed by solemn religious ceremonies. On that day, all fires were extinguished and images of household gods were discarded, along with cooking implements and the three traditional hearthstones of each household. As night fell, the people took up a vigil on their rooftops. At precisely midnight, a priest slew a captive by cutting out his heart. The priest then kindled a new fire in the open chest cavity of the sacrificed captive. If the fire burned successfully, the universe was safe for another 52 years; failure of the fire to light signaled the end of the present sun.

The ritual calendar was set down in the *tonalamatl,* or "book of days," one of several types of manuscripts compiled by Aztec scribes. The writing system was based on **glyphs,** or word pictures. Because Aztec writing relied on pictures rather than an alphabet, many details had to be filled in by the reader. Both reading and writing were arts taught only to nobles.

Using tools made of stone, Aztec sculptors carved numerous stone sculptures that far surpassed in quality anything produced by their predecessors. They executed realistic sculptures of gods, animal figures, masks, people, and replicas of temples and religious artifacts. Aztec relief sculpture adorned temples and other public buildings, often portraying a series of scenes depicting religious themes, military feats, or historical events.

The Aztecs were heirs to a long tradition of oral literature, and they created many epic and lyric poems, hymns, plays, and chronicles. Skilled orators were highly esteemed, and children of nobles were trained in this art. A good orator was described as one skilled at producing "pleasing words, joyful words, he has flowers on his lips. His speech overflows with advice, flowers come from his mouth. His speech, pleasing and joyful as flowers; from him come noble language and careful sentences" (Léon-Portilla 1969:27).

Many public religious ceremonies involved singing and dancing, requiring the participation of people from all walks of life, so both commoners and nobles were trained in these arts. Each deity had its own repertoire of songs, and long rehearsals preceded the public ceremonies. In addition, professional singers were employed by Aztec rulers to compose songs extolling their feats and those of their ancestors. When the Spaniards seized control of the Aztec empire, many of the books that preserved Aztec calendrical and literary knowledge were destroyed in the belief that they were "books of the devil." Much sculpture, which represented idolatry to the Spaniards, was also destroyed, and many of the exquisite gold and silver masterpieces were melted down for their metals and stones.

The Spanish Conquest

In February 1519, Hernán Cortés set sail from Cuba with six hundred men in eleven ships. The ships were armed with both light and heavy cannon and carried sixteen horses. Cortés's army was a varied lot, including mechanics, miners, sailors, and musicians. A few of the men were armed with crossbows, and some even carried muskets. Cortés was aided in his conquest of the rich and powerful Aztec empire by his alliances with subject groups who were growing restive under Aztec rule; by his relentless determination, which included destroying his own ships so his men could not return to Cuba; and by the Aztec leader Moctezuma's vacillation between confrontation and conciliation, due to his being uncertain whether Cortés was a man or a god.

When Cortés besieged Tenochtitlan on April 28, 1521, he had over nine hundred Spanish soldiers, untold thousands of Indian allies, eighty-six horses, fifteen cannon, and thirteen brigantines, small ships he had had constructed in Tlaxcalla and Texcoco. While the brigantines blockaded the city, Cortés's land forces approached Tenochtitlan along its three causeways. After several days of ferocious fighting, sixty-two Spaniards were captured alive and sacrificed, many others had been killed in the fighting, and large numbers of Cortés's Indian allies had deserted.

Cortés then concentrated on enforcing his blockade to prevent supplies from reaching Tenochtitlan. After seventy-five days, in which many Aztecs died of starvation or dysentery from contaminated water,

the Spanish and their Indian allies moved in and devastated what was left of the city. Entire quarters of the city were demolished, many Aztec survivors were slaughtered, and the city was sacked mercilessly. Of perhaps three hundred thousand original Aztec defenders, only about sixty thousand survived (Wagner 1944:355). Under the Spanish, Tenochtitlan was rebuilt as Mexico City, and stones from the razed Aztec capital were used to build a Catholic cathedral, which stands near the heart of Mexico City today.

THE NAYARS OF SOUTHERN INDIA

Anthropologists have long remarked on the unique features of marriage and family among the Nayars, a caste who inhabit what is now the state of Kerala in southwestern India. The Nayars of the nineteenth century were described as an exception to the universality of marriage because a woman and her children continued to reside with her matrilineal kin group after she assumed the title of married woman, and she was not required to maintain exclusive sexual relations with one man.

In recent times, however, many changes have taken place that have blurred or obliterated these distinctive features of Nayar domestic life. In the following essay, a Nayar describes what these changes mean in his own life and in the larger context of male–female relations in India. He notes that, though there are a few lingering remnants of the matrilineal system, the Nayar are moving toward the male-dominated systems characteristic of other parts of India.

NAYARS: TRADITION AND CHANGE IN MARRIAGE AND FAMILY

N. Prabha Unnithan*

I am a Nayar, but I was born and brought up in Malaysia. Other than the language we spoke at home (Malayalam, the language of Kerala), my childhood

---

*Adapted from Melvin Ember, Carol R. Ember, and David Levinson, *Portraits of Culture: Ethnographic Originals* (Upper Saddle River, NJ: Prentice Hall, 1995).

and family life in multiethnic Malaysia carried no trace of anything systematically different from that of other immigrant families from India. On a visit to India as a child, however, it appeared to me that my mother and I were spending most of our time at her family *taravad* (ancestral home based on descent group membership), which was described to me as my home. I preferred my father's place, where there were more children my age, but I remember my mother's family suggesting that I did not "really belong" to my father's family.

My first perception of the uniqueness of my heritage came as a college student in other parts of India. Reading about the various communities of India and discussing their similarities and differences with anthropology students formed my first experience with the exceptional traditions of the Nayars. This experience stimulated a curiosity that led me to read as much as I could about the Nayars and to discuss these matters with other Nayars. After coming to the United States, my wife and I discovered that we could attract the respectful and fascinated attention of any anthropologist by stating that we were Nayars.

Kerala and the Nayar

E. E. Evans-Pritchard once declared, "The people of Kerala in South Western India are amongst the most fascinating ethnic groups of the world. Their traditional claim to anthropological eminence rested on the once flourishing institution of matriliny among the Nayars and a special ritual bond of caste between the Nambudiri Brahmins and the martial Nayars" (1982:5). The Indian state of Kerala, where these groups have traditionally lived, has a history and culture that "is one of the major streams that have enriched the composite culture of the country" (Menon 1967:1).

The state of Kerala was created in 1956—nine years after India achieved independence from Britain—on the basis of a common language among its inhabitants following the linguistic reorganization of states in India. Kerala immediately gained prominence in 1957, when the local Communist party was elected to form the state government, the first time this had happened outside the Communist world (Mammen 1981). Known for its scenic beauty, Kerala has also attracted attention because of its high performance on various indicators of "development." Despite significant levels of poverty

and unemployment, Kerala has achieved high rates of life expectancy and literacy combined with low birth rates and infant mortality (Franke and Chasin 1990).

Geographically, Kerala is sandwiched between the thickly forested Western Ghats mountain range on the east and a 360-mile coastline on the Arabian Sea on the west. This isolation from the rest of the Indian subcontinent, combined with extensive contact with other countries across the seas, has facilitated the development of a distinctive culture, reflected in the complex Kerala caste system. Elsewhere in India, Hindu society has been divided into four major categories. The Brahmins were priests; the Kshatriyas were soldiers and kings; the Vaisyas were traders and landowners; and the Sudras performed various occupations of service to the castes above them. The traditional Hindu caste system of Kerala, which J. Puthenkulam refers to as "the citadel of caste rigidity and orthodoxy," came into being around the tenth century and is extremely complicated (1977:22). George Woodcock comments, "There were no less than five hundred castes and sub-castes, divided from each other by rigorous rules against inter-marriage and by an extraordinary pattern of pollution taboos" (1967:58). In Kerala, the Nayars, although Sudras, also carried out the functions of Vaisyas and Kshatriyas. The Kshatriyas and Samantans (local chieftains) are also thought to have originally been Nayars.

The Nayars once dominated Kerala through force as "a class of professional warriors who developed to a high level the art of swordsmanship, who formed themselves at time of battle into suicide squads" in the service of various kings and local chieftains (Woodcock 1967:60). More recently, their importance is based on ownership of land. Historically, the Nambudiri Brahmins were "never more than a thin insecure top crust on society" (Woodcock 1967:59).

Traditional Nayar Marriage, Family, and Kinship

Traditionally, Nayars, with minor exceptions, were matrilineal. In contrast, the Nambudiri Brahmins were patrilineal. Among the Nayars, two patterns of marriage and family life have been identified. In central Kerala and the upper region of southern Kerala, the first and (to social scientists) better-known pattern was practiced. Here, every Nayar girl before

This farmer of the state of Kerala in southern India is working a rich region once dominated by the Nayar. The Nayar were warriors and landowners who practiced an extreme form of matrilineality and matrilocality. As the Nayar have shifted to an economy based on wage labor, the formerly high status of women is gradually eroding.

puberty underwent a *talikettu-kalyanam* (literally, "tali-tying ceremony") as part of an elaborate celebration. After a short period of seclusion (supposedly indicating menstruation), a *tali* (a small leaf-shaped locket worn on a string or gold chain) was tied around the girl's neck by an "adult male who is a member of a superior caste, an unrelated member of the same caste, a cross-cousin, an aunt or the shaman of a local goddess" (Aiyappan 1982:226). Among Hindus in other parts of India, the tali indicated that a woman was married.

Some time following the talikettu-kalyanam, when the female in question had attained maturity, she became eligible to form more or less permanent sexual relationships with several men; each relationship was known as *sambandham* (literally, "alliance"). The sambandham was initiated without elaborate ritual. A proposal from either the parents or friends of either sambandham partner was followed by consultations with the *karanavan* (the eldest male, who was usually the head of the family) of each *taravad,* or ancestral home. To be considered eligible, males had to be of equivalent or higher caste than the woman.

On an auspicious day, the man went in procession to the woman's house, where there was a brief ceremony. The couple then spent the night together, and the man left for his taravad in the morning. A gift of clothes for the woman was sent by the man's family if this had not been part of the ceremony. A woman could consent to receive several men as sambandham partners with the approval of the head of her taravad. The various partners took turns visiting the woman at night. At the same time, men in the woman's taravad would be visiting their own sambandham partners. The men were also permitted to have more than one sambandham partner, but the children of these unions belonged in the mother's taravad. The man and woman in a sambandham partnership did not live together, and the man did not have any say in the upbringing of his biological children.

Ceremonial gifts, such as clothes, betel nut, and hair and bath oil, were given by the man to his sambandham partner during important festivals. The only other obligation of the man to his sambandham partner was to acknowledge paternity of his children and to assume a minimal portion of the expense of the midwife, who assisted at the birth of the children. The relationship between the man and the woman could be broken off by either partner without formality.

In attempting to account for this unique form of marriage, anthropologists have noted that there is symmetry between the Nayar matrilineal and Nambudiri Brahmin patrilineal systems. In most

Nambudiri *illams* (the equivalent of the Nayar taravads), only the oldest son was allowed to marry and inherit property, so that ancestral land and wealth would not be subdivided. Thus, younger Nambudiri sons would form sambandhams with Nayar women. Because the Nayar were matrilineal, the Nambudiri had no economic responsibility toward the children of their sambandham partners; therefore, the alliance did not challenge the estate of the oldest Nambudiri son. At the same time, the Nayar taravad gained status by being associated with the Brahmin caste.

The second and lesser-known pattern of marriage and family life was practiced mainly in northern Kerala (Fuller 1976:100). Here the talikettu-kalyanam was not considered an important rite, and greater emphasis was placed on the sambandham ceremony. The sambandham relationship here was similar to Hindu marriages in other parts of India and was meant to be a stable one. The man and woman lived together in his matrilineal taravad, along with his brothers and all their children. Alternatively, the woman would live with her own children in a separate house, where she would be visited by her husband. Women who were divorced or widowed moved back to their own taravad, where they (and their married sisters) retained property rights. Divorce and remarriage were permitted but rare.

Regardless of the marriage pattern, all Nayar families were characterized by three features: (1) descent and inheritance were matrilineal, so that female members and their male and female children possessed property rights, whereas the children of male members did not; (2) the taravads were exogamous, and members of one's own taravad were considered blood relatives, whereas members of the father's taravad were not; (3) a great deal of importance was attached to the wishes of the eldest male, or karanavan, who acted as head, manager, and public representative of the taravad.

In comparison with those of other Hindus, the traditional marriage and family arrangements of the Nayars provided relatively greater freedom and status for their female members. Women had a say in the initiation or termination of marriage relationships. Children, as long as their paternity was acknowledged, had to be taken care of by their taravad. Property rights were guaranteed for females. Women were accorded respect, and Nayar men expressed an "intensity of concern for mothers and sisters" as carriers of the taravad name (Aiyappan 1982:192).

Contemporary Nayar Marriage, Family, and Kinship

A number of factors that affected Kerala and its people in the nineteenth and early twentieth centuries eroded or extremely modified the traditional ceremonies, marriage patterns, and family relationships of the Nayar. The contemporary situation includes a decline in identification with the taravad as well as the expansion and increased importance attached to the sambandham ceremony, signifying an almost absolute conversion by Nayars to the ideal of a "strong" or stable monogamous marriage.

The Decline of the Taravad   With regard to family relationships and descent, one Nayar remarked that they had "left the mother's house but have not yet reached the father's home" (Puthenkulam 1977:216). This remark implies a transition to a more patrilineal system, with lingering remnants of identification with matrilineality and the taravad. This transition is manifested in three areas: property ownership, the increased influence of the father, and neolocal or patrilocal residence.

Property Ownership   Property used to be held jointly by the taravad and was administered by the eldest male in the matrilineal group (the karanavan). It was difficult, though not impossible, for the property to be divided against the wishes of the karanavan and older males in the matrilineal family. In the nineteenth and early twentieth centuries, a number of reports and court cases accusing karanavans of financial mismanagement, extravagance, or secret transfer of property to their own children led to more legal equality among taravad members with respect to property rights. Now, property is owned jointly by individual members, who may ask for their share of it on attaining adulthood. Puthenkulam notes that, given the legal bias toward individual property division, "it is not surprising that the vast majority of Nayar taravads have made use of it and partitioned their taravads" (1977:157). This is the case with my own matrilineal taravad. Obviously, after a few generations of division and subdivision, it is unlikely that any matrilineal property will remain.

Influence of the Father   A second measure of the decline of the taravad can be found in the increased influence of the father in the affairs of his children. Or, as Puthenkulam puts it, "The father has come to his own and the karanavan has been supplanted" (1977:162). Previously, as noted, children had very little to do with their fathers. Given the changed pattern of residence and declining economic importance of the taravad, the father is becoming increasingly important in the lives of his children.

Still, certain attachments to the karanavan or mother's brother continue. For example, my older brother spent much of his childhood with one of my maternal uncles because of proximity to better educational facilities. My uncle accepted his guardianship role, and others in the extended family viewed the arrangement as "proper."

Neolocal or Patrilocal Residence   It is now assumed that the wife will move permanently into her husband's home and live there with their children. Ironically, the house she moves into may sometimes be his ancestral taravad. A married son may bring his wife to live with his parents if he cannot afford a separate home. With employment opportunities mainly in the more urbanized areas of Kerala, elsewhere in India, or abroad, the couple is more likely to establish a new (neolocal) residence apart from kin.

However, the influence of the taravad does persist in some matters. Nayars continue to take their surnames from their mother's family and often include their taravad name, an expectation I have violated. Having spent a large part of my life in patrilineal or bilateral descent societies and wishing to avoid explanations of my matrilineal heritage, I have taken my father's surname (Unnithan) rather than my mother's (Nair), and I do not use the name of my taravad (Payanimvilayil). My decision to use my father's surname has led to some bemused questioning among some of my relatives as to how and when I had turned into a Unnithan!

The Expansion and Increased Importance of the Sambandham   While the talikettu-kalyanam and associated rituals have all but disappeared, those surrounding the sambandham have expanded. In comparison with marriage ceremonies of other Hindu groups, however, those of the present-day Nayars tend to be very short and simple. The actual marriage ceremony is the culmination of steps taken in advance that approximate an "arranged" marriage.

Marriages based on notions of romantic love do take place, but they are largely subject to family approval.

Marriages are mostly intracaste. The preference for intracaste marriage often causes middle-class Nayar families to look for potential partners in places far beyond the local village or district. Photographs of "eligible" young men and women are exchanged through professional matchmakers or friends and relatives to see if there is any interest on either side in a potential sambandham. Horoscopes are matched to consider whether the couple is astrologically compatible. The young man and his relatives may make a short visit to the woman's home for what is referred to as a *pennukaanal* (literally, "seeing the young woman"). Based on the consent of both the man and the woman and their respective families, arrangements are made for the wedding ceremony itself. Often a ceremony is also held to determine an astrologically auspicious date and time for the marriage ceremony. Invitations are mailed out by both families or are personally handed to close relatives who live nearby. Among some Nayars, wedding invitations are issued in the name of the karanavan, another vestige of the prestige that position once commanded.

Marriage ceremonies may be conducted at the bride's home or in an area built and used for that purpose at a temple nearby. The bridegroom, who arrives in a procession of his family and friends, is greeted at the entrance by members of the bride's family. His feet are washed and he is garlanded. The actual ceremony consists of the following rites: The couple sit next to each other facing (among other objects that signify auspiciousness and fertility) a pot of rice and a lighted oil lamp. The couple exchange rings and garlands (previously blessed by placing them in front of a temple god). The bridegroom places or ties the tali around the neck of the bride. The bridegroom then gives the bride a piece of cloth (almost always a *saree*). The bride and groom clasp hands and walk around the lighted lamp three times. They are then blessed by elders of both families. The ceremony is followed by a vegetarian feast in which both families participate. The bride then accompanies the groom to live with his family or to a new residence.

The contemporary Nayar marriage is continuous with tradition in that religious connotations are still minimal and the giving of clothing survives from the traditional sambandham. There are a number of changes, however. The tali-tying rite has been shifted from the talikettu-kalyanam to the sambandham ceremony. The sambandham ceremony and the process leading up to it have taken on features that underscore the desirability of monogamy and the stability of marriage. In addition, there are now elements suggesting increasing male dominance. For example, the male's family goes to view the bride-to-be, and the bridegroom's party is respectfully received at the wedding site. Increasingly, the groom's family demands from the bride's family a groomprice as a condition of marriage. The "groomprice" consists of "direct payments to the family of the groom" (Billig 1992). This was previously unknown among Nayars.

Stable Monogamy As an Ideal The importance of the sambandham relationship among contemporary Nayars is associated with the promotion of a family ideology based on stable monogamy. Nayars have substituted intracaste endogamy for the traditional pattern involving multiple visiting husbands and relationships with Nambudiri Brahmins. The practice of allowing Nambudiri sambandham partners has died out. Its demise can be attributed to the cessation of military service as the common occupation of Nayars; to changes within Nambudiri households that allow all males (not just the oldest) to marry Nambudiri; and to Nayar reformers who berated Nambudiris on their "religious" pretensions in separating sex and responsibility for its consequences (children).

A second aspect of the ideal of stable monogamy is the contemporary expectation that a husband and wife be sexually faithful to each other throughout their marriage. Not surprisingly, divorce is strongly discouraged. This focus on sexual exclusivity has led to the scrutiny of a potential bride's "character" (premarital virginity) before proceeding to an arranged marriage. Somewhat less intense attention is paid to a potential groom's "character."

A third expression of the stable, monogamous family ideal is the rise of essentially neolocal nuclear families resulting from emigration by Nayar men in search of employment. The state of Kerala has high levels of both education and unemployment. As men move to other parts of India or to other countries, it has become customary and accepted for their wives to live with them and raise their children in nuclear family units. If the couple returns to Kerala, they continue to live together.

It is difficult to find remnants of the old-order "weak" marriage ties among the Nayar. It is my observation that in comparison with other Hindu groups, Nayar women have greater freedom in consenting to or turning down marriage proposals. It is open to question whether this is due to Nayar traditions or because Nayar women possess relatively high levels of education and are more likely to work outside the home. Relative to other Hindu women, it also appears that Nayar women may choose to remain unmarried for longer periods of time. Furthermore, female children are not looked upon with disfavor even in the face of such new practices as groomprice. Michael S. Billig predicts that these practices "may actually enhance female autonomy and economic independence in Kerala by forcing women even further to pursue educational and career opportunities outside of marriage" (1993:211–212).

Factors for Change in Marriage and Family Customs

In general, three sets of influences—economic factors, reform movements, and legal changes—have contributed to the decline of the traditional Nayar patterns of marriage and family.

Economic Factors In the nineteenth century, after the British established control over the regions that constitute the present Kerala, they demobilized the armies of the local kings and chieftains. The Nayar men who controlled lands that had been given to them earlier by these rulers turned their attention to agriculture. There was more stability in their lives and more permanent contact with their sambandham partners, their relatives, and their biological children. This change may have led to greater identification with their family of procreation, which includes their children, rather than their family of orientation, or birth family. With this shift in emphasis, many Nayar men may have wished to transfer their property to their wives and children rather than to their matrilineal taravad.

An additional economic factor for change is the increasing role of the manufacturing and service industry sectors in India, and in Kerala in particular. Nayars, given their elite status, had greater opportunities to acquire the educational qualifications needed for these new jobs. At the same time, the past century saw population growth and economic competition from Ezhavas (a lower-caste group) and Syrian Christians who were also rapidly "modernizing." These groups began to aggressively buy up land that Nayar taravads and Nambudiri illams had owned. The rural agricultural economy that supported the caste structure and the place of Nayars in it was being dismantled. Puthenkulam observes, "Neither the taravad nor its kinship system or the sambandham could be imagined outside a village set-up. When the village economy crumbled, systems built on it had to follow suit" (1977:245).

Reform Movements   Reform movements among the Nayars themselves agitated for an end to matrilineality and the regularization of sambandham unions. Reformers disliked the grip of the karanavan on the property and affairs of the younger members of a taravad and wanted to end what they considered wasteful celebrations such as talikettu-kalyanam. They scorned the "status" associated with unions between Nayar women and Nambudiri men and pushed for the recognition of sambandham relationships as legal marriages, so that the husband could leave property he had accumulated during his lifetime to his children. The reformers, perhaps aided by changing economic and political circumstances, were successful in challenging almost every feature of traditional Nayar life that they disapproved of. Christopher J. Fuller suggests that these reformers were influenced by "the spread of Western ideas," most of it through education in English (1976:130). It is also true that, during this period, Kerala was becoming less isolated from the rest of India. Through migration, aided by the spread of rail travel, contacts multiplied with other, mostly patrilineal, Hindu and non-Hindu groups. In addition, Christian missionaries were able to instill Christian ideas of morality and monogamy, even though they may have failed to convert the Nayars. Some observers suggest that Nayar reformers were ashamed of their traditional way of life and its implied "immorality" in non-Nayar eyes. As A. Aiyappan puts it, "We grew ashamed of our matriliny and this affected even the thinking of scholars" (1982:222).

Legal Changes   Legal changes also hastened the decline of the taravad and matrilineality. In southern Kerala, this took the form of two pieces of legislation called the Nair Acts of 1912 and 1925. Together they had the effect of allowing for property division and bequeathing of individually acquired property to any individual's children. Similar legislation in central Kerala enacted in 1920 and 1938 severely curtailed the powers of the karanavan, legalized the sambandham relationship, prohibited multiple spouses, and declared the wife and children of a man his heirs. Most of northern Kerala, which was ruled directly by the British, enacted legislation in 1933 with similar provisions.

At the same time, laws subverting the economic basis that sustained traditional Nayar marriage and family structure were coming into effect. In the early twentieth century, land reforms that allowed tenants (primarily of the lower castes) to become owners of the lands they had cultivated for generations began to be enacted. Since the Nayars and to a lesser extent Nambudiris were the landholders, these reforms eroded the economic control of these two castes. Related reforms protected tenants from arbitrary eviction and from being required to pay excessive rents. The pace of these reforms picked up considerably after India's independence in 1947 and as a result of a string of Communist and leftist governments that have ruled Kerala since 1957. More recent legislation has given existing tenants the right to buy the land they have tilled, has banned the creation of new tenancies, and has proposed limits on the amount of land that can be owned by any one family.

Political Factors Promoting Change

Although at one time the "dominant caste" of Kerala, Nayars do not automatically occupy elite positions anymore. "The traditional Kerala society in which the caste of a person and the extent of the landed property owned by him determined his standing in the social scale is now a thing of the past" (Menon 1967:393). Instead, the disappearance of their patrons (rulers and local chieftains), democratization, and preferential policies favoring lower castes (implemented all over India) have eroded the powerful position that Nayars once held. They now have to compete with other groups or form coalitions with them to achieve power, wealth, and prestige. Caste, taravad, and matrilineality matter less in the public sphere than what can be gained or lost through interpersonal and intergroup transactions.

The structures that propped up Nayars and their particular way of life have been dismantled, making them, at least politically, not very different from other groups around them. Although Nayar women continue to have more say in their lives than other

Hindu women, there is a trend away from the female-centered family structure to the more male-dominated system characteristic of other Hindu groups.

THE HAN OF NORTHERN CHINA

More than one billion people live in China—one-fifth of the world's population, a proportion that would be even higher had not China instituted drastic population control measures in the 1970s. Much of China's population make their living in agriculture, a way of life that changed slowly over two thousand years, while China was ruled by powerful dynasties that closed its doors to foreign trade. After its defeat in the so-called Opium Wars in the 1800s, China's Qing dynasty was forced to open the country's ports to the British opium trade and to agree to many other unequal treaties that dealt crippling blows to the country's sovereignty and economy. In 1911 the dynastic system was overthrown by the revolutionary leader Sun Yat-sen.

Sun died in 1916, before he could stabilize China's economy and political system. Leadership passed to Chiang Kai-shek, but his government was challenged by Mao Zedong, a follower of Sun and leader of China's Communist Party. The rivalry between Chiang and Mao seethed under Japanese occupation of China from the mid-1930s until the end of World War II in 1945. In the autumn of 1949, Chiang's government was overthrown by Mao, and Chiang was forced to flee to the island of Taiwan, where he established a government dedicated to Confucian values of formal social relationships and an emphasis on traditional education in the arts. Taiwan also undertook a large-scale program of industrialization.

In mainland China, Mao seized land owned by landlords and organized agricultural production into farm cooperatives. In the capital city of Beijing, small-scale industries were turned into economic cooperatives. Ultimately, the system led to state and collective ownership of the key means of production. The Communist Chinese government pushed forward with a program of widespread mechanization, building of extensive irrigation canals, a rural health system, and education that ensured eight years of schooling for all resident children.

As were other rural Chinese, Han farmers who lived along the Great Wall on the northern frontier were caught between the push for collectivization and the force of traditions that emphasized family and village. The Han also had to cope with the competing needs of farmers and pastoralists, as well as with ethnic tension with indigenous nomadic Mongol pastoralists.

The competing needs of agriculturalism and pastoralism have plagued groups practicing these two forms of subsistence virtually since the rise of food production. In the Old Testament, Semitic pastoral nomads chronicled their battles with settled agriculturalists. Hollywood movies provide fictionalized accounts of encounters between ranchers and farmers in the settling of the American West. In the following essay, Burton Pasternak examines the divergent lifestyles of Han farmers and pastoralists near China's Great Wall.

HAN: PASTORALISTS AND FARMERS ON A CHINESE FRONTIER

Burton Pasternak*

When Han farmers first crossed the Great Wall in search of a better life, they found a setting where the climate was unmerciful, the land unyielding, and the local inhabitants unfriendly. Many eventually gave up and went home; only those prepared to alter their behavior were able to remain.

Whether they speak Mandarin or some other dialect, the Han have a common history and tradition. They use the same written language and share many goals and values. Their way of life is rooted in intensive farming. They transfer population pressure to land, applying ever more labor to squeeze marginal increments out of limited space. Male-headed extended families consisting of two or more married couples provide the workers. The history of Han expansion testifies to the success of their adaptation. But there have been limits, areas inhospitable to their way of life. It was at just such a frontier that they his-

---

*Adapted from Melvin Ember, Carol R. Ember, and David Levinson, *Portraits of Culture: Ethnographic Originals* (Upper Saddle River, NJ: Prentice Hall, 1995).

torically drew a line of stone, a "great wall," to mark the end of the "civilized" world. It was a frontier beyond which the Han believed they could not long survive as Han.

The Chinese state endorsed an ideology that encouraged homogeneity. Pressure to conform increased in post-1949 China, as the Communist state extended its apparatus downward to influence and control all aspects of life. Never before had government so controlled where people lived, where they worked, what they might grow, what they could eat or buy, when they could marry, and even how many children they might have, as well as when they could have them. Throughout the country, children learned Mandarin in school. Collectivization provided a common framework for the deployment of land and labor. By eliminating private property, regulating marriage, and stimulating class struggle within families, the state attempted to redirect orientation from family and locality to nation. Differences of wealth, lifestyle, and opportunity narrowed. People married, formed families, and even bore children in increasingly similar ways.

But older themes played on, along with their variations. In so vast and varied a country, with its multitude of climates, topographies, crops, and cultures, it could not have been otherwise. With the collapse of communes and restoration of family-based production, the potential for variation has increased.

The Setting

Inner Mongolia provides an exceptional setting in which to explore the way ecology shapes labor and, through it, marriage and family structure. We compare two modes of production, pastoralism and cultivation, each with subvariants. Our "laboratory," Hulunbuit League in northeastern Inner Mongolia, borders Heilongjiang province to the east, the former Soviet Union to the northeast, and Mongolia to the northwest. To the north, in the foothills of the Great Chingan mountain range, is an area rich in minerals and forest. East of the mountains, people farm (mainly maize, soybeans, wheat, potatoes, and sugar beets) or combine cultivation with limited dairying. Lush grasslands west of the mountains support sedentary and nomadic pastoralism (cattle and sheep).

The seasons are extreme; the winters cold and long, the summers cool and short. Because the frost-free period is less than 135 days, farmers produce only one crop. Large-scale cutting during the first half of this century left few trees; the loss has permitted erosion in the cultivated regions and threatens desertification on the grasslands. Seasonal windstorms sweep through. Soils are sandy. Nature is capricious, periodically providing either too much or too little rain. Rivers and streams flood, destroying crops and eroding farmland.

The climate is a problem for herdsmen as well. Sudden changes can dramatically reduce animal numbers, denying herders both the animals' products and their offspring. Most dangerous are "white disasters," heavy or early snowstorms that threaten lambs and prevent sheep from pawing through to grasses beneath the snow. Then there are "black disasters," when snowfall is so light there is little water for the animals and grasses are poor. Inner Mongolia is one of China's poorest regions, with a per capita income 20 percent lower than that of rural China in general. Income has risen in recent years, but much of the region continues to be undeveloped and sparsely populated.

The Han make up 80 percent of the population of Inner Mongolia, with a large ethnic minority population composed mostly of Mongols. Centuries of cultural and political separation have left a legacy of ill will. A massive intrusion of Han after the turn of the twentieth century, and the associated displacement of pastoral peoples, magnified the problem. Conversion of grassland into farms ruined traditional grazing lands, prompting a pastoral retreat. Heavy-handed attempts to create a Chinese version of socialist uniformity during the Cultural Revolution of the 1960s brought the problem to a head, and distrust remains on both sides.

Farming and Herding

Farming and herding differ in fundamental ways. Farmers depend on an essentially unexpandable resource: land. Labor is intensive, but not uniform. Each phase of the farming cycle—preparation, planting, maintenance, harvest—calls for a special kind of effort, and there are marked peaks and troughs in demand for labor. By farming near home, women can work alongside men, doing much the same tasks while still managing domestic chores.

The situation is different for pastoralists. Herds of cattle and flocks of sheep are expandable, and expansion may enable their managers to obtain great rewards. With sufficient grassland they can enlarge and diversify livestock, even cut hay for sale. The routine is more continuous and repetitive. Grazing, cutting hay, and most other pastoral work take place some distance from home. Women cannot do such work and at the same time milk the cows and run the household. The division of labor is therefore sharper.

The ideal herdsman is an adult male. Strength and experience are important. Mistakes can menace generations of animals. Therefore, youngsters contribute less among herding families than they do among farmers, while old people have more to offer and remain self-sufficient longer. An elderly couple would have a hard time plowing, building mounds, or harvesting on their own, so farmers gradually retire at about age sixty-five. They do not become idle even then. Old women free younger ones for work outside by looking after home and grandchildren. The elderly of both sexes lend a hand in the fields and process harvested crops when labor is badly needed.

Farming and herding differently shape family structure, the relationships of women and men and their access to education, the ages at which people marry and bear children, and even the number of children they have. These contrasts predate the commune and have outlasted it. Collectivization changed the way property and labor were used, and the state extended its control deeper, but differences rooted in ecology and technology have always precluded uniformity.

Frontier Farmers

Tranquillity Village and Middle Village in Inner Mongolia provide a baseline against which to measure changes that occurred when the Han moved into areas less hospitable for cultivation. The villages had been settled by parents or grandparents of the people we met, who came from impoverished regions across the Great Wall to scratch some sort of living out of the dry, sandy earth. Life was hard, even during the era of collectives. As before, the commune depended heavily on the labor of everyone. But the collective consciousness that endless political campaigns had tried to evoke proved hard to sustain. Some people, content to live on collective allotments and vegetables grown on small private garden plots, put few hours and little energy into collective fields. Others had to work harder simply to maintain output and work point value. Low productivity meant low work point value, so even with hard work there was little difference between what top and bottom earners brought home.

Families no longer owned land or major implements, but the number of family workers still governed income. Families with several men earned most because *cadres* (local Communist leaders)

Most Chinese agricultural production is based on rice. However, the Han farmers of China's Mongolian frontier subsist primarily on maize, soybeans, wheat, potatoes, and sugar beets. Here, a Chinese farmer plows his field in preparation for planting wheat.

reserved the best-paying jobs for men. To make a decent living, however, everyone had to do something. If there were not enough men, women or youngsters or old persons could substitute. Indeed, people claim that women did more during the collective period than before.

Women's Work In theory, women doing the same "heavy" jobs as men could earn as many work points, but in fact they earned less. The assumptions were that women are "not strong enough" to do the heaviest work and that they work "less well." Since the leadership defined women's tasks as "lighter," women were assigned fewer points. Women's workdays were also shorter because they had unremunerated household tasks to do. The fact that women worked fewer hours for lower wages only reinforced the traditional notion that men are "more valuable."

Women often found themselves torn between farming and domestic work. A mother-in-law relieved a younger woman of work in the fields. Or a young mother might leave her infant in a nursery, in the care of older siblings, or even alone constrained on the family sleeping platform, a solution that sometimes had tragic consequences when unattended infants rolled off onto the floor. Because women often worked far from home, nursing was inconvenient. A mother could not bring her infant to the fields.

After her sons married, a woman gradually reduced her outside work and remained at home more to care for grandchildren and manage lighter household chores. Her daughters-in-law replaced her in the fields. Even retired men and women did light field tasks, especially during periods of high demand. They could plant potatoes, pull weeds, turn compost, and help process the harvest.

The "Responsibility System" By 1979 communes were in serious trouble. People were not eager to work for low wages, and the value of the work point had fallen so low that many were in debt. Rumors of plans to replace the commune only increased uncertainty and worsened morale. Toward the end of 1982 the countryside shifted to a new system in which collective land was given to households under long-term contracts, the so-called responsibility system. After years of collectivization, the family returned to its role as the basic unit of production as well as consumption, but with an important difference. Land remained publicly owned; it still cannot be bought or sold and therefore cannot reconcentrate in fewer hands as in former times. Families may sink into poverty, but they cannot solve their problems by selling land.

Production of a food surplus through intensive agriculture gave rise to societies we think of as essentially modern, characterized by large populations settled primarily in cities, with stratified political organization. However, the shift from foraging to agriculture began about ten thousand years ago in different parts of the world, and centered on production of three crops that could be stored for extended periods of time: rice in Asia (as pictured here), wheat in the Middle East, and corn in North America.

DISCUSSIONS

The Red Wine of War:
The Manly Art of Dying for Honor

A young French soldier dying in World War I wrote these words to his parents: "If this letter comes into your hands it will be because I am no more and because I shall have died the most glorious of deaths. Do not bewail me too much; my end is the most to be desired."

P. H. Pearce, founder of the Irish revolutionary movement, wrote of the same war: "The last sixteen months have been the most glorious in the history of Europe. Heroism has come back to the earth. It is good for the world that such things should be done. The old heart of the earth needed to be warmed with the red wine of the battlefield. Such august homage was never before offered to God as this, the homage of millions of lives given gladly for love of country."

Why is the "old heart of the earth" warmed by the blood of dying soldiers? And why is one's country—an abstract concept—more important than human life? Why, in fact, are men in so many societies encouraged to put their lives on the line for glory?

Yanomamö males of Venezuela and Brazil engage in chest-pounding duels and other forms of aggressive display as women stand by urging them on, much as American cheerleaders urge football players on to glory. The Netsilik, who lived by seal hunting above the Arctic Circle of northern Canada, conducted song duels. Men involved in a dispute would compose derisive songs about

their opponents. The songs would be performed before the group by their wives, while the men kept time by drumming. The songs were often ribald, and the audience cheered the more biting and witty song. In one such song, a man accused his opponent of sexual excesses and impotence:

> When [your penis] really felt a
> yearning it needed no help
> And certainly, it could at that
> time—
> But towards your wife—the
> desired one
> You had to have [spirit] help.
> (Balikci 1970:185–186)

Because of the dramatic nature of male aggressive displays, it is often assumed that women are simply the victims of violence rather than the perpetrators and instigators. In fact, women in many societies attack each other physically, and husband beating is far from uncommon in the ethnographic literature. The work of Victoria Burbank (1994) and H. B. Kimberley Cook (1992), among others, suggests that female aggression is more widespread than previously thought.

In New Guinea, women stage ritual displays of aggression against men during adolescent male initiation rites and on some other occasions. Kenneth Read describes an attack by Gahuku women upon men returning from a pig exchange in another village:

> At once it was clear that the men were outmatched, taken aback by the venom of the women's attack,

retreating to stand defensively above their [pig]. . . . Another of the five women hurled a stone that caught Helekohe on the shoulder. The muscles of his neck tightened with rage as his shouts of unintelligible abuse were lost in the scuffle erupting around his effort to grab the assailant. Even with their greater numbers the women might not have prevailed, but the men were handicapped by the need to stay near the struggling pig, prevented by their concern for the animal from following up their advantage of strength. They could not guard it and themselves as well. The women broke through their defenses and the anguished squeals of the bludgeoned pig penetrated my ears like a needle. (1965:248)

The men had expected a "ritual" attack from the women but were outraged when the women "managed to kill three pigs, two mature and valuable animals as well as the small one intended to fall into their hands" (1965:249).

Female displays of aggression are viewed as atypical, dismissed as "cat fights," attributed to witchcraft, or defined as "ritualistic," rather than passionately felt. Why is female aggression downplayed and male aggressive display so often accepted, encouraged, or even glorified? David Gilmore (1993) suggests that males are urged to test their mettle by undertaking risky endeavors and engaging in competition to foster

Under the new system, farmers contract to sell a certain amount of grain to the government at a set price. In return they have the right to dispose of the rest of their crop almost as they choose. The intention was to assign land by contract for at least fifteen years to encourage improvement. But family division, population growth, and erosion created problems. In Tranquillity Village, two further

a "manly" form of nurturing, of sacrificing oneself for others. Women contribute to society by giving life through childbirth; men contribute to society by giving up their lives.

The role of warrior is glorified in pastoral societies and in horticultural societies, but the scope of warfare in state societies based on intensive agriculture is unparalleled. Armies are larger, prizes are richer, the power of generals is more absolute, the technology is more elaborate. The literature of state societies also suggests the victories are unexcelled in honor and the rulers in grandeur. The following poem, written in China in 800 B.C., extols the virtues of a Chou emperor who has repelled an invader:

> Fang-shu has come,
> He has bound culprits, captured chieftains.
> His war-chariots rumble,
> They rumble and crash
> Like the clap of thunder, like the roll of thunder.
> Illustrious truly is Fang-shu,
> It was he who smote the Hsien-yun,
> Who made the tribes of Ching afraid. (Waley [1937] 1960:129)

The ancient Persian empire also produced epic poetry recounting glorious triumphs on the battlefield. The tenth-century Persian poet Ferdowsi recounted the wonders of its rulers in the *Shah-Nama*, or *Epic of Kings*. One such king, Key Khosrow, reigned for sixty years. At the height of his glory, the victorious emperor surveys his accomplishments:

Wherever there is territory inhabited by man, from India and innermost China even unto Greece, from the West to the gateway of the East, lands mountainous or desert arid or rain-swept, I have denuded them of my enemies; command and sovereignty are mine and the entire world has ceased to fear any malevolent foe. . . . I have killed all who deserved death, all whose way was crooked and who behaved in barbarous fashion towards the pure gods. There remains no land, whether cultivated or waste, in which the proclamation of my sword is not recited. The great ones of the world are my vassals, though they be possessed of throne and diadem. Praise be to God, who granted me the *farr* [charisma similar to mana emanating from kings], this phase of the stars, my foothold and my power to give protection. (Ferdowsi ([10th cent.] 1985:174–175)

Faced with the unaccustomed idleness of peace, Key Khosrow fears he will become restless and turn to evil ways. The king announces to his chief general that he will withdraw from the affairs of men and turn to God: "Now that I have got vengeance for my father and adorned the world with triumph, have slain those who displayed their enmity towards me or through whom wrong and injustice were brought into the world, no further task remains to me in the world" (Ferdowsi [10th cent.] 1985:179).

Key Khosrow appointed his successor, bade farewell to his family and followers, and made his way to the frontiers of his realm, where he disappeared in a snowstorm among the mountains. The great Persian emperor is no longer in the world and, ironically, neither is the empire for which he fought so hard. By the time Ferdowsi chronicled Key Khosrow's victories, the Persian empire had already been overrun by Arab invaders.

Not all members of state societies view war so positively. Kings and generals may find honor and fame on the battlefield, but peasants forced to leave their crops dying in the fields so they can fight and die on those same fields often have no such visions of glory. Two thousand years ago, a weary Chinese soldier lamented his fate:

> Minister of War,
> We are the king's claws and teeth.
> Why should you roll us from misery to misery,
> Giving us no place to come to and stay?
> Minister of War,
> Truly you are not wise.
> Why should you roll us from misery to misery?
> We have mothers who lack food.

The red wine of the battlefield may warm "the old heart of the earth," but it does not nourish peasant mothers whose sons are providing the battlefield blood that so many heroes seem to feel the earth craves.

redistributions that occurred before the original contracts expired contributed to substantial peasant insecurity. Farmers who had worked hard, carefully rotating crops and applying compost and chemical fertilizers, lost plots they had struggled to improve. With tenure uncertain, many are reluctant to invest time and resources. The new system has also altered labor needs. Households are thrown back on their

Agricultural Societies

State societies, characterized by leadership based on office, stratification, and a bureaucracy, are typically based on intensive agriculture, which produces a food surplus necessary to support task specialization and ranking. In addition, agricultural societies have large populations, often densely settled in cities.

The vast accumulation of wealth made possible by intensive agriculture and concentrated in the hands of elites supports a class of artisans and soldiers, since elites provide a market for high-status goods and soldiers are necessary to protect goods that are not available to all. By way of contrast, the !Kung have no need of police officers or soldiers to protect their supply of mongongo nuts, since the plant and animal resources of foragers are available to all.

Task specialization and stratification of roles in state societies typically extend to the religious realm, so that priests preside over formal ritual complexes that support the status quo. Shamans treat illness and misfortune on an informal basis.

Anthropologists suggest that societies based on intensive agriculture follow a cycle of growth and decline, whereas forager societies are stable through time because they do not overtax the environment or accumulate stores of wealth that attract human predators. The three agricultural societies discussed in this chapter illustrate the organization and dynamics characteristic of agricultural societies.

The Aztecs of Central Mexico

Ecology	Varied; lakes, mountains, and hills of Valley of Mexico; coastal and other resources in other parts of empire.
Group Formation and Residence	Cities and communities organized around kinship, inherited status, and occupation.
Subsistence Base	Cultivate maize, beans, chiles, squash, cactus, maguey, cotton, cacao, and many other fruits and vegetables using irrigation and fallowing; gather wild plants and hunt land and water animals; exploit fish and other resources of rivers, lakes, and seashores.
Division of Labor	Gender division of labor; large degree of task specialization according to rural and urban occupations.
Exchange Systems	Generalized reciprocity; balanced reciprocity; tribute system; market system.
Kinship	Bilateral inheritance of property and patrilineal inheritance of position; arranged marriages and polygyny among nobility.
Status and Leadership	Society organized around inherited nobility and commoner status, as well as an intermediate group of artisans and merchants. High-status positions occupied by nobility; commoners could achieve status through military prowess; conquered areas pay tribute to series of increasingly high-ranking nobility, culminating in ruler of Tenochtitlan; differences in rank signified by dress, housing, education, and occupation; slaves by achieved status only.
Religion	Hierarchy of gods centering on the sun god; belief in five successive worlds culminating in disaster; ritual centering on human sacrifice, presided over by priestly class; male and female shamans heal, work sorcery.
Expressive Culture	Writing and calendrical system; books, poetry, and songs; dancing and singing; elaborate visual art complex.
Cultural Change	Spanish invaders under Cortés destroyed buildings, political system, art, and religious complex, as well as decimated the population.

The Nayar of Southern India

Ecology	Mountain range isolates Kerala from rest of India; coastline promotes interaction with other countries through shipping and trade.
Group Formation and Residence	Villages composed of several castes organized around unilineal descent groups.
Subsistence Base	Agriculture; Nayar subcaste is a hereditary class of warriors in service of Brahmins. The economic contribution of women centers on producing children of both sexes to increase the strength of the lineage.
Exchange Systems	Generalized reciprocity; balanced reciprocity; market system.
Kinship	Matrilineal descent; matrilocal residence; unilineal extended families; nonexclusive marriage endogamous to caste, exogamous to descent group; descent group solidarity.
Status and Leadership	State form of government; caste system; authority within descent group vested in oldest male.
Religion	Belief in hierarchical system of male and female deities; female fertility and clan status associated with goddess worship; priests; rituals conducted by priests and within families associated both with calendar and life cycle.
Expressive Culture	Writing; elaborate tradition of art and literature.
Cultural Change	Traditional matrilineal, matrilocal extended-family system eroded by British colonial rule and changes in legal system; shift to monogamous marriage, nuclear family, wage labor system.

The Han of Northern China

Ecology	Harsh climate with both mountains and plains; long, cold winters with short, cool summers.
Group Formation and Residence	Villages centered on descent group and occupational specialization of either farming or herding.
Subsistence Base	Intensive agriculture based on maize, soybeans, wheat, potatoes, and sugar beets; herding of cattle or sheep; combined agriculture and dairying.
Division of Labor	*Farmers:* men primarily responsible for fields, tending cows; women tend domestic chores, milk, work in fields; young people leave school to assist with subsistence chores; older women tend children and assist with domestic chores; family income supplemented with sideline involving providing services, marketing produce, dairying, or wage labor.
	Herders: men herd, women milk; women perform domestic chores and assist with herding; women and older men work collective gardens; both men and women engage in supplementary activities; women weave baskets; men make money by cutting hay, river fishing, construction and transportation enterprises.
Exchange Systems	Generalized reciprocity; balanced reciprocity; market system with cash.
Kinship	Patrilineal extended families of both stem and joint type; farm families have early patrilocal marriage with large families; herders have later marriages, patrilocal, with smaller families.
Status and Leadership	State system; village leadership based on government-appointed cadres; extended families headed by oldest male.
Expressive Culture	Writing; art; theater.
Cultural Change	Revolution overthrowing dynastic system; Han migration into Mongol territory; Communist revolution results in shift to economic cooperatives with subsequent return to family-based unit of production.

own resources. The family determines what, when, how, and where to plant; how to allocate labor; what sidelines to undertake; and with whom to cooperate.

Villagers occasionally repeat the old adage "Boys are precious, girls useless," but it has little substance in these farming villages. The restoration of family-based production and the development of new sidelines increased the variety and value of women's contributions. By age seventeen or eighteen, all teenagers have acquired basic farm skills. Even children under fourteen can help, which is why parents short on labor sometimes end a child's schooling early. Nearly all children finish elementary school now. However, most go no further than primary school because additional education has little to offer youngsters destined to replace their parents.

It is more important to have more than one woman in a household than more than one man. Women can make up for a shortage of men, but it is hard to make up for a lack of women. Women's work is held in lower esteem, so men avoid housework and are not trained for it. It is the multifaceted contribution of women that enables farmers to undertake sidelines without greatly cutting into farm work.

Since land cannot be enlarged and cultivation earnings are limited, sidelines provide an important supplement to farm income. In Tranquillity Village, people gather and transport gravel, collect and sift construction sand, process grain, make potato noodles and bean curd, tend a few sheep, fish, and manage small grocery stores. Such sidelines contribute about 19 percent of village income. In Middle Village, which is farther from substantial markets, these sidelines are less common (only 6 percent of income). Most families there (89 percent) raise a few dairy cows on limited grassland, providing 27 percent of village income. With dairying, there is no need to travel far, and men do not spend much time away cutting hay. Mostly they raise their animals in sheds, buying fodder from other places.

Men tend sheds, women milk cows, and families often hire local cowboys to graze their cows. Because of the heavy demand for labor from farming, however, the division of labor by sex cannot be hard and fast. Women often work in the fields, and men occasionally help with the milking. When men are busy in the fields, women may help in the sheds. In Middle Village, as in Tranquillity Village, cultivation remains central.

Income and Its Distribution Motivation and income improved once the responsibility system was in place. The view that modernization requires rewarding initiative replaced egalitarian notions at the foundation of collectives. But in a society that struggled to eliminate extremes of wealth and poverty, even a modest increase in inequality causes concern.

Land and labor are not the whole story. Wealthy families in both Tranquillity Village and Middle Village derive a greater percentage of their income from some sort of nonagricultural sideline, such as dairying. Wages do not make a significant contribution to income (less than 5 percent) or to income disparity in either farming village. There are few jobs, and people who take them cannot easily manage farm work.

There is still little money for emergencies, let alone for saving or investment, and many costs are rising. It costs more to feed, dress, educate, and marry off children. At the same time, youngsters spend more time in school and contribute later. Furthermore, many expenses once underwritten by the collective, such as education and medical care, are now the family's burden. As incomes rise, people are tempted to acquire the consumer goods increasingly available.

Marriage is no longer so simple as during the more Spartan years of Chinese communism. There has been a dramatic increase in cost, for bride as well as groom, especially since the shift to a privatized economy. Cadres tolerate greater display, and villagers spend more. In fact, getting children married is probably the greatest financial burden any family must bear. Traditionally more costly for the groom, even the expense of marrying a daughter has increased. Still, bridewealth without dowry is more common than the reverse, reflecting perhaps the importance of women's labor.

Children are costly even after marriage. At some point, every family divides; sons move off to live on their own, taking a share of family assets. This development has become more significant both because there is more to divide and because sons begin to live on their own sooner. On all fronts, farmers work harder to achieve ever-rising standards and expectations.

The New Herdsmen

In the farming area, Mongols adopted the Han mode of farming and way of life. Because of their smaller numbers and the demands of cultivation, they live interspersed with the Han and have become culturally indistinguishable from them. Few can speak Mongol. The two groups often intermarry, and, as do the Han, Mongols favor early patrilocal marriage, two or three children, and **stem families** consisting of parents and one married son.

As the Han adapted to the grassland, they abandoned farming for a pastoral life, which now shapes what they do and value. They did not cease to be Han, however, and despite the homogenizing efforts of the state, they forged another kind of Han Chinese society. In the pastoral region, there are more Mongols and more marked cultural and political differences. The Han and Mongols share public facilities and have many common interests, but they remain distinct subcommunities, as reflected in dress, speech, political competition, rarity of intermarriage, and occasional fights. More than among the cultivators, people speak their own languages and marry their own kind. Their children go to separate schools, where instruction is in their native tongue. Separate clinics treat illness according to distinct traditions.

There is an uneasy mix of traditions in the Inner Mongolian villages of Sandhill and Great Pasture. Mongols in town have homes like those of the Han, and, like them, grow vegetables in small gardens. They dress like Han and, like them, most speak Mandarin in addition to their native tongue. Few Han speak Mongol, but they too eat beef and mutton rather than pork, drink milk-tea, and share a regional penchant for hard liquor. When they cut hay or graze animals on the open grassland, they, too, live in *yurts*, circular domed tents made of skins stretched over a lattice framework.

When the Han first turned to pastoralism, dairying was more in keeping with their sedentary farming tradition. In Sandhill, wages supplement dairying, and in Great Pasture, many sell hay, raise sheep, or fish. Accustomed to a more nomadic way, the Mongols favor sheep. They rarely cut hay for sale and do not fish, because these activities would interfere with shepherding. Just as cultivation forged similarities, so too has pastoralism encouraged convergence. Old specializations blur as Han add sheep and Mongols expand into dairying. Han shepherds add yurts, while Mongol dairymen acquire fixed residences in or near town, close to schools and milk collection stations.

From Collective to Family Herding In herding, too, collective management ultimately turned out to be problematic. There was little incentive to carefully tend livestock, and cadres could not effectively control how people did their work. The problem was exacerbated during the Cultural Revolution

Task specialization by age and gender takes place in all societies, but production of a food surplus associated with intensive agriculture permits an extreme degree of task specialization. Agricultural societies typically have artisans, craftspeople specializing in production of different types of trade goods, such as shoes, clothing, and jewelry. These farmers of Xinjiang Province, China, still produce many goods at home. These men are dying yarn, which will be woven into cloth by women of the household.

(1966–1976), when cadres assigned points according to days worked, regardless of difficulty. Herdsmen then had every reason to avoid the hardest work. Many animals were lost, and livestock numbers expanded slowly if at all.

When the family became the basic unit of accounting, administrative responsibilities passed from commune to township. Families drew lots for cows and sheep, expecting to pay for them over time. Not many Han were interested in sheep, but everyone wanted cows, which do not require long periods far from home. Most Sandhill and Great Pasture Han lent their sheep to Mongol shepherds in exchange for meat. Pasture and grassland remain publicly managed and commonly shared.

Forms of Pastoralism and the Division of Labor

In Sandhill and Great Pasture, the shift from farming is complete. Grassland is now more abundant and herds are larger than in Middle Village. In 1988, most Sandhillers (83 percent of households) had cows. In Great Pasture, 98 percent of Han families had cows, and herds are larger than in Sandhill.

Pastoralism required adjustment of the Han way. Livestock require constant attention. The distances herdsmen travel and the need for skilled, experienced labor underlie sharper differences in the tasks of women and men, young and old. Even in collectives, the division of labor is very sharp. Teams of men pasture collective livestock; a smaller group of women earns points milking them.

Men earn points at a variety of tasks year round, but women and older men are "half labor," and their work is more limited. They often remain at home. For most tasks, cadres prefer men. Maturity, experience, strength, and endurance are crucial because harsh weather, mismanagement, wolves, and disease can quickly decimate herds and flocks. Herdsmen must be knowledgeable about animals, able to lift heavy animals and other objects, and prepared to spend long periods away from home, often in severe weather. Youngsters lack the necessary judgment, and women are inexperienced and have to remain close to home to run the household and care for children. With the collective gone, families depend more heavily on their own resources for the full range of tasks.

Sheepherding Sheep are risky and most efficiently managed in sizable flocks. Sheep need more substantial pasture and closer attention than cows; they must be moved often and watched constantly. Great Pasture Han were initially no more eager than Sandhillers to spend long periods on the open grasslands, so they, too, put the few sheep they obtained in the care of Mongol shepherds. But recently, as the selling price of sheep began to rise, a number of Han with sufficient male family labor have added sheepherding to dairying. Han shepherds have become the new nomads of China's northeastern frontier. Sheep, not assimilation to Mongol culture, encourage commonalties in behavior. While Mongols still prefer life in yurts on the open range, Han shepherds come from a sedentary tradition and still rely more heavily on dairying.

Division of Labor Among the herders, males and females have different work to do. Men work hardest in winter, when cows are penned much of the time. Women are busiest during the summer peak milking time. But compared with farmers, the tasks men and women do, and when they do them, change little during the year. Men have principal responsibility for work away from home and for tasks that demand great strength. In Great Pasture, they hitch up tank carts and haul water from the community well each day. They cut, haul, and pile hay. They shovel cow pens and feed livestock in winter. Pasturing sheep through the deep cold of winter imposes heavy demands, and only men fish in the nearby river. Women and men classify all these jobs as "heavy work," largely the domain of men.

Women do most of their work within compound gates. They care for children, build and maintain fires, clean, cook, wash, repair, and refill the padding in winter clothing, sew clothes, make shoes, garden, and put up vegetables. They milk cows in the courtyard. Women also convert cow dung into cooking fuel, shaping it into disks that they turn and dry in the winter sun, then pile for storage. They also make mud bricks used to fix houses. There are few tasks for which women and men readily replace each other.

The assignment of work by age is also different from that among farmers. Youngsters are too inexperienced to do much until about age fourteen, later than among the farmers. They lead calves to nearby pastures at daybreak and carry milk cans to the collection station twice a day. Girls help with milking. In general, people under twenty do not fully participate in herding sheep or cows, milking, cutting grass, or fishing. Like women, they may fill in but cannot replace men.

Because they start working later, children among the pastoralists go to school longer than among the farmers. More attend junior high, and the farmer–herder difference is especially marked for girls. Among the farmers, girls receive the least schooling, but among the herders they are better educated than males, in that more go to middle schools. That is because they do little in the way of herding, and milking takes place before or after school.

At the other end of life, retirement for pastoralists comes later than for cultivators. An elderly couple can make a living on their own until they are quite old. They can reduce the number of cows they manage, and thus the amount of pen cleaning and winter feeding they do. They may hire a cowherd to pasture their cows. Their children cut the hay they need, or they can trade grass-cutting rights for hay.

Income and Inequality: Herdsmen and Cultivators Compared

Privatization and diversification have increased income inequalities within and between communities. By allowing families to enlarge and diversify their enterprises, the new family responsibility system provided the basis for greater income inequality. Families that work harder, at a greater variety of tasks, see incomes rise. Inequality is on the increase, especially among the herders. Herders earn significantly more than farmers. Among herders, only the number of men is significantly related to income. Among farmers, both the number of women and the number of men are significantly related to income.

Income alone is not a sufficient indicator of wealth, however. It is especially imprecise for pastoralists because it does not consider capital assets such as savings, livestock, or machines. Animals are expendable as well as expandable capital; they represent wealth on the hoof. The herder invests care, feed, and capital, and if all goes well, animals multiply. Farmers also invest labor and capital, but their land does not expand, and their ability to increase crop yields is limited.

Nor does income reveal differences in risk or in ability to rebound from setbacks. Both herders and farmers experience difficult years. They may sustain losses or incur heavy expenses through marriages and funerals. However, whereas even a small rise in expenses can throw a farm family into debt from

which recovery is difficult, herdsmen can recover more quickly. Land cannot be sold to cover losses and be bought back later, but herdsmen can readily vary the size of their herds in response to the need for cash or a shortage of labor.

Economy and Family   Differences in the need for labor are reflected in the size and composition of families. Though individual family units could cooperate with others to meet changing needs for labor and resources, the preference is to place primary reliance on the family. Therefore farm families prefer early patrilocal marriage and extended families that allow one woman to work outside and another to work inside the home. Family division into neolocal units is a bigger problem for farmers than for herders because it reduces the number of women available for labor. At the same time, division of the family requires partition of the land, since parents give land to sons who establish their own families. In pre-Communist China, the preferred residence pattern was an extended family form known as the **joint family,** in which married brothers remained together. By maintaining an economically interdependent joint family, married brothers could economize on labor and capital to avoid borrowing or hiring labor. If they lived apart as separate households within a single property-owning family, they could avoid the strife that so often precipitated family division.

With collectivization, there was no longer any need to maintain the joint family to avoid partitioning the land, but it was still desirable to have more than one woman in the household, one to handle domestic duties while the other earned work points on the communal farms. The advantages of having more than one woman in the household encouraged a continuation of early patrilocal marriage and the stem form of extended family, composed of parents and one married son.

Among pastoralists, the labor of men is more important than the labor of women. Because there was no need to have more than one woman in the family to handle domestic chores, herdsmen married later and more often lived in neolocal households. Early marriage is less desirable to them because it is less important to acquire a daughter-in-law at an early age and more important to hold a son longer. Herdsmen still prefer the stem form of family because a married son takes livestock when he leaves. Since livestock multiply in a way land cannot, the sons' taking property is less of a problem for herders than for farmers.

Family Reproduction Throughout China the government has encouraged people to delay marriage and limit family size. Inner Mongolia has not escaped these efforts, although family planning has not been as strictly enforced there as in interior China. Parents continue to arrange marriages close to the legal age thresholds, although herdsmen still delay longer than farmers.

When infant and child mortality were high, many children increased the likelihood that some would survive to ensure the parents' care in old age. When collectives subsidized medical care and education, raising children cost less, and fewer children need to be born now to be certain some will survive. With the end of collectivization, the cost of raising and marrying children has increased.

Although pastoralists and cultivators are no longer eager to have as many children as they can, neither are they prepared to stop with one. Herders have more reason to avoid having many children, given their greater cost, longer school attendance, and later contribution to family subsistence, but even they have not embraced the one-child model urged by the state. Childbearing exceeds state recommendations in all sites, but farmers have more children than pastoralists. There is no significant difference in the average number of children born to Han and Mongol herders, but Han herders have fewer children than Han farmers do. These differences suggest that differences in economy and ecology are more important than ethnicity in regard to family size.

Herders, Cultivators, and the Status of Women

The Communist emphasis on mass participation brought large numbers of women into the labor force, and some observers suggest that it enhanced their leverage at home. In fact, the collectives also benefited from the contribution of women. If women enhance their value and voice by adding to income, then farm women should certainly be at an advantage, especially in the new economy because their work is essential to the household economy. But the connection between work and status is not straightforward. For one thing, women do not control their work, product, or income. Even when women work outside the home, their earnings are usually delivered to the family head. For a woman's labor to be considered "important," it must be visible and the economic advantage must be clearly linked to her efforts. Neither among farmers nor among herders do people consider women's work "important" in the sense of being central to the household economy. Both women and men share the perception that "men's work" is more important.

Under the new system, every person is entitled to an allocation of land at birth. Before a woman marries, her land is considered part of her family estate. When she marries, the land reverts to the community reserve until her husband's family requests an assignment on her behalf. Farm women enjoy a right to property that pastoral women do not. In the minds of farm family members, however, the land a woman brings with her is not identified with her. She does not decide what will be grown on it or who will use it. Therefore, it does not necessarily elevate her position.

The community does not assign herding women animals, pasture, or grassland when they are born or marry. If property conferred status or influence, then pastoral women would be disadvantaged. However, structural differences in the family and allocation of labor tip the scales the other way, enhancing the status of herding women. Cultivators are more often patrilocal, and a farm woman is more subject to her mother-in-law's judgments and moods. Since pastoralists are more often neolocal, we might expect that herding women would enjoy greater autonomy. In addition, herding women go to school longer, work and marry later, and bear fewer children, and many are better educated than their husbands. Is it not possible that these characteristics, which derive from their lesser contribution, confer a measure of influence or self-fulfillment?

In fact, the education advantage of pastoral girls does not lead to a better job or a better life. Most follow in the footsteps of their mothers. Indeed, the lower education of farm women, their earlier marriages, and their greater participation in work reflect their importance to the domestic economy. Nonetheless, it is doubtful that the earlier and more substantial input of farm women give them any great bargaining power. It may only make their lives more difficult.

Our observations in the field suggest that a variety of factors relating to ecology, subsistence, and the political structure shape the organization of the family, economic roles within the family, and relations between women and men. Changing political conditions in China that have had an impact on the allocation of land and resources have provided an ideal context in which to examine the interrelationships of all these factors. It is unlikely, however, that such complex variables could ever be reduced to a simple schema of causal relationships.

SUMMARY

Agricultural societies are characterized by large populations, cities, stratification, and warfare, all of which are associated with states. Whereas forager and horticultural groups remain stable through time, societies based on intensive agriculture appear to follow a cycle of florescence and collapse. The three agricultural societies discussed in this chapter—the Aztecs of central Mexico, the Nayar of southern India, and the Han of northern China—all reflect in varying degrees the effects of stratification, task specialization, and conflict centering on competition for control of the vast amount of wealth and power concentrated in the hands of the ruling class of agricultural states.

In the two-hundred-year history of their empire, the Aztecs developed a complex society based on cultivation of corn and other crops. They built great cities, including their capital of Tenochtitlan, near the heart of what is now Mexico City. The Aztecs had few domesticated animals, but they supplemented their diet through hunting, fishing, and gathering of wild plants. There were full-time artisans, professional merchants, and a military and religious bureaucracy employing great numbers of judges, governors, tax collectors, generals, warriors, teachers, and priests.

Political life was organized around a hierarchy of city-states, with rulers of conquered communities and city-states paying tribute to those higher up. Tenochtitlan was at the top of the tribute ladder. Since Tenochtitlan was not economically self-sufficient, it relied on almost continuous warfare to exact tribute from conquered areas so it could maintain its great wealth and obtain captives for human sacrifice, necessary to feed the gods and ensure the continuation of the universe. Aztec religious life was presided over by a hierarchy of priests, who performed the human sacrifices.

The intellectual accomplishments of the Aztecs included an accurate calendrical system based on astronomical observations, a writing system based on glyphs, magnificent sculptures, and various types of crafts, as well as poems, plays, and music. The Aztec Empire ended with Hernán Cortés's conquest of Mexico. Artworks and books were destroyed, gold and silver ornaments were melted down, and stones of the razed city of Tenochtitlan were used to build the new Spanish capital of Mexico City.

The Nayar of the state of Kerala in southern India were a warrior subcaste who have long interested anthropologists because of their residence pattern organized around matrilineal and matrilocal households. In the traditional system, women could enter into more or less permanent sambandham, or sexual relationships, with a number of "husbands" after undergoing a tali-tying ceremony at puberty. Males had no rights to their children, who remained in their matrilineal households, or taravads. In the lesser-known form practiced in northern Kerala, women moved into their husbands' matrilineal households after the sambandham ceremony. Both arrangements provided greater freedom and status for women, compared with other Hindu groups, in which descent is patrilineal.

In the nineteenth and twentieth centuries, a number of factors eroded or modified the traditional ceremonies, marriage patterns, and family relationships of the Nayar. One change was the decline in importance of the matrilineal household. Property was once held in common by the taravad and administered by the eldest male. Now, individual members may ask for their share upon attaining adulthood. Fathers have become more involved in the affairs of their children, and women now move permanently into their husband's home.

Another change is the decline of the tali-tying ceremony and the increased importance of the sambandham ceremony, which has become a marriage arranged by the families. It is now expected that the sambandham ceremony will result in a stable monogamous union with neolocal residence. These changes have resulted from economic, reformist, and legal challenges to the traditional system. Nayar marriage and family customs now conform more closely to those of other Hindus, in that there is a shift toward a male bias in inheritance and control. However, Nayar women continue to exert greater control over their lives than do other Hindu women.

China's long dynastic rule was overthrown by revolution in 1911. In 1949, Mao Zedong's Communist government made sweeping changes, converting clan-owned lands into farming collectives and small-scale industries into economic cooperatives. As have other rural Chinese, Han farmers who live along the Great Wall on the northern frontier have been swept along by these changes. Under the commune system, both men and women worked on collective farms. Though women were supposed to be equal in earning potential, commune leaders assigned them fewer "work points" for their labor, and their work hours were shorter because of domestic responsibilities.

In a move to increase productivity, China began to disband rural collectives in 1979 and now allocates land to individual families. Under the new "responsibility system," farmers contract to sell a certain amount of grain to the government at a set price; they can dispose of the rest of their crop as they wish. With restoration of the family-based system, everyone's labor is essential for farm families. Young people leave school early to help on the farm, and women often work in the fields. Since land cannot be enlarged and farm earnings are limited by the amount of land under a family's control, farmers increase their income by sideline activities, including providing services and dairying.

Among herders, the Mongol and Han lifestyles are merging to some extent, though the two groups continue to maintain separate languages and communities. As the Han adapted to the grassland, they abandoned farming for a pastoral life. Mongols who live in town have houses like the Han and grow vegetables in small gardens.

When the Han first turned to pastoralism, dairying was more in keeping with their sedentary farming tradition, whereas the Mongols favored sheep, which require long periods of time away from home. More recently, the Han have begun to herd sheep and Mongols have expanded into dairying. Both Han and Mongol herders marry later, are more often neolocal, and have smaller families than Han and Mongol farmers.

Whereas farming is seasonal, livestock require constant attention. Because herders must travel with their flocks, the division of labor by age and gender increases in importance. Because the labor of women is important in farming families, they tend to early patrilocal marriage, delayed family division, and extended families. Among pastoralists, the work of men is more important, so they tend to marry later and live in neolocal households.

The Communist emphasis on mass participation brought large numbers of women into the labor force, but women do not control their work and their earnings have usually been delivered to the family head. Neither farmers nor herders consider women's work central to the household economy, and both women and men view men's work as "more important."

The three agricultural societies described in this chapter represent adaptations to the social and climatic conditions of central Mexico, southern India, and northern China. Though the three groups are culturally dissimilar, they share traits associated with intensive agriculture, including hierarchical political organization and dramatic changes in their way of life resulting from population pressures, internal and external competition for access to resources, and disruption occasioned by war or revolution.

POWER WORDS

achieved status	**glyphs**	**stem family**
ascribed status	**joint family**	

INTERNET EXERCISE

1. Learn more about Aztec religion, medicine, and other aspects of their social life at **http://www.northcoast.com/~spdtom/aztec.html**. Choose a topic from among those available through the site and compare their information with that presented in this chapter.

2. India is going through many social changes, as is characteristic of stratified societies. On the website **http://www.mnet.fr/aiindex/kn.html**, a former Indian official, Kuldip Nayar, expresses concern over international perceptions of India after his country tested nuclear weapons. From an ethnographic perspective, briefly analyze Nayar's perspective in terms of the political dynamics of a stratified nation-state.

3. Most of what people in North America know about China is from media and government sources. The website **http://www.insidechina.com/** provides information about China from the perspective of mainland Chinese media and government sources. How does it differ from that of North Americans?

15
The People We Study

In this chapter . . .

Culture change

All cultures change. In fact, the ability to adapt to the environment through culture rather than biology has enabled human groups to survive in a variety of ecological contexts. Innovation, invention, and diffusion, or borrowing, are forms of culture change that originate from within a group. Colonialism, the subjugation of one group by another, is the most disruptive form of culture change.

Political and economic effects of colonialism

Colonized peoples lose control of their economic resources and become subject to the control of outsiders. Colonial governments impose a hierarchical form of political organization on formerly egalitarian groups and disrupt traditional social relationships that stabilized groups that were already hierarchical before colonization. In the process, indigenous peoples are marginalized or pushed to the fringes of society. In most cases, they are impoverished.

Population, economics, and health

The world's population is burgeoning. Population is growing fastest in the poorest regions of the world, and there is a strong relationship among poverty, malnutrition, and disease. Some suggest that population growth could be slowed by a redistribution of wealth. Even if that theory could be proved, there are no mechanisms in place for such a redistribution. Also, there is little international law to regulate transnational corporations and financial institutions in order to maintain minimal standards of wealth.

Culture change, culture loss, and "cocacolonization"

The lifestyles of indigenous peoples have been dramatically altered by various types of cultural colonialism, which include the effects of religious conversion and the introduction of Western consumer goods into traditional societies. Missionary activity erodes the confidence of indigenous peoples in their own traditions and disrupts the social order, and it can pave the way for commercial and political exploitation. Some indigenous peoples are fighting with some degree of success to take back their cultures.

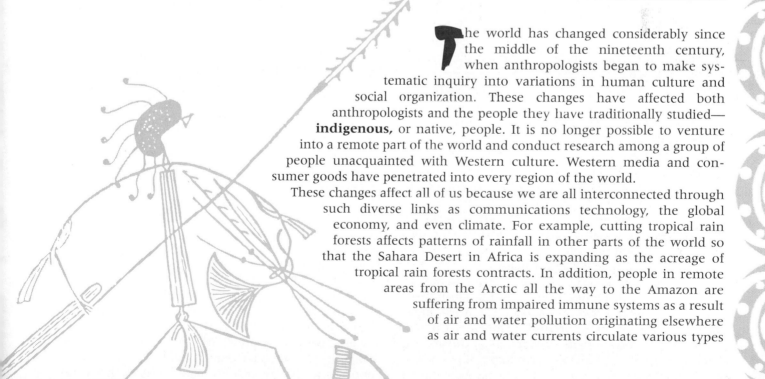

The world has changed considerably since the middle of the nineteenth century, when anthropologists began to make systematic inquiry into variations in human culture and social organization. These changes have affected both anthropologists and the people they have traditionally studied—**indigenous,** or native, people. It is no longer possible to venture into a remote part of the world and conduct research among a group of people unacquainted with Western culture. Western media and consumer goods have penetrated into every region of the world.

These changes affect all of us because we are all interconnected through such diverse links as communications technology, the global economy, and even climate. For example, cutting tropical rain forests affects patterns of rainfall in other parts of the world so that the Sahara Desert in Africa is expanding as the acreage of tropical rain forests contracts. In addition, people in remote areas from the Arctic all the way to the Amazon are suffering from impaired immune systems as a result of air and water pollution originating elsewhere as air and water currents circulate various types of toxins from the equator to the North and South Poles. There is no place left on the planet to hide.

Culture change is not always negative. In fact, the ability to change enhances human survival. As noted in Chapter 4, anthropologists such as Leslie White and Julian Steward have suggested that humans adapt to their environment primarily through culture rather than through biology. Culture allows humans to adapt more quickly to environmental changes than would be possible if they adapted solely through biology.

For most of human history, culture change took place gradually through the process of **innovation.** Innovation is change that results from variations in the customary way of doing things. It can produce changes in technology or cultural practices. For example, experimentation with flaking of various types of stone led to the production of sophisticated arrow points balanced by aerodynamically sound wooden shafts. Domestication of plants may have developed as foragers began to scatter seeds for harvesting later in their migrations. Innovation continues to be an important part of culture change, on both an individual level and a societal level, as we vary our daily routine or find a "better" way of doing things. If others adopt our better way, our innovation can effect subtle but widespread changes in a culture.

Invention is conscious innovation. We cannot transport ourselves back into the minds of prehistoric humans and determine how many of their vast number of innovations were conscious, but invention has certainly become an important part of modern culture change. In industrialized countries, many companies are established as the result of inventions. Often, large companies maintain a full-time staff charged with the responsibility of producing new products or improving existing products.

Many inventions are aimed at wooing consumers, as when computer companies find ways of processing increasingly large amounts of information more efficiently in a smaller space. The cosmetics industry employs small armies of people to invent new shades of lipstick, and commercial medical laboratories devote a large amount of their resources to developing new technology for treating disease.

Diffusion, or borrowing, has played a role in culture change throughout much of human history. Innovations in tool design spread over broad areas during the migrations of prehistoric foragers. Chinese bows were eagerly sought by warriors of the ancient Persian Empire. Techniques for making fine "china" and gunpowder were taken to Europe from China by medieval travelers. Pasta was also a Chinese invention, but after Chinese "noodles" were introduced into Europe they were subject to innovation by Italian chefs, so they have become linked in Western minds with Italian cuisine.

The typically "American" meal of hamburger and French fries represents a virtual United Nations of food. Cattle for the beef were domesticated in Africa; wheat for the bun was domesticated in the Middle East; varieties of lettuce, a common garnish, were cultivated by Greeks, Persians, and Moors; tomatoes were domesticated in North America; and potatoes for the "French" fries were domesticated in South America.

Innovation and diffusion are relatively benign forms of culture change. Because the impetus for adopting innovations and borrowing stems from conditions within the group, the new product or practice is usually consonant with its culture and social organization. Invention may also produce a relatively small amount of disruption. However, when corporate competition and advertising fuel entire industries based on invention, the process can produce dramatic culture change very quickly. Human beings are then forced to adapt rapidly to changes in technology, styles of dress, behavior, language, and values.

Colonialism, the subjugation of one group by another, produces the most disruptive form of culture change. The most pervasive and disruptive forms of culture change were produced by European colonialism. As noted in Chapter 1, the outward expansion of Europeans from the fifteenth to the nineteenth centuries altered the world's political map forever. In addition, the subjugation or domination of virtually all the people of the world by a few European countries produced profound changes in the world's economic systems, religions, kinship patterns, and expressive culture.

Virtually all aspects of human life have been affected by the expansion of European culture. In most places in the world, the role of midwife in childbirth has given way to doctors trained in concepts of modern Western medicine. Rice farmers drink Coca-Cola. Pacific Islanders learn English or French in schools patterned after European academies. Christianity has challenged the spiritual authority of traditional shamans.

In the pages that follow, we will explore some of the problems facing contemporary societies and examine some of their ingenious approaches to dealing with those problems. We will focus on three major issues that have dramatically altered the status and prospects of people in many parts of the world: (1) the political and economic effects of colonialism;

(2) the interrelationship of population, economics, and health; and (3) culture change, culture loss, and "cocacolonization."

POLITICAL AND ECONOMIC EFFECTS OF COLONIALISM

The most immediate and direct effect of colonialism is that indigenous people lose control of their economic resources and become subject to the political control of outsiders. In the process, traditional social relationships are disrupted. People who had been central to political and economic processes often become marginalized and impoverished. Colonized people in egalitarian societies become the bottom rung of a hierarchy imposed from outside. People in societies that were already hierarchical are displaced by outsiders, and the resources of the group are siphoned off for use by the colonizing power.

Societies that colonize other groups are by their nature hierarchical, since concentration of economic and political resources in the hands of an elite class provides both the means and the motive for colonial conquest. Hierarchical forms of government are supported by some form of tribute or taxes, made possible by the labor of a peasantry (in agricultural societies) or a working class (in industrialized societies). As illustrated by the examples of the Aztecs and Nayars in Chapter 14, the power of those in the higher levels of the hierarchy and the ability to exact taxes or tribute are supported by a class of warriors.

When European colonial powers began to dominate much of the rest of the world, they were sometimes able to supplant the indigenous hierarchy with their own bureaucratic apparatus, as when the Spanish conquered the Aztecs in central Mexico and the Incas in Peru. In both these cases, the transfer of power was devastating to the indigenous peoples. European diseases introduced to people who had not built up immunity to them produced epidemics that killed from 70 to 90 percent of the population in less than a century (Wilson 1992:186). This decimation of the labor force eroded the tax base. The Spanish also required tribute in a tangible and portable form that could be transported back to Europe. This meant that people who had been accustomed to paying their tribute in labor were now forced to pay in goods. The shift from a labor-based tribute system to a goods-based tax system destroyed the economy.

In other cases, European colonialists encountered peoples who had not developed a hierarchy similar to their own. These peoples were unaccustomed to paying taxes or tribute of any kind, since their subsistence-based economy would not support an elaborate hierarchy. In these cases, the indigenous people were killed, expelled from their lands, forced into slavery, or recruited into wage labor as miners, agricultural workers, or workers in other types of commercial operations. In all cases, the indigenous people formed the lower classes of the newly imposed hierarchical system.

Even in the post-colonial era, indigenous peoples are still losing rights to their land for a variety of economic and political reasons, including social reorganization after colonial powers returned rule to indigenous peoples. For decades, the !Kung of Africa have provided a model of the forager band lifestyle. Anthropologists have studied their dispersed residence patterns organized along bilateral kin lines, their customs of meat distribution based on generalized reciprocity, and their egalitarian political organization, which emphasized cooperation over competition.

Traditional !Kung lands are spread out over what are now the three African nations of Angola, Botswana, and Namibia. The fate of the !Kung has been intricately bound up in the political processes that transformed these former European colonial territories into modern nation-states. The emergence of Angola was particularly violent, as three rival rebel factions—each backed by foreign political powers—fought for control of the new government. By 1993, when the United States recognized the new government, the country's economy and many of its traditional cultures were in ruins.

The process of political change in Botswana was less devastating to the !Kung of that region, but it transformed many aspects of their way of life. It changed their subsistence economy into a cash economy, which in turn may have altered traditional modes of interaction. In 1966, the independent nation of Botswana was formed from the British protectorate of Bechuanaland. The new government encouraged the !Kung to enter the national economy and settle down as pastoralists or agriculturalists. The government provided economic rewards to the !Kung for abandoning foraging by buying their traditional handicrafts and giving them donkeys for pulling simple plows.

Innovations in communications technology have dramatically altered the lifestyles of people in many parts of the world. For this Masai cattle herder of Kenya's Rift Valley, however, the pastoral way of life continues undisturbed in the shadow of a satellite communications tower.

Meanwhile, !Kung in the neighboring country of Namibia—then still part of South Africa—were brought into the army. Their wages infused cash into the local economy. The Namibian !Kung soldiers' cash and goods flowed to Botswana !Kung through interactions with kin.

Ethnographer and archaeologist John E. Yellen (1991) argues that the transformation from a subsistence economy to a cash-based food-production economy in Botswana has eroded the traditional !Kung value of cooperation. Yellen conducted archaeological surveys of !Kung camps in the Dobe region of Botswana near the country's border with Namibia. Comparing camps occupied in the 1970s with those dating from the 1940s, Yellen noted several alterations in arrangements of huts and hearths that suggested the !Kung were withdrawing from interaction with their neighbors. Huts from earlier sites were set close together and arranged in a circle so that most entrances faced inward. That configuration allowed people in each of the huts to see into most of the others. This arrangement promoted interaction between people in the different huts. By the early 1970s, distances between huts had increased significantly, and huts were arranged in a linear pattern that gave families more privacy (Yellen 1991).

In addition, in earlier sites, hearths were located in front of huts, providing a center of social interaction. As people gathered around their hearths in the evening, traditional lore was passed from one generation to the next through story telling. Healing was conducted through trance dancing. Both activities promoted interaction among the group as a whole. Marjorie Shostak writes:

> The atmosphere of a ceremonial medicine dance is anything but reverential. It is an important social gathering, a time of general excitement and festivity, a time for people to ensure their safety, to suspend conflicts, and to act out and verify the common bond that unites them. People talk, joke, flirt, and comment on everything that happens. (1983:296)

Yellen notes that, beginning in the 1970s, hearths began to be located inside !Kung huts instead of in front of them, thus altering an important component of group solidarity.

> These changes occurred so abruptly that the pattern of camp design can be said to have been unambiguously transformed from "close" to "distant" within a few years. By implication, such changes in camp design indicate that major changes in social norms for openness and sharing occurred as well in the early to middle 1970s. (1991:210)

Another researcher, Diane E. Gelburd, compared !Kung ownership of personal property in the 1970s with the findings of a survey conducted by Richard B. Lee in 1963. Lee found that most people could carry all their worldly belongings with ease. Little more than a decade later, Gelburd noted that many !Kung owned large items that were difficult to transport, including plows and cast-iron pots. The !Kung were also using their newfound cash to hoard such goods as glass beads, clothing, and extra blankets. They often locked these items away in trunks, a departure from their previous pattern of cooperation and generalized reciprocity organized around sharing of game from hunting (cited in Yellen 1991).

In addition to these same pressures, the !Kung of Namibia were forced to adopt a more settled lifestyle, but government policies made it nearly impossible for them to flourish. Although the government policies were nearly disastrous for the !Kung, they have adapted to the changes and are increasingly successful in their new lifestyle. In 1971, the border between Namibia and Botswana was fenced, cutting off the !Kung residing in Namibia from 90 percent of their traditional foraging land and all but one of their permanent water holes. Under the Homelands Policy, the Namibian government gave much of !Kung land there to the Herero, another indigenous people whose traditional subsistence was based on cattle herding. Another large portion of !Kung land was designated as a game preserve. There was no longer enough land to support foraging, and the !Kung subgroup Ju/"huansi was forced to take up subsistence farming or herding.

Forced to settle down but cut off from many of their traditional water holes, Ju/"huansi attempts at food production were severely hampered. The people did not have sufficient water for themselves or their cattle. At the same time, the government supplied water for elephants and barred the Ju/"huansi from hunting elephants or lions. Lions found domesticated cattle easy prey, and elephants trampled crops and destroyed water pumps installed by the Ju/"huansi. Though the Ju/"huansi were prohibited from hunting elephants, the government Department of Nature Conservation opened the territory to wealthy trophy hunters from Europe and the United States. Enormous elephant carcasses were left rotting in the sun, attracting still more predators to Ju/"huansi land.

The enormous obstacles in the way of the Ju/"huansi's attempted transition from a foraging to a food-production economy inspired the Ju/"huansi to become involved in the decision-making process that was dictating their fate. Besieged by drought, lions, elephants, and government officials, the Ju/"huansi have become politically active. They voted for the first time in the 1989 elections. As a result, their rights to their lands are now recognized. When Namibia became an independent nation in 1990, the Ju/"huansi organized themselves into a farmers' cooperative. At one of the early meetings, the Ju/"huansi began developing rules for allocating their land and providing their people with water. A new leader of the cooperative is Tsamkxao, who began his career as a hunter, then became a cattle herder, and is now adapting his leadership skills to local government. Tsamkxao says:

> We've started our own drilling program, but we aren't satisfied to just have water holes for ourselves. We want to help people with no land, no water, nothing. First we must work to drill our own water holes. Some of us are

without water. Then we must search outside for our relatives who have no land or hope. Our local government must be like the father and mother of Ju/"huansi who have nothing, so we can give people more places and farms under our law. (Womack, *Faces of Culture,* video, 1994)

The Ju/"huansi are using traditional rules regulating foraging rights to lands to allocate land under the new system. As discussed in Chapter 11, rights to land are based on rules of kinship. A !Kung's *n!ore* is the land for which he or she holds foraging rights through bilateral descent, residence, or marriage. Basing land rights on traditional inheritance rules provides continuity between the old way of life and the new.

POPULATION, ECONOMICS, AND HEALTH

One of the most urgent and apparently insoluble problems affecting humanity is the dramatic rise in the world's population. It took more than four million years for the world's population to pass the one billion mark. It took about one hundred years to add more than four billion more people to that total. In 1999 the world's population passed the six billion mark. According to conservative estimates by the United Nations Department of International Economic and Social Affairs, there will be 8.6 billion people on the earth by the year 2025 (Figure 15.1). This population projection is based on the estimate that population growth will begin to decline from its present rate of 1.7 percent per year to 1.0 percent in 2025.

Most demographic experts agree that the continued rise in population will strain the earth's resources. Such large numbers of people are likely to increase already high levels of pollution and produce more armed conflicts arising from competition for land and other resources. Crowding in cities is expected to lead to increases in numbers and rates of infectious diseases. The predicted health crisis is likely to be exacerbated by expanded international travel, which introduces disease vectors from one population to others that have not developed an immunity to them.

Problems associated with increasing population are accentuated by international and regional disparities in the distribution of wealth and economic resources. Rates of population growth are greatest in nonindustrialized countries, which include some of

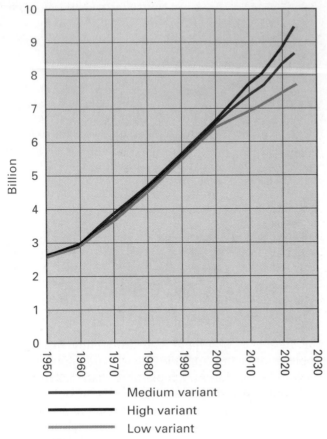

Medium variant
High variant
Low variant

FIGURE 15.1   United Nations Estimates of World Population Growth

In the mid-1990s, the world's population was growing at a rate of 1.7 percent per year. Most demographers predict a reduction in the growth rate due to wars, famine, disease, and the introduction of drastic population control measures in some of the most heavily populated regions of the world. The high variant on this chart is based on estimates of a decline in population growth to about 1.4 percent in the period between 2020 and 2025. The medium variant is based on estimates of a decline in population growth rates of 1.0 percent in the same period. The low variant is based on an estimated decline in population growth to 0.6 percent between 2020 and 2025.
Source: Adapted from United Nations, "World Population Prospects," *Population Studies* 120. New York: United Nations, 1991.

the poorest regions of the world (Figure 15.2). Africa has the highest rate of population increase, followed by Latin America. Africa also has the shortest life expectancy and highest infant mortality rate.

Growth rates have slowed for Asia, which faced the crisis earlier than other parts of the world. More than 50 percent of the world's people live in Asia, with China and India being the most critically overpopulated countries. Officials of both China and India

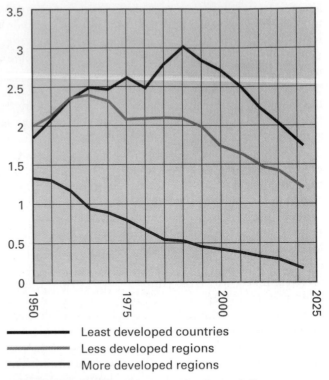

Least developed countries
Less developed regions
More developed regions

FIGURE 15.2   World Population Growth Rates According to Region

The world's annual rate of population growth is closely linked to economics. According to United Nations estimates, the highest rates of population growth are in what it calls the "least developed countries," whereas "more developed regions" evidence the lowest rates of population growth.
Source: Adapted from United Nations, "World Population Prospects," *Population Studies* 120. New York: United Nations, 1991.

have addressed the population issue with aggressive birth control measures, and both countries have been harshly criticized for adopting what has been considered extreme population control measures.

Europe has the lowest population growth rate. Even in industrialized countries, however, birthrates are highest among the poorest sectors of the population, which means that conditions associated with overpopulation fall most heavily on those least able to afford them.

Malnutrition and the Global Economy

Though demographics provide a dramatic picture of population pressures, high birthrates and infant mortality rates are more than numbers. They represent a great toll on human life. Nancy Scheper-Hughes (1991) describes the human cost of poverty and high

One of the most severe crises of the modern world is the precipitous increase in population, primarily among the poorest people of the world, such as those crowded together in this slum, or *favela,* in Rio de Janeiro, Brazil. In writing of a shantytown in northeastern Brazil, Nancy Scheper-Hughes notes that nearly half the children born to mothers in this shantytown die in the first year of life.

infant mortality rates among women and children of a shantytown in northeastern Brazil. On average, women of the shantytown experience 9.5 pregnancies, 3.5 child deaths, and 1.5 stillbirths. Seventy percent of all child deaths in the shantytown occur in the first six months of life, 82 percent by the end of the first year. Children under the age of five make up about 45 percent of all deaths in the community each year. As a result of such high infant mortality rates, Scheper-Hughes suggests, mothers in the shantytown make only a tentative commitment to their infants until a child has demonstrated a "knack" or "taste" for life by surviving its first year.

High infant mortality rates are usually associated with malnutrition, which also produces other types of health risks. A poorly fed pregnant woman is likely to give birth to children with greater-than-average rates and severity of birth defects. A malnourished infant or child becomes lethargic, uninterested in food, and subject to disease. Scheper-Hughes notes that women of the Brazilian shantytown selectively nurture more vigorous children and neglect those infants born "wanting to die." The women's custom of sorting their children into the binary oppositions of survivors and nonsurvivors is probably essential for providing maximum opportunities for survival to the stronger infants.

Malnutrition associated with poverty is a vicious cycle. Researchers have long known that malnutrition in children can result in a reduced ability to learn, and the lethargy induced by hunger interferes with an individual's ability to perform tasks. In a global economy increasingly geared toward wage labor, a poorly nourished worker may be unable to compete with workers from more fortunate circumstances. Poorly paid workers cannot provide adequate food for their children, thus producing another generation of nutritionally and economically disadvantaged individuals.

The area of northeastern Brazil studied by Scheper-Hughes was populated in large part by rural workers forced off their small subsistence-farming plots by large landowners wanting to use every available piece of land for sugar cultivation (1991:143–144). These workers became doubly disadvantaged in their ability to feed themselves and their families. They could no longer provide for their nutritional needs by subsistence horticulture, and their inability to feed themselves adequately placed them at a disadvantage in competing for jobs on sugar plantations.

Even when malnutrition does not directly cause death, it may damage an individual's immune system, so undernourished people are more subject to disease and less able to compete effectively in a labor market.

Can the Population Crisis Be Averted?

Some anthropologists feel the population crisis and related environmental problems could be averted through redistribution of wealth so that all people would have equal access to the earth's resources. Certainly, it is true that the poorest people have the most children because of lack of access to birth control and other forms of medical care. Even when they do have access to birth control, some poor people still choose to have many children. Because in many parts of the world they do not have access to social safety nets, children are their primary guarantee of being cared for in their old age or when sickness strikes. Thus, poverty and population growth are a self-perpetuating cycle.

It appears unlikely, however, that there will be a mass redistribution of wealth, since the people who control economic resources also control the political systems that regulate the economy. This is true on all levels: local, national, and international. Local politicians gain their position either by being affluent themselves or through financing by those who have a stake in the status quo. National political leaders acquire and maintain their position through dependency relationships with officials in business and finance.

As are other businesses, international corporations are operated according to the profit motive. Because no overarching agency controls the global economy, corporations best able to compete in international markets are those best able to negotiate effectively with local and national governments. Corporations are drawn to regions that are least likely to enact or enforce laws protecting the environment or the safety of workers at the expense of business.

Industries are best served by access to a large and cheap labor force and a large, affluent consumer market, but these often are not in the same country. For example, goods produced using cheap labor in Mexico or Asia may be targeted for consumers in Canada, the United States, or Europe. In the absence of some governing body with the power to coerce conformity to ethical business practices and employee safety standards, it is unlikely that international corporations will voluntarily adopt such policies. It is also unlikely they would voluntarily increase wages or take other measures that would redistribute the wealth of industrialized nations to people in poorer regions of the world. The efforts of some U.S. business leaders to have China permanently granted "most favored" trade status is not altruistic. American companies want to take advantage of an enormous, cheap labor force that is fast becoming an enormous commercial market with increasing quantities of disposable income to spend on prestigious U.S. products.

International law aimed at making businesses responsive to the needs of their employees, the local economy, and the environment is still in the process of being developed. The case of a toxic gas disaster at a Union Carbide plant in Bhopal, India, illustrates the legal and ethical complexities of doing business internationally. On the night of December 23, 1984, water was added to or leaked into a holding tank of methyl isocyanate, a chemical that when mixed with water produces a deadly gas. The Indian government estimates that 3,828 people died from the disaster and an additional 204,000 suffered some sort of injury. Most of the victims were lower class and uneducated, without political clout in India and no ability to sue in U.S. courts. Union Carbide claimed the disaster was due to sabotage by a disgruntled employee; the Indian government claimed it was caused by a faulty washing procedure. In any event, safety systems in the industrial plant were inadequate to prevent a crisis of such proportions.

Union Carbide chairman Warren M. Anderson immediately flew to Bhopal "with an open checkbook," according to a 1994 article in *Chemical and Engineering News*. Anderson was placed under arrest. Resolution of the case was hampered by jurisdictional disputes, because there is no international treaty covering this type of industrial disaster. The Indian government wanted the case tried in the United States, but the company fought for a trial in India. In 1989, Union Carbide settled out of court for $470 million, a figure that was lower than even the company expected, according to a 1994 article in *The Economist*. In 1994, Union Carbide sold its 50.9 percent share in Union Carbide India Ltd. to the government of India for $20 million and contributed the proceeds to the establishment of a hospital in Bhopal.

International issues involving environmental pollution can be just as difficult to resolve in the United States. Residents of Nogales, an Arizona town of twenty thousand residents located just across the border from an industrial region in Mexico, have experienced unusually high rates of multiple myeloma, a bone marrow cancer, and lupus, an autoimmune disorder in which the body's immune cells attack healthy tissue. According to studies by the University of Arizona and the Arizona Department of Health Services, multiple myeloma has occurred there at twice the rate expected for a town its size. Cases of lupus have occurred at four times the reported national average.

Nogales has no industry of its own, but about one hundred U.S.-owned electronics plants and other factories are located just across the U.S.-Mexican border.

These factories emit numerous toxic chemicals into the air, and the concrete-lined Nogales Wash carries a mixture of raw sewage and toxins from Mexico. It is difficult to identify a specific causal link between the toxins and the high rates of cancer and autoimmune disorders in Nogales. It is even harder to hold the U.S. owned companies accountable for pollution, since U.S. environmental laws do not apply to businesses operating in Mexico. The legal system may be stopped at the border but, as residents of Nogales say, "pollution does not carry a passport" (Cone 1996:A15).

Economics and Family Relationships

The economics of consumption also mediate against alleviating the population crisis through redistribution of wealth. The newly rich want the same access to consumer goods as is enjoyed by those who have long been in affluent circumstances. They may spend much of their recently acquired wealth on costly luxuries that drain their resources. In some cases, an influx of cash may disturb the balance of power between the sexes and further erode a woman's ability to practice birth control or prevent her husband from impregnating other women through extramarital affairs or **parallel marriages,** in which a man married to one woman sets up a second household with another.

Tracy Bachrach Ehlers (1993) describes the impact on the status of women after workers with the Peace Corps and the Catholic Church introduced commercial looms into the Guatemalan town of San Antonio Palopo. Gender relations had been skewed in favor of males even before the introduction of a cash economy because women were restricted in their interactions with people outside the family, including doctors, teachers, and traders. When not in the presence of men, however, women were eager to talk about sex and reproduction, freely expressing their negative feelings toward pregnancy and childbirth as well as their resentment at having to care for several small children.

Under the traditional subsistence economy, women and men were economically interdependent. Men worked in the fields and women processed grains, prepared onions for market, maintained the home, and used backstrap looms to weave clothing and other items for their families and for a small tourist industry. Both men and women traveled to the coast to pick cotton for wage labor. When production of woven goods was facilitated by the introduction of footlooms, men took up weaving for cash income. Women were relegated to nonpaying household chores, providing support services for their cash-producing husbands. With their new cash income, men could pay other men to do their work in the fields and devote their own time to entrepreneurial activities and hobbies. Bachrach Ehlers writes:

> Men have readily taken advantage of the opportunity to weave, as evidenced by the cash purchases of new tape decks, watches, roofs, and cement block houses. Several men have invested their earnings in motorboats, bars, tiendas (stores), and other businesses. (1993:311)

Whereas men have new social and economic mobility, the labor of women is now less obviously beneficial. Women are less able to prevent their men from fathering children by other women. Bachrach Ehlers writes: "San Antonio women are at a considerable disadvantage in maintaining themselves as partners in the family productive system" (1993:312). She notes that the incidence of parallel marriages is highest among the town's wealthiest men, and the influx of wealth has eroded women's ability to maintain their status within the family:

> While few men have the opportunity for more than casual affairs, men with money can take second wives, and they tend to flaunt their behavior. In a flagrant case of polygyny [in a traditionally monogamous society], one of the new contratistas [middlemen] built a house for his second wife and their children next to his first wife's house. The families involved have complained to the local authorities . . . , making the affair a public scandal. In another case, one of the town's well-to-do middlemen brought his parallel family to San Antonio's saint's day fiesta, an action so outrageous that his first wife tried to kill him. Both these wives took action to stop their husbands' infidelities, but neither has been successful. (1993:312)

In other words, the newly affluent males used part of their wealth to invest in additional wives, producing more children than would previously have been economically feasible. The reduced economic power of women limited their ability to curtail their husband's sexual activities outside the home.

Colonialism, Economic Exploitation, and the Environment

The world's upward-spiraling population and the unstoppably globalizing economy have seriously degraded the environment, meaning that more and more people must be supported on rapidly diminishing resources. As cities expand their boundaries, farmland is converted to industrial parks. The demand for wood is chopping down many of the earth's forests. Teak and rosewood are considered especially desirable for furniture, and the market for these woods is cutting deep, treeless swaths into tropical forests in Southeast Asia. The world's voracious consumption of oil and oil products is depleting the supply and polluting the environment.

Intensified food production has negative effects on the environment as well. Intensive farming techniques using fertilizer, pesticides, and irrigation can ultimately reduce the fertility of the soil by altering both its chemistry and its consistency. The world's rapidly increasing population is placing more demands on the earth's limited ability to sustain plants that can be consumed by humans, and improvements in agricultural technology do not always increase the productive capacity of the land.

As an example, for more than a thousand years farmers on the island of Bali have produced several crops of rice each year without pesticides or artificial fertilizer. Traditional systems of rice production were more than adequate to feed people in one of the most densely populated regions in the world. Formerly independent, Bali is now part of Indonesia, partly as the result of twentieth-century colonial expansion by the emerging nation-state of Indonesia.

Traditionally, rice cultivation in Bali is regulated by a hierarchy of Hindu priests living in the temple of the water goddess at Lake Batur. Located on top of a mountain, Lake Batur is the source of an elaborate system of springs, lakes, and canals that channel water into each farmer's fields. Timing of the irrigation and rice-planting cycle is regulated by temple priests who transmit their instructions through a series of regional leaders. The organization of the religious hierarchy mirrors the physical organization of the irrigation administrative system. Just as Lake Batur is the ultimate source of water, the temple at the lake is the source of the highest religious authority. Administration of the agricultural cycle is enforced through a graduated series of religious ceremonies culminating in the water ritual at Lake Batur.

The traditional system of a central administration regulating the irrigation and rice-planting cycle ensures that each farmer gets the water he needs at the appropriate time and reduces competition for the island's water and land resources. It also controls pests and replenishes soil nutrients. After each crop of rice has been harvested, ducks are released into the fields, where they feed off pests that might attack the next crop of tender rice shoots. The cycle of rice and ducks in the fields is an efficient system for feeding the ducks and keeping the pest population under control. In addition, duck manure provides fertilizer for the next rice crop.

Several decades ago, international developers undertook an intensive effort to improve Balinese rice yields with the aim of increasing exports. Outside contractors were called in to build new dams and new canals, change the cropping patterns, and introduce new rice varieties. The ducks were eliminated, and in their absence rice pests flourished. Pesticides were introduced to fight invasions of insects and disease. The innovations failed as soil fertility and productivity declined. Scientifically based technology proved to be a poor substitute for the agricultural expertise encoded in the traditional priestly culture.

A similar dilemma is to be found in southern Mexico. In order to provide for the nutritional needs of a population that virtually doubles every generation, Maya horticulturalists are using increasing amounts of modern artificial fertilizer to enhance the land's productivity. Eventually, this practice will result in diminishing returns. And, as a consequence of their efforts to produce more food, the Maya are poisoning another resource. Fertilizer is seeping into the water supply, making it unfit for human consumption. Artificial fertilizer, which is nutritious for corn and other crops, is poisonous to human beings.

Environmental pollution has become a global problem. The Inuit of northern Canada live in one of the most remote regions of the world, but they may be the most highly contaminated people on earth. Industrial and other pollutants from far parts of the world are carried north by air and sea currents. DDT, a pesticide, and polychlorinated biphenyls (PCBs), industrial chemicals, do not break down or wash away. Instead, they bind to sediments and collect in the bodies of marine mammals and fish, which are then eaten by humans.

Because they suppress the natural immune system, PCBs interfere with the body's ability to fight off disease. Children, the sick, and the elderly are especially subject to diseases since their immune systems are less efficient than those of healthy adults. If a pregnant woman is exposed to contaminated food or water, the developing fetus can suffer permanent damage to its thymus or bone marrow, where immune cells are produced. A child with a damaged immune system has impaired resistance to disease. In addition, the breast milk of Inuit mothers reflects high levels of contamination, so the PCBs in the breast milk are passed on to their nursing infants. Inuit children suffer from greater than average rates of meningitis, pneumonia, bronchitis, and ear infections, which may be related to their high exposure to PCBs.

Damage to the immune system associated with PCBs has also shown up in Russian and Taiwanese children as well as Swedish fishermen. These correlations are especially frightening since virtually everyone on earth has been exposed to at least low levels of pollution from PCBs, DDT, or dioxin, an herbicide. Some experts believe these three chemicals are present to some degree in the tissues of every living being on the earth (Cone 1996).

The Yanomamö of Brazil have been subjected to both environmental degradation and economic exploitation. With the discovery of gold in Yanomamö territory, miners invaded the area in large numbers. They brought with them destabilizing consumer goods and diseases for which the Yanomamö had not built up immunity. But their negative impact did not end there. The miners extracted gold by diverting streams and rivers through sluices, or man-made channels, where mercury was added to the water. Mercury amalgamated the gold, causing it to sink to the bottom, where it could be more easily collected. The mercury-contaminated water was then channeled back into the rivers and streams, where it entered the organs and tissues of fish, plants, and other organisms. Consumption of contaminated fish or plants by humans can then lead to kidney disease or autoimmune disorders, in which the immune system becomes hyperactive and attacks healthy tissues.

The Yanomamö have also become economically dependent on the miners. According to Napoleon Chagnon, who has studied the Yanomamö for many years, the miners supply the Yanomamö with rice and other goods, disrupting the traditional subsistence economy based on horticulture. When the miners leave, taking much of the region's marketable resources with them, many Yanomamö will be left much poorer, subsisting in a degraded environment without the cash income to buy the consumer goods to which they have become accustomed (Womack 1994).

The Yanomamö in Venezuela have been more fortunate. Much of their land has been set aside as a "biosphere" reserve by the Venezuelan government. This experimental approach to preserving traditional ways of life protects the Yanomamö and their environment from incursions from outside, so that the people and the plants and animals on which the people depend can remain in balance.

This approach differs from the establishment of reservations for Native Americans by the U.S. government one hundred years ago. In those cases, American Indian groups were driven off their lands, which were converted for use by white settlers. Indians were forced to adapt to the most marginal of environments, ones not coveted by colonials. This forced relocation stripped Indians of their subsistence base and made them economically, politically, and culturally dependent on the U.S. government.

In the case of the Yanomamö and the Venezuelan government, Yanomamö rights to their land and traditional way of life are protected. Since the subsistence base is intact, the Yanomamö are left with more options than were available to the North American Indians. The establishment of a biosphere reserve remains an experiment, however. The Yanomamö may be protected from political and economic exploitation, but it remains to be seen whether they can resist cultural incursions.

CULTURE CHANGE, CULTURE LOSS, AND "COCACOLONIZATION"

Even where contact between outsiders and indigenous peoples appears peaceful and relatively nonexploitative, the intrusion can profoundly disturb a group's sense of "safety" in their traditional world. Thomas Gregor (1992) gives the example of the Mehinaku, who live in a single village along with eight other single-village groups on a large, government-protected reservation at the headwaters of the Xingu River in central Brazil. Although the Mehinaku live in one of the remotest areas of Brazil, Gregor notes, "The flotsam and jetsam of industrial society"—battery-operated radios, aluminum pots, and discarded items of Western clothing—have found their way into Mehinaku culture (1992:213). Despite this incursion, Gregor writes, these items "affect only the appearance of Indian culture. They catch the eye of the visitor, but they do not break the rhythm of traditional subsistence, ritual, and trade that are the heartbeat of Xingu life" (1992:213).

The Mehinaku regard outsiders with anxiety, however. In the past, Indians of the region were subject to incursions by Europeans bringing diseases and by Brazilian bounty hunters, reducing the indigenous population of the region to one-tenth its former size. Today, visions of white men invade Mehinaku dreams. Dreams are especially significant to the Mehinaku, who believe that their nightly visions predict future events. In dreams, they believe, the soul wanders into the dream world of the community and surrounding forest, meeting the wandering souls of animals, spirits, and other villagers. Gregor writes:

> Many Mehinaku dream symbols are gloomy forecasts of death or misfortune. The grimmest omens of all, however, are those that deal with the white man. Any dream about a Brazilian is a bad omen. Even a dream prominently featuring an object associated with Brazilians, such as an airplane, is distressing. (1992:214)

One of the most prominent dream associations is between Europeans and disease. In the early 1960s, nearly 20 percent of the Mehinaku died in a measles epidemic. Villagers continue to suffer from imported diseases. According to Gregor: "Dreams of the white man are, for the Mehinaku, 'pictures' of disease. A person who has such a dream is likely to become sick" (1992:214). White men are also associated with danger, aggression, and anxiety in Mehinaku dreams. Many dreams recorded by Gregor express fears of rape, kidnapping, or assault with guns or other weapons. Gregor concludes: "Mehinaku lands and culture remain largely intact, but a part of their inner tranquillity

has been laid to waste. Neither geographic isolation nor heroic efforts at protection could save it" (1992:216).

Anthropologists and others have adopted the term **cocacolonization** to describe the process by which products and customs associated with Western culture are introduced into indigenous groups, thereby challenging, altering, or displacing the traditional culture. The term refers to the fact that Coca-Cola was one of the first corporations to establish "colonies" of markets and plants in small-scale societies. It reflects the idea that Western firms—especially those of the United States—aggressively market their products throughout the world, altering local economies and disrupting traditional cultures. In fact, however, cultural colonialism takes a number of forms. This section deals with the effects of religious conversion through missionary activity as well as introduction of Western consumer goods.

Missionary Activity

The immediate effect of religious conversion through missionary activity is that indigenous people lose faith in their traditional world view. As noted in Chapters 1 and 9, a coherent world view provides a group with a clearly defined place in an ordered universe. Loss of a sense of order and meaning can result in psychological distress and confusion on the part of the individual. In most cases of contact with missionaries, indigenous people must yield their central place in the universe to white outsiders, who present themselves as possessing a superior point of view. For

As a result of tourism, Masai culture is for sale. Traditional people all over the world are finding a lucrative market for the products of their culture. This Masai woman is bargaining with an American tourist over a length of colorful woven cloth.

example, Karl Heider reports that Christian missionaries used Western medicine as a tool of conversion among the Dani of New Guinea:

> I, like most outsiders, gave penicillin shots, which were to treat yaws [a type of tropical skin ulcer]. It is a sure cure. One missionary told me that when he gave penicillin shots, he had the patient pray with him to Jesus. Then, when the yaws were cured, he would point out that the Dani owed the cure to Jesus. (1991:13)

By taking over the healing function of traditional religious leaders, the missionary eroded the status of the traditional leaders in the community while increasing his own status in the group.

The missionary's intentions were no doubt magnanimous, since he believed that Christianity was superior to the religions he was attempting to displace. However, this type of culture change has far-reaching and long-lasting consequences, many of them unintended. Undercutting traditional authority disrupts the social order. Since merchants and military personnel often operated alongside missionaries, outsiders representing secular institutions introduced European diseases and prostitution at the same time missionaries introduced a new religion. Young people can be attracted to the power of the outsiders as represented by their superiority in healing, military prowess, and control over trade goods.

The activities of missionaries can also open the door to economic exploitation, as they did in Hawaii. Hawaii became a trade stop for European sailors after Captain James Cook came upon the islands in 1778. Native Hawaiians succumbed to a range of diseases introduced by the outsiders—from syphilis to smallpox to cholera—because they had not built up immunity to the foreign diseases. In less than twenty-five years, the population of native Hawaiians had fallen almost 90 percent from about three hundred thousand to thirty-five thousand. The old social ties were severely disrupted, and the Hawaiians became subject to despair and drunkenness, a process of dissolution experienced by many colonized peoples throughout the world.

Christian missionaries there speeded the process of social and cultural disintegration by attacking the roots of the native way of life—the religion, dress, art, dances, and language. Many descendants of missionaries joined with merchants in commercial exploitation of the people and their land. The Great Mahele, a land allotment act of 1848, permitted the purchase of land by private persons so that within a few years most Hawaiian land was owned by outsiders. Subsistence farms operated by Hawaiians were replaced by plantations owned by whites, who imported cheap labor from China, Japan, Korea, and the Philippines. This importation of labor changed the demographics of the islands, throwing native Hawaiians into minority status. Today, only 0.9 percent of the population is of unmixed Hawaiian blood; part-Hawaiians make up only 18.3 percent of the population.

There are efforts to restore some aspects of the traditional Hawaiian culture. The Bishop Museum (established by descendants of early merchants and missionaries, ironically) sponsors programs to teach Hawaiians their traditional art of woodcarving. Mormon missionaries have established the Polynesian Cultural Center, which attempts to preserve the expressive art traditions, not only of Hawaii, but of

This ritual performance at Xoken Chapel in Central America combines Christian symbolism with that of traditional Mayan culture. Though the aim of Christian missionaries is to convert indigenous people to a different way of life, the result is more often the emergence of a form of religious and cultural syncretism incorporating the new beliefs and practices into traditional ways of life.

other Polynesian groups as well. In their own behalf, Native Hawaiians are attempting to increase their political and economic influence. For the most part, however, traditional Hawaiian culture has largely disappeared. Its most public manifestation is in the form of hula dances staged for tourists. As the traditional Hawaiian religions have given way to commercial exploitation, beautiful carved representations of tiki spirits have degenerated into crude figurines produced primarily as souvenirs.

The Yanomamö in Venezuela and Brazil have been subjected to religious conversion by Christian missionaries, both Catholic and Protestant. Though the Yanomamö in Venezuela have not been subject to the devastation brought on by mining as have their Brazilian counterparts, missionary activity has produced subtle but far-reaching changes in their traditional patterns of subsistence, residence, and intergroup conflict. Missions have been established near navigable rivers. Yanomamö villages are becoming increasingly dependent on these mission posts, where missionaries have started schools and economic cooperatives. The Yanomamö are lured away from traditional subsistence activities by wage labor at the missions, which allows them to buy trade goods introduced by the outsiders. Missionaries also train Yanomamö men as teachers and send them to outlying villages. The missionaries encourage the Yanomamö in remote areas to move closer to the missions to increase their accessibility (Chagnon 1993).

Missionaries have also introduced shotguns into Yanomamö territory, providing a powerful weapon for missionized groups to use against people in more remote areas. Chagnon writes:

> Significant numbers of Yanomamö in the remote villages are being shot and killed by raiders from mission villages who, now that they have an arms advantage, invent reasons to get "revenge" on distant groups, some of which have had no historical relationship with them. (1993:220)

Chagnon notes that missionaries distribute the shotguns to the Yanomamö for "hunting." However, he records a number of incidents in which missionized Yanomamö killed men in less missionized villages or used the weapons to conduct raids in which they abducted women. The missionaries deny any knowledge that the weapons are being used in raiding. This denial may be disingenuous in some cases, though. Chagnon quotes the reaction of Protestant missionaries when he complained to them about a raid conducted by Yanomamö using shotguns to attack and kill a group of men from a remote village:

> They weren't sure which guns were used in the killings and were not going to ask, adding: "If we ask and find out that our guns were used, we would have to confiscate them from the Yanomamö. They would then move away from the mission. You don't know how hard we worked to establish our mission here. My husband carried our kerosene refrigerator on his back from the top of that mountain over there where the cargo plane dropped it off!" (1993:220)

Protestant and Catholic missionaries compete for the loyalty of Yanomamö groups by offering trade goods. Chagnon describes the case of one Catholic priest who lured a faction of a Yanomamö village away from the Protestants by offering them shotguns and outboard motors. Missionaries initially distribute Western goods freely, then gradually require the Yanomamö to work for the missions doing wage labor, such as hauling sand for making the cement blocks used in the construction of mission facilities (Chagnon 1993:221).

As the Yanomamö are drawn into a wage labor economy through dependence on Western trade goods, their traditional pattern of subsistence—based on horticulture supplemented by foraging—collapses. Their relatively nonhierarchical society becomes highly stratified since only a few Yanomamö men can achieve high status in the new mission-based economy. Yanomamö men and women become impoverished and dependent on the missions and outside entrepreneurs. Even the most successful Yanomamö man cannot rise above a secondary role in the newly imposed hierarchy, which will always maintain the status of outsiders at the top.

Not only do missionaries impose a system that maintains their own power; they themselves choose the Yanomamö's native leaders. Chagnon writes that leaders of missionized groups no longer develop out of the traditional system of kinship and building of alliances within and between villages. Instead, the leaders are chosen by missionaries. As a result:

> In [an area studied by Chagnon], these emerging young leaders invariably come from one of the three Salesian mission posts and have been carefully groomed for these roles. The exotic experiences and privileges they have been afforded by the Salesians who selected them enable them to take a commanding lead in the process of the developing native leadership. (Chagnon 1993: 217–218)

Chagnon notes that some of the leaders developed by missionaries have used the authority of their new position to punish their traditional rivals. He provides the example of one Yanomamö mission-appointed law officer who attempted to use his position to arrest and jail some members of his village who had sought retribution against him for leading a gang rape against a young woman of the village (1993:218).

The missionaries disrupt traditional lines of authority and influence by favoring younger men over the elders, who are viewed as being too resistant to change. Chagnon notes that leadership is now based on the ability to get along with outsiders:

> Younger men were emerging as leaders, their prominence being determined by new, nontraditional factors, such as ability to speak Spanish, doing personal favors for the local Salesian [Catholic] missionary, willingness to give up freedoms and traditions, willingness to enter a market economy and exchange labor or products for material items from the outside world. (1993:217)

Culture change nearly always produces tensions between the generations, as young people question the customs of their elders and seek ways to throw off their authority. Religious conversion is especially problematic if the convert is led to believe that his or her relatives will be condemned to hell for their traditional cultural practices.

In many cases, missionary activity encourages young people to rebel against the authority of their elders and in so doing disrupts relations within the family. While teaching a course on Asian Americans in Los Angeles, I discovered that missionary activity erodes traditional family relations even in the urban context. A Korean student approached me with the idea of writing his research paper on his father's practice of ancestor reverence. Each year, on the anniversary of his parents' deaths, the elder Korean American conducts traditional rites that include offering food and other gifts to his deceased parents. The son seemed uneasy as he described the practice, then confessed that he felt guilty about taking part in a "pagan" rite since he had converted to Christianity. The young man said his Christian sister refused to take part in the ritual. I pointed out to the young man that Christ had always stressed the importance of respecting one's parents and that his father's ritual was a way of showing respect. I said, "Your father is not worshipping his parents; his 'sacrifice' is a way of showing the respect due them for all the sacrifices

they made for him." I noted that people in the United States also consider it important to remember their dead relatives by putting flowers on their graves and by setting aside one day a year—Memorial Day—as a day of remembrance.

The work of missionaries is not entirely negative. Many have compiled dictionaries and grammars of native languages, helping to prevent the languages from being completely lost as a result of culture contact. Missionaries also use modern medicine to treat some indigenous diseases that previously resulted in death or disfigurement. In addition, education provided by missionaries prepares many young people to deal with incursions by outsiders.

Even under the best of circumstances, however, the work of missionaries and other outsiders erodes traditional knowledge and social structure. Father Frank Mihalic, a Jesuit missionary in New Guinea, notes that education has alienated young people from their "one talks," the term used to describe kinsmen. Father Mihalic says, "They don't like history because history is embarrassing. They wince when I talk about the way their dad or their mom lived" (cited in Linden 1993:224).

Father Mihalic and other members of the Jesuit order have intervened to prevent the government from burning spirit houses used during initiation rites. However, other missionaries tell young people that their customs are primitive and barbaric (Linden 1993). John Maru works in Papua New Guinea's Ministry for Home Affairs. As a result of his missionary education, he says, he came to view traditional gift exchanges and other traditions as a waste of time and money. Now, however, he has come to see that "such customs serve to seal bonds among families and act as a barrier to poverty and loneliness" (Linden 1993:224).

"Cocacolonization"

The Westernization of the world has already penetrated into virtually all traditional cultures. Writing in the *Cultural Survival Quarterly*, Noreene Janus notes:

> No one can travel to Africa, Asia, or Latin America and not be struck by the Western elements of culture—automobiles, advertising, supermarkets, shopping centers, hotels, fast food chains, credit cards, and Hollywood movies give the feeling of being at home. Behind these tangible symbols are a corresponding set of values and attitudes about time, consumption, work relations, etc. (1991:229)

As early as 1952, Lauriston Sharp observed that adoption of Western consumer goods subtly transforms traditional social relations in ways that are ultimately pervasive and irreversible. Sharp described the effects of introducing steel axes among the Yir Yiront of Australia at the end of the nineteenth century and early in the twentieth century. The steel axe gradually displaced the traditional stone axe. Sharp noted that stone axes were central to the organization of relations within the family and between groups. Men made the stone axes, but women and children could use them for cutting firewood and other chores. To acquire the stone for the axes, a man had to set up trade relationships with men in other groups, establishing a network that ultimately extended four hundred miles to the south. The axes and spears were important in male initiation rituals and other ceremonial observances. The stone axe was an important symbol of masculinity among the Yir Yiront in general and a totemic emblem for one Yir Yiront clan (Sharp [1952] 1994). As noted in Chapter 1, totemic emblems provide a tangible symbol of solidarity for clans in Australian aboriginal societies.

Missionaries rewarded the "better" aboriginals with steel axes, which set them apart from their fellows. In many cases, the steel axes went to younger men, women, and children, undercutting the status of older men. Since the steel axes were distributed by missions, trade relationships throughout the area were disrupted, and, in turn, regional celebrations centering on male initiations were disrupted. Distribution of the steel axes at ceremonial occasions organized by missionaries or cattle ranchers emphasized the subordinate status of aboriginals and the superordinate status of whites. Sharp writes:

> The most disturbing effects of the steel axe, operating in conjunction with other elements also being introduced from the white man's several subcultures, developed in the realm of traditional ideas, sentiments, and values. These were undermined at a rapidly mounting rate, with no new conceptions being defined to replace them. The result was the erection of a mental and moral void which foreshadowed the collapse and destruction of all Yir Yiront culture, if not, indeed, the extinction of the biological group itself. ([1952] 1994: 386–387)

Missionaries are not the only Westerners to use manufactured goods to draw indigenous peoples into their sphere of influence. For most of the history of Western contact with indigenous peoples of other cultures, trade goods have been introduced to reinforce the superior social status of whites. This has been the case whether the outsiders have been missionaries, merchants, or military personnel. Katherine Milton (1992) notes that officials of the Indian Protection Service in Brazil have long used pots, machetes, axes, and steel knives as a way of inducing uncontacted Amazonian groups to become dependent on manufactured goods. At first these items are hung from trees or laid along trails frequented by Indians. When a group drawn by the prospect of additional "gifts" submits to "pacification," all its members are presented with trade goods. Once the Indians have become accustomed to the goods, they are told they must work to earn money to buy additional goods or manufacture goods for trade so they can buy new or additional items. Those who are not drawn into working for non-Indian bosses begin to produce extra goods of their own for trade to the outsiders (Milton 1992). In this way, a subsistence economy geared toward domestic needs is transformed into a political economy based on a class of entrepreneurs whose status rests on controlling the production of others. As noted in Chapter 4, the shift from a subsistence economy to a political economy results in an upward spiral of increased population, stratification, and production of a surplus because the role of non-food-producing entrepreneurs is justified and supported by controlling the surplus produced by a number of workers (Johnson and Earle 1987).

Among Amazonian Indians, the switch to a market economy based on production of a surplus reduces the time they can spend foraging, and the variety of foods in their diet is, in turn, reduced. They also begin to cultivate new crops, such as coffee and rice, which can be traded or sold easily, further reducing the variety in their diet. Clearing larger fields for cultivation of surplus crops increases the risk of such diseases as malaria because cleared areas with standing water permit proliferation of disease-bearing mosquitoes and flies (Milton 1992). Thus, introduction of trade goods subjects indigenous people to the same upward spiral of disease, stratification, and increasing population experienced by the early settled food producers described by Jared Diamond, as discussed in Chapter 4.

The extension of Western influence into all parts of the world is not a process of diffusion but of various types of conquest—political, cultural, and economic. In her *Cultural Survival* article, Janus notes that modern cultural conquest is based in the economics of advertising:

Some believe global culture has resulted from gradual spontaneous processes that depended solely on technological innovations—increased international trade, global mass communications, jet travel. Recent studies show that the processes are anything but spontaneous; that they are the result of tremendous investments of time, energy and money by transnational corporations. (1991:229)

Janus suggests that television advertising in particular has a disproportionately negative effect on the self-image of poor people in non-Western societies. Children learn to associate happiness with consumer products, being young and white, and wealth. The emphasis on youth and individual activities in Western advertising erodes the traditional authority of elders and the solidarity of the group. Janus describes an example when she comments: "Traditionally, drinks are consumed only in social settings. . . . Yet, the advertising of Coca-Cola and Heineken portrays drinking as an individual act rather than a collective one" (1991:230). This advertising subtlety promotes Western values of individualism over the solidarity of the community.

Indigenous Peoples Fight Back

Despite the almost overwhelming force of Western colonialism, it would be a mistake to view indigenous peoples as passive victims of external aggression. In some cases, they have fought back with whatever military force they possessed, with the strength of their traditional social and cultural forms, and with the power of their ideas. In recent years, many indigenous groups have fought to maintain their cultural identities and increase their political voices with some of the same weapons that were formerly used to subjugate them.

Earlier in this chapter, we saw how the !Kung used the political power of the vote to ensure their traditional land rights and are drawing on traditional rules of kinship to extend those rights to the dispossessed members of their group. The Navajo of the southwestern United States illustrate a different form of adaptation to colonial contact. Before contact with Spanish explorers in the sixteenth century, the Navajo were one of a number of Apache forager bands who hunted bison, elk, and a variety of smaller game with the powerful sinew-backed bow. They gathered nuts, seeds, berries, roots, and other plant foods. Though their pattern of descent appears to have been bilateral, some researchers suggest there may also have been a pattern of matrilineality and matrilocality (Downs 1972).

Linguistic analysis indicates that the Apache are related to the Athapaskans of Canada. Some linguists suggest that the Athapaskan language may have developed out of a Sino-Tibetan branch of the Asian languages; if it did, then the Athapaskans must have migrated across the Bering Strait into North America from the region of western China and Tibet. The name Apache was given to the southern Athapaskan speakers by the Spanish (Downs 1972). By early in the seventeenth century, one group of Apaches had learned farming from the Pueblo Indians. The Spanish called this group the Navajo Apaches, meaning "Apaches of the big fields." These farmers lived in

With the introduction of communication satellites, television has become available to villages formerly out of reach of national and international programming. Here, people of a village in India are viewing an educational program via satellite. Similar technology has made commercial television programs produced in the United States available to people who are otherwise unfamiliar with American culture.

DISCUSSIONS

Who Owns Culture?

One of the primary objectives of the earliest American anthropologists was to document native cultures before those cultures were inalterably changed by contact with Europeans or even wiped out altogether. In this discussion we look at the effects of various forms of culture change on indigenous peoples, including change caused by outside agents, as in colonialization, global marketing, and missionary activity. But seldom does anthropology look at its own history of influencing change in native culture. Anthropology has played an important role in the United States' exploitative relationship with Native Americans.

It is against that backdrop that a modern drama between anthropologists and Native Americans unfolds. It is a fight for who shall control ancient Indian material culture and human remains, and therefore the authority to interpret those remains. The battle is often reported as a struggle between science and sentiment; in the context of Western culture, science is assumed to have the morally superior claim. Upon closer examination of the history of relations between scientists and American Indians, the issue may really be whether anthropologists can do better than they have in the past at putting aside their own sentiments when studying indigenous peoples. In his book, *Skull Wars: Kennewick Man, Archaeology, and the Battle for Native American Identity,* David Hurst Thomas examines anthropology's past and how that is affecting the battle over the Kennewick skeleton. In her discussion of his work, writer Laura Womack says Thomas's book shows how early anthropologists contributed to

the devastating changes forced on Native Americans by European settlers.

ANTHROPOLOGISTS AS AGENTS OF CHANGE

Laura Womack

American Indians have long objected to their ancestors' remains being displayed in museums like curiosities. As a result of their objections, Congress passed the Native American Graves Protection and Repatriation Act (1990), which required museums and universities to audit their collections of Indian artifacts and return some items to affiliated tribes. Then, in 1996, a human skeleton was discovered along the banks of the Columbia River in Washington state. Scientific dating methods placed the skeleton 9,000 years ago, in the murky prehistory of the continent among the earliest remains excavated in the new world. Although racial typing has been dismissed as invalid by many scientists, the skull was determined to exhibit morphological characteristics more commonly associated with European "Caucasoid" populations than with Native Indian groups often classified as "Mongoloid" populations presumed to have come to the North American continent via the Bering Straight. The ancestry of the skeleton could have a profound impact on the sensitive discussion over who the first Americans were.

The fight for who shall take possession of the ancient skeleton, named "Kennewick Man," is often reported in popular media as a simple battle between those who would further the cause of Science through a determined pursuit of the Truth, versus the descendants of a spiritual

people who place ancestral relationships before analytical thought. That the conflict is thought of in those terms is ironic. Anthropologists no longer credit distinctions drawn between so-called rational and primitive cultures, but the dichotomy was embraced by early anthropologists. In the nineteenth century E.B. Tylor wrote, "Even in healthy waking life, the savage or barbarian has never learnt to make that distinction between subjective and objective, between imagination and reality, to enforce which is one of the main results of scientific education" (1871:445).

Presumptions of different modes of thought persist in nonscientific circles. But the battle over Kennewick Man is more complicated than that. David Hurst Thomas writes in *Skull Wars: Kennewick Man, Archaeology, and the Battle for Native American Identity,* "It is a political struggle over who will control the interpretation of ancient American history—government, academia, or Native Americans" (2000:xxv). That battle is the most recent in a long history of conflict among these groups. The U.S. government's history of abuse of American Indians is already well documented. What few people know is the role scientists played in that history of abuse. The modern Indian demand for control of early American artifacts is the reaction of a people who have been repeatedly robbed of their land, their ancestral remains, and even their culture by invaders who have often used pseudo-science, including very flawed early anthropology, to justify these thefts.

Thomas describes how the discovery of sophisticated cultural achievements associated with the

ancient, man-made mounds that dot the Midwest were used to justify pushing Native Americans off their land. The mound builders belonged to the Mississippian culture that dates back to about 800 A.D. At Cahokia, Illinois, the mound builders created a sprawling city of over 30,000 people and constructed over one hundred mounds. The largest mound, Monk's Mound, is as tall as a ten-story building and covers 16 acres (Fagan 1983:258). Thomas writes that scholars thought the mound builders must have been more advanced than the Indians settlers encountered. The mound builders were thought to be most likely white, perhaps related to the relatively sophisticated indigenous peoples in modern-day Latin America. Thomas notes that President Andrew Jackson laid the basis for forced removal of southeastern Indians to Oklahoma by telling Congress in 1830, "In the monuments and fortresses of an unknown people, spread over the extensive regions of the west, we behold the memorials of a once powerful race, which was exterminated, or has disappeared, to make room for the existing savage tribes." Thomas argues that if the modern "savages" who occupied North America had wiped out an earlier—probably white—people, then the white settlers were justified in appropriating Indian lands (2000:128).

This thinking is eerily similar to that of the Asatru Folk Assembly, one of the present-day groups fighting for possession of the Kennewick skeleton. According to Thomas, the Asatruans, self-described descendants of the early Scandinavian and Germanic tribes in Northern Europe, believe the Kennewick skeleton and

its purported Caucasian characteristics support the theory that America was first settled by whites and, Thomas writes, "by implication, rightfully 'belongs' to their Aryan ancestors" (2000:xxii).

The persistence of race politics in the fight over the Kennewick skeleton is a long, dark shadow of anthropology's history in the United States. Anthropology evolved out of the study of natural history. In the nineteenth century, American Indians were conceived of as belonging to the skeletons and cultural artifacts collected along with fish, game, and other animals to begin some of the United States' most prestigious natural history museums. In addition to Native Americans, other indigenous people, such as Tasmanians and Africans, were displayed in Europe.

To collect native skeletons, some museums relied on paid scavengers, grave robbers, and even soldiers. Despite many Native Americans' attempts to stop them, skeleton hunters haunted burial grounds for the remains of Indians recently dead from European diseases or the sites of "Indian massacres," where Indians were the victims rather than the aggressors. Thomas describes the "trophies" collected by soldiers after Methodist minister and Civil War hero Major John Chivington lead an assault on two Cheyenne villages in a land dispute with settlers:

> Fleeing children became moving targets for marksmen, and several still-living Cheyennes were scalped. One woman's heart was ripped out and impaled on a stick. Several soldiers galloped around the battleground, sporting bloody vaginas as hatbands.

One trooper cut off White Antelope's testicles, bragging that he needed a new tobacco pouch. Later, nobody could remember whether White Antelope was wearing the peace medal given to him by President Lincoln. Returning to Denver, the Sand Creek heroes paraded through the streets, to the cheers of throngs. Theatergoers applauded an intermission display of Cheyenne scalps and women's pubic hair, strung triumphantly across the stage.

Several of the Cheyenne dead received special treatment. After the corpses were beheaded, the skulls and bones were defleshed and carefully crated for shipment eastward to the new Army Medical Museum in the nation's capital. (Thomas 2000:53)

The horrifying circumstances under which skeletons were sometimes collected undoubtedly add to the offended sensibilities present-day Native Americans feel about museum collections of their ancestors' remains. But there's more to the story. Even before some of these vast collections of American Indian skeletons were assembled, researchers had extensively measured and analyzed skulls from various peoples, with a mind to delineate differences between the races. As Thomas reports, in the first half of the nineteenth century, American doctor Samuel George Morton amassed an incredible collection of 600 skulls—mostly Indian. Based on cranial capacity, which he assumed indicated a superior intellect, Morton concluded that Caucasians were the most intelligent, followed by Indians and then blacks. Morton's theory was that the races had been created separately by God, allowing Euroamericans to

(*continued*)

DISCUSSIONS

Who Owns Culture? (*continued*)

justify subjugating non-whites, according to Thomas.

> By transferring the study of race from theology to science, Morton mounted an elegant and empirical defense of manifest American destiny: Euroamerican-style civilization was fated to control the Western Hemisphere, but America's indigenous people stood in the way. Although an outright policy of extermination would be decidedly un-Christian, the Indian problem might just resolve itself, since America's native inhabitants were doomed by their own biology. (2000:42)

Morton's hierarchical view of the different ethnic groups' physical capabilities was complemented by the ideas of Henry Lewis Morgan. Morgan, who is sometimes called the father of American anthropology, based his hierarchical theory of human cultural development on his detailed study of the marriage patterns of the Seneca in New York and on similar data from a questionnaire he distributed around the world. Morgan decided that the lowest state in human cultural evolution was the first of three stages of "savagery," which progressed through three stages of "barbarism" and culminated in "civilization" and monogamous marriage. According to Morgan, American Indians had attained either lower or middle status barbarism.

Of course, Europeans had attained civilization. Thomas writes, "The conquest of Indian people by Euroamericans could now be seen not as the aggression of one people against another but as part of the inevitable, inexorable expansion of civilized people around the world" (2000:48). Their interpretations of both biology and culture reassured Europeans that it was only "natural" that they should dominate Native and African Americans.

Modern anthropologists have rejected these ideas, including cranium size as a predictor of intelligence and hierarchies of culture that presume progress over time. Even the concept of race has been largely discredited. In fact, a skull collector himself and another "father" of American anthropology, Franz Boas was the first to promote the theory that it was not a set of inherited "racial" characteristics that most influenced an individual's behavior, but rather socialization, or "nurture" in the "nature–nurture" debate. As noted in Chapter 3 of this text, Boas died of a heart attack while delivering an impassioned plea for vigilance against racism.

Though the field of anthropology rejected these Eurocentric theories that served to justify the elite's dominance over other groups, similar theories persist in scientific as well as nonacademic circles.

Richard J. Herrnstein and Charles Murray ignited an inflamed debate in 1995 when they published *The Bell Curve: Intelligence and Class Structure in American Life.* The authors argued that intelligence, rather than environment, was the most important factor influencing an individual's socioeconomic status. Critics said the theory was racist because a disproportionate number of minorities are poor, uneducated, and/or in jail.

In the context of the enduring relationship between scientific theories and political agendas, the battle for possession of Kennewick Man is not just a conflict between American Indians' desire to bury their dead and scientists' desire for access to data that may help our understanding of how the Western Hemisphere was populated. The battlefield is awash in the politics of a more recent immigration by Europeans—politics that were advanced by the racist theories of early anthropologists. This enduring relationship between science and politics shows the anthropologist's potential to inadvertently affect dramatic change upon the peoples they study.

Source: David Hurst Thomas, *Skull Wars: Kennewick Man, Archaeology and the Battle for Native American Identity* (New York: Basic Books, 2000); Brian M. Fagan, *People of the Earth: An Introduction to World Prehistory* (Boston: Little, Brown, 1983).

---

semisubterranean houses consisting of a hole dug into the ground with a domed roof of timber and earth built over it. Farming was supplemented by hunting and gathering.

Navajo life changed dramatically as a result of diffusion from both the Pueblo Indians and the Spanish. From the Pueblos, the Navajo adopted farming and weaving, clothing styles, and many religious ideas and ceremonies. From the Spanish, the Navajo and the Pueblo people acquired domesticated animals, including sheep, goats, cattle, and horses. Sheep were especially suited to the high, arid country of New Mexico and Arizona occupied by the Navajo. Combining farming with seminomadic sheepherding, the

Navajo lived in relatively permanent villages in the winter and migrated to a series of grazing grounds throughout the rest of the year. By the early 1800s, the Navajo began to be known for their woolen blankets and baskets, which they traded to the Spanish and Pueblos, and later the Anglos.

The Navajo supplemented their subsistence, organized around herding, weaving, hunting, and farming, by raiding the Pueblos and the Spanish. Because the Navajo lived in remote areas of the region, retribution against them was difficult. James F. Downs writes, "Hogans were located on mesa tops, in little out-of-the-way canyons, or other hard-to-find places. Structures were built so that they blended into the landscape" (1972:13–14). In 1846, as a result of the Mexican War, New Mexico and much of what is now Arizona came under the control of the United States, but U.S. soldiers were no more effective against the Navajo than were the Spanish.

Downs notes that the Civil War, from 1861 to 1865, "provided a period of rest for many tribes on the frontier, as troops were withdrawn for fighting in the East" (1972:14). After the war, however, the United States had a large army of volunteers with nothing to do, so they mounted a large-scale campaign against the Navajo and other Apaches. An army under the command of Kit Carson led the campaign against the Navajo. Downs writes:

> Too wise to attempt to force a pitched battle, Carson attacked the economic base of Navajo life. Wherever his command rode, they burned cornfields, slaughtered livestock, [and] cut down peach trees. . . . Finally the Navajo, starving and unable to grow food, withdrew into the almost impenetrable reaches of Canyon DeChelle in eastern Arizona. Here for a while they held out, but starvation did what battles could not, and they were forced to surrender. (1972:14–15)

The Navajo who surrendered were taken to Fort Sumner in New Mexico, where they were encouraged to settle down and take up sedentary farming. Though the plan was intended to be humanitarian, the Navajo suffered a great deal (Downs 1972). Their crops were ruined by bad weather, and they were raided by Comanches from Texas. Finally, Navajo leaders requested that they be allowed to take their people back to their homelands. In 1868, the U.S. government set aside about one million acres centered on Canyon DeChelle as a reservation. Downs comments, "By this time the captive Indians had virtually no horses, and the trip was made on foot. In Navajo tradition, it is referred to as the Long Walk" (1972:15).

Unlike Indian groups of the Great Plains, the Navajo were encouraged to become self-sufficient through government grants of seed, farm implements, and livestock. They incorporated much of what they had learned at Fort Sumner into their culture. Forced to depend on gifts of unbleached muslin or castoff Anglo clothing, the Navajo began to model their clothing on European styles. Women began to wear long, wide skirts with a shirtwaist, making them of velvet or velveteen instead of muslin. Men adopted the shirtwaist, wearing it with long muslin trousers. Both sexes continued to wear moccasins, but men began to abandon the turban for felt hats.

Established in an area that no one else wanted, safe from raids by others, and having learned the harsh consequences of raids themselves, the Navajo devoted themselves to rebuilding their culture and acquiring wealth. Their herds made them self-sufficient, and they produced goods for trade to whites: raw wool, hides, rugs, livestock, and silver jewelry. According to Downs:

> Population increased from perhaps twelve [thousand] to fifteen thousand in 1868 to nearly fifty thousand in the 1930s. From a handful of sheep and goats given to them in 1868, the Navajo increased their livestock holdings to well over a million head. Safe from excessive Anglo pressure in an area without roads or lines of communication, they expanded and developed what the Navajo have come to think of as the true old style of life. Until Arizona's entrance into the Union as a state prevented further expansion, the reservation was repeatedly increased from one [million] to sixteen million acres in size and formed the foundation for the development of modern Navajo culture. (1972:16)

Downs adds, "Although not all Navajo today live on the reservation, nor have they ever done so, the reservation is the heartland of Navajo life" (1972:17). He notes that Navajo life today is organized around what he calls "the female principle." Descent is matrilineal and residence is matrilocal. The most important figure in Navajo mythology is Changing Woman, who gave birth to the hero twins, the source of what the Navajo consider their own particular culture. Women may greet any man of whatever age as "my son," and men can greet any woman of whatever age as "my mother." Though men occupy public positions, they view themselves as acting on behalf of their mother's kin group. The Navajo integrated Western practices into their community to achieve success on their own terms.

Today Navajo on the reservation emphasize their distance from outsiders. Relations with the U.S.

The Bitter Fruits of War and "Ethnic Cleansing"

In Chapter 1, the concept of ethnicity was introduced and the case of ethnic violence in some nation-states that were formerly part of Yugoslavia was discussed. Anthropologist Robert M. Hayden notes, "The collapse of the former Yugoslavia has been accompanied by violence that has shocked the world" (1996:783). Headlines around the world chronicled "ethnic cleansing," especially attempts by Serbian extremists in Bosnia to exterminate their Muslim neighbors. But headlines cannot convey the grief, rage, and terror engendered when former friends, coworkers, and neighbors find themselves enemies in a war conducted in their homes, streets, and marketplaces.

Sarajevo, a once-beautiful city in the mountains of Bosnia, was torn apart by violence, in part because it was home to Serbs, Muslims, and Croats. Before the collapse of the strong central Yugoslav government, these groups had lived peacefully with each other despite their disparate languages, religions, cultures, and histories. After a period of

violence in the early 1990s following the collapse of the Yugoslav government, Sarajevo came under the control of Muslims, and Serbs withdrew to the area around the town of Pale (PAH-lay), fifteen miles away. Most Muslims in the Serbian-controlled region were killed, but some Serbs continued to live in Sarajevo.

In the following essay, Dan Bernstein, a columnist for the *Press-Enterprise* in Riverside, California, writes about a journalist born in Yugoslavia who returned to his country to tell the story of war's devastation. On his journey between Pale and Sarajevo, the journalist brought joyful news—and a grapefruit—to an impoverished old Serbian woman whose son had been killed in the violence. The woman assumed that her daughter, who had remained in Sarajevo, had also been killed. Even though she lived only a few miles from Sarajevo, the woman had no way of traveling there, so she did not learn that her daughter was still alive until the journalist arrived bearing the grapefruit.

THE GRAPEFRUIT STORY
Dan Bernstein

He took his tape recorder to the open-air market, but kept it hidden in a bag. He asked about the price of eggs and the price of fruit. He thought it might seem suspicious if he didn't buy anything, so he bought a grapefruit.

He bought the grapefruit as he recorded ambient, open-air sounds for the broadcasts he planned to make for the Voice of America. Bela Skopal was far from home. He lives in Jurupa [California], near a golf course. But in a way, Bela Skopal was home: an "ethnic Hungarian" born in Yugoslavia. Skopal, his wife, and his little boy came to the United States in 1980. They are now American citizens. Bela, forty-six, is a correspondent for the Hungarian Language Service of Voice of America. He just spent nearly a month traveling through Bosnia and nearby climes, speaking to Muslims, Croats, Serbs, Bosnians, taking the pulse of a region that has ripped itself to shreds.

He bought the grapefruit in a town called Pale, which is controlled by the

government are conducted through the Tribal Council. Downs notes, however, that the council has little authority in the eyes of most Navajos, who continue to make decisions at the level of the homestead or independent nuclear unit. Still, the outside has been brought closer to the Navajo by paved roads, electricity, and the establishment of schools. A junior college on the reservation has made higher education more accessible, and Navajos are increasingly acquiring college degrees. As are many other indigenous groups, the Navajo are being forced into political activism by the discovery of natural resources on

their land, including oil, uranium, natural gas, coal, and other minerals. In general, however, outsiders—including anthropologists—are not welcomed on the Navajo reservation.

In the mid-1990s, Akiko Arita, a graduate student in photojournalism from Japan, completed the circle of cultural migration by conducting a photographic study of the Navajo. She was welcomed into the community at Window Rock because she resembled them in appearance. She photographed their daily lives, including family celebrations and economic activities. She also participated in some of their ceremonies,

Serbs. He had come from Sarajevo, not more than fifteen miles away. Sarajevo is largely controlled by Bosnian Muslims.

It would never have occurred to Bela to make this short trip alone. He hired a "fixer." Anybody with any sense (and a wad of hard currency) hires a fixer. A fixer takes care of everything—from the armor-plated Land Rover, to finding lodging, to setting up interviews for American correspondents.

After Bela had covertly recorded his sound bites at the Serb-controlled open-air market, he and Miki, the fixer, headed back to Sarajevo. But first, Miki wanted to stop at a country house where he used to spend weekends. The owner of the house had been killed in the war, but Miki wanted to stop anyway. An old woman lived there—the dead owner's mother.

She was poor and frightened—and shocked to see that Miki, a Serb, had survived in Muslim-controlled Sarajevo. She was certain he had been killed. That was the logic of this war. Certain people in certain places were certain to die. People clung to this logic. It was one of the few ways they could make sense of the war.

The eighty-four-year-old woman apologized to Bela. She wanted to "bake" him coffee. She had nothing. She received the equivalent of ten dollars a month from her dead husband's pension. Bela felt sorry for her. He gave her the grapefruit.

They talked a while longer. They talked about the old woman's daughter, who still lived in Sarajevo. Miki, the fixer, knew the daughter, knew where she lived. We are going back to Sarajevo, he told her. We can bring your daughter a message, a present—anything. We'll take it to her.

The old woman began to cry. She had nothing to give her daughter. Nothing. Except, of course, the grapefruit.

The next evening, Bela and Miki rode the elevator (this one worked, others didn't) to a high-rise apartment in downtown Sarajevo. The apartment is heated by gas, but the regular gas lines are faulty, so they run the gas through rubber hoses from one apartment to the next. It is just one of the many humdrum inconveniences people live with. Like plastic windows. So many windows have been blown out that glass has

become a luxury. Many people just use plastic.

The daughter was stunned to learn that Bela and Miki had seen her mother. The daughter hadn't seen her own mother for at least two years. They gave the daughter the gift from her mother. They gave her the grapefruit.

To the outsider, it is an incomprehensible conflict. The geography lesson from hell. A war in which the goal was not merely to vanquish enemies but destroy entire cultures. But through the shards of fear and destruction, a few truths emerge:

A grapefruit can be a precious jewel. It is all some people have left. A grapefruit can travel farther and in greater safety in two days than a mother and daughter can travel in two years.

As Bela Skopal told his grapefruit story—his war story—the clutter of maps and fresh boundaries and international agreements gave way to pained images of ordinary people. A mother. A daughter. And a fixer who couldn't quite fix everything.

Source: Reprinted with permission from the *Press-Enterprise.*

usually closed to outsiders. She allowed her Navajo subjects to choose the events to be photographed, then allowed them to select the pictures to be displayed in an art gallery on the California State University–Northridge campus. One remarkable finding in the study is that the Navajo repeatedly chose pictures in a series rather than in isolation, as is characteristic of mass media. They did not choose the "best" photos of a particular event. Instead, they chose a series that depicted the event in its entirety. They also chose photos that depicted the interactions of family members, especially those of women. Arita (1994)

concluded that, though the Navajo have undergone many transformations in their circumstances, their way of viewing the world still reflects traditional values emphasizing the importance of women. Furthermore, she notes, the Navajo still emphasize the importance of process rather than completion of an event.

The Kwakiutl of Alert Bay, on the western coast of Canada, have used Western political activist techniques to restore cultural objects taken away from them by colonial authorities. They are also drawing on the skills of linguists and the memories of elders to

Navajo women turned the tables on Japanese photographer and anthropologist Akiko Arita by arraying her in Navajo dress and using her camera to photograph her in one of their homes. Since their devastating contact with the U.S. government in the nineteenth century, Navajo have tried to remain aloof from outsiders. Though they were once the subject of intense anthropological scrutiny, the Navajo have resisted even this incursion in recent years. Arita was able to bridge the gap because of her similarity to them in physical appearance and culture.

document traditionally oral aspects of their culture and transmit them to future generations.

Early in the twentieth century, government officials banned the potlatch, a system of redistribution that provided an important focus for leadership within the community and a context for transmission of culture through dances and story telling. At the time the potlatch was banned, Kwakiutl masks were taken away for display in Canada's National Museum of Man. After years of negotiation, the museum agreed in the early 1970s to return the masks to the Kwakiutl of Alert Bay if they agreed to build a museum in which to house them (Womack 1994).

The Kwakiutl built a museum patterned after the traditional ceremonial big house, adapting it to exhibit collections of art. The Kwakiutl call the new museum the Box of Treasures. The masks returned to them by the National Museum form the nucleus of the exhibit, but the Kwakiutl have supplemented the display by adding their own treasured objects handed down through the generations (Womack 1994).

The Box of Treasures has become a center for renewal of Kwakiutl culture. Linguists are interviewing Kwakiutl elders to construct a grammar of the language; the interviews are videotaped to provide a resource for the community. Children are taught the Kwakiutl language and the ceremonial dances. They learn about their traditions through recounting of folktales and religious myths. A woman actively involved in the process assesses the results:

> We've won some victories, the people in this area. The masks have come home. The old people are teaching the children what they know. We're rebuilding and growing stronger in all sorts of ways. . . . All the time we are doing these things with our kids, we realize there are all sorts of things happening outside of this center over which we have no control. . . . We celebrate the good things that have happened for us. But, most of all we celebrate the fact that we're still alive, we're still here. We've survived and will continue to survive, and we're always going to be here. (Womack 1994)

Camcorders, portable video recorders, have become an important weapon for Indians in Brazil's tropical rain forest (Zimmer 1991). Pressed by increasing demands for electricity, Brazil is increasingly turning its attention to the development of hydroelectric projects, which involve damming rivers to harness their energy. Many towns in Brazil now get their electricity from diesel-fired generators powered by fuel that has to be hauled in over poor roads or by barge. Electronorte, the regional power company, plans to accommodate increasing demands for electricity by constructing eleven dams that would cover 3,800 square miles, a region twice the size of Delaware but representing only two-tenths of 1 percent of the Brazilian Amazon.

The Kayapo of central Brazil blocked construction of an additional dam on their territory by videotaping the results of an existing dam in eastern Brazil. The Tucurui hydroelectric dam, built on the Tocantins River, had flooded eight hundred square miles of rain forest that had once been the home of the Parakanan and Gavioes Indians (Zimmer 1991:223). Electronorte was planning to build a series of dams in the middle of

Sometimes the old ways provide the foundation for the new. The theme for the design of this building for the Navajo Community College was taken from the eight-sided hogan (front), a traditional Navajo dwelling.

Kayapo territory, including one that would flood an area more than twice as large as the Tucurui reservoir. Carl Zimmer describes the visit of Kayapo chiefs to the Tucurui reservoir:

> Wearing full ceremonial costume, with brilliantly feathered headdresses and black body paint and, in some cases, enormous disks in their lower lips, the Kayapo chiefs toured the Tucurui dam. They took a boat trip on the new lake. They looked out at the dead trees that still rose, bleached and bare, above the water, and they wanted all their kin to see what a dam could do. So they videotaped it. (1991:223)

The video was shown to hundreds of Kayapo on a videocassette recorder hooked up to a gasoline-powered generator (Zimmer 1991:223). United by the dramatic footage, the normally dispersed Kayapo staged demonstrations at the site of the largest of the proposed dams and in the nearby town of Altamira. The Altamira dam project was put on hold (Zimmer 1991:223).

In San Francisco, a teenaged refugee from Cambodia used a video camera to document his senior year in high school and his life in a housing project. The result was broadcast on PBS in 1996 as "a.k.a. Don Bonus." Don Bonus was the name Sokly Ny chose for himself to fit in better. He chose the name Don "because it sounds macho, and 'Bonus' from the packs of gum I buy that give you a second pack free as a bonus" (Coburn 1996). Sokly lived with his mother, stepfather, grandmother, and siblings. His biological father was killed by the Khmer Rouge during their deadly slaughter in Cambodia in the 1970s, after the United States had withdrawn from the Vietnam War. Sokly was carried out of Cambodia by his older brother when he was only three.

In the U.S. housing project, neighbors stole the family's possessions—from their furniture to their food—and broke their windows with rocks. The terrified family of ten was forced to move twice within a year, and Sokly nearly flunked out of school because of his involvement with a group of young Asians trying to fit in by being "cool." When Sokly asked his former high school teacher to describe what he was like in his junior year, the teacher replied flatly, "You were a vegetable."

Sokly was provided with the camcorder by filmmaker Spencer Nakasako, who also edited and adapted the resulting work for television. For many people in the United States, the Vietnam War is a remote memory and life in a housing project a remote source of anxiety, but the camcorder allowed a confused teenager to document a largely forgotten group of people—Southeast Asian refugees. Sokly told an interviewer he used the video to counsel himself: "I'd watch scenes of my life and then talk about how I was feeling and then watch that and try and change. Sometimes the camera was my only friend" (Coburn 1996).

According to Buddhist philosophy, change is an inevitable part of human life. This Buddhist monk has incorporated that philosophy into his daily life, as he uses a sewing machine to preserve an old tradition. The monk's robes must be formed of patches to symbolize poverty, and he makes use of Western technology to streamline the process of sewing the patches together.

THE IMPACT OF CULTURE LOSS

Ultimately, the effects of culture loss are incalculable. And increasingly it is becoming clear that loss of indigenous customs and knowledge subtly impoverishes all of humanity. The most direct effects are to those who no longer have access to their traditions.

For example, youths of Papua New Guinea who have been educated in Westernized schools no longer have survival skills suitable for their natal villages, no longer knowing which rot-resistant woods to use to build huts or which poisonous woods to avoid when making fires for cooking (Linden 1993:223).

Earlier in this chapter, we noted that traditional Balinese rice cultivation practices are more effective in allocating water, maintaining the quality of the soil, and controlling pests than are modern "scientific" agricultural techniques. In many other parts of the world, traditional farmers are proving to be a valuable resource for modern food production because of the wide variety of crops they produce. Reliance on one crop or strain makes a farmer vulnerable to diseases and pests that become adapted to that particular variety of corn, rice, potatoes, or other crop. By cultivating a number of strains of corn, rice, or potatoes, traditional farmers provide a genetic reservoir for scientific research on disease-resistant varieties of plants. Traditional knowledge of medicinal plants and healing techniques can be even more directly applicable. During the Persian Gulf War of 1991, European doctors treated some wounds with a sugar paste used in Egyptian battlefield medicine four thousand years ago (Linden 1993:225).

Culture is not infinitely flexible, and human beings are not entirely malleable. Though changing one's mind certainly occurs faster than altering one's genetic makeup, our ability to respond to the demands placed on us by accelerated rates of culture change in the past few decades is limited by our culturally programmed assumptions about what is possible, appropriate, or "good." In other cases, our culturally programmed view of "new" as being necessarily better than that which is traditional causes us to undervalue some cultural knowledge and ways of life that could enhance the survival of all human beings.

SUMMARY

All cultures change through time. These changes may result from processes originating within the society. Innovation results from variations in the customary way of doing things, variations either in customs or technology. Invention is a conscious process of innovation. Diffusion of technology or cultural practices results when one group borrows from another.

The most disruptive form of culture change is colonialism, the subjugation of one group by another.

Though Europeans were not the first to practice colonialism, the outward expansion of Europe from the fifteenth to the nineteenth centuries is the most extensive example of colonialism in human history. This period of European expansion has influenced or transformed traditional societies all over the world politically, economically, and culturally.

In the process of being colonized, traditional cultures lose control of their political and economic systems. As a result, indigenous peoples become marginalized in the new colonial society. People in egalitarian groups become the bottom rung of the colonial hierarchy, and people who have carved out a niche in societies that are already hierarchical are replaced by colonial authorities. Subjugated societies are exploited for their economic potential.

One of the most serious problems facing human beings is a dramatic rise in population beginning around one hundred years ago, an increase closely tied to economics. The rate of increase is greatest in the poorest regions of the world, and, in industrialized countries, population growth is greatest among the poorest segments of society. Poverty combined with population growth results in malnutrition and high rates of disease. One consequence of malnutrition and disease is a reduced ability to compete for wage labor jobs. This produces a cycle of poverty, malnutrition, and disease. Some anthropologists feel the population crisis could be averted by redistribution of the world's wealth. It is unlikely, however, that wealth will be redistributed because political and economic institutions are controlled by the wealthy rather than by those who would benefit from redistribution. In addition, international law is inadequate to ensure redistribution or to regulate international corporations to protect the environment and the safety of workers.

The rising population and expansion of the global economy have seriously degraded the environment so that more and more people must subsist on less farmland and shrinking environmental resources. Environmental pollution resulting from pesticides and industrial chemicals has penetrated to all areas of the earth, since wind and air currents carry pollution around the globe and across national boundaries. Pollution has compromised the health of indigenous peoples even in very remote places.

Indigenous peoples are threatened also by various kinds of cultural colonialism. Missionary activity reduces the confidence of indigenous people in their own culture and often disturbs the traditional social organization by encouraging young people to rebel against their elders. Missionary activity can also open the door to economic exploitation. The term *cocacolonization* has been used to describe the process by which products and customs associated with Western culture displace aspects of traditional culture.

Many indigenous groups are now resisting outside domination, attempting to regain control of their economic base and to preserve their cultural traditions. They are drawing on the experience of their elders, ethnographies compiled by anthropologists, and technology. They may use tape recorders to record their language and camcorders to document their way of life and to protect it from incursions from outsiders.

POWER WORDS

cocacolonization	indigenous	parallel marriages
colonialism	innovation	
diffusion	invention	

INTERNET EXERCISE

1. The United Nations Population Information Network (POPIN) provides a wealth of information about international population trends on their website at **http://www.undp.org/popin/popin. htm**. What issues does this organization identify as significant in considering world population trends?

2. The International Political Economy Network website (**http://csf.colorado.edu/ipe/**) is hosted by the organization Communications for a Sustainable Future in Boulder, Colorado, USA. Taking an ethnographic approach, address the following questions: What kinds of themes are identified as important by this group? To what demographic group does the IPEnet seem designed to appeal?

3. The American Anthropological Association maintains a website apprising members of issues relating to government affairs and public policy. Visit their website at **http://www.ameranthassn.org/ gvt/govafar.htm** to find out what government and public policy issues anthropologists consider relevant to the discipline.

16
The People We Are

In this chapter...

Anthropology and academics

Anthropology is most commonly encountered by students in the context of academia, but academia is more complex than most students realize. Anthropology as a career differs in research universities, four-year colleges and universities, and community colleges. Much of the difference centers on the often-competing demands of research and teaching. Anthropologists also work at research institutions and in museums, where the difference between teaching and research is continually redefined.

Anthropology and medicine

Western medicine has produced treatments for illnesses once viewed as fatal or debilitating, but medical practitioners have much to learn from traditional healers about the importance of the psychological and social context of illness. Medical anthropologists address a variety of issues in health care, including how to incorporate the wisdom of traditional healers into Western medical science. Medical anthropologists also note the importance of cultural factors in treating indigenous people and members of minority groups.

Anthropology and the political economy

As indigenous people are drawn into the global economy and the political turmoil of emerging nation-states, anthropologists may become caught up in the process of mediating between the people they study and outsiders. In some cases, anthropologists become advocates for the people they have studied. In other cases, they have become consultants for businesses, helping to adapt the corporate culture to the needs of human beings or assisting families of workers employed by international organizations.

Anthropology and media

Almost by definition, anthropologists are interpreters and communicators, both in terms of understanding people unlike themselves and in conveying that understanding through ethnographic reports. Visual anthropologists contribute to the ethnographic enterprise through film. Anthropologists can also extend the educational range of anthropology through mass media by bringing their expertise to bear on contemporary social and cultural issues.

*U*nlike students who have majored in some other disciplines, anthropology majors are not besieged by recruiters seeking to lure them into secure careers with lucrative offers of employment. Few people outside of colleges and universities have a clear idea of what anthropology is, and fewer still are aware of its applications to contemporary society. Though this picture is rapidly changing, and anthropologists are becoming increasingly attractive to medical schools and businesses, it is generally incumbent on the anthropologist to demonstrate the value of his or her training.

While still in graduate school, I was approached by a young man at a party who asked, "What do you do?"

"I am an anthropologist," I replied proudly.

"How can you justify that?" he demanded.

I then inquired about his profession and discovered that he was a lawyer. As an anthropologist schooled in cultural relativism and the insider perspective, I found both his profession and his indictment of my own chosen career to be more informative than offensive.

Anthropologists are lured to the field by fascination with the subject rather than by the prospect of a guaranteed prestigious, high-paying job. Still, anthropologists do find gainful employment in a variety of contexts. The traditional occupation for anthropologists, as for majors in other theoretical and research-oriented disciplines, is that of college or university professor. However, fewer than 30 percent of people with degrees in anthropology make their careers in academia. In most cases, this is because there are too few professorial jobs to employ all the people qualified to fill them.

On the positive side of this equation, anthropological training enables one to adapt readily to a variety of contexts, and anthropologists are carving out careers in a wide variety of fields. As I was nearing completion of the doctoral program at UCLA, one of my peers bemoaned the fact that he would be unable to find a job as a professor because he was unable to conduct a countrywide search. His wife had a lucrative and prestigious position with the city of Los Angeles, and she would understandably be unwilling to give up her job to relocate with him for less money. My colleague abandoned his dreams of an academic career and began to carve out a career in public administration. Within six years, he had risen to the position of president of a humanitarian organization. Ten years after receiving his Ph.D., the man was interested in making a career change, and I suggested that he consider returning to his original dream of teaching anthropology. He replied, "I'm priced way out of that market. They can't afford me, and I don't want to go back to it."

In general, anthropologists build careers in four main contexts: (1) at colleges and universities, (2) at research institutions, (3) in a variety of applied fields, and (4) in related fields, by integrating their anthropological expertise with the specialized knowledge of that field. Within the profession, anthropologists distinguish between academically oriented and applied branches of the field. Academically oriented anthropologists are employed by colleges, universities, or research institutions; they focus on teaching, training future anthropologists, and conducting research according to the disinterested scientific model. Applied anthropologists focus on adapting anthropological theory and methods to contemporary issues and problem-oriented contexts.

ANTHROPOLOGY AND ACADEMICS

During the nineteenth century, anthropology developed as a theoretical discipline. In the twentieth century, the field became adapted to three primary contexts: (1) colleges and universities, (2) research institutions, and (3) museums. In the United States at the beginning of the twentieth century, anthropologists moved among these contexts, and there was no clear dividing line between academically oriented anthropology and what is now called applied anthropology. Franz Boas, often called the father of American anthropology, both taught at Columbia University and was active in a variety of causes. He pushed for reform of museum designs to reflect the integration of particular cultures and was politically active in the fight against racism.

Boas's student Ruth Benedict conducted highly theoretical research but also applied her theories in conducting research on Japanese culture for the U.S. War Department during World War II; the result was a work titled *The Chrysanthemum and the Sword* (1946). Margaret Mead taught at Columbia University and directed the Columbia University Institute for Contemporary Cultures, but she centered her professional life at New York's American Museum of Natural History. Her work for the War Department during World War II focused on an analysis of American character structure and culminated in the book *And Keep Your Powder Dry* (1942).

During the 1960s, increased public interest in cultural issues, fueled in large part by Mead's popular writings and television appearances, drew funding for anthropological research and professorial positions at U.S. colleges and universities. At the same time, anthropologists became concerned over the possibility of unethical use of information collected by anthropologists. The intimate knowledge of a wide variety of indigenous groups could be used for military, commercial, or political purposes. The new abundance of academic jobs, combined with ethical concerns, led anthropologists to withdraw from seeking practical applications for anthropological knowledge and methods. For the next thirty years, anthropology became primarily an academic discipline.

Anthropology in Academia

Though anthropologists generally view careers in the field as being either academic or applied, in fact, there is a range of job possibilities in both contexts. For one thing, not all colleges and universities have specialized anthropology departments. At these institutions, it is possible to be the sole anthropologist in a department of sociology and anthropology, for example. Anthropologists at these institutions say they value the opportunity to interact with their colleagues in other disciplines, whereas the usual organization of college departments into discrete units minimizes interdisciplinary contact. At the same time, anthropologists in departments that combine disciplines miss the interaction with their anthropology colleagues. They find the annual meetings of the American Anthropological Association of great value in maintaining contacts within the discipline and keeping abreast of current research.

In general, professorial jobs in departments of anthropology are available at three levels: (1) research-oriented universities, (2) four-year and liberal arts colleges, and (3) two-year or community colleges. Having taught at all three levels, I am basing this discussion of professorial careers on my own experience and that of my colleagues.

Research-Oriented Universities Tenure-track jobs at research-oriented universities are eagerly sought and hard to come by. Universities that emphasize research and grant doctoral degrees are the most prestigious contexts in which one can carve out a career in anthropology. Thus, these universities can have their pick of each new class of Ph.D.s. The most desirable candidates are those who have already presented papers, who have published journal articles, and who have a book contract for publication of their doctoral research.

The ideal first job is a **tenure-track** position, which means the anthropologist is hired for a trial period of from five to seven years. During this time, the tenure-track candidate works on publishing journal articles and at least one book to become eligible for tenure. This process is the source of the famous academic dictum "publish or perish." **Tenure** is granted when an individual's colleagues grant permanent and guaranteed employment on the basis of his or her contributions to the field. When the tenure review comes up, the individual either acquires permanent status at the university or is rejected and must search for another position. This is a grueling process that subjects the candidate to considerable stress and anxiety.

In many cases, tenure-track positions are unavailable, and anthropologists seeking to establish themselves in academic jobs take one-year appointments, which may or may not be renewable. In these cases, the individual is subjected to the process of seeking new employment each year and in most cases must undergo the expense and upheaval of relocation.

Whether seeking tenure or holding a series of one-year appointments, the anthropologist undergoes a great deal of job insecurity at the same time he or she is attempting to pay off college loans and, in many cases, establish a family. Many individuals abandon academia at this point, seeking more lucrative or stable jobs in fields that allow them to apply their anthropological expertise.

Once past the tenure process, however, anthropologists in professorial positions gain both job security and the opportunity to conduct research and instruct others in the field that has captured their interest since early in their college careers. Though anthropologists at research institutions must struggle to balance their research, teaching, and institutional duties, most consider themselves fortunate to have survived the harsh selective process. It is not uncommon to hear anthropologists marvel at their good fortune: "I can't believe I get paid to talk about the subject I love most!"

Four-Year and Liberal Arts Colleges Whereas prestigious research universities typically emphasize specialized research interests, the primary mission of four-year and liberal arts colleges is educating undergraduate students. In the case of liberal arts colleges, which are generally privately rather than publicly funded, the object is to provide a broad-based education rather than a specialized one.

The undergraduate education one receives at a four-year or liberal arts institution is not necessarily inferior to that provided by research institutions. Classes are typically smaller, so there can be more interaction with instructors. The educational advantage of attending a research university is the opportunity to be taught by individuals who developed the theories under discussion. However, many outstanding scholars are drawn to the less competitive atmosphere of four-year or liberal arts colleges, and college and university professors at these institutions are expected to make a research contribution as well.

Professors at public four-year colleges typically carry a heavier teaching load than those at research institutions, and the pressure to publish is not as intense. Still, the tenure system is in effect at four-year and liberal arts colleges, and full-time jobs are hard to get, as funding has shifted away from the social sciences to the physical sciences.

Many four-year colleges cut costs by making extensive use of part-time instructors. Part-time instructors are paid less than full-time or tenured professors and may not receive many of the insurance benefits. In addition, part-time instructors usually do not have job security. The career of Geri-Ann Galanti is characteristic of many, though she is unusually successful in combining academic and applied anthropology. Galanti was drawn into anthropology by the discovery that thinking is fun:

> The moment I "became" an anthropologist . . . I was in the bowels of the college library, researching a term paper. It suddenly struck me that anthropology was like a good mystery novel. Elements of culture and environment were the clues. If you had enough clues, you could make predictions about other aspects of the culture—because they all fit. (pers. comm. 1996)

Despite her fascination with research, Galanti's primary goal was to teach: "Unlike many anthropologists who love to do research, my heart is really in teaching. Teaching is what I love doing—and since anthropology is my favorite subject in the world, I'm delighted to be teaching anthropology" (1996:2).

Galanti feels her decision to remain in her hometown of Los Angeles prevented her from getting a position that could lead to tenure because she does not have geographic mobility. She teaches physical, cultural, and medical anthropology in the anthropology department at one California State University campus and commutes to another California State University campus to teach in a school of nursing. She notes:

> It's hard when you've gone through a system that puts "tenured full professor" at the top of the list of values, to be in a position where that is not a possibility. But if I look at what I want in a career—the freedom to teach a variety of courses to a variety of students, and to do the kind of work I want to do, when I want to do it—I've pretty much got it. The job insecurity is the worst feature, but then, I never take my job for granted, as many full-timers do. I always appreciate it. (1996:3–4)

Galanti has published a book titled *Caring for Patients from Different Cultures* and has developed a consulting business, presenting workshops at hospitals and medical conferences. In addition, her class for the nursing program is carried nationwide on cable television. Galanti says she likes the feeling that her instruction in anthropology helps her students in their own lives:

> Overall, I make a decent living as an anthropologist, between my two part-time positions, book royalties, and lecture fees. I'm happiest when I'm in front of a group, trying to convey some information, and see that they really get it. The feedback from my nursing students is especially gratifying. What I teach them about different cultures actually helps them provide better patient care,

as well as lowers their stress on the job. I feel like I'm making a difference in the world. It's not the traditional role I imagined, and it's not without aggravation, but I'm happy. And as a side benefit, when I'm asked at a party what I do, I'm always proud to say I'm an anthropologist. (1996:4–5)

Two-Year and Community Colleges Two-year and community colleges serve the needs of students who need additional preparation before transferring to four-year colleges, who seek training in a technical field, or who wish to return to college after working or raising a family. Community college students are a diverse population with a variety of educational needs. For this reason, there is a strong emphasis on teaching at these institutions, with research playing a secondary role.

Because anthropologists at two-year colleges often carry a heavier teaching load than those at four-year colleges and universities, they find it difficult to make time to focus on research. For this reason, positions at two-year colleges are more attractive to anthropologists who prefer teaching to research. In the past, community colleges were an important job market for anthropologists with master's degrees. Now, however, there is an abundant supply of anthropologists with Ph.D.s; therefore, it is difficult to get a professorial job at a junior college without a doctoral degree.

The mission of two-year colleges is twofold: (1) to provide a broad-based education equivalent to the first two years at a four-year college, and (2) to offer specialized training in a technical field within a collegiate context. Because coursework at two-year colleges is almost exclusively lower division, anthropology classes are typically offered only at the introductory level. For instructors, this means teaching a large number of introductory classes with little opportunity to offer more specialized classes that draw on one's research expertise.

On the other hand, many anthropologists, including myself, feel a certain missionary zeal in introducing students to a discipline that has changed our lives so profoundly. Most anthropologists never quite lose their passion for the field, and we experience great satisfaction when students tell us, "You've changed my life. Now I understand so much more about my family (or my work or my motivations)."

Many anthropologists are drawn into the field when they take an introductory class at a junior college. Joan Barker has set more fledgling anthropologists on this path than most. She began teaching anthropology part-time with a master's degree when she was still in her twenties. In addition to parenting her younger brother and sister, she conducted research in West Africa. While Barker was teaching at Santa Monica College in the Los Angeles area, one of her students challenged her to study closer to home. The student, a policeman, dared her to apply the anthropological approach of cultural relativism and insider perspective to a study of the Los Angeles Police Department (the LAPD).

That challenge led to Barker's Ph.D. research on the Los Angeles Police Department. She studied the stages of the police career, beginning with the recruits' early idealism at the Police Academy, their subsequent disillusionment when they tried to apply their training to the streets, their mechanisms for coping with the danger of police work, and their readjustment to civilian life upon retirement. Barker's study was conducted during a period when the LAPD was implementing affirmative action programs that emphasized the hiring of women and minorities, thus providing important insights into police attitudes about their work and their relations with the public. Barker's work subsequently became important when the LAPD became involved in a series of scandals.

Barker's research is also directly applicable to teaching at a community college. Not only do police officers take her classes, but all her students benefit from learning about an important component of a complex and diverse city. In addition to her introductory classes in cultural anthropology, she also offers courses on gender and traditional peoples and cultures of Africa.

As is the case at most community colleges, Santa Monica does not have a separate anthropology department. However, Santa Monica College serves a large student population, so Barker and her colleagues have been able to develop a comprehensive anthropology program. Barker, a full-time cultural anthropologist, and a full-time physical anthropologist form the nucleus of the anthropology program. They call on part-time instructors to cover the spectrum of anthropological subfields. Barker notes:

> Those of us who teach anthropology in two-year colleges wince when we hear the term "junior college," because there is no question there is [the] implication of reduced status. But there is no reduction in quality of education. I teach anthropology in [a] community college the same way I taught at a four-year college. (pers. comm. 1997)

With such a comprehensive anthropology program, Santa Monica College produces a number of students who transfer to four-year colleges and universities. It is an important feeder school to UCLA. Barker notes: "We have some very good students. We also have some not-so-good students. I am proud of the fact that one of our graduates is a Rhodes Scholar." Barker is referring to Alvan Ikoku, who was born in the United States but whose family were Ibos from Nigeria. When he was eleven years old, Ikoku returned with his family to Nigeria. He says, "I knew then I had to be a doctor. My six-year stay in Nigeria revealed the serious health problems facing the world and made me sensitive to the excruciating results of disease." After returning to the United States, Ikoku enrolled at Santa Monica College before going on to become a premed student at Stanford University.

Though Barker has conducted significant research, she finds many rewards in teaching. She says, "I have been teaching anthropology for twenty-four years and I still get excited by it. I am just as excited as when I first began teaching, only now I teach it better."

A Bird's-Eye View of the Three Levels of Academia Having taught at all three levels of academia, I am in a good position to compare the advantages and disadvantages of each. Students at research universities are generally more focused and better prepared academically than are those at four-year and two-year colleges, since the prestige of research institutions allows them to select their students from among the upper 5 to 10 percent of high school graduates.

In my occasional role as visiting scholar at UCLA, I enjoy the opportunity to focus on anthropology, since most of the students I teach are anthropology majors. Because these students are, by and large, dedicated to the field, they are knowledgeable about anthropology, so I must stay abreast of current issues. In terms of job conditions, teaching at a research university is luxurious compared with teaching at other types of educational institutions. Being employed exclusively for one's specialized knowledge of a particular subject is like being a rare bird sought for one's plumage. It is hard not to preen under such admiring regard.

To continue the avian imagery, teaching at a four-year college forces one to be a more utilitarian bird. I think of myself in this role as a chicken, producing eggs for the next generation. At California State

DISCUSSIONS

Issues of Access and Power—Contrasting Ethnographic Examples

As it has been for most other anthropologists, one of the greatest lures to the discipline for me was my dream of traveling to some exotic place to live "like the natives." Though I have conducted limited fieldwork in Mexico and among indigenous people on the east coast of Taiwan, I found my most exotic populations in two widely differing areas of Los Angeles. Research for my master's thesis was conducted among a group of Spiritualists in a poor, ethnically mixed neighborhood in the South Central area of Los Angeles. Research for my doctoral dissertation was carried out among affluent, internationally recognizable professional athletes.

The two groups represent greatly differing fieldwork conditions with respect to the kinds of access I was permitted, the nature of the anthropologist–informant relationship, and the theoretical issues I was able to address. In both cases, my field site was chosen, not by me, but by my research subjects. In both cases, I was invited to conduct the study by an insider to the group. The two cases illustrate fieldwork issues relating to problems of access and the differential power relationship between anthropologists and the people they study. These problems also arise in conducting research at the village level, but the complexity and fluidity of the urban research setting require that they be addressed immediately and directly in the process of carrying out the research. Otherwise, access to the field site can be quickly withdrawn. Both research sites allowed me to test the validity of anthropological research methods.

Power Balance Favors the Anthropologist

My research among the Spiritualists began by happenstance when I casually remarked to an acquaintance that I was interested in studying faith healing. The acquaintance replied, "We do that." She then invited me to conduct my research at her church. I was not familiar with Spiritualism at the time, and, at first, I was reluctant to commit myself to doing ethnography in what appeared to me to be a mundane setting. Largely in response to her eagerness, I accompanied my acquaintance to a Sunday morning service at her church. Thus began a two-year study of a Spiritualist church.

The basic tenet of Spiritualism is that people survive in spirit form after death. Spiritualist practice is organized around contacting spirits of the dead to gain their assistance in healing or dealing with everyday life or to obtain information about life after death. Spiritualism is a branch of Christianity, but Spiritualists do not view Christ as God, but as a more "highly evolved" person, whom they refer to as "elder brother." Spiritualists believe that spirits of good and bad people go to the same place after death. The place is called Summerland, because it is just like this world except that Summerland is a place of continual sunshine and flowers. Because

Most anthropologists are employed in teaching at the college or university level, an occupation that requires a specialized knowledge of anthropology reflected in having earned a Ph.D. Here, author Mari Womack teaches a class at Santa Monica College, a community college having a large international student population.

Summerland is inhabited by both good and evil spirits, spirits of the dead should be contacted only by trained mediums who have acquired a spirit guide to help them to safely receive messages from the spirits.

The Spiritualist religion began in the first half of the nineteenth century in upstate New York, at a time when a number of new religions were developing in that area. Spiritualism was quickly adopted by intellectuals of the time, attracting such prominent supporters as the journalist Horace Greeley. At the same time, some Spiritualists set themselves up as mediums, using trickery to get money from grieving people seeking to contact their recently dead relatives. In his grief over the death of his son Todd, President Abraham Lincoln attempted to contact his son's spirit through use of a medium.

As the result of charlatanism by mediums, Spiritualism had fallen into disrepute in the United States by the end of the nineteenth century. It did not entirely disappear, however. It had spread into England, where it was adopted by Sir Arthur Conan Doyle, author of the Sherlock Holmes novels. Traces of Spiritualism are found in detective novels by Agatha Christie. Spiritualism also spread into Latin America, where it is known as Spiritism.

Spiritualism continues in North America today in two forms: (1) a New Age intellectualist movement, popular among the affluent, that continues the Spiritualist practice but does not use the Spiritualist name, and (2) a means of dealing with illness, poverty, and family problems utilized by a disenfranchised underclass. The group of Spiritualists I studied fell into the second category.

As an anthropologist in training at a well-known university, I was seen as a member of a class of privileged elites by my Spiritualist informants. Thus, my participation in the group was eagerly sought. Whereas anthropologists studying in other societies must overcome barriers posed by cultural differences relating to outsider status, my main problem was in resisting conversion attempts. My presumably superior status made me an especially desirable convert, and my presence in the group validated both their religion and their claims to social authenticity. In addition, the woman who had invited me to conduct the study was the daughter of a prominent member of the group, so I was allowed access to all levels of the group, and my questions were freely answered.

As required by the American Anthropological Association code of ethics, I stated my intention to study the group from the anthropological perspective at the outset and reiterated this position whenever it appeared that my status as marginal "native" was becoming obscured. This problem arose often as my study continued. Near the end of my first year of study, it was suggested that I undertake the training to become a healer. I declined on the basis that I did not have faith in my ability to heal. "You don't have to believe," I was told. "If you learn to heal, the healing will take place regardless of what you believe."

From the methodological perspective of participant observation, I could have ethically undertaken the training to be a healer. However, it would have violated my personal ethics. On the basis of my observations of healing and the course of illnesses among

church members, I had concluded that healing served as a mechanism for recruitment to the group and planned to make this point an important part of my ethnography (Womack 1977). I felt that consenting to become a healer would misrepresent my intentions both to the Spiritualists and to the people who came to the group seeking their healing rituals.

When I repeatedly declined to become a healer, my presence in the group was no longer validating since I had, in their view, rejected their religious beliefs and practices. As the pressure on me progressed, I became concerned that my developing role as "nonbeliever" might reflect negatively on the family of the woman who had sponsored me into the group. After two years of research, I concluded my study and severed my connection to the group.

As my experience among the Spiritualists indicates, defining one's boundaries is an important issue for an anthropologist studying a religious group. The anthropologist must gain the insider perspective without "going native," which would mean confusing one's role of professional insider for that of the true insider. For members of religious groups, the anthropologist's declining to "go native" can be seen as rejection of their beliefs and practices.

Power Balance Favors the Subjects

In studying professional athletes, I was faced with other issues in boundary definition. My study of ritual use by professional athletes began when a friend who was a professional hockey player invited me to watch a Los Angeles Kings game in which he was playing. For anthropologists,

(*continued*)

DISCUSSIONS

Issues of Access and Power—
Contrasting Ethnographic Examples (*continued*)

wherever there are people to be observed, there are data that can be collected.

Anthropological researchers are trained to look for patterns of behavior, as well as for behavior that seems to deviate from a standard pattern. When the players skated onto the ice before the game, I noted that each player skated in a stylized pattern while warming up for the game but that the pattern was different for each player. The fact that each player skated a different pattern was a probable indicator that the pattern was dictated not by the team but by player preference. Immediately, my anthropological training kicked in and I started to ask "Why?"

Fascinated, I watched the players warm up before the game. Then, as they skated off the ice one by one, each player stopped to tap the goal or the goalie's knee pads. Even one who knew nothing about hockey could figure out that the goal and the goalie are important to the outcome of the game and, therefore, could become power objects, or *fetishes*. As I observed the players making contact with the goal or goalie, I thought I might be witnessing ritual.

It is important in anthropological research not to jump to conclusions. In order to understand whether the behavior I had observed actually was ritual, I needed the insider perspective. Over dinner after the game, I asked my friend and several of his teammates about the practice of tapping the goal or the goalie. I was quickly provided with a great deal of information about power spots in the locker room, rituals in the locker room, lucky clothes, and lucky

meals—much more than I could digest at one sitting. Before dinner was over, I had my field site for my Ph.D. research.

The first phase of my research was carried out informally among hockey players and their families. This informality allowed me to get a holistic look at the social world of athletes in this sport. At this initial stage, I was thinking more in terms of a journalistic than an academic article, and I so informed the people with whom I was spending time. At this stage, I was able to learn about the stresses of team membership, player-management relationships, and the problems of keeping families together when athletes are continually on the road during a season and are subject to frequent trades. I was also able to observe how a player's performance on the ice affected a wife's status with the wives of other players.

About this time, I was commissioned to write a magazine article on sports magic, which provided me with press credentials to expand my study. It also led to different problems of access. I was able to interview such athletes as Jackie Stewart, the auto racer, and Chris Evert, the tennis player, among many others. Though I was able to talk freely with athletes, as well as their managers and trainers, on any subject relating to sports performance (including rituals), it would have been professionally inappropriate to inquire about their personal lives.

At this point, I decided to shift from an ethnographic methodology to a comparative study. Without access to data that would support a holistic

analysis, it is difficult to conduct ethnographic research. On the other hand, a comparative approach would allow me to track one or a small number of variables in a variety of contexts, attempting to answer such questions as: How does a particular variable change in different contexts? What factors are constant among different contexts?

My initial plan for these interviews was to compare rituals of team sport athletes with rituals of individual sport athletes. After about six months of interviewing individual and team sports athletes, I realized that there are so many differences in the lifestyles, schedules, and practice priorities of these two groups that the variables involved would be impossible to sift through. I decided that team sport athletes would provide the perfect laboratory to test a long-standing debate in anthropology: Do social or psychological factors play a greater role in ritual?

Anthropologists have long noted that risk and use of ritual are positively correlated, but it is difficult to test such complex variables in a controlled environment. Two great anthropologists in the British tradition of the field—Bronislaw Malinowski and A. R. Radcliffe-Brown—had begun the debate early in the twentieth century. Malinowski had argued that anxiety was the key factor in use of ritual and that ritual magic was most likely to be used in conditions of physical danger or when the outcome of an enterprise was uncertain. Radcliffe-Brown argued that ritual was aimed at reinforcing the solidarity of the group by enhancing the social role of ritual specialists.

All the factors of psychological danger and social complexity identified by anthropologists were present in varying degrees in the team sports of baseball, football, and hockey, thus providing an ideal laboratory for a comparative study of the relationship between risk and ritual. The danger of losing was a constant for the three sports. At the same time, there was a continuum of risk of physical danger represented in the three sports, with baseball having the least risk of disabling injury and football and hockey both being high-risk sports. Baseball was the most individual of the three sports; football was the most socially coordinated of the three sports; and hockey ranked in the middle on this variable. All three sports involved a high degree of social complexity involving team members and people on the periphery of the team.

This was the most sensitive phase of the study. Most athletes consider it bad luck to talk about their rituals, and they do not like hangers-on. At the same time, they are surrounded by groupies who want to be seen hanging out with athletes. Most also have rigidly defined categories of behavior appropriate to male and female roles. Male athletes make sharp distinctions between "good" and "bad" women, and they scorn women whose behavior is ambiguous with respect to these categories. Had my behavior challenged any of these categories, I would not have been able to complete the study. I have noted elsewhere that athletes repeatedly tested my ability to recognize their concepts of appropriate behavior (Womack and Barker 1993).

I chose to play the role of "soft" professional woman. I verbally distanced myself from sportswriters when seeking an interview by identifying myself as a social scientist. I never used language the athletes would consider inappropriate for a woman, and I always wore clothing appropriate for working in an office. Further, I restricted my contact with the athletes to the field or stadium. I obtained access by being accredited by the teams' press office, and this allowed me to hang out with athletes during practice or, depending on the sport, before games. During this phase of my research, I never socialized with the athletes away from the professional setting, though I had many casual conversations with them on the sidelines.

A Balance of Power

As this phase of the study was winding down, two circumstances changed my relationship with the athletes: I went to work for *Voice of America,* the international radio broadcaster, and Los Angeles was picked to host the 1984 Olympic Games. I was assigned to cover the negotiations and many international athletic competitions leading up to the Games.

As I became increasingly an insider with sportswriters, my relationship with the athletes shifted once again. Journalists and athletes operate in separate, equal, and interlocking realms, and there is always an uneasy relationship between the two groups. Though journalists and athletes are mutually interdependent, they operate in two very different and very public realms that reflect Western assumptions about the mind–body dichotomy. Journalists consider their association with words—conceptually connected with the mind—to give them superiority over athletes. Athletes are sensitive to cultural stereotypes about "dumb jocks" and resent what they call "jocksniffers," hangers-on to the team.

With my identity vis-à-vis the athletes more clearly defined as a journalist, I had much greater access to information about them, and I was able to observe and interview athletes from a variety of sports and from most countries in the world. In some cases, I was able to interview them about their rituals, but typically they do not welcome such inquiries from journalists. For journalists, the most important information about athletes is related to training and performance, and I could not deviate too far from this norm without endangering the journalist–athlete relationship. However, I was able to confirm my theory that rituals used by athletes are shaped more by the culture of the sport than by the culture of the country of origin.

Beginning with my coverage of the Los Angeles Olympics and continuing until the 1988 Winter Olympics in Calgary, Canada, my duties included covering a variety of sporting events—ranging from international gymnastics championships, Super Bowls, and All-Star Games to professional boxing. I covered all of Mohammed Ali's retirement events except the last one, but I did cover his training leading up to his last fight. By the end of that era, most of the athletes I had studied earlier were retiring, and I was feeling that my research roots were beginning to wither. Anthropologists develop strong ties to the people they study, and during my early days of research, I had come to view the athletes as "my people." Anthropologists grow older, and so do the people they study. I

(*continued*)

DISCUSSIONS

Issues of Access and Power— Contrasting Ethnographic Examples (*continued*)

had never been interested in sports as a purely voyeuristic enterprise, and I was ready to get back into anthropology.

In 1989, a private foundation funded by a Mexican media corporation hired me to conduct a study of sporting art, covering as many regions of the world and as many eras as possible to fit into the budget and the time frame provided for the study. I was back in the business of research on the social context of sports, but with an entirely altered perspective. I had begun my research as an insider, albeit on the sidelines, and had progressed through shades of participant observer negotiation.

This study put me solidly in the camp of the observer. At the same time, my research focus shifted from a study of the social interaction of athletes to the social role of athletes as hero, a study presaged in my dissertation. I had also shifted from ethnography to *ethnology*, cross-cultural comparison.

University–Northridge, most of my students were not anthropology majors. They took anthropology as a general education requirement to supplement their training in psychology, economics, engineering, or some other field. Because anthropology was not their primary focus, they were less willing to devote their time to exploring the deeper and more inaccessible aspects of the field. However, it was richly satisfying to extend the range of anthropology beyond the confines of a particular department.

Teaching at a community college requires one to become a wilder sort of bird. Students at two-year colleges are a much more heterogeneous group than are students at research institutions and four-year colleges. In general, they are in the process of becoming accustomed to college, and they represent a wide variety of age, skills, commitment, and preparation. Some are just making the transition from high school; others have been working for a number of years and are returning to college to complete their college degree; still others have a degree and are taking classes to enhance their work skills or to pursue a particular interest. In Los Angeles, many community college students are from foreign countries and must contend with a language barrier or the pressures of adjusting to life in the United States.

Teaching anthropology to such a diverse group is both challenging and exhilarating. Many community college students are unusually dedicated because they have made economic and personal sacrifices to pursue their education. On the other hand, they may be constrained by their economic or personal circumstances from dedicating their full attention to the class. For some students, language or inadequate preparation in high school is a barrier to understanding some of the more sophisticated anthropological concepts. At the same time, their particular and sometimes unusual circumstances make anthropology especially relevant to them.

In one class, which included several international students, I was discussing woman–woman marriage in an African cattleherding group. As noted in the discussion of the Nandi in Chapter 12, woman–woman marriage permits the female husband to acquire the status of a male and continue her family's patrilineal line. Most U.S.-born students are skeptical of this practice, perhaps suspecting the concept to be an anthropological fantasy. In this class, however, a female student from Africa interrupted my description of this type of marriage with the remark, "My aunt was involved in one of those marriages." In another class, a student from Africa shared his experience of male puberty rites. In yet another class, a Russian émigré enhanced our discussion of Marxist economics with his own experience of the Soviet system.

Such a broad range of life experiences represented in the classroom lifts anthropology off the printed page and brings it vividly to life. As an anthropology instructor, I am always exhilarated to see the look of recognition on the face of a Chinese student as I describe a patrilineal system of kinship, or the look of

Traditionally, anthropological studies took us to other parts of the world in search of cross-cultural evidence of what it means to be human. Today, the anthropological approach is relevant for people all over the world, since the barriers to cross-cultural understanding are no longer geographical. Instead, the adventure of anthropology may now consist of breaking down barriers to understanding arising from cultural isolation.

wonder on the face of a student from India as I describe the Nayar marriage system, or the look of pride on the face of an African American student as I describe the intricacies of the Nuer segmentary lineage system.

Barker reports a similar classroom experience. She was discussing Ethiopian marriage rules and the punishment for breaking them when one of her students interrupted with a story of her own. The student had emigrated from Ethiopia to the United States with a male cousin. When the cousin got married in the United States, he broke some Ethiopian marriage rules that were considered inviolable. A group of elders in his natal village gathered around a tape recorder and recorded a series of **curses,** ritual chants aimed at bringing harm to the errant individual. Barker found this to be a wonderful illustration of the "wedding" of tradition and technology.

Research Institutions and Museums

Not all research-oriented anthropologists carve out careers at colleges and universities. Some are employed at institutions either entirely dedicated to research or having only a minimal teaching function. One of the best known of these is the Smithsonian Institution, which employs anthropologists focusing on various aspects of culture from folk music to folklore. Another institution devoted solely to research, the Human Relations Area Files, based in New Haven, Connecticut, maintains data on more than three hundred cultures studied by anthropologists.

Some research institutions focus on a specific aspect of culture. For example, anthropologists at the Philadelphia Geriatric Center study such issues as folk models of aging and beliefs associated with death and dying. The Amerind Foundation, located in Arizona, deals with a variety of issues relating to Native Americans.

All these research institutions depend on grants from government sources, private foundations, or a variety of sponsors. Because grant donors typically fund specific types of research, the priorities of the granting foundation may shape the type of research the anthropologist can do. In most cases, the anthropologist requesting a grant must be affiliated with a university or research institution. A number of anthropologists have established their own research institutions, much as entrepreneurs in business establish their own companies, and a great deal of creative research in applied fields has been undertaken in this way.

Museums Museums are a traditional context in which anthropologists employ their expertise. These jobs include such diverse roles as planning and finding grants for exhibits, caring for collections of cultural artifacts, and overseeing operations of the museum as director or in some other managerial capacity.

Museums have long played an important role in preserving cultural **artifacts,** the material products of culture, and placing them on public display. They serve an important educational function in permitting nonanthropologists to become aware of the

Two cultural traditions of the U.S. Southwest converge in this display of Navajo silver-decorated belts and Hopi kachina figures. Both the Navajo and the Hopi occupy the "four corners" area of Arizona, New Mexico, Utah, and Colorado, but they are from very different cultural traditions. For Navajo sheepherders, silver jewelry and belts indicate status and comprise a readily convertible form of wealth. For Hopi horticulturalists, kachina figures represent spirit beings associated with the ancestors and with rain essential for growing corn.

tremendous diversity in world cultures. In recent years, however, museums have come under fire by some indigenous people. In the early days of European colonial contact, explorers and anthropologists took for display in museums many cultural artifacts, including religious objects, from groups with whom they came into contact. This practice enhanced the physical preservation of the objects but removed them from their cultural context. It also meant that descendants of the people who had produced them and had given them meaning had little access to them and no control over them. In Chapter 15, we discussed the example of the Kwakiutl of Alert Bay, who negotiated with Canada's Museum of Man to have many of their masks returned to them.

In response to the pleas and demands of indigenous groups intent on repatriating their traditional artifacts, a number of anthropologists engaged in work at museums are trying to develop programs that will allow these groups to retain rights to their artifacts. **Repatriation,** the process of returning control over artifacts to the descendents of the people who produced them, is now a major concern for museums. Christopher Donnan, formerly director of UCLA's Fowler Museum of Cultural History, worked with Walter Alva of Peru to unearth one of that country's richest coastal archaeological finds. The American media referred to the occupant of the chief tomb as "the King Tut of the Western Hemisphere." After a national tour of the United States organized by Donnan, the artifacts were returned for permanent display at the Bruning Archaeological Museum in Lambayeque, Peru. This was a pioneering effort that combined the advantages of widespread international media exposure with repatriation of the objects to the people who are most entitled to view them and benefit from the attention they have drawn to this important cultural area.

APPLICATIONS OF ANTHROPOLOGY

As college and university budgets become increasingly strained and research funds are increasingly being dedicated to specialized subjects with direct applications, anthropologists have been forced to seek careers outside the traditional educational and research contexts. As a result, they are gaining employment in a variety of positions: as workers with international organizations, both institutional and corporate; as advocates for the rights of indigenous people; as consultants for educational institutions and businesses; and in a wide range of capacities relating to medicine and health care delivery systems. This type of work is known as **applied anthropology.** According to a 1996 survey by the American Anthropological Association, from 30 to 50 percent of anthropologists work in applied fields. This number varies from year to year.

In fact, the line between research-oriented anthropology and applied anthropology is blurred. Many anthropologists in academia conduct research or work in applied fields; applied anthropologists may have strong research interests. In practice, the distinction is based in large part on whether the anthropologist is employed by an academic institution or by an organization oriented toward application of research results.

Though the applications of anthropology are limited only by the imagination of the anthropologist, in this chapter, we focus on three areas in which anthropology can make important contributions: (1) medical systems, including epidemiology, health care delivery systems, and integration of traditional healing systems with Western medicine; (2) economic systems, including advising indigenous people on development projects that might affect their way of life; and (3) mass media as a means of implementing the educational role of anthropology.

Anthropology and Medicine

The applications of anthropology to various aspects of medicine are far-reaching. Research-oriented anthropologists study such issues as the social context of Western medicine and traditional healing techniques. As noted in Chapter 8, a number of anthropologists have focused on psychotherapeutic aspects of shamanic healing. Applied anthropologists have been employed in a wide range of medically oriented tasks, from evaluating the effectiveness of health care delivery systems to exploring social and cultural factors in the transmission of epidemic diseases. **Medical anthropology** is a large and growing component of applied anthropology, and medical anthropologists are employed by a variety of organizations, including medical centers and health management

organizations (HMOs), the U.S. Centers for Disease Control and Prevention, the National Institutes of Health, state and federal organizations, and pharmaceutical companies.

The "Rituals" of Western Medicine It is common to speak of the "miracles" of modern medicine, and indeed some results of Western drugs and medical practices appear miraculous. However, anthropologists are well aware that herbs and techniques of traditional shamans result in what appear to be "miraculous" cures as well. Increasingly, anthropologists are studying both Western medicine and shamanic healing, and they are learning that both traditions combine knowledge of physiology with psychotherapy to produce healing results. In this section, we discuss the work of some anthropologists who are assisting Western medical personnel in providing the appropriate social context for treating people unaccustomed to treatment according to the scientific model, which seems to them cold and sterile. In some cases, the anthropologist bridges the gap between Western and indigenous healers to improve the context of healing for patients of both types of practitioners.

In all societies, an important component of healing is the credentials of the healer. Shamans sometimes establish their credentials through dramatic displays of visitations from spirits. On a long-term basis, however, their claim to effectiveness in healing must rest on their ability to alleviate the distress—both psychological and physical—of their patients. A shaman who fails to heal cannot build a clientele. Western doctors, as well, must establish their healing credentials. In this case, the source of authority is a degree from a recognized medical school, a license to practice medicine, and, often, affiliation with an accredited medical facility. Thus, Western doctors practice their craft backed by the authority of science. Anthropologists have noted, however, that even Western doctors draw on symbolic emblems and rituals to underscore their authority. Dan Blumhagen notes that the doctor's white coat is a symbol of power and competence:

> The image of power and protection emerge: While wearing a white coat the physician is able to handle safely the deadly scourges that plague mankind and is able to render them innocuous. One result of this perception of power is that physician-scientists were granted tremendous authority. ([1979] 1991:197)

Blumhagen suggests that the authority of science transfers power to the physician and reduces the autonomy of patients: "No mere individual desires or beliefs were allowed to stand in the way of the public's health as determined by medical laboratories" ([1979] 1991:197).

Pearl Katz suggests that surgical procedures aimed at preventing viral or bacterial contamination of the operating room serve to distance medical personnel from ordinary social norms and values: "The boundaries which separate the operating room from the outside contribute to a particular mental set for the participants, which enables them to participate in a dispassionate manner in activities they would ordinarily view with strong emotion" ([1981] 1991:214).

Though distancing mechanisms protect medical personnel from strong emotions and enhance their authority as healers, the emphasis on sterile procedures can be perceived by patients and their loved ones as lack of caring. Robbie Davis-Floyd argues that obstetrical procedures surrounding childbirth practices in the United States remove the locus of control from the woman giving birth and transfer it to hospital staff, which is generally organized around patriarchal models of hierarchy. At the same time, the emphasis on technology, considered superior to the biology of childbirth, leads women to view their bodies as defective machines. Davis-Floyd quotes one woman who describes her childbirth experience:

> It's almost like programming you. You get to the hospital. They put you in this wheelchair. They whisk you off from your husband, and I mean just start in on you. Then they put you in another wheelchair, and send you home. And then they say, well, we need to give you something for the depression. [Laughs] Get away from me! That will help my depression! (1994:339)

Davis-Floyd suggests that technologically oriented childbirth procedures socialize a woman at a time she is vulnerable into seeing herself as dependent on science and technology. In turn, the woman will socialize her child in the same culturally constructed world view:

> Obstetrical interventions . . . attempt to contain and control the process of birth, and to transform the birthing woman into an American mother who has internalized the core values of this society. Such a mother believes in science, relies on technology, and recognizes her inferiority (either consciously or unconsciously) and so at some level accepts the principles of patriarchy. (Davis-Floyd 1994:339)

Medical anthropologists have noted that medical procedures that reinforce the authority of the medical establishment and emphasize technology over the psychological and social dimensions of illness do not provide the best possible context for healing. Members of minority groups and people accustomed to relying on shamans or other traditional healers may be reluctant to call on medical personnel who do not take account of their close relationship with extended family members or respect their religious customs.

Detoxifying Western Medicine Writing in the *Western Journal of Medicine*, anthropologist Anne Sutherland notes that medical personnel find American Gypsies difficult to work with for a variety of reasons relating to Gypsy culture:

> Gypsies . . . are assertive in seeking medical care. . . . Gypsies often request specific "famous name" physicians and demand specific treatment they have heard of even when the treatment or specific physician is inappropriate. Gypsies frequently request specific colored pills that they share with their relatives. They prefer older, "big" (well-known) physicians over younger ones. They often do not comply with preventive and long-term treatment. When a relative is sick, they come to the hospital in alarmingly large numbers, sometimes camp on hospital grounds, disregard visiting rules, and generally create chaos in the corridors of the hospital. ([1992] 1994:408)

Sutherland developed guidelines for medical personnel to help them understand aspects of Gypsy culture that affect treatment:

- Older relatives have an important role in the decision-making process of a patient. Try to include them and treat them with the respect they are due as elders in the community. Older relatives can be of great help in ensuring the cooperation of younger ones.

- Gypsies can alternate rapidly between moods or styles of interpersonal interaction from extreme assertion to plaintive begging. Medical personnel should appeal to the strong desire of Gypsies to obtain the best medical treatment and assure them that cooperation will work best.

- English is a second language. Explain clearly without resorting to too many technical terms the procedures the patient will undergo. Then ask if there is anything that is against the patient's religion. If there is something the patient and family do not want done, explain why it is necessary or allow the patient to forgo it.

- Many Gypsies cannot read, but it would be a mistake to assume that they are therefore less intelligent. Read important instructions (particularly at the time of patient screening) to a patient or ask a translator to read out loud to the patient.

- Gypsies accept emergency measures more readily than they accept instructions to undertake changes in diet or lifestyle; however, instruction in long-term health goals is crucial. They need education on the connection between diets high in animal fats, heavy smoking, drinking, and no exercise and the health problems they cause.

- A Gypsy patient does not want to be alone and will be fearful and agitated if forced to be without family. Allowing some relative in the room with the patient on a rotating basis will keep the chaos to a minimum. Allow someone to stay overnight with the patient. If the patient is dying, it is essential that relatives be allowed to be present at the moment of death. ([1992] 1994: 417–418)

Many applied anthropologists work with medical organizations and health care professionals to develop ways of making Western medicine more "user friendly" for patients from a variety of backgrounds. In some cases, this means mediating between Western medical personnel and traditional healers. Edward C. Green ([1987] 1991) went to Swaziland in southern Africa to serve as an anthropologist on the Rural Water-Borne Disease Control Project for the U.S. Agency for International Development. His job as an anthropologist was to study the relationship between cultural beliefs and practices and the status of water and sanitation. However, the scope of his study expanded.

In the process of learning about health-related beliefs and attitudes, Green interviewed traditional healers. He discovered that the healers were interested in learning more about Western medicine and working cooperatively with doctors and nurses. He also learned that the traditional healers distinguished between "African" diseases, those treatable only by African medicines and rituals, and new or foreign diseases more treatable by Western medicine. The Swazi healers referred the latter cases to clinics and hospitals.

Green notes that the World Health Organization had recommended that "poorer nations try to find ways for indigenous healers to work cooperatively

with modern health sector personnel" ([1987] 1991:202). In view of that recommendation, Green worked with the Swaziland Ministry of Health to develop a program to integrate the two systems of healing by conducting a series of workshops aimed at bringing together medical practitioners and traditional healers.

Such programs are becoming increasingly important, not only in such areas as Africa and Latin America but in industrialized countries as well. Significant portions of the population in affluent countries call on the services of healers using a wide variety of techniques, from laying on of hands to applications of various kinds of herbs. As anthropologists contribute their expertise in the importance of the social and cultural dynamics of illness, Western medical practitioners are learning that traditional healing practices, once dismissed as superstition, can contribute an important dimension to treating disease.

Anthropology and the Political Economy

Anthropologists have long dealt with political and economic systems as research topics. In recent decades, the economies of many indigenous groups have become turbulent in the wake of national or international political upheaval, the rise of international corporations, and development attempts aimed at drawing formerly isolated regions into the global economy. As a result, many anthropologists have applied their expertise to easing the transition for indigenous groups and, in many cases, as advocates on behalf of these groups' economic rights. At the same time, there is increasing awareness on the part of both anthropologists and members of the business community that anthropological theories and methods are an important aid to understanding the "culture" of modern corporations.

Aiding Indigenous People   As the people anthropologists study become increasingly drawn into the global economy—either as targets of development or as recruits in wage labor economies—the line between anthropological research and advocacy may become blurred. David Turton was conducting fieldwork among the Mursi, a pastoral group on the Ethiopia–Sudan borderlands, during the famine of 1971–1973. During the same period, the Mursi were caught up in armed conflict among several groups in the region. Many Mursi died—"most from disease

A Bird's Eye View of Applied Anthropology

As the people anthropologists have traditionally studied are increasingly drawn into a global economy, some anthropologists have declared the field to be on its way down. Other anthropologists have taken flight, inaugurating the fledgling field of aviation anthropology. Allen W. Batteau notes that Airbus Industrie of Europe "is unique among commercial aircraft manufacturers in its use of anthropologists and anthropological insight to design flight decks for the world aviation market." In the following article, Batteau discusses the emerging field of aviation anthropology, along with its implications for airline safety.

ANTHROPOLOGY WITH AN ALTITUDE
Allen W. Batteau

Aviation anthropology—unlike aviation psychology, which is a substantial and well-respected subdiscipline with annual conferences and an international journal—is still at the gate.

Most of the world's aviation anthropologists gathered in September 1998 in a small room to discuss the issues of cultural contexts of flight automation and aviation safety. Despite this inauspicious start, anthropology has a critical role in aviation, both to improve flight safety and to understand how aviation transforms world culture.

Cultures in the Air

Within the aviation industry and safety studies, there is extensive discussion of the effects of a national culture on safety and of "safety culture," an elusive concept embracing attention to detail, adherence to procedures, and open communication within non-adversarial relationships. Despite considerable discussion of the effects of "culture" on operations, it is not anthropologists but political scientists, organizational theorists, and social psychologists who contribute to studies of culture and aviation.

Studies questioning whether cultural differences among flight crews enhance or degrade safe flight suggest, for example, that airlines using multicultural crews should select pilots for their ability to adapt to cultural differences. Other studies examining the significance of individualism and power distance for Crew Resources Management observe that psychological conceptions such as these embody Western folk models that may not contribute to safe flight in an international context.

Psychological researchers are also concerned about the impact of organizational culture and "safety culture" on flight operations. Results of a Flight Management Attitudes Questionnaire conducted by a team of psychologists reveal how "cultures" can affect the acceptance or rejection of crew coordination goals. They also describe a "safety culture" consisting of demonstrated commitment to safety, open channels of communication, and a bias toward

and hunger, some violently and a few from suicide by starvation" (de Waal 1996:242). Turton wrote that the Mursi "came through this experience with their social and economic institutions intact and an undiminished sense of their cultural identity" (cited in de Waal 1996:242).

The Mursi later became victims of a massacre. A rival neighboring group was provided by the Sudanese government with modern Soviet-made guns to use in the fight against southern rebels. The Mursi had only a few obsolete rifles. In February 1987, between six hundred and eight hundred Mursi were killed in a surprise attack (de Waal 1996:242). The surviving Mursi were forced to evacuate the southern part of their territory. As a result of the susceptibility of the Mursi to both famine and political upheaval, Turton found his role shifting from that of ethnographer to advocate on behalf of a group of people threatened with the destruction of their society and perhaps of their physical survival (de Waal 1996:242).

In Pocatello, Idaho, a cultural anthropologist was called in to evaluate the English-speaking ability of six elderly Bannock-Shoshoni Indian women in a dispute over Social Security payments. The women were accused of fraud in failing to report rental of some farmland to Euro-Americans. The women had rented the land in January, but they didn't receive

safety in tradeoffs between safety and profitability.

Diversity at Flight Level 350

Anthropology has been of particular use by contributing insights on technology transfer to the study of aviation. There are currently two major manufacturers of large commercial aircraft, with another dozen manufacturers of commuter-size airliners. Counting the EU [European Union] as a single entity, seven countries monopolize the production of passenger aircraft. These aircraft are flown by airlines from over 80 countries in more than 160 airspaces by pilots whose diversity reflects that of the world's cultures. What may seem obvious in Toulouse can become opaque to pilots in Guanajuato. Designs optimized for the airspaces of North America or Europe crash more frequently in Africa or South America. Safety devices incorporating American cultural assumptions have proven totally ineffective in China and the Far East. Procedures refined in the United States mystify and confuse pilots from other countries. Some airlines, such as Cathay Pacific, perhaps reflecting the crossroads and cosmopolitan character of Hong Kong, effectively adopt these technologies. Others do not

Related to this issue are the emerging international alliances beginning to dominate commercial aviation. Alliances such as Star Alliance and One World bring together airlines from multiple countries, cultures, and regions, usually in an opportunistic fashion. Within the alliance there can be code-sharing, sharing of facilities, crews, and even resources such as training, maintenance, and ramp services. How effectively two separate corporate cultures can integrate their operations while maintaining separate corporate and national identities is an untested idea which is ripe for anthropological study.

International operations is a third issue of increasing prominence. In the future, foreign or expatriate flight crews in national or foreign airspaces will be the rule, not the exception. Both on the flight deck and between aircraft and ground, effective coordination will become more difficult as communication crosses multiple cultural boundaries. Despite the emergence of a common industry culture within the aviation industry, pilots themselves reflect increasingly diverse backgrounds.

Industrial anthropology is booming, to judge from the financial pages of *The New York Times* or *USA Today*. Companies from Motorola and Apple Computer to Proctor & Gamble and General Motors have found that anthropology lends unique insight to the global aspects of their operations. The U.S. Air Force looks to anthropologists to understand the cultural aspects of a changing environment. Companies and countries that are likewise ready to understand the cultural complexity and diversity of today's world will be those that emerge as leaders in the twenty-first century.

Given the headlong rush toward global integration in commercial aviation—unmatched by any other industry touching large segments of the public—there is an urgent need to bring anthropological understanding to bear in the commercial aviation industry.

Source: "Anthropology with an Altitude," *Anthropology News* (May 2000).

payment until December. Officials of the Pocatello Social Service Agency claimed the income should have been reported as soon as the land was rented in January. The officials stopped all checks to the women and demanded that they pay back money they had already received.

Barbara Joans, a cultural anthropologist at Idaho State University, was called in to determine whether the women were able to understand instructions given to them by Pocatello Social Service officials. The women technically spoke English, but they used either Bannock or Shoshoni in their daily interactions. Adapting techniques of participant observation, Joans engaged the women in conversation on a range of subjects in a variety of contexts. She determined that all the women could communicate in English on the level of everyday common speech, such as comprehending the statements "Are you cold?" and "Are you hungry?" Only one of the women could understand English at the level of joking or comprehending nonliteral sentences. None of the women could understand English at the level of completely comprehending laws and regulations governing their lives. Joans also learned that Social Service officials had conveyed information about Social Security rules during a group lunch on the reservation when many activities were competing for the women's attention. As a result, the judge trying the case ruled that the women did not have to return the Social Security money sent them and required the Pocatello Social Service Agency to use a Bannock-Shoshoni interpreter when describing program requirements at the reservation (Joans [1984] 1991).

There are also attempts by anthropologists to prevent indigenous people from becoming victims of exploitation by helping them offer some commodity to the global economy more significant than their wage labor or nonrenewable resources. Jason Clay is one of the organizers of an advocacy group for indigenous people and their cultures called Cultural Survival, based in Cambridge, Massachusetts. Clay has been promoting renewable products of the Amazon such as nuts, oils, medicinal plants, and flowers. He believes that marketing these products could fuel a multimillion-dollar retail industry that could convince governments to leave the forests standing (Linden 1993).

The results of marketing efforts such as Clay's are yet to be evaluated. One by-product of the shift to a global economy, however, is that indigenous people are increasingly using international distribution systems, such as the Internet, to market their own cultural products.

Consulting with Businesses Laura Nader once chastised anthropologists for "studying down," whether working among the exotic "other" or the perhaps even-more-exotic "us":

> If we look at the literature based on field work in the United States, we find a relatively abundant literature on the poor, the ethnic groups, the disadvantaged; there is comparatively little field research on the middle class and very little firsthand work on the upper classes. (1974:289)

Nader suggests that anthropologists "study down" because they see themselves as champions of the oppressed. However, she notes that studying the poor and disenfranchised also places the anthropologist in a position of power with respect to the people he or she is studying. Nader urges anthropologists to study powerful institutions in the United States, such as the U.S. Congress.

Relatively few research-oriented anthropologists have heeded Nader's call, but many applied anthropologists have rushed to fill the gap. According to a 1996 survey conducted by the American Anthropological Association, 12 percent of applied anthropologists are employed by for-profit organizations.

Writing for *Business Week,* Sana Siwolop notes:

> More and more companies agree that there is a payoff in being subjects [of anthropological research]. Many turn to anthropologists when they want to change their corporate culture. Others call on anthropologists when a new top executive wants the lowdown on his employees or needs insight into a company being merged or acquired. GM, for example, hired a staff anthropologist soon after it acquired Electronic Data Systems Corp. in 1984. Demand for anthropologists is particularly strong in Silicon Valley, where job-hopping and rapid changes in management often wreak havoc in an organization. ([1986] 1991:35)

In studying corporations, anthropologists apply the traditional approach combining holism, insider perspective, and cultural relativism to understand the dynamics of corporate culture. Sunny Baker, co-founder of Corporate Anthropology Group, which numbers Microsoft among its clients, often conducts participant observation by taking a job at the company she is studying so she can observe how employees interact with each other (Siwolop [1986] 1991).

Eleanor Herasimchuk Wynn became a market analyst at Bell Northern Research, a telecommunications research and development laboratory, through a series of serendipitous events. As a student in linguistic anthropology at the University of California–Berkeley, Wynn collected tape recordings of a Los Angeles engineering firm to use in analyzing status relationships implicitly expressed in conversational styles. While at Berkeley, she was hired by the Xerox Palo Alto Research Center to study patterns of interaction in the office. On the basis of that study and with funding from Xerox, Wynn wrote her dissertation on the transmission of information through office conversations and the social component of knowledge brought to clerical tasks. At Bell Northern Research, she conducted market research on the introduction of new products into office automation and communication. Wynn notes:

> I feel that I have discovered "my people": communications and data processing managers in Fortune 500 companies and state government. I suppose I could have stayed in research, which would have been like academic work, with equally interesting colleagues and "pure" projects. But marketing forces you into the big real world, to look ahead at large-scale technology trends which will eventually have a massive social and technological impact. (From *Anthropology Newsletter* 24:5, 1983)

For many people, the North American workplace has changed, and with it, the pattern of social interaction. These office workers, virtually isolated from co-workers in other cubicles, may simultaneously be in contact with people all over the world through the Internet. Will this change the nature of being human? Many anthropologists are now conducting research on the cultural dynamics of corporations and are applying that understanding to producing a more "user-friendly" corporate environment.

Easing "Culture Shock" for Corporate Families
In the mid-1990s, a U.S. teenager living with his mother and stepfather in Singapore became the subject of international headlines when he was sentenced to whipping for participating in vandalism with several other expatriate youths. In the United States, this particular form of corporal punishment is prohibited, and acts of vandalism by young men from affluent families are often downplayed as being due to youthful high spirits. In Singapore, however, such transgressions are severely punished.

This international incident, which strained relations between the United States and Singapore, was based on a series of misunderstandings. It could have been ameliorated had anthropologists been involved at several points along the way: (1) preparing the teenager's family for differences in cultural values; (2) working with Singaporean officials to develop a system to deal with vandalism involving foreign visitors; (3) working with international companies to develop programs to ensure that the behavior of employees and their families is culturally appropriate; and (4) educating the U.S. news media to understand that "American" values are neither universal nor necessarily more humane than those of other societies. Vandalism that might be tolerated in U.S. cities is considered a serious crime in many other parts of the world. An anthropologist trained in Chinese values could have informed the boy's parents and officials of the company that sent them to Singapore that breaking social norms is especially severely dealt with in this particular city.

Drawing on the experience of anthropologists studying cross-culturally, Lillian Trager developed a workshop designed to prepare individuals and families for the issues they will encounter in living abroad (Trager [1987] 1991). Though the Singapore case was unusual in the sense that it created a sensation in the U.S. press, families of workers in international corporations often find themselves caught up in cultural

Unlike many other groups studied by anthropologists, Trobriand Islanders have managed to absorb some aspects of culture change without abandoning their traditional way of life. They still participate in the Kula ring, a form of ceremonial exchange studied by Bronislaw Malinowski early in the twentieth century. Here, Trobriand Islanders play their own version of the British game of cricket, adapted to customs associated with their traditional style of warfare.

misunderstandings or suffering from depression and anxiety due to loneliness or **culture shock,** the stress of coping with unfamiliar social and cultural contexts. Anthropologists, who may spend much of their lives in unfamiliar contexts, are experts on the subject of culture shock, in terms of both their training and their cross-cultural experiences in adaptation.

ANTHROPOLOGY AND MEDIA

By its very nature, anthropology is intrinsically linked to communication. Not only do anthropologists observe the daily lives of the people they study; they must also rely on those people's reports about what their experiences mean to them. Anthropologists must then find words to communicate an understanding of the people's experience to other anthropologists and to nonanthropologists. It is becoming increasingly clear that anthropology has much to contribute to understanding the intricate processes of social interaction and cultural construction that underlie complex contemporary societies.

When anthropologists turn to communicating their understanding of social and cultural processes to their colleagues and members of the public, they must rely on various forms of mass media. Their traditional reliance on publication of ethnographies and articles in professional journals has limited reporting of data to anthropological colleagues. However, anthropology has much to contribute to public policy and public understanding of social issues. In this section, we discuss various aspects of anthropology's relationship to media: (1) visual anthropology, a subdiscipline that focuses on techniques for recording and communicating ethnographic information through visual images, (2) the mass media and anthropology, which deals with the application of anthropology to contemporary issues, and (3) anthropology and journalism, which focuses on the contribution anthropology can make to understanding the social and cultural construction of news events.

Visual Anthropology

Excerpts from Franz Boas's early films of the Kwakiutl can still be seen on PBS stations in the United States. Margaret Mead pioneered the use of visual media, both still photography and films, as a research tool. Film, still photography, and video continue to flourish as important means of documenting the diversity of cultures throughout the world. Not only do ethnographic films enliven anthropology classes; they also make up a significant portion of the programming for PBS and cable television.

Visual anthropology, a subfield of anthropology aimed at exploring visual techniques for documenting cultures, has become an important part of the anthropological enterprise. John Collier Jr. and Malcolm Collier note: "The critical eye of the camera is an essential tool in gathering accurate visual information" (1986:5). The "ethnography" of the visual anthropologist is typically an **ethnographic film,** in which the ethnographer attempts to communicate his or her understanding of a particular culture through visual images. Most ethnographic films find their way into the college classroom, but increasingly emphasis is on presenting such materials in a way that will appeal to a popular audience.

Photography and film are sometimes considered a more accurate means of data collection than note taking, since the visual image portrays something that is evidently "real." In fact, visual media are as subject to selective editing as verbal media. The photographer or filmmaker decides what events are worthy of recording, as does the anthropologist relying on audio tape and note taking. Clifford Geertz writes: "The ethnographer 'inscribes' social discourse: *he writes it down*. In so doing, he turns it from a passing event, which exists only in its own moment of occurrence, into an account, which exists in the inscriptions and can be reconsulted" (1973:19).

Though a visual image may seem more "real" than a written account, the act of filming is actually far more constricted than writing, because film is usually in more limited supply than paper or audio tape and filming an event does not allow for digressive discourse. In addition, both visual images and words must be edited to a length suitable for their audience. Even the most dedicated anthropologist would be less willing to watch a year-and-a-half-long film documenting someone else's field site than to read someone else's field notes covering the same period. One magnificent attempt to let the visual image speak for itself was a classic two-part film called *The Nuer,* about an African cattleherder group studied by E. E. Evans-Pritchard. Though acclaimed for its sweeping vistas of the Nuer in their homeland in the southern Sudan, it is now seldom shown because its length and lack of commentary make it unsuitable for classroom viewing.

In updating the PBS series on cultural anthropology, *Faces of Culture,* producer John Bishop and I found ourselves inadvertently perpetrating a revolution. Our goal was to present a balanced picture of the range of cultural anthropological topics through a series designed to substitute for an introductory course on cultural anthropology. We sought to integrate contemporary research on gender, ethnicity, and other issues currently attracting the attention of anthropologists. We also wanted to avoid presenting an idiosyncratic view that primarily reflected our own political perspective. We decided to let the people speak for themselves by minimizing commentary and presenting a range of viewpoints.

We were startled by the results. After putting together the video, titled *Sex and Marriage,* in which people from several cultures presented their views on marriage, Bishop called me to say, "We've made a powerful political statement here." When I viewed the completed documentary, I was compelled to agree. The heartfelt views of people from such areas as Morocco and West Africa added up to a powerful portrait of marriage customs. In addition, we combined ethnographic footage with fast-paced commercial timing, which increased the visual impact.

Mass Media and Anthropology

The various forms of mass media extend the educational range of anthropology far beyond the classroom, though many anthropologists are uneasy about "going public" with respect to social issues that require a great deal of sensitivity. However, awareness of the applicability of anthropology to contemporary issues and problems is increasing, and one of the most effective ways to influence public policy and public opinion is through mass media.

Margaret Mead made effective use of mass media by producing anthropological films, appearing on television, and addressing her books to a popular audience. She also influenced American culture indirectly through her association with others who helped to shape public opinion. Paul Bohannan suggests that Margaret Mead shaped U.S. culture in powerful and pervasive ways that often go unacknowledged (pers. comm. 1997). He notes that the pediatrician for her daughter, Mary Catherine Bateson, was Dr. Benjamin Spock, the physician who wrote the definitive book on parenting for the 1950s and 1960s. As anyone familiar with Mead's vivid and forceful personality would attest, Spock could not have failed to be impressed with her views on cultural relativism, developed in her years of study with Franz Boas and finely honed by her years of research on child rearing in several parts of the world. Bateson writes of her mother: "Margaret's ideas influenced the rearing of countless children, not only through her own writings but through the writings of Benjamin Spock, who was my pediatrician and for whom I was the first breast-fed and 'self-demand' baby he had encountered" (1984:23). Bateson adds, "Spock was blessedly relaxed about letting my mother do as she wanted, abandoning the fixed schedules that were regarded as essential to health, but he seems to have been only partly aware of the innovation taking place in front of his eyes" (1984:23).

During 1991 and 1992, David Givens, editor of the *Anthropology Newsletter,* emphasized the theme "Projecting Anthropology to the Public." In the November 20–24, 1991, issue of that publication, American Anthropological Association president June Buikstra noted the importance of anthropology in addressing contemporary issues:

> Like many of you, I am frequently amused by the range of subjects anthropologists are thought to command. I have, for example, aggressively sought information concerning the recently discovered Tyrolean "Iceman from the Similuan" not only out of academic interest but with the certainty that I will be questioned by family, friends and fellow airline travelers. While dinosaurs have not disappeared entirely from the menu of such casual queries, I am delighted to note that anthropology appears to be increasingly perceived as playing an important role in contemporary issues.

In some cases, anthropologists make use of the mass media to advocate human rights causes for indigenous people. Some cultural anthropologists, including myself, are often interviewed by journalists, who call upon us to apply anthropological insights into the organization of the family and other social institutions to problems that are prevalent in Western society. In other cases, anthropology in the mass media is "underground." A number of filmmakers are fans of anthropology, and anthropologists may work as advisers on films that are set in a context traditionally studied by anthropologists. Science fiction films and television shows, including *Star Wars* and *Star Trek,* are influenced by the anthropological view that one's own understanding is enhanced by contact with others unlike ourselves and that understanding is enhanced through application of the principle of cultural relativism.

Anthropology and Journalism

When I first applied my Ph.D. in anthropology to a career as an international radio broadcaster, my journalistic colleagues viewed my academic specialization with skepticism. "It's too bad she didn't get her doctorate in a relevant field like political science or economics," one said. At the same time, my ability to quickly gain information about a wide variety of topics—from the economic to the esoteric—won the admiration of other journalists. They attributed my reporting skill to some innate ability or "talent." I always responded, "It's because of my training as an anthropologist. This is what anthropologists do: they observe, interview, and write reports about what they have seen and heard." Since few people outside the field know what anthropology is, it is up to the anthropologist to demonstrate the value of the discipline.

I consider the approach and methods of anthropology virtually indispensable to a career in communications. I have taught courses on the theory of mass communications to journalism students and exhorted them to take anthropology classes. I encouraged my journalism students to do "ethnographies" of journalism and journalistic reports. In all

The world has changed a great deal since anthropology emerged as a discipline amid the intense period of intellectual debate during the mid-nineteenth century. However, some things remain constant, including ironies arising from the human condition. The message scrawled on this phone booth, "reverence for life," evokes the words of a Turkana cattle-herder: "Sometimes you sacrifice cattle to thank God for giving you life."

cases, they were astonished to discover how much the culture and social organization of journalism shape the way news events are reported. At the same time, I trained future journalists in anthropological techniques of interviewing so they could report on the event rather than on their own cultural biases.

For nonjournalists, a clear understanding of the anthropological approach enhances one's ability to be an insightful consumer of mass media in general. Popular forms of entertainment, including films and television programs designed to entertain, are vehicles of modern myths. Application of anthropological concepts relating to symbols and world view allows the viewer to comprehend the values and meanings that lie beneath the surface of the story. Understanding the social organization and culture of journalism allows one to realize that a news report is not simply a collection of "facts" but is a cultural product shaped by its social context. Journalists are not dispassionate observers of objective events; they, like anthropologists, are working professionals who must carve out a career in a demanding but rewarding field.

SUMMARY

Anthropology is little known or understood by people who have not studied the discipline, which means that anthropologists often must develop entrepreneurial skills to support themselves. Anthropologists are lured to the field by fascination with the subject rather than by the prospect of a lucrative career. However, anthropological training adapts readily to a variety of contexts, and anthropologists find jobs in a wide variety of applied fields as well as in academia.

Early in this century, there was no clear dividing line between academic anthropology and its applied aspects. Franz Boas and his students, especially Ruth Benedict and Margaret Mead, applied anthropological analysis to a variety of social issues. During the 1960s, however, concern over ethical issues in applied research and an increase in funding for university positions drew most anthropologists into academia.

The most prestigious teaching jobs are at research-oriented universities that grant Ph.D. degrees. However, these jobs are eagerly sought and hard to come by. Whereas the most prestigious Ph.D.-granting universities emphasize research over teaching, four-year and liberal arts colleges typically emphasize undergraduate education. The teaching load is heavier in four-year colleges than in research-oriented universities, but classes are typically smaller and the pressure to publish is not as intense. Two-year or community colleges serve a diverse population, including students who need additional preparation before transferring to four-year colleges, those who seek training in a technical field, and those who wish to return to college after working or raising a family. Thus, teaching is strongly emphasized at two-year colleges, teaching loads are heavy, and there is usually little time or incentive to do research.

Anthropologists are also employed at research institutions, some of which focus on a specific area of culture. All research institutions are funded by grants of various kinds, and the topics being studied are strongly influenced by the available funding. Museums employ anthropologists in a variety of positions, from planning exhibits to overseeing museum operations. Museums play an important role in preserving cultural artifacts and educating the public about the range and diversity of the world's cultures. However, they have come under fire by a number of indigenous groups, who note that displaying objects in museums remote from the objects' places of origin removes them from their cultural contexts. In recent years, some museums have worked with indigenous groups to help them establish their own locally controlled and operated museums.

Theories and methods of anthropology are being applied in a variety of contexts. Many anthropologists are employed in a variety of medical contexts, by medical centers and health maintenance organizations, by the U.S. Centers for Disease Control and Prevention, and by the National Institutes of Health, as well as by many other medically oriented organizations. Some anthropologists work with Western medical practitioners to make treatment more "user friendly." Using participant observation and drawing on their knowledge of indigenous cultures, anthropologists help develop ways of transcending the doctor–patient barrier that often accompanies the Western medical emphasis on scientific authority and technology.

Anthropologists also work in a variety of economic contexts. Some anthropologists become advocates for the people they study when those people are drawn into political or economic upheaval. Others help indigenous people market their renewable products, enabling them to participate in the global economy without becoming victims of it. Anthropologists also work as consultants to businesses, helping to improve lines of communication, develop more humane workplaces, and in some cases ease the culture shock of families of workers who undergo international transfers.

Anthropology has long made a strong contribution to the mass media. Ethnographic films provide much programming for PBS and cable television, in addition to enlivening anthropology classes. Anthropologists are increasingly contributing their expertise to the media in exploring contemporary social issues. In some ways, they are following in the footsteps of Margaret Mead, who used mass media to promote anthropology and address social concerns.

Anthropologists still rarely use their training to carve out careers as professional journalists, though the anthropological approach has much to contribute to reporting of news events. In this chapter, I argue that anthropology should be a required part of a journalist's training. As is clear from the range of topics and issues covered in this book—and in most introductory anthropology classes—anthropology has much to contribute to an understanding of what it means to be human, whatever the social and cultural context.

POWER WORDS

applied anthropology	curses	repatriation
artifacts	ethnographic film	tenure
culture shock	medical anthropology	tenure track
		visual anthropology

INTERNET EXERCISE

1. Find out about careers in anthropology by visiting the American Anthropological Association website at **http://www.aaa.org/careers.htm**.

2. The National Association for the Practice of Anthropology maintains a website for people interested in applied anthropology. Visit their website at **http://www.aaa.org/napa/index.htm** to find out whether your interests and career goals match those of professionals in the discipline.

3. The International Union of Anthropological and Ethnological Sciences (IUAES) maintains a website at **http://www.icsu.org/Membership/SUM/iuaes.html**. Based on their description of their purpose, briefly discuss why it is important that anthropologists be organized on an international level.

GLOSSARY

achieved status   Social ranking attained by an individual on the basis of skills or personal qualities.

affines   Individuals related through marriage ties.

age grade   A category of people who fall into a culturally distinguished age range. Some examples in the United States are teenagers, thirtysomethings, and senior citizens.

age set   A group of individuals, usually males, who move through all of life's stages together.

agemates   Males who have been initiated in puberty rites together and who go through all of life's stages together.

agnates   Individuals who are related to each other through males, especially through patrilineal descent.

agrarian   Relating to the agricultural way of life.

altered state of consciousness   Perceptual and cognitive experience differing from "ordinary" experience, such as dreams, trance, or feelings of being "in the zone."

ambilineal descent   A form of reckoning descent in which an individual may affiliate with either the mother's or father's kin group. This practice provides great flexibility for the distribution of resources. Also known as *cognatic descent.*

ambilocal or **bilocal residence**   A form of residence pattern in which a married couple may choose to live with or near either the wife's or the husband's parents.

ancestor reverence   Symbolic beliefs and practices in which a relationship of kinship and reciprocity is marked through ritual observances.

ancestor spirits   Spirits of the dead who retain their ties of kinship and reciprocity to close relatives.

androcentrism   A male-centered perspective.

animism   The belief in a spirit essence that animates people, animals, plants, and sometimes geographical features.

anthropomorphism   Attributing human characteristics and motivations to things that are not human.

applied anthropology   The application of anthropological theory, methods, and research findings in nonacademic contexts, such as business, medicine, or forensics.

arbitrary   Socially constructed meanings associated with symbols, signs, and language.

archaeology   A subfield of anthropology centering on the study of cultures of the past through analyzing their material remains.

artifact   An object manufactured or modified by humans.

artisan   A skilled worker trained in a trade or craft.

ascribed status   The quality of having social ranking assigned to an individual at birth.

avunculocal residence   A residence pattern in which the groom brings his new wife to live with or near his mother's brother after marriage.

balanced reciprocity   A form of exchange in which goods or services are provided without expectation of a return in kind.

band   A type of political organization that is autonomous at the local level; bands are kin-based and egalitarian.

barter   An exchange of goods or services considered to be of equal value.

Big Man   In Melanesia a man who aims to increase his status by redistributing pigs and other goods at a feast and giveaway.

bilateral descent   A form of reckoning kinship in which descent is traced through both the male and female lines. Literally "two sides."

bilingualism   The ability to speak two languages fluently.

binary oppositions   Contrasting pairs, such as male/female, young/old, sun/moon, by which people organize their social and conceptual worlds. This idea is associated with the French anthropologist Claude Lévi-Strauss.

biological determinism   A school of thought that believes that personality is biologically encoded and cannot be altered by environment or education.

Black English or **Black English Vernacular (BEV)**   A variant of English believed to be spoken by many African Americans that follows a somewhat different set of rules for forming words into sentences.

body language   Communication through posture and gestures.

bound morpheme   A morpheme, or smallest unit of sound that contains meaning, that cannot stand alone. It must be combined with other morphemes to generate meanings.

bride capture   A marriage custom in which the groom makes a great show and pretense of stealing the bride from her family.

brideservice   Labor or service owed by the groom to the bride's family in compensation for the loss of their daughter's labor.

bridewealth   Goods given by the groom and/or the groom's kin to the family of the bride. This is the most common form of marriage payment. Also known as *brideprice.*

brother-sister exchange   A form of marriage exchange in which two brothers marry two sisters, thus avoiding the need to provide bridewealth, brideservice, or dowry.

cargo cult   A form of religious movement characteristic of Melanesian groups, in which rituals are undertaken to acquire cargo or material goods believed to have been sent by the ancestors that have gone instead to whites.

cash   A medium of exchange with a culturally assigned value.

caste   A ranked group, often associated with a certain occupation, membership to which is assigned at birth. Associated with a hierarchical society.

chiefdom   A type of political organization that is regional, kin-based, and hierarchical.

circular migration   A type of migration that involves travel to other nations to work while maintaining one's place of origin as the primary residence base.

clan   A kin group whose members trace their relationship to a founding ancestor but cannot specify the links to that ancestor.

class   In a hierarchical society, a category of people who have approximately the same access to power and resources.

classificatory kin terms   Kin terms in which genealogically distinct relatives are merged into one term. In English, the term "uncle" includes siblings of one's parents as well as spouses of parental siblings.

clitoridectomy   Genital surgery in which all or part of the clitoris is excised; performed during female puberty rituals.

closed system   A property considered characteristic of nonhuman communication forms in which sounds or other communications cannot be recombined to generate infinite new meanings.

Cocacolonization   A form of cultural and economic colonialism in which one group dominates another through marketing of consumer products such as soft drinks and hamburger chains.

code-switching   Combining linguistic sequences from two or more languages within a conversation.

cognates   Individuals who are related to each other by links of descent to a common ancestor through either the male or female line.

cognition   The process of acquiring information about the world, then reordering and interpreting it so that it can be used to operate within that world.

collaterals   Individuals related to a given Ego either through a connecting female relative or a connecting male relative but not through a direct line of descent. For example, one's father is in the direct line of descent in a bilateral or patrilineal system, but the father's brother is a collateral.

collective nurturance or **community-as-parent**   Childrearing practice in which the entire community is involved in child care and nurturance.

colonialism   The process by which one group subjugates another, imposing on the dependent group its own political authority, economic system, culture, and in most cases religion. The process is typically accomplished through establishment of a colony or occupying force.

complex society   A society characterized by a great deal of task specialization and differences in access to power and resources.

compound family   A residence pattern consisting of a man, his wives and children, and dependent relatives.

consanguines   Individuals related through biological ties.

contagious magic   A type of magic characterized by the principle that the part controls the whole. An example of contagious magic is using hair or nail clippings in a charm designed to kill or to evoke love.

corporate   Having the ability to make decisions or own property as a group.

cosmology   A symbolic description of the universe.

couvade   A childbirth custom in which the father of the child behaves as though he were giving birth, including observing all the rituals associated with birth.

creation myth   Symbolic story that describes how the universe and the people, plants, and animals that inhabit it came to be. Creation myths provide a social charter that justifies customs and social relationships.

cross cousins   Cousins who are related to each other through an opposite-sex parent sibling link.

cross-cultural   Phenomena or mode of comparison not limited to a particular culture or group.

Crow kinship terminology   A form of designating kin, associated with matrilineal descent, in which Ego's mother is merged with her female siblings, and Ego's father is merged with his male siblings. The mother's kin group is distinguished according to gender and generation; the father's kin group is distinguished according to gender only.

cultural anthropology   A subfield of anthropology centering on the study of contemporary human groups through the anthropological method of participant observation.

cultural ecology   Associated with Julian Steward, an approach to anthropological analysis that focuses on the relationship of a culture to its environment.

cultural materialism   Associated with Marvin Harris, a school of thought that attempts to explain culture as a strategy for making material resources available for human use.

cultural relativism   The belief that cultures should be valued according to their own standards.

culture   According to E. B. Tylor, "The complex whole which includes knowledge, belief, art, law, morals, custom and any other capabilities and habits acquired by man as a member of a society."

culture-and-personality school   A branch of cultural anthropology that developed in the first half of the twentieth century among students of Franz Boas, whose primary aim was studying the relationship among culture, childrearing practices, and adult personality.

culture shock   A sense of disorientation resulting from being suddenly immersed in a culture having values and practices that are markedly different from one's own.

curses   Imprecations or incantations aimed at bringing harm to a person who has caused offense.

data   Information acquired in the process of conducting systematic or controlled observations.

deities   Spirit beings with varying degrees of motivation and power to affect human affairs.

democracy   A political system under which all citizens are supposed to have a voice in government.

demons   Malevolent beings with varying degrees of motivation and power to affect human affairs.

descriptive linguistics   Also known as *structural linguistics*, the specialization in linguistics that focuses on the grammatical structure of language.

deviant   Individual behavior that varies from the norm to a degree that is considered to be disruptive to the group.

diachronic analysis   A type of analysis that tries to understand the present in terms of the past.

dialect Systematic variation in a language, related to geographic region or social class.

diffusion Culture change through borrowing, or the change that results from borrowing.

disinterested A desired property in science in which research is not affected by the researcher's personal opinions or hope of gain.

displacement The ability of language to communicate concepts remote in time and space.

distribution system System for allocating access to goods and services in a society.

divination A ritual that uses secret knowledge to call on spirits or signs to aid in diagnosing illness or the causes of group crisis, or to determine a course of action.

dominant symbol A symbol that stands for a number of important values in a group and is used on a variety of ritual or other formal occasions.

dowry The transfer of goods or money from the bride's family to the bride upon her wedding.

econiche A specific environment to which a species adapts.

economic system System for organizing the production and distribution of goods and services within a group.

egalitarian Characteristic of a society in which social roles are allocated by gender or age, but are otherwise undifferentiated.

Ego Individual for whom a genealogy is constructed.

Ego-centered In kinship terminology, refers to a characteristic of bilateral descent, which can only be figured from a specific Ego.

emic The insider's perspective on a particular culture.

enculturation The process by which an individual acquires knowledge of a particular culture.

empiricism In scientific research, the practice of relying upon observation and experimentation.

endogamy A marriage practice according to which people are expected to take mates from within the group.

Eskimo kinship terminology A form of kinship terminology associated with bilateral descent that distinguishes relatives by gender and generation but not by whether they are related on the mother's or father's side.

ethnic group A biologically self-perpetuating group of individuals who share basic cultural values, language, and customs and identify themselves as belonging to a particular group.

ethnocentrism The belief that one's own culture is superior to all others.

ethnographic film A film or video that seeks to document a particular group either in part or holistically.

ethnography A descriptive account of a particular culture, usually containing an analysis of its social structure, including kinship, economic and political organization, and religion.

ethnology The comparative study of human groups. In Europe, the practice of cultural anthropology.

etic The outsider's perspective on a culture.

Eurocentrism The belief that all aspects of European culture represent the best forms of culture.

evolution The process of development or growth in a group; technically, the change in allele frequency in a population from one generation to the next.

exogamy A marriage practice according to which people are expected to take mates from outside the group.

expressive culture The visual and performance arts, festivals, play, sports, and games.

extended family Form of family organization that extends beyond the reproductive unit of parent or parents and children to include the grandparent generation or siblings of one or both parents.

family An economically interdependent unit consisting of people related by consanguineal or affinal ties.

festival A sacred or secular period of celebration that includes cultural performances, usually associated with an important person, event, or point in the calendar.

fetish An object believed to have magical power.

fictive kin People who are not blood relatives of an individual but occupy the place of biological kin and are referred to by kinship terminology.

folktales Stories that express values and social dynamics of a group in symbolic form.

foragers People who do not produce their own food but instead rely on wild plants and animals for subsistence.

forensic anthropology Application of knowledge of human anatomy and physiology to gaining evidence for solving crimes or identifying human remains.

fraternal polyandry The marriage of one woman to more than one brother at the same time.

free morpheme A morpheme, the smallest unit of sound that has meaning, that can stand alone as a word or be combined with other morphemes to generate compound words.

functionalism Associated with Bronislaw Malinowski, an anthropological approach that emphasizes the synchronic and holistic approaches.

gender Cultural meanings, values, and social roles assigned with respect to sex differences.

genealogy A diagram of social relationships within a kin group.

general evolution Associated with Leslie White, a theory of social evolution that argues that cultures evolve through a series of universal stages as a result of increasing use of technology to capture energy.

generalized reciprocity System of exchange in which services or material goods are provided without expectation of return in kind.

genetics The study of the mechanisms of heredity and variation in organisms.

ghosts Spirits of the dead who no longer have reciprocal rights and responsibilities with living humans and are expected to sever their ties as a result.

gift exchange A form of marriage exchange in which the families of a bride and groom provide each other with gifts of relatively equal amounts.

glyphs Stylized characters often incised in stone that convey information through signs or symbols.

gods Spirit beings conceived of as having varying degrees of motivation and power to affect the course of human events.

grammar Set of rules for combining sounds into meaning and including a lexicon of meaningful words.

hallucinogens Substances such as peyote and certain mushrooms that cause altered states of consciousness. Shamans may use hallucinogens for medicinal purposes or for divination.

Hawaiian kinship terminology A form of kinship terminology that distinguishes only by generation and gender.

hierarchy A form of social organization in which some roles are associated with more power, higher status, and greater access to resources than others.

historical linguistics A specialization of linguistics that focuses on studying the development, divergence, and relatedness of human language.

historical particularism A school of thought that favors the study of specific cultures and their history, without reference to social evolutionary concepts.

holism An attempt to understand attitudes, behavior, and social institutions within their social and cultural context.

horticulturalists People who cultivate crops and tend cultivated crops without the use of plows or irrigation, typically a self-sufficient mode of subsistence.

household A group of people who live together in a single dwelling or group of dwellings and are considered an economic unit.

icon Image or emblem. In popular usage, may refer to an image that has religious significance.

iconography A pattern of imagery or design associated with a particular culture.

illiterate Description of members of a society with a written language who have not learned to read and write.

imitative magic A type of magic characterized by the principle that like controls like. An example would be a voodoo doll in which the figure of the doll represents the human it is intended to control.

incest taboo A social rule that prohibits sexual relations with certain categories of relatives.

indigenous Related to the original inhabitants of a place or to their culture.

indirect dowry A form of marriage exchange in which the groom provides goods to the bride or her father with the expectation that the goods end up with the new conjugal couple.

industrialized Having an economic system heavily dependent upon manufacturing.

infanticide The practice of killing infants; female infanticide is the practice of killing female infants, usually for purposes of population control or as a result of economic factors.

infibulation A practice associated with northern Sudan that involves the partial sewing shut of the vaginal opening.

innovation Change resulting from variations in the customary way of doing things.

insider A member or native of a culture.

intensive agriculture A mode of subsistence that produces a food surplus through cultivation of land with the aid of plows, fertilizers, and irrigation. Some intensive agricultural societies are also industrialized.

intersubjectivity In scientific research, the idea that independent researchers observing the same phenomena and following the same methodology will arrive at the same conclusions.

Inuit A linguistic grouping that includes all of the peoples of the far north from Alaska to eastern Canada.

invention Change resulting from conscious or deliberate innovation.

Iroquois kinship terminology A form of kinship terminology that merges Ego's father with his male siblings and Ego's mother with her female siblings and distinguishes cross cousins from parallel cousins on both sides. The Iroquois system further distinguishes between father's and mother's relatives.

joint family A living arrangement in which married brothers, with their wives and children, share a household.

key informant A particularly observant and articulate member of a group who assists an anthropologist in his or her research.

kin-based society A group characterized by a political organization in which functions are traditionally allocated on the basis of kinship.

kindred In a bilateral descent system, a group comprised of relatives to whom a particular Ego claims kinship.

kinesics The study of communication by posture and gesture, or *body language.*

kinship system A system for organizing biological relationships within a group.

Kula ring A system of exchange among Trobriand Islanders in which balanced reciprocity in the form of ceremonial gift exchange established lifelong alliances between male trading partners.

land tenure A system for establishing who has access to a particular area of land and its resources.

language A sound-based form of communication in which meaning is conveyed by combining sounds according to a set of rules.

langue All that a particular set of speakers can potentially know about their language.

law A formal system of rules recognized by a society as binding on its members.

legends Stories about the past purporting to tell the history of a particular group, often recounting the adventures of a folk hero.

levirate A practice in which a widow marries her deceased husband's brother.

lexicon The vocabulary of a language or group of speakers.

lineage A kin group whose members trace descent matrilineally or patrilineally from a common ancestor through known links.

lineal kin People who are related to an individual through a direct line of descent, either through the male or female line.

linguistics A subfield of anthropology that centers on the study of all forms of human communication, especially language.

literate Having the ability to read and write.

magic A symbolic system aimed at gaining control over one's environment, condition, or associates.

mana An impersonal force that can be associated with persons, places, or objects.

market system A form of exchange which is concluded in a single transaction at a public place either through barter or transfer of cash.

marriage A publicly recognized social contract that establishes an economic contract, sexual rights, social identity of offspring, and an alliance between kin groups.

Marxism Associated with Karl Marx and Friedrich Engels, a school of thought that argues that the social organization and ideology of a particular society are determined by its economic base.

material culture The material products of a group, including its art, tools, ritual objects, utilitarian goods, and dwellings.

matriarchy A mythical system under which women were heads of families and controlled society and the political system.

matriclan A clan, or kin group claiming descent from a common ancestor, tracing descent through the female line.

matrikin People related to Ego through his or her mother.

matrilineage A unilineal descent group composed of members related through the female line.

matrilineal descent A form of kinship reckoning in which descent is traced through the female line.

matrilocal residence A residence pattern in which a man leaves his family of birth and moves into his wife's family's household at marriage.

medical anthropology A specialization applying anthropological theories and methods to the field of medicine, addressing such issues as health care delivery and epidemiology.

medical model An approach to diagnosing and healing disorders based on the assumption that illness is a biological condition that can be eliminated by treating symptoms and prescribing medications.

mercantilism An economic policy associated with European colonialism whereby a colonizing power was favored in trade relationships with its colonies.

metaphor A form of imagery in language and symbols based on *analogy*, a comparison between two objects or concepts according to their perceived similarity.

methodological relativism A methodological stance that involves setting aside one's own values for the purpose of conducting a study.

metonymy A form of imagery in language and symbols based on contiguity (contact) or the idea that the part stands for the whole.

millenarian movement A religious movement based on the idea that a corrupt society signals the end of the world, which can be avoided if members are purified through a prescribed set of beliefs and ritual practices.

moiety A form of kinship in which a society is divided into two unilineal descent groups.

monogamy A system of marriage involving one husband and one wife.

mores Informal formulations of social values.

morpheme The smallest unit of sound that has meaning in a language.

morphology In linguistics, the study of the internal structure of words according to the meanings contained in their morphemes.

multilinear evolution Associated with Julian Steward, a theory of social evolution that suggests that parallel cultural patterns may develop in different societies as a result of similarities in adaptation to the environment.

multivocal A characteristic of symbols referring to the fact that they convey a number of meanings, both conscious and unconscious, at the same time.

myths Symbolic stories about the nature of the universe and the role of human beings in it.

national character Associated primarily with Ruth Benedict, the idea that members of a nation or cultural group manifest an aggregate personality characterized by consistency in attitude and behavior through time.

nation-state A political entity with territorial boundaries and government recognized as autonomous by its neighbors.

nativistic movment A social movement, which may be religious or take some other form, that aims to restore power to groups disempowered by colonialism or other social disruption.

natural selection Associated with Charles Darwin, a principle of evolution that asserts that members of a particular species that are especially well suited to a particular environment will thrive and reproduce, thus passing on their inheritable adaptive traits to their offspring.

neo-evolutionism A school of thought that attempts to refine the process of analyzing change in human groups by isolating factors that affect culture and social organization.

neolocal residence A residence pattern in which a bride and groom establish a new residence apart from relatives of both families after marriage.

network analysis A form of social science research based on analyzing the pattern of interaction within a group by drawing on the social network of a particular individual or family.

nonliterate societies Societies in which the language does not have a written component.

normative In social science research, characteristic of a majority of people in a group. More generally, conforming to social values and expectations.

nuclear family An economically interdependent unit consisting of a parent or parents and their dependent offspring.

objectivity In scientific research, basing one's analysis on observable behavior or other phenomena rather than on emotion or subjective opinion.

Omaha kinship terminology A form of kinship terminology associated with patrilineal descent that merges Ego's father with his male siblings and Ego's mother with her female siblings. Members of Ego's mother's descent group are distinguished by gender but not by generation, whereas members of the father's descent group are distinguished by gender and generation.

open system A characteristic of human language in which infinite new meanings can be generated by combining a limited number of sounds according to a set of rules.

paradigm Conceptual model on which scientific investigation is based.

parallel cousins Cousins who are related to each other through a same-sex parental sibling link.

parallel marriage   A pattern of marriage in which a man married to one woman sets up a household with another.

parole   A linguistic act in which a speaker of a particular language draws on his or her knowledge of a language to engage in a conversation or other form of discourse.

participant observation   The preferred anthropological method, it involves living as a member of the society under study and sharing in day-to-day activities, usually for an extended period of time.

pastoralists   People dependent primarily on domesticated animals, such as cattle, for subsistence.

patriarchy   A system of male control of the political system.

patriclan   A clan, or kin group claiming descent from a common ancestor, tracing descent through the male line.

patrikin   People related to Ego through his or her father.

patrilineage   A unilineal descent group composed of members related through the male line.

patrilineal descent   A form of kinship in which descent is traced through the male line.

patrilocal residence   A residence pattern in which a woman leaves her family of birth when she marries and moves into her husband's household.

perception   The biological and conceptual processes of apprehending and interpreting environmental stimuli.

personality   A pattern of consistency in attitude and behavior through time that is characteristic of an individual.

philosophical relativism   The belief that all cultures and ways of life are equally valid.

phonemes   The smallest units of distinctive sound that make up the basic building blocks of language.

phonology   The study of rules for combining sounds in a language.

phratries   Unilineal descent groups composed of clans considered to be related to each other but in which the connecting links are not specified.

physical anthropology   A subfield of anthropology that focuses on the study of nonhuman primates, the physical characteristics of humans, and evolution.

pig feast   A redistribution form of exchange characteristic of Melanesia, in which a man hoping to become a Big Man draws on his kin networks to host another village at a ceremonial feast and give away pigs and other valuables.

plural society   Society made up of more than one cultural tradition or ethnic group.

political system   The organization and allocation of power within a society.

polyandry   A system of marriage in which a woman may have more than one husband.

polygamy   A system of marriage in which a person of either sex may have more than one mate.

polygyny   A system of marriage in which a man may have more than one wife.

postindustrial society   A society, having once been industrialized, that has become sufficiently affluent to contract out manufacturing of goods to a less affluent society.

postpartum sex taboo   A population control practice banning sex between married partners for a culturally defined period of time, typically backed by beliefs about supernatural sanctions.

potlatch   A redistribution form of exchange characteristic of native peoples of the northwestern coast of North America in which a lineage head collects art objects and other valuables to be given away to members of another lineage at a ceremonial feast and dance performance.

priest   A religious leader whose authority is conferred by the office.

primatology   The study of nonhuman primates.

primogeniture   A custom of inheritance in which the eldest child has first claim to a family's wealth and power. *Male primogeniture* is the system in which the first male child inherits his family's wealth and power.

production   The process of converting material resources for human use.

psychological anthropology   A specialization in anthropology that studies the relationship between the individual and the group.

redistribution   A form of exchange in which an individual seeks to enhance his status through a ceremonial feast and giveaway of valued objects.

referent   The thing that a symbol or sign stands for.

religion   A symbolic system involving beliefs and practices aimed at directing the relationship of human beings to the supernatural.

repatriation   Returning control over artifacts or other cultural products to members of the society that produced them.

revitalization movement   A religious movement aimed at bringing about social change.

rite of intensification   A regularly occurring ritual that reinforces the solidarity of the group.

rite of passage   A ritual that accompanies a change from one social status to another.

ritual   Symbolic behavior associated with religion and magic that is repetitive, sequential, non-ordinary, and believed to be powerful.

ritual inversion   Ritual or other form of symbolic behavior in which ordinary statuses and roles are reversed. For example, a king may be ridiculed or subjected to other forms of humiliation.

sanction   A means of social control designed to enforce conformity to social rules.

Sapir-Whorf hypothesis   A theory advanced by Edward Sapir and Benjamin Whorf that language shapes thought.

scarification   The process of decorating the body by inflicting wounds and allowing the wounds to heal into scars.

science   A framework for systematically acquiring information about the physical world and testing that information through controlled observations.

segmentary lineage   Associated with African cattle herders, a system of unilineal descent that allows segmentation along the lines of brothers. This permits orderly division of the group and provides a model for political alliances among near and far lineage mates.

semantics   Rules for generating meaning in constructing words and sentences.

serial monogamy   A form of marriage in which an individual is married to only one partner at a time but may form monogamous relationships with other partners over his or her lifetime.

shaman   A religious person whose power resides in the demonstrated ability to control spirits or supernatural forces.

shifting agriculture   A form of cultivation in which a plot of land is cleared, usually burned, planted for a few seasons, then allowed to lie fallow to enable the soil to replenish itself. Also called *swidden* or *slash-and-burn agriculture.*

sib   A group of people who trace descent to a founding ancestor. There is some disagreement among anthropologists over this term; some view it as being the same as a *clan;* others view it as a synonym for *lineage.*

sign   An image, word, or behavior that stands for a referent in a one-to-one relationship; as opposed to a symbol, which is multivocal.

sign language   A system of language in which meaning is communicated through gestures. Unlike body language, sign language is rule-based, and the meanings of gestures are arbitrary, or socially assigned.

sister exchange   A practice in which a groom's sister is given to the bride's family in compensation for the bride.

slash-and-burn agriculture   A cultivation technique in which an area of forest is cut down and then burned, allowing the ashes to serve as fertilizer for crop production. Because the soil is only fertile for a few seasons, this technique requires that the land be allowed to lie fallow after a few seasons. Also called *shifting* or *swidden agriculture.*

social charter   A property of creation myths that explains and justifies social statuses and roles by tracing them to a divine origin.

social Darwinism   Application of the theory of natural selection to social organization, involving a misinterpretation of Darwin's biological theory of evolution.

social structure   The formal organization of a society, including politics, economics, kinship, and religion.

socialization   The process of transmitting appropriate cultural values and social behavior from one generation to the next.

society   A group of people occupying a territory and sharing a language or culture.

sociolinguistics   A specialization of linguistics that focuses on studying the social context of language use.

sorcerer   Religious practitioner who uses his ability to control the spirits to cause harm.

sororal polygyny   A form of marriage in which a man marries two or more sisters at the same time.

sororate   A practice in which a woman marries her deceased sister's husband.

souls   The animating spirits of living beings.

specific evolution   Associated with Julian Steward, a theory of social evolution that holds that the changes in each culture must be studied as adaptations to a specific environment rather than with reference to universal stages.

spirit possession   The belief that a disembodied spirit may inhabit the body of a living person.

Standard American English (SAE)   The form of English in the United States most commonly heard on mass media, as well as in schools and other public institutions.

state   A type of political organization that is regionalized, bureaucratic, and hierarchical.

stem families   A living arrangement in which parents reside with one married son, his wife, and children.

stratified   Characterized by a system of social organization in which some social roles or positions are associated with more power, higher status, or greater access to resources than others.

structural functionalism   Associated with A. R. Radcliffe-Brown, an approach to anthropology that argues that social institutions exist to maintain the social order.

structural linguistics   Also known as *descriptive linguistics,* the specialization in linguistics that focuses on the grammatical structure of language.

subcaste   A division of a caste.

subincision   A form of genital surgery in which the underside of the penis is slit open to the urethra; performed during male puberty rituals.

subsistence   The means by which human groups convert environmental resources to human use.

swidden agriculture   A shifting pattern of cultivation. Also called *shifting* or *slash-and-burn agriculture.*

symbol   An image, word, or behavior that expresses ideas too complex to be stated directly.

synchronic analysis   A type of analysis that emphasizes the present.

syntax   The rules of sentence formation for a language.

taboo   Cultural rules or practices of avoidance.

task specialization   A system in which not everyone performs the same type of work.

tattooing   A form of body decoration produced by inserting pigment or dye under the skin.

technology   Knowledge of tool manufacture and use.

tenure   Rights to property, a position, or an office.

tenure-track   In academic terminology, a professorial position that does not guarantee employment but may lead to a guarantee of employment.

terms of address   Terms used in discourse that indicate the relationship of the speaker to the person being addressed, such as "Mom" or "Dr."

theory   In science, a general statement about the relationship between variables.

totem   An animal or other figure symbolizing the unity of the kin group; typically viewed as the founding ancestor of the group.

trance   An altered state of consciousness characterized by some degree of dissociation from ordinary experience and, in some cases, by loss of consciousness.

transhumance   The practice of moving herds to different pastures depending on seasonal availability of resources.

unilineal descent   A system of kinship in which descent is traced through either the male or the female line, but not both. Literally "one line."

variables   In scientific research, measurable factors that may assume any of a number of values. For example, the variable "age" may assume values ranging from 0 to more than 100.

visual anthropology   A specialization in anthropology aimed at collecting and presenting data through use of film, videotape, and still photography.

witch   A powerless individual, unable to meet his or her needs through normal social interactions, whose frustration, anger, and jealousy invites evil into a society.

world view   A generally coherent system of cultural beliefs and values shared by members of a culture.

writing   A form of communication that transforms the grammar of human language into icons capable of transmitting information at a distance and through the generations.

REFERENCES

Adler, Margot. *Drawing Down the Moon*. New York: Penguin, 1979.

Agar, Michael. *The Professional Stranger*. New York: Academic Press, 1980.

Aiyappan, A. *The Personality of Kerala*. Trivandrum, India: University of Kerala, 1982.

Allen, Catherine Wagner. *Coca, Chica and Trago: Private and Communal Rituals in a Quechua Community*. Ann Arbor, MI: University Microfilms, 1978.

———. *The Hold Life Has*. Washington, DC: Smithsonian, 1988.

Alvard, M. "Testing the 'Ecologically Noble Savage' Hypothesis: Conservation and Subsistence Hunting by the Piro of Amazonian Peru." Ph.D. diss., University of New Mexico, 1993.

Amadiume, Ifi. *Male Daughters, Female Husbands: Gender and Sex in African Society*. London: Zed Books, 1987.

Aschenbrenner, Joyce. *Lifelines: Black Families in Chicago*. New York: Holt, Rinehart and Winston, 1975. (Reprinted by Waveland Press, Prospect Heights, IL, 1983.)

Babbie, Earl. *The Practice of Social Research*, 5th ed. Belmont, CA: Wadsworth, 1989.

Bachofen, J. J. *Mother Right*. In *Myth, Religion, and Mother Right: Selected Writings of J. J. Bachofen*. Translated by Ralph Manheim. Bollingen Series. Princeton, NJ: Princeton University Press, 1967. (Originally published 1861.)

Bachrach Ehlers, Tracy. "Debunking Marianismo: Economic Vulnerability and Survival Strategies among Guatemalan Wives." In Mari Womack and Judith Marti, eds., *The Other Fifty Percent: Multicultural Perspectives on Gender Relations*. Prospect Heights, IL: Waveland Press, 1993.

Bailey, F. G. *The Tactical Uses of Passion: An Essay on Power, Reason and Reality*. Ithaca, NY: Cornell University Press, 1983.

Balikci, Asen. *The Netsilik Eskimo*. Garden City, NY: Natural History Press, 1970.

Barker, Joan C. *Danger, Duty, and Disillusion: The Worldview of Los Angeles Police Officers*. Prospect Heights, IL: Waveland Press, 1999.

Barnard, Alan. *Hunters and Herders of Southern Africa: A Comparative Ethnography of the Khoisan Peoples*. Cambridge: Cambridge University Press, 1992.

Barnes, John A. "Genitrix : Genitor :: Nature : Culture." In Jack Goody, ed., *The Character of Kinship*. Cambridge: Cambridge University Press, 1973.

Barnouw, Victor. *Culture and Personality*. Chicago: Dorsey Press, 1985.

Barth, Fredrik. *Nomads of South Persia*. Oslo, Norway: Universitetsforlaget, 1961. (Reprint. Prospect Heights, IL: Waveland Press, 1986.)

———. *Ethnic Groups and Boundaries: The Social Organization of Culture Differences*. Boston: Little, Brown, 1969. (Reprint. Prospect Heights, IL: Waveland Press, 1998.)

Bastide, Roger. *Sociologie et psychoanalyze*. Paris: Presses Universitaires, 1950.

Bateson, Mary Catherine. *With a Daughter's Eye*. New York: Washington Square Press, 1984.

Beeman, William O. "Revitalization Drives American Militias." In James P. Spradley and David W. McCurdy, eds., *Conformity and Conflict: Readings in Cultural Anthropology*. New York: Longman, 1997.

Benedict, Ruth. *Patterns of Culture*. New York: Mentor, 1946a. (Originally published 1934.)

———. *The Chrysanthemum and the Sword*. Boston: Houghton Mifflin, 1946b.

Benjamin, Gail R. *Japanese Lessons*. New York: New York University Press, 1997.

Berdan, Frances F. *The Aztecs of Central Mexico: An Imperial Society*. Fort Worth, TX: Holt, Rinehart and Winston, 1982.

Berlin, Brent, and Paul Kay. *Basic Color Terms: Their Universality and Evolution*. Berkeley: University of California Press, 1969.

Bettelheim, Bruno. *Symbolic Wounds: Puberty Rites and the Envious Male*. Glencoe, IL: Free Press, 1954.

Billig, Michael S. "The Marriage Squeeze and the Rise of Groomprice in India's Kerala State." *Journal of Comparative Family Studies* 23 (1993):197–216.

Bishop, John Melville, with Naomi Hawkes Bishop. *An Ever-Changing Place*. New York: Simon and Schuster, 1978.

Bloomfield, Leonard. *Language*. New York: Holt, Rinehart and Winston, 1933.

Blumhagen, Dan. "The Doctor's White Coat: The Image of the Physician in Modern America." In Aaron Podolefsky and Peter J. Brown, eds., *Applying Cultural Anthropology: An Introductory Reader*. Mountain View, CA: Mayfield, 1991. (Originally published in *Annals of Internal Medicine* 91 [1979]:111–116.)

Boas, Franz. "A Journey in Cumberland Sound and on the West Shore of Davis Strait in 1883 and 1884." *Journal of the American Geographical Society of New York* 14 (1884):258–261.

———. "The Social Organization and the Secret Societies of the Kwakiutl Indians." *Annual Report of the United States National Museum for 1895*. Washington, DC: Smithsonian Institution, 1897.

———. "The Kwakiutl of Vancouver Island." *Memoirs of the American Museum of Natural History* 8 (1909).

———. "Geographical Names of the Kwakiutl Indians." *Columbia University Contributions to Anthropology* 20. New York: Columbia University Press, 1934.

———. "Kwakiutl Culture As Reflected in Mythology." American Folk-Lore Society, Memoir 28. New York: G. E. Stechert, 1935.

———. *The Mind of Primitive Man*. New York, Macmillan, 1944.

———. *Kwakiutl Ethnography*. Edited by Helen Codere. Chicago: University of Chicago Press, 1966.

Bock, Philip K. *Rethinking Psychological Anthropology*. Prospect Heights, IL: Waveland Press, 1988.

Bodley, John H. *Anthropology and Contemporary Human Problems*. Mountain View, CA: Mayfield, 1985.

Bohannan, Laura. "Shakespeare in the Bush." In James P. Spradley and David W. McCurdy, eds., *Conformity and Conflict: Readings in Cultural Anthropology*. Glenview, IL: Scott, Foresman, 1990. (Originally published 1966.)

Bohannan, Paul. "Artist and Critic in African Society." In Morton H. Fried, ed., *Readings in Anthropology*, 2d ed., vol. 2. New York: Thomas Y. Crowell, 1968. (Originally published in Marian W. Smith, ed., *The Artist in Tribal Society*. Proceedings of a symposium held at the Royal Anthropological Institute. New York: Free Press, 1961.)

Bohannan, Paul, and Mark Glazer, eds. *High Points in Anthropology*, 2d ed. New York: McGraw-Hill, 1988.

Bolton, Ralph. "The Qolla Marriage Process." In Ralph Bolton and Enrique Mayer, eds., *Kinship and Marriage in the Andes*. Washington, DC: American Anthropological Association, 1977.

Bonvillain, Nancy. *Language, Culture, and Communication: The Meaning of Messages*. Upper Saddle River, NJ: Prentice Hall, 1997.

Bourguignon, Erika. "The Self, the Behavioral Environment, and the Theory of Spirit Possession." In Melford E. Spiro, ed., *Context and Meaning in Cultural Anthropology*. New York: Free Press, 1965.

———. *Possession*. San Francisco: Chandler and Sharp, 1976.

Bowen, Elenore Smith. *Return to Laughter*. Garden City, NY: Doubleday Anchor, 1964. (Originally published in 1954.)

Boyd, Robert, and Joan B. Silk. *How Humans Evolved*. New York: W. W. Norton, 2000.

Bray, Warwick. "The City State in Central Mexico at the Time of the Spanish Conquest." *Journal of Latin American Studies* 4 (1972):161–185.

Brenneis, Donald. "Shared and Solitary Sentiments: The Discourse of Friendship, Play, and Anger in Bhatgaon." In Catherine A. Lutz and Lila Abu-Lughod, eds., *Language and the Politics of Emotions*. Cambridge: Cambridge University Press, 1990.

Brewer, John, and Albert Hunter. *Multimethod Research: A Synthesis of Styles*. Sage Library of Social Research # 175. Newbury Park, CA: Sage, 1989.

Briggs, J. L. *Never in Anger: Portrait of an Eskimo Family*. Cambridge, MA: Harvard University Press, 1970.

Buechler, Hans C., and Judith-Maria Buechler. *The Bolivian Aymara*. New York: Holt, Rinehart and Winston, 1971.

Burbank, Victoria K. "Fight! Fight!: Men, Women, and Interpersonal Aggression in an Australian Aboriginal Community." In Dorothy Ayers Counts and Judith K. Brown, eds., *Sanctions and Sanctuary: A Cultural View of the Beating of Wives*. Boulder: Westview Press, 1992.

———. *Fighting Women: Anger and Aggression in Aboriginal Australia*. Berkeley: University of California Press, 1994.

Burling, Robbins. *Man's Many Voices: Language in Its Cultural Context*. New York: Holt, Rinehart and Winston, 1970.

Calnek, Edward. "The Sahagún Texts as a Source of Sociological Information." In Munro S. Edmundson, ed., *Sixteenth Century Mexico: The Work of Sahagún*. Albuquerque: University of New Mexico Press, 1974.

Campbell, Bernard G., and James D. Loy. *Humankind Emerging*, 7th ed. New York: HarperCollins, 1996.

Cannell, Fenella. "Concepts of Parenthood: The Warnock Report, the Gillick and Modern Myths." *American Ethnologist* 17 (1990): 667–686.

Carroll, John B., ed. *Language, Thought, and Reality: Selected Writings of Benjamin Lee Whorf*. Boston: Technology Press of Massachusetts Institute of Technology, 1956. (Originally published 1940.)

Carter, William E. "Trial Marriage in the Andes?" In Ralph Bolton and Enrique Mayer, eds., *Kinship and Marriage in the Andes*. Washington, DC: American Anthropological Association, 1977.

Cashdan, Elizabeth. "Property and Social Insurance among the Gllana." Paper presented at the Second International Conference on Hunting and Gathering Societies, Montreal, 1980.

Cassels, R. "Faunal Extinction and Prehistoric Man in New Zealand and the Pacific Islands." In P. Martin and R. Klein, eds., *Quaternary Extinctions*. Tucson: University of Arizona Press, 1984.

Cerroni-Long, E. L. *Anthropological Theory in North America*. Westport, CT: Bergin & Garvey, 1999.

Chagnon, Napoleon A. *Yanomamö*, 4th ed. Fort Worth, TX: Harcourt Brace Jovanovich, 1992.

Chance, Norman A. *The Eskimo of North Alaska*. Fort Worth, TX: Holt, Rinehart and Winston, 1966.

———. *The Inupiat and Arctic Alaska*. Fort Worth, TX: Holt, Rinehart and Winston, 1990.

———. *China's Urban Villagers: Changing Life in a Beijing Suburb*. Fort Worth, TX: Holt, Rinehart and Winston, 1991.

Chivers, David. "The Siamang in Malaysia: A Field Study of a Primate in a Tropical Rain Forest." *Contributions to Primatology* 4. Basel, Switzerland: S. Karger, 1974.

Chodorow, Nancy. "Family Structure and Feminine Personality." In Michelle Zimbalist Rosaldo and Louise Lamphere, eds., *Woman, Culture and Society*. Stanford, CA: Stanford University Press, 1974.

Coburn, Judith. "Harsh Life Comes to Life on Video." *Los Angeles Times*, June 25, 1996.

Cole, M., and S. Scribner. *Culture and Thought: A Psychological Introduction*. New York: Wiley, 1974.

Collier, Jane, Michelle Rosaldo, and Sylvia Yanagisako. "Is There a Family? New Anthropological Views." In Barrie Thorne and Marilyn Yalom, eds., *Rethinking the Family: Some Feminist Questions*. New York: Longman, 1982.

Collier, John, Jr., and Malcolm Collier. *Visual Anthropology: Photography As a Research Method*. Albuquerque: University of New Mexico Press, 1986.

Cone, Marla. "Human Immune Systems May Be Pollution Victims." *Los Angeles Times*, May 13, 1996.

Cook, H. B. Kimberley. "Matrifocality and Female Aggression in Margariteño Society." In Kaj Björkqvist and Pirrko Niemelä, eds., *Of Mice and Women: Aspects of Female Aggression*. New York: Academic Press, 1992.

———. *Small Town, Big Hell: An Ethnographic Study of Aggression in a Margariteño Community*. Antropologica Suplemento No. 4. Instituto Caribe de Antropologia y Sociologia, Fundacion La Salle de Ciencias Naturales, 1993.

Cordere, Helen. "Kwakiutl: Traditional Culture." In Wayne Settles, ed., *Northwest Coast Handbook of the North American Indians*, vol. 7. Washington, DC: Smithsonian Institution, 1990.

Cortés, Hernán. *Five Letters of Cortés to the Emperor*. Translated by J. Bayard Morris. New York: Norton, 1928. (Originally written 1519–1526.)

Courlander, Harold. *The Fourth World of the Hopis*. Albuquerque: University of New Mexico Press, 1971.

Csikszentmihalyi, Mihaly. *Beyond Boredom and Anxiety*. San Francisco: Jossey-Bass, 1975.

Cuddon, J. A. *The International Dictionary of Sports and Games*. New York: Schocken Books, 1979.

Culbert, T. Patrick. *The Lost Civilization: The Story of the Classic Maya*. New York: Harper and Row, 1974.

Curtis, Edward S. *The North American Indian* 10, 1915. (Reprint. New York: Landmarks in Anthropology, Johnson Reprint Corporation, 1970.)

Darwin, Charles. *On the Origin of Species,* 1859. (Facsimile. Cambridge, MA, and London: Harvard University Press, 1964.)

David, Nicholas, Judy Sterner, and Kodzo Gavua. "Why Pots Are Decorated." *Current Anthropology* 29 (1988):365–379.

Davies, Ian, and Greville Corbett. "A Cross-Cultural Study of Color-Grouping: Tests of the Perceptual-Physiology Account of Color Universals." *Ethos* 26 (1998):338–360.

Davis-Floyd, Robbie. "The Ritual of Hospital Birth in America." In James P. Spradley and David W. McCurdy, eds., *Conformity and Conflict.* New York: HarperCollins, 1994.

DeBoer, Warren. "Response to Why Pots Are Decorated." *Current Anthropology* 29 (1988):381–382.

De Fuentes, Patricia, ed. and trans. *The Conquistadors.* New York: Orion, 1963.

Degérando, Joseph-Marie. *The Observation of Savage Peoples.* Berkeley: University of California Press, 1969. (Originally published in French as *Considerations on the Diverse Methods to Follow in the Observation of Savage Peoples,* 1800.)

Deren, Maya. *Divine Horsemen: The Voodoo Gods of Haiti.* New York: Delta, 1970.

Desjarlais, Robert. "The Makings of Personhood." *Ethos* 27 (2000): 466–489.

Diamond, Jared. "The Worst Mistake in the History of the Human Race." *Discover,* 1987. (Reprinted in Aaron Podolefsky and Peter J. Brown, eds., *Applying Cultural Anthropology: An Introductory Reader.* Mountain View, CA: Mayfield, 1991.)

Díaz del Castillo, Bernal. *The Discovery and Conquest of Mexico.* Translated by A. P. Maudsley. New York: Noonday, 1956. (Originally written 1560s.)

Dolgin, Janet. "Just a Gene: Judicial Assumptions about Parenthood." *UCLA Law Review* 40 (1993).

Donald, Leland, and Donald H. Mitchell. "Some Correlates of Local Group Rank among the Southern Kwakiutl." *Ethnology* 14 (1975):325–346.

Doob, Leonard W. *Becoming More Civilized: A Psychological Exploration.* New York: Holt, Rinehart and Winston, 1960.

Douglas, Mary. *Purity and Danger: An Analysis of the Concepts of Pollution and Taboo.* London: Routledge and Kegan Paul, 1966.

———. *Natural Symbols.* New York: Random House, 1970.

Downs, James F. *The Navajo.* Fort Worth, TX: Holt, Rinehart and Winston, 1972. (Reprint. Prospect Heights, IL: Waveland Press, 1984.)

Draper, Patricia. "!Kung Women: Contrasts in Sexual Egalitarianism in Foraging and Sedentary Contexts." In Rayna R. Reiter, ed., *Toward an Anthropology of Women.* New York: Monthly Review Press, 1975.

Drucker, Philip, and Robert F. Heizer. *To Make My Name Good: A Reexamination of the Southern Kwakiutl Potlatch.* Berkeley: University of California Press, 1967.

Durán, Diego. *The Aztecs: The History of the Indies of New Spain.* Translated by Doris Heyden and Fernando Horcasitas. New York: Orion, 1964. (Originally written 1581.)

———. *Book of the Gods and Rites* and *The Ancient Calendar.* Translated by Fernando Horcasitas and Doris Heyden. Norman, OK: University of Oklahoma Press, 1971. (Originally written 1570 and 1579.)

Durkheim, Emile. *The Elementary Forms of the Religious Life.* Translated by Joseph Ward Swain. London: Allen and Unwin, 1915. (Reprint. New York: Free Press, 1965.)

Edgerton, Robert B., and L. L. Langness. *Methods and Styles in the Study of Culture.* San Francisco: Chandler and Sharp, 1974.

Ellefson, J. O. "Territorial Behavior in the Common White-Handed Gibbon *Hylobates lar.*" In Phyllis Jay, ed., *Primates.* New York: Holt, Rinehart and Winston, 1968.

Erikson, Erik H. *Childhood and Society,* 2d ed. New York: Norton, 1963. (Originally published 1950.)

Evans-Pritchard, E. E. *The Nuer: A Description of the Modes of Livelihood and Political Institutions of a Nilotic People.* Oxford: Oxford University Press, 1940.

———. *Man and Woman among the Azande.* London: Faber and Faber, 1974.

———. *Witchcraft, Oracles, and Magic among the Azande.* Oxford: Clarendon Press, 1976. (Originally published 1937.)

———. Foreword to *Slow Flows the Pampa: Socio-Economic Changes in a Kuttanad Village in Kerala,* by K. E. Verghese. New Delhi: Concept, 1982.

Fagan, Brian M. *People of the Earth: An Introduction to World Prehistory.* Boston: Little, Brown, 1983.

———. *World Prehistory: A Brief Introduction,* 3d ed. New York: HarperCollins, 1996.

Falassi, Alessandro. "Festival: Definition and Morphology." In Alessandro Falassi, ed., *Time Out of Time: Essays on the Festival.* Albuquerque: University of New Mexico Press, 1987.

Faris, James C. *Nuba Personal Art.* Toronto: University of Toronto Press, 1972.

Ferdowsi. *The Epic of Kings (Shah-Nama).* Translated by Reuben Levy. London: Routledge and Kegan Paul, 1985. (This translation originally published 1967; Persian original written 10th century.)

Firth, Raymond. "Malinowski As Scientist and As Man." In R. Firth, ed., *Man and Culture.* London: Routledge, 1957.

———. *Symbols: Public and Private.* Ithaca, NY: Cornell University Press, 1973.

Fowler, Loretta. *Shared Symbols, Contested Meanings: Gros Ventre Culture and History, 1778–1984.* New York: Cornell University Press, 1987.

Franke, Richard, and Barbara Chasin. "Development without Growth: The Kerala Experiment." *Technology Review* (April 1990):43–51.

Freeman, Derek. "Everything Got a Moral . . ." *Pacific Islands Monthly* (1983a):7.

———. "Inductivism and the Test of Truth: A Rejoinder to Lowell D. Holmes and Others." *Canberra Anthropology* 6 (1983b): 101–192.

———. *Margaret Mead and Samoa: The Making and Unmaking of an Anthropological Myth.* Cambridge, MA: Harvard University Press, 1983c.

Freilich, Morris, ed. *Marginal Natives: Anthropologists at Work.* New York: Harper and Row, 1970.

Freud, Sigmund. *Totem and Taboo.* New York: Norton, 1950. (Originally published 1901.)

———. *Civilization and Its Discontents.* Translated by James Strachey. New York: W. W. Norton, 1961.

Friedl, Ernestine. "Society and Sex Roles." In James P. Spradley and David W. McCurdy, eds., *Conformity and Conflict: Readings in Cultural Anthropology,* 7th ed. Glenview, IL: Scott, Foresman/

Little, Brown Higher Education, 1990. (Reprinted from *Human Nature,* April 1978.)

Fromkin, Victoria, and Robert Rodman. *An Introduction to Language,* 4th ed. Fort Worth, TX: Holt, Rinehart and Winston, 1988.

Fromm, Erich. *Escape from Freedom.* New York: Farrar and Rinehart, 1941.

Fuller, Christopher J. *The Nayars Today.* Cambridge: Cambridge University Press, 1976.

Gailey, Harry A., Jr. *History of Africa,* vol. 3. Malabar, FL: Krieger, 1989.

Geertz, Clifford. "Deep Play: Notes on the Balinese Cockfight." In Clifford Geertz, ed., *Myth, Symbol, and Culture.* New York: Norton, 1971. (Also in Clifford Geertz, *The Interpretation of Cultures.* New York: Basic Books, 1973.)

————. *The Interpretation of Cultures.* New York: Basic Books, 1973.

————. "Art As a Cultural System." In Susan Feagin and Patrick Maynard, eds., *Aesthetics.* Oxford: Oxford University Press, 1997. (Originally published in *Modern Language Notes* 91 [1974]: 1473–1483, 1488–1490, 1497–1499.)

Gilligan, Carol. *In a Different Voice: Psychological Theory and Women's Development.* Cambridge, MA: Harvard University Press, 1982.

————. "Adolescent Development Reconsidered." In C. Gilligan, J. V. Ward, and J. M. Taylor, eds., *Mapping the Moral Domain.* Cambridge, MA: Harvard University Press, 1988.

Gilmore, David D. "Manhood." *Natural History,* June 1990. (Reprinted in James P. Spradley and David W. McCurdy, eds., *Conformity and Conflict.* New York: HarperCollins, 1994.)

————. "Men and Women in Southern Spain: 'Domestic Power' Revisited." In Mari Womack and Judith Marti, eds., *The Other Fifty Percent: Multicultural Perspectives on Gender Relations.* Prospect Heights, IL: Waveland Press, 1993.

Glazer Schuster, Ilsa M. *New Women of Lusaka.* Mountain View, CA: Mayfield, 1979.

Gleason, Henry A. *An Introduction to Descriptive Linguistics,* rev. ed. New York: Holt, Rinehart and Winston, 1961.

Goldman, Irving. *The Mouth of Heaven: An Introduction to Kwakiutl Religious Thought.* New York: Wiley, 1975.

Goldschmidt, Walter. *The Sebei: A Study in Adaptation.* New York: Holt, Rinehart and Winston, 1986.

Goldstein, Melvyn C. "Polyandry: When Brothers Take a Wife." In James P. Spradley and David W. McCurdy, eds., *Conformity and Conflict.* New York: HarperCollins, 1994. (Originally published as "When Brothers Take a Wife." *Natural History* [March 1987].)

Gone, Joseph P. "Gros Ventre Cultural Identity as Normative Self: A Case Study." M.A. thesis, University of Illinois at Urbana, 1996.

Good, Kenneth, with David Chanoff. *Into the Heart: One Man's Pursuit of Love and Knowledge among the Yanomama.* New York: Simon and Schuster, 1991.

Goodale, Jane Carter. *Tiwi Wives: A Study of the Women of Melville Island, North Australia.* American Ethnological Society Monographs no. 51. Seattle and London: University of Washington Press, 1971. (Reprint. Prospect Heights, IL: Waveland Press, 1994.)

Goody, Jack. *The Logic of Writing and the Organization of Society.* Cambridge: Cambridge University Press, 1986.

Gough, Kathleen. "Nayar: Central Kerala" and "Nayar: North Kerala." In Christopher J. Fuller, ed., *The Nayars Today.* Cambridge: Cambridge University Press, 1976.

Graburn, Nelson H. H. "Introduction: The Arts of the Fourth World." In Nelson H. H. Graburn, ed., *Ethnic and Tourist Arts: Cultural Expressions from the Fourth World.* Berkeley: University of California Press, 1976.

Green, Edward C. "The Integration of Modern and Traditional Health Sectors in Swaziland." In Aaron Podolefsky and Peter J. Brown, eds., *Applying Cultural Anthropology: An Introductory Reader.* Mountain View, CA: Mayfield, 1991. (Originally published in Robert Wulff and Shirley Fiske, eds., *Anthropological Praxis.* Boulder, CO: Westview Press, 1987.)

Gregor, Thomas. "Dark Dreams about the White Man." In *Anthropology: Annual Editions 92/93.* Guilford, CT: Dushkin, 1992. (Originally published in *Natural History* 92, no. 1 [1983].

Gregory, James R. "The Myth of the Male Ethnographer and the Woman's World." *American Anthropologist* 86 (1984):316–327.

Hamblin, Robert L., and Brian L. Pitcher. "The Classic Maya Collapse: Testing Class Conflict Theories." *American Antiquities* 45 (1980):246–271.

Hanna, Judith Lynne. *Dance, Sex and Gender.* Chicago: University of Chicago Press, 1988.

Harkin, Michael. "Carnival and Authority: Heiltsuk Cultural Models of Power." *Ethos* 24 (1996):281–313.

Harner, Michael. "The Ecological Basis for Aztec Sacrifice." *American Ethnologist* 4 (1977):117–135. (Also published as "The Enigma of Aztec Sacrifice." In James P. Spradley and David W. McCurdy, eds., *Conformity and Conflict: Readings in Cultural Anthropology,* 4th ed. Boston: Little, Brown, 1980.)

Harris, Marvin. *The Rise of Anthropological Theory.* New York: Harper and Row, 1968.

————. *Cows, Pigs, Wars and Witches: The Riddles of Culture.* New York: Vintage Books, 1974.

————. *America Now: The Anthropology of a Changing Culture.* New York: Touchstone, 1981.

Hart, C. W. M., Arnold R. Pilling, and Jane C. Goodale. *The Tiwi of North Australia,* 3d ed. New York: Holt, Rinehart and Winston, 1988.

Hartsock, Nancy. *Money, Sex, and Power: Toward a Feminist Historical Materialism.* Boston: Northeastern University Press, 1983.

Hayano, David M. *Poker Faces: The Life and Work of Professional Card Players.* Berkeley: University of California Press, 1982.

Hayden, Robert M. "Imagined Communities and Real Victims: Self-Determination and Ethnic Cleansing in Yugoslavia." *American Ethnologist* 23 (1996):783–801.

Hays, H. R. *From Ape to Angel: An Informal History of Social Anthropology.* New York: Capricorn Books, 1958.

Heider, Karl. *Grand Valley Dani: Peaceful Warriors,* 2d ed. Fort Worth: Holt, Rinehart and Winston, 1991.

Heizer, R. "Primitive Man As an Ecologic Factor." *Kroeber Anthropological Society Papers* 13:1031. Berkeley: Kroeber Anthropological Society, 1955.

Herdt, Gilbert. *The Sambia.* New York: Holt, Rinehart and Winston, 1987.

Herskovits, Melville J. *Life in a Haitian Valley.* New York: Knopf, 1937.

Hewlett, Barry S. *Intimate Fathers: The Nature and Context of Aka Pygmy Paternal Infant Care.* Ann Arbor: University of Michigan Press, 1992.

Hogbin, Ian. *The Island of Menstruating Men.* Prospect Heights, IL: Waveland Press, 1996. (Originally published 1970.)

Homans, George C. "Anxiety and Ritual: The Theories of Malinowski and Radcliffe-Brown." *American Anthropologist* 43 (1941):164–172.

Hrdy, Sarah Blaffer. *The Woman That Never Evolved.* Cambridge, MA: Harvard University Press, 1981.

Huizinga, Johan. *Homo Ludens: A Study of the Play Element in Culture.* Boston: Beacon Press, 1950.

Huntingford, G. W. B. *The Nandi of Kenya: Tribal Control in a Pastoral Society.* London: Routledge & Kegan Paul, 1953.

Hurston, Zora Neale. *Tell My Horse.* New York: Lippincott, 1938.

Jaffe, Hosea. *A History of Africa.* London: Zed Books, 1985.

Jahoda, Gustav. "Geometric Illusions and Environment: A Study in Ghana." *British Journal of Psychology* 57 (1966):193–199.

Janus, Noreene. "Advertising and Global Culture." In Aaron Podolefsky and Peter J. Brown, eds., *Applying Cultural Anthropology: An Introductory Reader.* Mountain View, CA: Mayfield, 1991. (Originally published in *Cultural Survival Quarterly* 7[2] [1983]: 28–31.)

Jeffrey, Robin. *The Decline of Nayar Dominance: Society and Politics in Travancore, 1847–1908.* New York: Holmes and Meier, 1976.

Joans, Barbara. "Problems in Pocatello: A Study in Linguistic Misunderstanding." In Aaron Podolefsky and Peter J. Brown, eds., *Applying Cultural Anthropology: An Introductory Reader.* Mountain View, CA: Mayfield, 1991. (Originally published in *Practicing Anthropology* 6[6] [1984]:8.)

Joensen, Joan Pauli. *Faerøske sluppfiskere: Etnologisk undersogelse at en erhvervsgrupes liv.* Tórshavn, Faeroe Islands: Føroya FróDskaparfelag, 1975.

Johnson, A. "How the Machiguenga Manage Resources: Conservation or Exploitation of Nature?" *Advances in Economic Botany* 7 (1989):213–222.

Johnson, Allen W., and Timothy Earle. *The Evolution of Human Societies: From Foraging Group to Agrarian State.* Stanford, CA: Stanford University Press, 1987.

Johnson, Allen W., and Douglass Price-Williams. *Oedipus Ubiquitous: The Family Complex in World Folk Literature.* Stanford, CA: Stanford University Press, 1996.

Joseph, George Gheverghese, Vasu Reddy, and Mary Searle-Chatterjee. "Eurocentrism in the Social Sciences." *Race and Class* 31 (1990):1–26.

Kahn, Miriam. *Always Hungry, Never Greedy: Food and the Expression of Gender in a Melanesian Society.* Prospect Heights, IL: Waveland Press, 1994.

Katz, Pearl. "Ritual in the Operating Room." In Aaron Podolefsky and Peter J. Brown, eds., *Applying Cultural Anthropology: An Introductory Reader.* Mountain View, CA: Mayfield, 1991. (Originally published in *Ethnology* [1981].)

Kearney, Michael. *World View.* Novato, CA: Chandler & Sharp, 1984.

Keesing, Roger M. *Kin Groups and Social Structure.* New York: Holt, Rinehart, and Winston, 1975.

Kiev, Ari. "Spirit Possession in Haiti." *American Journal of Psychiatry* 118 (1961):133–138.

———. "The Psychotherapeutic Value of Spirit-Possession in Haiti." In Raymond Prince, ed., *Trance and Possession States.* Montreal: R. M. Bucke Memorial Society, 1966.

Klima, George J. *The Barabaig: East African Cattle-Herders.* New York: Holt, Rinehart and Winston, 1970. (Reprinted in Arthur C. Lehmann and James E. Myers, eds., *Magic, Witchcraft, and Religion: An Anthropological Study of the Supernatural,* 4th ed. Mountain View, CA: Mayfield, 1997.)

Kluckhohn, Clyde. *Mirror for Man.* New York: Premier, 1957.

Koven, Michèle E. J. "Two Languages in the Self/The Self in Two Languages: French-Portuguese Bilinguals' Verbal Enactments and Experiences of Self in Narrative Discourse." *Ethos* 26 (1998): 410–455.

Kramer, Augustin. *Die Samoa-Inselm,* vol. 1. Stuttgart: E. Naegle, 1902.

Kulick, Don. "Anger, Gender, Language Shift and the Politics of Revelation in a Papua New Guinean Village." *Pragmatics* 2 (1993):281–296.

Kuper, Adam. *Anthropology and Anthropologists: The Modern British School.* London: Routledge, 1989.

Kuper, Hilda. *The Swazi: A South African Kingdom.* Fort Worth, TX: Holt, Rinehart and Winston, 1963.

Labov, William. *The Social Stratification of English in New York City.* Washington, DC: Center for Applied Linguistics, 1966.

Lakoff, George, and Mark Johnson. *Metaphors We Live By.* Chicago: The University of Chicago Press, 1980.

Lamphere, Louise. "Strategies, Cooperation, and Conflict among Women in Domestic Groups." In Michelle Zimbalist Rosaldo and Louise Lamphere, eds., *Women, Culture and Society.* Stanford, CA: Stanford University Press, 1974.

Langer, Suzanne. *Philosophy in a New Key.* Cambridge, MA: Harvard University Press, 1942.

Langer, Walter C. *The Mind of Adolf Hitler.* New York: Signet, 1973.

Langness, L. L. *The Study of Culture.* San Francisco: Chandler and Sharp, 1974.

———. "Oedipus in the New Guinea Highlands?" In Mari Womack and Judith Marti, eds., *The Other Fifty Percent: Multicultural Perspectives on Gender Relations.* Prospect Heights, IL: Waveland Press, 1993.

Lattimore, Owen. *Inner Asian Frontiers of China.* Boston: Beacon Press, 1962.

Leach, Edmund. *Social Anthropology.* Oxford: Oxford University Press, 1982.

Lederman, Rena. *What Gifts Engender: Social Relations and Politics in Mendi, Highland Papua New Guinea.* Cambridge: Cambridge University Press, 1986.

Lee, Dorothy. "Codifications of Reality: Lineal and Nonlineal." In James P. Spradley and David W. McCurdy, eds., *Conformity and Conflict: Readings in Cultural Anthropology,* 4th ed. Boston: Little, Brown, 1980. (Originally published as "Lineal and Nonlineal Codifications of Reality." *Psychosomatic Medicine* 12 [1950]: 89–97.)

Lee, Richard. *Subsistence Ecology of !Kung Bushmen.* Ph.D. diss., University of California, Berkeley, 1965.

———. "What Hunters Do for a Living; Or, How to Make Out on Scarce Resources." In Richard B. Lee and Irven DeVore, eds., *Man the Hunter.* Chicago: Aldine, 1968.

———. *The !Kung San: Men, Women, and Work in a Foraging Society.* Cambridge: Cambridge University Press, 1979.

———. "Eating Christmas in the Kalahari." In James P. Spradley and David W. McCurdy, eds., *Conformity and Conflict.* New York: Longman, 1997. (Originally published as "A Naturalist at Large: Eating Christmas in the Kalahari." *Natural History,* December 1969.)

Léon-Portilla, Miguel. *Pre-Columbian Literatures of Mexico.* Norman: University of Oklahoma Press, 1969.

Lessa, William A., and Evon Z. Vogt, eds. *Reader in Comparative Religion: An Anthropological Approach,* 4th ed. New York: Harper and Row, 1979.

Lester, Rebecca J. "Embodied Voices: Women's Food Asceticism and the Negotiation of Identity." *Ethos* 23 (1995):187–222.

LeVine, Robert A. "Cross-Cultural Study in Child Psychology." In Paul H. Mussen, ed., *Carmichael's Manual of Child Psychology,* 3d ed., vol. 2. New York: Wiley, 1970.

Lévi-Strauss, Claude. *Structural Anthropology.* New York: Basic Books, 1963.

Leyburn, James G. *The Haitian People.* New Haven, CT: Yale University Press, 1966.

Linden, Eugene. "Lost Tribes, Lost Knowledge." In *Anthropology: Annual Editions 93/94.* Guilford, CT: Dushkin, 1993.

Lizot, Jacques. *Tales of the Yanomami: Daily Life in the Venezuelan Forest.* Translated by Ernest Simon. Cambridge: Cambridge University Press, 1991.

Lomax, Alan. *Folk Song Style and Culture. American Association for the Advancement of Science Publication No. 88.* Washington, DC, 1968.

Lowie, Robert. *The History of Ethnological Theory.* New York: Rinehart, 1937.

Lutz, Catherine, and Lila Abu-Lughod, eds. *Language and the Politics of Emotion.* Cambridge: Cambridge University Press, 1990.

Maimonides, Moses. *The Guide for the Perplexed,* 2nd ed. Translated by M. Friedländer. New York: Dover, 1956.

Maine, Sir Henry. *Ancient Law: Its Connection with the Early History of Society and Its Relations to Modern Ideas.* London: John Murray, 1861.

Malinowski, Bronislaw. *Magic, Science and Religion and Other Essays.* Garden City, NY: Doubleday Anchor, 1954. (Originally published 1948; the essay "Magic, Science and Religion" was originally published in James Needham, ed., *Science, Religion and Reality.* New York: Macmillan, 1925.)

———. *Sex and Repression in Savage Society.* London: Routledge and Kegan Paul, 1955. (Originally published 1927.)

———. *A Diary in the Strict Sense of the Term.* London: Routledge and Kegan Paul, 1967. (Reprint. Stanford, CA: Stanford University Press, 1989.)

———. *Argonauts of the Western Pacific.* Prospect Heights, IL: Waveland Press, 1984. (Originally published 1922.)

Mammen, P. M. *Communalism vs. Communism: A Study of the Socio-Religious Communities and Political Parties in Kerala, 1892–1970.* Columbia, MO: South Asia Books, 1981.

Mangin, William. *Peasants in Cities: Readings in the Anthropology of Urbanization.* New York: Houghton Mifflin, 1970.

Maquet, Jacques. *The Aesthetic Experience.* New Haven, CT: Yale University Press, 1986.

Marcus, George E., and Michael M. J. Fischer. *Anthropology As Cultural Critique: An Experimental Moment in the Human Sciences.* Chicago: University of Chicago Press, 1986.

Marglin, Frederique Apffel. *Wives of the God-King: The Rituals of the Devadasis of Puri.* Oxford: Oxford University Press, 1985.

Marshall, Lorna. *The !Kung of NyaeNyae.* Cambridge, MA: Harvard University Press, 1976.

Marti, Judith. "Introduction: Economics, Power and Gender Relations." In Mari Womack and Judith Marti, eds., *The Other Fifty Percent: Multicultural Perspectives on Gender Relations.* Prospect Heights, IL: Waveland Press, 1993.

Martin, Emily. "Gender and Ideological Differences in Representations of Life and Death." In James L. Watson and Evelyn S. Rawski, eds., *Death Ritual in Late Imperial and Modern China.* Berkeley: University of California Press, 1988.

Martin, P. "Prehistoric Overkill." In P. Martin and R. Klein, eds., *Quaternary Extinctions.* Tucson: University of Arizona Press, 1984.

Marx, Karl. "The German Ideology." In E. Hobsbawm, ed., *Precapitalist Economic Formations: Karl Marx.* Translated by J. Cohen. New York: International Publishers, 1965.

Marx, Karl, and Friedrich Engels. *The Communist Manifesto.* New York: Washington Square Press, 1964. (Originally published in German in 1848.)

McCorkle, T. *Fajardo's People: Cultural Adjustment in Venezuela; and the Little Community in Latin American and North American Contexts.* Los Angeles: University of California at Los Angeles; Latin American Center, Caracas, Venezuela: Editorial Sucre, 1965.

McLennan, John Joseph. *Primitive Marriage.* London, 1865.

Mead, Margaret. *Coming of Age in Samoa: A Psychological Study of Primitive Youth for Western Civilization.* New York: Morrow, 1928. (Dell Laurel Edition published 1968.)

———. *Sex and Temperament in Three Primitive Societies.* New York: William Morrow, 1935.

———. *And Keep Your Powder Dry: An Anthropologist Looks at America.* New York: William Morrow, 1942.

Menon, A. Sreedhara. *A Survey of Kerala History.* Kottayam, India: National Book Stall, 1967.

Mernissi, Fatima. *Dreams of Trespass: Tales of a Harem Girlhood.* Reading, MA: Addison-Wesley, 1994.

Merrill, William L. "Religion and Culture: God's Saviours in the Sierra Madre." In James P. Spradley and David W. McCurdy, eds., *Conformity and Conflict: Readings in Cultural Anthropology,* 6th ed. Boston: Little, Brown, 1987. (Originally published as "God's Saviours in the Sierra Madre." *Natural History* [1983].)

Métraux, Alfred. *Le Vaudou Haitien.* Paris: Gallimard, 1958.

Milton, Katharine. "Civilization and Its Discontents." *Natural History* 101 (1992):37–42.

Min, Pyong Gap. *Changes and Conflicts: Korean Immigrant Families in New York.* Boston: Allyn and Bacon, 1998.

Mishler, Elliot G. "The Analysis of Interview Narratives." In T. R. Sarbin, ed., *Narrative Psychology: The Storied Nature of Human Conduct.* New York: Prager, 1986, pp. 233–255.

Moore, Omar K. "Divination: A New Perspective." *American Anthropologist* 59 (1957):69–74.

Morgan, Lewis Henry. *Ancient Society.* New York: Henry Hold & Co., 1877.

Motolinía de Benavente, Toribio. "History of the Indians of New Spain." In Elizabeth A. Foster, ed. and trans., *Documents and Narratives Concerning the Discovery and Conquest of Latin America.* New Series, no. 4. Berkeley, CA: Cortés Society, 1950. (Originally written ca. 1536–1543.)

Nader, Laura. "Up the Anthropologist: Perspectives Gained from Studying Up." In Dell Hymes, ed., *Reinventing Anthropology.* New York: Vintage Books, 1974.

Namboodiripad, E. M. S. *Kerala Society and Politics: An Historical Survey.* New Delhi: National Book Centre, 1984.

Nanda, Serena. *Neither Man nor Woman: The Hijras of India,* 2nd ed. Belmont, CA: Wadworth, 1999.

Nash, June. "Gender Studies in Latin America." In Sandra Morgen, ed., *Gender and Anthropology: Critical Reviews for Research and Teaching.* Washington, DC: American Anthropological Association, 1979.

Newman, Philip L. *Knowing the Gururumba.* New York: Holt, Rinehart and Winston, 1965.

Nicholson, H. B. "Religion in Pre-Hispanic Central Mexico." In *Handbook of Middle American Indians,* vol. 10. Austin: University of Texas Press, 1971.

Nietschmann, Bernard. "When the Turtle Collapses, the World Ends." *Natural History* (June–July 1974).

Nohara, Komakichi. *The True Face of Japan.* London: 1936.

Obeyesekere, Gananath. "Methodological and Philosophical Relativism." *Man* 1 (1966):368–374.

Ohnuki-Tierney, Emiko. *The Ainu of the Northwest Coast of Southern Sakhalin.* New York: Holt, Rinehart and Winston, 1974.

Olmstead, A. T. *History of the Persian Empire.* Chicago: University of Chicago Press, 1948.

Ostrander, Susan. *Women of the Upper Class.* Philadelphia: Temple University Press, 1984.

Paige, Karen Ericksen, and Jeffery M. Paige. *The Politics of Reproductive Ritual.* Berkeley: University of California Press, 1981.

Parker, Philip. "Motivation of Surrogate Mothers: Initial Findings." *American Journal of Psychiatry* 140 (1983):117–119.

Parsons, Elsie Clews. *Pueblo Indian Religion.* Chicago: University of Chicago Press, 1939.

Parsons, Talcott. "On the Concept of Power." *Proceedings of the American Philosophical Society* 107 (1963a):232–262.

———. "On the Concept of Influence." *Public Opinion Quarterly* 27 (1963b):37–62.

Peters-Golden, Holly. *Culture Sketches: Case Studies in Anthropology.* New York: McGraw-Hill, 1994.

Pilcher, William W. *The Portland Longshoremen: A Dispersed Urban Community.* New York: Holt, Rinehart and Winston, 1972.

Plattner, Stuart. *Economic Anthropology.* Stanford, CA: Stanford University Press, 1989.

Pollack, R. H. "Müller–Lyer Illusion: Effect of Age, Lightness, Contrast and Hue." *Science* 170 (1970):93–94.

Powdermaker, Hortense. *Stranger and Friend: The Way of an Anthropologist.* New York: Norton, 1966.

Price-Williams, Douglass R. *Explorations in Cross-Cultural Psychology.* San Francisco: Chandler and Sharp, 1975.

———. "In Search of Mythopoetic Thought." *Ethos* 27 (1999): 25–32.

Puthenkulam, J. *Marriage and the Family in Kerala: With Special Reference to Matrilineal Castes.* Calgary: University of Calgary, 1977.

Radcliffe-Brown, A. R. *The Andaman Islanders.* Cambridge: Cambridge University Press, 1922.

———. *Taboo* (The Frazer Lecture). Cambridge: Cambridge University Press, 1939. (Reprinted in William A. Lessa and Evon Z. Vogt, eds., *Reader in Comparative Religion: An Anthropological Approach,* 4th ed. New York: Harper and Row, 1979.)

———. *Structure and Function in Primitive Society.* London: Routledge, 1952.

Raemakers, J. "Synecology of Malaysian Apes." Ph.D. diss., Cambridge University, 1977.

Rai, N. "From Forest to Field: A Study of Philippine Negrito Foragers in Transition." Ph.D. diss., University of Hawaii, 1982.

Ravenscroft, Kent. "Voodoo Possession: A Natural Experiment in Hypnosis." *International Journal of Clinical and Experimental Hypnosis* 13 (1965):157–182.

Read, Kenneth E. *The High Valley.* New York: Scribner's, 1965.

Redfield, Robert. "The Primitive World View." *American Philosophical Society, Proceedings* 96 (1952):30–36.

———. *The Primitive World and Its Transformations.* Ithaca, NY: Cornell University Press, 1953.

Redford, K. "The Ecologically Noble Savage." *Orion* 9 (1991): 24–29.

Roberts, John M., and Brian Sutton-Smith. "Cross-Cultural Correlates of Games of Chance." *Behavior Science Notes* 3 (1966): 131–144.

Rosaldo, Renato. *Culture and Truth.* Boston: Beacon Press, 1989.

Rubin, Gayle. "The Traffic in Women: Notes on the Political Economy of Sex." In Rayna R. Reiter, ed., *Toward an Anthropology of Women.* New York: Monthly Review Press, 1975.

Rubin, Lillian Breslow. *Worlds of Pain: Life in the Working-Class Family.* New York: Basic Books, 1976.

Sacks, Karen. "Engels Revisited: Women, the Organization of Production, and Private Property." In Rayna R. Reiter, ed., *Toward an Anthropology of Women.* New York: Monthly Review Press, 1975.

Sahagún, Bernardino de. *Florentine Codex: General History of the Things of New Spain.* Translated by Arthur J. O. Anderson and Charles E. Dibble. Salt Lake City, UT and Santa Fe, NM: University of Utah and School of American Research, Santa Fe, 1950–1969. (Originally written ca. 1569.)

Sahlins, Marshall. "Evolution: Specific and General." In Marshall Sahlins and Elman Service, eds., *Evolution and Culture.* Ann Arbor: University of Michigan Press, 1960.

Sahlins, Marshall, and Elman Service, eds., *Evolution and Culture.* Ann Arbor: University of Michigan Press, 1960.

Salisbury, R. F. *From Stone to Steel.* Melbourne, Australia: Melbourne University Press, 1962.

Salzman, P. C. "Political Organization among Nomadic People." In Y. A. Cohen, ed., *Man in Adaptation.* Chicago: Aldine, 1974.

Sapir, Edward. "The Status of Linguistics As a Science." In D. Mandelbaum, ed., *Selected Writings of Edward Sapir.* Berkeley: University of California Press, 1949.

Saussure, Ferdinand de. *Cours de Linguistique Generale* (Course in General Linguistics). New York: McGraw-Hill, 1966. (Originally published 1916.)

Schebesta, P. *Revisiting My Pygmy Hosts.* London: Hutchinson, 1936.

Scheper-Hughes, Nancy. "Lifeboat Ethics: Mother Love and Child Death in Brazil." In Aaron Podolefsky and Peter J. Brown, eds., *Applying Cultural Anthropology: An Introductory Reader.* Mountain View, CA: Mayfield, 1991. (Originally published 1989.)

Schieffelin, B. B. *The Give and Take of Everyday Life.* Cambridge: Cambridge University Press, 1990.

Schieffelin, E. L. *The Sorrow of the Lonely and the Burning of the Dancers.* New York: St. Martin's Press, 1976.

Schiffrin, Deborah. "Narrative as Self-Portrait: Sociolinguistic Constructions of Identity." *Language in Society* 25:167–203.

Schlegel, Alice. "Status, Property, and the Value on Virginity." In Mari Womack and Judith Marti, eds., *The Other Fifty Percent: Multicultural Perspectives on Gender Relations.* Prospect Heights, IL: Waveland Press, 1993.

Schlegel, Alice, and Herbert Barry III. "The Cultural Consequences of Female Contribution to Subsistence." *American Anthropologist* 88 (1986):142–150.

Schneider, David. *American Kinship: A Cultural Account.* Englewood Cliffs, NJ: Prentice Hall, 1968.

Segall, Marshall H., D. T. Campbell, and M. J. Herskovits. *The Influence of Culture on Visual Perception.* Indianapolis: Bobbs-Merrill, 1966.

Selsam, H., and H. Martel. *Reader in Marxist Philosophy.* New York: International Publishers, 1963.

Service, Elman. *Primitive Social Organization: An Evolutionary Perspective.* New York: Random House, 1962.

Seymour, Susan. "Expressions of Responsibility among Indian Children: Some Precursors of Adult Status and Sex Roles." *Ethos* 16 (1992):355–370.

Shankman, Paul. "The History of Samoan Sexual Conduct and the Mead–Freeman Controversy." *American Anthropologist* 98 (1996): 555–567.

Shepher, Joseph. *Incest: A Biosocial View.* New York: Academic Press, 1983.

Shore, Bradd. "Sexuality and Gender in Samoa: Conceptions and Missed Conceptions." In S. Ortner and H. Whitehead, eds., *Sexual Meanings: The Cultural Construction of Gender and Sexuality.* Cambridge: Cambridge University Press, 1981.

———. *Sala'ilua: A Samoan Mystery.* New York: Columbia University Press, 1982.

Shostak, Marjorie. *Nisa: The Life and Words of a !Kung Woman.* New York: Vintage Books, 1981.

Siemens, Stephen David. "Access to Women's Knowledge: The Azande Experience." In Mari Womack and Judith Marti, eds., *The Other Fifty Percent: Multicultural Perspectives on Gender Relations.* Prospect Heights, IL: Waveland Press, 1993.

Silberbauer, George. *Hunter and Habitat in the Central Kalahari Desert.* Cambridge: Cambridge University Press, 1981.

Simmel, Georg. *The Philosophy of Money.* London: Routledge and Kegan Paul, 1978.

Siwolop, Sana. "What's an Anthropologist Doing in My Office?" In Aaron Podolefsky and Peter J. Brown, eds., *Applying Cultural Anthropology: An Introductory Reader.* Mountain View, CA: Mayfield, 1991. (Originally published in *Business Week* [1986].)

Slocum, Sally. "Woman the Gatherer: Male Bias in Anthropology." In Rayna R. Reiter, ed., *Toward an Anthropology of Women.* New York: Monthly Review Press, 1975.

Somers, Margaret R. "The Narrative Constitution of Identity: A Relational and Network Approach." *Theory and Society* 23 (1994): 605–649.

Spencer, Herbert. *Social Statics.* New York: Appleton, 1883. (Originally published 1850.)

———. *Principles of Sociology.* New York: Appleton, 1896. (Originally published 1876.)

Spiro, Melford E. *Oedipus in the Trobriands.* Chicago: University of Chicago Press, 1982.

Spradley, James P. *You Owe Yourself a Drunk: An Ethnography of Urban Nomads.* Boston: Little, Brown, 1970.

———. *Participant Observation.* New York: Holt, Rinehart and Winston, 1980.

Steadman, Lyle B., Craig T. Palmer, and Christopher F. Tilley. "The Universality of Ancestor Worship." *Ethnology* 35 (1996):63–76.

Steward, Julian. *Theory of Culture Change.* Urbana: University of Illinois Press, 1955.

———. "Review of White's *The Evolution of Culture.*" *American Anthropologist* 62 (1960):144–148.

Stocking, George W. *Race, Culture, and Evolution: Essays in the History of Anthropology.* New York: Free Press, 1968.

Strathern, Marilyn. "The Pursuit of Certainty: Investigating Kinship in the Late Twentieth Century." Paper presented at the 90th American Anthropological Association Annual Meeting, Chicago, 1991.

Sutherland, Anne. "Gypsies and Health Care." In James P. Spradley and David W. McCurdy, eds., *Conformity and Conflict.* New York: HarperCollins, 1994. (Originally published in *The Western Journal of Medicine* [September 1992].)

Sutton-Smith, Brian. "The Two Cultures of Games." In G. S. Kenyon, ed., *Aspects of Contemporary Sports Sociology.* Chicago: Athletic Institute, 1968.

———. "Games: The Socialization of Conflict." In Ommo Grupe, Dietrick Kurz, and Johannes Marcus Teipel, eds., *Sport in the Modern World: Chances and Problems.* Heidelberg, Germany: Springer-Verlag Berlin, 1973.

Sutton-Smith, Brian, and John Roberts. "The Cross-Cultural and Psychological Study of Games." In G. Luschen, ed., *The Cross-Cultural Analysis of Games.* Champaign, IL: Stipes, 1970.

Swadesh, Morris. "Linguistics As an Instrument of Prehistory." In Dell H. Hymes, ed., *Language and Society.* New York: Harper and Row, 1964.

Takuan Soho. *The Unfettered Mind.* Tokyo: Kodansha, 1986.

Talmon, Yonina. "Mate Selection in Collective Settlements." *American Sociological Review* 29 (1964):491–508.

Taub, David. "Female Choice and Mating Strategies among Wild Barbary Macaques (*Macaca Sylvanus L.*)." In D. Lindburg, ed., *The Macaques: Studies in Ecology, Behavior and Evolution.* New York: Van Nostrand-Reinhold, 1980.

Tax, Sol. *An Appraisal of Anthropology Today.* Chicago: University of Chicago Press, 1953.

Thomas, David Hurst. *Skull Wars: Kinnewick Man, Archaeology and the Battle for Native American Identity.* New York: Basic Books, 2000.

Thomson, David S. "Worlds Shaped by Words." In James P. Spradley and David W. McCurdy, eds., *Conformity and Conflict.* New York: HarperCollins, 1994. (Originally published in *Human Behavior: Language.* New York: Time Life, 1975.)

Tierney, Helen, ed. *Women's Studies Encyclopedia. Vol. 1: Views from the Sciences.* New York: Peter Bedrick Books, 1991.

Torquemada, Juan de. *Los Veinte i un libros rituales i monarchia Indiana,* 3 vols. Mexico City: Editorial Porrua, 1969. (Originally published 1615.)

Trager, Lillian. "Living Abroad: Cross-Cultural Training for Families." In Aaron Podolefsky and Peter J. Brown, eds., *Applying Cultural Anthropology: An Introductory Reader.* Mountain View, CA: Mayfield, 1991. (Originally published in *Practicing Anthropology* 9[5] [1987]:11.)

Turnbull, Colin M. *The Forest People.* New York: Touchstone, 1962.

———. *The Mountain People.* New York: Touchstone, 1972.

Turnbull, Stephen. *The Book of the Samurai: The Warrior Class of Japan.* New York: Gallery Books, 1982.

———. *The Lone Samurai and the Martial Arts.* London: Arms and Armour Press, 1990.

Turner, Victor. *The Forest of Symbols.* Ithaca, NY: Cornell University Press, 1967.

———. *The Ritual Process: Structure and Anti-Structure.* Ithaca, NY: Cornell University Press, 1969.

———. *Dramas, Fields, and Metaphors: Symbolic Action in Human Society.* Ithaca, NY: Cornell University Press, 1974.

———. "Carnival, Ritual, and Play in Rio de Janeiro." In Alessandro Falassi, ed., *Time Out of Time: Essays on the Festival.* Albuquerque: University of New Mexico Press, 1987.

Tutin, Caroline. "Sexual Behavior and Mating Patterns in a Community of Wild Chimpanzees (*Pan troglodytes*)." Ph.D. diss., University of Edinburgh, 1975.

Tylor, E. B. *Primitive Culture.* London: Murray, 1871.

———. "Animism." In William A. Lessa and Evon Z. Vogt, eds., *Reader in Comparative Religion: An Anthropological Approach,* 4th ed. New York: Harper and Row, 1979.

———. "Primitive Culture." In Paul Bohannan and Mark Glazer, eds., *High Points in Anthropology,* 2nd ed. New York: McGraw-Hill, 1988.

United Nations. *World Population Prospects 1990.* New York: United Nations, 1991.

Vancouver, George. *Voyage of Discovery to the North Pacific Ocean and around the World,* I–III. London: Robinson and Edwards, 1798.

Van Gennep, Arnold. *The Rites of Passage.* Translated by Monika B. Vizedom and Gabrielle L. Caffee. Chicago: University of Chicago Press, 1960.

Vanstone, James W. *Athapaskan Adaptations: Hunters and Fishermen of the Subarctic Forests.* Chicago: Aldine, 1974.

Vickers, W. "Size, Life-History, and Ecology in Mammals." *African Journal of Ecology* 17 (1988):185–204.

Volosinov, V. N. *Marxism and the Philosophy of Language.* Cambridge, MA: Harvard University Press, 1973. (Originally published 1929.)

Von Furer-Haimendorf, C. "Priests." In Richard Cavendish, ed., *Man, Myth, and Magic,* vol. 16. London: BPCC/Phoebus, 1970.

Waal, Alex de. "In the Disaster Zone: Anthropologists and the Ambiguity of Aid." In William A. Haviland and Robert J. Gordon, eds., *Talking about People: Readings in Contemporary Cultural Anthropology,* 2d ed. Mountain View, CA: Mayfield, 1996. (Originally published in *Times Literary Supplement,* July 16, 1993.)

Wagner, Henry R. *The Rise of Fernando Cortés.* Berkeley, CA: Cortés Society, 1944.

Waley, Arthur, trans. *The Book of Songs.* New York: Grove Weidenfeld, 1960. (Originally published 1937.)

Wallace, Anthony F. C. "Revitalization Movements." *American Anthropologist* 58 (1956):264–281.

——. *Religion: An Anthropological View.* New York: Random House, 1966.

——. *The Death and Rebirth of the Seneca.* New York: Vintage Books, 1969.

Ward, Martha C. *Nest in the Wind: Adventures in Anthropology on a Tropical Island.* Prospect Heights, IL: Waveland Press, 1989.

——. *The Hidden Life of Tirol.* Prospect Heights, IL: Waveland Press, 1993.

Warner, W. Lloyd. *A Black Civilization: A Social Study of an Australian Tribe.* Gloucester, MA: Peter Smith, 1969.

Watson, E. L. Grant. *But to What Purpose? The Autobiography of a Contemporary.* London: 1946.

Watson, J. B. *Tairora Culture: Contingency and Pragmatism.* Seattle: University of Washington Press, 1983.

Weber, Max. *The Theory of Social and Economic Organization.* Translated by A. M. Henderson and Talcott Parsons. New York: Oxford University Press, 1947.

——. *Economy and Society: An Outline of Interpretive Sociology.* Ephraim Fischoff, et al, trans. Guenther Roth and Claus Wittich, eds. Berkeley: University of California Press, 1978.

Weismantel, Mary. *Food, Gender and Poverty in the Ecuadorian Andes.* Philadelphia: University of Pennsylvania Press, 1988.

——. "The Children Cry for Bread: Hegemony and the Transformation of Consumption." In Benjamin S. Orlove and Henry J. Rutz, eds., *The Social Economy of Consumption.* Society for Economic Anthropology Publications 6 (1989).

Weissner, Polly. "Hxaro: A Regional System of Reciprocity for the Reduction of Risk among the !Kung San." Ph.D. diss., University of Michigan, 1977.

Westermarck, Edward. *The History of Human Marriage.* London: Macmillan, 1894.

White, Leslie. *The Science of Culture.* New York: Grove Press, 1949.

——. "Review of Steward's *Theory of Culture Change.*" *American Anthropologist* 59 (1957):540–542.

Whiting, Beatrice B., and John W. M. Whiting. *Children of Six Cultures: A Psycho-Cultural Analysis.* Cambridge, MA: Harvard University Press, 1975.

Whorf, Benjamin Lee. "Science and Linguistics." In John B. Carroll, ed., *Language, Thought, and Reality: Selected Writings of Benjamin Lee Whorf.* Boston: Technology Press of Massachusetts Institute of Technology, 1956. (Originally published 1940.)

Willey, Gordon R., and Demitric B. Shimkin. "The Collapse of Classic Maya Civilization in the Southern Lowlands: A Symposium Summary Statement." *Southwestern Journal of Anthropology* 27 (1971):1–18.

Wilmsen, Edwin. *Land Filled with Flies: A Political Economy of the Kalahari.* Chicago: University of Chicago Press, 1989a.

——. "Those Who Have Each Other: Land Tenure of San-Speaking Peoples." In Edwin Wilmsen, ed., *We Are Here: Politics of Aboriginal Land Tenure.* Berkeley: University of California Press, 1989b.

Wilson, Samuel M. "Death and Taxes." In *Anthropology: Annual Editions 92/93.* Guilford, CT: Dushkin, 1992. (Originally published in *Natural History* [1991]:22, 24–25.)

Winterhalder, B. "Foraging Strategies in the Boreal Forest." In B. Winterhalder and E. Smith, eds., *Hunter–Gatherer Foraging Strategies.* Chicago: University of Chicago Press, 1981.

Wolf, Arthur. "Adopt a Daughter-In-Law, Marry a Sister. A Chinese Solution to the Problem of the Incest Taboo." *American Anthropologist* 70 (1968):864–874.

Womack, Mari. ". . . His Truth Shall Endureth Unto All Generations: A Study of the Transfer of Leadership in Eternal Truth Church, a Spiritualist Church in Southeast Los Angeles." Unpublished master's thesis, UCLA, 1977.

——. "Sports Magic: Symbolic Manipulation among Professional Athletes." Ph.D. diss., University of California, Los Angeles, 1982.

——. "Why Athletes Need Ritual: A Study of Magic among Professional Athletes." In Shirl J. Hoffman, ed., *Sport and Religion.* Champaign, IL: Human Kinetics Books, 1992.

——. Introduction to "Why Not Ask the Women?" In Mari Womack and Judith Marti, eds., *The Other Fifty Percent: Multicultural Perspectives on Gender Relations.* Prospect Heights, IL: Waveland Press, 1993.

——. *Faces of Culture.* PBS television series. Coastline Community College, Costa Mesa, CA, 1994.

——. "Studying Up and the Issue of Cultural Relativism." In E. L. Cerroni-Long, ed., *Insider Anthropology. National Association for the Practice of Anthropology Bulletin* 16 (1995):48–57.

Womack, Mari, and Joan C. Barker. "Adventures in the Field and in the Locker Room." In Mari Womack and Judith Marti, eds., *The Other Fifty Percent: Multicultural Perspectives on Gender Relations.* Prospect Heights, IL: Waveland Press, 1993.

Womack, Mari, and Judith Marti, eds. *The Other Fifty Percent: Multicultural Perspectives on Gender Relations.* Prospect Heights, IL: Waveland Press, 1993.

Wong, Bernard P. *Chinatown: Economic Adaptation and Ethnic Identity of the Chinese.* New York: Holt, Rinehard and Winston, 1982.

Woodburn, James. "Discussions, Part V—Population Control Factors: Infanticide, Disease, Nutrition, and Food Supply." In Richard B. Lee and Irven DeVore, eds., *Man the Hunter.* Chicago: Aldine, 1968.

Woodcock, George. *Kerala: A Portrait of the Malabar Coast.* London: Faber and Faber, 1967.

Worsley, Peter. "Cargo Cults." In James P. Spradley and David W. McCurdy, eds., *Conformity and Conflict*. New York: HarperCollins, 1994. (Originally published 1959.)

Yanagisako, Sylvia Junko. "Family and Household: The Analysis of Domestic Groups." *Annual Review of Anthropology* 8 (1979): 161–205.

Yellen, John E. "The Transformation of the Kalahari !Kung." In *Anthropology: Annual Editions 91/92*. Guilford, CT: Dushkin, 1991. (Originally published in *Scientific American* [April 1990]:96–105.)

Young, Serinity. *An Anthology of Sacred Texts by and about Women*. New York: Crossroad, 1993.

Zelizer, Vivian. *Pricing the Priceless Child*. New York: Basic Books, 1985.

Zimmer, Carl. "Tech in the Jungle." In *Anthropology: Annual Editions 91/92*. Guilford, CT: Dushkin, 1991. (Originally published in *Discover* [August 1990]:42–45.)

Zorita, Alonso de. *Life and Labor in Ancient Mexico*. Translated by Benjamin Keen. New Brunswick, NJ: Rutgers University Press, 1963. (Originally written 1570s or 1580s.)

PHOTO CREDITS

Chapter 1   2 Ken Heyman/Woodfin Camp & Associates 5 Marvin E. Newman/Woodfin Camp & Associates 10 Art Resource, N.Y. 15 Irven Devore/Anthro-Photo File 18 Dennis Budd Gray/Stock Boston

Chapter 2   22 Jason Laure/Woodfin Camp & Associates 25 Kristen Loftsdottir 26 Richard Kahn 28 David Blundell 33 Napoleon Chagnon/Anthro-Photo File

Chapter 3   46 Odyssey Productions 50 Smithsonian Institution 53 Tony Howarth/Daily Telegraph Magazine/Woodfin Camp & Associates 55 Chuck Fishman/Woodfin Camp & Associates 59 Yale University Library 60 Bell/Anthro-Photo File 65 American Museum of Natural History 67 Ken Heyman/Woodfin Camp & Associates

Chapter 4   72 David Blundell 75 Peter Menzel/Stock Boston 76 David Austen/Stock Boston 77 Peter Menzel/Stock Boston 78 Robert Aschenbrenner/Stock Boston 81 Gerry Howard/Stock Boston 88 W. Lynn Seldon, Jr./Omni-Photo Communications, Inc.

Chapter 5   98 David Blundell 101 Shostak/Anthro-Photo File 105 David Blundell 113 David Austen/Stock Boston 114 Owen Franken/Stock Boston 115 Jean-Claude LeJeune/Stock Boston 121 Scala/Art Resource, N.Y.

Chapter 6   126 Robert Harding Picture Library Limited 131 (top) Marc and Evelyne Bernheim/Woodfin Camp & Associates; (bottom) David Blundell 134 SuperStock, Inc. 135 Bareg Schuler/Anthro-Photo File

Chapter 7   152 Sheila Nardulli/Liaison Agency, Inc. 154 Corbis 160 Jim Anderson/Woodfin Camp & Associates 165 David Blundell 172 Peter Menzel/Stock Boston

Chapter 8   176 Dorothy Little/Stock Boston 179 Jean-Claude Lejeune/Stock Boston 185 Laman/Anthro-Photo File 187 David Blundell 188 L. Birmingham/Liaison Agency, Inc. 192 Elizabeth Crews/Stock Boston 197 Halpern/Anthro-Photo File 201 John Bishop/Media Generation

Chapter 9   206 David Blundell 208 Don Farber/Woodfin Camp & Associates 213 Sujoy Das/Stock Boston 217 AP/Wide World Photos 218 Etter/Anthro-Photo File 219 David Maybury-Lewis/Anthro-Photo File 220 SuperStock, Inc. 229 Kal Muller/Woodfin Camp & Associates

Chapter 10   236 Jason Laure/Woodfin Camp & Associates 239 Mark J. Terrill/AP/Wide World Photos 240 David Blundell 241 K. Rosenthal/Stock Boston 245 C. Jopp/Robert Harding Picture Library Limited 249 John Bishop/Media Generation 255 John Bishop/Media Generation 256 David Blundell 257 Robert Frerck/Odyssey Productions

Chapter 11   260 John Bishop/Media Generation 262 Ewing Galloway, Inc. 264 Irven DeVore/Anthro-Photo File 265 John Bishop/Media Generation 270 Gavin Hellier/Robert Harding Picture Library Limited 271 David Blundell 283 Alaska Division of Tourism 284 SEF/Art Resource, N.Y. 286 Alaska Division of Tourism

Chapter 12   290 Lila Abu-Lughod/Anthro-Photo File 293 J.F.E. Bloss/Anthro-Photo File 294 David Hiser/Stone 296 Robert Harding Picture Library Limited 298 Smucker/Anthro-Photo File 309 N. Keddie/Anthro-Photo File 315 John Bishop/Media Generation 317 John Bishop/Media Generation

Chapter 13   324 David Holdsworth/Robert Harding Picture Library Limited 328 Robin Hanbury-Tenison/Robert Harding Picture Library Limited 330 Victor Englebert/Photo Researchers, Inc. 336 David Austen, Stock Boston 337 Bell/Anthro-Photo File 342 SuperStock Inc.

Chapter 14   356 Peter Menzel/Stock Boston 358 F. Jordan/Explorer/Photo Researchers, Inc. 360 The Granger Collection 364 The Granger Collection 369 Cheryl Sheridan/Odyssey Productions 376 Robert Harding Picture Library Limited 377 David Blundell 383 David Blundell

Chapter 15   390 Michael Dwyer/Stock Boston 394 Adrian Arbib/Anthro-Photo File 397 Edith G. Haun/Stock Boston 402 Bruce Gelvin 403 Macduff Everton/Corbis/Sygma 407 SuperStock, Inc. 414 Akiko Arita 415 David Blundell 416 David Blundell

Chapter 16   418 David Blundell 424 Don Farber Photograph 429 Dorothy Littell/Stock Boston 430 Grace Davies/Omni-Photo Communications, Inc. 437 David Graham/Black Star 438 D.K. Holdsworth/Robert Harding Picture Library Limited 440 John Bishop/Media Generation

NAME INDEX

SUBJECT INDEX

464